THE JOURNALS AND
LETTERS OF
FANNY BURNEY

'Camilla Cottage', built in West Humble, Surrey, by Alexandre d'Arblay in the years 1796–7

THE JOURNALS AND LETTERS OF

FANNY BURNEY

(MADAME D'ARBLAY)

VOLUME IV
WEST HUMBLE 1797–1801
LETTERS 251–422

Edited by

JOYCE HEMLOW

OXFORD
AT THE CLARENDON PRESS
1973

Oxford University Press, Ely House, London W. 1

GLASGOW NEW YORK TORONTO MELBOURNE WELLINGTON
CAPE TOWN IBADAN NAIROBI DAR ES SALAAM LUSAKA ADDIS ABABA
DELHI BOMBAY CALCUTTA MADRAS KARACHI LAHORE DACCA
KUALA LUMPUR SINGAPORE HONG KONG TOKYO

© *Oxford University Press 1973*

*Printed in Great Britain
at the University Press, Oxford
by Vivian Ridler
Printer to the University*

CONTENTS

opinion de celui qui l'a ecrite. Tu n'as donc pas encore vu Charle? — Le lundy et le Mardy j'ai diné à Norbury, et la correspondance du Chev^r Shaub[3] a fait les frais de la soirée. Elle est reellement tout a fait interessante, et souvent trés piquante. Mais tu n'etais pas là! et puis Amelia n'y etait pas non plus. Elle a eu de la fievre (C'est à dire une fièvre de rhume) depuis ton depart. [xxxxx *3 lines*] Ce qui ׀ me fâche c'est [d'avoir] fait trop bonne chere!!! Et puis ce diable de Lally parait si content des bons morceaux et de leur quantité, qu'il n'y a pas moyen de songer à une reforme. Cependant il est phisiquement impossible que cela ne nuise au desir qu'on aurait de le voir plus souvent. S'il pouvait s'en douter! Je suis sur qu'alors il prefererait ne manger que du pain et des pommes de terre. La Princesse est à chaque moment plus aimable, et je dois te prevenir que même Melle Upton[4] est presque gaie, et qu'elle a fait ma conquête. Il est vrai que c'est en me parlant beaucoup de toi—Adieu *toi*! sans qui je ne suis plus moi. Je baise tendrement hersel[f]

Mes tendres respects à ton Pere. j'embrasse Sally.׀

[xxxxx *3 lines marginal writing, top* p. 1]

253   Chelsea College, 1 November 1797

To Charles Burney

A.L. (Osborn), 1 Nov. 1797
Single sheet 4to 2 pp.
Docketed and dated in pencil, p. 1: Fanny Burney to her brother Charles (1797)

My dearest Carlos—

In the midst of packing[1]—alas, not of paying!——I received my royal summons,[2] to announce that my interview would be held in Town—I set off as quick as possible therefore for

---

[3] Whether or not Sir Luke's letters survive, they seem not to have been known to his biographer Rudolf Massini (iii, L. 122 n. 6).
[4] Elizabeth Albana Upton (iii, L. 216 n. 16), who was to marry (1798) Frederick William Hervey (1769–1859), *styled* Lord Hervey. See L. 269 n. 11.

Chelsea, where I now am, in waiting & constant expectation of my promised honour.

I just write this to hope you will find occasion to *peep in* while here I stay. I should so rejoice to shake hands with you!

I am uncertain wholly of my time. But this new regulation will make us postpone our frolic for Greenwich & for Richmond till after your own at Christmas. Our removal makes it intensely inconvenient to leave home just now, & I must return as soon as my grand object is fulfilled. ᴵ Would I could see you first. Poor M. d' A. is obliged to remain solo. It was impossible to qui[t] our loaded Trunks & Boxes wholly to themselves. But the *Idol of the World* accompanies me.

Great complaints (entre nous) are made here of your *non visits*.

I hope Rosette is well. My kind Love to her, & to Carlino. & best Comp^ts· to Mrs. Bicknell.

I shall really much & truly rejoice if you can let me see your goodly Countenance—which is—some how or other—much to my taste.—

Nov. 1. 97.
Chelsea College.

254   Chelsea College, [*pre* 3 November 1797]

To M. d'Arblay

A.L. (Berg), *n.d.*
Single sheet 4to   2 pp.   wafer tear
Edited by FBA, p. 1, *annotated and dated in error:* 4th Novr 1796   (13)
From Chelsea College whither I went alone on news my dear Father feared he might lose his apartments there.ᴵ

                                        Bookham.²

J'étois toute agitée ce matin jusqu'à l'heure de l'arrivée de la poste—I feared my dearest ami might not write till he heard from me,—& I regretted I had not drawn from him a promise

253. ᴵ More exactly, *un*packing, perhaps, as the move from the Hermitage, Great Bookham, to Camilla Cottage, in West Humble, seems to have been in progress (see L. 263, pp. 50–2).   ² See iii, L. 242 n. 9 and L. 249 n. 1.

254. ᴵ An editorial error (see also L. 251 n. 1).
    ² An inadvertent error in writing.

I now rejoice I did not mention. I entreat every day to see your hand—till I give you mine. The day wants its sanction & blessing ⌐with me¬ till you have communed with me.

I have no news yet from the Queen's House. Her Majesty is probably much occupied, as this week is a very full one for her. I remain wholly within till her commands arr[ive] though my dear Father offers me his carriage for my comm[issions.] But he is within also himself, & therefore I have not to murmur, you will believe. He is now reading to me his great poem,[3] which I really & sincerely think admirable.

James has just brought me Mr. Mathias's account. He is most industrious to serve & oblige. I never saw him look better, nor in better humour: he is resigning the fruitless & baleful study of politics for the more useful & calm one of mathematics: & 'tis amazing the good effect | already produced.

I am extremely glad you have done with Mrs. Bailley.[4] ⌐The *extra* was a most happy idea.¬ I tremble a little at the Memoir of Mr. Ochlie[5]—but heartily wish to know the worst. I want all the Memoirs immediately. We can then calculate fairly our income,—& what will it be that we cannot contentedly live within, if our darling preserves his health, & our Cottage may still afford us its beauty?

Be careful of *me* in yourself, mon bien aimé!—I find [nothing] any where to recompense me for separation.

I know not why you have sent me M. de la fayette's declaration,[6] though I am much pleased to read it again. I always see his name with deep interest, & true admiration, but not, at this period, without alarm even to affliction—yet I will never endeavour to interfere with any step you plan in consequence of your ideas of right, & your instinctive feelings. The *name* here must not be pronounced!—The C^t de Rivaroli[7] is a reigning favourite!—*alas, that* prejudice can be so powerful!—Adieu!—

[3] CB's poem on Astronomy (iii, L. 221 n. 6).

[4] Catherine Bailey (iii, L. 124 n. 2), owner of The Hermitage at Great Bookham.

[5] The carpenter (iii, L. 122 n. 7).

[6] Lafayette, liberated from Olmütz on 19 Sept. 1797, had been required to declare that he would not re-enter Austrian territories without special permission. M. d'A's copy of this Declaration (signed 26 July 1797) is preserved in the Scrapbook (Berg) 'Fanny d'Arblay and friends. France. 1679–1820', p. 89. A translation was published in *The Times* (28 Sept. 1797).

[7] Antoine Rivaroli (1753–1801), who in 1792 had attacked Lafayette and the Constitutionalists in *De la vie politique, de la fuite et de la capture de M. Lafayette* (ii, L. 94 n. 3).

255   *for* 3 November 1797

For Mrs. Phillips

A.J.L. (Diary MSS. vi. 5028–[51], Berg), written at West Humble on 20 Mar. 1798 for SBP, at this time at Belcotton, County Louth

Three double sheets and six single sheets 4to foliated (1) (2) (3) (4) (5) (6) The first four pages (5028–[31]) are in the hand of M. d'A   24 pp.

Edited by FBA, the 2nd. ds. or p. 5 (5032), *annotated and dated*: Court Letter —97.

Edited also by CFBt *and the* Press.

A second version of this Court Journal, a copy in hand of M. d'A, is extant in the West Humble Letter Book (Osborn), pp. 16–47   33 pp.

Westhamble, March 20. 1798.

Though I have so lately sent off a close Scribbled sheet to my most beloved Susan, I will begin again, that I may endeavour to have any long promised Court history ready for the next pacquet. It must be a mere abridgment of my first design, for so much time has since passed, that my memory has had fresh gleanings that have taken place of the earlier, but what I can recollect currently, I will no longer leave to the chance of escaping me.

Nov. 3ᵈ 1797.

I went up stairs to Miss Planta's room, where while I waited for her to be called, the charming Princess Mary passed by attended by Mʳˢ Cheveley.[1] She recollected me, & turned back, & came up to me with a fair hand graciously held out *to* me. 'How do you do Madame d'Arblay?' She cried 'I am vastly glad to see you again. And how does your little Boy do?'

I gave her a little account of the Rogue, & she proceeded to

255. [1] Louisa Laetitia Niven (d. 18 June 1807) was one of the daughters of John Niven (d. 1771), a page who had served at Court since 1748 (R.H.I., Windsor). Louisa had married *pre* 1771 Jerningham Cheveley (d. 26 Mar. 1786) 'of Gray's Inn, one of the cursitors for London and Middlesex' (*GM* lvi¹. 270). The mother of three children, she was employed from 5 June of that year as wet nurse to Prince Ernest Augustus at an annual salary of £200 and she continued in the royal service until her death (R.H.I., Windsor; Stuart, *Dtrs. Geo. III*, pp. 261, 326–31; and Papendiek, i. 61–2).

enquire about my new Cottage, & its actual state. I entered into a long detail of its bare walls & unfurnished sides, & the gambols of the little man unincumbered by cares of fractures from useless ornaments, that amused her good humoured interest in my affairs very much; & she did not leave me till Miss Planta came to usher me to Princess Augusta.

That adorable Princess received me with a smile so gay & a look so pleased at my pleasure in again seeing her, that I quite regretted the *etiquette* which prevented a *chaste embrace*. She was sitting at her toilette having her Hair dressed. The Royal Family were all going, at night to the Play.[2] She turned instantly from the glass to face me & insisted upon my being seated immediately. She then wholly forgot her attire & ornaments & appearance, & consigned herself wholly to conversation, with that intelligent animation which marks her character. She enquired immediately how my little Boy did, & then with great sweetness after his Father—& after my Father.

My first subject was the Princess Royal, & I accounted for not having left | my hermitage in the hope of once more seeing her R[l] Higness before her departure.[3] It would have been, I told her, so melancholy a pleasure to have come merely for a last view, that I could not bear to take my annual indulgence at a period which would make it leave a mournful impression upon my mind for a twelve month to come. The Princess said she could enter into that, but said it, as if she had been surprised I had not appeared. She then gave me some account of the ceremony; & when I told her I had heard that her R[al] H[ss.] the Bride had never looked so lovely,[4] she confirmed the praise warmly, but laughingly added 'T'was the Queen dressed her!— You know what a figure she used to make of herself, with her odd manner of dressing herself; but Mama said: 'Now really, Princess Royal, this one time is the last; & I cannot suffer you to make such a Quiz of yourself; so I will really have you dressed properly. And indeed the Queen was quite in the right, for every body said she had never looked so well in her life.

---

[2] *The Merchant of Venice* was to be played that evening at the Theatre Royal, Covent Garden.   [3] On 2 June (iii, L. 238 n. 2).

[4] Cf. *The Times* (19 May 1797): 'The BRIDE looked extremely well; indeed, it was generally remarked, that her Royal Highness never appeared to so much advantage.'

The dress was described in the *Morning Chronicle* (19 May 1797) as 'a most

The word *Quiz*, you may depend was never the Queen's! I had great comfort however in gathering, from all that passed on that subject, that the Royal Family is persuaded this estimable Princess is happy. From what I know of her disposition I am led to believe the situation may make her so. She is born to preside; & that with equal softness & dignity; but she was here in utter subjection, for which she had neither spirits nor inclination. She adored the King, honoured the Queen, & loved her sisters, & had much kindness for her Brothers: but her style of life was not adapted to the royalty of her nature, any more than of her Birth; & though she only wished for power to do good, & to confer favours, she thought herself out of her place in not possessing it. |

I was particularly happy to learn from the P^ss Augusta that she has already a favourite friend in her new Court, in one of the Princesses of Wirtemberg wife of a younger Brother of the hereditary Prince,[5] & who is almost as a widow, from the Prince her husband being constantly in the Army. This is a delightful circumstance, as her turn of mind & taste, & employments accord singularly with those of our Princess.

I have no recollection of the order of our conversation; but will give you what morsels occur to me as they arise in my memory.

The terrible mutiny[6] occupied us sometime. She told me many anecdotes that she had learnt in favour of various sailors, declaring with great animation, her security in their good hearts, however drawn aside by harder & more cunning heads. The sweetness with which she delights to get out of all that is tremendous or forbidding in her rank is truly adorable. In speaking of a sailor on board the St Florenzo,[7] when the

superb and beautiful embroidery of white and silver', the sleeves, 'tastefully decorated with quilted lace, and silver embroidered bands'. The train was of 'silver tissue, trimmed with silver fringe'. Over this the Princess 'wore a superb mantle of scarlet velvet, trimmed all round with the finest ermine'; and on her head, 'a coronet, set with brilliants'.

[5] Prince Louis, Duke of Würtemberg (1756–1817), had married in 1797 Henriette of Nassau-Weilburg (1770–1857).

[6] The Mutiny at the Nore, virtually at an end by 13 June 1797.

[7] Originally a French ship *La Minerve*, which, sunk on 19 Feb. 1794 at St. Fiorenzo, Corsica, by the English batteries, was later weighed and commissioned as the *San Fiorenzo*. A ship of 42 guns, she was placed under the command of Sir Harry Burrard Neale (1765–1840), 2nd Bart. (1791), Admiral of the White (1830), and figured largely in histories of the Mutiny at the Nore as one of the loyal ships. Though forced for a time to sham mutiny, she escaped under fire on 30 May 1797.

Royal Family made their excursion by sea from Weymouth, she said: 'You must know this man was a great favourite of mine for he had the most honest countenance you can conceive; & I have often talked with him, every time we had been at Weymouth, so that we were good friends: but I wanted now in particular, to ask him concerning the mutiny; but I know I should not get him to speak out while the King & Queen & my sisters were by; so I told Lady Charlotte Bellasyse[8] to watch an opportunity when he was upon deck & the rest were in the cabin; & then we went up to him, & questioned him. And he quite answered my expectations; for instead of taking any merit to himself from belonging to the St Florenzo which was never in the mutiny, the good creature said he was sure there was not a sailor in the navy that was not sorry to have belonged to it, & would not have got out of it as readily as ǀ himself, if he had known but how.'

We had then a good deal of talk about Weymouth:[9] but it was all local; & as my Susan has not been there it would be too long to scribble.

'One thing,' cried she, her eyes brightening as she spoke, 'I must tell you, though I am sure you know it a great deal better than me; that is about Mr Locke's Family, & so I think it will give you pleasure. General & Mrs Harcourt[10] went lately, to see Norbury Park & they were in the neighbourhood somewhere near Guildford, sometime, the General's Regiment being quartered there abouts. And the family they were with knew the Locke's very well & told them they were the best people in

See, e.g., James Dugan, *The Great Mutiny* (1965), pp. 215, 242–3, 247, 250. The ship was again placed in the service of the King at Weymouth in October 1798 (*Later Corr. Geo. III*, iii. 146).

[8] Lady Charlotte Belasyse (1767–1825), eldest daughter and co-heiress of Henry (1743–1802), 3rd Earl Fauconberg of Newborough (1774). According to the R.H.I., Windsor, she was a Lady of the Bedchamber (1798–1806) to the younger daughters of George III and later (1819–1825) to Mary, Duchess of Gloucester. She was to marry in 1801 Thomas Edward Wynn *later* Belasyse (*fl.* 1801–26) of Newburgh Priory, Yorkshire.

[9] In the summer of 1789 (6 July–14 Sept.) FB had accompanied the royal family to Weymouth (*DL* iv. 293–324).

[10] William Harcourt (1742/3–1830), who was to succeed his brother George Simon (1736–1809), Viscount Nuneham, as 3rd Earl Harcourt. With a parliamentary and military career (see *DNB*), he held a succession of appointments at court, e.g., extra Groom of the Bedchamber (1766), Master of the Robes (1808–9), Master of the Horse to the Queen Consort (1809–18), Keeper of Windsor Great Park (1815). At this time he was Colonel of the 16th (Queen's) Regiment of Light Dragoons.

On 3 Sept. 1778 he had married Mary (*c.* 1750–1833), daughter of William

the world. They said Mr Locke was always employed in some benevolent action; & all the family were good: & that there was one daughter quite beautiful & the most amiable creature in the World & very like Mrs Locke.'

'The very representative, cried I, of *both* Parents!' And thus encouraged, I indulged myself without restraint or conciseness in speaking of the sweet Girl & her most beloved & incomparable Parents, & Mr William, & all the house in general.

This led to the young couple, M^r & Mrs Charles,[11] & I had great pleasure in affirming the perfectly amiable & domestic life of the latter, & how unspoiled retirement had found her, though it had taken her from shew & dissipation. 'I think that quite natural, cried the sweet Princess, when any one knows what the Country & retirement are.

And she then related one mighty interesting anecdote of a daughter of Lady Sidney[12] who since her mariage, has never returned to Town, but to lie in, though she had lived continually at public places before.

The Princess Elizabeth now entered but she did not stay. She came to ask something of her sister relative to a little fête she was preparing, by way of a collation in honour of the Princess Sophia, who was twenty this day. She made kind enquiries after my health, &c—& being mistress of the Birth-day fête, hurried off, & I had not the pleasure to see her any more. |

[*Here ends the part that was copied by M. d'Arblay; the remainder of the Journal is in Madame d'Arblay's hand.*]

I must be less minute, or I shall never have done.

My charming Princess Augusta had just renewed conversation, when the Princess Sophia came in, to speak to me. She had a pair of spectacles on, which, with her uncommonly

---

Danby (1712–84), of Swinton, Yorks., and widow of Thomas Lockhart (*c.* 1740–75) of Craig House near Edinburgh.

[11] Cecilia Margaret Locke *née* Ogilvie (iii, L. 171 n. 10; L. 177 n. 4), daughter of the Duchess of Leinster (1731–1814) and half-sister to the Irish radical Lord Edward Fitzgerald (1763–98). On more than one account, therefore, a person of interest.

[12] Elizabeth Powys (1736–1826), who had married in 1760 Thomas Townshend (1732/3–1800), cr. Baron Sydney (1783), Viscount Sydney (1789). The daughter may have been Frances (1772–1854), who had married in 1794 George Talbot Rice (1765–1852), Dynevor Castle, County Carmarthen, M.P. (1790–3) and Lord Lieutenant of the County (1804–52). By this time she was the mother of three children who, born in London, were baptized at St. George's Chapel, Hanover Square.

young Face,—its shape being as round as a baby's, & its colour as rosy,—had a most comic & grotesque appearance. She came up to me with an air of droll good humour, & was beginning a chat, when the Princess Augusta expressively told her she should see me again afterwards,—& then she scampered gaily off. She is so near-sighted, that she is almost blind; & the Queen now permits her always to wear spectacles. 'And I want her, said Princess Augusta, to wear them at the Play, where we are going to Night; but she is afraid, she says, of some paragraph in the News-papers: but what, I ask her, can they say? *That the Princess Sophia wears spectacles!* Well, & what harm can that do her? Would it not be better they should say it, than she should lose all sight of the performers?'

Admiral Duncan's noble victory[13] then became the theme— but it was interrupted by the appearance of the lovely Princess Amelia,—now become a model of grace, beauty, & sweetness in their bud.[14] She gave me her hand, with the softest expression of kindness, & almost immediately began questioning me concerning my little Boy, & with an air of interest the most captivating. But again Princess Augusta declined any interuptors; 'You shall have Mad^e d'Arblay all to yourself, my dear, soon!' she cried, laughingly; &, with a smile a little serious, the sweet Princess Amelia retreated.

It would have been truly edifying to young ladies living in the great & public world to have assisted in my place at the Toilette of this exquisite Princess Augusta. Her ease, amounting even to indifference, as to her ornaments & decoration shewed a mind so disengaged from vanity, so superior to mere personal appearance, that I could with difficulty forbear manifesting my admiration of such rare excellence. She let the Hair Dresser proceed ǀ upon her head, without comment, & without examination, just as if it was solely his affair, & she only supported a block to be dressed for his service. And when the man, Robinson,[15] humbly begged to know what ornaments he was to prepare the Hair for, She said 'O—there! my feathers,—& my

[13] See nn. 17, 24, below.

[14] H.R.H. the Princess Amelia was at this time a little over 14 years of age.

[15] Daniel Robinson (*fl.* 1793–1817), hairdresser, appears in the Treasurer's Accounts of Her Majesty Queen Charlotte (Add. MSS. 17871–2 and 17889–93, for the years 1793–4 and again from 5 Apr. 1812–1 Jan. 1817, for which service he was paid an annual salary of £150).

Gown is blue—so take what you think right.' And when he begged she would say whether she would have any ribbons, or other things, mixed with the Feathers & Jewels, she said '*You* understand all that best, Mr. Robinson, I'm sure,—there are the things—so take just what you please.' And after this, she left him wholly to himself, never a moment interrupting her discourse, or her attention, with a single direction.

She had just begun a very interesting account of an officer that had conducted himself singularly well in the mutiny,—when Miss Planta came to summon me to the Queen. I begged —& most willingly obtained—permission to return afterwards for my unfinished narrative, & then proceeded to the White Closet.

The Queen was alone, seated at a Table, & working. Miss Planta opened the Door, & retired without entering. I felt a good deal affected by the sight of Her Majesty again, so graciously accorded to my request;—but my first & instinctive feeling was nothing to what I experienced, when, after my profoundly respectful reverence, I raised my Eyes, & saw in hers a look of sensibility so expressive of regard, & so examining, so penetrating into mine, as to seem to convey—involuntarily— a regret I had quitted her,—This, at least, was the idea that struck me, from the species of look which met me,—& it touched me to the Heart, & brought instantly, in defiance of all struggle, a flood of Tears into my Eyes. I was some minutes recovering,—& when I then entreated her forgiveness, & cleared up, the voice with which she spoke, in hoping I was well, told me she had caught a little of my sensation, for it was by no means steady. Indeed, at that moment, I longed to kneel & beseech her pardon for the displeasure I had felt in her ⎮ long resistance of my resignation; for I think, now, it was from a real & truly honourable wish to attach me to her for-ever. But I then suffered too much from a situation so ill adapted to my choice & disposition to do justice to her, opposition, or to enjoy its honour to myself.—Now—that I am so singularly—alas, *nearly* singularly!—happy, though wholly from my perseverance in that resignation, I feel all I owe her, & I feel more & more grateful for every mark of her condescendsion either recollected, or renewed.

She looked ill,—pale & harrassed; the King was but just

returned from his abortive visit to the Nore,[16] & the inquietude she had sustained during that short separation, circumstanced many ways alarmingly, had evidently shaken her: I saw with much—with deep concern her sunk Eyes & spirits. I believe the sight of me raised not the latter. Mrs. Schwellenberg had not long been dead;[17] & I have some reason to think she would not have been sorry to have had me supply the vacancy: for I had immediate notice sent me of her death by Miss Planta, so written, as to persuade me it was a Letter by command. But not all my duty, all my gratitude, could urge me, even one short fleeting moment, to weigh any interest against the soothing serenity—the unfading felicity of a Hermitage such as mine.

We spoke of poor Mrs. Schwelly, & of her Successor, Mlle Bachmeister,[18] & of mine, Mrs. Bremyre:[19] & I could not but express my concern that Her Majesty had again been so unfortunate; for Mlle Jacobi had just retired to Germany, ill, & dissatisfied with every thing in England.[20] The Princess Augusta had recounted to me the whole narrative of her retirement & its circumstances. The Queen told me that the King had very handsomely taken care of her. But such frequent *retirements* are heavy weights upon the royal bounty! I felt almost *guilty* when

---

[16] A triumphal procession down the Thames to the Nore to celebrate Admiral Duncan's victory and to view the captured Dutch ships was planned for 30–31 Oct., on the first of which days His Majesty proceeded as far as Greenwich. Fitted up superbly, his yacht had 'in the fore cabbin . . . a chair and rich canopy of crimson velvet, with gold fringe, for the KING to sit on; the floor is covered with carpeting, and the chairs for the Noblemen who attend him are mahogany, with Morocco leather-seats. In the after-cabin is the State-bed for his MAJESTY to sleep in, with sofas covered with crimson damask in the apartments adjoining for the Gentlemen in waiting' (*Morning Chronicle*, 30 Oct. 1797).

Unfortunately on 31 Oct. the winds grew boisterous and on the heaving Thames the boats pitched and tugged at anchor. 'If the wind had happily been favourable', the *Morning Chronicle* reported on 1 Nov., 'the spectacle would have been beautiful; but they [the ships] durst not carry their canvas, and the storm was so great that the effect on the fresh-water Sailors was extremely ludicrous:—it sickened many a Beau of a water excursion' and few hearts could be found hardy enough to continue the jaunt.

[17] Elizabeth Juliana Schwellenberg, for thirty years Keeper of the Robes to Queen Charlotte, had died on 7 Mar. 1797, aged 69 years (*GM* lxvii. 261–2, 348), and was buried in the German Chapel in the Savoy.

[18] Sarah Charlotte Bachmeister was appointed Keeper of the Robes to Queen Charlotte on 11 Oct. 1797 and continued at a salary of £200 per annum until 2 (?Feb.) 1802. (R.H.I., Windsor).

[19] Margaret Bremeyer (d. 29 Dec. 1806), Keeper of the Robes to Queen Charlotte at a salary of £200 a year from 11 Oct. 1797 to her death (Add. MSS. 17876–84; and R.H.I., Windsor). See also *GM* lxxvi (1806)², 1254.

[20] See i, L. 7 n. 3.

the subject was started.[21] But not from any reproach, any allusion,—not a word was dropt ⏐ that had not kindness & goodness
for its basis & its superstructure at once.

'How is your little Boy?' was one of the earliest questions,—
& how sweet a one to my feelings?—'Is he here?' she added.

'O yes, I answered, misunderstanding her; he is my shadow.
I go no where without him.'

'But—*here*, I mean?'

'O no, Ma'am!—I did not dare presume—'

I stopt, for her look said it would be no presumption! And
Miss Planta had already desired me to bring him to her next
time; which I suspect was by higher order than her own
suggestion.

She then enquired after my dear Father, & so graciously,
that I told her not only of his good health, but his occupations,
—his new work,—a poetical history of Astronomy,—& his
consultations with Herschal.

She permitted me to speak a good deal of the Princess of
Wirtemberg,—whom they still all call Princess Royal. She told
me she had worked her wedding Garment, & *entirely*,—& the
real labour it had proved, from her steadiness to have no help,
well knowing that 3 stitches done by any other would make it
immediately said it was none of it by herself. 'As the Bride of a
widower,[22] she continued, I knew she ought to be in white &
Gold; but as the King's eldest Daughter, she had a right to
white & silver, which she preferred.'

A little then we talked of the late great naval victory; &
she said it was singularly encouraging to us that the 3 great
victories at sea had been 'against our 3 great Enemies, suc-
cessively; Lord Howe against the French, Lord St. Vincents
against the Spaniards,—& Lord Duncan against the Dutch.'[23]

---

[21] The generosity of the pension perhaps depended in part on length of service.
Miss Planta, who was to serve twenty years in all (1792–1812) at a salary of £100,
was retired with a pension of £200. FB's with five years at court was £100. In this
year (see the Treasurer's Accounts of the Queen's Household, 1 Jan. 1797–1 Jan.
1798, Add. MSS. 17875), the Queen paid £700 in pensions.

[22] The Princess Royal had married (18 May 1797) Frederick, the Hereditary
Prince of Würtemberg (1754–1816), a widower, whose first wife (11 Oct. 1780)
had been Augusta (1764–88), niece of George III and sister of Caroline, Princess of
Wales.

[23] Three naval victories were thankfully celebrated at the time: the battle of
the First of June 1794, when Richard Howe (1726–99), cr. Earl Howe (1788),
Commander of the Channel Fleet (1790) defeated the French; secondly, the battle
of St. Vincent, fought on 14 Feb. 1797, when Admiral John Jervis (1735–1823),

PLATE I

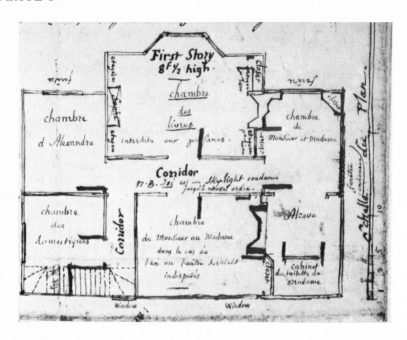

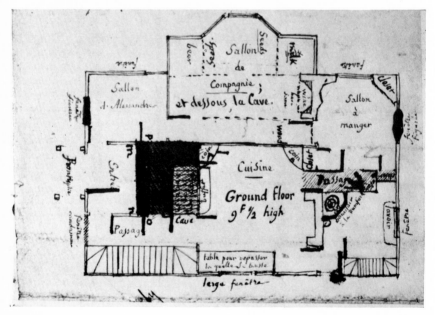

Plans of the interior of 'Camilla Cottage', drawn by M. d'Arblay for Susan Phillips

She spoke very feelingly of the difficult situation of the Orange family now in England,[24] upon this Battle: & she repeated me the contents of a Letter from the Princess of Orange,[25] whose character she much extolled, upon the occasion, to the Princess Elizabeth; saying she could not bear to be the only person in England to withhold her congratulations to the King upon such an occasion, when no one owed him such obligations; but all she had to regret was that the Dutch had not fought *with*, not *against* the English, & ┃ that the defeat had not fallen upon those who ought to be their *joint* enemies. She admired & pitied inexpressibly this poor fugitive Princess.

I told her of a Note my Father had received from Lady Mary Duncan,[26] in answer to his wishing her joy of her Relation's prowess & success, in which she says 'Lady Mary, has been, for some Days past, like the rest of the Nation, drunk for joy.—'! This led to more talk of this singular lady, & reciprocal stories of her oddities.

She then deigned to enquire very particularly about our new Cottage; its size, its number of rooms, & its grounds. I told her, honestly, it was excessively comfortable, though unfinished & unfitted up, for that it had innumerable little contrivances & conveniences just adapted to our particular use & taste, as M. d'Arblay had been its sole architect & surveyor.[27] 'Then I dare say, she answered, it is very commodious, for there are no people understand enjoyable accommodations

Commander-in-Chief in the Mediterranean (1795), defeated the Spanish fleet; and thirdly, the battle of Camperdown, fought on 11 Oct. 1797, when Admiral Adam Duncan (1731–1804), Commander-in-Chief in the North Sea (1795–1801), defeated the Dutch navy.

In 1797 all three were awarded high honours. Admiral Howe was made a Knight of the Garter; Admiral Jervis, cr. Earl of St. Vincent; and Admiral Duncan, Viscount Duncan of Camperdown.

Popular applause is reflected in the newspapers of the day, e.g., the *Morning Chronicle* (18 Oct. 1797) with its account of the occasional stanza added to 'Rule Britannia' and sung with lusty encores at Drury Lane the preceding evening.

[24] In England at this time were William V (1748–1806), Stadtholder of the Netherlands, Prince of Orange-Nassau-Dietz, his wife the Princess Frederica Sophia Wilhelmina (1751–1820), his younger son Frederick William George (1774–99), his elder son William Frederick (1772–1843), and the wife of the latter Frederica Wilhelmina (1774–1837), daughter of King Frederick William II (1744–97) of Prussia.

[25] Apparently, as will be seen, the Princess Frederica Wilhelmina (see above).

[26] Lady Mary's late husband Sir William Duncan (1707–74), Physician in Ordinary to George III (c. 1760), a brother of Alexander Duncan (1703–71) of Lundie, was Admiral Duncan's uncle.

[27] For a picture of the exterior and plans of the interior of Camilla Cottage, see frontispiece, and Plate II.

more than French Gentlemen, when they have the arranging them themselves.'

This was very kind; & encouraged me to talk a good deal of my Partner, in his various works & employments; & her manner of attention was even touchingly condescending, all circumstances considered. And she then related to me the Works of two French Priests,[28] to whom she has herself been so good as to commit the fitting up one of her apartments at Frogmore. And afterwards she gave me a description of what another *French* GENTLEMAN—elegantly & feelingly avoiding to say *emigrant*—had done in a room belonging to Mrs. Harcourt, at Sophia Farm,[29] where he had the sole superintendence of it, & has made it beautiful.

When she asked about our Field,[30] I told her we hoped, in time, to *buy* it, as Mr. Locke had the extreme kindness to consent to part with it to us, when it should suit our convenience to purchase instead of renting it. I thought I saw a look of peculiar satisfaction at this, that seemed to convey pleasure in the implication thence to be drawn that England was our decided, not forced or eventual residence. And she led me on to many minute particulars of our situation & way of living, with a sweetness of interest I can never forget. |

Nor even here stopt the sensations of gratitude & pleasure she thus awoke,—she spoke then of my beloved Susan,—asked if she were still in Ireland, & how the *pretty Norbury* did. She then a little embarrassed me by an enquiry *Why Major Phillips went to Ireland?* for my answer, that he was persuaded he should improve his Estate by superintending the agriculture of it himself, seemed dissatisfactory; however, she pressed it no further. But I cannot judge by what passed whether she concludes he is employed in a military way there, or whether she has heard that

---

28 Unidentified.

29 Sophia Lodge (or Farm), shown in coloured lithographs in the *Repository of Arts, Literature, Fashions* (3rd ser., 1823), ii. 249–50, was situated in the parish of Clewer. Refurbished by Wyatt, it was acquired in 1781 by William Harcourt (n. 10 above) and became part of the Harcourt estates of St. Leonard's Hill near Windsor. During the French Revolution, General Harcourt, and his brother, the 2nd Earl Harcourt, entertained many of their French relatives (see v, Ll. 513, 515), some of whose retinues doubtless provided the gifted interior decorator here referred to.

The editors are much indebted to Mrs. J. K. Batey of Oxford for interesting information about Sophia Farm and the Harcourts.

30 See iii, L. 136, p. 48 and n. 14.

he has retired. She seemed kindly pleased at all I had to relate of my dear Norbury, & I delighted to call him back to her remembrance.

She talked a good deal of the Duchess of York,[31] who continues the first favourite of the whole Royal Family. She told me of her beautiful works, lamented her indifferent health, & expatiated upon her admirable distribution of her time, & plan of life, & charming qualities & character.

She asked me about Mr. Locke & his family, & honoured me with an Ear of uninterrupted attention while I made an harangue of no small length upon the Chief in particular, & the rest in general. She seems always to take pleasure in the quick gratification this subject affords me.

Of her own royal Daughters she permitted me also to talk—especially of my two peculiar idols, the name sakes of our dear female Lockes. And she gave me a long & copious description of the new improvements still going on at Frogmore, with an interesting detail of some surprises the King had given her, by orders & buildings erected in the Gardens during her absence.

But what chiefly dwells upon me with pleasure, is, that she spoke to me upon some subjects & persons that I know she would not for the world should be repeated, with just the same confidence, the same reliance upon my grateful discretion for her openness, that she honoured me with while she thought me established in her service for life. I need not tell my Susan how this binds me more than ever to her. [1]

Very short to me seemed the time, though the whole conversation was serious, & her air thoughtful almost to sadness, when a Page touched the Door, & said something in German. The Queen, who was then standing by the Window, turned round to answer him, & then, with a sort of congratulatory smile to me, said 'Now you will see what you don't expect—The King!—'

I could indeed not expect it, for he was at Blackheath at a Review[32]—& he was returned only to Dress for the Levee. I was so sensible of her sweetness in having me with her at this moment, & seeming to felicitate me that she was able, that,

---

[31] See i, L. 11 n. 22 and iii, L. 199 n. 19.

[32] Cf. *The Times*, 4 Nov. 1797: 'Yesterday morning the KING reviewed the East Kent Regiment of Militia on Blackheath.'

when the dear King entered, & she condescendingly said herself as he came in 'Madame d'Arblay,' I was again over-powered with sudden emotion,—& as the King benignly came up to me, with an 'How do you do, Mad^e d'Arblay?' I was forced to cover my Eyes with both hands, & my Mouth, too, almost convulsed with endeavours to restrain an agitation I wished to feel less palpably. But their goodness is more touching to me than ever, from the knowledge I have how much inconvenience & disturbance they have had renewed from my resignation; for I have no room to tell you long histories I have gathered from Miss Planta—& from the encreasing general distrust of French Emigrants, from which, with such impressive goodness, they seem to mark, by every demonstration of favour, their opinion that my dear & honoured partner deserves exemption. *Imagine* all this & its concomitancies clearer than I have expressed it, my Susan, & you will not wonder I was thus moved by his gracious entrance, & loved voice, & benign Countenance.

The King instantly turned away, & spoke with the Queen, to give me time to recover, but in a manner that shewed his right interpretation of an emotion that must have been misunder-stood indeed to have offended him. He then came back to me, & in a low, but most kind tone of voice, said 'And how does your little Boy do?' Dear, dear King! how sweet was the enquiry! & in how many ways precious to me! It did not, however, much contribute to my stoicism! And again he talked to the Queen, addressing me only between times. He related very pleasantly a little anecdote of Lady Elgin,[33] the Governess of the little Heiress presumptive of these Kingdoms: 'She brought the little Princess, he said, Charlotte, to me just before the Review. She hoped, she said, I should not take it ill; for, having mentioned it to the Child, she built so upon it that she *had thought of nothing else!* Now this, cried he, laughing heartily, was pretty strong! how can she know what a Child is *thinking* of before it can *speak*? But this must be *between ourselves*.'

How dearly condescending this last phrase! My Susan will remember it, & keep the Courtly trait to the singular number.

[33] Martha White (*c.* 1740–1810), daughter of 'Thomas Whyte, Esq. of London, merchant, deceased', had married on 1 June 1759, Charles Bruce (1732–71), 9th Earl of Kincardine (1740), 5th Earl of Elgin (1747). See *Scots Magazine*, xxi. 272. On 18 Jan. 1797 (see *GM* lxvii. 535) she was appointed Governess to Princess Charlotte of Wales, which post she held until 1805 (R.H.I., Windsor). The Princess was 2 years old at this time.

The chearfulness excited by this just derision of overstrained adulation, restored me completely. I was very happy at the fondness they both expressed for the little Princess. A sweet little Creature, the King called her; A most lovely Child, the Queen turned to me to add; & the King said he had taken her upon his Horse, & given her a little ride, before the Regiment rode up to him. ' 'Tis very odd, he added, but she always knows me on Horse back, & never else.' 'Yes, said the Queen, when his Majesty comes to her on Horse back, she claps her little hands, & endeavours to say *Gan pa*' immediately.'

I was much pleased that she is brought up to such simple & affectionate acknowledgement of relationship.

The King then enquired about my Father, & with a look of interest & kindness that regularly accompanies his mention of that most dear person. He asked after his health, his spirits, & his occupations, waiting for long answers to each enquiry; the Queen anticipated my relation of his astronomic work, & he seemed much pleased with the design, as well as at hearing that his *protegé*, Dr. Herschal, had been consulted, & would close the plan. |

He then spoke of My dear Father again, & his present way of life, & said he had been concerned by his not looking well at the ancient music; I told him he had suffered from an incessant cough, but was now quite recovered, & in even remarkably good looks.

I was then a little surprised by finding he had heard of 'Clarentine':[34] he asked me, smilingly, some questions about it, & if it were true, what he suspected, that my youngest sister had *a mind to do as I had done*, & bring out a work in secret? I was very much pleased then when the Queen said 'I have seen it, Sir, & it is very pretty.'

There was time but for little more,—as he was to change his dress for the Levee. But their extreme goodness enabled me, in taking my leave, to express unrestrainedly the warm gratitude I felt for their inappreciable graciousness in permitting me this annual indulgence. Their kindest smiles accepted my homage, & I left their presence more attached to them, I really think, than ever.

I then, by her kind appointment, returned to my lovely &

[34] SHB's novel. See iii, L. 204 n. 9.

loved Princess Augusta. Her Hair dresser was just gone, & she was proceeding in equipping herself. 'If you can bear to see all this nasty work, cried she, pray come & sit with me, my dear Madame d'Arblay.'

Nothing could be more expeditious than her attiring herself, nothing more careless than her examination how it succeeded. But judge my confusion & embarrassment, when, upon my saying I came to petition for the rest of the story she had just begun, & her answering by enquiring what it was about, I could not tell! It had entirely escaped my memory! & | though I sought every way I could suggest to recall it, I so entirely failed, that, after her repeated demands, I was compelled honestly to own that the commotion I had been put in by my interview with their Majesties, had really driven it from my Mind.

She bore this with the true good humour of good sense; but I was most excessively ashamed.

She then resumed the reigning subject of the Day, Admiral Duncan's victory; & this led to speak again of the orange Family: but she checked what seemed occurring to her about them, till her wardrobe woman had done, & was dismissed. Then, hurrying her away, while she sat down by me, putting on her long & superb Diamond Earrings herself, & without even turning towards a Glass, she said 'I don't like much to talk of that family before the servants, for I am told they already think the King too good to them! Besides one is obliged to be so cautious not to have what one says repeated.'

I ventured here to say I flattered myself my Name never would be cited as retailing any information from the royal houses—but she interrupted me with an 'O *you*!' that seemed, sweetly, to say all profession from *you* is superfluous—

She then told me several anecdotes concerning the poor exiled family,—some of which I will venture to give my dearest Susanna—from whose dear & faithful bosom nothing yet ever transpired that had been lodged there in confidence.

The Princess of Orange[35] is, I find, a great favourite with them all; the Prince Frederick[36] also, I believe, they like very much; but the Prince himself[37] | she said, has never, in fact,

[35] Frederica Louise Wilhelmina (1774–1837) of Prussia, wife of William Frederick (below).
[36] Frederick William George (1774–99).
[37] William Frederick (1772–1843), hereditary Prince of Orange.

had his education finished. He was married quite a Boy,[38] but, *being* married, concluded himself a man, & not only turned off all his instructors, but thought it unnecessary to ask, or hear, counsel or advice of any one. He is like a fallow field, that is, not of a soil that can't be improved, but one that has been left quite to itself, & therefore has no materials put in it for improvement.'

She related me several comic stories of his *naiveté*: among others, 'one, said she, I must tell you, that will shew you how little he knows the World, from letting nobody give him any lessons. And he told this to the King himself! He went, he said, to Vauxhall, *incog*:—but, sitting down to supper, they brought him some very good wine, which he did not expect, & drank so much the more from the surprise: & then, he said, there came some very pretty ladies, who were very agreeable; & he got into such spirits, that he talked a great deal with them, & liked them extremely: & he kept with them, chatting & laughing, & very well pleased, & drinking their healths, till, all at once, when he was quite unsuspicious, these pretty ladies became so free, that he saw he was with improper Company! But he determined, he said, to tell it to the King himself, because he knew, else, somebody would make a story of it, & relate it to his Majesty to his disgrace & derision! Now you see, my dear Madame d'Arblay, what sort of a simple man he is, in the ways of the World, to betray such a ridiculous adventure to the King, & get himself laughed at, when, if he had not told it himself, how could it be known? for who else would have told such an anecdote of the Prince of Orange to the King?'

Many people! thought I; but it would not have been so characteristic. ⎪

She then told me that she had hindered him, with great difficulty, from going to a great dinner, given at the Mansion House, upon the victory of Admiral Duncan.[39] It was not, she said, that he did not feel for his Country in that defeat, but that he never weighed the impropriety of his public appearance upon

[38] At the age of 19.

[39] In reporting on the general illuminations, tolling church bells, and 'the joy inspired in the nation by the late glorious Victory', *The Times* (17 Oct. 1797) mentioned celebrations in 'The Admiralty-Office in particular, . . . the Theatres and Opera House, the Mansion House, and that belonging to the Hudson's Bay Company'.

an occasion of rejoicing at it, nor the ill effect the history of his
so doing would produce in Holland. She had the kindness of
heart to take upon herself preventing him; 'for no one, says she,
that is about him dares ever speak to him, to give him any hint
of advice; which is a great misfortune to him, poor man: for it
makes him never know what is said or thought of him.' She
related with a great deal of humour her arguments to dissuade
him, & his *naive* manner of combatting them. But though she
conquered at last, she did not convince.

The Princess of Orange, she told me, had a most superior
understanding, & might guide him sensibly & honourably; but
he was so jealous of being thought led by her counsel, that he
never listened to it at all. She gave me to understand that this
unhappy Princess had had a life of uninterrupted indulgence &
prosperity, till the late revolution; & the suddenness of such
adversity had rather soured her mind, which, had it met sorrow
& evil by any gradations, would have been equal to bearing
them even nobly; but so quick a transition from affluence
of power, & wealth & grandeur, to a fugitive & dependent
state, had almost overpowered her.

A Door now was opened from an inner apartment, where,
I believe, was the grand Collation for the Princess Sophia's
birth Day,[40] & a tall thin young Man[41] appeared at it, peeping,
& staring, but not entering.

'How do do, Ernest? cried the Princess, I hope you are well;
only pray do shut ǀ the Door.'

He did not obey, nor move, either forwards or backwards,
but kept peering & peeping ludicrously enough. She called to
him again, beseeching him to shut the Door; but he was
determined to first gratify his curiosity, & when he had looked
as long as he thought pleasant, he entered the Apartment; but
Princess Augusta, instead of receiving & welcoming him, only
said 'Good by, my dear Ernest. I shall see you again at the
Play.'

He then marched on, finding himself so little desired, & only
saying 'No, you won't; I hate the play.'

I had risen, when I found it one of the Princes; & with a

[40] The *Morning Post and Gazetteer* (3 Nov. 1797) had announced that 'This being
the Birth-day of Her Royal Highness Princess Sophia, who compleats the 20th year
of her age, Their MAJESTIES will receive the congratulations of the nobility.'

[41] Prince Ernest, Duke of Cumberland (1799). See iii, L. 197 n. 13.

motion of readiness to depart; but my dear Princess would not let me.

When we were alone again, 'Ernest, she said, has a very good Heart; only he speaks without taking time to think.'

She then gave me an instance;—the Orange family, by some chance, were all assembled with our royal family, when the news of the great victory at sea arrived—or at least upon the same day. 'We were all, said she, distressed for them upon so trying an occasion; & at Supper we talked, of course, of every other subject: but Ernest, quite uneasy at the forbearance, said to me, "you don't think I won't drink Admiral Duncan's health tonight?" "Hush!" cried I,—"That's very hard indeed!" said he, quite loud. I saw the Princess of orange looking at him, & was sure she had heard him. I trod upon his foot, & made him turn to her. She looked so disturbed, that he saw she had understood him, & he coloured very high. The Princess of Orange then said "I hope my being here will be no restraint upon any body! I know ¹ what must be the subject of every body's thoughts, & I beg I may not prevent its being so of their discourse." Poor Ernest now was so sorry, he was ready to die, & the tears started into his Eyes, & he would not have given his toast after this for all the World.'

The play they were going to was the Merchant of Venice, to see a new Actress just now much talked of, Miss Betterton;⁴² & the indulgent King, hearing she was extremely frightened at the thoughts of appearing before him, desired she might chuse her own part for the first exhibition in his presence. She fixed upon Portia. How I wished for a place to have seen the honoured group as well as the excellent Play & new Actress!

In speaking of Miss Farren's marriage with the Earl of Derby,⁴³ she displayed that sweet mind which her state & station has so wholly escaped sullying; for, far from expressing either resentment or derision at an actresses being elevated to the rank of 2ᵈ Countess of England, she told me, with an air of satisfaction, that she was informed she had behaved extremely well since her marriage, & done many generous & charitable actions.

⁴² Julia Betterton (1779–1850) had made her London debut at Covent Garden on 12 Oct. 1797, when she played Elwina in Hannah More's *Percy* (1777). For her career, see *DNB* under Glover, Mrs. Julia.

⁴³ See iii, L. 231 nn. 4, 5.

She spoke with pleasure, too, of the high marriage made by another Actress, Miss Wallis, who has preserved a spotless character, & is now the Wife of a man of fortune & family, Mr. Campbell.[44]

In mentioning Mrs. Siddons, & her great & affecting powers, she much surprised me by intelligence that she had bought the proprietorship of Sadler's Wells. I could not hear it without some amusement; it seemed, | I said, so extraordinary a combination—so degrading a one, indeed, that of the first Tragic Actress, the living Melpomene, & something so burlesque as Sadler's Wells.[45] She laughed, & said it offered her a very ludicrous image,—for 'Mrs. Siddons, & Sadler's Wells, said she, seems to me as ill fitted as the dish they call a Toad in a hole; which I never saw, but always think of with anger,—putting a noble sirloin of Beef—into a poor paltry batter pudding!'

The Door now again opened, & another royal young man put in his head. He did not stare as long, nor as hard as Prince Ernest, but he looked examining the domain & its contents, &, upon the Princess's saying 'How do do, William?' I recollected the Duke of Clarence.

I rose, of course, & he made a civil Bow to my courtsie. The Princess kept her seat, & spoke to him with a voice of kindness, but a look of absence, that seemed to decline any discourse that might detain him. He loitered about, however, chatting leisurely, & in no haste. She asked him about the house of lords the preceding Evening,[46] where, I found, he had spoken very handsomely & generously in eulogium of Admiral Duncan, of

---

[44] Tryphosa Jane Wallis (*fl.* 1789–1814), a child-actress in Dublin, who, after appearances in Bath, was first seen on the London stage on 10 Jan. 1789 in the title role of *Tancred and Sigismunda* and applauded in many roles thereafter (*DNB*). Her career was suspended on 11 June 1797 when she married at Gladmuir, Haddington, James Elijah Campbell (*fl.* 1795–8), an ensign in the 3rd Regiment of Guards (9 Dec. 1795).

[45] William Siddons (d. 10 Mar. 1808), who in 1773 had married the actress Sarah Kemble (1755–1831), owned in the years 1792–1802 one-quarter of Sadler's Wells, as did Richard Hughes Sr. (d. 1815). Though the first two years of the Hughes–Siddons management had been highly profitable, there were losses in 1796 of *c.* £339 and in 1797, of *c.* £250. Dennis Arundell, *The Story of Sadler's Wells* (1965), pp. 56–7, deduced from the remarks in FBA's text above (*DL* v. 372–3) that Mrs. Siddons had 'probably put up the money to save her husband and the Wells'.

[46] On the opening of Parliament on 2 Nov. an order was tabled in the House of Lords proposing that a Resolution of thanks be presented to Admiral Lord Viscount Duncan for his 'decisive Victory over the *Dutch* Fleet' (*LJ* 41. 422). On 8 Nov. the Duke of Clarence moved that the speech of thanks by the Lord Chancellor and Admiral Duncan's reply be entered in the Journals.

whom they both talked some time. The King, she said, was to
see him that Day. How good, thought I, of the King to see me
too! & I gathered, by their conversation, his Majesty had not
been able to indulge the Princess Sophia with partaking of her
Birth Day collation, so much he had been hurried & engaged,
by the Review, Levee, & Admiral.

Finding he was inclined to stay, the Princess said to me
'Madame d'Arblay, I beg you will sit down.'

'Pray, madam, said the Duke, with a formal motion of his
hand, let me I beg you to be seated.'

I thanked them, but, as he stood himself, declined obeying;
but the Duke then, coming up to me, said 'I must insist,
Madam,—You force me else to leave the room!' & took hold of
me to seat me himself. Of course I then resisted no longer.

'You know—You recollect Madame d'Arblay, don't you,
William?' said the Princess.

He bowed civilly an affirmative, & then began talking to me
of Chesington; & how I grieved poor dear Kitty was gone![47]
how great would have been her gratification to have heard that
he mentioned her, & with an air of kindness, as if he had really
entered into the solid goodness of her character. I was much
surprised, & much pleased, yet not without some perplexity &
some embarrassment, as his knowledge of the excellent Kitty
was from her being the dupe of the *mistress* of his aid de Camp,
Colonel Dalrymple;[48] & as I had heard from her, in a Letter not
long before her death, that the Duke had carried *Mrs. Jordan*[49]
to Chesington, where the poor simple soul had received her as
an honour, & accompanied her about the village, &c!—

The Princess, however, saved me any confusion beyond
apprehension, for she asked not one question; whether from any
previous knowledge of circumstances, or general prudence, or a
desire to shorten the discourse, I cannot tell. She certainly did
not strive to detain him: she never asked him to be seated, nor
spoke when he was silent: & when he moved in towards the
next apartment, she said, with vivacity, 'Pray shut the Door,
William!' which was not violently inviting his stay, or return; I
& shut it, therefore, he did & we were again alone.

---

[47] See iii, L. 247, p. 354 and n. 17.   [48] See iii, L. 247 n. 21.
[49] Dorothea or Dorothy Jordan (1762–1816), generally considered 'the first
actress of her day', became in 1790 the mistress of the Duke of Clarence (*DNB*).

She then talked to me a great deal of him, & gave me, admirably, his character. She is very partial to him, but by no means blindly. He had very good parts, she said, but was so indolent that he never did them justice: 'If he has something of high importance to do, she continued, he will exert himself to the utmost, & do it really well; but otherwise, he is so fond of his ease, he lets every thing take its course. He must do a great deal,—or nothing. However, I really think, if he takes pains, he may make something of a speaker by & by in the house.'

She related a visit he had made at Lady Mary Duncan's at Hampton Court, upon hearing Admiral Duncan was there: & told me the whole & most minute particulars of the Battle, as they were repeated by his Royal Highness from the Admiral's own account. But you will dispense with the martial detail from me! 'Lady Mary, cried she, is quite enchanted with her gallant nephew. I used to look, says she, for honour & glory from my *other* side, the Thanets,[50]—but I receive it only from the Duncans!—As to the Tuftons, what good do *they* do their country?—Why they play all day at Tennis, & learn with vast skill to *notch & scotch & go one!*—And that's what their Country gets from them!'

I thought now I should certainly be dismissed, for a Page came to the Door, to announce that the Duke of York was arrived: but she only said 'very well,—*pray shut the Door.*—' which seemed her gentle manner of having it understood she would not be disturbed, as she used the same words when messages were brought her from the Princesses Elizabeth & Mary.

She spoke again of the Duchess of York with the same fondness as at Windsor. 'I told you before, she said, I loved her like one of my own sisters,—& I can tell you no more! And she knows it; for one Day she was taken ill, & fainted, & we put her upon one of our Beds, & got her every thing we could | think of our-

---

[50] Lady Mary Tufton (1723–1806), eldest daughter of Sackville Tufton (1688–1753), 7th Earl of Thanet, had married in 1763 William Duncan (i, L. 21 n. 5; see also n. 27 above). A brother of Alexander, he was Admiral Duncan's uncle. 'The Tuftons', so slightingly referred to by Lady Mary, must have been the children of her brother Sackville Tufton (1733–86), the 8th Earl (1753), six of whom were living at this time and in their twenties (Lodge, 1845, and Burke's *Extinct Peerage*).

selves, & let nobody else wait upon her,—& when she revived, she said to my Brother 'These are *my* sisters! I am sure they are! They *must* be my own!—'

Our next,—& last interruption I think, was from a very gentle tap at the Door, & a 'May I come in?' from a soft voice, while the lock was turned, & a youthful & very lovely female put in her head.

The Princess immediately rose, & said 'O yes!' & held out her two hands to her; turning at the same time to me, & saying 'Princess Sophia.'

I found it was the Duke of Gloucester's Daughter.[51] She is very fat, with very fine Eyes, a bright even dazzling bloom, fine teeth, a beautiful skin, & a look of extreme modesty & softness & feminine sweetness of character.

She courtsied to me so distinguishingly, that I was almost confused by her condescendsion, fearing she might imagine, from finding me seated with the Princess Augusta, & in such close conference, I was *somebody*.

'You look so fine, & so grand, cried she, examining the Princesse's attire, which was very superb in silver & Diamonds, that I am almost afraid to come near you!'

Her own dress was perfectly simple, though remarkably elegant. 'O!—I hate myself when so fine! cried Princess Augusta; I cannot bear it,—but there is no help,—the people at the play always expect it.'

They then conversed a little while, both standing, & then Princess Augusta said 'Give my love to the Duke, (meaning of Gloucester) & I hope I shall see him by & by; & to William,—' (meaning the Duke's son.)[52]

And this—which was not a positive request that she would prolong her visit,—was understood, & the lovely Cousin made her Courtsie, & retired.

To me, again, she made another, so gravely low & civil, that I really blushed to receive it, from added fear of being mistaken. I accompanied her to the Door, to shut it for her;—& the moment she was out of the room, | & out of sight of the Princess Augusta, she turned round to me, & with a smile of extreme civility, & a voice very soft, said 'I am so happy to see you!—

---

[51] Sophia Matilda (1773–1844).
[52] Prince William Frederick (1776–1834). See also i, L. 3 n. 8.

I have longed for it a great, great while—for I have read you with such delight—& instruction—so often!——'

I was very much surprised indeed,—I expressed my sense of her goodness as well as I could, & she courtsied again, & glided away.

'How infinitely gracious is all your royal highnesses house to me! cried I, as I returned to my charming Princess; who again made me take my seat next her own, & again renewed her discourse—

But I can write no more,—for I have far exceeded my proposed limits; my beloved Susan's call upon me for Letters[53] invigorated my memory, & my slackened Pen, & I have now given my Court account I hope at as full length as she can desire.

I stayed on with this delightful Princess till near 4 o'clock,—when she descended to Dinner. I then accompanied her to the head of the stairs, saying 'I feel quite *low* that this is over! How I wish it might be repeated in *half a year* instead of a year!—'

'I'm sure & so do I!' were the last, & most kind words, she condescendingly, & with energy uttered.

I then made a little visit to Miss Planta, who was extremely friendly, & asked me why I should wait another year before I came. I told her I had *leave* for an Annual visit, & could not presume to encroach beyond such a permission. However, as she proposed my calling upon her, at least, when I happened to be in Town, or at Chelsea, I begged her to take some opportunity to hint my wish of admission, if possible, more frequently.ⁱ

This was no black Day, for its end answered to its beginning: I went from the Palace to our good & dear James, who, notwithstanding his democratic quarrels with Mr. Pitt & the Administration, is always sincerely pleased at the graciousness he sees me experience from the Royal family, & takes great delight in hearing any particulars of my reception. I was engaged to meet our dear Esther there, & found also Sally, Marianne, Edward, our good aunt, & Letty Brookes. Mr. Burney was engaged. My visit occupied all the discourse, except some sad & stolen, & yet soothing minutes with dear Esther upon a subject always nearest & dearest to our hearts!—

---

[53] SBP's request is missing but printed in *FB & the Burneys*, pp. 265–93, is her gratitude for the Journals that FBA sent in 1798 (the above journal was not written until *c.* 20 Mar. 1798).

In the Evening, I went to the Play with James & Marianne. It was a new Comedy called Cheap Living, by Reynolds, or Morton;[54] & full of absurdities,—but at times irresistibly comic. I found, upon returning to Chelsea, that my dearest Father had been as happy as myself: he had had *Mr. Windham* with him for an hour or two. It was singular he should come while I was at Chelsea, yet on the only Day I was abroad.

The next Day I returned to my Cottage & Cottager—with my dear bantling,—& found all here smiling & dear.——

Very soon afterwards, I had a Letter from Miss Planta, saying she had mentioned to Her Majesty my regret at the long intervals of annual admissions;—& that Her Majesty had most graciously answered *'She should be very glad to see me whenever I came to Town.'* Think of my gratitude for a sweetness of condescendsion so flattering to my sincerely devoted feelings of affectionate reverence towards this most truly gracious & benign Queen!—I am sure I need not paint them to my Susanna—nor tell what so well she will conceive as the warmth of my acknowledgements in answer.

256   [West Humble, *c.* 10 November 1797]

For Mrs. Francis (*later* Broome)

Copy in hand of CBF (Barrett, Eg. 3693, f. 69–b) of a part of a conversation between FBA & CB *c.* 10 Nov. 1797 on the subject of CBF's intended marriage to Ralph Broome

Single sheet 8vo   2 pp.   written on a cover *addressed*: To / Mr Hoole Senr / N° 7. Pavement / Moorfields   wafer

I come on an Embassy to ⟨to⟩ demand one of the y^r *princesses* in Marriage—
The princesses!—
'I come to demand one of y^r royal *daughters* in Marriage
'1. of my daughters
why there is but one—what Sall?—w^t does any body want Sall?—⟨sh⟩ Charlotte
CHARLOTTE

[54] It was not Thomas Morton (*c.* 1764–1838) but Frederic Reynolds (1764–1841) who wrote *Cheap Living*, a play first performed at Drury Lane on 21 Oct. 1797.

even so. Charlotte is demanded in Marriage & I am come the ambassadress on the occasion.

for Gods sake w^t does this mean!—

I come f^{rm} her wth the most dutiful duty that ever ⌐ was dutified —& at the desire of the gentleman with the most respectfull respects & a ⌐demand of y⌐ request for y^r friend^p—

A person you don't know—

dont know.

nor I—

does James.

nor James. nobody knows him, & yet a person very generally known—even eminently known—

No less than Mr Broome the celebrated author of — — — — Simkin[1]—

'a compleat smile played all over his features.

a long acquaintance renewed—

he held back—on acc^t of the children

I don't see that—they are so well off.[2] & the £4000 is very handsome—

---

256. [1] On Wednesday evening (8 Nov.) FBA's widowed sister Charlotte Francis had 'contracted herself' (see FBA's full history of the affair, L. 273, pp.118–24) to Ralph Broome (1742–1805), author of the *Letters of Simpkin the Second, Poetic Recorder, of all the proceedings upon the Trial of Warren Hastings* (1789); *An Elucidation of the Articles of Impeachment preferred by the last Parliament against Warren Hastings, Esq., late Governor of Bengal* (1790); *A Comparative Review of Mr. Hastings and Mr. Dundas, in War and Peace* (1791); and *An Examination of the Expediency of continuing the Present Impeachment* (1791). Though in *Observations on Mr. Paine's Pamphlet Entitled the Decline and Fall of the English System of Finance* . . . (1796) Broome argued for the stability of the Bank of England, he made use of the occasion to introduce levelling or 'democratic' sentiments with respect to society—ideas by no means pleasing to CB—and not more palatable to the Burneys at this time were his personal attacks on Burke in *Strictures on Mr. Burke's Two Letters. Addressed to a Member of the Present Parliament* (1796). Alluded to by CB and FBA are Broome's 'democratic' or radical publications which, probably unsigned, the editors have not been able to identify. On the next day CBF went to West Humble and, after apprising FBA of the event, asked her to inform CB and JB and to beg their concurrences and good offices with respect to settlements. On the next morning (10 Nov.), the sisters went to London, and FBA, finding her father alone at Chelsea, broached the subject in a dialogue, part of which she later wrote down or possibly dictated for CBF's information and comfort.

[2] By the will of her first husband Clement Francis (P.C.C., Fountain 607), CBF was provided with an annuity of £100 a year with added annuities of £100 a year for each of her three children. She was therefore quite independent.

To James Burney

A.L. (PML, Autog. Cor. bound), 10 Nov. 1797
Double sheet 4to   4 pp.   trimmed   wafer
Addressed: To / Capt Burney, / N° 26. James Street, / Westminster
Also L., incomplete copy in hand of CBF (Barrett, Eg. 3700A, f. 122–b)
single sheet folio   2 pp.   [*begins*:] I went to Town this morning   [*ends*:]
& so on ad infinitum.

Westhumble,
Nov. 10. 97.

My dear Brother,

I went to Town this Morning Express upon business of deep
importance¹   My first embassy was to our dear Father; my
second, & last, to my dear James. I had the good fortune to find
the one, at home, alone, & kindly comfortable; but the other
I missed wholly.

What I communicated verbally to the one, I must now write
to the other.

In one of your last Letters to me, written upon the birth of
Your little Daughter,² you asked 'Which of us will be the next to
add to our Family?'

I now Answer,—Charlotte.

Not, indeed, by a Son & Heir,—for that she has; nor yet by
a fair Daughter, for that she has also: but by a full grown new
Relation, commonly known by the appellation of a Son in Law.

Now who do you think it is?

What say you to Mr. Mathias?³

But no,—he can't determine upon Matrimony.

What say you to young Hoole?⁴

But no,—he's rather too much in the dumpus way.

257. ¹ The sisters in their mission to London (see L. 256 n. 1) missed James, but,
returning on the same day to West Humble and arriving at 10 o'clock, they 'set
about Letter writing immediately' (L. 273, pp. 120), FBA composing the 'long
epistle to James' (above).

² JB's letter of 1 Dec. 1796 (iii, L. 217 n. 14), announcing the birth of his daughter
Sarah, had concluded with such a query.

³ Thomas James Mathias (iii, L. 148 n. 5), one of CBF's oldest friends. Cf. i,
L. 28 n. 2.

⁴ The Revd. Samuel Hoole (*c.* 1758–1839; see i, L. 33 n. 31).

What say you to Benjamin La Trobe[5]

O No,—he's gone to America.

What say to John Repton?[6] |

No,—he lives too far from London.

What say you to Mr Broome?[7]

Why I never saw him in my life.

What say you to Mr. Tremmels?[8]

He's rather too short.

What say you to Dr. Crighton?[9]

Why I don't like rhubarb & Jollop.

Why you are so difficult there's no knowing how to satisfy you. But what say you, once more, to this Mr. Broome?

Why, I tell you, I never saw him.

Why no more Did I.

Then what puts him into your head again?

Nay, nay, he i'n't in *my* head! Not but what he might be without much offence, for he has a pretty good one of his own.

Pho, pho,—what's his head,—or your's,—to the business? Tell me if you mean any thing,—or nothing, about Charlotte?

Why Charlotte will have it *his* head is in conjunction with her heart, so that, some how or other, I can't tell how to separate them.

Well, then, the case stands thus:

Last Wednesday,[10] this gentleman demanded her opinion of their passing the winter together: &, if agreeable, the next winter also, & the next: Spring, Summer, & Autumn included: & so on, ad infinitum.

Charlotte smiled, & said an Agreeable Companion by a fire side was exactly to her taste. |

Why then, says he, ask your sister d'Arblay to ask your papa's consent, & your Brother's approbation.

So I will, says she.

So on Thursday (yesterday) she comes post to Westhamble.

5 Benjamin Henry Latrobe (i, L. 11 n. 27).

6 John Adey Repton (1775–1860), son of Humphry Repton (i, L. 7 n. 25), whom CBF would have known in Aylsham.

7 Ralph Broome (L. 256 n. 1).

8 Conjecturally Robert Tremmels (*c.* 1742–1802) of Northumberland Street, the Strand, a 'gentleman' coal-merchant and lately a widower (*GM* lxvi (1796), 445; and lxii (1802), 274).

9 Alexander Crighton (1763–1856), M.D. See iii, L. 164 n. 8.

10 On 8 Nov.

And Friday (this Day) off we set together post for the Metropolis.

one stopt by the way, incog: the other proceeded to Chelsea & to James Street.

Thus much for Prelude.

Now for *Seriosity*.

This Gentleman was of Mr. Hastings' Coterie in India,[11] & returned thence the same year as Mr. Francis did, who was intimately acquainted with him, & very fond of him. Charlotte has known him many years, & with much regard. He is a widower, &, she thinks, about 50. He was Judge Advocate in India, & Persian Translator. She does not know what his fortune is, but it is evidently above a mere competency, & he proposes settling upon her an Estate he inherits from his Father worth 4 thousand pounds. He is the author of the admirable & celebrated Simkin's Letters, & of more serious tracts relative to Mr Hastings' trial, & to Indian finances.

Now all else I have been able to gather I have told my dear Padre, & you may converse with him, privately, upon the affair: but you must withold it from *all others* till she has informed Esther & Charles & Susanna of her new prospects. This she has made me, also, promise.

I was excessively vexed indeed at missing you, as I wished earnestly to discuss the business with you: but if you can go to

[11] Ralph Broome (1742–1805) was the third son of Ralph Broome (1714–68) of Bushton, Wiltshire (see L. 261 n. 3).

In the Scrapbook (Berg) 'Fanny Burney and family. 1653–1890', p. 68, there is an editorial note (supplied by JCBTM for her mother CFBt, FBA's first editor) stating that Ralph Broome 'had been sent to India as a Cadet' and that 'his rapid acquirement of the Oriental languages (and his superior talents) caused him to be employed in that country as Judge Advocate. He had no personal acquaintance with Mr. Hastings but returning to England during the progress of the Trial . . . he attended . . . every afternoon formed his own judgment upon the arguments brought forward, and the next morning . . . Simpkin's humorous & versified narration always appeared in *Bell's Weekly Messenger*' (see L. 256 n. 1). By an extramarital relationship with 'an Indian lady', he had a daughter Miriam (*c.* 1781–*c.* 8 Sept. 1840), whom he brought to England with him *c.* 1785 and later (1803) married to his nephew Ralph Broome (1781–1838), a lawyer or advocate like most members of the family. On 24 Feb. 1790 Broome himself had married Lucy Jeffreys, one of the daughters of 'the late Rich. J. esq. of Penkelly, Brecknock' (*GM* lx (1790), 179); and she must have been the Mrs. Ralph Broome who died at Hot Wells, Bristol, on 15 Nov. 1796 (*GM* lxvi (1796), 971).

Such are some of the relevant facts. Broome was a great versifier with a flair for occasional poetry. His Persian translations, however, seem not to have reached print. His publications of 1796 (see L. 256 n. 1) were, from CB's point of view, offensively 'democratic' in tone.

Chelsea on Sunday Evening, she means to be there, & will be particularly happy to meet you.

My Father has been infinitely kind, & said Charlotte had conducted herself so unexceptionably since she was in her own power, that he would not interfere in her decision. |

I saw your very sweet Babe this morning, & kissed her for my Alex. Give my love to Mrs. B[urney] & many thanks for her kindness in my runaway visit. Adieu, my dearest James.

I believe him to be a remarkably agreeable man. His poetry, certainly, is full of Wit, & of the first comic cast.

258   West Humble, 14 November [1797]

To Mrs. Phillips

A.L. (Berg), 14 Nov.
Double sheet 4to   3 pp.   wafer
[*Not addressed but sent with a pacquet of letters, probably franked.*]

Westhamble—Nov. 14th

The immense pacquet I enclose from our Esther will give my beloved Susan the grand regale of this dispatch—My royal adventures must be postponed,[1] & my alexandriana, & wait till I can sit down for an Hour to my pen,—which I have never done since my arrival hither,[2] nor yet for one quarter of that time. The quantities of new arrangements, making & re-making in succession, from various changing motives for the alterations, with the helplessness of poor Betty in never satisfying the dear Boy away from me, occasion my whole Day to be regularly occupied by domestic employments: & the afternoon we devote to each other, my Monsieur working incessantly till then in his field. Thus, since here I have been, *not a Letter* have I written!— this delicious little Plague, now in my arms & pretending to drive a phaeton *ike Mitty Locke*—must soon learn a new lesson, or adieu to all but himself for his Mammy! since at present, he

258. [1] FBA's account of her audience of 3 Nov. 1797 with the Queen was written only on 20 Mar. 1798 (see iii, L. 255).
    [2] At Camilla Cottage, West Humble, to which the d'Arblays had moved in mid October 1797.

so accustoms his little person to be always with me, that 'tis nearly a tragedy to get rid of him. And the little Soul, even now, while he torments my Pen, & distracts my attention every second, by jumping up & down every other minute from my lap, looks so guiltless of mischief, there is no being very enraged, & such a picture of perfect happiness there is no help for loving to look at it. — — — Ah my Susan!—if an idea that has struck Esther is founded—how must I dwell in perspective upon such another little winning angel to endure what precedes its appearance! My dearest—dearest Susan!—what a flood of tears the very idea cost me when first started to me! yet only at first—for your Children are all three just what should make one wish for ˡ a fourth,—only that their *travelling* is so cumbersome, & so cruel—However, let the real truth be known to us at once, for a thousand reasons, I beseech: Surely—surely, *if so*, the English Journey will be in time for the confinement!— I die to hear more, & for this greatest of all satisfactions—

I have a long history also to relate, of *surprising adventures* not my own,³—but a commission given me for that purpose has been withdrawn, & lies now dormant for further orders.

As to M. de la F[ayette], m. d'A. reserves to write wholly upon that subject himself. An idea he has formed of visiting him⁴ is the only *personal* draw back I experience to even perfect happiness!—but the thought of the Sea—& the feelings of my Father—& the possible ill-will & false suggestions & imaginations which may be raised at C[our]t give me dreadful uneasiness when this scheme is agitating. Mr. Locke thinks it ill-judged, ill-timed, & wholly unnecessary. It cannot but be ill-thought of *here*, perhaps to serious mischief, in times so critical —for where now do Emigrés find refuge out of Great Britain? They are to be banished even from Hamburgh!—

Poor M. de N[arbonne] was on the point of returning to his Country—when this barbarous new revolution broke out.⁵ We have had, at least, the satisfaction to hear he is still safe in Swisserland. This news does not come from himself! nor ONE WORD!—but, lastly, from M. le Baron de Cadignan,⁶ aide de

³ Doubtless CBF's plans for remarriage.
⁴ Presumably at Wiltmold *près* Ploën in Holstein (ii, 'Commentary', pp. 186–7). M. d'A's letter to SBP was written 16 Nov.–17 Dec. 1797 (Berg).
⁵ See iii, L. 247 n. 10.
⁶ Ann-Gérard Dupleix de Cadignan (*c.* 1772–*pre* 1815), falconer to the comte de

Camp to M. de la F[ayette], who writes it to M. d'A. from Hamburg, whither he had voyaged to meet & embrace the liberated General & his fellow Captives.

This morning M. Bourdois[7] has been here, to a *lunch dinner*, & M. d'A is walked off with him, to accompany part of the way back—He is clever & gay & pleasant, & seems entirely friendly & well disposed | to good,—& he has brought the most welcome news to M. d'A That he has procured the passage of a few lines to his uncle, acknowledging the receipt of the sweet Letters we have mentioned to you.[8] The lines were sent unsealed, unsigned, undated, & written as from a mere acquaintance: but the hand will be known, & the caution understood, & therefore they will give great satisfaction to that excellent uncle.

It was cruelly provoking to me, that the week I was called upon to spend at Chelsea, preparatory to my royal interview,[9] was just the week the very charming Princesse, & the dear M. de Lally spent at Norbury. once I saw them here, whither they came through all the mud, & once at Norbury, (morning & Eve of the only day I had left) & I thought them more interesting than ever. And her tender affection for my Susan is as warm & as sweet as when she saw her almost daily.

I have now an opportunity to send this, & will not lose it, as Esther's pacquet she tells me is pressing,—

God bless my own dearest & ever most beloved Susanna!— & send her fortitude for all as well as patience!—

Love to the Major—

& to my dear Fanny & Norbury & Willy.

I shall impatiently indeed wait for your next!—my own dear —dear Susan!—

remember me to your good Susan[10] too—

Her poor sister[11] is not well—but is removed to Mickleham— with her Family. The other house was found too damp, I believe. Betty's Sister[12] is removed to Mickleham also.

Provence, Lt.-Col. of dragoons and aide-de-camp to General Lafayette, was the son of Charles Dupleix (1738–79), *dit* baron, *puis* comte de Cadignan.

[7] See iii, L. 245 n. 10.

[8] See iii, Ll. 245 and 246.

[9] From Saturday 28 Oct. to 3 Nov. 1797.

[10] SBP's servant Susan Adams (iii, L. 216 n. 11).

[11] Ann *née* Adams, wife of Robert Newton (iii, L. 237 n. 6; iv, L. 262 n. 1).

[12] Mary *née* Parker, the wife of John Woodyear (iii, L. 237 n. 5).

To Mrs. Francis (*later* Broome)

A.L. (Diary MSS. vi. 5016–[19], Berg),   16 Nov. 1797
Double sheet 4to   4 pp.   *pmks* DARKING   17 NO 97   17 NO 97
red wafer
Addressed: Mrs. Francis, / Hill Street, / Richmond, / Surry.
Endorsed by CBF: Sister d'arblay / 1797.
Edited by CFBt *and the* Press.

Westhamble,
Nov. 16th 1797—

Your Letter[1] was most welcome to me, my dearest Charlotte,
& I am delighted Mr. Broome & my dear Father will so
speedily meet. If they steer clear of politics, ⌐any pose Mr.
Broome takes must no doubt dismay terribly, in opposition
⟨total⟩ to his¬ there can be no doubt of their immediate exchange of regard & esteem. At all events, I depend upon Mr.
B[roome]'s forbearance of such subjects, if their opinions clash.
Pray let me hear how the interview *went off*. And how it was
managed with Sarah & Marianne. And whether you have *come
to the point* with Charles & Etty, or if You wish me to write to them.
And what you determine upon with respect to our sweet Susan.
And a thousand (at least) other things, which I am very impatient to hear. And how our ever good & trusty James has
performed since the commencement. & whether the Egyptian
Pyramids had a proper attention paid them on the Monday's
conference.[2]

I need not say how I shall rejoice to see you again, my
dearest Charlotta—nor how charmed we shall both be to make
a nearer acquaintance with Mr. Broome—but ¦ for Heaven's
sake, my dear Girl, how are we to give him a Dinner? Unless
he will bring with him his poultry,—for our's are not yet arrived
from Bookham:—& his Fish,—for our's are still at the bottom of
some pond we know not where;—& his Spit, for our Jack is yet

259.   [1] This letter is missing.
      [2] Unexplained. Probably a family allusion or joke.

without one;—& his Kitchen Grate,—for our's waits for Count Rumford's next pamphlet[3]—

Not to mention his Table Linnin, for he will think else we have borrowed Mr. Givyn's[4] to begin a fresh 6 weeks with.—

And not to speak of his knives & forks, some ten of our poor original twelve having been massacred in M. d'Arblay's first essays in the art of Carpentering.—

And to say nothing of his large spoons, the silver of our plated ones having feloniously made off under cover of the whitening brush.—

And not to talk of his Cook,—our's being not yet hired—

And not to start the subject of Wine,—ours, by some odd accident, still remaining at the Wine Merchant's!

With all these impediments, however, to *convivial* hilarity, if he will eat a quarter of a joint of meat (his *share*, I mean!) tied up by a packthread, & roasted by a log of wood on the Bricks,— & declare no potatoes so good as those dug by M. d'Arblay out of his Garden,—& protest our small beer gives the spirits of Champaign,—& make no enquiries where we have deposited the Hops he will conclude we have emptied out of our Table-Cloth—& pronounce that bare walls are superior to Tapestry —& promise us the first sight of his Epistle upon visiting a new built Cottage— —We shall be sincerely happy to receive him in our Hermitage—where I hope to learn, for my dearest Charlotte's sake, to love him as much as, for his own, I have very long admired him.

Manage all this, my dear Girl, but let us know the day, as we have resumed our Norbury Park excursions, where we were yesterday. God bless you, my love, & grant that your happiness may meet my wishes: ever & ever yours most affectionately— F. d'A.

N.B. Mr. Broome will have full scope left to his Imagination to furnish our rooms, as well as to paper our Walls.

direct, Westhamble, near Dorking, Surry.

---

[3] Count Rumford's much-advertised essay 'On the Construction of Kitchen Fire-places' (iii, L. 218 n. 10), published eventually in three sections between 1799 and 1802, contained matter on jacks and kitchen grates (*Works*, iii. 235 ff., and 462–7).

[4] This allusion is lost.

To Mrs. Waddington

L. printed in 'A Burney Friendship', *Monthly Review*, viii (Sept. 1902), 160–1.

My Dear Marianne,—

You will accept me then, according to my offered condition, *for better for worse*; I, too, must *accept the acceptance*, though not without some unpleasant feelings in finding how strongly the worser part seems to you the larger.

I thank you for your bathing advice and anecdotes, and rejoice with my whole heart in the flourishing state of your lovely little ones.[1] I know how much yours is wrapt up in them, nor can I wonder that your invariable excessive tenderness to them should have produced the effect you mention, in the terrible test to which you put my heroic little namesake. Gratitude is not a taught, but an instinctive feeling, and its operations are commonly among the earliest promises from which we may flatter ourselves with future good. Much of this delightful anticipation is already accorded me, and I cherish all its offerings and its augurs as my (almost) first happiness.

M. D'Arblay is much gratified that you are an enthusiast for Count Rumford, whom he studies night and day.[2] Our few chimneys in our little cottage are all of his construction, and the tiny laundry is so also, with alterations which we flatter ourselves will be improvements by M. D'Arblay himself: for in studying both the Count's works and his own convenience *con amore* he thinks he has still ameliorated the new economy. Passionately fond of every species of architecture, however humble, he has given his whole mind to the business, in the progress of our lilliputian home, and I own I think most prosperously. The only drawback to the (apparently *minor*, but, from their daily use, *major*) comforts of his ingenuity is, that it has made it impossible to settle any previous estimate for the undertaking. In being his own and sole surveyor, so many

---

260. [1] Of four daughters born, there were surviving at this time Frances, aged 6, and Emelia, aged 3.
  [2] Volume i of *Essays, Political, Economical, and Philosophical* (1796) had included a treatise 'of Chimney Fireplaces' (iii, L. 218 n. 10).

contrivances and alterations have occurred to him in the course of the building, and so many mistakes to rectify from inexperience, that I own I look forward with some tribulation to the sum total of the affair.[3]

A very short time ago my Architect had reason to expect some justice from his own country that might have rendered his extravagance a mere bagatelle, for he was much pressed by a friend,[4] to endeavour to recover something from the shipwreck of his family's fortunes during the late seemingly favourable turn for moderate and just characters. But what a reverse from all such prospect is now produced by the banishment unheard of almost all in public life who had manifested virtue of principle, or courage against tyranny.[5] M. D'Arblay has had the grief to learn, within these few months, the death of his only brother,[6] who was extremely dear to him, though adverse fate and circumstances had separated their interests like their persons.[7]

I have not met with the poem 'Leonora.'[8] We have lately read Watkin's 'Tour to Constantinople,'[9] and find in it much entertainment. We are preparing a place for the chimney-piece so kindly sent me by your Uncle Bernard (Dewes),[10] and which I shall so love to look at! I am obliged most reluctantly to have it shortened from the impossibility of having a chimney to fit its size in so small a habitation. But I shall touch nothing of *Her* work—it would be sacrilege. . . .

Did I mention to you that when I was at Windsor[11] General Manners[12] inquired most *tenderly* after *Miss Port?* assuring me

[3] Some seventeen years later M. d'A estimated the cost of Camilla Cottage at £1,300, not including his own labour as architect and 'surveyor'. See a copy (Berg) by AA of a draft letter 'never sent' to William Locke, Jr. [May 1814].

[4] Felix Ferdinand (iii, L. 245 n. 3; L. 247 n. 13).

[5] The *coup d'état* of 18 Fructidor (4 Sept.). See iii, L. 247 n. 10.

[6] François Piochard, Sʳ de Blécy, had been killed in 1795 (iii, L. 245, p. 340).

[7] M. d'Arblay laments his losses and disappointments in a letter (Berg) to SBP, 16 Nov. 1797.

[8] In the years 1795–6 no less than five poets, including Sir Walter Scott, published English translations of Gottfried August Bürger's poem 'Lenore' (1773). Both the Hon. William Robert Spencer and Sir John Thomas Stanley had entitled their versions 'Leonora'.

[9] Thomas Watkins, *Travels through Swisserland, Italy, Sicily, the Greek Islands to Constantinople* . . . (1792).

[10] A work in 'stained Paper' by Mrs. Delany recently sent by her nephew Bernard Dewes (iii, L. 124 n. 8). It is described in vol. iii, L. 191; its eventual disintegration, in vol. iv, L. 315.

[11] Evidently in her visit of July 1796 (iii, L. 199).

[12] Robert Manners (1758–1823), Equerry to the King (1784–1800), was a grandson of the 2nd Duke of Rutland.

he should never call her by any other name. Your late admirer, whom you yclept Taffy,[13] was *not* there, nor any of that set you remember, but Mr. Digby[14] and Lord Walsingham.[15] But the Rutland swain[12] spoke your virgin name, which he has determined shall live with you for ever, with his very softest smile.

Mrs. Locke and all her charming family always inquire about you with unceasing interest. You will say, with a little uneasy smile, I am sure you cannot *unceasingly* answer them! But they know me too well to be hurt by my want of writing punctually, and too ill, woe is me! to expect from me in that respect anything better. You amuse yourself very much with playing upon me what you call my approbation of brevity; but you mistake widely; I do not recommend to you to *practise*, but to *excuse* it. Mark that, dear Marianne!

261

West Humble,
10 December 1797

To Doctor Burney

A.L.S. (Diary MSS. vi, not numbered, Berg), 10 Dec. [17]97
Double sheet 4to   4 pp.   *pmks*   DARKING   12 DE 97   12 DE 97
wafer
Addressed: Dr. Burney, / Chelsea College, / Middlesex.
Endorsed by CB: Fanny—ab^t / Charlotte's 2$^{d.}$ match
Annotated, p. 1: ⟨Saratina⟩—O [*out?*]

Decr 10.th —97 West Hamble.

My dearest Padre,

I am shocked inexpressibly—nay, alarmed, at poor Charlotte's situation. A confidential Letter from good James has just given me an insight into the present apparent posture of affairs.[1] James has behaved with the courage & probity that,

---

13 Unidentified.
14 The Hon. Stephen Digby (i, L. 21 n. 8; iii, L. 199).
15 Thomas De Gray, 2nd Baron Walsingham (iii, L. 199 n. 10).

261. 1 Family letters on the subject of Ralph Broome were in later years searched for at the request of CBFB and destroyed. Missing from the Burney Papers therefore are letters of this time from JB, EBB, and CB to FBA, as well as family letters to CBF.

from his infancy, you have so often told me were the marked features of his first opening character. But this poor thing is *fascinated,*—& *how,* from your joint pictures of the Object, & from a few words of Hetty's (who says 'I know only the exterior of this Gentleman, which is neither striking for elegance nor gentility') *how,* I say, I cannot well imagine. His first attraction, the Fame of his sportive Genius, I can easily enter into; indeed it *more* than reconciled my mind at the beginning to the thoughts of the union; but how that can operate against all charm of manner, all sympathy of taste, & all *liberality* of kindness,—can only be attributed to that eternal wonder-raiser, *the wanton God who pierces Hearts.* Charlotte, of a truly chaste & gentle mind, never has been inflamable—never, before, lost sight of the conveniencies of life from any system that could approach to romance.—She may now, indeed, suppose this Match will only enlarge those conveniencies,—but I did not believe she would ACT upon mere supposition; & both you & James use nearly the same words in stating He MAY be rich—but he MAY be poor. ——I have been so ill at ease about her, that, having accidentally a long téte à tete with Mr. Locke, who called to take me, with only my little Alec, an airing the other morning, that I related to him the affair, in order to beg his opinion as to the money transactions, & your power as a Trustee.[2]

His opinion confirmed my worst fears—my dearest Father will burn what I shall write. After most attentively hearing me, 'Depend upon it, he said, he is *not* a rich man. If there *can* be a *doubt,* treat it as a *certainty.* A rich man never leaves a doubt.'

I told him Charlotte had informed me, that though he proposed to settle upon her an hereditary estate worth £4000, he could not do it, he had said, till *after marriage,* from a clause in his Father's Will.[3]

---

[2] CB was a Trustee of 'the Norfolk marriage settlement' dated 18 Jan. 1786, whereby Clement Francis had settled £7,500 on his wife Charlotte Ann *née* Burney.

A document (BM Eg. 3708, ff. 105–9) goes on to recite that '£2000 Consols (part of the £7,500) was sold out by Charles Burney and Robert Francis at the request and for the benefit of Broome & wife under a Decree in Chancery leaving £5,500 stock no more in the name of the Trustees'. This sum was to be divided equally among the three Francis children. CB remained a Trustee until his death (1814).

[3] In a will dated 30 Dec. 1767 and proved 30 May 1768 in the Archdeaconry Court of Wiltshire (a copy of which the County Archivist has kindly supplied), Ralph Broome 'the elder' (d. 1768) of Bushton bequeathed to his third son, Ralph,

This was a thing quite new to his Ears, he answered, & added, 'It is so singular, that he OUGHT to produce the Will, & to give personal security for his own conduct *after marriage* in keeping to his professions.'

As to your power as a Trustee, he said he had no doubt of its validity: & that no change could be made in the disposition of the money to which you were Trustee, without your consent. 'It would else, he said, be *no* trust. The word *Trustee* would lose its meaning.' And he added 'I think Dr. Burney will be *perfectly right* to refuse his consent while any mystery remains as to an adequate settlement, or any mistery as to his *positive* situation.'

Mr. Locke is so extremely lenient in his judgement, that I could not forbear writing you this opinion, my dearest Padre, though I ˡ entreat you to quote it to *no one*, unless you should think proper to do it to James, in your mutual confidential consultations. Mr. L[ocke] thinks no better of a *stock-jobber* than you do,—& fears his ultimate aim is but to possess what he can obtain for the dangerous, destructive purpose of gaming with it in the alley! — —

I have ventured to write *twice* to this poor thing—endeavouring to excite her own caution, & awaken some surmises, though without naming them,—for I believe she shews her Letters to Mr. B[roome]—at least I know she wishes to have only such as she can shew: I have therefore been very circumspect, & not hinted at the terrible conjectures I have just written you, lest they might blast all her future comfort in our intercourse. I have earnestly begged, however, to see her again, either here or at Richmond. I would then venture further. My first Letter of this kind has been sent near a fortnight, yet remains unanswered. My second is only written now, since the receipt of what I have mentioned to you from James. They both are worded in the most softening manner as to the Man I could devize—for I have

the freehold estate of Tytherton Kellaways in the parish of Bremhill and that of Nuthills in the parish of Calne.

Though special clauses of the will gave leave to settle Nuthills as a jointure on a wife or wives (as conjecturally it may have been settled on Broome's first wife, L. 257 n. 11), no such clauses were inserted with respect to the Tytherton estates, which, nevertheless, seem eventually to have been settled on Charlotte (Burney) Francis, presumably by the deed she mentions in her letter (Berg) of 1 Mar. 1798 to FBA. In any case a survey and evaluation of the Tytherton estates, dated 1820, are to be found among the legal documents relating to Ralph Broome (d. 1805), his widow (d. 1838), and her family (Barrett Collection, Eg. 3708, ff. 86–144).

NO hope the marriage will not take place, I can only wish her to leave *money matters* to better heads.

How I pity her, from all I can gather, I cannot express! Simple, Unsuspicious, unforseeing as she is, what may not a man of his deep & acute abilities, well studied, too, in the law,[4] do with her? Just what he pleases. She is proud of being his choice, & thinks it an honour to obey him already. This I saw at first, but with an idea it might give mutual happiness: he loves to declaim; she is contented to listen & admire; he wants adulation, not sociality,—she pays ⏐ the homage as his due, without feeling its exaction. All this, therefore, might have done well, had he been the Man of perfect worth & honour his elucidation made me expect to find him.—But—helas!—

Let me now thank you very much for the Examiner,[5] which I think most satisfactorily done for the Information in politics, & most deservedly for the slaps at Morning Chronic. I should like to see how the latter bears such blows.[6] It is rather more used to *INFLICTION*, as yet, than to *endurance*. The comparison of the Chief *seceder* to Mart. Scrib: made me laugh heartily.[7] Nevertheless, I would not pique those Gentlemen to return again. All goes so much more smoothly from their retreat, that I wish them Green fields & rural walks to the end of the Session. I was glad of the Letter to Lord Moi[ra], with whom

---

[4] See L. 257 n. 11.

[5] CB had sent FBA the four opening numbers of the new weekly periodical *The Anti-Jacobin; or, Weekly Examiner*, the Prospectus of which (20 Nov. 1797) explained its chief purpose and function as a defence of government against 'JACOBINISM' in all its shapes.

Conceived by George Canning and his friends (who wrote as well the brightest of the satirical verses), contributed to by knowledgeable members of the government, including Pitt himself, and edited by William Gifford (1756–1826), later editor of the *Quarterly Review*, who had as his special responsibility the sections headed LIES, MISREPRESENTATIONS, and MISTAKES, as culled from the opposition papers the *Morning Chronicle*, *Morning Post*, and *Courier*, the *Anti-Jacobin* continued as an effective defence of government policy until July 1798. Accounts of it are given by Dorothy Marshall, *The Rise of George Canning* (1938), pp. 175–89; and by Draper Hill, *Mr Gillray* (1965), pp. 64–71.

[6] Discovering by 17 Jan. 1798 who their assailants were, the *Morning Chronicle* soon enlisted satirists whose essays sometimes, in contemporary opinion, rivalled those of the anti-Jacobins. See Draper Hill, op. cit., p. 69; and *Lord Granville Leveson Gower | (First Earl Granville) | Private Correspondence | 1781 to 1821*, ed. Castalia, Countess Granville (2 vols., 1916), i. 197–8.

[7] The chief 'seceder' or absentee from Parliament at this time was Charles James Fox. In the first number of the *Anti-Jacobin* he had been compared to '*Jack*, in SWIFT's History of *John Bull*—who, by the advice of his friend *Habakkuk* [i.e. Erskine], fairly hangs himself, in hopes that certain persons will come with the greatest possible eagerness to cut him down'. '*Jack* has hung some time: we do not yet understand that there is any probability of his being cut down.'

I was extremely angry indeed. Mrs. Cooke had just been with
me, & had told me she had never read so mischievous &
abominable a speech in Parliament.[8] We will take the utmost
care of the papers, & thankfully return them by the next
opportunity.—Poor Mrs. Rishton's pacquet is a cruel history.[9]
It ought to be addressed to our poor *Charlotte*, to let *her*, while
yet free, see what incessant torment & anguish a lordly,
domineering, selfish Husband occasions. Your Collection of
learned Wights at the Royal Society stopt my breath—though
the '*Nothingists*' gave it me back.[10] But I delight in the comf.
Letter from Hershall.[11] There, indeed, is knowledge & pre-
eminent merit breath-ful!—But how frightened I am at your
idea of 80£ for the new assessment![12]—we have never yet paid
any Tax, but for Powder,[13] & quite tremble in the dark.—

I doat on your carrying Mrs. Crewe to Burlington House.[14]—
My Chevalier & notre Petit want to embrace you—*velly much*—

FBA, unaware of the modern attribution to Arbuthnot of 'Law is a Bottomless
Pit', part 1 of *The History of John Bull*, yet knew that it was written by one of the
Scriblerians.

[8] The *Anti-Jacobin* of 30 Nov. (as well as those of 4 and 11 Dec.) took issue with
the Earl of Moira, who in the House of Lords on 21 Mar. 1797 had given notice of
a motion respecting Ireland and who on 22 Nov. had urged more lenient
measures than those advocated and practised by government (*Parl. Hist.* xxxiii.
1058–63; and *AR* xxxix (1797), 238–43). The motion was rejected 72 against 20.
As the Earl's recommendations stretched to Catholic Emancipation for Ireland,
the reaction of the Mrs. Cookes (i.e. the vicars' wives) of the land could be expected.

[9] Maria's 'cruel history' is extant in the series of confidential letters she addressed
to FBA (see *Catalogue* and iii, L. 222 n. 10; L. 242 n. 4). The 'pacquet' here referred
to is missing but in a letter (Eg. 3697, ff. 293–6b) of 25 [Apr. 1799] she explains
that by the terms of separation her husband had allowed her '£300 Clear' per
annum.

[10] Lost with the relevant letter is CB's account of the meeting of the Royal
Society, on Thursday 30 November at Somerset Place, with a dinner following at
the Crown and Anchor (*Morning Chronicle*, 1 Dec.).

[11] In Burney idiom the word *comfortable* meant *friendly* in a homely, hospitable,
trusting, and family fashion; and William Herschel's letter of 28 Nov. 1797
(Osborn) provided, besides solicited technical information on astronomy, invitations
for a repetition of CB's visits to Slough.

[12] On 4 Dec. 1797 Pitt had proposed a trebling of the assessed taxes on houses,
windows, dogs, clocks, and watches (*Parl. Hist.* xxxiii. 1068). The Triple Assessment, extended and modified in various ways later (see L. 263 n. 3), received its
third reading on 3–4 Jan. 1798 in the Commons, where it carried by 202 against
127, and was assented to by the Lords, after long debate, on 12 Jan. 1798. See *AR*
xl (1798), chap. xiii.

[13] Pitt's new Ways and Means Bills, see *AR* xxxvii (1795), 178–9, had included
a tax on powder. The only exemptions were 'clergymen not possessing one hundred
a year, subalterns in the army, and officers in the navy, under the rank of masters
and commanders'.

[14] This was the beginning of many visits by CB to the Duke of Portland.

My love to Sally—Dearest sir Yours ever & ever most dutifully
& affectionately

F. d'A.

I hope you had [*wafer*] at Mrs. Ma [*wafer*]

262   [West Humble,]—17 December 1797

To Mrs. Phillips

A.L. (Berg), –17 Dec. [17]97
Originally a double sheet 4to, of which the first leaf is cut away and
missing 2 pp.   wafer
Addressed: Mrs. Phillips, / Belcotton, / Drogheda

. . . [Mrs. Newton] seems a most good & gentle creature, &
reminded me of my favourite Susan [Adams] very much.[1] She
said that her sister who is lately dead had been long in ill
health, & could not be expected to recover. She spoke with
great affection of your Susan [Adams], but kindly said she could
not wonder she could not leave her good mistress & the fine
child, though she knew it was hard to her to quit her friends &
country. I was very glad to see her, & she had an ardent desire
to see our cottage. I told her I knew Susan would be very
happy she had found her way to us, & she seemed delighted I
should convey an account of her to her dear sister. I introduced her little Richard to my Alex,—but though almost
exactly of an Age, they each hung back, ashamed, & afraid of
one another. Nevertheless, a few Cakes passed between them,
which though the one gave, & the other received, by holding
out the little hand as distant as possible from the body, would
soon have brought them into greater intimacy, had more time
been allowed. Mr. Newton, she said, was very well.— — —
My beloved Susanna's *Decr 7th* is just arrived—it is now

262. [1] The caller was Ann *née* Adams (iii, L. 237 n. 6) of Epsom, who had
married Robert Newton of Mickleham. Their son Richard William, baptized at
Dorking on 27 May 1795, was five months younger than AA.
   The third Adams sister, who had died at Swansea, was either Elizabeth or
Rebecca (iii, L. 222 n. 27).

Decr 17th—97 What satisfaction & ease its opening has occasioned I cannot express—I was just writing to Esther, & instantly mentioned my relief[2]—which will be her's truly *de même*.—Thank God! — — It was truly kind, my dearest darling, to write so speedily, for the fear was haunting me—& however I might have sought consolation had my apprehensions been verified, I again *thank God*! they are not.— —Yet—sorrows *told & untold*—& sleepless nights! — — — alas—alas!—that health so precious—a life so invaluable—a Being so beloved — — I must run—run—run—

This long pacquet will make amends, I trust, for the two short ones. As to the sweet Amelia's history[3]—it is ill worth recounting, reading, or remembering. It was *strange* in all ways, in some unaccountable:—I must not dilate uncommissioned—but probably some Notes upon the subject will now be sent you. If not, at least assure yourself that *she* was concerned in it is all that could give it interest. The affair given for you, & withdrawn,[4] must make another pacquet, either before or after the royal. According as I am desired. It will be too long for any joint business.

I cannot understand the draw-backs there are to seeing Janey Paney[5]—nor why ¦ my Susan should fear loving anew—Shut not your heart from whatever would call forth its affections, my beloved Susanna—I should rejoice with *all* mine in finding you had met with a new claimant worthy exciting its sensibility—Tell me about this, & tell me you will not resist your impulse for the deserving & affectionate friend of your Norbury. About him, too, we are quite in arrears.

Love to the Major, & to my Fanny, & Norbury & Willy. All our Race is well.

God bless you, my most dearly loved—take more care of yourself than a *Bride Elect*, or you are cruel indeed! to *me* far from alone, though I can never help putting *me* first—but it is not because I see not my partners—our Etty—our Mrs.

---

[2] SBP's letter of 7 Dec., apparently dispelling the fears her sisters had conceived of her pregnancy (see L. 258), is missing.

[3] Probably the preliminaries to the marriage arranged between Amelia Locke and John Angerstein (*c.* 1774–1858), which was to take place on 2 Oct. 1799.

[4] Preliminaries to CBF's marriage to Ralph Broome (1742–1805), which was to take place on 1 Mar. 1798.

[5] Molesworth's jealousy was the difficulty, as SBP was to explain in her letter (Berg) of 5–19 Jan. 1798, printed in *FB & the Burneys*, pp. 265–72.

Locke—our Padre—but you will *not* be cruel—you *will* take care of your Children's invaluable mother—& *try*, at least, to sleep—try to *repeat* something by heart,—that has often helped me in my days of toil & nights of watchfulness.[6] If you have not regular poems ready, try *songs*,—Italian airs—nay, overtures & sonatas. *Pray* try, my Susan! My Eyes ache to think of yours! God forever bless & preserve you!

Not one word *in haste* for reading in this Packet—

263   West Humble, December 1797

To Mrs. Phillips

A.J.L. (Diary MSS. vi. 5020–[27], Berg), Dec. 1797
Originally three or more double sheets large 4to, of which only the first two are extant 8 pp. numbered [1], 3, 5, 7
Edited by CFBt *and the* Press.

Westhamble—Dec^r——97

This moment I receive, through our Heart's dearest Friend, my Heart's own Susanna's Letter.[1] I grieve to find she ever waits anxiously for news—but always imagine All things essential perpetually travelling to her, from so many of our House, all in nearly constant correspondence with her. This leads me to rest quiet as to *her*, when I do not write more frequently—but as to *myself*, when I do not *hear* I am saddenned even here—even in my own new Paradice—for such I confess it is to me;—& were my most beloved Susan on this side the Channel—& could I see her most dear—dear Face, & fold her to my breast—I think I should set about wishing nothing but to continue just so.—For circumstances, pecuniary ones I mean, never have power to distress me, except I fear exceeding their

---

[6] To this advice SBP was to reply in her letter of 5–18 Jan. 1798 (Berg): 'I do *try* to sleep with all my power; I am very thankful when I succeed—I have not left untried all you propose—but *en fait de vers*, one poem constantly forces itself on my recollection nearly to the exclusion of every other—the Hymn to Adversity—I think I *feel the Iron hand scourge*—and the train of thoughts wch follow are not friendly to rest—.'

263. [1] Possibly SBP's letter of 28 Nov., of which only a copied excerpt survives (Berg).

security. And that fear these times will sometimes inflict. We know not yet what will be our taxes, &c—nor what our means of answering such calls. Our great Bills are yet unsettled,[2]—& all promised to be discharged next January. This, at least, will let us know our situation, & that is always the first point towards accommodating ourselves to its demands. But I very much apprehend our Building will ALL ways be dear to us! So many ideas were awakened during its raising that inevitably occasioned extra-work, that our first estimates can but little avail us. The new threefold assessment of taxes has terrified us rather seriously: though the necessity, & therefore justice of them, we mutually feel. My Father thinks his own share will amount to 80 pounds a Year![3] —— We have, this very Morning, decided upon parting with 4 of our new windows. A great abatement of *agremens* to ourselves, & ¦ of ornament to our appearance; & a still greater sacrifice to *l'amour propre* of my Architect, who indeed, his fondness for his edifice considered, does not ill deserve praise that the scheme had not his mere consent, but his own free proposition.

My Babsy was not *at Court*, my Susan, but I shall defer that narrative to give first what I am sure will have first place with you, our own & our family's history; as I have already briefly hinted all went well.[4]

Your idea that my Builder was not able to conduct us hither I thank God is wholly unfounded. His indiscretion was *abominable*, but so characteristic of his constant fearlessness that any thing can annoy his health, that I will tell it you. Some little time before, he brought me home a Dog, a young thing, he said, which had hit his fancy at Ewell, where he had been visiting M. Bourdois,[5] & that we should educate for our new House Guard. It is a *barbette*, &, as it was not perfectly precise in cleanliness, it was destined to a Kitchen residence till it should be trained for the Parlour. This, however, far from being resented

---

[2] See L. 260 n. 3.

[3] On 20 Dec. 1797 proposals were made to extend the Triple Assessment (L. 261 n. 12) to include male servants, carriages, and pleasure horses. The bill, entitled 'An Act for granting to His Majesty an Aid and Contribution for the Prosecution of the War', was given Royal Assent on 12 Jan. See *CJ* 53: 137, 178–9, 229; also *The Times* (21 Dec. 1797).

[4] The narrative of FBA's audience with the Queen on [3 Nov. 1797], although here inserted chronologically, was not written until 20 Mar. 1798.

[5] See iii, L. 245 n. 10.

by the young stranger, as an indignity, appeared to be still rather too superb, for *Muff* betook to the Coal hole, & there seemed to repose with native ease. The Purchaser, shocked at the rueful appearance of the curled Coat, once white, but now of Jetty blackness, & perhaps piqued by a few flippancies upon the delicacy of my Present, resolved, one night, to prepare me a divine surprise for the following Morning: &, when I retired to my downy Pillow, at Eleven o'clock, upon a time severely cold, walked forth with the unfortunate delinquent to a certain Lake you may remember ¹ nearly in front of our Bookham habitation, not very remarkable for its lucid purity, & there immersed poor Muff, & stood rubbing him Curl by Curl, till each particular one was completely bathed. This business was not over till near midnight,—& the impure water which he agitated, joined to the late hour, & unwholesome air, sent him in with a kind of shivering, which was speedily succeeded by a dreadful attack of pain in the head, & a violent & feverish & rheumatic cold. This happened just as we were beginning to prepare for our removal.[6] You will imagine, untold, all its alarm, & all its inconveniencies; I thank God it is long past, but it had its full share, at the moment, of disquieting & tormenting powers.

We quitted Bookham with one single regret—that of leaving our excellent neighbours, the Cookes.[7] I do not absolutely include the fair young Lady in my sorrow!—but the Father is so worthy, & the Mother so good, so deserving, so liberal & so infinitely kind, that the world certainly does not abound with people to compare with them. They both improved upon us considerably since we lost our dearest Susan,—not, you will believe, as substitutes! — — — Heavens! how wide, how wide! — — but still for their intrinsic worth, & most friendly partiality & regard. The eldest son, too, is a remarkably pleasing young man: the younger seems as sulky as the sister is haughty. They may easily get neighbours to supply my regard for either.

We languished for the moment of removal with almost infantine fretfulness at every delay that distanced it—& when

---

[6] Apparently about mid October.

[7] The Revd. Samuel Cooke and his wife Cassandra *née* Leigh (iii, L. 122 n. 8); their daughter Mary (b. 14 Mar. 1781—*post* 1820); their sons Theophilus Leigh (1778–1846), M.A. Oxon. (1801), B.D. (1812), rector of Brandeston, Norfolk (1812); and George (1779–1853), M.A. Oxon. (1804), B.D. (1812), Sedleian Professor of Natural Philosophy (1810).

at last the grand day ǀ came, our final packings, with all their toil & difficulties & labour & expence, were mere acts of pleasantry: so bewitched were we with the impending change, that though from 6 o'clock to 3 we were hard at work, without a *kettle* to boil for Breakfast, or a knife to cut bread for a luncheon, we missed nothing, wanted nothing, & were as insensible to fatigue as to hunger. M. d'A. *then* set out on foot, loaded with remaining relics of things, to us, precious, & Betty afterwards with a *remnant* Glass or two; the other maid had been sent 2 Days before. I was forced to have a Chaise for my Alex & me, & a few looking Glasses, a few folios, & not a few other *oddments*,— & then, with dearest Mr. Lock—*our Founder's*—Portrait,[8] & my little Boy, off I set—& I would to God my dearest Susan could relate to me as delicious a journey!—My Mate, striding over hedge & ditch, arrived first, though he set out after, to welcome me to our New dwelling,—& we entered our new *best Room*, in which I found a glorious fire of wood, & a little Bench, borrowed of one of the departing Carpenters. Nothing else. We contrived to make room for each other, & Alex disdained all rest. His spirits were so high, upon finding 2 or 3 rooms totally free for his horse (alias any stick he can pick up) & himself, unincumbered by chairs & Tables, & such-like lumber, that he was merry as a little andrew, & wild as twenty Colts. Here we unpacked a small Basket, containing 3 or 4 loaves, & with a Garden knife, *fell to work*; some Eggs had been procured from a neighbouring Farm, & one saucepan had been brought by the Maid. We dined, therefore, exquisitely, & drank to our new possession from a Glass of clear water out of our new Well. At about 8 o'clock, our goods arrived—We had our Bed put up in the middle of our Room, to avoid risk of damp ǀ Walls, & our Alex had his dear Willy's crib[9] at our feet.

We none of us caught cold. We had fire night & day in the maid's room, as well as our own—or rather in my Susan's room, for we lent them that, their own having a *little* inconvenience against a fire, because it is built without a Chimney.

We continued making fires all around us, the first fortnight;

[8] A copy by Edward Francesco Burney of the Lawrence of William Locke, Sr. Cf. the portrait described in Sotheby's Catalogue (1960, item 295), now the possession of Mr. Philip Spencer, of Norbury Park.

[9] A crib formerly used by Susan's son, John William James Phillips, now aged 6 (i, L. 6 n. 1).

& then found Wood would be as bad as an apothecary's Bill—
so desisted.—But we did not stop short so soon as to want the
latter to succeed the former, or put our calculation to the proof.

Our most beloved & precious Friends came together to
welcome our entrance the same day—but before our arrival.
I thus missed the only time my sweet Mrs. L[ocke] has been
able to visit our new domain: she has had a Cold since, which
though *indeed* only a cold, has forced her to extreme Care, to
avoid wh⟨at⟩ she suffered from want of care last Winter. Mr
Locke has blessed our habitation with his most smiling benediction, given by every feature of his face, repeatedly, & our
lovely Amelia has almost always accompanied ⟨him⟩. She is
more caressing, sweet, amiable than ever,—at least than ever
since she entered in the World. She is, indeed, a third angel of
the ⟨Meridian⟩, & she loves my Susan with *enthusiasm* as well
as truth,—tenderly, indeed, & with all her fair soul.

Our first Week was devoted to unpacking, & exulting in our
completed plan. To have no one thing at hand—nothing to eat
—no were to sit—all were trifles—rather, I think, amusing than
incommodious.—The house looked so clean—the distribution
of the rooms & closets is so convenient, the prospect every where
around is so gay, & so lovely, & the Park of dear Norbury is so
close at hand, that we hardly knew how to require any thing
else for existence than the enjoyment of our own situation.

At this period, I received my summons.[10] I believe I have
already ǀ explained, that I had applied to Miss Planta for
advice whether my best chance of admission would be at
Windsor, Kew, or London; I had a most kind Letter of answer,
importing my Letter had been seen, & that Her Majesty
would herself fix the time when she could admit me. This was
a great happiness to me, indeed! And the fixture was for The
Queen's House in Town.

The only draw back to the extreme satisfaction of such
graciousness as allowing an *Appointment* to secure me from a
fruitless journey, as well as from all doubt of impropriety, &
all fear of intrusion, was that, exactly at this period, La Princesse d'Henin & M. de Lally were expected at Norbury. I hardly
could have regretted any thing else, I was so grateful,—& so
delighted by my summons: but this I indeed lamented. They

[10] See L. 251, p. 1.

arrived to dinner on Thursday[11]—I was involved in preparations, & unable to meet them; & my Mate would not be persuaded to relinquish aiding me. The next Morning, *through mud, through Mire*, they came to our Cottage. The poor princesse was forced to change Shoes & stockings. M. de Lally is more accustomed to such expeditions. Nothing could be more sweet than they both were, nor, indeed, more grateful than I felt for my share in their kind exertion. The house was re-viewed all over—even the little *Pot au feu* was opened by the princesse, excessively curious to see our manner of living in its most minute detail. I have not heard if your Letter has been received by M: de L[ally][12] but I knew not then you had written, & therefore did not enquire. The princesse talked of nothing so much as you, & with a softness of regard that quite melted me. I always tell her warmly how you feel about her. M. de Lally was most melancholy about France—the last new & | most barbarous revolution[13] has disheartened all his hopes—Alas— whose can withstand it? They made a long & kind visit, & in the afternoon we went to Norbury Park, where we remained till near Eleven o'clock, & thought the time very short. M^e d'Henin related some of her adventures in this second flight[14] from her terrible Country, & told them with a spirit, & a power of observation, that would have made them interesting if a tale of old times—but now, all that gives account of those events awakens the whole mind to attention. M. de Lally, after Tea, read us a beginning of a new Tragedy, composed upon an Irish story,[15] but bearing allusion so palpable to the virtues & misfortunes of Louis 16. that it had almost as strong an effect upon our passions & faculties as if it had borne the name of that Good & unhappy Prince. It is written with great pathos, noble sentiment, & most eloquent language. I parted from them with extreme reluctance—nay, vexation. Mon Ami visited them daily in my absence, & twice M. de Lally spent a morning with him here.

---

[11] On Thursday 26 October.   [12] This letter has not survived.

[13] That terminating in the *coup d'état* of 18 Fructidor (4 Sept.) and the defeat of Royalist hopes (iii, L. 247 n. 10).

[14] For the Princesse d'Hénin's forced return to England after 18 Fructidor, see Madame de Latour du Pin's *Journal*, ii, chap. vii.

[15] 'Tuathal-Teamur, ou, la restauration de la monarchie en Irlande', never printed, though completed in five acts by 1824, when Lally is reported (*NBG*) to have read it to the French Academy.

I set off for Town early the next Day, Saturday.[16] My time was not yet fixed for my royal interview, but I had various preparations impossible to make in this dear quiet obscure Cottage. Mon Amico could not accompany me, as we had still two Men constantly at work, the house *without* being quite unfinished. But I could not bear to leave his little representative, who, with Betty, was my companion to Chelsea. There I was expected, & our dearest Father came forth with open arms to welcome us. He was in delightful spirits, the sweetest humour, & perfectly good looks & good health. My little rogue soon engaged him in a romp, which conquered his rustic shyness, & they became the best friends in the world. Sally soon after joined us, & was gay & comfortable. I was obliged to go to Town for some purchases, &c, & took my happy Boy & his admiring Nurse to the great streets & great shops about Pall Mall. At our return, I had the true pleasure to find our ever good James, who spent the day at Chelsea. In the Evening, We left him & Sally at Chess, & my dear Father took me to his Study, where he began me his new work,[17] which I think I really excellent—at once instructive & elegant. I know not if he has told you its subject, or if he wishes to have it left to his telling. You may enquire *Sunday* we had our Esther, her Marianne, Aunt Beckey & Miss Brookes, & Edward. Mr. Burney was prevented by some engagement, which I heartily regretted. James came to Tea. Esther looks tolerably well, & was in spirits—whenever we talked not of Exiles——— Marianne is good & lively; Aunt Beckey was affected inexpressibly, good & kind soul, by the sight of my Alec, who was *the thing* of the Day. In the Evening we had some sublime Music of Haydn's; though a little à contre coeur to Hetty, who had not practiced it, & not being *quite* at ease herself, could not be convinced what exquisite delight she gave others. Poor Aunt Beckey, indeed, who wanted to spend the evening in chatting with me, after our long & eventful absence, was terribly vexed there was Music at all, & has since owned to Charlotte she was ready to cry at every bar.—

Monday I had a very kind Letter from Miss Planta,[18] in

[16] On Saturday 28 Oct. The journey and the arrival at Chelsea was reported in L. 251.   [17] The versified history of Astronomy (see Lonsdale, pp. 384–94).
[18] Miss Planta's letters have not survived but the audience took place on 3 Nov. (see L. 255).

return to an enquiry on my part, acquainting me no appointment could be yet made, but that I should have timely notice. I deemed it necessary, therefore, never to stir abroad, as a summons might be expected every moment. James came again, & again the study & reading with my dear Father ended the day. Tuesday, & Wednesday, were in every respect the same. Thursday morning I had a Letter from Miss Planta, written with extremest warmth of kindness, & fixing the next Day at Eleven o'clock for my royal admission.

I then went to Town, shopping upon various important articles for our Hermitage,—& called in Titchfield Street, & shook hands with all its good & dear personages, & took Marianne with me to Grocers & Drapers, & then called for my Father in Brooke Street & returned to his study with his dear self for the Evening.

Friday I leave to my next pacquet. I cannot write it without making minutes.

I must now add, with my kind remembrance to your good Susan, that I have had the satisfaction of seeing her Sister. She came hither a fortnight ago, & brought her fine little Boy.[19] She accompanied Betty's sister,[20] with whom she resides at Mickleham. She seems quite recovered from her cruel accident, which was being thrown down, & stunned, by a Horse, on the road from Leatherhead Fair. Fortunately no serious hurt has happenned, though she was much bruised, & terrified out of her senses. But she feels nothing from it now. I |

[*the concluding pages are missing*]

[*top margin,* p. 1]

we don't know of whom to enquire about Christ⟨yne⟩,[21] nor any circumstance relative to that affair?

19 The visit of Ann *née* Adams and her son Richard William Newton was reported in L. 262.
20 Mary, wife of John Woodyear (see iii, L. 237 and n. 5).
21 Unidentified.

To Esther (Burney) Burney

A.L. (Berg), 4 Jan. 1798
Double sheet 4to 4 pp. *pmks* DARKING 6 JA 98 wafer
Addressed: Mrs. Burney, / Upper Titchfield Street, / Portland Place, /
London.

West Hamble, Jany 4. 1798

I feel inclined to write you a very long Letter, my dearest
Esther, from the impression made upon my mind by the pacquet
I have just read for our beloved Exile[1]—& which is truly
interesting to me. I am much vexed, however, to inform you I
cannot send it immediately, as, most provokingly, Mrs. Lock
has but just forwarded a pacquet. Depend, however, upon its
safety, & that it will set off the first moment it can *decently*
follow its predecessor, which will be in about a Week. It is
always quite a joy to me to have a Letter from you to enrich our
cargo, for I know there is no one the sweet soul will *more* tenderly
receive.

But now, I must speak of your own affairs, my dearest Etty, &
tell you how *doubly* you have touched me by your relation,—
first with deep concern in the thought of your relinquishing
your favourite habitation,[2]—nearly as dear to you as our little
self-raised structure is to ourselves;—& next at the most unexpected philosophy with which you bear it—Pardon the word
unexpected, for I will confess I had feared such a necessity would
half have demolished you: you have had it so long, you have
made it so pretty, it has cost your excellent Mr. B[urney] so
much money, that it has uncheared *me* ever since I read the
paragraph. And my mate is *truly* My mate in his sympathy. I
took an airing this morning with Mr. Locke & my alex, & my
mind was so full of it, I could not forbear mentioning it; he was
very sensibly concerned, & looked even *sorrowful*; but not at all

264. ¹ EBB's letter has not survived, though doubtless it was safely delivered in
Ireland through franking privileges of friends of the Lockes, apparently Windham
and Thomas Pelham, chief secretary to the Lord Lieutenant of Ireland (see
L. 279 n. 2).
    ² EBB was to move *c.* 21 June 1798 from 2 Upper Titchfield Street, Portland
Place, where she had lived since 1785, to 43 Beaumont Street, Devonshire Place.

surprised, he told me, for he had, this very morning, been *foretelling* the event to Mrs. Locke; he sees the pressure of the new assessments so hard upon everybody,[3] that you had occurred to him, & he had just predicted what he now heard. He is himself forced to retrenchments that enable him but too well to judge the retrenchments of others. The *new* assessment alone will stand him in 407 pounds a year.

We are ignorant, yet, how we shall fare ourselves, our House not having yet been visited by the Tax-Agents. However, the probability of an Invasion appears so very striking,[4] that, severe as are the means for Individuals, I do most truly believe the general safety demands them—& God grant they may but prove effectual!

You will have *NO* turn, my dear Etty, to pay for your pacquets, till you seal them,—remember that!—& remember, too, amongst all the expences of the times, *you* have not MUCH to reproach yourself with consuming my income by postage.—

We were quite charmed with your Bull—for I could not but read to M. d'A. an account so flattering in many particulars to his national feelings. What upon Earth will all those poor injured people, *les emigrés*, now do? how can they support all these additional duties? they will not fall upon many, indeed, as Housekeepers, but all species of existence will become dearer. For ourselves, we watch the opening of the 3 p^r Cents with inexpressible anxiety, as we must then sell out to finish all our building accounts.[5] We have wholly set aside all plans of fitting up the house, & are determined to try at introducing the new system of œconomy, suitable to the times, of bare walls.

I must not longer defer speaking of the maiden you have procured me,—she appears to me to justify all the kind hopes you entertained for us. She has only to continue steadily as she has begun, & we shall *both* become even *fond* of her, for we have been so long tormented with *extravagant dawdles*, that to find a

---

[3] See L. 261 n. 12; L. 263 n. 3.

[4] With Fishguard (iii, L. 228 n. 1) and Bantry Bay (iii, L. 220 n. 3) in mind, together with the threats of the Directory, it was not difficult to fear a third attempt on the part of the French to land an army in the islands.

[5] The 3 per cent consols went on sale on 9 Jan. 1798 at 47¾ ⅞ ex. div. 48¼. In June–July 1796 the d'Arblays had probably invested some of the proceeds of *Camilla* in 3 per cents, which at that time were selling for 65¾–59¼ (*AR* xxxviii (1796), 'Appendix to the Chronicle', p. 110). For investments in 5 per cents see iii, L. 193 n. 3; L. 250 n. 1.

servant who will be careful & active if she is capable of attaching herself to those she serves, we shall consider as a treasure. At all events, I am much obliged for your kindness: & she says *she hopes she shall answer to your goodness in recommending her.*— I am sure I hope so too!—

I hesate whether to talk of poor C—or not—poor—poor C! —I find you observe the same total silence to Ireland that I do:[6] & I am now very glad it was demanded, for the affair so situated as to have required Letters without end, or to have occasioned a suspense the most anxious to our dearest Susan. I was better reconciled when I wrote last—I am now *quite the reverse*. I had a Letter from our most worthy James yesterday Morning that made me quite *sick* about her.[7] The MAN, as you expressively call him, seems to have no species of value for her ⌐ independent of her little wealth. I do, however, see some glimmering of hope she may yet escape this blind *martyrdom.*— Certainly, though in a different manner, I will do my utmost to aid J[ames] in saving her,—if my influence may be counteracted by one more powerful it shall not be, at least, from want of exertion.—

How much pleasanter a theme—& a prospect, is there *in* & *for* the new Reverend![8]—I read the history of the Bishop's *manner* of making the examination, & ordination, with extreme pleasure. It is so *good*, & so like him. But I feel much disappointed about the 2 years—yet perhaps there may be reasons to make the degrees *ultimately* the more desirable, & profitable.— I trust there are. Yet—in the meantime, how *very* hard upon you & Mr. B[urney] is the interval!—I told Mr. Locke this morning the last kindness of the Bishop, & he said 'It was very c[onsi]derate, & very good;—yet it is very likely his young Protegé is better prepared for his new office than half the young clergymen in the kingdom,—since two years *willing* study & application, at his time of life, frequently make greater advance-

---

[6] SBP was still to be kept in ignorance of Mrs. Francis's (CBF's) unsettled plans of marriage.

[7] Most of the letters about and from Ralph Broome were later destroyed (L. 261 n. 1).

[8] According to the 'Worcester Journal', EBB's son Richard Allen Burney (1773–1836) had been ordained deacon on 1 Jan. 1798 by the family friend of the Burneys, Brownlow North (i, L. 3 n. 10), Bishop of Winchester (1781). Richard was to graduate B.A. (Oxon.) in 1799 and to be ordained priest in midsummer of that year.

ment in any serious pursuit, than a whole youth spent upon it in the *common* way,—that is to say, the *idle way.*'

Cecilia's 4 seasons amused me excessively,[9]—yet, comic as they are, they have *promise* of something *serious*, for the thoughts are innocently her *own*, & not borrowed from the little Songs & odes she may have read. I hope, if I go to Norbury Park before the pacquet is sent off, you will not quarrel with me if I read it there. she still continues fresh in their remembrance & admiration as one of the most singularly sweet Children in the world. And *you*, my dear Etty, are a scarcely ever failing subject with Mrs. Locke in almost every meeting. That sweet Creature suffers with rheumatic colds, & is so perpetually confined, she has been only twice at our little dwelling. Her incomparable Partner delights us with a call 2 or 3 times a week—indeed whenever he can—& takes true pleasure in seeing M. d'Arblay, in a Barber's ⏐ flannel Waistcoat,—(such a one as our Padre dresses in—) laboriously planting & digging his own Potatoes— &c. my alex is already enchanting his rising fancy with promises that, when he is Taller, he is to share in this delicious regale.

— — — I read with great chagrin indeed the account of the *respectable Relative*, both for *his* sake & your's,[10]—but as to *your* diminishing, I think, I must frankly say, it is even *conscientiously* out of all question, your calls & claims considered. I grieve about him in every particular—I always imagine there is some concealed uneasiness pressing upon his mind, & operating,

---

[9] Cecilia Charlotte Esther Burney (1788–1821), brought as an infant to be nursed in a cottage at Mickleham, had won the hearts of both SBP and Mrs. Locke (iii, L. 132 n. 5).

A copy of verses entitled 'On the four seasons of the year' by 'Cecilia Burney aged 9 years' is extant in a Commonplace book of poetry, 1771–1806, 90 f. (170 pp.), 4to, pp. 75–6, in the Houghton Library, Harvard University. Though catalogued under Charlotte (Burney) Francis Broome, these verses at least seem to be in the hand of her granddaughter Julia Charlotte (Barrett) Thomas, *later* Maitland (1808–64). Eight stanzas in all, the first and fourth read respectively:

> In the lovely months of spring
> I like to walk, to dance, to sing
> And then the garden's full of beauty
> A sign the gard'ner does his duty
>
> . . .
>
> When day shuts in & night's approaching
> The Bats are apt to be encroaching
> And frighten people from the garden
> For which they never ask their pardon

[10] Edward Francesco Burney (1760–1848), the artist, EBB's cousin and brother-in-law, who had never learned to collect money owed to him.

unconsciously to himself, upon his conduct. I have long thought this, & with true concern, from the esteem & love I bear him. But how *he* can be pecuniarily distressed I cannot devise, his expences so few, & his talents so acknowledged & superiour. Has he never the courage to demand & be paid? I wish he would consult with his *old friend & crony* formerly, *Cousin Charles* of Greenwich. He would soon learn how to spur slack pay-masters. And it is truly scandalous he should not, by this time, be even *rich*, with his works, his merit, & his virtuous life. —As to that flippant, vulgar Bête, Mr. R^y I really don't think him worth the smallest resentment, & dare say what he said was not only without fear or Wit, but without meaning. There are people in the World who MUST *say* something, whether they can *think* of anything to say or not, merely from the urgency of an unruly tongue, that won't lie still.

My kind Love to dear Mr. Burney, & Marianne & Sophy. I hope *Amela* is getting well. God bless you dearest Esther— don't plague yourself to write till another pacquet. our joint congratulations to the Reverend & kindest remembrances to Edward.

265   West Humble, 11 January 1798

To M. d'Arblay

A.L. (Berg), 11 Jan. [17]98
Double sheet 4to   3 pp. *pmks* DARKING JA 13 JA 98 2 wafers
Addressed: Alexander d'Arblay Esqr, / at Dr. Burney's, / Chelsea College, / Middlesex
Docketed in unknown hand: 1796
Edited by FBA, p. 1, *annotated and dated*: 1798— (15)

Thursday
Camilla Cottage. Jany 11th —98

Tell me if ever any thing was half so vexatious? ⌐The Baker¬ did not come this morning, & the bread was sent over from

265. ¹ Mail to and from the Dorking Post Office was obligingly carried by the Dorking bakers, Mary Pullen, widow, and William Pullen, as listed in *The Universal British Directory of Trade, Commerce, and Manufacture* (5 vols., 1790–8), ii (1791), 840. The life histories of two sisters Mary and Sarah *née* Brown, both bakers, who died

William's where it had been left last night! I could not bear the uncertainty whether or not I might see you—or at least your writing & I sent Jenny to Dorking—she was caught by the sudden change of weather before she left the field, but took the umbrella, & seeing me uneasy would not be stopt—but was detained, however, by the rain, so late that she only came back at 4 o'clock.—she then brought me your most disappointing letter, but she returned in a shower, which continues still, & robs me of means of returning the Receipt till tomorrow. Mrs. Pullen has given the information, by Jane, that she can no longer send *every day* either Cream or butter, as almost all the other families lived close & made that Journey indispensable, for her Boy was departed for the winter—But we can be sure of being served 3 times a week.

Well—& I cannot fret about that now, I am so much engrossed by great disappointment[7]—not till *Dimanche au soir!*—!!

— — —

I had not formed an idea of such a delay.

However, I have no doubt it is indispensable[2]—but I am a very bad single Hermit—though single I can scarcely be called with my gay little Alex— | who is gayer, brighter, brisker than any thing else that ever was human. I think his spirits encrease every moment. He always says you are to return to Dinner, & bring with you '*Gan pa & illill/Little/aunt SALL,*' as he now most facetiously calls his reverend kinswoman, laying a stress upon the monosyllable the most saucily comic imaginable.

Yesterday we strolled as far as Chapel Farm.[3] The Lanes were perfectly dry & clean. But our little field looked so melancholy without it's Workman, that I will go that way no more— before — — *lundi!*—

on the same day (17 Mar. 1811) at the ages respectively of 80 and 79 years, can be traced in the parish registers of Mickleham and Dorking. Mary had married on 2 Feb. 1754 Jonathan Pullen (d. 9 May 1773); and her sister Sarah, on 20 Feb. 1757, William Pullen (baptized 5 Feb. 1736), possibly the William Pullen of Mickleham, where the loaves were left. See also L. 290, p. 166.

² M. d'Arblay had gone to London to sell out stocks and settle the expenses of Camilla Cottage.

³ A farm of 260 acres occupied by William Williter (1736–1816) of Mickleham, being a part of the large holdings (1,500 acres) inherited by Sir William Geary (*c.* 1755–1825), a detailed description of which is given in *Particulars | of Sundry | Freehold & Copyright Estates,* . . . *the late property of | Admiral Sir Francis Geary, Bart. Deceased: Which will be Sold by Auction* . . . *the 12th of May 1797* (extant in the Surrey Archaeological Society, Castle Arch, Guildford). By 1801, as the Tax Assessments show, the property had been acquired by Sheridan, Williter remaining the farmer.

All looks melancholy—& feels melancholy—even in this dear Cottage without my runaway—& I have employed myself only *upon melancholy subjects*, since I saw him—except when with our Alex, whose delicious gaiety is irresistibly contagious.

a most kind, kind Letter arrived after your departure from my dearest Father,[4] with an invitation for you the most sweetly affectionate. Pray thank him, with my best of Loves & Duties. ⌐I am sadly mortified he wants the Reviews,[5] you may ⌐ ask if they shall be sent by the stage—& whether if not, they should be left till called for at the Inn.

James was very good to get the receipt so exactly. Pray love & thanks—

My love also to Sarah mate.

No one has been here since your departure, but a poor woman & in the same state less willingly—a poor *dumb* Beggar, whom you may remember in our walks [at] Bookham.⌐

Adieu,—je vous aime a little—

il me semble — —

I live entirely in the Book Room—

The Parlour is intolerable. But I am used to b[eing] without you in the Book Room, & the opposite Chair does no[t] look so forlorn.

Muff sends his duty. He barks & behaves well.

Jane says the house is but solitary without you.

Betty is ashamed to talk of her fears.

Another person sees you are determined to try her courage.—

& Puss has stolen some milk, & is in disgrace.

[4] This letter is missing, but the contents are reflected in FBA's reply (L. 266).

[5] As may be seen from the references (L. 266, p. 66) the d'Arblays had been lent numbers 27, 28, and 29 of what must have been *The European Magazine and London Review*, Jan.–June 1795, July–Dec. 1795, Jan.–June 1796.

To Doctor Burney

A.L.S. (Barrett, Eg. 3690, ff. 93–4b), 15 Jan. [17]98
Double sheet 4to   4 pp.   *pmks*   DARKING   18 JA 98   JA 98   wafer
Addressed: Dr. Burney, / Chelsea College, / Middlesex.
Edited by FBA, p. 1, *annotated*:   al.—O   [*all out?*]   O [*out?*]
Docketed: Sarah Harriet
Edited also by CFBt.

West Humble—
Jany 15. —98.

My dearest Padre,

Your most kind invitation to my dear Partner was very consolatory to my first widowed morning[1]—the 4 following were *vary dule*, though not for want of a *fiddle*; Alex is the most *étourdi*, gay, romping, riotous little monkey now living. His disposition is full of enjoyment, & his heart of happiness, &, when the violence of his spirits are tired out by their own mad frolicking, he is bewitchingly tender & carressing. There is no wanting employment with such a little wretch—but *participation* is wanted for every thing, & I almost grudge the little Rogue's amusing powers when enjoyed only by myself.

My Mate is returned full of satisfaction from his kind fare at Chelsea, & only regretting he could not spend more time there with you, though not free from fears what *he* thought so little was for *you* too much.

You do not tell me one word in the last 3 Letters of Moons, Stars, & such little branches of the Heavens. Yet I feel sure you do not *flag*, for you are now in the part of the work where your materials are easiest to obtain & authenticate, & where you are endowed with a pleasure so very great to a Heart like yours— that of giving to living merit the meed so almost always reserved to lawrel its Manes.[2]

I will not again enter upon the affairs of C[harlotte]—as I have nothing new to relate, but I cannot help hoping your resentment will subside into pity, if not kindness, upon further

266. ¹ CB's letter of *c.* 10 Jan. is missing.
  ² Cf. William Cowper's 'Charity': 'Verse, like the laurel, its immortal meed, / Should be the guerdon of a noble deed.'

consideration of the good as well as weak side of her character, &
upon hearing she thinks she has behaved to you heroically, for,
without internal conviction, & against her own | inclination;
she resists Mr. B[roome] merely from her Duty to ⟨you⟩—for
the suspension seems to hang entirely upon her telling him that
both *now*, & when his wife, she should resolutely adhere to her
determination never to withdraw the trusteeship by a contest.
What the Man must be who could desire it—I have begged *her*
to consider.[3]—

But—I am very much now engrossed by another subject—
Mrs. Crewe.—I feel ashamed—yet deeply penetrated by her
appeal; The difficulty, the nice delicacy of her situation makes,
indeed, a but too *Reasonable affliction*—& the terror of seeing
'laxity of morals' descend,[4] where such goodness of principle
& of Heart ought to be maternally hereditary, is sufficient to
distress the strongest mind, & embarrass the best understanding.
Inadequate as I am to counsel in so intricate a labyrinth, I
cannot, so called upon, hold coldly back from speaking; on the
contrary, I ask myself what, if so situated, I would do,—& I find
I answer—I would seek to fulfil my *plighted* duty, in forbearing
to weaken filial respect, by pointed animadversions; & there,
therefore, I would compel myself to be *passive*. But I would
unhesitatingly fulfil my *maternal* call, in openly discussing right
& wrong, unsparingly condemning every deviation, however
disguised, from moral rectitude, & marking, with all the effect
in my power, the nearly insensible gradations by which a spirit
of ridicule upon serious subjects leads to | lightness of principle;
& how imperceptibly, yet indelibly, a want of exactitude, even

---

[3] See L. 261 n. 2.

[4] Mrs. Crewe's son John (i, L. 24 n. 29), 'a most gentlemanly, good-natured
young man' but also described as 'hanging loose on society and a frequenter of the
gaming-table', emerges in Sir John Barrow, *An Auto-biographical Memoir* (1847),
pp. 51–2, as one of the attachés in Lord Macartney's embassy of 1792 to China
(i, L. 24 n. 30). Before acceding to Mrs. Crewe's request that he be taken on the
voyage, Lord Macartney had insisted that he give ' "a most solemn pledge, on his
honour, that he will not touch either cards or dice or other instruments of gambling,
either on board ship or at any place where we may stop." He gave the pledge and
broke it—lost . . . it was said, some thousand pounds, not any part of which could
he pay; and it was also said he had compounded the debt for an annuity of as
many hundred pounds as he had lost thousands. My cabin on the passage home
was on the lower deck, and scarcely a night passed in which I was not disturbed by
the rattling of dice, or by Mr. Crewe's scraping on the bass-viol.'
  After some army service (see L. 332 n. 7; L. 337 n. 11) he married in 1807
Henrietta Maria Anne Hungerford (*c.* 1772–1820), succeeded his father as 2nd
Baron Crewe (1829), but spent most of his life on the Continent (*Barthomley*, p. 323).

in trifles, of truth, disturbs the whole œconomy of Honour: &
there, therefore, I would permit myself to be active. That this
forbearance of personality could not alltogether avert censure
by implication, I readily see; but it must be checked from all
utterance, & learn, from example, to be silent. And, where some
risk must be run, it is surely less terrible to have the Eyes opened
to failures in a character that ought to be held up to respect
from its position, than to have them habitually blinded, till the
same errours are fallen into, or even unconsciously adopted.

The fear of saying any thing offensive to such near affinities
may have made me obscure, but I have endeavoured to answer
Mrs. C.'s call upon me as a Casuist *frankly*, though I cannot so
as to merit the distinction with which her call honours me. My
dearest Father will judge for me whether or not to transcribe it,
& kindly burn what I have written, if he thinks the fire a better
place for it than Crewe Hall.

I am very curious to see this *Miss Sourby*,[5] that either *you* or
yours must be suspected to have written. Mrs. C.'s ideas of the
various Jacobins are all excellent; I am amazed she does not
connect them into use herself.[6] Her wishes for *my* pen are truly
flattering to me—& almost tempt me to own to *Her* what I had
nearly vowed to own to no one but my Mate, you, & Mr. Locke
& our Susanna—namely, that I am just now immersing once
more deeply into a scribbling business[7] that fills all my
scribbling ideas, & takes me up all I can exist from my little

[5] Letitia Sourby was a fictitious correspondent (perhaps in fact CB), who,
writing in the *Anti-Jacobin* on 18 Dec. 1797, described the effects of the new radical
or Jacobinical ideas in the domestic circle. Letitia's father, a newly converted
enthusiast of Freedom, but a great Tyrant at home, had left off church attendance
in favour of *natural* Religion, made light of marriage vows in favour of 'Concu-
binage', and opposed war and all measures taken for the defence of the realm.

[6] Mrs. Crewe had evidently asked CB to solicit contributions from FBA for the
Anti-Jacobin, as at a previous time she had suggested that FBA write a satiric
commentary on manners of the times for the projected periodical, the *Breakfast
Table*.

[7] As was customary with FBA when she was alone, she had evidently taken to her
pen again, and the 'scribbling business' in hand was probably the comedy 'Love
and Fashion', a draft of which (235 8vo pages), sewn in a mottled paper cover, is
extant in the Berg Collection, as are also preliminary notes and revisions of the
play.

In the autumn of 1799, the play was offered to Thomas Harris, the Manager of
Covent Garden Theatre by her usual 'Agent' CB Jr. Harris offered £400 and
proposed to produce the play the following March; but at FBA's request, motivated
by CB's objections and SBP's death in Jan. 1800, he returned the manuscript. The
play remained unproduced. (See A. L. S., Berg, from CB Jr. to FBA, 30 Oct. 1799
and Ll. 345, 364, 366, and 407). See also, the editor, 'Fanny Burney: Playwright',
UTQ xix no. 2 (Jan. 1950), 170–89.

occupying Alec. The fear of ¦ raising expectation, & the uncertainty of the time I may require, make me extremely
unwilling to *expand* upon this subject: yet the exceeding kindness, upon so many—upon all occasions, indeed, of Mrs. C.
makes me wish to shew her, at least, the gratitude of confidence. I cast into your hands, however, my dearest Padre,
to communicate or not—as also to add, or not, that the *nature*
of the Work is the same as that to which she was so strenu-
ously & flatteringly friendly & good.

I was much vexed not to have had your Letter in time for M.
d'A.'s taking back the Reviews. We have volumes 27. 28. &
29.[8] They are very full of instruction & entertainment, &
particularly so for those who have but a few Books: for it lets us,
at least, know the *existence* of others. Mrs. C[rewe] little imagines
the *excess* of our retirement! For *periodical* essays, I must repeat,
the *World* is the scene for the Writer.[9] To gather nothing but by an
occasional news-paper, or an occasional Letter, would soon make
so manifest a paucity of materials, that the Cause could not be
served, though the attempter might be disgraced. I wish she
could see our Hermitage! & its secluded situation. Adieu, most
dear Sir—my kind Love to that wicked dumb Girl, & my Mate's,
—& his most cordial respects & true affection to my dear Padre
join sincerely & heartily with

your F. d'A.'s

No news lately from Ireland.—How frightful is the King's
ad⟨dress to⟩ the Parliament![10]—

---

[8] Cf. L. 265 n. 5.   [9] Cf. iii, pp. 277–8, and n. 2.
[10] In an address of 11 Jan. 1798 the King had acquainted the House of Lords
with reports he had received of 'preparations made, and measures taken, in
France, apparently in pursuance of a design openly and repeatedly professed, of
attempting an invasion of these kingdoms'. He therefore thought it necessary to
implement the militia act of 2 Nov. 1797, see *AR* xl (1798), 'State Papers', 209.

267   West Humble, [18 January 1798]

To Mrs. Phillips

A.J.L.S. (Diary MSS. vi. 5052–[5], Berg), *n.d.*
Double sheet 4to   4 pp.   wafer
Addressed: Mrs. Phillips, / Belcotton, / Drogheda. / Ireland.
Edited by FBA, p. 1 (5052), *annotated and dated*: Jan^ry 18. 1798.[1] God Save
the Queen!
Edited also by CFBt *and the* Press.

West Hamble.

I had meant to hear again from my beloved Susan before I
wrote—but no Letter comes, & the decency of the thing seems
now satisfied with respect to time for venturing another pacquet:
I will therefore beg our darling friend to forward this pacquet
from Esther without further delay.[2] It came, unluckily, too
recently after our last sending to be forwarded sooner. Yet I
think the mode so good & useful, that I always encourage our
Etty to make me her conveyor.—

Her letter is extremely full of interest, of every kind—she
allowed me to read it, & I take the allowance as a Letter to
myself.

I am very impatient to know if the Invasion threat affects
your part of Ireland. Mr Oracle is of opinion the French
soldiers will *not* go to Ireland, though there flattered with much
help, because they there can expect but little advantage, after all
the accounts spread by the opposition of its starving condition:
but that they *will* come to England, though sure of *contest*, at
least, because there they expect the very road to be paved with
gold.

Nevertheless—how I wish my Heart's beloved here!—to
share with us at least the same fears, instead of the division of
apprehension we must now mutually be tormented with. I own
I am sometimes affrighted enough. These sanguine, & sanguinary wretches will risk all for the smallest hope of plunder; &

267.   [1] The Queen's birthday (19 May) was celebrated on 18 Jan.
          [2] Cf. the opening paragraph of L. 264.

Barras[3] assures them they have only to enter England to be Lords of wealth unbounded.

But Taleyrand —— ! how like myself must you have felt at his conduct! indignant—amazed—ashamed!—our first prepossession against him was instinct—he conquered it ⎮ by pains indefatigable to win us,—& he succeeded astonishingly, for we became partial to him almost to fondness. The part he now acts against England,[4] may be justified, perhaps, by the spirit of revenge; but the part he submits to perform of coadjutor with the worst of villains, with Barras—Rewbel[5]—Merlin[6]—marks some internal attrocity of character that disgusts as much as it disappoints me: & now, a last stroke,[7] which appears in

---

[3] Paul-Jean-François-Nicolas, comte de Barras (1755–1829), who, having taken a strong part in the *coup d'état* of 18 Fructidor, had become *président du Directoire*. With a military career culminating in his appointment (4–5 Oct. 1793) as Lt.-Gen., Commander-in-Chief of the Army of the Interior, he had in 1797 taken a great interest in the invasion of England, the spoils in view providing enticing motives for soldiers like those in the *Légion Noire* who had landed in Feb. 1797 in Pembrokeshire (iii, L. 228 n. 1).

[4] Talleyrand's late sentiments and intentions with respect to England had recently emerged, for instance, in the letter that, as Minister of Foreign Relations, he had addressed to 'ALL THE DIPLOMATIC AND CONSULAR AGENTS OF THE FRENCH REPUBLIC', a translation of which had been given prominence in the editorial columns of *The Times* (8 Jan.). Characteristic of the English, the rallying indictments alleged, were craft, 'mercantile avarice', 'shameful and criminal Machiavelism', 'dark intrigues', 'black calumnies', 'perfidious seductions', and 'frightful projects'. 'England . . . is our eternal enemy . . . . This Colossus with earthen feet, must now be overthrown.' And the advice he went on to give the consuls perhaps reflects the seductions he had practised with such evident success in Mickleham: Make yourselves 'beloved, esteemed, and respected'. 'Do not fly in the face of the usages, of the manners, or of the prejudices of the countries where you reside . . . in the room of unmeaning etiquette, substitute the sauvity of temper, polite frankness, which flow from the soul of virtue, and from the consciousness of native dignity . . . above all, beware of . . . noisy and irascible fierceness. . . .'

[5] Jean-François Reubell (1747–1807), a member of the Directory from its inauguration on 13 Brumaire of the year IV (3 Nov. 1795) until Prairial of the year VII (June 1799), and an implacable enemy of *émigrés*, refractory priests, and Royalists.

[6] Philippe-Antoine, comte Merlin de Douai (1754–1838), long an associate of Reubell (above). Made Minister of Justice in Sept. 1795, he was notorious for his abuses of the law ('C'est la raison d'État qui dicte la jurisprudence') and his aggrandizement of a huge fortune. In Sept. 1797 he had been appointed a Director, losing his place only with the *coup d'état* of 30 Prairial (18 June 1799).

[7] Evidently FBA had now seen the leading article in *The Times* (15 Jan. 1798) reporting Talleyrand's representation to the King of Prussia with respect to the French exiles to the number of 4,000, who, settling in the Duchy of Brunswick, were likely to make it a 'new Coblentz'. The King of Prussia was asked to request the Duke of Brunswick 'to expel from his Duchy, without distinction of age or sex, the proscribed and emigrated French refugees' who had settled there. Among those to be ruthlessly uprooted, *The Times* went on to say, were Talleyrand's uncle and mother, namely, Alexandre-Angélique de Talleyrand-Périgord (1736–1820), archevêque duc de Reims (1777–90, 1815–17), cardinal (1808), pair de France,

Yesterday's paper, gives the finishing hand to his Portrait in my Eyes,—*he* has sent (& written) the Letter which exhorts the King of Prussia to *order* the Duke of Brunswick to banish & drive from his Dominions All the Emigrants there in asylum!——& among these are the archbishop of Rennes, his uncle—&—— his own Mother!——

Poor M. de N[arbonne]!—how will he be shocked & let down! where he now is we cannot conjecture—all Emigrants are exiled from the canton of Berne, where he resided[8]—I feel extremely disturbed about him—If that wretch Taleyrand has not given him some private intimation to escape, & *where to be safe*, he must be a *monster*.

We have no further news from France, of any sort.

M. de Lally, in a beautiful Letter to Mrs. Locke, speaks of my Susan—in terms so grateful to my Heart, that my dear *Partner in All* will copy for her the Letter.[9] I don't exactly know *when*, indeed—for his intentions are rather quicker than his execution. But he will do it.

He has lately been in Town, to sell out for our final workmen[10]—It was a terrible time, when the stocks were so low— but we had no choice. You will have seen the fruitless attacks made upon Mr. Shirley[11]—though, once again, his promises keep off violent measures. Indeed with *me* they would always; but M. d'A. is sometimes irritated beyond listening.

He spent some days upon this occasion at Chelsea, where he saw our dearest Father quite well, & excessively kind. our poor Esther was cruelly tormented with the tooth ache, & he could not see her: all else were well, & the young Divine[12] in good looks & good health. |

You tell us nothing lately of Norbury,—pray make amends. My little Man has conceived a passion for Amelia that is no small trait of the resemblance I covet. She is the only person to whom he will go willingly, & unbribed. He is good if we but

archevêque de Paris (1817); and Alexandrine-Victoire-Eleonore (de Damas d'Antigny) (*c.* 1728–1809), who had married in 1751 Charles-Daniel, comte de Talleyrand-Périgord (1734–88).

[8] As may be deduced from the date lines of the comte de Narbonne's letters (see *Catalogue*), he was living in Jan. 1796 at 'Glairesse' (Glaris) in Switzerland. In Aug. 1797, however, he wrote from 'Tubingen . . . en Souabe', Würtemberg, saying that he had been reading only German for a year.

[9] The letter and the copy are missing.
[10] Cf. L. 265, p. 61.
[11] See iii, L. 193 n. 7 and L. 234 n. 2.
[12] Richard Allen Burney (L. 264 n. 8).

name her, & he cries bitterly at her departure, though un-
moved by that of any other human being. Pray ⟨tell⟩ Norbury
to love his little Cousin for this early sympathy of taste.

I should be much pleased to hear you could see again Mrs.
Hill[13]—your account of that meeting makes me grieve it should
not be repeated. Do the Kiernans never come to Belcotton?
probably you could not accommodate them; but I I am disappointed you do not go sometimes to Dublin. I was so much
pleased with your description of that family, & the Maturins,[14]
that I should think you less lost if more amongst them.

This very day—I thank God! we paid the last of our workmen—our House now is our own fairly,—that it is our own
madly, too, you will all think, when I tell you the small remnant
of our income that has outlived this payment. However if the
Carmagnols do not sieze our *walls*, we despair not of enjoying,
in defiance of all *straitness* & *strictness*, our dear dwelling to our
Heart's content. But we are *reducing* our expences, & way of
life, in order to go on, in a manner you would laugh to see—
though almost cry to hear!—We know nothing yet of our
Taxes—nothing of our assessments—but we are of good courage,
& so pleased with our maisonnette, we think nothing too dear
for it, provided we can but exist in it.—

I should like much to know how you stand affected about the
assessment—& about the Invasion.—

M.d'A. saw Mr. Maturin[15] while at Chelsea, where, as well
as at the ever hospitable James's, they were invited to dine
together. Mr. Shirley had said he should put the long contested
affair into his hands; but he meant *your* Mr. Maturin, we now
learn, who is still to be expected, & who is to bring the interest
of the last half year upon the bond. This Gentleman was extremely polite & pleasing. You had paved the way for a good
reception of any one of his name to all of ours.

The communication to which I alluded I am charged to
hold back. It is a thing I liked better at first than afterwards, &
hope will *blow over.* |

O that all these public troubles would accellerate your
return! private blessings they would then, at least, prove,—

---

[13] See iii, L. 216 n. 3; also *FB & the Burneys*, pp. 236–7.
[14] See *FB & the Burneys*, pp. 237–9; also iii, L. 215 nn. 2, 7.
[15] Gabriel Maturin (iii, L. 215 n. 7), elder brother of Norbury's tutor.

ah my Susan!—how do I yearn for some little ray upon this subject!—

Charles, & his family, are at Bath: & Charlotte is gone to them for a fortnight.[16] All accounts that reach me of all the House & race are well. Our Ange of anges, Mr. Lock gives us very frequent peeps indeed—& looks with such benevolent pleasure at our dear Cottage & its environs—& seems to say— *I brought all this to bear!*—& to feel happy in the noble trust he placed in our self-belief that he might venture to shew that kind courage without which we could never have been united[17]— All this retrospection is expressed by his penetrating Eyes at every visit. He rarely alights, but I frequently enter the phaeton, & take a conversation in an airing: And when he comes without His precious Amelia, he indulges my Alex. in being our third. Our other ange has been here with him 3 times lately, & looks most bloomingly, & in all she is sweetness & goodness. They bear this heavy new loan most chearfully, nay heroically, though relinquishing some comfort daily, as it will amount to 507 pounds *additional* yearly. They are going to part with one Coach & Coachman.[18] Augusta behaves in the most amiable manner upon this trial, & continues & contributes & arranges new œconomies daily. I am sure you will have been affected as I was by poor dear Esther's history on this subject.[19] Her heroism I own I did not expect. But a great stroke is sometimes better borne than a small one, from shewing the necessity of fortitude. My Father says the new assessment will stand him in above 80 pds. a year!—Adieu, my ever beloved—dear—dearest Susan! God preserve you! & restore you to your

F. dA.

My Love to the Major—& to my dear Fanny—& to Norbury where you can—& Willy. I think Cecilia's verses charming. I amused dear Mr. Lock very much with them. I am *every Day* hoping for news of you, my own Susan!—pray remember me to your good Susan—Her sister Newton is well. one of my Maids saw her last Sunday.

My Mate's tenderest Love to you.

16 The opposition of CB and JB to Charlotte's marriage to Ralph Broome held sway for the moment and she had gone to Bath to 'divert her chagrin' (L. 273).
17 Mr. Locke had thought FBA and M. d'A could live on £120 a year (ii, L. 101 n. 1).   18 See L. 263 n. 3.   19 Cf. L. 264 and n. 1.

268   [West Humble, *pre* 1 March 1798]

To Ralph Broome, Sr.

L.S., copy in hand of M. d'A (West Humble Letter Book, pp. 14–15, Osborn), *n.d.*

Annotated, p. 15, *by* FBA *in her editorial capacity*: BROOME

Answer to a highly improper, nay, impertinent Letter of appeal against a deservedly beloved and nearly infatuated Sister, with whom Mr. B[roome] was on the point of marriage, though completely unworthy——of so pure, so sweet, so innocent, & so estimable a companion. M. d'A took this Copy for his Son.

To Ralph B — Esqr

Sir,

The alacrity with which I undertook to prepare your reception at Chelsea resulted from an impulsive belief I was promoting the happiness of my sister. You were not, indeed, personally known to me, but my inferences were drawn from what appeared to me the most promising probabilities.

Had we met first, I might, possibly, have formed a different idea; my sister has one of the purest of hearts & the most amiable & affectionate of dispositions; her intentions are always upright, & her principles are blameless; but as an excess of timidity robs her of the courage to assert herself, she has not perhaps a character of that decision & force which the severity of your sounder judgement may make requisite to your perfect confidence & unalienable approbation. Yet she would be wretched without them. She is unused to any difficulties, & accustommed to the extreemest lenity: I must frankly, therefore, confess, that now, from all I have been able to gather through others, & yet more from the censures conveyed in your own letter & statement; I also '*retract*,' and am no longer persuaded that either party would be the happier for the union.[1]

268. [1] Ralph Broome's letter to which this is the reply, though missing, is described by FBA in L. 273, p. 121, as 'a very long double Letter, full of complaints against my Father—Brother—& Charlotte herself,—& only civil to *me* of all the family: speaking of all else with the haughtiest resentment'. FBA (loc. cit.) characterizes her reply (above) as 'the most keen . . . I ever composed in my life,—declining all argument, justifying my Father and James, & warmly *panegyrizing* Charlotte'.

With regard to my family, I shall enter into no arguments, since the affair is closed: but I much regret the quick misunderstanding which prevented your seeing even a second time two Gentlemen whom you could not, I will venture to affirm, have known without respecting. The *predictions*[2] which you acknowledge to have preceded your interview made your penetration give place to prejudice & prepared the way to the hard opinions thence imbibed. |

You will excuse the little reserve with which I have written, from recollecting what you have given me to read. Personally, nevertheless I must always feel flattered by your obliging acceptance of the early though I believe mistaken zeal, with which I was actuated. I remain, Sir, your ob^dt Servt

A. d'Ary

P.S. I am extreemly glad you have forborn naming this affair amongst your friends; you can afford to send one thing to oblivion—

As has been said (L. 261 n. 1), Broome's irascible letters to the Burneys were later, at CBFB's request, searched for in the accumulated hoards of manuscripts and destroyed, as well evidently, as the replies, the above surviving from the circumstance of its having been copied into a Letter Book, where it eluded the search.

2 *Predilections?*

269   [*for* 21–23 February 1798]

For Mrs. Phillips

A.J.L. (Diary MSS. vi. 5056–[67], Berg), written at West Humble in [Dec. 1798]

Three double sheets and one single sheet 4to   foliated 1, 2, 3, 4 *verso* of p. 5056 was stuck with two wafers to the next page [5057] 14 pp.

Edited by FBA, p. 1 (5056), *annotated and dated*: 2ᵈ account 1798

p. 12 [5065], *top margin*: 2ᵈ accᵗ

Edited by CFBt *and the* Press.

Also J.L., copy in hand of M.d'A (West Humble Letter Book, pp. 53–67, Osborn), dated: Westhamble December—1798

And now I have to prepare another Court Relation for my dearest Susanna.

In February, I received one Wednesday Morn,[1] a Letter from our dearest Father, telling me he feared he should be forced to quit his Chelsea apartments, from a new arrangement among the officers, & wishing me to represent his difficulties, his Books, health, *time of life*—!—& other circumstances, through Miss Planta, to the Queen. M. d'Arblay & I both thought that if I had any chance of being of the smallest use to this dearest of Persons, it would be by endeavouring to obtain an audience; not by Letter; & as the most remote hope of success was sufficient to urge every exertion, we settled that I should set out instantly for Chelsea; & a Chaise, therefore, we sent for from Dorking, & I set off at Noon. M. d'A. would not go, as we knew not what accomodation I might find; & I could not, uninvited & unexpected, take my little darling boy: so I went not merrily, though never more willingly.

My dear Father was at home, &, I could see, by no means surprised by my appearance, though he had not hinted at

---

269. [1] On Wednesday morning 21 Feb. 1798. CB's letter is missing but for his fears that he might lose his apartments at Chelsea, see Lonsdale, pp. 392–3, and Captain C. G. T. Dean, 'Dr. Burney's Connection with the Royal Hospital, Chelsea', *Transactions of the London and Middlesex Archaeological Society*, N.S. viii, pt. iii (1944). See also the editorial explanations that FBA mistakenly appended to Ll. 251 and 254.

desiring it. of course he was not very angry—nor sorry,—& we communed together upon his apprehensions, & settled our plan. I was to endeavour to represent his case to the Queen, in hopes it might reach his Majesty, & procure some order in his favour. The particulars of this business I do not enter upon, as I doubt not but our Padre transmitted them to you at the time. I wrote to Miss Planta, merely to say I was come to pass 3 days at Chelsea, &, presuming upon the gracious permission of her Majesty, I ventured to make known my arrival, in the hope it might possibly procure me the high honour of admittance. She was not at home, but the Note was left. |

I was greeted at Chelsea not alone by Sally, but by Mrs. Rishton, & Soph[y.] Mrs. Rishton's history is long;[2] but it's catastrophe is brief: & brie[fly t]herefore I will relate it. When I was with her at Thornham, after quitting my Court service, she first opened to me her heart, & her misery; relating that she had never known real happiness with Mr. Rishton for more than a few weeks, though occasionally, & even frequently, she had had gleams of sunshine upon her discontent. Nevertheless, she had found his character austere, haughty, irascible, & impracticable. He had compelled her to relinquish, as her own act, all her early connexions—myself alone excepted, by some whim, I suppose,—& even exacted that she should never invite her Brother, nor his Wife nor family, to her [hou]se, as he disliked & despised them all! Upon this terrible subject I have had innumerable Letters;—but from the death of my Mother they became not only innumerable, but — —

An interruption in breaking off my phrase, makes me forget what I meant it should be. Briefly, however, after her Mother's Death she conceived a hope of effecting a total separation from Mr. Rishton, & obtaining from my Father an honourable asylum under his roof, with such an allowance from her husband as her own fortune gave her a right to claim. This scheme was hanging—now off, now on, for many months, & she wrote to me almost incessantly, & came to me twice, to consult & counsel. I was [alw]ays clearly of opinion that whatever were her wishes she had forfeited, by her marriage vow, the right of positively quitting him, if she could not obtain his consent. And, far otherwise, he opposed the project | with his utmost

2 Cf. iii, L. 222 n. 10; and iv, L. 270 n. 3.

might, through all means possible, save of force; persuasion was exhausted, promises of a changed conduct were unbo[und]ed, & menaces of ill consequences were frightful: nevertheless, he e[xpen]ded all his store of good in professions; none remained for action, & after repeated engagements, of seeing her Brother, &c, all violated, she one good morning left her house, while he was visiting at Lynn, whence he was to travel upon business to London. !!!

This step, you will easily believe, was not of my recommendation! It's vehemence & determination really startled me. I found her, however, now at Chelsea,—whence she had despatched James to communicate the tydings to Mr. Rishton, on his arrival at an hotel.

They were received, you will imagine, most furiously: however he declared he would no longer fight against her resolution & antip[athies], but merely desire she would accompany him back for a few days, in which he would arrange his affairs for a total separation, & publicly, & in some measure amicably agree to it. This James counselled her not to refuse, & I frankly told her I thought she had no right to hesitate about. She acquiesced, though in terror of what might ensue, & agreed to go to Thornham again, & in the same Chaise with him, upon his own return.

I am too much in arrears for comments upon this very extraordinary history,—but Mr. R[ishton]'s unspeakable efforts to keep, yet regular [wish] to deprive her of every happiness, rob her of every comfort, & refuse her every wish — — will make any body sigh, that such should be human nature! |

James joined us in the Afternoon, which was spent in perfect harmony & comfort. Sally was urgently desirous to ⟨h⟩elp Mrs. Rishton, who told me she was determined to attach her future existence to that only sister she could now claim real kindred with—the unhappy, wretched & culpable Mrs. Meeke having more deeply than ever repeated all the provocations of worthlessness & hollowness which have so often been practiced & pardonned in vain.[3]

The next morning, Thursday, I had a Note from Miss Planta, to say that she had the pleasure to acquaint me Her

[3] See i, Intro., p. lxxiv; and iii, L. 122 n. 12.

Majesty desired I would be at the Queen's House the next day at 10 o'clock.[4]

How sweetly condescending so immediately to admit me!

My Father, of course, lent me his Coach, & I went up the well known stairs to seek Miss Planta, to announce me.

⟵————⟶

This has laid by so very long, my dearest Susan, from hopes of verbal communication, that, to arrive at the subjects & interest of the present moment, I shall not attempt the minuteness I gave my last account with. I believe it will be more comfortable to yourself to advance quicker, & I am sure it will be more easy as well as pleasant to me.

Miss Planta conducted me immediately, by order, to the Princess Elizabeth, who received me alone, & kept me Tête à tête till I was summoned to the Queen, which was near an hour. She was all condescendsion & openness, & enquired into my way of life & plans with a sort of kindness that I am sure belonged to a real wish to find them happy & prosperous. When I mentioned how much ׀ of our time was mutually given to Books & writing, M. d'Arblay being as great a scribbler as myself, she good-naturedly exclaimed 'How fortunate he should have so much the same taste!'

'It was that, in fact, I answered, which united us, for our acquaintance began, in intimacy, by reading french together, & writing themes, both french & English, for each other's correction.'[5]

'Pray, cried she, if it is not impertinent—may I ask to what religion you shall bring up your Son?'

The Protestant, I replied; telling her it was M. d'Arblay's own wish, since he was an Englishman *born*, he should be an Englishman *bred.* with much more upon the subject that my Susan knows untold.

She then enquired—why M. d'Arblay was not naturalised.

This was truly kind, for it looked like *wishing* our permanently fixing in this his adopted Country. I answered that he found he could not be naturalised as a Catholic, which had made him relinquish the plan: for though he was firmly persuaded the real difference between the two religions was trifling, & such as even

---

[4] On 23 Feb. 1798.   [5] See ii, Appendix II, pp. 188 ff.

appeared to him, in the little he had had opportunity to examine, to be in favour of Protestantism, he could not bring
himself to study the matter with a view of changing that seemed
actuated by interest. Nor could I wish it, earnest as I was for his
naturalisation. But He hoped, ere long, to be able to be naturalised as an Irishman, that clause of Religion not being there
insisted upon: or else to become a Denizon, which was next
best, & which did not meddle with Religion at all. She made me
talk to her a great deal of my little Boy, & my Father, &
M. d'Arblay. And when Miss Planta came | to fetch me to Her
Majesty, she desired to see me again before my departure.

The Queen was in her White Closet, working at a round
Table, with the four remaining Princesses, Augusta, Mary,
Sophia, & Amelia. She received me most sweetly, & with a look
of far better spirits than upon my last admission. She permitted
me in the most gracious manner to enquire about the Princess
Royal—now *Duchess* of Wirtemberg,[6]—& gave me an account
of her that I hope is not flattered; for it seemed happy, & such
as reconciled them all round to the separation. When she
deigned to enquire, herself, after my dear Father, you may be
sure of the eagerness with which I seized the moment for
relating his embarrassment & difficulties. She heard me with a
benevolence that assured me—though she made no speech, my
history would not be forgotten, nor remembered vainly. I was
highly satisfied with her look & manner.

The Princesses Mary & Amelia had a little opening between
them, & when the Queen was conversing with some lady who
was teaching the Princess Sophia some work, they began a
whispering conversation with me about my little Boy. How tall
is he? how old is he? Is he fat or thin? Is he like you or M.
d'Arblay? &c, &c, with sweet vivacity of interest, the lovely
Princess Amelia finishing her listening to my every answer with
a 'dear little thing!' that made me long to embrace her as I have
done in her Childhood. She is now full as tall as Princess Royal,
& as much formed,—she looks 17,—though only 14,—but has
an innocence, an Hebe blush, an air of modest candour, & a
gentleness so carressingly inviting of voice & Eye, that I have
seldom seen a more captivating young Creature.

Then they talked of my new house, & enquired about every

6 See iii, L. 238 n. 2; and iv, L. 255 n. 4.

Room it contained, | & narrowly, I wished I had had a Copy of the little plan[7] of it M. d'Arblay made for my dearest Susan. And then of our Grounds, & they were mightily diverted with its mixtures of Roses & Cabbages, sweet briars & Potatoes, &c.

The Queen, catching the domestic theme, presently made enquiries herself, both as to the building & the Child, asking, with respect to the latter '*Is he here?* as if she meant in the Palace!—I told her I had come so unexpectedly myself, upon my Father's difficulties, that I had not, this time, brought my little Shadow: I believed, however, I should fetch him, as, if I lengthened my stay, M. d'Arblay would come also. *To be sure!* she said—as if feeling the trio's full objections to separating.

She asked if I had seen a play just come out, called 'He's much to blame'.[8] & on my negative began to relate to me its plot & Characters, & the representation & its effect, &, warming herself by her own account & my attention, she presently entered into a very minute history of each act, & a criticism upon some incidents, with a spirit & judiciousness that were charming. She is delightful in discourse when animated by her subject, & speaking to auditors with whom, neither from circumstance nor suspicion she has restraint. But when, as occasionally she deigned to ask my opinion of the several actors she brought in review, I answered I *had never seen them*—neither Mrs. Pope—Miss Betterton, Mr. Murray, &c she really looked almost concerned; she knows my fondness for the Theatre, & I did not fear to say my inability to indulge it was almost my only regret in my Hermit-life. 'I, too, she graciously said, prefer plays to all other amusements.'

By degrees, all the Princesses retired, except the Princess Augusta. She then spoke more openly upon less public matters: in particular upon the affair | then just recent, of the Duke of Norfolk; who you may have heard had drunk, at the Whig Club, To the Majesty of the People: in consequence of which the King had erased his name from the privy counsel: & the Queen, laughing, told me one of her Sons had told her his

---

[7] See Plate II.

[8] *He's Much to Blame*, attributed to Thomas Holcroft and to John Fenwick, was first performed at Covent Garden on 13 Feb. 1798. Maria Ann Campion (1775–1803), who had recently (24 Jan.) married Alexander Pope (1763–1835), played the part of Maria; Julia Betterton (L. 255 n. 42), Lady Jane; and Charles Murray (1754–1821), Doctor Van Gosterman.

Grace had been caricatured drinking it from a silver tankered, with the burnt bread still in flames touching his mouth,—& exclaiming—Pshaw!—*my* TOAST *has burnt my Mouth*![9]

This led me to speak of his great brick house which is our immediate vis à vis,—& of Lady Burrel, who now inhabits it.[10]

And then of the marriage of Miss Upton, which was then being kept at Norbury Park, with Lord Hervey: & sundry anecdotes followed of the Bishop of Derry (Earl of Bristol) Lord Hervey's Father.[11] And much then ensued upon Lady Templetown: concerning whom she opened to me very compleatly, allowing all I said of her uncommon excellence as a Mother, but adding 'Though she is certainly very clever, she thinks herself so a little too much: & instructs others at every word. I was so tired with her beginning every thing with *I think*, that, at last, just as she said so, I stopt her, & cried O, I know what

[9] Charles Howard (1746–1815), Duke of Norfolk, Earl of Arundel, Surrey, and Norfolk, and Earl Marshal (1787), etc. (*DNB*).

Widely publicized at this time were the celebrations at the Crown and Anchor marking the 49th birthday of Charles James Fox (24 Jan.), when at the close of an inebriated and somewhat abandoned evening the Duke had proposed a toast to '. . . OUR SOVEREIGN THE MAJESTY OF THE PEOPLE'.

His apologetic letter, sent to the King (*Later Corr. Geo. III*, iii, 1680), on learning that he was deprived of the Lord Lieutenancy of the West Riding and of the command of the Militia of the Riding, proved inefficacious; and he was removed as well from the Privy Council. These events, reported with malicious gusto in the *Anti-Jacobin* (29 Jan.), were noted as well by James Gillray (1756–1815) and other caricaturists, though the caricature here described has not been found.

[10] This was Deepdene, evidently discernible from West Humble.

[11] Elizabeth Albana Upton (1775–1844), eldest daughter of Lady Templetown (iii, L. 216 n. 16), had married on 20 Feb. 1798 Frederick William Hervey (1769–1859), *styled* Lord Hervey (1796), 5th Earl of Bristol (1803), cr. Earl Jermyn of Horningsheath and of Bristol (1826).

He was the surviving son of Frederick Augustus (1730–1803), 4th Earl of Bristol (1779), Bishop of Cloyne (1767–8), of Derry (1768). The Earl Bishop had tried to forestall the penniless 'love match' (above) in favour of a match with 'a real Cornucopia', 'one of the prettiest, sweetest, most delicate, and innocent, as well as accomplished little women I ever saw, endowed with £100,000 down, besides the reversion of landed property in Germany, with the promise of an [English] Dukedom'. The lady so endowed was the comtesse de la Marche (*fl.* 1780–98), a natural daughter of Frederick William II of Prussia; and in a series of seven letters (1 Aug.–26 Sept. 1796) the Bishop urged his daughter Lady Elizabeth Foster (i, L. 3 n. 122) to put the two prospects to her brother: 'No fortune. / Wife and children beggars for want of settlement. / No connexion. / A love match. . . .' *as against* '£5000 a year down. / £5000 a year in reversion. / An English Dukedom. . . . / Royal connexion—Princess of Wales, and Duchess of York.' The letters are printed in *The Two Duchesses*, ed. Vere Foster (1898), pp. 119–29. See also William S. Childe-Pemberton, *The Earl Bishop* (2 vols., 1925), ii, chap. 51.

The Bishop's splendid travels in Prussia and Italy, his fabulous collections of paintings and *objets d'art*, his wit, grandiose schemes, cynical interference in politics, and finally his arrest as a spy (*AR* xl (1798), 'Chronicle', 34) provided anecdotes for every ear.

you think, Lady Templetown!—Really, one is obliged to be quite sharp with her to keep her in her place!'

How curious!

Then we spoke of Mrs. Charles Lock, & I had great pleasure in praising her, where I found a general idea conceived unfavourably of all her race. However, Her M[ajesty] much blamed the Duke of Richmond¹² for not doing something essential for them: rich as he is, & fond of Mr. Charles, as I told her, in a very extraordinary manner. 'However, he will never, said she smiling, hurt himself ¹ very much by his *generosity*, I believe we may depend!'

Lady Camelford,¹³ she told me, she had been informed had a considerable sum in the French Funds, which she endeavoured, from time to time, to recover; but upon her last effort, she had the following query put to her agent by order of the Directory: how much she would have deducted from the principal as a contribution towards the loan raising for the army of England.!

If Lady Camelford were not Mother in Law to a Minister who sees the King almost daily, I should think this a made story.

When, after about an Hour & half's audience, she dismissed me, she most graciously asked my stay at Chelsea, & desired I would inform Miss Planta before I returned home.

This gave me the most gratifying feeling, & much hope for my dearest Father.

Returning then, according to my permission, to Princess Elizabeth, she again took up her netting, & made me sit by her. We talked a good deal of the new married Daughter of Lady Templetown, & she was happy, she said, to hear from me that the ceremony was performed by her own favourite Bishop of Durham,¹⁴ for she was sure a blessing would attend his joining their hands. She asked me much of my little Man, & told me several things of the Princess Charlotte, her niece, & our future Queen¹⁵—She seems very fond of her, & says 'tis a lovely

---

¹² Brother to the Duchess of Leinster (iii, L. 171 n. 11) and an uncle to Cecilia Margaret *née* Ogilvie, the wife of Charles Locke.

¹³ Anne Wilkinson (1738–1803), who had married in 1771 Thomas Pitt (1736/7–93), cr. Lord Camelford, Baron of Boconnoc (1784). Their daughter Anne (1772–1864) had married on 18 July 1792 William Wyndham Grenville (1759–1834), Foreign Secretary (June 1791–Feb. 1801) and Auditor of the Exchequer (1794).

¹⁴ Shute Barrington (1734–1826), Bishop of Llandaff (1769), of Salisbury (1782), of Durham (1791).   ¹⁵ Charlotte Augusta of Wales, born 7 Jan. 1796.

Child, & extremely like the Prince of Wales. 'She is just 2 years old, said she, & speaks very prettily, though not plainly. I flatter myself Aunt *Liby*, as she calls me, is a great favourite with her.'

My dearest Princess Augusta soon after came in, &, after staying a few minutes, & giving some message to her sister, said 'And when you leave Elizabeth, my dear Madame d'Arblay, I hope you'll come to me.'

What a sweet Creature!—This happenned almost immediately, & I found her hurrying over the duty of her toilette, which she presently dispatched, though she was going to a public Concert of Ancient Music,[16] & without scarcely once looking in the Glass from haste to have done, & from a freedom from vanity I never saw quite equalled in any young woman of any class,—& then dismissed her hairdresser & wardrobe woman, & made me sit by her in the same condescending & confidential manner as upon my last admission; & entered immediately, & with a smile that acknowledged her view & feeling of the pleasure she imparted, into conversation with the same grace, openness, & kindness.

Almost immediately we began upon the Voluntary Contributions to the support of the War;[17] & when I mentioned the Queen's munificent donation of five thousand pounds a year for it's support, & my admiration of it, from my peculiar knowledge, through my long residence under the royal roof, of the many claims which Her Majesty's benevolence, as well as state, had raised upon her powers,—she seemed much gratified by the justice I did her royal Mother, & exclaimed eagerly, 'I do assure you, my dear Madame d'Arblay, people ought to know more how good the Queen is, for they don't know it half!' And then she told me that she only by accident had learnt almost all ⏐ that she knew of the Queen's bounties. 'And the most

[16] The Royal Family attended the Antient Music on 23 Feb. (*The Times*, 24 Feb. 1798).

[17] Voluntary Subscriptions or Contributions, invited with the object of raising £16 million for the conduct of the war and the payment of debts, were authorized by the Act for the Increased Assessments (L. 261 n. 12). *The Times* (16 Jan.) gave prominence to the plan and 'for the information of the Public', outlined the contributions expected. 'The Great, the very Rich, the Men in Power and Place' might offer one-fifth of their incomes, and so on down the scale.

The Queen's contribution of £5,000 out of the £58,000 that, according to the Treasurer's Account (Add. MSS. 17871), she was allowed in the year 1797–8, would come to 7 per cent.

I gathered, she continued, laughing, was, to tell you the real truth, by my own impertinence! for when we were at Cheltenham, Lady Courtown (the Queen's Lady in waiting for the Country)[18] put her pocket Book down on the Table, when I was alone with her, by some chance open at a page where Mama's name was written: so not guessing at any secret commission, I took it up, & read—*Given by Her Majesty's commands*——so much, & so much, & so much,—And I was quite surprised. However, Lady Courtown made me promise never to mention it to the Queen. So I never have. But I long it should be known, for all that; though I would not take such a liberty as to spread it of my own judgement.'

I then mentioned my own difficulties, formerly, when Her Majesty, upon my ill state of health's urging my resigning the honour of belonging to the royal household, so graciously settled upon me my pension, that I had been forbidden to name it.[19] I had been quite distressed in not avowing what I so gratefully felt, & hearing questions & surmises & remarks I had no power to answer. She seemed instantly to comprehend that my silence might do wrong, on such an occasion, to the Queen, for she smiled, &, with great quickness, cried 'O—I dare say you felt quite guilty in holding your tongue!' And she was quite pleased with the permission afterwards granted me to be explicit.

When I spoke of her own & her royal sisters contributions, 100 per annum, she blushed, but seemed ready to enter upon the subject, even confidentially, & related its whole history. No one ever advised, or named it to them, as they have none of them any separate establishment, but all hang upon the Queen, from whose Pin money they are provided for till they marry, or I have an household of their own granted by Parliament.

[18] Lady Mary Powys (*c*. 1737–1810), who had married in 1762 James Stopford (1731–1810), 2nd Earl of Courtown (1770), cr. Baron Saltersford (1796), was appointed Lady-in-Waiting in 1788 (R.H.I., Windsor). In attendance on the Queen at Cheltenham in the summer of that year, Lady Courtown proved so useful and pleasant, reported FB (*DL* iv. 14–74), that she had 'a new place not merely given, but created for her', that of 'Lady in Waiting in the Country'. Since 'the Country' was interpreted to include Windsor and Kew (*DL* iv. 100), she was in residence at Kew during the King's illness of 1788–9, and she accompanied the Royal Family on the ensuing visit in August to Weymouth (*DL* iv. 188, 190, 194, 310, 313, 358, etc.).

[19] FB's pension of £100 a year had been announced in *St. James's Chronicle*, 4–6 Oct. 1791 (i, L. 7, p. 69).

'Yet we all longed to subscribe, cried she, & thought it quite right, if other young ladies did, not to be left out. But the difficulty was how to do what would not be improper for us, & yet not to be generous at mamma's expence; for that would only have been unjust. So we consulted some of our friends, & then fixed upon an hundred pounds a piece; & when we asked the Queen's leave, she was so good as to approve it. So then we spoke to the King; & he said it was but little, but he wished, particularly, nobody should subscribe what would really distress them; & that if that was all we could conveniently do, & regularly continue, he approved it more than to have us make a greater exertion, & either bring ourselves into difficulties, or not go on. But he was not at all angry.'

How condescending the simplicity of this recital!

She then gave me the history of the contribution of all her Brothers, & that the Prince of Wales—alas! the more the shame! —could not give in his name without the leave of his Creditors, to whom his income is now mortgaged![20]—'But Ernest, said she, who is very little in debt, & will soon be cleared, gives £.300 a year; & that's a 10th of his income; for the King allows him £.3000.'[21]

All this leading to discourse upon loyalty, & then its contrast, democracy, she narrated to me at full length a lecture of Thelwall's,[22] which had been repeated to her by M. de Guiffardiere.[23] It was very curious from *her* Mouth! But she is candour in its whitest purity wherever it is possible to display it, in discriminating between good & bad, & attracting rays of light even from the darkest Shades. So she did even from I Thelwell—so she did even from the Duke of Bedford,[24] in

[20] With improvements to Carleton House and to the Pavilion at Brighton the Prince's debts had mounted to £630,000 by 1795. The arrangements by which on his marriage (8 Apr.) an attempt was made to liquidate the sum, the debentures floated, the parts of his income reserved, etc., are described in part by E. H. Coleridge, *The Life of Thomas Coutts, Banker* (2 vols., 1920), ii. 59–61, 64, 91). The debts of the Prince of Wales in Mar. 1797 were still £432,344.

[21] The sum is correct, as see Anthony Bird, *The Damnable Duke of Cumberland* (1966), p. 63.

[22] John Thelwall (1764–1834), a poet, a radical (tried on charges of sedition in 1794, but acquitted), and a popular lecturer who commented 'freely upon contemporary politics through the medium of "Lectures upon Roman History"' (*DNB*).

[23] See i, L. 3 n. 4.

[24] Francis Russell (1765–1802), 5th Duke of Bedford (1771), who had taken his seat in the House of Lords on 5 Dec. 1787. A Foxite Whig, he had opposed a bill for

relating to me an interesting & curious scene between him & one of her own ladies—Lady Charlotte Bellasyse; whom he had formerly been intimately acquainted with, while she belonged to the opposition family of the Duke of Norfolk, whose Heir, Mr. Howard, had married her Sister, Lady Elizabeth Bellasyse:[25] but who, now, divorced from him, & married to Lord Byng, Lord Lucan's son, is in a species of disgraceful retirement, & no more in the way of such meetings as occasioned Lady Charlotte's intimacy with his Grace. Lady Charlotte, after long losing sight of him, from being appointed of the household of the Princesses, & consequently, mixing with a wholly different set, accidentally met him at the playhouse, whither she went with her Aunt, Lady Melbourne:[26] & he had so little delicacy, or indeed decency, as to start democratic subjects, & sport witticisms against courts & courtiers, in so pointed a manner, even occasionally asking 'What says Lady Charlotte to that?' as to make it impossible for her to miss his inferences at her situation. 'And though she was so nervous, said the Princess, as to be really ill afterwards, with her vexation at being so marked by him, she had the spirit & spunk to treat him with a contempt at the time that, in the end, disconcerted him, & made him obliged to give up his attack with confusion.' This anecdote she related in all its details, & in so entertaining a manner, that I am sorry to be so long in arrears as not to have courage to give the tale at length, & in her own words.

the security of the King's person (*Later Corr. Geo. III*, ii, L. 1229), and consistently an oppositionist and no friend of the Court, he had been lately caricatured by Gillray (for his Francophilia) and much castigated by the *Anti-Jacobin* for tax evasion.

[25] Lady Elizabeth Belasyse (1770–1819), sister of Lady Charlotte (L. 255 n. 8), third daughter of the 2nd Earl Fauconberg of Newborough (1774), had married on 24 Apr. 1789 Bernard Edward Howard (1766–1842), 12th Duke of Norfolk (1815), the legitimate son of this marriage being Henry Charles Howard, born 12 Aug. 1791. Divorced in May 1794, see the 'TRIAL *for* ADULTERY' in the court of King's Bench, 24 Feb. 1794, *AR* xxxvi (1794), 'Appendix to the Chronicle', 121–30, Lady Elizabeth married on 26 May 1794, the co-respondent Richard Bingham (1764–1839), *styled* Lord Bingham (1795), 2nd Earl of Lucan (1799), with whom she had been living since 24 July 1793. Their only child was Lady Elizabeth (1795–1838). In 1794, however, it had been feared that, under certain circumstances, their issue might succeed to the dukedom of Norfolk, at which 'the whole house of Howard had a right to complain', for what, apart from a divorce or proved adultery, could, at the death of the legitimate heir, 'prevent him from being duke of Norfolk?'

[26] Elizabeth Milbanke (*c.* 1753–1818), who had married in 1769 Peniston Lamb (1745–1828), 2nd Bart. (1768), cr. Lord Melbourne, Baron of Kilmore (1770), cr. Viscount Melbourne (1780). Her husband's sister Lady Fauconberg, *née* Charlotte Lamb (1743–90) was Lady Charlotte's mother.

She made me, as usual, talk of my little Boy, & was much amused by hearing that, imitating what he heard from me, he called his Father '*mon ami*' & *tutoiyed* him, drinking his health at dinner, as his Father does to me, '*à ta santé*.

Our conversation was interrupted, at last, by the entrance of Princess Mary, who, after a little chat about the play, & the Queen's admirable account of it, sat down to write a note to '*Cousin Sophy*,' as she most unaffectedly said, meaning, as I found, the Princess Sophia of Gloucester.[27]

When, at length, the Princess Augusta gave me the bow of *congée*, she spoke of seeing me again soon; I said I should therefore lengthen my stay in town, & induce M. d'Arblay to come & bring my Boy.

'We shall see you, then, certainly, said she smiling, and — — do pray, My dear Madame d'Arblay,—bring your little Boy with you.'

Imagine if this, which finished my visit, made its termination melancholy & disagreeable?

'And—don't say any thing to him!' cried she, as I was departing; let us see him quite—*natural*!'

I understood her gracious—& let me say rational desire, that the Child should not be impressed with any awe of the royal presence. I assured her I *must* obey, for he was so young, so wild, & so unused to present himself except as a plaything, that it would not be even in my *power* to make him orderly.

And here ends my second Court narration, my dearest Susan. I am sure you will want a *third*, when you see to what an event it leads, & therefore I will begin preparing it against the next pacquet without delay.

---

[27] Sophia Matilda, Ranger of Greenwich Park (1773–1844).

270   [*for c.* 26 February–8 March 1798]

For Mrs. Phillips

A.J.L. (Diary MSS. vi. 5068–[87], Berg), written at West Humble in Dec. 1798.

Five double sheets 4to, numbered 1, 2, 3, 4, and 5 (though of number 5, the conjugate leaves have been separated)   20 pp.

Edited by FBA, CFBt, *and by* ?Colburn's editors, *see* Textual Notes.

Also J.L., copy in hand of M. d'A (West Humble Letter Book, pp. 92–115, Osborn) dated: Dec. 1798.

Third Account.

I will not give the real date when I resume my narrative,[1] my most beloved Susan—but I never know how to do more than prepare a pacquet from conveyance to conveyance, be the materials of what antiquity they may. You will pardon, however, as well as conceive why, that I must infinitely abridge my relations.

My dear Father was extremely pleased with what I had to tell him; & hurried me back to West Hamble,[2] to provide myself with baggage for sojourning with him till Mrs. Rishton's return, when there would no longer be a spare room. Mrs. R[ishton] had set off for Thornham with her *cara sposa*, as I have mentioned, that they might have, at his request, an AMICABLE PUBLIC SEPARATION.[3] My two Alexanders, you will believe, were

270. [1] The references in these Court Journals to Lord Edward Fitzgerald indicate that they must have been written *post* 4 June, though, like L. 271, L. 270 may have been written even later, i.e. *post* 18 Dec. 1798.

[2] This would have been on Friday 23 Feb., and over the weekend FBA apparently went to West Humble, returning to Chelsea *c.* 26 Feb. with M. d'A and Alexander for a visit concluded on 10 Mar., the day before Maria Rishton's return to Chelsea (see L. 271 n. 28).

[3] In letters of 18 Mar. [1798] and May 1798 (Eg. 3697, ff. 258–9b, 261–6b) Maria Rishton mentions Rishton's unexpected appearance in London, her return with him to Thornham, and his renewed efforts to keep her ('Threat, Supplications —promises—Carte Blanche Offerd—of Change of residence, choice of Friends Companions—endeavours to Allarm my Conscience'). Finally, stipulating that she keep a manservant (at a salary of £50 a year), he unwillingly agreed to a separation with the generous allowance of £350 a year.

now warmly invited to Chelsea,—& we all returned thither together, accompanied by Betty Nurse.

I shall complete my next Court visit before I enter upon aught else.

I received, very soon, a note from Me Bremyere,[4] who is my successor,—(I have told you poor Mlle Jacobi[5] is returned to Germany, I think? & that her Niece, *la Bettina*,[6] is to marry a rich English Merchant, & settle in London?) This note says— 'Mrs Bremyere has received the Queen's commands to invite Madame d'Arblay to the play to-morrow night[7]—with her own desire I would drink Coffee in her Apartment before we went to the Theatre.

Could any thing more sweetly mark the real kindness of the Queen, than this remembrance of my fondness for plays & of what had dropt from me in my last Audience of my present removal from *seeing* them? To *think* of me in this manner was a gratification I felt most ⎮ singularly; & to let me, once more, go in my own old place—opposite to Herself, the dear King, & all her lovely Daughters, was inhancing the condescendsion, & doubling my gratitude.

My dear Father lent me his Carriage; & I was now intro-duced to the successor of Mrs. Schwellenberg, *Mlle Bachmaister*,[8] a German, brought over by M. de Luc,[9] who travelled into Germany to accompany her hither. I found she was the lady I had seen with the Queen & Princesses, teaching some work. Not having been to these long known apartments since the death of Mrs. Schwellenberg, I knew not how they were arranged, & had concluded Me Bremyere possessed those of Mrs. Schwellen-berg. Thither, therefore, I went,—& was received to my great surprise, by this lady—who was equally surprised by my entrance, though without any doubt who I might be, from having seen me with the Queen, & from knowing I was to join

---

[4] See L. 255 n. 19.   [5] See i, L. 7 n. 3; and L. 12 n. 6.

[6] This is 'Betti' Winkelmann, who was described in i, L. 12 n. 6. The record of her marriage has not been found.

[7] The play (see p. 90) was a command performance on 1 March of George Colman's *The Heir at Law* (1797). See *Morning Chronicle*, 1 Mar. 1798.

[8] See L. 255 n. 18.

[9] M. de Luc (i, L. 3 n. 3), a scholar of some repute and Reader to the Queen (1774–1818), had been sent in November 1797 on 'a secret mission to Brunswick with the idea of inducing the Duke to support the scheme of a Second Coalition (of Russia, Austria, Britain and Prussia) against France' (*Later Corr. Geo. III*, iii, L. 1670 n. 4 and Ll. 1673, 1675, 1689, 1693, 1719).

the play party to my *ci-devant* Box. I enquired if I had made any mistake, but though she could not say no, she would not suffer me to rectify it, but sent to ask Mᵉ Bremyere to meet me in her room.

Mˡˡᵉ Bachmeister is extremely genteel in her figure, though extremely plain in her face; her voice is gentle & penetrating, her manners are soft, yet dignified, & she appears to be both a feeling & a cultivated character. I could not but lament such had not been the former possessor of an Apartment I had so often entered ⎮ with the most cruel antipathy. I liked her exceedingly; She is a marked Gentlewoman in her whole deportment; though whether so from Birth, Education, or only Mind, I am ignorant.

Since she gave me so pleasant a prejudice in her favour, you will be sure our acquaintance began with some spirit. We talked much of the situation she filled; & I thought it my duty to cast the whole of my resignation of one so similar upon ill health. Mrs. Bremyere soon joined us, & we took up Miss Barbara Planta[10] in our way to the Theatre.

When the King—the dear—dear King entered, followed by the Queen & his lovely Daughters, & the orchestra struck up God save the King, & the people all called for the Singers, who filled the stage to sing it—the emotion I was suddenly filled with so powerfully possessed me, that I wished I could—for a minute or two—have flown from the Box, to have *sobbed*!— I was so gratefully delighted at the sight before me, & so en-raptured at the continued enthusiasm of the no longer volatile people for their worthy, revered Sovereign—that I really suffered from the restraint I felt of being forced to behave decourously. The thoughts of his dreadful illness—his miracul-ous recovery—his constant benignity—to *me* his even partial goodness—& the knowledge I was indulged with this view of him by the Queen, & with his certain consent, filled my heart so full, that, though ⎮ only with joy, I was almost in an hysteric. M. d'Arblay, who went into the Pit, to see the Royal family,— & who forgot not his *Athanase*, told me afterwards he was quite frightened by the motion of my shoulders, I so shook. Every royal Eye deigned to look up to me—with my Opera Glass I caught them all; & my Companions all pointed out to me that the King himself fixed his Glass upon me.

[10] See i, L. 23 n. 81.

[*Here M. d'Arblay interpolated*]

Oui, à 3 fois différentes et pendant assez longtems. La reine en souriant lui avait fait remarker les pleurs de l'Athanase, les Princesses se la montraient l'une l'autre dabord en riant, mais ensuite deux d'entr'elles joignirent leurs larmes à celles qu'elles voyaient couler. C'etait je crois la Princesse Augusta et la p^esse Mary. Je suis encore à concevoir comment cela n'a pas fait une sorte de scene. A chaque instant je m'attendais à voir tout le spectacle occupé du même objet, et je redoutais les suites de cette attention si générale.

[*Madame d'Arblay continued*]

I am sure they could not wonder, after so long an Absence from such a sight, with such recollections as it revived, that I was so much touched. God bless them! long & ALL!—The King, in his own Family, is as Mr. Lock to me in his!—a chief so inestimable as well as venerable!

The Play was the Heir at Law, by Colman the younger. I liked it extremely. It has a good deal of character, a happy plot, much interest in the under parts, & is combined, I think, by real Genius, though open to innumerable partial criticisms.

I heard a Gentleman's voice from the next Box call, softly, to Miss Barbara Planta 'who is that lady?' & heard her answer my Name, & him rejoin 'I thought so!—' I found is was Lord Aylsbury,[11] who, also, has resigned, & was at the Play only for the pleasure of sitting opposite his late Royal Mistress.

I was brought back to the Queen's House by Miss Bachmeister, where I found I our dear Padre's Carriage was appointed; but not arrived; & therefore I made still further acquaintance with Mlle Bachmeister, & still more to her advantage.

Again I pass over, for the present, intervening accounts, to finish my Court narration.

About a Week after this theatrical regale,[12] I went to the

---

[11] Thomas Brudenell-Bruce (1739–1814), 2nd Baron Bruce of Tottenham (1747), cr. 4th Earl of Ailesbury (1776), K.T. (1786), Governor to the Prince of Wales (1776), Chamberlain to the Queen (1780), Lord Chamberlain (1781–92), Treasurer (May 1792–19 Apr. 1814). See R.H.I., Windsor, *The Royal Kalendar*, and BM Add. MSS. 17871.

[12] This must have been on 4 or 5 Mar. The Royal Family attended the Chapel Royal on 4 Mar. and were reported to have returned from Windsor on 6 Mar. (*Morning Chronicle*, 5, 7 Mar.).

Queen's house, to make known I had only a few more days to remain at Chelsea. I arrived just as the Royal Family had set out for Windsor; but Miss Bachmeister, fortunately, had only ascended her Coach to follow. I alighted, & went to tell my errand. Mrs Bremyere, Mrs. Cheveley,[13] & Miss Planta were her party. The latter promised to speak for me to the Queen; but gathering I had my little Boy in my Father's carriage, she made me send Will for him. They took him in, & loaded him with *Bon-bons*, & admiration,—& would have loaded him with carresses to boot, but the little wretch resisted that part of the Entertainment!

Upon their return trom Windsor,—You will not suppose me made very unhappy to receive the following Billet—

8. March, 1798[14]

My dear Friend,

The Queen has commanded me to acquaint You that she desires you will be at the Queen's House on Thursday morning at 10 o'clock, with your lovely Boy. You are desired to come up stairs in Princess Elizabeth's Apartments, & Her Majesty will send for you as soon as she can see you.

Adieu, yr^s most affect^ly.
M. Planta.

A little before ten,—you will easily believe—we were at the Queen's House, & were immediately ushered into the apartment of the Princess Elizabeth, who, to shew she expected my little man, had some play things upon one of her many Tables. For Her Royal Highness has at least 20 in her principal room. The Child, in a new muslin Frock, sash, &c. did not look to much disadvantage, & she examined him with the most good humoured pleasure, & finding him too shy to be seized, had the graciousness,—as well as sense,—to play round, & court him by sportive wiles, instead of being offended at his insensibility to her royal notice. She ran about the room, peeped at him through Chairs, clapped her hands, half caught, without touching him, & shewed a skill & a sweetness that made one almost sigh she should have no call for her Maternal propensities.

13 See L. 255 n. 1.
14 Apparently FBA had transcribed here not the date of the invitation but that of the actual audience (Thursday 8 Mar. 1798).

There came in, presently, Miss Dashwood,[15]—a young lady about 13, who seems in some measure under the protection of Her Royal Highness, who had rescued her poor injured & amiable Mother, Lady Dashwood, from extreme distress, into which she had been involved by Her unworthy Husband's connexion with the infamous Lady Wallace, who, more hard hearted than even Bailiffs, had forced certain of those gentry, in an execution she had ordered in Sir Harry Dashwood's house, to seize even all the Children's play things!—as well as their Cloaths,—& that, when Lady Dashwood had but just lain in, & was nearly dying! This charming Princess, who had been particularly acquainted with Lady Dashwood during her own illness at Kew Palace, where the Queen permitted the inter-course, ⏐ came forward upon this distress, & gave her a small independant house, in the neighbourhood of Kew, with every advantage she could annex to it; & afterwards, through her influence, procured her the place of sub-Governess to the Princess Charlotte. But she is now lately no more—& by the sort of reception given to her daughter, I fancy the Princess transfers to her the kind benevolence the Mother no longer wants.

After a little talk with her, & shewing her a Work Box, to ask if she thought it could be repaired, saying 'I hope it can, for I have a great value for it,—it was given me by your Mother!—' She pointed to my Alex, adding 'Look at that Child!'

'A very pretty *little Girl*, indeed, ma'am!' said Miss Dashwood.

Just then, Miss Planta came to summon us to the Princess Augusta. Princess Elizabeth said she would see us again, &

[15] Anna Maria Dashwood (1785–1857), daughter of Henry Watkin Dashwood (1745–1828), 3rd Bart. (1779), M.P. (1775–80, 1784–1820), who had married in 1780 Mary Helen (*c.* 1763–96), daughter of John Graham (d. 20 June 1776) of Kinross. Dashwood 'seems to have been very extravagant' (Namier), his father in 1775 having had to pay £25,000 to settle his debts. In the years 1789–93 he became indebted to 'Lady Wallace', *née* Eglantine Maxwell (*c.* 1750–1803), who had married on 4 Sept. 1772 Thomas Dunlop-Wallace (d. 1835), from whom she had been divorced in 1778, retaining, however, the title (above). It was she who in 1793 sent 'a sheriff's officer to execute judgment on the property of the Dashwoods' (Walpole, xii (2) 87 and notes).

Lady Dashwood died on 6 Oct. 1796—too soon to profit from appointments at Court arranged by the Queen and the Princesses, i.e. Lady of the Bedchamber to the Princesses and Governess of the Royal Nursery, Carleton House (the Princess Charlotte had been born on 7 Jan. 1796). Lady Dashwood's daughter Anna Maria (above) was Maid of Honour to Queen Charlotte from 12 Dec. 1805 to 21 May 1810 at a salary of £300 per annum (R.H.I., Windsor).

made [Alex] take off with him a skipping Frog, which had mightily struck his fancy.

We found my darling Princess [Augusta] at her Toilette—&, with her usual carelessness of her attire, she instantly turned from the Glass,—& gave it not another glance; leaving wholly to her Hair-Dresser to deck her to her own taste! She received me with her customary sweetness, & called the little Boy to her. He went, fearfully, & cautiously, yet with a look of curiosity at the state of her head, & the operations of her *Friseur*, that seemed to draw him on more powerfully than her commands. He would not, however, be touched, always flying to my side at the least attempt to take his hand. This would much have vexed me, if I had not seen | the ready allowance she made for his retired life, & total want of use to the sight of any body out of our family, except the Locks—amongst whom I told her his peculiar preference for Amelia. 'Come, then, cried she, come hither, my dear, & tell me about her,—is she very good to you?—do you like her very much?'

He was now examining her fine Carpet,—& no answer was to be procured. I would have apologised; but she would not let me. ' 'Tis so natural, she cried, that he should be more amused with those shapes & colours, than with my stupid questions.'

Princess Mary now came in, &, earnestly looking at him, exclaimed 'He's beautiful!—What Eyes!—do look at his Eyes! —O what Eyes!—He's beautiful!'

'Come hither, my dear! again cried Princess Augusta, come hither,—' and, catching him to her for a moment, & holding up his Hair, to lift up his Face, & make him look at her, she smiled very archly, & cried 'O! horrid Eyes!—Shocking Eyes!—take them away!'

Princess Elizabeth then entered, attended by a Page, who was loaded with play things, which she had been sending for. How extremely sweet! You may suppose him caught now! He seized upon Dogs, Horses, Chaise, a Cobler, a Watchman, & all he could grasp,—but would not give his little person, or Cheeks,—to my great confusion,—for any of them!

I was fain to call him a little Savage,—a wild Deer,— a creature just caught from the Woods—& whatever could indicate his rustic life, | & apprehension of new faces, to prevent their being hurt,—& their excessive good nature helped all my excuses,—nay, made them needless, except to Myself.

Princess Sophia appeared next,—with *Spectacles* on!—She has had a danger of squinting, as well as extraordinary near-sightedness, & Ramsden[16] has made her some glasses to draw her Eyes right, which she now always wears, except in Public.

These spectacles excited so great a curiosity, again, in my little ungovernable urchin, that he suffered Her Royal Highness to take both his hands, & satisfy herself with looking at him, from his own desire to return stare for stare.

'How do you like that old lady, in her spectacles, my dear? cried Princess Augusta, laughing; is not she a good old soul?— Come hither, & let me look at those shocking Eyes again.'

This order was obeyed— —for,—I am ashamed to add,—it was accompanied by the offer of a Bonbonière!

'And what, cried I, when he had served himself, do you say, you little Savage, to Princess Augusta?'

He looked up to her, &, very gravely, answered '*Sanky, Pincess Adusta.*'

Pleased to have made him at length speak, she eagerly tried to draw him on into some discourse. 'How does M. d'Arblay do? she cried, (how sweet that!) I hope he is very well?—Your Papa, my dear, I mean?—What does he call *his* Papa?' *Mon ami*, I told her, sometimes, when he heard me say so; &, much diverted, She cried 'How does Mon ami do?' |

The Child understood her perfectly, & quietly answered 'He's very well.'

'And where is he, my dear?'

'He's in his oom/room/.'.

'And where do you live, my dear? Can you tell?'

'O, his Father teaches him that every morning, cried I, for fear of Gipseys!' & he pretty readily answered himself 'I live at West Hamble, Box Hill, Suddy/Surry/.'

'And what's your Name, my dear?'

'My Name's Ales*s*ander d'Arblay, & Master d'Arblay, & Charles Louis.'

This ended the conversation, for Princess Elizabeth began playing upon an Organ she had brought him, which he flew to

---

[16] Jesse Ramsden (1735–1800), a skilled optician and experimental scientist, whose shop was at 2 Piccadilly.

seize. 'Ay, do! that's right, my dear! cried Princess Augusta, stopping her Ears at some discordant sounds,—take it to Mon ami, to frighten the Cats out of his Garden!—'

Miss Gomme[17] was now kindly sent for, to see my Urchin—& only, in such a presence, presumed to *kiss his hand*,—which was fortunate, as I am sure he would have rebelled, had she attempted his Face. But he was wild now with his play things, dancing, pulling, & rioting about with them in all directions, the sweet Princess forbidding me to check him, & giving him full licence to run, not only all around, but to open the door, & caper about the adjoining & more spacious Apartment, at his pleasure.

And now, last of all, came in Princess Amelia,—&, strange to relate the Child was instantly delighted with her! She came first up to me, &, to my inexpressible surprise & enchantment, she gave me her sweet ǀ beautiful Face to kiss! An honour I had thought now for-ever over, though she had so frequently gratified me with it formerly. Still more touched, however, than astonished, I would have kissed her hand,—but, withdrawing it, saying 'No, no,—You know I hate that!' she again presented me her ruby lips,—& with an expression of such ingenuous sweetness & innocence as was truly captivating. She is—& will be—another Princess Augusta.

She then turned to the Child, & his Eyes met hers, with a look of the same pleasure that they were sought. She stooped down to take his unresisting Hands, &, exclaiming 'Dear little thing!' took him in her arms—to his own as obvious content as her's.

'He likes her! cried Princess Augusta; a little Rogue!—see how he likes her!'

'DEAR little thing!' with double the emphasis, repeated the young Princess, now sitting down, & taking him upon her knee. 'And how does Monsieur d'Arblay do?'

The Child now left all his new play things, his admired Carpet, & his privilege of jumping from room to room, for the gentle pleasure of sitting in her lap, & receiving her Carresses. I could not be very *angry*, You will believe; yet I would have given the World I could have made him equally grateful to the Princess Augusta.

This last charming Personage, I now found, was going to sit

17 See i, L. 7 n. 5.

for her Picture.[18] I fancy to send to the Duchess of Würtemberg. She gave me leave to attend her, with my Bantling. The other Princesses retired to dress for | Court.

Miss Barbara Planta, who had been ordered to read to Her Royal Highness while sitting to be painted, now came; &, like Princess Mary, as soon as she looked at the Child, exclaimed 'He's beautiful!—'

The Princesses Jewels were just placing; 'O! she added, how he must like to see such fine things! How he must be struck! Look, Master d'Arblay! look at her royal Highnesses head! how he must like it!'

'More than *I* do, I am sure, then! cried she, for I hate it!' & gave her Friseur just the first that came to hand.

We now followed Her Royal Highness to the Apartment where the Canvass & Pallet were prepared, & the Painter in waiting. I had no opportunity to ask his name, & cannot tell who he was. But his Picture promised much resemblance.

The little fellow, in this half darkened room, clung to me entirely, without any desire to play about; but the Princess, again lifting up his Hair to raise his Face, said to the Painter 'What do you think of this Child?'

'I think him beautiful!' he answered,—& just then a page came to call us to the Queen.

But I have forgot to mention that the Princess Augusta had already informed me, & with a pleasure sparkling in her kind Eyes, that the Queen again designed me the high regale of sitting opposite to them All at the Play this Evening.[19] Need I tell you how penetrated I felt? |

It was with great difficulty I could part my little love from his grand collection of new play things, all of which he had dragged into the Painting room, & wanted now to pull them down stairs to the Queen's Apartment. I persuaded him, however, to relinquish the design without a quarrel, by promising we would return for them.

Upon the Stairs I was met by Mlle Bachmeister, with an invitation to Coffee, previous to the Play.

[18] Possibly to Sir William Beechey (1753–1839), whose full-length portrait of Princess Augusta, exhibited at the Royal Academy in 1802, hangs now in Buckingham Palace.

[19] *Secrets Worth Knowing* by Thomas Morton (*c.* 1764–1838) was given a command performance at Covent Garden on 8 Mar. (*Morning Chronicle*, 8 Mar. 1798).

I was not a little anxious, you will believe, in this presentation of my unconsciously honoured Rogue, who entered the
White Closet totally unimpressed with any awe, & only with a
sensation of disappointment in not meeting again the gay young
party, & variety of play things, he had left above. The Queen,
nevertheless, was all condescending indulgence, & had a
Noah's Ark ready displayed upon the Table for him.

But her look was serious & full of care, &, though perfectly
gracious, none of her winning smiles brightened her Countenance, & her voice was never chearful. I have since known that
the Irish Conspiracy with France was just then discovered, &
O'Connor that very morning taken.[20] No wonder she should
have felt a shock that pervaded her whole mind & manners! If
we ALL are struck with horrour at such devellopments of Treason,
danger, & guilt—what must they prove to the Royal Family,
at whom they are regularly aimed? How my Heart has ached
for them in that horrible business! |

'And how does your Papa do?' said the Queen, most graciously, & in a manner to call for one of my lowest & most
grateful Reverences.

'He's at *Telsea*.' answered the Child.

'And how does Grand Papa do?'

'He's in the *toach*,' he replied.

'And what a pretty Frock you've got on! Who made it you?
Mama?—or little Aunty?'[21]

It was Mama;—poor little Aunty has not the most distant
idea of such an exertion; nor, here, was it either necessary, or
to be expected. The Queen asked a few questions about her
then, as if willing to know what kind of character she had;—
very clever, I answered; a little excentric, but good in principles,
& lively & agreeable.

The little Boy now grew restless, & pulled me about, with a
desire to change his situation; I was a good deal embarrassed,
as I saw the Queen meant to enter into conversation as usual;

---

[20] Arthur O'Connor (1763–1852), the Irish rebel (*DNB*), had been arrested at
Margate on 28 Feb. (*The Times*, 2, 3 Mar.) with a number of conspirators. 'In one
of their great coats was found a most seditious paper, purporting to be an address
from a secret Committee of United Irishmen to the Executive Directory of France.
Drawings and bearings of the English coast were also found on them; with a list
of the houses where the Meetings of the Corresponding and other Democratic
Societies are held in this country.'

[21] Sarah Harriet Burney.

which I knew to be impossible, unless he had some entertainment to occupy him. She perceived this soon, & had the sweetness & goodness immediately to open Noah's Ark herself, which she had meant he should take away with him to examine & possess at once. But he was now soon in raptures; & as the various animals were produced, looked with a delight that danced in all his features; and when any appeared of which he knew the names, he capered with joy; such as 'O! a *Tow*/Cow/!' But at the Dog, he clapped his little hands, & running close to her Majesty, leant upon her lap, exclaiming 'O! it's Bow Wow!—'

'And do you know this, little Man?' said the Queen, shewing him a Cat.

'Yes, cried he, again jumping as he leant upon her, 'it's name is *talled* Pussy!' And at the appearance of Noah, in a green mantle, & leaning on a stick, he said 'At's That's / the Shepherd's Boy!'

The Queen now again attempted to discourse, & enquired about my dear Father, & heard all I had to say relative to his Apartments with an air of interest, yet not as if it was new to her. I have great reason to believe the accommodation then arranging, & since settled, as to his continuance in the College,[22] has been deeply influenced by some royal hint: I know they are extremely kind to my dear Father, & though they will not openly command any thing not immediately under their controul, I have no doubt they have made known they wished such an accommodation might be brought about.

She then asked if my dearest Susan was still in Ireland, & gave me an opening to speak of Belcotton, & its loyalty; & enquired again after '*pretty little Norbury*.' Ireland, then, was touched upon,—& the Fitzgeralds; & Mrs. Charles Lock & Miss Ogilvie—& afterwards Mr. & Miss Angerstein.—She openly said she pitied poor Mr. Lock for his connexion with the Fitzgerald family.[23] I was surprised,—because ignorant Lord Edward had just then avowed his guilt by his sudden flight.[24]

[22] See Lonsdale, pp. 392–3.
[23] See i, L. 9 n. 5; iii, L. 177 n. 4; L. 203 n. 10. Charles Locke was formerly engaged to Juliana Angerstein (iii, L. 197 n. 7).
[24] Lord Edward Fitzgerald (1763–98). For a sympathetic account of the rebel and his family at this time, see Brian Fitzgerald, *Emily, Duchess of Leinster . . .* (1949), pp. 212–59.

I spoke warmly of Mrs. Charles; 'I am glad, she said, mildly, she proves deserving; She has been very— — ⏐ *fashionable*! Both the sisters have been brought up completely to be—*fashionable*. I fear poor Mr. Lock will regret the first business had not rather taken place!'

She said this with a real voice of concern for our beloved oracle—& I loved her for it, though I wondered—but alas!— since then I have too forcibly felt the truth of her fears,—for so bewitched, so blinded, so infatuated, have all the Sisters been by that cruel Brother, that he has nearly destroyed all their happiness, & touched all their principles!—It is indeed a blessing for them—& for *nos anges* that he is no more. The Queen was much more deeply informed that I was, for long afterwards.—

I imagine she had just heard of the marriage of Charlotte,[25] for she enquired after my *sister Francis*, whom she never had mentioned before since I quitted my post. I was obliged briefly to relate the transaction, seeking to adorn it, by stating Mr. Broome's being author of Simkins' Letters. She agreed in their uncommon wit & humour, but, I fancy, has heard of some more recent publications, which savour of democracy, as such there are, I believe, though not positively avowed.[26]

My little Rebel, mean while, finding his animals were not given into his own hands, but removed from their mischief, was struggling all this time to get at the Tunbridge ware of the Queen's Work Box, &, in defiance of all my efforts to prevent him, he seized one piece, which he called a Hammer; & began violently knocking the Table with it. I would fain have taken it away silently; but he resisted such grave authority, ⏐ and so continually took it back, that the Queen—to my great confusion, now gave it him. Soon, however, tired also of this, he ran away from me into the next room,—which was their Majesties' Bed room,—& in which were all the Jewels ready to take to St James's for the Court attire.

I was excessively ashamed, & obliged to fetch him back in my arms, & there to keep him. 'Get down, little Man; said the Queen, you are too heavy for your Mama.'

[25] Charlotte Ann Francis *née* Burney had married Ralph Broome (L. 257 n. 11) at Marylebone Church on 1 Mar. 1798.
[26] See L. 256 n. 1 and L. 272 n. 1.

He took not the smallest notice of this admonition; the Queen, accustomed to more implicit obedience, repeated it; but he only nestled his little head in my Neck, & worked about his whole person so that I with difficulty held him.

The Queen now imagined he did not know whom she meant, & said 'What does he call you? Has he any particular name for you?'

He now lifted up his head, &, before I could answer, called out, in a fondling manner 'Mama! Mama!'

'O! said She, smiling, he knows who I mean!'

His restlessness still interrupting all attention, in defiance of my earnest whispers for quietness, she now said 'Perhaps he is hungry?' And most condescendingly rang her Bell, & ordered a page to bring some Cakes.

He took one, with great pleasure, & was content to stand down to eat it. I asked him if he had nothing to say for it; he nodded his little *head*, & composedly answered 'Sanky, Queen!'

This could not help amusing her,—nor me neither, for I had no expectation ˡ of quite so succinct an answer.

The Carriages were now come for St James's,[27] & the Princesses Augusta & Elizabeth came into the Apartment. The little wretch, in a fit of renewed lassitude, after his Cake, had flung himself on the floor, to repose at his ease. He rose, however, upon their appearance, & the sweet Princess Augusta said to the Queen 'He has been so good, up stairs, Mama, that nothing could be better behaved.' I could have kissed her shoe-strings for this sweetness, as it seemed the instinctive kindness of a momentary view of my embarrassment at his little airs & liberties.

'And have you seen, Mama, she added, what a pretty bow he makes?'

He has a way, when so disposed, of holding down his little head after a Bow, that passed, probably, for respect—though it was mere whim. And then she again recounted how *sensible* he was, from some half imagined circumstances her sweet mind & fancy had put together to do him such honour, for my relief & delight.

---

[27] The attendance of the Princesses Elizabeth and Augusta at the Drawing Room to be held at St. James's Palace that day is mentioned in the *Morning Chronicle* (9 Mar.).

The Queen heard her with an air of approving as well as understanding her motive, & spoke to me with the utmost condescendsion of him, though I cannot recollect how, for I was a good deal fidgetted lest he should come to some disgrace, by any actual mischief, or positive rebellion. I escaped pretty well, however, & they all left us with smiles & graciousness.

I followed them from the White Closet, & went up stairs for the toys, & with the Ark, & the *Hammer*, (which when I had replaced in the Work ⎸ Box, the Queen a second time put upon his ark for him) a Watchman which Princess Augusta desired might be *her's*, & a Cobler, an organ, a chaise, & a Frog, of Princess Elizabeths, we returned to Chelsea. We could carry no more, & Horses, Dogs, & other animals were left, most reluctantly, in the Princesses' Apartments.

You will not be much surprised to hear that *Papa* came to help us out of the Coach at our return to Chelsea, though down two pair of stairs, so eager was he to know how our little Rebel had conducted himself, & how he had been received. The sight of his play things, you will believe, was not very disagreeable! The Ark, Watchman, & Cobler I shall keep for him till he may judge their *worth beyond their price* himself.

I returned to the Queen's House in the Afternoon, to drink Coffee with Mlle Bachmeistre, whom I found alone, & spent an half hour with very pleasantly, though very seriously, for her character is grave & feeling, & I fear she is not happy. Afterwards we were joined by Me Bremyere, who is far more chearful; & we then called for *Mrs. de Guiffardiere*, who, with a young Niece, a rather pretty Girl, were ordered by the Queen of the party.[28]

Me de Guiffardiere is an extremely gentle & pleasing woman. She seemed delighted in being of the party, & not sorry to see me again. I Need not say how many strange scenes her sight brought back to my recollection. I have never seen her *caro sposo*[29] since I changed my Name: though, in the short time we were at Windsor, he called thrice at our lodgings. The Play

[28] Jeanne-Adrienne Peschier (i, L. 17 n. 18), wife of the Revd. Charles de Guiffardière, had two nieces, Françoise-*Henriette* Peschier (1771–1817) and *Charlotte*-Adrienne (1774–1849), daughters of Pierre-François Peschier (1730–78) of Geneva. *Charlotte*-Adrienne remained in England, marrying in 1800 the Revd. Alexander Sterkey (*c.* 1767–1838), Minister of the Helvetic Church in Soho, London.

[29] The Mr. Turbulent of the Court Journals of 1785–91 (i, L. 3 n. 4).

was called Secrets worth Knowing.[30] A new piece:—it will never, I dare prophesy, become an old one. In the ⏐ next Box to ours, sat Mrs. Ariana Edgerton,[31]—the Bed-Chamber woman to Her Majesty who used so frequently to visit me at Windsor. She soon recollected me, though she protested I looked so considerably in better health she took me for *my own younger sister*, & we had a great deal of chat together, very amicable & cordial. I so much respect her warm exertions for the Emigrant ladies, that I addressed her with real pleasure, in pouring forth my praises for her kindness & benevolence. But—of course, my first delight was my opposite sight. The dear King & Queen & their five Daughters were received with testimonies of loyal joy that went warm to my heart,—& I saw that they again all deigned to look up for me, & seem pleased in my pleasure. It is a most delicious family—& I love & honour every part of it more, I think, than ever.

When we returned to the Queen's House, my Father's carriage was not arrived, & I was obliged to detain Mlle Bachmaister in conversation for full half an hour while I waited; but it was not at all to her disadvantage, except in keeping her from rest, as it served to encrease my good disposition to her. She is really an interesting Woman.—Had she been in that place while I belonged to the Queen—Heaven knows if I had so struggled for deliverance!—for poor Mrs. Schwellenberg so wore, wasted, & tortured all my little leisure, that my time for repose was, in fact, my time of greatest labour. So all is for the best! I have escaped offending lastingly the Royal Mistress I love & honour, & — — I live at West Hamble with my two precious Alexanders. — —

[30] See n. 19 above.
[31] See i, L. 13 n. 16; and *DL* iii. 99, 103, 123, 273; iv. 111, 464.

271   [*for c.* 26 February–10 March 1798]

For Mrs. Phillips

A.J.L. incomplete (Diary MSS. vi. 5088–[99b], Berg) with a detached fragment (Barrett, Eg. 3690, f. 181–b, foliated [5099c–d]), written at West Humble [*post* 18 Dec. 1798], and including copies of FBA's correspondence with Mrs. Chapone.

Originally five or more double sheets 4to, numbered by FBA [1], 2, 3, 1, [2], mutilated and prepared for publication, as see Textual Notes   16 pp. plus the fragment *recto* and *verso*   18 pp. in all

Edited by FBA, 2nd and 3rd double sheets annotated and postdated: Chelsea—1798; *4th double sheet*: II   West Humble—1798

Edited also by CFBt and the Press.

[*Here a leaf (two pages) is missing, but the real introduction to this Journal of the Chelsea visit of Feb.–Mar. is the introduction to the* COURT JOURNAL *for 26 Feb. to 8 Mar. 1798 (L. 269). The visits at Court recounted at the beginning and much enlarged in the telling, play havoc with the chronological sequence of events as a whole. When editing the Journals Madame d'Arblay herself perceived this and tried to remedy it by inserting the headings* Chelsea *and* West Humble *and by numbering these sections* [Part] I *and* [Part] II. *She also supplied the introductory sentence, probably derived from the bottom of the discarded leaf:*]

[But I have not told you of my renewed intercourse with Mrs Chapone, who had repeatedly sent me kind wishes & messages of her desire to see me again.] [1]

She was unfortunately ill, & I was sent from her door, without being named. But she sent me so kind a Note to Chelsea that I will copy it for my dear Susan, who will like to see it for her sake, as well as mine.

My dear Madam,

You can hardly imagine the vexation I felt from losing the pleasure you so kindly intended me,[1] after having so long—& so much desired to see you. I was very ill, & obliged to refuse all visitors that morning,—& indeed I am still but a poor

---

271. [1] In a review of Mrs. Chapone's constant kindness, FBA goes back a year to the occasion of her visit to Chelsea in the fortnight 23 Dec. 1796–6 Jan. 1797 (iii, L. 220 and n. 1).

Creature, though better.—but I would have borne a week's illness to have been well when you called—& the rather, because I cannot hope for another opportunity of seeing you here, as your stay is so short, & I am quite unable to go to you. Be assured I always think of you with great regard, & take a sincere interest in all that concerns you. I was very sorry to hear of Dr. Burney's severe loss.[2] I hope his health has not suffered. I hope M. d'Arblay, & your little Boy, are well. I heard it said that he was gone abroad; but I know not whether it is true. If it be, I hope it is on some advantageous errand. A line from you, with as much information as you think fit would be most welcome to dear Madam, your obliged

> & affect[e] servant, H. Chapone.

They have put my *name* in your list,[3] with *Mr.* before it, leaving out the S.—so that it appears not to be there, a disgrace I could not bear.—
Jan[y]. 97.

This little letter, but strong & undoubted mark of constant regard, from one whose character & writings I so sincerely respect & admire, gave me very great pleasure. Indeed she had always behaved towards me with affection, as well as kindness, & I owe to her the inestimable blessing, never to be remembered without gratitude and delight, of my first acquaintance with my ever most dear Mrs. Delany. It was Mrs. Chapone who took me to her first,[4]—whose kind account had made her desire to know me, & who always expressed the most generous pleasure in the intimacy she had brought about, though it soon took place of all that had preceded it with herself. I wrote a very long answer, with a little history of our way of life, & traits of M. d'Arblay by which her quick discernment might judge both of that & my state of mind.

When we came again to Chelsea, at this period,[5] our Esther desired—or was desired by Mrs. Chapone, to arrange a meeting, which she particularly wished might include M. d'Arblay, who, on his part, also desired to make the acquaintance—in consequence of which I had again a little Letter which I will Copy.

---

[2] The death of Mrs. Burney on 20 Oct. 1796.
[3] This is the subscription list to *Camilla*, where *Mr.* in place of *Mrs.* indeed appears.
[4] See *DL* ii. 167, 193–202.   [5] The period 21 Feb.–15 Mar. 1798.

'You are very good, my dear Madam, to afford me an Evening of your precious time, & to promise to prevail on M. d'Arblay to favour me also. I cannot say how much I shall rejoice to see you. It is a pleasure I have longed for several years. If it is agreeable to Dr. Burney, I shall be flattered by his accompanying you. When Mrs. Burney[6] asked me whether I had answered your Letter,[7] my treacherous, superannuated Memory, retaining only the pleasure that Letter gave me, led me to answer that I was persuaded I had: but I afterwards recollected that considering yours was a reply to a set of questions I had put to you it would seem as if I meant to draw you into a continued correspondence, which I had no right to, were I to follow it with another: | I therefore refrained upon principle, & real respect for your superior avocations. I believe this to be the real truth of what passed in my mind at the time, though, without *meaning* a *fib*, I could not, at the moment your sister asked me, recollect any thing that could have prevented my thanking you for the great satisfaction I felt in your kindness, & in the picture you gave me of your domestic happiness. I should like much to see your dear Boy if it were possible; & shall always take a sincere interest in all that is interesting to you.

Ever, my dear Madam,
Your affect^e serv^t H. Chapone.

I was really sorry I could not call upon her with my urchin, as she was so very kind as to wish it, but I could only get conveyed to her one Evening, when I went with our Esther, but was disappointed of M. d'Arblay, who, most unfortunately, had been obliged to go to West Hamble, for the *Shirley Bond*,[8] as Mr. Maturin was to meet him the next morning. This really mortified me, & vexed Mrs. Chapone.

We found her alone, & she received me with the most open affection. I had the utmost pleasure & gratification in the meeting. If I have always respected her character & talents, & been sensible of the honour done me by her partiality, imagine if I did not gratefully feel all this now doubled, nay trebled, by the worth & soundness she evinces by thus coming forward to demonstrate her solid regard, while so many | caught, or warped, Heaven knows how, by Mrs. ord, have taken no steps

---

[6] EBB.   [7] This letter to Mrs. Chapone is missing.

[8] See iii, L. 193 n. 7 and L. 234 n. 2. Gabriel Maturin (iii, L. 215 n. 7) was acting as Walter Shirley's agent (see Ll. 283–91).

whatever to shew me the smallest mark of remembrance. Mrs. ord herself, in particular — — if I did not regularly believe she was duped by another who loved nothing so much as weakening friendship, & sewing ill ideas & ill will amongst friends,— I should feel a resentment towards her to cancel all softer thoughts, & all former obligations.[9] But I always think she was not left to herself.

Mrs. Chapone knew the day I could be with her too late to make any party, & would have been profuse in apologies, if I had not truly declared I rejoiced in seeing her alone. Indeed it would have been better if we had been so completely, for our dearest Esther knew but few of the old connexions concerning whom I wished to enquire & to talk, & she knew too much of all about myself & my situation of which Mrs. Chapone wished to ask & to hear. I fear, therefore, she was tired, though she would not say so, & though she looked & conducted herself with great sweetness.

Mrs. Chapone spoke warmly of Camilla,—especially of Sir Hugh, but told me she had detected me in some *gallicisms*, & pointed some out. She pressed me in a very flattering manner to write again,—& dear Hetty, forgetting our relationship's decency, seconded her so heartily you must have laughed to hear her, *hoping* we could never furnish our House till I went again to the Press! When Mrs. Chapone heard of my Father's difficulties about Chelsea,[10] & fears of removal, on account of his 20.000 ǀ Volumes—'20.000 Volumes! she repeated; 'bless me! why how can he so encumber himself? Why does he not burn half? for how much must be to spare, that never can be worth his looking at, from such a store! And can he want to keep them all?—I should not have suspected Dr Burney, of all Men, of being such a Dr. Orkborne!'[11]

I came away much impressed with her goodness, & promising never to be in town without waiting upon her.

The few other visits which opportunity & inclination united for my making during our short & full fortnight were—to

[9] Mrs. Ord's sentiments on FB's marriage are reflected in SBP's comments: 'but if you forgive Mrs Ord one abominable word—you are a better Christian than I am—*albeit* I mean to pray for the amendment of her heart & intellect. . . .' (A.L.S., Berg, *c.* 1793.)

[10] See Journal-Letter 269 and Lonsdale, pp. 392–3.

[11] The pedant in FBA's *Camilla* (1796).

Mrs. Boscawen, whither we went *all* THREE, for I knew she wished to see our little one, whom I had in the coach with Betty, ready for a summons. Mrs. Boscawen was all herself, that is all elegance & good breeding. Do you remember the verses on the *blues* which we attributed to Mr. Pepys—

> Each art of conversation knowing,
> High-bred, elegant Boscawen.—[12]

The visit, however, was a good deal spoilt by the entrance of Mr. Goodenough, a placid smiling Clergyman,[13] who interrupted her questions about *Camilla Cottage,* a name she has heard from Miss Cambridge that my wicked Mate has given to our little dwelling, *Camilla raised,* & in which she seems to take singular interest. She has been, indeed, a principal builder, and therefore should love the edifice.[14] My good & ever kind Miss Cambridge sent me, afterwards, a note she wrote to her upon our visit, in which she speaks of it in terms that could not but be highly gratifying to us.

Miss Thrales,—where I also carried my little Alex, & grieved I could not spend a day, for none of my old friends are—*can be* more cordial, more warm, more animated, indeed, than these three persons. Susan & Sophy ⏐ preserve for me inviolably the strong, nay fond affection they loved me with while yet Children,[15] & always meet me with open arms & tender embraces, & will not suffer me to call them otherwise than in those days, *Susan & Sophy.* They are very charming Girls, not positively handsome, but peculiarly agreeable in their persons, gay, open, liberal, informed, & entertaining. Miss Thrale, from me, deserves the highest encomiums, for I believe her friendship & esteem of the most tried fidelity. With me, too, when we are alone, she is never reserved; her Letters are all confidential, & she has solemnly assured me I shall be the first to whom she will

---

[12] As shown by the handwriting (Osborn), the verses, printed in *DL* ii. 78, were composed by CB (see Lonsdale, pp. 266–7).

[13] Samuel Goodenough (1743–1827), B.A. (Oxon., 1764), M.A. (1767), D.C.L. (1772), F.R.S. (1789), vice-president of the Linnean Society (*DNB*), Dean of Rochester (1802), Bishop of Carlisle (1808). In 1772 he established a school in Ealing, which he carried on for twenty-six years.

[14] See iii, L. 171 n. 8.

[15] For Mrs. Thrale's daughters, see i, L. 11 n. 4; or Clifford, Appendix A. FB had spent many months at Streatham in the years 1778–82 when Susanna and Sophia were schoolgirls (*DL* i. ii).

ever communicate any thing of importance. It is impossible to *like* her as much as her sisters, they are so infinitely more engaging in their manners, but it is a real justice which I really pay her in loving her as much, from her solid high principles, her excellent & noble conduct in the dispensation of her fortune, & her unalterable constancy of friendship.

Alex was mighty well received, particularly by Susan, who exclaimed, like Princess Mary, 'Why he's *beautiful! quite* seriously *beautiful!*' The little rogue, however, would not go to any of them, nor suffer one of them to touch him, though he looked at them with great pleasure. But he took a strange fancy into his head, of strutting up & down their room with very *succinct* drapery, hoisting up his peticoats as high as he could hold them, to see how far he could reach his little legs in stepping from compartment to compartment of their carpet. It was impossible to scold him, he performed the feat so innocently; but ¦ I stopt him as soon as I was able, assuring him the Miss Thrales never walked with their *Cloaths so short*; & Susan, laughing heartily, said 'No, my dear, that is not *the way!*' I am glad he performed not this freak at the Queen's house, nor before Mrs. Boscawen! For, having once adopted it, he was no sooner released from my *putting him to rights*, & saw us engaged in chat, than he gravely re-commenced his course, with the same curtailing ceremonies.

Lady Strange,[16]—whom I had not seen for more years than I know how to count, but from whom I had had extremely kind messages by Miss Bell, when at Chelsea before Alex's Birth, & whom I had promised, through Bell, to wait upon whenever I should find opportunity. She was at home, & alone, except for her young Grand Child, another Bell Strange,[17] daughter of *James*, who is lately returned from India with a large fortune, is become Member of Parliament, & has married, for his second wife, a niece of secretary Dundas's.[18] Lady Strange received me

[16] For these early friends of the Burneys, Lady Strange and her daughter Isabella, see i, L. 21 n. 13. Sir Robert had died on 5 July 1792.

[17] Isabella Katherine Strange (*c.* 1785–1847), daughter of James Charles Edward Stuart Strange (1753–1840), M.P. (1796–1804), and his first wife Margaret *née* Durham of Largo, Fifeshire (d. *pre* Oct. 1791 in Madras). James had married on 18 Dec. 1798 as his second wife Anne Drummond *née* Dundas (1767–1852), widow of Henry Drummond (d. 4 July 1794).

[18] This Journal-Letter must have been composed after the event above, i.e. *post* 18 Dec. 1798.

with great kindness, &, to my great surprise, knew my person instantly, though she expected to see a stranger, from the servant's ill pronunciation of my name. I found her more serious & grave than formerly; I had not seen her since Sir Robert's death, & many events of no enlivening nature; but I found, with great pleasure, that all her native fire & wit & intelligence were still *within*, though less voluntary & quick in flashing out, for every instant I stayed, she grew brighter, & nearer her true self.

Her little Grand Child is a delightful little Creature, the very reverse ¹ of the other Bell in appearance & disposition, for she is handsome & open & gay; but I hope, at the same time, her resemblance in character, as Bell is strictly principled & upright. I was sorry she was out.

Lady Strange enquired if I had any family, & when she gathered I had a little one down stairs in the Carriage, she desired to see it, for little Bell was wild in the request. 'But— have *naé mair*! cried she; the times are bad; & hard,—ha' naé mair! if you take my advice, you'll ha' naé mair! you've been vary discreet, &, faith, I commend you!—'

Little Bell had run down stairs to hasten Betty & the Child, & now, having seized him in her arms, she sprang into the room with him. His surprise, her courage, her fondling, her little form, & her prettiness had astonished him into consenting to her seizure; but he sprang from her to me the moment they entered the drawing room.

I begged Lady Strange to give him her blessing,—she looked at him with a strong & earnest expression of examining interest & pleasure, & then, with an arch smile, turning suddenly about to me, exlaimed 'Ah! faith & troth, you mun ha' some mair!—if you can make 'em so pratty as this, you mun ha' some mair! Sweet Bairn!—I gi' you my benediction! be a *con*fort to your pappa & Mamma!—Ah! madam!—(with one of her deep sighs) I must gi' my consent to your having some mair! if you can make 'em so pratty as this, faith & troth I mun let you have a Girl!—'

I write all this without scruple to my dearest Susan, for *prattiness* like this little urchin's is not likely to spoil either him or ourselves by *lasting*. 'Tis a juvenile Flower—yet one my Susan will again, I hope, view while still in its first bloom. ¹

Miss Gomme[19]—I also visited in particular, while the royal family were at Windsor, & we renewed our old contract of faithful friendship, however apparently broken by little inter-course: for we both hate Letter-writing, & have, insensibly, dropt corresponding, yet both, I am really persuaded, feel for each other unfailing regard & good opinion.

I called at Chelsea upon Mrs. Hagget, Mrs. Hammond, Miss Grant, & Mrs. Keate,[20] but could stay with only a few minutes each. And I do not recollect any other visit I was able to make, except to Mrs. James Burney. Charles was at Bath, & I only saw him for a few instants, with his wife, Mrs. Bicknell, & his son, in their way on the road.

But I was extremely pleased in having an interview again with my old, & I believe very faithful friend Mr. Seward,[21] whom I had not seen since my Marriage, but whom I had heard, through the Lockes, was indefatigable in enquiries & expressions of good will upon every occasion. He had sent me his compilation of anecdotes of distinguished characters, & two little Letters have passed between us upon them. I was un-luckily engaged, in one of my few engagements, the morning he was at Chelsea, & obliged to quit him before we had quite overcome a little awkwardness which our long absence, & my changed name had involuntarily produced at our first meeting, & I was really sorry, as I have always retained a true esteem for him, though his singularities, & affectation of affectation always struck me. But both those & his spirit of satire are mere *quizziness*; his solid mind is all solid benevolence & worth.

I forgot to mention that Stephen Allen[22] was in town, & is a very more tolerable personage as a middle-aged Clergyman than he was as a *young youth*; | though the improvement is by no means such as I had been taught to expect, for he is still formal, not natural, & a little *what you may call* tiresome.

Mr. Maturin, Gabriel,[23] we saw one morning, & he seemed a very honest & honourable young Man, & gained M. d'Arblay's esteem & confidence immediately upon our affairs. He spoke

[19] See i, L. 7 n. 5.
[20] In April 1792 FBA had made a similar series of calls on the wives and daugh-ters of the staff at Chelsea College. The ladies here mentioned are identified respectively in i, L. 21 nn. 18, 17, 16, 20.
[21] See iii, L. 171 n. 16.
[22] See i, Intro., lxxiv.
[23] See n. 8 above.

highly of dear little Norbury—& somewhat *frankly ladipas* of what you may call—*abrompt!*[24]

Good Mr. punning Townshend[25] called upon us twice, & shewed me the Telegraph,[26] that is fixed up at Chelsea, & was as simple, & sensible, & gentle, & odd as ever.

And now I must finish this Chelsea narrative, with its most singular, though brief adventure. One morning, at Breakfast, my Father received a Letter, which he opened, & found only contained a blank cover, with a Letter enclosed, directed À Madame, Madame d'Arblay.

This, upon opening, produced a little bank note of £5.—& these words—

'Mad[me] d'Arblay need not have any scruple in accepting the enclosed trifle, as it is considered only as a small tribute of Gratitude & Kindness,—so small, indeed, that every precaution has been taken to prevent the least chance of discovery: & the person who sends it even, will never know whether it was received or not. Dr. Burney is quite ignorant of it.—'

This is written evidently in a feigned hand—& I have not the most remote idea whence it can come. But for the word *Gratitude*, I might have suggested many——but, upon the whole, I am utterly unable to suggest any one Creature upon Earth likely to do such a thing. I might have thought of my adorable Princess, but that it is so little a sum—Be it as it may, it is certainly done in great kindness, by some One who Knows £5. is not so small a matter to Us as to most others;——&, after vainly striving to find out, or conjecture whence it came, we determined to devote it to our *Country!*—There's Patriotism! We gave it in *voluntary subscription* for the War.[27] And it was very seasonable to us for this purpose.

---

[24] A term used by Mrs. Schwellenberg in describing Molesworth Phillips.

[25] Identified by C. G. T. Dean, *The Royal Hospital Chelsea* (1950), p. 250, as 'a civil Lord of the Admiralty' and if so, possibly the Hon. John Townshend (1757–1833), Lord of the Admiralty (1782–3).

[26] In 1796 'an Admiralty telegraph', a primitive device consisting of 'a wooden frame and six large shutters', had been erected on the roof of the East Wing of Chelsea Hospital, near the Governor's house. 'A clumsy apparatus, then newly invented', it made part of the signalling system of the time whereby, in clear weather, messages could be transmitted from the Admiralty House to Portsmouth in fifteen minutes. See Dean, p. 250; also H. P. Mead, R.N., *The Mariner's Mirror*, xxiv (1938), 184–203.

[27] See L. 269 n. 17.

This magnificent patriotic donation was presented to *The Bank of England* by Mr. Angerstein, through Mr. Locke: & we have had *thanks from the Committee* which made us blush. Many reasons have prevented my naming this anecdote—the principal of which were fears that if it should be known such a thing was made use of—&, as it chanced, when we should otherwise have really been distressed how to come forward or hold back,—any other Friend might adopt the same method,—which, gratefully as I feel the kindness that alone could have instigated it, has yet a depressing effect, & I would not have *become current*. Could I, or should I ever trace it, I *Must*, in some mode or other, attempt *retaliation*.

Behold us, now, back again at our dear West Hamble. And let me call back what I can of the little events I think my Susanna might like to hear. I must not attempt order of time, but trace & narrate as they arrive to my Memory's researches, till I come to the present year.

Mrs. Rishton took our apartment at Chelsea the Day after our return.[28] We could not stay to see her, as we could not all be accommodated together; but she wrote me a long detail of her adventures, which, after innumerable difficulties, happily ended in her calling upon me *to congratulate her on being permanently settled with 'our dear Father,'* as she calls my Father, *at Chelsea, & with Sally, to whom she fears not uniting her destiny for-ever, as she is exactly to her taste, & to reside with her always, & share fortune & time & fate with her, is her destination, as well as wish.* Sally, also, wrote me word that Mrs. Rishton made Chelsea as much paradise as *Chelsea* could ever be made.[29] I was truly glad, auguring all good to poor Sarah from the superior experience & | & prudence, & general manners of Mrs. Rishton, joined to such warm & even enthusiastic affection: though that it would *so* last, I more than doubted, from my knowledge that poor Sarah is capricious, & only loves, or likes, where & while she is served or amused.

I do not enter upon our renewed happiness in Norbury Park, as all of that passes in our current Letters;—but this was soon blighted of its gay bloom, by a Letter from our beloved Mr.

---

[28] Maria Rishton states in her letter of 18 Mar. (Eg. 3697, ff. 258–9b) that she had arrived at Chelsea 'last Sunday' (i.e. 11 Mar.). The d'Arblays therefore returned to West Humble on Saturday 10 March.

[29] This letter is not extant.

Locke, informing me of the seizure of Messrs Sheers, &c,[30] in
Ireland, & the absconding of Lord Edward FitzGerald.[31] I
need not enter upon all this melancholy business,—we were so
much shocked, at the time, for the whole family, that we went
every morning, & had notes every Evening, to satisfy our
extreme anxiety, for poor Mrs. Charles, who was big with
Child,[32] & for the unhappy Duchess, who doated on this
wretched son, as well as for his sisters Lady Lucy & Lady
Sophia, & Miss Ogilvie.[33] He was the general darling of all.
How culpability is encreased by his unfeeling resolution to
brave such ties, such affections, in pursuit of his inordinate
ambition of signalising himself, stimulated by personal revenge
for having been degraded from his rank in the Guards,[34] as a
punishment for his heading Clubs openly adverse to Government!

A short time after, the family gave out that Lord Edward was
safely landed on some shore not at war with England; in-
sinuating, but not affirming, Guernsey. They then appeared
rather more easy; though the first despair they betrayed, upon
his elopement, had manifested their terror of his danger, &
given rise to fruitful suggestions of their knowledge of his
criminality. Lady Lucy, in particular, had been immersed in
unceasing sorrow, till this report called her to some recollec-
tion; & Mrs. Charles was in agonies that menaced | her own &
her unborn Infant's life. Her whole soul seemed wrapt up—
lost—in that unhappy Brother & his situation. At this period,
a foreign employment was seeking for Mr. Charles,—but the
distress of his lovely wife's family superseded the application,
now, & the desire. *Lord Craven*,[35]—of whom you must remember
La Bonne's[36] account—came to Norbury Park, to visit Mr.
Charles there; Mrs. Charles went to Lady Henry FitzGerald's.[33]

30 Henry Sheares (1755–98) and his brother John (1766–98) were to be publicly
executed on 14 July 1798.
31 Lord Edward Fitzgerald was hiding in Dublin at this time (see L. 270 n. 24).
32 Georgina Cecilia Locke, born on 11 June and baptized on 19 Aug. (see the
registers of the Mickleham parish church).
33 See iii, L. 171 n. 11; L. 175 n. 3; L. 177 n. 4; and L. 203 n. 8.
34 Lord Edward Fitzgerald was never in the Guards, but he had been dismissed
from the army in 1792 for his participation in the English Festival held in Paris
when he drank a toast to 'The speedy abolition of all hereditary titles and feudal
distinctions' (Thomas Moore, *The Life and Death of Lord Edward Fitzgerald* (2 vols.,
1831), i. 131, 137). See also Brian Fitzgerald, op. cit., p. 202; and *The Times* (3, 5 Dec.).
35 William Craven (1770–1825), 7th Baron Craven (1791), cr. 2nd Earl of Craven
(1801).   36 Madame Monbrun, French governess.

Miss ogilvie continued with the Duchess in town, & was ill-judged enough to persuade herself to be about in public as usual, by way of concealing an alarm which her Brother's flight alone shewed she could not be without. Mrs. Charles & Lady Lucy then came for a few days to Norbury Park; Lord Craven, with Mr. Charles, rode by our Grounds, & stopt to present M. d'Arblay to his lordship, in his flannel Garden Jacket, while he was digging & planting Potatoes!—But Lord Craven seemed to understand his situation & condition, & to respect both, for he entered into conversation freely, upon politics, & shewed himself completely loyal; & he came again in a few days, in the same manner, & stopt for another discourse. And soon after, Lady Lucy, Mr. & Mrs. Charles, Augusta, Amelia, Lord Craven & George all came to the house, to visit us. M. d'Arblay was unfortunately confined with a fit of the rheumatism, caught in his arduous toils. I received them as well as I could, in our best parlour, which is quite unfurnished, & unpapered; & having given them leave to admire the prospect from the windows, took them to our little sitting & dining room,—which could but just hold them, & where I was obliged to send for Chairs from up stairs, having never had occasion to prepare for so *LARGE* a party before!—

The novelty, & little inconveniences of all this were here useful, as they ⌐ occupied our minds, as well as our manners & our chattery, & distanced the fearful subject of our thoughts. They had heard from Mrs. Locke of our true interest & concern in their situation & distress, & Lady Lucy seemed anxious to express a kind sense of it by her soft & melancholy manner, & Mrs. Charles embraced me, with a look that spoke 'you feel for our Edward!—' But I did not!—it was for her, her Mother, her sisters, I felt—not for a wanton young madman, who could risk all their happiness for his wild & pernicious schemes & enter-prizes. Lord Craven is a very handsome young man, & very fashionable, though he seems sensible, informed & shrewd. But nothing did I see to authorise *reports*—or *hopes*!—by no means. —though in the lady no small appearance of believing herself the object of both. She was silent, bashful, downcast, timid, & embarrassed.[37] Amelia was chearful, natural, gentle, & beautiful.

[37] Perhaps Mr. Locke's elder daughter Mary Augusta (1775–1845), who according to the *Locks of Norbury*, pp. 220, 241–2, 245, and Oman, pp. 132,

When she has walked, she is still in her first bloom, which, otherwise, young as she is, she does not appear—so widely different is the duration of first beauty in *her* & her incomparable mother, who is still blooming & lovely—I had almost said as ever.

Alex was immediately called for, & in very good looks—& pronounced by Lady Lucy to resemble nothing alive—& only to remind her of some beautiful portrait of a Child by some great old Painter. Lord Craven said he had some likeness to his Brother Keppel.[38] Mr. Charles played with him, & shewed him off, & Amelia made to, & received court from him. He, also, helped off the cruel feelings all parties were suppressing; for he was very popular indeed.

We purposed returning this visit as soon as M. d'Arblay could quit his ^l Room:—But before that happenned, they all set off for Town, & all our friends accompanied them, where they stayed at least 3 weeks—& then had but just returned when they were summoned back, by information that Lord Edward was seized.[39] He & Mrs. Locke came to us with this intelligence, & with the private account of the dreadful particulars of the seizure, & their sad forebodings of the calamitous catastrophe. We parted from them in much dejection: & the event was suited to the worst prognostics. They stayed till it was all over; Mr. Locke & Amelia then came first, those dear persons requiring the one fresh air, the other the delight of nursing her adored Father in quiet. They had passed a most disturbed time—& my dearest friend could hardly breathe for happiness when once able to join them. She had suffered inexpressibly—& in all ways,—she had nursed Mrs. Charles in her unhappy lying in,[40] when

[The lower part of this page was cut away]

165, 337, 363, 450, 'wasted the best years of her life on a romantic attachment for Graham Moore' (1764–1843). The youngest son of Dr. John Moore (ii, L. 68 n. 41) and brother of the hero of Corunna, he had a distinguished naval career, Commander of the Mediterranean Fleet (1820), Admiral (1837), G.C.B. (1836), and died unmarried. Eventually (29 May 1815) Augusta became the second wife of Sir George Martin (1764–1847), Admiral (1821), G.C.B. (1821).

38 Keppel Richard Craven (1779–1851), son of William (1738–91), 6th Baron Craven (1769), who had married on 30 May 1767 Elizabeth Berkeley (1750–1828). After the separation of his parents in 1783 he had been brought up in France. See *The Beautiful Lady Craven . . .*, ed. A. M. Broadley and Lewis Melville (2 vols., 1913), i, Intro., p. xxvi.

39 Lord Edward was seized on 19 May and, wounded fatally, he died in prison on 4 June.   40 See n. 32 above.

| to delight either in her own sweet little Children, or her adopted family, so recently idolized. Lord Edward seemed to have abolished all ties, all tenderness, for all but himself! This was wearing off, however—& is now, I think, looked back to as a dream. But it has been a miserable & dreadful business in all its circumstances.—We afterwards saw her when ever we could go to Norbury Park during her visits, & she came, with Charles & Augusta, to see us, & stayed some time, & was extremely kind & courteous, always appearing to retain her first disposition & partiality towards us both. Poor thing! how sincerely & from our Hearts we pitied her. I really believe she both saw & felt sensations such as are the most deplorable. Mr. Charles, too, deserved the utmost compassion, for he seemed deeply wounded by the extravagance of her nearly frantic sufferings, & has been much altered. It was truly unbearable to see such a reverse of almost

[*The lower part of this page was cut away*]

272   Chelsea College, 2 March 1798

To Mrs. Broome

A.L.S. (Berg), 2 Mar. [17]98
Single sheet 4to   2 pp.

March 2ᵈ—98
Chelsea College

To feel, as well as say that I wish to both all joy & happiness is now all that remains,[1]—& as dissension is at an end, & retrospection would be useless, I will waft to the winds whatever

272. [1] This is the reply to an announcement of 1 Mar. (Eg. 3693, ff. 70–1b) in which CBFB explained that the 'Marriage articles' having proved satisfactory, her marriage to Ralph Broome (L. 257 n. 11) had taken place that day at Marylebone Church. The 'Deed' (probably that relating to the Tytherton estates, L. 261 n. 3), her friend Mr. [Samuel] Hoole had thoroughly approved in all respects, and to FBA she relegated the awkward task of making the news known to the family (she herself being about to depart for Bristol):

Having so totally fail'd in *my* part of the negotiation with my Father & Broʳ on this Subject, I despair of success in introducing the Subject to them again—I therefore entreat you, my kind Sister, to judge & act for me, when & how you can—& I also request you to be so kind as to write an explanatory Letter to my Sister's Burney & Phillips, to Charles, & to Miss Cambridge, not saying a word, to the three latter, of any opposition being made, as I mean to sink that part of the Story—

does not spring from the fairest hopes, & settle in the warmest wishes. I need not tell my dearest Charlotte how affectionate & how sincere they are,—nor with what pleasure I shall hasten back to the first period of my best *prognostics* & ideas.

I saw Esther this morning, & had an explanatory discourse with her, & she will herself write you her kind feelings.

James I have seen this afternoon, & he charges me to send you his Love, & that he heartily wishes you happy, & that whenever you & Mr. Broome come to Town, he shall cordially shake hands with you both if you call upon him in James Street or, should he first find occasion to go to Richmond, he will call upon you himself.

I have no message from my Father,—but a little time must be allowed for passing away his surprise, which, as he was wholly unprepared for this event, has been extreme.

I will write to Charles to-morrow, & to our Susan very quickly, & to Miss Cambridge immediately. |

M. d'Arblay charges me with joining him in all I can say, to *both*, that is most cordial in kindness, & tender interest for my dearest Charlotte's happiness. Mr. B[roome] can confer upon me no favour so great as changing my late fears into a security they were ill-founded.

I should have much more to say in answer to many important points,—but all of *approbation* with respect to what you have confided to me of the new treaty, if I were more composed. But I will not lose a post at a time such as this. I must hasten, before I can even attempt to rest, this sincere offering of my ever faithful affection for my ever dearest Charlotte.

Heaven bless you!

F. d'A.

I direct by the *old* name, from uncertainty if your new one is declared at Richmond.

I am very glad you make a little tour.

Our stay here is for about another week; but we are yet unable to fix whether we can make our long promised visit before *May* to my dear Charlotte, & from still *impending* causes. We came away at this time with inconvenience & hurry, from the motives I mentioned in my last.[2]

---

[2] For the motives of the hurried visit to CB, see L. 269. The d'Arblays were to return to West Humble on 10 March.

To Mrs. Phillips

A.L. (Berg), 12 Mar. 1798
Double sheet large 4to   4 pp.   [*the cover missing*]
Annotated in an unknown hand, p. 1, *top margin*: Charlotte Broomes Marriage—

pray remember *Dorking* not *Leatherhead* in the directions.

West Hamble near Dorking
March 12. 1798. Surry.

What a world of materials have I for my beloved repository! but time always moves so quick, & the Pen so slow, that I can never keep pace with my designs, or my desires. All, however, must yield to my thanks for the last most touching, but exquisitely interesting folio addressed to myself.[1] I can never tell you how much it moved me,—with admiration—sympathy—& INDIGNATION—I conceive the object to be delightful—but there is something so singular in the mutual situation, that the friendship so ready to reciprocate would move one even in fiction,—how much more thus circumstanced!—my dear, & *excellent*, I must say, Susanna!—my Heart seems to *bleed* & to *boil* in turn for you—Tell me always all you can upon this subject, I beg,—for *I—we* am & are as singularly interested as the personages are singularly situated. I must now hasten off to another affair, which I am, at length, commissioned to unfold, after having been charged to relate, & then to withhold communication long since. The *result* you know from Esther—but the particulars I am sure you will be glad to have more at large.

About the middle of November, I was surprised as well as much pleased by a visit from Charlotte. Her little namesake was with her, but soon consigned to my Alex, as I saw her bursting with desire of private conference. She then informed me that she came to ask my assistance,—but not my advice,—

---

273. [1] This is the folio letter (Berg) of 5–19 Jan. 1798, most of which is printed in *FB & the Burneys*, pp. 265–72. Annotated by FBA: 'extraordinary History of Miss B or Janey Paney 1798', it gives a full account of Phillips's infatuation for Jane Brabazon (iii, L. 222 n. 20) and of the mutual affection and admiration of the two women—a curious triangle.

that she had contracted herself the very NIGHT before to Mr. Broome, author of Simkens' Letters, &c, & that they jointly wished to have my Father & James informed of their purpose through me,[2] from a persuasion I should use my utmost endeavours to smooth over any difficulties, & pave the way to general happiness from the connexion. As I had never seen Mr. B. it was impossible for me to be otherwise than very anxious at this unexpected confidence; but as his Simkens' Letters are delicious in humour & pleasantry & cleverness, I augured only good, & most promptly undertook to make every exertion in my power to avert coldness or displeasure on the part of our dear Father, with whom my only fear was from my own doubts of the *politics* of Mr. B. My Mate gave his chearful benediction to her, & full consent to my immediate mediation. The next Morning, therefore, after she had given the first airing to my Susanna's destined Chamber—we set out together for Chelsea. She went to a house in Sloane Street, while I stopt upon my embassy.

My dear Father was at home, &, most fortunately, alone: the business was a little awkward, but the name was brilliant, the works had been high in favour,—by *me* almost adored—& my courage all hung upon *Simken*. I was heard with a smile, as soon as that name was pronounced, & the little I had to say of money matters was completely satisfactory. When I was returing, however, to proceed with the same embassy to James, he characteristically said 'Tell her I must leave her to her own judgement,—& she has conducted herself so irreproachably since she has been wholly her own mistress, that I have great reliance upon her prudence—but —— tell her I earnestly desire she will first enquire whether he is not a Democrat—for I have some suspicion he has turned that way.'

Thence I set off for James,—accompanied by Sally, who was just returned from a walk, & good-humouredly | distressingly, proposed the junction. I was saved, however, any difficulty, by the absence of James from his home: & though I missed some embarrassment, I was very seriously sorry not to meet him. He is the best good fellow, & kindest Brother imaginable, & I wished to discuss many matters with him. In returning, I had extreme need of address & management to part from Sally,

[2] See Ll. 256 and 257.

without offending her, or awakening suspicion; for I had promised to see Charlotte in Sloane Street, where I knew she was waiting for me in agonies of impatience. I contrived it, however, with some absurdity of invention & rhodomontade, & relieved poor Charlotte's mind by a few words of comfort. I then returned to the College, where my dear Father had ordered me a hot little half dinner, of which he partook, & we had a very chearful tête à tête meal, Mrs. Young[3] occupying Sally in the other room. This part of my enterprize ended completely to my satisfaction, & I left my dear Father in excellent health & spirits & good humour.

I went in for a moment to Mrs. Young, whom I saw with true commiseration, as she was in deep mourning for her lovely little Girl, Patty, but a few months lost to her.

I re-joined Charlotte, who came back with me to West Hamble, & my Susan's room, in order to hear at leisure the history & detail of all that had passed.

Here we arrived about 10 at night, & set about Letter writing immediately. I composed a long epistle to James,[4] with the history of the business, & a short one to my Father with Charlotte's contentment with my account of his reception of her design. She then said I should write to Etty, & you, & Charles,—but afterwards stopt me to wait *further progress*.

It was settled Mr. B. should visit my Father the following Sunday, & meet James.—

I had no news of the interview for some time—& then I heard from Charlotte that she believed James, by his interference in money transactions, would *break off the Match*; & from my Father, that he was in *horrour* of the plan, as he was now convinced Mr. B. was a Democrat, if not Jacobin,—& from James that he had every species of doubt that could render the connexion terrifying & disagreeable:—& soon after from Esther, who had gathered the state of the affair through Charlotte's bewilderments, that she thought nothing could have brought it to bear but total want of common sense & reason.

This was very comfortless, & I was truly uneasy & disturbed

---

[3] Arthur Young's wife, the late Mrs. Burney's sister (i, L. 23 n. 29), whose youngest daughter Martha Ann, 'Patty' or 'Bobbin' (b. 5 May 1783) had died on 14 July 1797 (see his *Autobiography*, chap. xii).
[4] See L. 257.

for my poor Charlotte; but I must now be more concise & general, or I shall never have done.

The *settlements*[5] caused such contestation & ill blood, that I really thought (& *wished*) they would prove the bane of the proceeding: I had long Letters to write to all round, without end, to try to conciliate, & at least prevent the added evil of a family quarrel. Charlotte came to me 5 times, abruptly, but in a distress of mind how to decide & act that won all my pity, & obtained my every moment of thought. Whatever of advice or consolation I could suggest was her's, & much she needed ALL that she could meet; for she was unable to judge for herself two Hours following; she was incenced with James for his interference, piqued against my Father for his cold withdrawing from concurrence, & though warmly defending Mr. B. from every attack, unskilful how to vindicate his conduct, & miserable with unacknowledged fears lest it was really wrong or unkind. I felt a compassion for her wretched state & unceasing doubts that made me devote to her & her affairs ! almost my whole thoughts. At length—the *breach* was declared,—& she went to Bath[6] to endeavour to divert her chagrin.

Speedily after, Mr. B. addressed himself to *me*,[7]—in a very long double Letter, full of complaints against my Father— Brother—& Charlotte herself,—& only civil to *me* of all the family: speaking of all else with the haughtiest resentment.

Provoked by a confidence so extraordinary, I wrote the most keen reply I ever composed in my life,—declining all argument, justifying my Father & James, & warmly *panegyrizing* Charlotte.

This had an answer full of civility to ALL! with excuses the most obsequious, & a general tenour of extreme humility, even to melancholy, at his disappointment.

Much surprised, but always irresistibly melted by humility & concession in a proud & fiery character, I instantly sent a softening answer—wishing him happy, but still frankly declaring I did not think his character & that of Charlotte *congenial*.

Another Letter came now, calling upon me to enter into

---

5 See L. 261 n. 3.

6 This was around 18 Jan. (see L. 267, p. 71).

7 This must have been the letter to which FBA's L. 268 is the reply. Saved from the circumstance of its having been copied into a Letter Book, it (alone of the correspondence here mentioned) is extant.

particulars, attacking my acquiescence in the breach, & seeming to think me *reprehensible* for not taking sides with *him*, who had done me the honour to claim me for his advocate & champion, against the faulty & inferior characters that ventured to oppose him.

My answer was now most concise, not more than 4 lines—positively declining to enter any further into the business, or to vindicate even myself.

Almost immediately after, arrived a Letter from Charlotte, to inform me that all was renewed, & settlements then making out between them, in which no one was to take any part; & conjuring me to let nothing transpire till I heard more.

This was unpleasant enough;—but I could not forfeit her confidence: it would have been still more useless than treacherous, as she is wholly independent.

We were just setting out for Chelsea,[8] upon news I had received from our dear Father that he feared losing his apartments at the College, & wished me to try if I could write in his behalf to the highest Powers,—highest & most benign. My dear Partner thought I had best go to him instantly, to consult in person: I did so, & I will tell you hereafter more of all that passed in consequence.

At Chelsea I received, a day or two after, a Letter from Charlotte Broome.[9]

I was called upon to declare this marriage to my Father & the family.

I give you leave to envy me!—I was truly concerned with a thousand fears for *her*, & perfectly uncomfortable to make so unwelcome a communication to my Father. He was very angry indeed,—& vowed he would see neither of them.

·I knew passion such as that must pass, & let it cool—but I felt—& feel still what will not so easily pass of inquietude for my poor Charlotte.

She next sent me the deeds, &c, last drawn up,—&, though I seem to stand alone, I own I think them perfectly honourable & satisfactory & fair. But a prejudice is gone abroad that time only can clear away. Should he prove kind, all will be forgotten —my only hope is in *her* adoration of his wit & parts, which, if it lasts, may engage his tenderness, as it must gratify his vanity.

---

[8] On 21 Feb. 1798.   [9] The letters referred to in L. 272 n. 1.

If it lasts *not*—what can they have in ˡ *common*, with abilities &
pride such as his, simplicity & timidity such as her's?—

You will write to her, I am sure, my dearest Susanna, your
kind wishes—but say not a word, not a hint of this history, as
she flatters herself the difficulties will never reach you!—!—
from *ME* they shall reach no other,—but to *you* I *can* only write
openly. It is therefore that I felt but little alacrity to begin the
tale.

I have still never seen him; but we shall probably soon meet,
as *he* is earnest to make the acquaintance personal, & she, I
know, wishes few things so ardently. It is singular that he has
taken various measures for a meeting ever since he came from
the East Indies,—which was the same year that Mr. Francis
arrived;[10] but they have always been frustrated. I have long
known of this, & desired it also myself,—from admiration of
Simkens' Letters,—though I little imagined the *rencounter* was to
be deferred till I met a Brother!

He was married about 7 years ago to a Miss Jeffereys, with
whom he lived very unhappily. She has been dead about a year
& a half. She had two little ones, but both of them expired in
Childhood. Mr. B. has a natural daughter, whose Mother was
an Indian of high rank. She has been educated in England, &
now resides with her Father, & Charlotte, most kindly, has
consented to her continuing with them. She is 17.![11]—

They are just now at his house, at Lisson Green; but you will
direct still as formerly at Richmond. They have not yet fixed
where they shall permanently settle. I am assured little
Charlotte is extremely pleased with the marriage. Marianne &
Clement will be so of course.

She was given away by Mr. Hoole,[12] the Lawyer, Brother to
the Ariosto Hoole; Miss Morton[13] was her Bride-Maid, & Mr.
Morton[14] performed the Ceremony, in Marybone Church.

I have written all these particulars, because I can judge the
true interest you will take in an event of such extreme & lasting
importance to this perfectly *good* Soul, who can never have any

---

[10] In 1785 (*ED* ii. 273).   [11] See L. 257 n. 11.
[12] Samuel Hoole (d. *post* 1803), a lawyer and brother of John Hoole (1727–1803)
the translator (iii, L. 140 n. 4).
[13] The governess Elizabeth Morton (iii, L. 212 n. 4).
[14] Probably the Revd. Joshua Morton (*fl.* 1778–1825), later (1800) vicar of
Riseley, Beds.

errour of heart, whatever she may have of Head; never any of design, whatever she may have of execution. I am very solicitous about her,—& have no hope for her, but on the principle I have hinted at that flattered talents may find a pleasure from her gentle adulation that may soften a rigid nature.

The history of my late expedition I defer,[15] as this is so closely long, & as I shall have no other narrative for many a Month to give,—for these are no travelling times! & my Gardener is no where happy for more than 3 days away from his champ & chaumiere. I leave you to conjecture how much & long his rib would enjoy herself away from him. Our bantling has the same rustic & homely taste, & is in raptures to be returned to '*Papa's new House*;' which he could not love more, if his share in the construction of it was as great as in its possession. If I can possibly get time, I will write my promised court account for this pacquet;[16] but as Mr. Bourdouis[17] comes to-morrow for a few Days, perhaps I must be obliged to postpone it. God bless —&bless my sweetest—dearest—dearest Susan!—How dear a Letter this last of all, addressed to our best Friend!—but where —O where is our anchor!—Guard your Health, my beloved Sister—of all things, & most of all, guard your *Health*!—

274   West Humble, 18 March 1798

To Charles Burney

A.L.S. (John Comyn, grangerized *Diary*, vol. vi. 14), 18 Mar. [17]98
Double sheet 4to   4 pp.   *pmks*   DARKING   20 MR 98   20 MR 98
wafer mended
Addressed: Dr. Charles Burney, / Greenwich, / Kent.

WestHamble near
Dorking—
March 18—98

How very provoking, my dearest Carlos, to be so near you, yet wholly miss you! I cannot yet get the better of that dis-

---

[15] That is, the Journal Letters 269, 270, and 271, which were not written until December 1798.
[16] The Court narrative, L. 255, completed by 20 March.
[17] Lambert Antoine Bourdois (iii, L. 245 n. 10).

appointment, it so thoroughly chagrined me. My better Half, who had better luck, explained, I trust, how inevitably I was confined *in waiting*, & prevented going to you.

But I feel extremely anxious for news of your poor Rosette— & for news of your own fortitude upon such repeated trials. Bear up, against them, dearest Charles,—the disorder will in time wear itself out, & that without wearing out its poor Patient, who has certainly more internal strength of resistance than she believed, or than seemed apparent. Take—& if, or when she is well enough, give my kindest wishes, with true sympathy in her sufferings, & your cruel view of them, & hard disappointment at their so unexpected renewal.[1]

The Wife of Bath[2] is now, I believe, at Bristol. I am sure she will be much pleased at your Brotherhood of Broom & Birch. I have never yet seen him but hope to like | him, ere long, as well as his verses. He need wish nothing more.

My Father was *delighted to pardon* the omission so honourably caused to his Sunday's hope of you. I have heard of Lord Spencer's kindness about some *rare Book* with great pleasure: But I have never caught its name. Whether it is too heathenish for the pronunciation of those who mentioned it, or for the Ear of her who heard it, I know not, but I rejoice just as well,—for 'twas the deed, & the donor, that charmed me.

M. d'A. returned so happily laden with food for his 5 or 6 shelves, that believe me Lord Spencer gave you not more enjoyment. Suppose yourself but without the Iliad & Odyssey (whether in greek or English) & imagine your rapture at their sudden possession. You can then judge what you have done.

The many-named youth[3] was not left to silent solitude—he accompanied us to Chelsea—& he was singularly honoured by the highest of presentations. He behaved tolerably well upon the occasion.—& when Her Majesty gave him, most sweetly & graciously, a play thing called Noah's ark, containing little representations of all sorts | of animals, & I asked him what he had to say for it, he most simply answered, looking innocently in her Face, '*Sanky | Thankee |, Queen!*'

274. [1] Sarah (Rose) Burney or 'Rosette' was subject to fits of depression, difficult at this distance to analyse, but often alluded to in the correspondence between CB Jr. and his son CPB (see *Catalogue*).

[2] Charlotte Ann (*née* Burney) Francis, who had married secondly (1 Mar.) Ralph Broome (L. 272 n. 1).

[3] Alexander Charles Louis Piochard d'Arblay.

If you think—as *I* certainly do,—that the 2ᵈ edition of Camilla is retarded on account of the last payment,[4] I beg you will relinquish that payment to a further period, for me,—M. d'Arblay has given me his consent to this proposition—sooner than thus injure the sale. The Book is never advertised, not even in lists of Cadell or Payne of a whole columns length in the news papers. We all know there are modes of slackening, as well as of accelerating sales; & I would rather, plumply & openly, enter into a new contract for the remaining sum, than see a 2ᵈ Edition thus postponed, though the first was gone, *within a few hundreds*, by the Publisher's own acknowledgement, 4 or 5 months after publication. Think this over for me, my dear Charles, & open upon the subject candidly & frankly with the parties when you next see them. But without troubling yourself to go to them on purpose, as nothing presses. I have an account, also, with Mr. Payne, which I imagine he remits till his own & Mr. Cadell's can be arranged. I have several corrections for the new Edition & not a little curtailing here & there. Don't let them print without sending for my prepared copy. *Entre nous*, I have, also ǀ some other things to talk to you of, *thereto relative*,[5] when we meet.

I heard from little Martin of your loyalty—& of *his*.—which he was properly proud of. I think him very much improved.[6]

I fear to enquire how the school, & matters of such serious sort go on—nothing prospers that I hear of, in any line at present. Heaven, as you say, send us more auspicious times!

We rarely hear from our dear Susanna—but how do I grieve to have her at such a period in that dangerous country!

Adieu, my dear Carlucci—This is a little chattery, to relieve my vexation at losing something so near an opportunity of a dearer one. My Love to Carlino,—& best compts. to Mrs. Bicknell,—& all that is kindest to your poor Patient, when you think her well enough to name to her

your most truly affecte
F. d'A.

Most cordial Love from my Partner.

[4] See L. 314 n. 5.

[5] The play 'Love and Fashion', which FBA was then writing.

[6] JB's son Martin Charles Burney was attending CB Jr.'s school at Greenwich.

To Mrs. Broome

A.L.S. (the first leaf and a segment (1·5 × 7·2″) cut from the second leaf, Berg: and the remainder of the second leaf (7·4 × 7·2″), Barrett, Eg. 3693, f. 72–b), 3 Apr. 1798

Originally a double sheet 4to (8·9 × 7·3″), mutilated as described in Textual Notes *pmks* DARKING 5 AP 98 5 AP 98 wafer

Addressed: Mrs. Broome, / at Ralph Broome's Esqr, / Queen Charlotte Row, / New Road

Endorsed by CBFB: Sister / d'arblay / April — — — 1798 / ans^d april 7th—

Docketed in pencil, p. 1: 98

Edited by CFBt.

April 3^d 1798
West Hamble, near
Dorking.

Now that I see my dearest Charlotte again happy, that she has dismissed my inquietude—I might indeed truly say my sorrow for her conflicts & disturbance—my old vile habits creep back, & I put off writing from day to day, till the desire to again hear forces my Pen into my hands.

And now it is there—before I touch upon any thing else, let me cordially thank my new Brother for giving me sight & possession of the truly kind lines addressed to his beloved[1]—& I am sure grateful Bride. I, too, feel grateful for them, & even venture to take myself a little meaning in the *eloge* to Truth at the conclusion.

Nothing can make me happier than the whole style of your Letter, my dearest Charlotte, it seems written with such perfect, such unaffected ease of mind & happiness of Heart. Pray tell Mr. Broome that not all my wicked propensity to procrastination could have deferred so long my answer to his kind idea of coming hither, were we in better plight for his reception: but we have only a shell of a House,—& not so much as a shell of

275. [1] This was the poem of four stanzas, preserved in the Scrapbook (Berg) 'Fanny Burney and family. 1653–1890', p. 68, entitled 'Three Weeks after Marriage', in which, taking issue with the thesis that 'Love grows daily weaker by possession', Broome affirms (stanza 3) that '. . . Charlotte's Charms deep rooted in Affection / Shall daily flourish like the spreading Vine / Whilst all her Virtues shall afford protection / And everlasting Happiness be mine.'

Culinary materials. And though I have accustomed myself to love, not dread his Wit, I have hardly courage to say to him—as I have done to his Partner—*We have nothing to offer you but ourselves—yet come!* — — I leave the matter in your hands, however, ⏐ for you know exactly not only what you shall find, but what he can *bear to want.*

It must have been a great pleasure to you to see Mrs. Barnewall[2] again; though I know you had rather have met Mrs. Hill. As to our dearest Susan—I don't find that she has seen ANY of her friends since the first fortnight after her arrival in Ireland. She has remained constantly at Belcotton, & there no one seems to visit her. I fancy there is no accommodation for any visitor.—Ireland is in so dreadful—so menaced a State, that my Heart aches when I reflect upon her residence there. The conduct of Lord Edward FitzGerald has stabbed the peace of all the best part of his family. You know, I suppose, he is Brother to Mrs. Chas. Locke Jr—You would feel, I am sure, to hear of the sufferings of the Mother & Sisters upon his accusation & non-appearance.—

A kind Letter from our excellent Miss Cambridge speaks highly of the conversation powers & pleasantness of Mr. Broome,—speaks, in short, according to my imagination of them. You don't tell me you have heard from Charles, yet I sent you off his Letter myself.

Not one line have I heard from our dear Padre since I left him.[3] I fancy his removal occupies him wholly. One Letter from Mrs. Rishton is all I have had from Chelsea.[4] You ⏐ know, I suppose, she is now going to live with my Father & Sally? Long unhappiness, from dissimilarity of disposition & opinions at home, have at length subsided into this decided, yet amicable separation. I think it may be a serious comfort to my Father, whom she adores,—I am sure it may be of infinite use as well as pleasure to sally; & she herself is relieved from a bitter weight of affliction.

If it should be possible for you to change my Lace, I shall be

---

[2] Maria-Theresa Kirwan (d. 13 Oct. 1824), eldest daughter of Richard Kirwan (1733–1812) of Craig Castle, Galway, had married in 1793 John Thomas Barnewall (1773–1839), 15th Baron Trimleston (1813). Her sister 'Bessy' (Mrs. Hill, see iii, L. 216 n. 3) had been in earlier times a great favourite of the young Burneys.

[3] On 10 March.

[4] The letter of 18 March (L. 270 n. 3).

vast glad, for reasons which, were we to meet, you would see to be *pretty obvious*: but I am less anxious about the *breadth* than the *fineness*. It was a *small* Shop, with a Bow window. But as it is very possible you may have nothing to do that way, let it not torment you; if you find it inconvenient, pray give to Titchfield Street to be kep[t] for me till I can discover how to change it. It is somewhere nearly opposite to *Bond Street*, but *how* nearly I cannot recollect. Perhaps Marianne⁵ will have the kindness to try to negociate it for me, if your avocations are all another way; & I do most seriously beseech you not to undertake it through any difficulty. I well know your promptitude to oblige, & that it always more wants repressing than urging. Our sister Esther has the one pᵈ Note which we settled to have unpaid you here when we last made up our accounts. Should the commission devolve upon Marianne, whose kindness will make her, I am sure, undertake to be your deputy for me, I must beg you to let me still owe you the £1. that she may take it for executing the bargain. Excuse all this tiresome detail. |

M. d'A. is Gardening all day long, with a laborious perseverance that procures us Cabbages, potatoes, & soupe meagre every Day. What can the times do to people *revelling* in such luxuries? If they will but leave us our Field, & our Cottage, & *de quoi* to buy bread & small beer, we almost defy them.

I am almost afraid to ask if *you* have heard from Chelsea—? But I wish much to know if you have heard from Ireland, as my Letters are all unanswered for some time, though pacquets must so often pass at this eventful period for that agitated country.

My evening was extremely to my *gust* with the exemplary Mrs. Chapone. And I went to 6 plays from Chelsea, The Belles' Stratagem—The Castle Spectre—He's much to blame—Cheap Living—Secrets Worth Knowing—& the Heir at Law.⁶ The two last by *royal favour*, in my old place. After my long abstinence from the Theatre, this was pretty full fare. We are both very fond of Plays & Operas, & very indifferent to all other public places. My little Boy is *all alive*. My kindest Love to

---

⁵ EBB's daughter.

⁶ FBA saw *Cheap Living* on 3 Nov. 1797 (L. 255 n. 54), *The Heir at Law* on 1 Mar. 1798 (L. 270 n. 7), and *Secrets Worth Knowing* on 8 Mar. (L. 270 n. 19). She could have seen Hannah Cowley's *The Belle's Stratagem* (1780) on 22 Feb., Matthew Gregory Lewis's *The Castle Spectre* (1797) on 26 Feb. or 5 Mar., and Thomas Holcroft's *He's Much to Blame* (1798) on 26 or 27 Feb. or on 3, 5, or 6 Mar.

Charlotte the little, Marianne & Clement. M. d'A. bids me add Charlotte the big for him. Our joint kindnesses to Mr. B[roome] —& long may my dearest Charlotte preserve the ease she has given to her most affec^te F. d'A. for then she must preserve *her* happiness like that of her Mate—& make *'Everlasting happiness'*⁷ be the portion of *both*.

276   West Humble, 20 April 1798

To Sarah (Rose) Burney

A.L.S. (The Fitzwilliam Museum, Cambridge, Ashcombe v. 61), 20 Apr. [17]98

Double sheet small 4to (?)   3 pp.   *pmks*   DARKING   21 ⟨ ⟩ 98 seal

Addressed: Mrs. Burney, / Greenwich, / Kent.

I most truly rejoiced at sight of your hand, my dear Rosette, for I had truly been grieved by the account of your illness: & the serene & composed style in which you write does you real honour in my Mind, after trials so very severe, so often repeated. I could not have wondered if a murmuring spirit had displayed itself; but I need not, I think, say how much higher you stand with me for being calm, & even rising, at times, to chearfulness. Your fortitude has seemed to me considerably encreased of late; but though I admire the goodness of providence in strengthening your mind to your burden, I sincerely & earnestly lament the sad occasions & sufferings that call such firmness forth.

The first week in May, my dear Rosette, is sooner than it ˡ will be possible for us to see you, from important agricultural & horticultural businesses, which demand M.d'A.'s active presence in his field. But the visit so long designed, & so often deferred, will constantly dwell in view till we can accomplish it. Give us credit for this. My dear Brother I am sure cannot doubt it.

M. d'Arblay is much obliged to dear little Carlos for remembering his pictures, & he will not fail to claim them.

---

⁷ See note 1 on p. 127.

I am in great & incessant uneasiness for my beloved sister Phillips, whose residence in Ireland, at this rebellious & frightful epoch, is an unremitting drawback to my happiness.

Pray give our joint kindest Love to my Brother, & to Charles, & our Comp^ts to Mrs. Bicknell.

And add our joint thanks for the newspapers, without which, at this critical period, I think we should *burst.*

Adieu, my dear Rosette, & long may you be spared any new griefs or trials—

affect^ly Yours—
F. d'A. |

Pray make my congratulations to Mrs. Rose¹ on her recovery. I hope to hear as good news of poor Mrs. Foss.²

April 20.—98
West Hamble, near *Dorking*, not *Leatherhead.*

277   West Humble, 25 April 1798

To Doctor Burney

A.L.S. (Diary MSS. vi. 5102–[5], Berg), 25 Apr. [17]98
Double sheet 4to 4 pp. *pmks* DARKING 27 AP 98
Addressed: Dr. Burney, / Chelsea College, / Middlesex.
Edited by FBA, p. 1 (5102), *annotated*: ❖ (1) *Charlotte's 2^d marriage—Astronomy Poem. West Hamble*
Edited also by CFBt *and the* Press.

West Hamble, Dorking—
April 25.—98

*Bouder,*¹ my dearest Father?—But I am sure you do not think it, therefore I will not disgrace myself with a defence. But I have

276. ¹ Probably Rosette's mother Sarah (*c.* 1726–1805), eldest daughter of Samuel Clarke (1684–1750), D.D., and widow of William Rose (1719–86), who had conducted a school at Chiswick. 'Mrs. Rose' could also be Rosette's sister-in-law Sarah *née* Farr (*c.* 1759–1848), who in 1790 had married Samuel Rose (1767–1804).
 ² Rosette's sister Anne *née* Rose (d. 26 May 1808), who had married (1780) Edward Smith Foss (*c.* 1756–1830), a solicitor.
277. ¹ A term evidently used by CB in his letter of 24 Apr. (Berg), of which, however, the first leaf was torn away and discarded by FBA in her editorial capacity. Part of the text remaining on the second leaf is printed in *DL* v. 407–8. See also Lonsdale, pp. 391–2.

intended writing every Day, & the constant glimmering hope that *to-morrow* I should hear, with the idea you were always packing up & removing, have made another to-morrow & to-morrow always keep off *to Day*. Indeed that is the cruel trick of *to-morrow*, which does more mischief to ones fair resolves than any philosophy of *TO DAY* ever rectifies.

I delight in the account of your *conviviality*; nobody was ever so formed for society in its best state as my dearest Father,[2] ⌐& I think I never so much enjoyed his partaking of it thus abundantly as now that he ⟨seems but quite⟩ swept from such iminent danger of being separated from those who make it most pleasant to be in.

What a charming hope you open to me of escaping the change of Apartments.[3] I must not dwell upon it, as it would only add force to the disappointment if it should be blighted but there will want no spur to rejoicing, should it be fulfilled.⌐

I am excessively pleased at the Coterie for reading my admirable Poem,—& that it will be finished to so much advantage in the quiet attic retreat & society of Hampstead. I laughed heartily at the judges that got you on to be sole purveyor, & all the more for the pleasure I receive in hoping my favourite poem is felt by such hearers to be too good to be read in scraps, with alternate quotations or fragments of other works. I wish I could hear from somebody else how the reading took: you are prodigiously stingy upon the subject. However, I may judge a little from the setting aside all *tocca lei's*.

How interesting is your account of M. Clery!—I should like extremely to meet with him. If your list is not closed, of scrip, my Chevalier begs you | will have the goodness to trust him with the 6ˢ & enter his name. Your description of him is just

---

[2] The unprinted part of the second leaf (see above) carries one part at least of CB's social calendar (see nn. 7, 8, 9 following).

[3] This hope, however, proved nugatory (see Lonsdale, pp. 391–2).

what his conduct had made my mind describe him.[4] But I am a good deal disappointed, my dearest Father, you cannot bring yourself to see Charlotte[5]—so much of what you disapprove in her conduct was the mere effect of timidity & simplicity, that it seems as if her perfectly spotless, nay exemplary life to that period might be set in a balance that would rise in her favour. They have incessantly pressed our visit to them, promised so long before he was in question—but many circumstances make us firm in defering it: the principal of which causes we cannot say, for it is the awkward position we could be in at Chelsea: ⌐to visit from their house, her Father, whom she could not see, would be cruel,—to be so near that dear & most dear personage, & refuse ourselves the high gratification of his sight, would make the rest vain to us & the visit truly tormenting. We have, therefore, also put off Charles, whose wife has now written to propose performance of our engagement early in May,⌐ but we hope our delay, which also ⌐serves productive notions, &⌐ is extremely serviceable to our horticultural avocations, will be terminated by a reconciliation that will make the excursion all we can wish. The Br[oome]'s have invited themselves here to pass next Sunday.[6] We should never have dreamt of inviting them—we are so little stored in hospitable materials, that a perfect stranger to us has something terrific to our poor fare & its tackle: however, there was no saying a positive nay, & so if he puts us into an *Epitre*, & does it with the fun & good humour of his Simken, we must only be the first to laugh—But alas—the *stock-jobbing Politician* gives so different an idea! I hear he is extremely kind to the Children, ⌐& my dread of him will end once given over to our inspection. Charlotte the younger is to accompany them.⌐ |

I am very glad to hear of your sweet hearts, old & new—

[4] Jean-Baptiste Cant Hanet de Cléry (1759–1809), for whose forthcoming work *Journal de ce qui s'est passé à la tour du Temple pendant la captivité de Louis XVI, roi de France* (Londres, 1798), CB had obtained '30 subscribers', which names, he explains to FBA in his letter of 4 June (Osborn), he had kept back in hopes of increasing until he received notice that all lists were wanted, 'wch notice . . . never came'; thus CB failed to submit his list of subscribers (including the d'Arblays) in time for the printing. His account of his meeting with M. Cléry is lost with the discarded leaf (see n. 1).

[5] See L. 272 n. 1. CB had been very angry indeed at the announcement of the Broome marriage (1 Mar.), as FBA, who had been asked by CBFB to divulge the matter, well knew (L. 273, p. 122).

[6] Sunday 29 April.

but of Mrs. Garrick chiefly.[7] I rejoice Mrs. Carter is so well again. Does L[y] Rothes tell you how nearly we are neighbours? We see her house where ever we see our own.[8] It is a constant object. But we have not yet been very sociable, for the weather would not do for *my* Carriage, though hers, before she went to Town, kindly found its way to us 3 times.

L[y] *Northwick* makes me *grin*—for I thought it my own table, when I held the Assizes at *Northwick*,[9] to give a little hint against dancing around Thieves, Highwaymen, & poor wretches going to the Gallows. Pray when next you can indulge me, tell me how the dinner went off at L[y] Inchiquin's,[10] & if she seems happy. All you find time to name of those my old connexions is peculiarly interesting to me.

I have some hope the public affairs may now wear a better aspect, from the tremendous danger so narrowly escaped of utter destruction, & so notorious as to defy the plausibility & sophistry of contest. We have had papers, through dear Charles, up to Monday—& the King's Message[11] made me thrill through every vein: but the sight of Mr. Sheridan seconding Dundas[12] struck me as a *good* to undo many an evil: M. d'A. thinks it will shew the Carmagnols the *Species* of *Friends* who were to abet them beyond all the speeches of all the Ministers; for if even the opposition, even the supporters of the War being our Aggression, & the Republic So Glorious &c &c—point out the real aim of our Enemies, that our money & credit is all they

[7] CB names as his 'old sweet hearts' Mrs. Garrick, Hannah More, and Betty Carter. His new love was 'the Speaker's sister', Anne Addington (d. 1806), who had married on 2 Jan. 1770 William Goodenough (*c.* 1743–8 Aug. 1770), M.A. (Oxon. 1764), B.Med. (1767). He was a brother of Samuel, Bishop of Carlisle (L. 271 n. 13). [8] See iii, L. 123 n. 5.

[9] Rebecca Bowles (d. 1818), who had married (1766) Sir John Rushout (1738–1800), 5th Bart. (1773), cr. Baron Northwick (1797). It was in Northwick (*Camilla*, i, bk. ii, chap. 4) that FBA had contrived a fictional breakfast on the day of the assizes.

[10] Sir Joshua Reynolds's niece, formerly Mary Palmer (i, L. 1 n. 9), whom the Burneys knew before her marriage to the elderly Lord Inchinquin (i, L. 23 n. 26).

[11] On 20 Apr. His Majesty had informed the House of 'increasing activity in the ports of France, Flanders, and Holland' and of the preparation of 'troops and warlike stores' with the 'avowed design' of invading England (*AR* xl, 'State Papers', 211–12). 'His Majesty places the firmest reliance . . . on the bravery of his fleets and armies and on the zeal, public spirit, and unshaken courage, of his faithful people, already manifested in the voluntary exertions of all ranks, more than ever necessary, at a moment when they are called upon to defend all that is most dear to them.'

[12] On 20 Apr. Sheridan had seconded Dundas's motion than an address of thanks be presented to His Majesty for his message (*Parl. Hist.* xxxiii. 1423–8), at the same time affirming his full support of the Ministry in the defence of the country (see also *The Times*, 20, 21 Apr.).

want, that their pretences of giving US liberty &c are incapable of duping even their admirers—surely they must see that their chance of reception here through *our own means* is shallow & unfounded, ⌐if only the basest & meanest of adventures are engaged in the conspiracy that invites them. We are extremely impatient to know if Mr. Fox will follow ¦ the same steps. If not, Mr. Sheridan surely stands the highest, & I remember he behaved the most handsomely about the Meeting. Indeed I was so much pleased with his speech, & so charmed at the idea of the effect it may produce in France, as well as amongst the evil disposed here, that I began to be as pleased as heretofore I have been frightened at his vicinity.[13] We are almost equally near to him as to Mr. Locke & L^y Rothes.

I am sorry to say we have not Pennant,[14] and it must be searched elsewhere—nor have we now ANY Books of my dear Father, but the 3 first vols. of the Monthly Review. We returned all others except the poem. I am⌐ so little generous or noble, that I feel almost vexed, instead of glad, that the 12th Book is finished, for I had made a sort of regale to myself that something should have been written of it in our *Chaumière*. Don't forget what we build upon this summer. We shall dare *YOU* with our *fare & tackle*—our Alex, & our Prospects, with our true joy in your sight, & your own view of my virtuous Companion at the daily cultivation of his Garden, will supply, to your kind paternal Heart, all deficiencies, & make you partake of our pleasure.

Adieu, most dear Sir—my Mate embraces you with cordial ⌐respect & true affection. My Alex often talks of you, & bids *me* talk of you. He is most grown, & not yet ugly. My Love to Mrs. Rishton & Sally—ever & ever

most dutifully & most affectionately⌐
Your F. d'A

⌐*The ⟨Irish⟩ affair is very explosive*⌐
⌐No very late news from sweet Susanna—⌐

[*marginal writing top* p. 1]

⌐Could you be so kind as to let James know we have received the Notes for the last Mr. Mathias's receipt. We did what we told you about the vol. of essays.⌐

---

13 Sheridan had acquired Polesden Lacey in 1796–7 (iii, L. 242 n. 18) as part of the dowry of his second marriage. See Robin Fedden, *Polesden Lacey* (1953).

14 Doubtless one of the works of Thomas Pennant (1726–98).

278 [West Humble, 2 May 1798]

To James Burney

L., copy in hand of M. d'A (West Humble Letter Book, p. 16a, Osborn),
2 May [17]98

To James. May 2ⁿᵈ—98.

I shᵈ have been very glad to have had yʳ letter on Sunday[1]
before our visitants: for though I desire nothing less than any
further interference with their concerns, if I had been previously
apprised that you wished for a meeting, I am sure by what I
feel within at such a wish of yours, I should have proposed it with
an energy not to have been *amicably* [re]sisted,—& in his visit
here, he seemed perfectly determined upon entire amity. He
spoke civilly, almost kindly of whoever he named of the family,
made no sort of allusion to past combats & contests except in
joke, & was so good humoured & so desirous to please, that,
had I seen him without the biass of uncomfortable accounts
I shᵈ have spent the day with extreme satisfaction. Had he even
hinted at any complaint against my dear Father or my dear
James, my altered countenance would have distroyed *his*
comfort as effectually as my offended feelings would have distroyed
my own. But he put me to no such trial. All that passed *here*
was in his favour; he seems extremely kind to Cha[rlotte]—&
really very fond of the children. They brought charlotte, & he
regretted not having clement all day.

I was extremely glad at the re-appearance of my letter,[2] for
it was rather too detailed a picture to be risked in a magazine or
news paper. And nothing now gets out of the first hands but to
fall into those of all the World. Since, therefore, it buoyed up so
lightly from a watery grave, by now it will irradiate your
'blazing earth' in a fiery one.

278. ¹ On 29 Apr. JB's letter is missing as is also the original of FBA's reply, this
letter on Broome surviving only from the circumstance of its having been copied
into a Letter Book.
² An unidentified letter.

Conjointly with M. d'Arblay
To Mrs. Phillips

A.L. and PS. (Berg), 13 May 1798
Double sheet 4to   4 pp.   wafer
Addressed: Mrs. Phillips, / Belcotton, / Drogheda / Ireland

West Hamble *near Dorking* Surry,
May 13. 1798

I begin to feel so compleatly uneasy at this VERY long silence
of my best beloved Susan that I shall send this forthwith to
Town, in hopes my dearest Mrs. L[ocke] will be able to forward
it,—though we had neither of us purposed writing again till we
heard. But *why* is my Susan silent?——I always feel my first
fright for her precious health—my next, lest the tempestuous
times / tems—¹ / should have annoyed her.—The public state of
things in Ireland makes any want of intelligence uncomfortable,
were there no private motives whatever for solicitude. Write—
my dearest, dearest Susan!—If you are not well, let my dear &
good Fanny write for you, & immediately. I conclude the Major
too much occupied.

our earnest petition to see you & the dear Children, till safer
times, we *more* earnestly than ever repeat—Is there no hope for
us?—May we address the Major?—The day does not pass in
which we ever fail to sigh for your sight. I have no doubt but
James would fetch you, if the Major will consent. & surely he
might as well be disincumbered of such helpless personages at a
period when he can be so little certain of not being called away
from protecting them to distant service.

Here, at least, all who are engaged in the service are liable to
such calls.

Some times I fear you have not received the last pacquet,
through Mr. Pelham's illness.² It had the first sheet of my Court
Anecdote—here I send two more sheets—&, ¹ will have the

279. ¹ The coded allusion to Phillips's ungoverned rages. Cf. SBP's reports on 'le
temps' ('quelquefois assez mauvais, mais nous n'avons pas eu de grands orages et à
l'heure qu'il est tout est tranquille'). See *FB & the Burneys*, pp. 240, 276, 294–5.

² The Hon. Thomas Pelham (1756–1826), who, at this time chief Secretary to
the Lord Lieutenant of Ireland (see *DNB*), would have been in a position to oblige
the Lockes in the delivery of pacquets.

remainder ready for next pacquet. But this I forward, in uncertainty of its opportunity of departing, to our beloved friend,
who has been above 3 weeks in Town.

When I heard last from our Padre,[3] he was well, & in great
spirits, notwithstanding Invasions—for he had been of parties
with Mr. Windham & Mrs. Crewe, & so busy with his new
work, that his Mind was occupied compleatly. We expect
Invasion here or in Ireland Daily!—*We* are alarmed—*I* am
very much indeed—at times quite to sickness at heart,—but yet
all seems fair for our ultimately well doing, from the encreasing
spirit of all conditions, & even all parties of Men to resist these
cruel Spoilers. Their treatment of the Swiss has lost them more
friends than any of their other subduing conquests.[4] The Swiss
were so confessedly free—the assault so palpably for plunder, &
the conduct So indisputably tyrannical & oppressive, that their
warmest former defenders are ashamed & silenced. Even Mr.
Sheridan has given them up as *rapacious & unjust*, & offered his
best services to aid in their defeat, if they effect a landing.[5]

I want to know from you if you gather any thing relative to
L^d E[dward] F[itzgerald] in Ireland. His friends have been half
demolished with terror about him—but now say he is in a
neutral country,[6] & will re-appear & vindicate himself from all
charge of treason, as soon as the time for his trial | arrives: &
that he only absents himself to avoid previous confinement.
I hope they do not flatter themselves!—*ha*—!—

Charlotte & Mr. Broome & little Charlotte spent a Day here
a fortnight ago.[7] I liked him much better than I had of late
expected. He is full of information upon various subjects, &
seems *innately* good humoured. He is very fond of Charlotte, &
almost doats upon Clement, as well as seems *proud* of little
Charlotte, & very kind to Marianne. With all this, I again hope
she will be really & permanently happy; for though I see he
does not believe the human being was ever created who equalled
himself in knowledge or parts, that he esteems himself to be all-

---

[3] On 24 AP 98 (see L. 277 n. 1).

[4] In February 1798 the French armies had entered the Vaud and on 5 Mar.
maréchal Brune had occupied Berne itself. The conquered cantons were plundered of
millions found in the coffers; and 'the booty was to be increased to fifteen millions
by means of imposts levied on the country' (Madelin, p. 569).

[5] See L. 277 n. 12.

[6] A false report. Lord Edward was in hiding in Dublin.

[7] On Sunday 29 Apr. (cf. L. 278 n. 1).

knowing, & nearly all others to be all ignorant,—yet, with the constant adulation his vanity will receive from his adoring Wife, who thinks just the same both of him & of others, I doubt not but his love will be kept alive, & his desire to *shew* her happy will conduce to his pleasure in making her so.

I am excessively concerned to tell you my Father has not yet seen them, & refuses to listen to any thing I can represent in their favour: yet *why* so much anger, & wherefore its blaze to the World, it is difficult to explain: except upon the terrible score of *politics*, in which he has no mercy for a dissentient opinion.

We have not yet had our assessed taxes demanded. But our Cottage is so ¹ compleatly comfortable, & its situation so sweetly beautiful, that we care less & less. We *only* fear the *Carmagnols!*—I hate to call them *French*. M. d'A. is writing to M. de Narbonne—William Locke undertakes to have a Letter conveyed to him through Mr. Arbuthnot,⁸ a Gentleman with whom—strange to tell, he has been in *constant correspondence!* what may have caused his silence here & at Norbury Park becomes more & more wonderful! yet to hear of him—of his very existence, even, is a great joy.

Our sweet friend will tell you, when she has time, her own adventures in London—I shall only anticipate her having seen our Etty, & giving me a good account of her. James I have heard from lately. He kindly transacts our business with Mr. Mathias. Charles I have not seen nor heard from this age—but I have a Letter from Mrs. B[urney] who has been desperately ill again, but is recovering. We are much pressed to their house, & to Charlotte's.—but cannot conveniently travel for sundry reasons. And we are listeners to, not makers of objections to quitting our Hermitage. Mrs. L[ocke] writes us word she & dearest Mr. L[ocke] & the two dear Girls are all well. God bless my dearest beloved—

I am sure she will not receive & read this without snatching a pen to write again to her

F. d'A.

How is Janey Paney?—How I do love her!—Tender Love to my Fanny. & little Willy—I hope Norbury is well?

⁸ Charles Arbuthnot (1767–1850), M.P. (1795–6, 1808–31), diplomat, and politician (*DNB*).

Love to the Major—
My Mate's truest tenderness. My dear Boy is not free from his obstinate foes, Worms, but otherwise well, & *always* in spirits.

[*By M. d'Arblay*]

Je suis tellement faché de votre silence que je suis tenté de ne pas même vous dire que je vous aime de tout mon coeur — Ne seriez vous pas bien punie si j'allais m'aviser de vouloir faire un secret de ce qui est depuis longtems si bien connu de tout le monde —

280   [West Humble, 4 June 1798]

To Doctor Burney

A.L.S., two fragments (Barrett, Eg. 3690, f. 95–b and Berg, Diary MSS. vi. 4996), *n.d.*

Presumably in the original a double sheet 4to, of which the first leaf is missing, as are strips from the top and from the bottom of the second leaf. The middle part of the second leaf is extant in two segments, the upper in the Barrett, the lower in the Berg Collection. 2 pp. *pmks* DARKING 4 JU 98   4 JU 98

Addressed: Dr. Burne[y] / Chelse[a College] / M[iddlesex]

Edited and mutilated by FBA *and possibly by* CFBt. *See* Textual Notes.

[*first leaf missing, top of second leaf cut away and missing*]

& much pitied & respected. What a gallant [*cut*]
What is become of Bonaparte?[1] I can never suppose the *Egyptian* Scheme real,—nor that *he* will go any where but to *Vienna* or *England*; & I fancy the other reports are only to keep him out of sight, in hope to put us off all guard, till his name shall be announced *Landed*, & heading the March to the Bank: If *You* think all this over, comfort me with saying so, for I never look forward to such an expedition without freezing.

How firm & steady is Lord Camden![2] what he says of en-

280. [1] Bonaparte had set out for Egypt on 19 May, had seized Malta on the way, and landed on 30 June at Alexandria (Madelin, pp. 569–70).

[2] John Jeffreys Pratt (1759–1840), 2nd Earl Camden (1794), who had been appointed 11 Mar. 1795 Lord Lieutenant of Ireland (see *DNB*), had recently sent a reassuring dispatch to the Secretary of State, assuring him of the safety of Dublin (see *The Times*, 1 June, as reprinted from the *London Gazette Extraordinary*). The Yeomanry, and the Regular and Militia forces had evinced 'steadiness, discipline, and bravery' such as must 'inspire the best-grounded confidence in their exertions should they have a more formidable enemy to contend with'.

countering *a more formidable Enemy if needful* did me good, &
raised my courage; for surely if ever the Carmagnols mean to
make their attempt, either here or in Ireland, this wretched
time of disorder & distress & rebellion will be what most will
suit them.—But what, dearest Sir, could bewitch Mr. Pitt to
fight

[bottom of page cut away, top of p. 4 cut away]

Imagine my surprise the other Day, My dearest Padre, of
receiving a visit from *Mr. & Mrs. Barbauld!*[3]—We had never
visited, & only met one Evening at Mr. Burrows,[4] by appointment, whither I was carried to meet her by Mrs. Chapone.
They are at Dorking, on a visit to Dr. Aikin, her Brother, who is
there at a lodging for his health. I received them with great
pleasure, for I think highly both of her talents & her character,
& he seems a very gentle, good sort of man.

I am told, by a French Priest[5] who occasionally visits
M. d'Arblay, that the commanding officer at Dorking[6] says he
knows you very well; but I cannot make out his name.

[bottom of p. 4 cut away]
[crosswriting on p. 4, beginnings of lines cut away]

⌐poor, poor Lady! / —My Mate longs to send you his /
[cut] wholly delighted—to our great /
*[cut]*ings then say sweet words /

[M]y Love to Mrs. R. & Sally
ever & aye most affect^{ly} & dutifully⌐
your F d'A.

3 The Revd. Rochemont Barbauld (d. 1808), a dissenting minister, and his wife,
Anna Letitia *née* Aikin (1743–1825), the well-known writer and editor. Her brother
John Aikin (1747–1822), M.D. (Leyden, 1784), his wife Martha *née* Jennings
(*c.* 1747–1830), and his daughter Lucy (1781–1864) were to remain four months in
Dorking. Lucy described the visit and the country about Dorking in *Memoir of
John Aikin, M.D.* . . . (2 vols., 1823), i. 210–12 and ii. 311–20; while her father's
descriptions were printed in the *Monthly Magazine*, vi (Sept. 1798), 161–3, 255–7.

4 The Revd. John Burrows (1733–86), a family friend of the Mulsos and of
Mrs. Chapone, see John Cole, *Memoirs of Mrs. Chapone* . . . (1839), pp. 54, 63. He
had married 28 Dec. 1762 Maria Smith (1739–91), daughter of Thomas Smith
(d. 1744) of Hadley, Middlesex. Cf. L. 292, pp. 187–8.

5 Possibly Nicolas Daniel, prêtre, who appears in the supplementary *Liste* . . .
des Emigrés (1794) as having emigrated on 4 Oct. 1793. See also iii, L. 179 n. 10
and iv, L. 292, p. 189.   6 Unidentified.

To Esther (Burney) Burney

A.L.S. (Berg), 5 June [17]98
Double sheet large 4to   4 pp.   *pmks*   EPSOM   6 JU 98   wafer
Addressed: Mrs. Burney, / Upper Titchfield Street, / Portland Place, / London
Scribbling, musical notes, p. 4

West Hamble,

My dearest Esther,   June 5.—98

How delighted am I to have a Commission from our Susan!—
I have this morning a Letter from that beloved Creature, from
whom I have not had one before since *March*[1]—& she charges
me to make you, as well as our dear Father, to whom I have
this moment written, acquainted with its chief contents—for she
is sure you must be a full sharer of the extreme anxiety the
situation of Ireland has given me,[2] & she assures us all that she
believes herself in perfect safety, that all her neighbourhood are
friendly & good & loyal, & all the poor people about, & all the
Major's workmen are even kindly attached to them. And—
which is truly consolatory—that if the rebellion continues, the
Major has promised to take them to Dublin—whence, she says,
the passage is very short to *Wales*, &, should it still not be
crushed, she & her 3 loves are all to come over—

I hope my dear Esther will not feel quite the *contrast* that
encreases *my* joy upon this Letter, for I hope she has escaped the
terror that I have been seized with. Mrs. Locke tells me you
have had a Letter from her of the 17 of April; you could not,
therefore, have an equal suspense to torment you,—I had not
myself when I heard that, till yet another Week passed without
a word that was fresh, & till the opening of the downright
rebellion, & the declaration of Martial Law awakened every
fear I could feel, & gave me a heart-ache & dread that cast a
gloom over all my happiness, & first brought dejection &
disturbance within the dear walls of my tranquil Hermitage.—

281. [1] These letters are missing, as is also the letter sent to EBB on 17 Apr.
    [2] Open rebellion had broken out on 23–4 May in Dublin, its environs, and in
many parts of the country. Lord Camden's Proclamation of 30 Mar., *AR* xl (1798),
'State-Papers', 233–4, had declared the kingdom in actual rebellion and directed
officers and soldiers to take action without magisterial authority.

The ǀ thankful gratitude with which this Days post has filled me I cannot express. Yet I have the mortification to hear that all my own Letters since March have been lost!—at least that they have never come to hand. And the style in which I write to that dear soul, upon *all subjects* but the one of her own captivity, is so utterly unguarded, so detailed, so sincere, that it is impossible for me to know to what such Letters may expose me, if they fall into any hands that make them public, for it is impossible for me to recollect who or what I have spoken of, nor how nor in what manner I have treated either persons or things. Nevertheless, I was becoming so wretched about this darling Creature, that to be relieved from my dreadful apprehensions makes me too grateful for long or strong vexation about any thing else.

Since the rebellion has broken out, I have lived with news papers & Maps—& when I saw that the Insurgents have been within 8 miles, as well as I can calculate, of Belcotton, I was taken with a tremor her hand & a later date alone could put an end to: for the account of this conflict at *Lusk*;[3] which I found on a Map at the distance I have mentioned, is on the 24th—& her Letter is dated the 27th—She will write to you, she says, soon, but would not have you wait for her Letter to be relieved from the alarm which she is sure the public accounts must have given us all.

The only Letter she has received of mine I am happy to tell you is that which your last, of 4 Sheets, accompanied: this she ǀ expressly mentions.[4] She has had a bilious attack—but protests it is over—& a Nervous cruel pain in her face & head, & Willy to nurse for a rash, & for Worms. But, as usual, she declares all is over, & that she is well. And tries whatever is possible to diminish our fears for her situation, by assurances she generously gives of its security—

You must be sure our dear Friends at Norbury Park are deeply grieved for the Fitzgerald Family,—they had but just returned to their charming home when the news of L$^{d.}$ E[dward]'s seizure,[5] & the misery it had occasioned, carried them again to Town, where they now are, exerting all their

---

[3] Among the villages in the environs of Dublin where fighting occurred, FBA selected Lusk, probably from its position to the north of Dublin, though in fact only eight miles from it and hardly constituting a threat to Belcotton.

[4] This must have been FBA's letter of 4 Jan. (L. 264).

[5] Lord Edward was seized in the evening of 18 May.

powers in consoling & fortifying the unhappy Mother & sisters. Yet, in a Note I have received since I began the first line of this Letter, M^rs L[ocke] says they have now great hope that the circumstances of guilt which have been circulated are false, or exaggerated, & that he will be cleared of all capital criminality. I had feared & believed the contrary so entirely, that I have seldom been more surprised; but indeed should it prove they do not flatter themselves, I shall truly rejoice, for they are all, as far as I have seen of them, peculiarly pleasing & interesting.

Mrs. Locke, in a Letter from London[6] during her first residence, says 'I have had the happiness to spend a comfortable half Hour with sweet Mrs. Burney & her charming Girls—' &c &c & in her only visit here between the journies, she said 'She is so amiable as to make light of her removal,[7] because she must be sure how I felt it for her,—but she chearfully declared it was to a very pretty Apartment, eligibly & genteely situation, & would not let me be uneasy—' | when, my dearest Esther, is this to take place?

Mr. & Mrs. Barbauld, whose names I am sure you must know, (she was Miss Aiken) called upon me last Week, & gave me a good account of dear Mrs. Chapone, from whom they had heard of our trio visit, & to whom she had kindly said *That she had been agreeably disappointed* of a party that she had invited to meet us. When you see her, don't forget my affectionate Respects, which are most sincerely & gratefully her's.

Pray give my Love to dear Mr. B[urney]—& to Marianne, Fanny when you see her, & Sophy, & Edward—& tell my dear Marianne I shall be much obliged to her to write a line to her Uncle James, to tell him the date & good news of our Susan's last Letter, in case he may have shared any of my inquietude. M. d'A. gardens unremittingly, & is now making me shady Walks for the summer that will be delicious. My little Boy grows daily, & strengthens, & is well, though he has very little appetite, & a worm complaint. God bless you, my ever dearly loved sister—

Yours most affecly

F d'A

M. d'A. sends his Love—.

---

[6] The letter is missing.   [7] To 43 Beaumont Street (L. 264 n. 2).

To Doctor Burney

A.L. incomplete (Diary MSS. vi. 5106–[7], Berg), 7 June [17]98
Originally a double sheet 4to (8·5×8″), of which the second leaf, torn away, is still missing   2 pp.
Edited by FBA, p. 1 (5100), *annotated*: ⁜ (2) on M. Clerys account of Louis 16 in the Temple.
Edited also by CFBt *and the* Press.

West Hamble, June 7ᵗʰ·—98

Indeed, my dearest Father, your Book[1] has half killed us—We have read it together, & the deepest tragedy we have yet met with is slight to it.—The extreme plainness & simplicity of the style, the clearness of the detail, the unparading yet evident worth & feeling of the Writer make it a thousand times more affecting than if it had been drawn out with the most striking eloquence. What an Angel—what a Saint yet breathing was Louis 16ᵗʰ — — the last meeting with the venerable M. de Mallesherbes,[2] & the information which prostrate at his feet he gives of the King's condemnation, makes the most soul-piercing scene, & stopt us from all reading a considerable time,—frequently, indeed, we have been obliged to take many minutes respite before we could command ourselves to go on.— But the last Scene with the royal family—the final parting—& it tore us to pieces! — — 'tis the most heart-breaking picture that ever was exhibited.—

How much we are obliged to you for it, dearest Sir, infinitely as it has pained & agitated us!—It arrived by the very same Messenger that took my last Letter to you, with an account of our sweet Susanna. | How interested it leaves one for the good writer, the faithful, excellent, modest M. de Clery! I want a 2ᵈ part—I want to know if he was able to deliver the King & Seal[2]—if he saw the unhappy Queen, the pious Princess

282. [1] In a letter (Osborn) of 4 June 1798 CB had reported the arrival of a complimentary copy of 'good M. Cléry's most interesting & afflicting' *Journal* (see L. 277 n. 4). CB's 'superb' copy was in English, i.e. the translation by R. C. Dallas (see *DL* v. 408 n. 1), but he had procured for the d'Arblays a French copy in 'papier velin', which, after reading with 'an aching & almost broken heart' he had sent on to West Humble.   [2] See ii, L. 68 n. 9.
[3] See Austin Dobson's note, *DL* v. 411 n. 1.

Elizabeth, the poor Madame Royale whom he left fainting, & that fair lovely blossom, the sweet Dauphin, any more.—I feel extremely dissatisfied to be left in the dark about all this.

I am shocked not to see your name in the subscription, after an interest such as you have both felt & shewn for this worthy man—it is infinitely provoking you knew not in time of the publication. M. d'A. is vexed, too, not to have his own name there, in testimony of respect to this faithful Creature, who will be revered to his last hour by whoever has any Heart for fidelity, gratitude, & duty.

⌐His Note to you was very gratifying to me.³ It is a side of the character I have formed of him.¬

Have you Mr. Twining still?⁴ O that he would come & mortify upon our bread & cheese, while he would *gladify* upon our pleasure in his sight!—The weather, now, is such as to make bare Walls *rather agreeable*—& *without* he would see what he loves in fair views, & what he so strikingly denominates *God's Gallery* of Pictures. — — & our one little live piece would not, I think, excite in him much black bile—If he is still with you, do speak for us.—*do-y.*—*will-y?*—⌐and our yellow ⟨flowers⟩¬

---

283   **West Humble, 20 June 1798**

Conjointly with M. d'Arblay
To Mrs. Phillips

A.L. & A.N.S. (Berg), 20 June 1798
Double sheet small 4to (7·8 × 6·5″)   3 pp. wafer
Addressed: Mrs. Phillips, / at Mr. Kiernan's, / Henry Street, / Dublin / Ireland [*franked ? but cover missing*]
Endorsed by SBP: June 20ᵗʰ 98

West Hamble,
June 20—98.

What I suffer from finding you receive none of my Letters— & make no preparations for listening to their urgent prayers for your immediate return to share our Hermitage with your 3

³ The polite note of 2 June 1798 accompanying the gift (see above) CB had copied in his letter to FBA. The original, along with a letter of 16 June, is extant in the Comyn Collection.
⁴ The Revd. Thomas Twining (iii, L. 133 n. 7), at this time visiting in London, had dined with CB on Sunday 3 June.

Children, my dearest—dearest—darling sister I cannot write—
I would not afflict you with writing if I could——If this should
arrive—for God's sake answer it in Person, if not utterly impossible!—We can arrange you ALL HERE PERFECTLY WELL—
our Garden would fed *20 such*—O Come! —— I pine to see
you in such safety——We have written *twice* to the Major[1]—
this entreaty—& included himself, if his affairs made it possible.

In the last, my love, we besought him, if — as we cannot
doubt, there are any money difficulties in arranging such a
journey so suddenly, he would be kind to us enough to make
use of £100 which he had just written me word he had paid into
Mr. Maturin's Hands in part of Mr. Shirley's Bond.[2]—If he is
at Drogheda, you, my beloved, will receive it,—& for pity's
sake use it for ME in bringing to me my Heart's dear Sister &
her three dear Children without waiting to answer other wise.
It was my true Heart's partner's *OWN* suggestion—& he will
substantiate it better for Mr. Maturin's sight. |

So many of my Letters are lost, I will now enter upon nothing
more—but write a duplicate of this by the common post.
Esther—James—& this Morning my dear Father have sent me,
severally, their Letters[3]—I should else run wild—the last to me
is *May 27.* since when We have written *3*—& *2* before that I
find have never arrived.—

God bless you, my own Susan!—& grant me to embrace you
in my peaceful retreat speedily—speedily!—My rest is broken
by your residence there—if you return the instant all is quiet,
still COME!—We join in supplicating you to let this happy
chance for facilitating obvious & unavoidable obstacles be the
means of giving rest again to my Heart, & Joy beyond all joy to
my beloved & sympathising Partner's—Listen, My own Susan,
as indeed, *so situated*, I would listen to *YOU*—Love to the Major—
& the 3 dear ones.— |

June 20. 1798
Westhamble—

[*By M. d'Arblay*]

What a happiness my dearest sister if you could without any
delay answer our wishes. I hope the Major has now received the

---

283. [1] These letters are missing.   [2] See L. 271 n. 8.
 [3] Of SBP's letters written from Ireland at this time there survive a letter of
25 June (Berg) to CBFB; and another (also Berg) of 2⟨6⟩ June to FBA.

letter in which I entreated him to ask Mr. Mathurin for the hundred pounds he wrote to me he had deposited for me in his hands, and to apply them to the purpose your sister has spoken you of. He cannot oblige me in a most friendly way than by making that commission for me. Je me tais pour avoir trop à dire. Adieu dearest dearest Sister—

Alexandre d'Arblay

284   West Humble, 20 June 1798

Conjointly with M. d'Arblay
To Mrs. Phillips

A.L. & A.L.S. (Berg), 20 June 1798
Double sheet small 4to 4 pp. *pmks* EPSOM 21 JU 98 25 JU 98
wafer
Addressed: Mrs. Phillips, / at—Kiernan's Esqr, / Henry Street, / Dublin. / *IRELAND*
Endorsed by SBP: June 21st .98
Docketed, p. 4: June 20th / M^e d'Arblay / & General—

June 20. 1798
West Hamble.

O my beloved Susan how cruelly unaccountable that my Letters should thus all miscarry!—I have this moment only written to you in the hopes of having my lines forwarded through Mr. Windham, but my terror of the failure induces me to address you again instantly by Post—that my chance may be double, at least,—for it is Heart-breaking to see you resigned to continuing in Ireland at such a period, without even the consciousness of the anguish your residence there occasions. If indeed it is inevitable—we must submit as well as you,—though not as patiently—but if it is *any thing* short of inevitable—Come to us, my beloved Sister! my dear & dearest beloved—come with your three lovely Children, & live with us upon our roots, & share our peaceful roof,—we have contrived Beds & Bedding for you ALL—the Major also included if his residence in Ireland is not indispensable. Tell him so, & that we are sure he will pardon all homeliness of fare & paucity of accommodation. The good Susan | too will be most welcome—she has earned a welcome from All my beloved sister's Friends, & will ever have it.

We have acquainted Mrs. Newton[1] she is safe—&c—

If any Money difficulties arise to a journey so sudden & unprepared, we wrote to the Major to entreat he would take up the £100 which he wrote us word he had paid to Mr. Maturin for us from Mr. Shirley.[2] This we must now beg may be repeated to him, if the Letter still is not arrived. 5 I calculate to be lost!—the 2 last directed to the Major.—This will cause us no inconvenience—& bring us the most exquisite happiness—O use it, my Susan, if only to bring you here during the very great storm, & to take you back instantly after! To *ME* it will purchase peace, health, strength, & Joy—to my own Partner a pleasure beyond *ALL* other—it was his *OWN* suggestion entirely—Think nothing at all, in these dreadful times, of when or how to re-settle—let it be the last account upon yr. Books—we must always be yr. Debtors if it procures us your sight! Dearest sweetest soul come instantly!—all will contend to possess you —but This still & tranquil spot will be my Susan's Home.— Love to the Major—If he cannot bring, he will at least fetch you—Love to the 3 dear Children—how I shall be transported to embrace You & them— |

I only know even the miscarriage of my Letters by the enclosures made me by Esther, James, & our Padre. They are all well. Norbury Park still empty. Charles was here on Sunday— very anxious, & affectionate. Come! Come! Come!

[*By M. d'Arblay*]

Yes, my dearest Sister Come & come without delay. The Major wrote to your sister & commissioned her to enquire at Bookham after the cottage we have left, in order to know if it were let. I flew instantly to Mrs Bayley;[3] & sent him word it was empty; entreating him at the same time to accept *bonne-ment* the offer we had already twice made of our own cottage in which you will be *all* welcome without the smallest inconveniency, and on the contrary with the most heart felt happiness

284. [1] See iii, L. 237 n. 6.　　　　　　　　　[2] See L. 271 n. 8.
　　[3] Catherine Bailey (iii, L. 124 n. 2), owner of 'The Hermitage', Great Bookham.

on the part of the two he[rmits]. I begged also from him the favour to ask to Mr Mathuri[n if] the hundred pounds he wrote he had deposited in his hands for us, & to apply them to the use your sister speaks you of. Pray, my dear sister, Tell the Major He can never do any thing for which we should be—so much obliged to his kindness, than to take again that money & use it to make the commission to which We entreat him to give a speedy end. my love to him & the dear Children *Sans oublier leur mere*

Alexandre d'Arblay

Westhamble June 20—1798

[*Madame d'Arblay added*]

I hope that sweet J[aney] P[aney] is in Dublin?

285   West Humble, 21 June 1798

To Esther (Burney) Burney

A.L.S. (Berg), 21 June [17]98
Double sheet 4to   4 pp.   *pmk*   22 JU 98   wafer
Addressed: Mrs. Burney, / N° 2. Upper Titchfield street, / Portland Place. / London / or Beaumont street, / Devonshire place, N° 43.
Endorsed by EBB: 1898

My dearest Esther,   Westhamble,
                                             June 21.—98

I am almost distract to find none of my Letters received by our darling sister—the reason is beyond all conjecture—save one of a very dark nature which I will not dwell upon—for it may be only cruel accident. — — *two* have *miscarried* previously to that in which yours through Mrs. Locke arrived to her,—the *first* of which contained my first entreaty to see her here—& the 2^{d.} of which invited *him* too.—A long journal account of my *visit royal* was also included.—[1]

Most unfortunately, the one which was *received*, (with *yours*,) only speaks by allusion & retrospection of this urgent entreaty: she has not, therefore, enough understood to answer it.—

<hr>

285. [1] Probably L. 270.

Upon finding these two lost, I wrote by the common post to *Belcotton*, & addressed it to the Major himself,[2] earnestly begging them *all* to come over, & partake of our homely fare till better times.

Soon after, I had a Letter from the Major,—but of near a month old, & not in answer,—yet to say *they were coming*, & bid us enquire if our cottage at Bookham was empty.—

Mr. d'A. flew thither, & wrote all its particulars instantly, again to the Major, & directed to him at Mr. Kiernan's, Dublin.[3]

One other, also, went in the interval, but I wholly forget in | which interval, to herself at Belcotton, by private conveyance. 5 in all I account to have missed her! — —

And I have not heard from her since the 27th May,—except through you—James—& our dear Father.

But Mr. Locke has had a Letter from the Major, positively saying Susan & Fanny should come over immediately. Mrs. Locke has answered it, requesting to see them at Norbury Park.

All this failure at such a time harrasses me beyond all words— it is inconceivable & afflicting to excess — —

But now to the principal subject of your Letter this moment read.—My dearest Esther!—kind, generous!—Thank God your Heart may here be at rest, without torturing your so widely claimed income for this beloved object at this moment.—The Letter I have mentioned from the Major was to announce, also, that he had just paid into M[r] Maturin's hands one out of the four hundred guineas due to us from Mr. Shirley[4]—& it so strongly occurred to us that *Money* was the real obstacle to the sweet soul's removal, that my true partner himself immediately proposed | lending this Money, in any manner, & without any security, &c, to aid the Journey,—& to this effect he wrote instantly to the Major himself, begging it might be used without scruple or delay.—

Now as this is *in Ireland* already, & has only to be re-claimed from Mr. Maturin, to whom it will be sufficient to shew M. d'Arblay's Letter, it will be readier than any thing we can send over: &, besides, more likely to be accepted, because the

[2] The letters to and from the Major are missing.
[3] Phillips's brother-in-law (iii, L. 215 n. 2) lived in Henry Street, Dublin.
[4] For FB's loan to the Shirleys, see iii, L. 193 n. 7; L. 234 n 2; and iv, L. 271 n. 8.

transaction has always gone through the Major's hands. To *me* it has be[en] a relief, persuaded that *this* was the efficient obstacle, beyond all expression—& such has been my long inquietude about this darling Creature, that it will be the *cheapest purchase* ever made of returning tranquility & happiness if it is accepted. And I little doubt its acceptance at a time so dreadfully difficult for raising money. My M. d'Arblay loves her so tenderly, that the action is as *necessary* to him, as it is sweetly kind to me.

But you will understand, my dearest Esther, it must by no means be mentioned: the Major would fire & resent its being known, & it would be unkind even to our angel; but to *you* it is impossible for me to be silent, since I see you will else be straining your very vitals to do what our EXTREME RETIRED ŒCONOMY enables us to do so much more easily. I assure you I cried over every line of your Letter[5] from the tender generosity of such an idea, with so large a family, & in *such times!*— knowing as I know that I were the times ten times worse, & the family thrice as large, you would still put it in practice, unless convinced it might be dispensed with without injury to that dearest object. — — Yesterday I wrote again, & again M. d'A. upon finding the Letter not yet received, through that you sent addressed to our dear Father. This we directed to *her* with the same proposal, &c. And to Day *again* all over again, by Mrs. Locke's Agent.[6] What upon Earth to suggest more to get at her, I cannot devise! but we are really miserable at such miscarriages. We send or go every Day to Dorking in hopes of news—&—but to you I need not describe the restlessness of such uneasiness, suspence & doubt.—

I should have answered your former kind Letter, & given my congratulations upon Richard's happy commencement,[7] but that I have daily hoped to have a Letter to recount to you from Ireland—the same to my dear Father—& to James.—The moment I hear, depend upon my writing. We have the more reason to hope the offer will be accepted by the Maj—because,

---

[5] EBB's letter is missing.

[6] Perhaps Thomas Pelham (L. 279 n. 2), or perhaps the Agent of Mr. Locke's estates in County Kerry (see his will, proved 3 Nov. 1810, P.C.C. Collingwood, 554).

[7] Richard Allen Burney (i, Intro. lxix; iii, L. 229 n. 7; iv, L. 264 n. 8) was recently ordained priest ('Worcester Journal').

in his own Letter announcing the £100, he complains openly of *being very poor himself*. I think exactly with you as to her real danger, & but apparent calmness, & I would not hear of her return to that defenceless Belcotton for all I am worth in the World literally. How I rejoice we wrote when we did to the Major.—he certainly now *can* let her come, when he thinks it expedient. Those Letters addressed to *him* have probably been travelling after him—every Day, therefore, notwithstanding such incessant disappointment, I have fresh hope. I am indeed your Debtor for your Letter at such a period. God bless you, dearest Esther—I wish I could help you—the removal must be dreadfully fatiguing[8]—Heaven grant it may not affect your health.

My Mate's kindest remembrances to *all*—with those of
your truly affe^{tte}
F. d'A.

M. d'A. will run with this himself to the post, in [ho]pes it may quiet *ONE* of your many solicitudes.—& perhaps the *greatest* just now.

pray thank dear Marianne for her kind words. My dear Child is now well again.

286   [West Humble, *c.* 24 June 1798]

To Mrs. Broome

A.L.S., part of one leaf only (Barrett, Eg. 3693, f. 73–b), *n.d.*
Originally a double sheet, or at least a single sheet 8vo, of which the top has been cut away leaving the fragment (5·9×4·6″) 2 pp.

[top of leaf cut away]

But I thank my dearest Charlotte for her Letter, & her *footing* to my little one, which suit extremely well. And if you can possibly be so good as to get me the paper from Mr. Mat[hias] to sign, speedily—that is immediately—I can have a conveyor for the *monish* in M. d'A. himself, who must be in town, to go to the Bank, the beginning of the Week—& only

[8] See L. 264 n. 2.

for a few Hours. He cannot, therefore, I fear, call *any* where. But if you can contrive, my dear Churlott, to send me the paper to sign, he can do the rest, as I shall make it over to him.

[*top of leaf cut away and a line split*]

season ⟨   ⟩. I dare not [suggest a] Night, our accomodations being such as you know, & such as Mr. Broome would think us mad to offer. But if you can be extravagant enough to *Carriage it* for a day, you will make us very happy—& with all the Loves you can crowd into your laps.

Alex is now really well, I thank Heaven, & growing robust. He sleeps soundly, at last, & just as a Child ought to do, with one Sleep.

Best regards to Mr. Broome, & Compt⁵ to Miss B[room] & Miss M[orton]¹—& Love to the dear little ones—

Dearest Charlotte, Adieu, ever & ever

Yours F d Ar.

287   West Humble, July 1798

To Hester Maria Thrale
later Viscountess Keith

L. copy in hand of M. d'A (West Humble Letter Book, pp. 49–52, Osborn), July 1798

To Miss Thrale

Westhamble

July 1798

Your kind idea of ornamenting my little cottage with some of the work of your own hands, gave me great pleasure,¹ & as I do not fear being obliged by you, after the long test of the many years our friendship has stood unbroken though battered at by Time, absence, silence, & various events,—Why I will

286. ¹ See iii, L. 212 n. 4.

287. ¹ Miss Thrale's letter is missing, but for the culmination of the friendship between her mother and FB, see *HFB*, pp. 169–83, and Clifford, chap. x.

not lose the gratification merely because I cannot return it: though that, I confess, is ordinarily sufficient reason with me for starting even insuperable objections.—Alas—I regret, at this moment, I did not make them *insuperable* to the continual exertions of this sort of Mrs Piozzi from the commencement of our acquaintance to its most unprovocked breach! She loaded me with obligations, which, even at the time, were oppressive to me, dearly as I loved her; & which, even then, when I considered her fondness to be unalterable, I thought the least pleasant part of it, from an inherent dislike to all sort of presents, & from an innate spirit of contentment with what I naturally possessed, however small its proportion to what surrounded me. The things, indeed, from her were trifles, her affluence considered,—but my pride was dearer to me than her gifts, which were forced upon me, whether I would or not, & which hurt me inexpressibly, even, in private, to tears of vexation, as sometimes they were accompanied with a raillery ǀ that shewd she discredited the sincerity of my resistance. But I valued her friendship too much for any *serious* dispute & all other she over-powered.—What she can invent to amuse her fancy with in fashioning any just enmity towards me, I cannot devise. That *he* be offended I opposed his marriage with all my might, is natural enough, though unjust & unwise; for I could mean him no harm—I thought not of him, personally at all: it was She I thought of; & I ran all risks to serve, not to dis-oblige. But I am convinced from the moment of their Nuptials, she shewed him all my letters, & probably attributed to me every obstacle that he had found in his way. It is the common mode upon such occasions, by which the 'fond married dames' repair their cruelties & hesitations; & the counsellors who, however urged to openness, have declared adverse sentiments, are almost uniformly sacrificed at the hymeneal shrine. Of this I was aware, generally speaking, all the time I worked so strongly against the match: but I thought her so superior to such ǀ common, poor, paltry, fifteen years old Girlishness, that I never abated my courage.— And indeed, she bore all my oppo-sition, which was regularly the strongest the utmost efforts of my stretched faculties could give, with a gentleness nay a *deference* the most touching to me, till the marriage was over—And then, —to my never ending astonishment, in return to the constrained

& painful letter I forced myself to write of my good wishes, she sent me a cold, piqued, reproachful answer, in entirely a new style to any I had ever received from her, to upbraid me that my *congratulations were not hearty*! As if I could write *congratulations* at all! or *meant* to write them! How gross must have been such hypocrisy!—And for what? Not to please *her*, for she must have seen their falsehood & despised them.—And had *he* any claim upon me?—Had any human being, indeed, a claim upon my veracity?

I wrote then, indeed, an answer somewhat high, for I felt injured, & far from averse to letting her see my resentment. She sent | me a reply *All kindness & returning affection*. To that, you may believe I wrote with warmth & friendship,—but I *NEVER* have heard from her since, in any way good or bad! And sometimes I have thought, as my next news was that she had left England, that my letter was some how lost, as she was continually changing place, & had a maid, I have heard from Mr Seward, who used to sometimes keep or destroy her letters.

I did not mean to let this grievous subject swallow up all my paper—but it is one always near my heart when it recurs, & I am not sorry to have you know how the strange total breach of intercourse began, as far as I know it myself. She must have motives of her own which I cannot fathom, or our acquaintance never could have dropt, though its pristine warmth & pleasure could no more have been revived. — — —

288   West Humble, 6 July 1798

To Mrs. Phillips

A.L.S. (Berg), 6 July 1798
Double sheet 4to   4 pp.   wafer
Addressed: Mrs. Phillips, / at ⌐Henry⌐ Kiernan's Esqr, / Henry Street, / DUBLIN. [*franked? but cover missing*]
Endorsed by SBP: July 6th / —98—

West Hamble, July 6th 1798.

I seize with avidity the hope that a Letter may now really reach you, my best beloved Susan, & *comfortably*: two most dear

Letters I have now to acknowledge, one of June 21. received 5 days ago, the other of June 27.¹ received this very Hour—& which *we* have read with an agitation of spirits inexpressible. Much I confess myself disappointed at what relates to the Maturin business²—I had thought my Susan would have listened to my prayers if she *could*—that at least she would not have hesitated as to the means of the two *journies*, if taken with a certainty of return, & for only one dear MONTH—Good God, my Susan! if I could make you *feel* what to ME—to US let me say, would be the obtaining you though only for a *WEEK*, to be sure you did not return till the rebellion was *really over*, & not merely crushed from powers of immediate effort, you could not refuse to set apart scruples about that miserable sum, while you nourish those that keep alive an uneasiness of restless terror that affects a tranquility till now unruffled. Dear darling Sister! will not this thought move you? Never suppose I do not enter completely into your horrour of incurring new difficulties— (*debiti*) but this must be considered as *none*: it is our fervent—our truly united supplication you would consider it in its true light —namely as spent for *us*, not for yourself, since you are so satisfied to run all risks, that I plainly see if we can succeed in dragging you away, it will be entirely for our sakes, & not to shock & afflict us by a resistance of entreaty not more grievous to me than to my Partner it is *astonishing*, nay, nearly un-intelligible. He would not a moment, he says, hesitate, in any embarrassment, to share Bed, Board, & cloathing with M. de Narbonne nor would M. de N. with *him*: & he asks why *notre soeur* should hold out from similar participation. Are *you* less dear to us? Are we to you?—Did you blame their sentiments or did you love & honour it? I well remember the *last* was your feeling,—why *then*, my beloved Susan!—why not adopt it where the ties of nearest blood are joined to those of fondest affection? ǀ You will say would I?—, my *YES*, dearest Susan,

---

288. ¹ This letter is missing but surviving in the Berg Collection is SBP's folio letter, dated Dublin, 2⟨6⟩ June [1798], which in later years FBA numbered 'N⁰ 4 June 1798' and annotated: '·※· ·※· Exquisite forbearing virtue with exquisite dis-interested & touching tenderness!' Of this letter FBA obliterated some 57 lines. The residue is printed in *FB & the Burneys*, pp. 272–7.
    ² Giving as a reason 'the probable approach of certain ruin' and 'the great *im*probability . . . of [Phillips's] being able to replace any fresh sum that he might borrow', SBP had refused the aid offered by JB and the d'Arblays. 'If I am un-happy, I wᵈ not be forced into becoming voluntarily despicable.'

where equally certain not to distress, nor even perplex by compliance, & where I saw I really injured happiness by refusal.

I could not upon *less* grounds, I confess: but our situation is truly singular: We have paid all our House bills, & found out new methods of œconomy, by practice & retirement, & my dear gardener's encreasing skill in his art, by which we live upon so little as keeps us free from all debt. We defer fitting up our house till some new means occur, & we find ourselves so comfortable in it with all its nakedness, that we have no sort of anxiety for that period, though we have signals in contemplation by which we mean, ere long, to look forward to it. This 100 being out of the stocks, makes no disadvantage in selling, & it is so little, after all, that, separately, it can add to our revenue, that we may fairly say we shall scarcely miss it. I could say much more in this plain way, but that I hate to state any thing in addition to the petition of our happiness.

I will stop, therefore, with only this one thing more: we are both ready to enter into any bond whatever to partake *all your worldly Goods* with *you*, if at any period in this ever changing life *you* should be easy, when *we* are embarrassed.

Your embarrassments, too, my Susan, so innocently incurred, should still less be a restraint—the *most* exalted of female characters I ever knew, the *most* perfect, Mrs. Delany, when deprived of great part of her jointure by frauds practiced by trustees, consented to let the D^s of Portland treat her as a sister,[3]—supply her with all she had herself from her Country houses of vegetables, Fish, & Poultry, & lend the the complete use of a Carriage & Coachman for herself & her friends. And this that noble-minded creature only did because, had the case been reversed, she felt what she must have suffered had the D^s

---

[3] New light on the vexed question of Mrs. Delany's indebtedness to the Duchess of Portland, touched on in *Memoirs*, iii, 45–9, and denied by Lady Llanover (see *HFB*, pp. 461–2 and 494 n. N.), is provided by Mrs. Delany's will (P.C.C. Calvert 239), pr. 7 May 1788: 'The Duchess Dowager of Portland was so good on my buying my House in St. James Place to lend me unasked four hundred pounds for which she has my Bond. I desire it may be discharged her Grace would not accept the Interest.'

To the analogy between herself and Mrs. Delany, SBP was to reply in her letter (Berg) of [20] July, *pmk* 30 JY 98, of which FBA had obliterated some 53 lines, the residue being printed in *FB & the Burneys*, pp. 277–81: 'I will not . . . tell you I am *not Mrs Delany*, nor my Fanny the D^{ss} of Portland that Mrs Delany had neither a husband nor a child—that the D^{ss} in the midst of affluence and prosperity c^d in no way so highly have enjoyed the blessings of—as—I will not proceed—.'

resisted her. This she has told me herself. And how tenderly did the D^s pay back the high trust this marked that their friendship could never know change! — | This REVERED PERSON I may quote as a pattern to you, & to Mrs. Locke—though I know NO OTHER I ever for a moment place above you.

I said I would have done—yet know not how to go to any thing else, my Heart is so completely with this subject.—I have just been interrupted by dearest Mr. & Mrs. Locke—we have talked of nothing else—my Eyes were so red with your dear Letter, & my Naso so troublesome, I saw I should wound her tender affections by concealment, & told her, therefore, our petition, & she approves it every way, & so does Mr. Locke, & I am sure they would neither of them, *so situated*, be hard hearted. If you can but come, you & the 3 dear Children, for a few months—how it will lighten what else of exile must ensue! our dearest Padre—Esther—James & Charles will insist upon your passing some time with them—We would meet you instantly for the certainty you were indeed here & safe, & then wait your time for settling you here,—Charles is heartily & cordially earnest to have your dear Boys at his school, Fanny must always be by your side—& we can lodge ALL at vacations. And when every body sails over to some friend during this storm, why should my Susan, for whom so many are combatting, not bless us with her sight & her safety? We would never interfere with the Major's after-plans. We feel all the duties as well as virtues of your sacrifices & compliances. We only entreat that the *two voyages*, for a little repose of security to yourself, & the exquisite joy of holding you to our Hearts after the terrors we have suffered for your danger, may be *our affair*.

The words you ask for are precisely what follow.—'I have just put a bill of a £100 into Mr. Maturin's hand for part of payment of your bond. The remainder, I hope, will soon be remitted to you.'

Is the direction to Mr. G[abriel] M[aturin] at Mrs. Browne's, Beaumaris,[4] sufficient? Will it be best to write to *him* to remit it back, or wait the M[ajor]'s answer to our entreaty he would claim it? we thought him then in Ireland, & that shewing

---

[4] Gabriel Maturin (iii, L. 215 n. 7), an intermediary in the business of FBA's loan to the Shirleys (L. 271 n. 8), resided as a tutor with the family of Dominick Geoffrey Browne (1755–1826) of Castle Macgarrett, County Mayo, who had married in 1785 Margaret *née* Browne (d. 1838). See also L. 294 n. 15.

M. d'A.'s signature would be enough. For god's sake let nothing be omitted from *mistake* in this business! That would, indeed, be too afflicting. We write all round at every Letter you send, & a secret committee is now formed upon your affairs, & to deliberate upon the measures for your return, at which we cabal by word of Mouth or word of Pen weekly. One who for particular reasons appears not is at la tête—& ought to be. we went together to Mrs. Newton, tell good Susan, & saw ˡ her & her two Children well,[5] & made her smile irresistibly by telling her Susan's dignified title of ma'am. She is sure, she says, Susan will never wish to come over without you & Willy. She desires her kind love to her dear Sister.—Do remember me to Mrs. Hill,[6]—I always loved her more than I *saw* from what I heard. But your J[aney] P[aney] has got all our hearts. What a sweet Character![7] we want to make up *another mattrass* for her at West Hamble! She would little guess what a proof that is of extraordinary regard. I quite love her. I think I know her intimately, & see your arms open to receive her, & your spirits revive, & your natural feelings have some vent, when she toils so far & through such difficulties to embrace You. Embrace her for *ME* that she knows you worth such exertion. My sweet Mrs. Locke says we may renew our Mr. W[indham]'s conveyance. I am most thankful, for I long so always to *hear*, yet make such conscience of telling you so often, when I know every body is writing to you, that I want to have 2 or 3 Letters for one always. The difference, just now, of the eagerness *must* be so great— Esther dies to bring you over, & thinks of expedients with all her might. I shall immediately forward to all round that I have fresh news of your actual safety. Charlotte's Letter arrived at the same time with mine.[8] I hope she goes on happily. As long as she can demonstrate invariable admiration, I have no fear for her. She expresses her warm wishes for your return. A very kind interest is kept up for you in Mickleham, & all around it, & a general desire is still alive for your return to these parts.

Adieu, my dearest, my darling Susan! I will own I do not send off this letter without hope from its effect. I should be too

---

[5] Of Mrs. Newton's children, Richard alone is identified (iii, L. 237 n. 6; and iv, L. 262 n. 1).   [6] See iii, L. 216 n. 3.

[7] In a letter of 2⟨6⟩ June, op. cit., SBP had expatiated on Jane Brabazon's sensibility and kindness.

[8] SBP's letter (Berg) of 25 June 1798 to CBFB.

much grieved to oppress you with entreaty, if I did not think my pleas *reasonable* as well as earnest: I would not for the UNIVERSE involve any new expence to gratify my longing wishes or restless fears: but I claim from my tender Susan what Mrs. Delany granted to HER friend, & what M. d.Arblay, without even regret granted to his. Heaven bless you, sweetest Sister, & guide you & *yours* 1.2.3. to your faithful

F. A. d'A.

our beloved Friend will write herself, or I should have entered into her affairs—& return, &c—M. d'A. says he has been composing you a vehement scold. |

My kindest love to my dear Fanny & Norbury & Willy. I conclude the Major at Drogheda—otherwise add ditto. I can't wonder at poor Norbury's joy swallowing up his concern.⁹ My Boy is quite well, & as merry as a Grig |

289   West Humble, 1 August 1798

To Esther (Burney) Burney

A.L.S. (Berg), 1 Aug. 1798
Double sheet 4to   4 pp.   *pmks*   EPSOM   2 AU 98   wafer
Addressed: Mrs. Burney / Nº 43. Beaumont Street, / Devonshire Place / London.
Scribbling in pencil, p. 4.

westhumble Aug. 1ˢᵗ 1798

My dearest Esther, I earnestly hope, has not been so unfortunate as to believe in the apparent promise of seeing our beloved Sister?—My own previous disappointment, which was greater than I can express, saved me at least from *this*. — — the Letter which our good James transmitted to me, from the Major,¹ & upon which he seems himself to rely, did not delude me into any other hope than that—if the rebellion keeps her

⁹ Norbury was seldom allowed to visit Belcotton. His joy at seeing his mother in Dublin notwithstanding the dangers that brought her there may be in the part of the letter later suppressed by FBA.

289. ¹ This is SBP's letter (Berg) of [20] July [1798], *pmks* 26 JY 98 30 JY 98, of which the parts left unobliterated by FBA are printed in *FB & the Burneys*, 277–81.

from Belcotton, & the Cartland's cannot longer press her stay from any family reasons at Dublin, she would *then* be permitted to come to her friends & her Country. And I have now just got a Letter from her to this purpose. She desires me to communicate it to you & James, to prevent any expectations she does not think will be fulfilled—alas!—Not an Hour, she says, had passed, after this favourable answer to James, & much such another to Charles, before the Major let her see he had *no plan* whatever of keeping to the engagement into which he had entered. It seems as if he liked to trifle with her & our feelings— yet she says he is *really* in an undecided & embarrassed state, that makes his inconsistencies to be pitied, however they may be blamed. She cannot [|] attempt, she says, to enter into a discussion of their circumstances, but they are such, that were it not for the anxiety *we* all manifest at her stay in Ireland, she should think it her duty to *insist* upon *remaining*, not *removing*, to guard, as much as in her lies, his & her Children's property & credit.—

This is so dreadfully serious, that it damps, in every way, all & every species of hope. Yet I am so persuaded Belcotton, & all other places in the vicinity of the Metropolis, will be dangerous for inhabiting many months to come, from the hoards of Banditti which the straggling & flying remnants of the rebellion will leave to infest the Mountains with, that it is IMPOSSIBLE for me to yield to any of her representations for continuing upon such a spot. To return to it would be bitter enough—but still that, after the nation is really tranquil (should that period arrive in our days,) would not be more cruel than the separation we have already submitted to. But now, her absence is a thousand times more grievous than at first, from the terror of her personal safety joined to her general suffering. She says there have been 2 engagements within 9 Miles of Drogheda[2]— & does not, herself, pretend now to assert that all may be relied upon in her neighbourhood for loyalty & safety.— [|]

Consult with dear James—we must ALL still, *I* think, as far as in us lies, represent to her that her LIFE must be more precious than the Major's, or even than her Children's property,—& that it seems as if from day to day, & Hour to Hour

---

[2] Two 'engagements were fought the 21ˢᵗ & 22ᵈ near Slane . . . about 9 miles from Drogheda', SBP had reported in a suppressed portion of her letter (op. cit.) 'Almost all the regular troops participated' and 'the yeomen for the town'.

it must be in danger, if she goes to so defenceless a place in this turbulent season of smothered, but not vanquished rebellion, whose embers are ready to be lighted by the first match that touches them.

About what I mentioned to you, she is obdurate so as to make us nearly quarrel with her,—& the M[ajor] *declines* it, but not, I think, so inexorably. We shall continue, therefore, presenting our petition, as much as we *dare*. We hear, by this last Letter, that the money is actually in the hands of Mr. G. Mathurin, tell my dear James, who knows the transaction, & will be glad to have this intelligence. At least, so Susan *believes*, she says.

I expect to see our dearest Padre here shortly, & shall then discuss the subject with him; but not write first, as I know not his present address.³

M. d'A. was much vexed he missed you, in his London peep —but he rejoices me with his description of your new apartments, which he tells me are charming—gay, fashionable, & tout à fait *gentille*. He thinks the change, also at Chelsea, all for the best, which I little expected to hear. How are your NIGHTS now, my dearest Esther? Do you sleep any better since this change? The street seems quiet, M. d'A. says, & not likely to disturb you. How melancholy Edward must be!⁴ I hope Richard frequently visits him, if now with you. And Amelia? is she better? M. d'A. says he likes her Balcony as well as she does herself. Was your visit *comf.* at Pow's?⁵ & was Mrs. Rish[ton] in her old funny style? I rejoiced to hear Mr.

³ CB had begun his 'summer rambles' on 21 July with a visit to Bulstrode and planned to go into Hampshire, doubtless for his usual visit to Richard Cox at Quarley. See a letter (Osborn) from CB to William Herschel, dated Bulstrode, 22 July 1798. He was to visit West Humble later in August (see L. 290, p. 166; and L. 292, p. 176).

⁴ Charles Rousseau Burney, as long as he occupied the large house on Titchfield Street (L. 264 n. 2), had been able to accommodate his brother Edward Francesco.

⁵ EBB had set off to Gravesend with Maria Rishton on 11 July for a visit of a fortnight with a friend of their early King's Lynn days, namely, 'Pow', the widowed Mrs. John Allen, *née* Mary Turner (*c.* 1745–1815), daughter of Charles Turner (bur. 12 May 1792), Mayor of King's Lynn (1759, 1767), later Collector of Customs (by proxy), with a residence in Queen Square, London (see burial registers of St. George the Martyr, Queen Square; and his will, P.C.C. Fountain 305).

In February 1773 Mary Turner had married at King's Lynn the Revd. John Towers Allen (*c.* 1735–87) of Wiggenhall St. German, Norfolk. His M.I., with that of his widow, can be seen in the church at Terrington, St. Clement. In the winter of 1799–1800 Maria Rishton spent some months with 'Madame A—', whom she described in a letter of 7 Jan. [1800] (Eg. 3697, ff. 297–8b).

B[urney] was of the party. My kind love to him, & to your Girls dear. How I wish we had accommodations to press you, my dearest Esther, to view our little Hermitage with Mr. B[urney]!—but we have no double bed—& I fear putting you, as I have done Charlotte, in a single one without curtains, in a bare walled Chamber. Yet this what I do *not* fear offering to Susan—nor should I to *YOU*, were you in Ireland—& with M[ajor]—but I dread your rheumatic seizures. However, we live in hopes for another year. *This* we have been obliged to stop short. My dear *Father* we shall trepan into our own room— but not let him know it.—We spent yesterday at Norbury Park, where all were well, & where I rarely go without my dear Esther's being a part of our best discourse. *Mrs. L[ocke]* speaks so EXACTLY as you do about the M[ajor]—that I could not forbear regretting to her you did not hear her. 'Twould have solaced you a little.—

o yes, she said, I know dear Mrs. Burney & I have the very same shade of opinion about him!—My Boy is well, & not very dullifying to us.—God bless you, dearest Esther—ever & aye faithfully & most affectionately yours

F. d'A. [|]

M. d'A.'s kindest remembrances.

Certainly, as you say, the death of L^d E[dward] F[itzgerald] was a very great Mercy to his family. Things *now* are proving against him that render his very memory horrible.[6]

---

[6] As FBA could have seen in *The Times* (2 Aug.), a bill had been brought forward on 27 July 1798 for the attainder of Lord Edward Fitzgerald. 'The bill passed the house of lords in . . . September, and received royal assent in . . . October' (Thomas Moore, *The Life and Death of Lord Edward Fitzgerald*, ii. 155, 170 ff.).

To Mrs. Broome

A.L.S. (Berg), 14 Aug. [17]98
Double sheet 4to   4 pp.   *pmks*   P.P.P. RICHMOND   15 AU 98
15 AU 98   AUG 98   wafer
Addressed: Mrs. Broome, / ⌐Hill Street, / Richmond, / Surry.⌐
Readdressed in unknown hand: Nº 113 / High Street / Southamton
[*On fold*:] Mʳˢ Broome / Nº 113—High Street / Southa[mp]ton
[*With the message*:] all well & happy at Richmond
Endorsed by CBFB, p. 1: Sister d'arblay—/ Augᵗ,—1798/ ansᵈ — — augᵗ—
30ᵗʰ

WestHamble near Dorking
Surry.—Augᵗ 14. / 98

I have deferred writing, my dearest Charlotte, because your
Letters called for Answers which I could not make, but yet
hoped to acquire materials for making by some delay.—In one
—& the chief point, my hopes are at this instant verified—for
I have *just* received news that our beloved Sister is, at length,
preparing to set out for England.—Heaven grant that no new
reverse may again blight our expectations! The Letter is to my
Father,[1] & he has transmitted me the particulars, which I
forward to my dear Charlotte by the Post which brought them.

I dare not build *absolutely* upon any event which may be
directed by the Major, from the fluctuating propensities
which lead him so often from the straight line: however, she
seems to think she shall not again be disappointed, nor disappoint us all again so bitterly,—for she expressly desires that
no more Letters may be sent to her, unless she writes again, as,—
if she comes,—she shall be sailed before they can arrive. Heaven
speed her, sweet soul!—*for* though the real rebellion is crushed,[2]
there are so many worthless ⏐ Adventurers engaged in it, who
had rather live by plunder than by labour, that no lone &
undefended house will be thought secure for many months to
come. This has been represented to the Major by his Irish
friends, & by all the neighbourhood of Drogheda, & therefore

290. ¹ Both letters are missing.
    ² The Rebellion was crushed when on 21 June 1798 General Gerard Lake (see
DNB) routed the rebel forces entrenched at Vinegar Hill. The next day he
marched into Wexford itself.

he yields to the necessity of letting her come over to her own friends till tranquility is restored, & security may be relied upon.

I wish I could as satisfactorily answer about Russia; you must tell Mr. Broome I have not the smallest knowledge of the funds of that Country,—nor, indeed, of any other!—All I ever knew, I told you,—that a *Lady LOST* her all in a *Russian Negociation*— I *thought* in the *Russian Funds*; but it might perhaps be be some private transaction: I only know that the Money was entrusted to the Chaplain of the British Factory at Petersburg, Dr. King;[3] —whom you must remember; but the particulars I heard too briefly for relating, or retaining, with any certitude & ᐟ precision. When I saw my Father, a few days since, I tried to ask him something of *Russian Funds*, as a general question; but he looked thoughtful, without answering, & the subject & the recollections are all so delicate, I could not press the matter.

I heard with infinite pleasure that he will now be glad to see you & Mr. Broome whenever you will at Chelsea. He intended, also, calling upon you in a visit he purposes to Mrs. Boscawen at Kew: but I gather, by a Letter to day, you are not at Richmond. I think that extremely provoking. The Day is not my Father's fixing; but Mrs. Boscawen's, for some particular meeting.

Dear Norbury is to remain in Dublin—this is a cruel drawback to our Susan's comfort.—Fanny & Willy are to accompany her, & her faithful Susan. Tell all this to our dear Miss Cambridge, should you see her before I write. You do not let me know where to direct, so I trust this to Richmond. But I entreat you to omit *Leatherhead* in our Address, & say West Hamble near *Dorking*, Surry,—as we have no communication of Letters from Leatherhead, except by Messengers who come over purposely. ᐟ We thank you about the alien Bill—but think the only articles which can concern us are in the News-papers; & M. d'A. has waited upon the Magistrate of the Parish, & *given an account of himself*.[4]

[3] John Glen King (1732–87), D.D. (1771). The investment by which in 1767 Mrs. Burney lost £5,000 is explained in Scholes, i. 307; ii. 131 n. 1.

[4] The Alien Bill of 1793 (see iii, L. 136 n. 11) was reviewed in the House in April 1798 (*The Times*, 20, 28 Apr.) and a revised bill, to be effective until 1 Jan. 1800, had passed its third reading on 2 May (*CJ* 53: 530).

M. d'A. had evidently complied with clauses requiring re-registration of emigrants, though the document in question is not to be found.

How glad I am you have seen so much of Mr. Seward—
when you meet next, pray give him my best Comp^ts & if he
should be in a very kind humour—such as I have been wont to
see him in—I could almost be tempted to wish you would hint
to him that 3 volumes look *rather ODD* in our little Book case, of a
work that has *4* extant⁵—however, don't *insinuate this plot* into
the discourse, unless his Eyebrows have their best arches in
order. I most heartily rejoice you so often see dear Mr. Cambridge, & that he retains for me all his primitive kindness.

When the *grand meeting* is over, pray let me know—I long for
the period, for a thousand reasons. I think, & hope, it will pass
as if accident only had retarded it. We had a few days here of my
dear Father, much damped by *Gout* & Cold,—but still most
dear to me. My little Man is well, but again has lost his appetite,
& were he not gay, & bright-Eyed, 'twould be most alarming.
As it is, it gives but occasional fright, or uneasiness.—M. d'A.
joins me in kindest remembrances to Mr. Broome, & your dear
little ones.

God bless you, my dearest Charlotte—& preserve you as like
as possible in two Things Happiness & Affection to yours

faithfully & truly

for-ever F. d'A.

If I knew how to form you a better wish, I would.

291   West Humble, [28]–29 August [1798]

To Mrs. *and* Major Phillips

A.J.L. (Diary MSS. vi. 5130–[3] and two discarded leaves, Berg),—
29 Aug.

A double sheet and two single sheets 4to   8 pp.   wafer

Addressed: Mrs. Phillips, / to the care of Mr. Kiernan, / Henry Street, /
Dublin. / To be forwarded / with speed.

Endorsed by SBP: F d'A. / rec^d Sept 6 or 7th

Docketed, p. 8: C. 24

Edited by FBA, p. 1 (5130), *annotated and dated*: our PADRE—Aug^st. 28.—
98

Edited also by CFBt *and the* Press.

If I could find words—but the language does not afford any—
any—My dearest—dearest Susan—to tell what this final blow

⁵ See iii, L. 171 n. 16.

has been to me,[1] I am sure I should be a brute to make use of them—but after so much of hope—of fear, of doubt, of terror,— to be lifted up, at length, to real expectation—& only to be hurled down to disappointment — — & You—sweetest soul!— that can think of any body else in such a situation!—for though your neighbours are so good,[2] Ireland is so unsettled, in *our* estimation, that I believe there is hardly one amongst us would not at least have parted with a little finger by the Hatchet to have possessed you for a few Months in England—

I write because I MUST write, but I am not yet fit for it—I can offer no fortitude to my Susan, & it is wrong to offer any thing else—but I must write, because I must let her see my hand, to tempt a quicker sight again of her own to Eyes which yearn after it incessantly.

Why did the Major desire me to look after our old Cottage at Bookham? & so obligingly, so pleasantly, so truly say he was certain of the pleasure he gave me by the commission?—Can you tell?—

We had heard so much of the scarcity of cash, & difficulty to raise it in these times, in Ireland, that we ventured, in return to the friendly address & correspondence he began himself so good humouredly, to entreat his making use of the 100 he told us he had just placed with Mr. Maturin: & the hope that has lived with us to this Minute that it still might be found convenient, has determined M. d'A. never to write about it, nor take the smallest notice of the Major's kind intelligence, while any ray of light yet remained that it might be rendered so clear to us. GOD knows thousands coming in any other shape would not enrich us like the sight of my Susan in this! — — — *us* I may indeed say, for James & Charles, with all the true love they have proved, cannot go further than my partner in what he feels.—

291. [1] As the text goes on to explain, this was a letter from Phillips annulling plans and promises recently made of bringing his family to England. Cf. *FB & the Burneys*, p. 276.

[2] 'Nothing of Rebels around about Drogheda', reported SBP in one of the suppressed sections of her letter (Berg) of 2⟨6⟩ July (op. cit.), 'the vigilance of Government & the activity of the yeomanry have been admirable'.

Apropos the landing of the French on 22 Aug., in a letter of 8–11 Sept. (Berg), printed in part in *FB & the Burneys*, pp. 281–5, SBP testified to her 'present secure & undisturbed existence'. 'The people around us work on tranquilly, & shew no alarm except when they conceive we are likely to leave them—so little is known about the Invasion that they conclude the French to have been *all killed*, & they seem perfectly content with the supposition.'

Guard your *health*, my Susan—that is my first prayer,—you must see what a round of happiness depends upon it.—

I am very glad, indeed, the people of Belcotton are so worthy & so grateful. But—is your return not reckoned premature by others besides *US*?

I know your strength of mind, my beloved Susanna,—I only fear for your weakness of body.

My Father I hear is deeply affected by this unexpected disappointment. Sally writes me word so. Neither he nor Esther could bring themselves to inflict what they felt here.

But M. d'A bids none of us murmur,—he says he thinks the Major means, at last, to give us all a sudden & generous surprise.—How I should bless him for it!

I had had great pleasure indeed in the thought of seeing my dear Fanny—my kindest love to the sweet Girl, & tell her so. I am sure she will bear the change better than almost any other young person & try to forget it. Dear Norbury's generosity was beautiful. Mrs. Wall[3] says he is a lovely Creature, inside & out. Certainly I will ǀ endeavour to think of your nearness to have tydings of him. Dear Boy!—What a blessing he has been to you from his birth!—

In a Letter I have just got from Charles,[4] he says 'I am cut to the soul by this unexpected disappointment of Susan,— I had contrived good accommodation for Norbury & Willy, though my School is not merely full, but *overflowing*. I have 3 out-standers.'

I have not heard from or of James —but perhaps, like M. d'A he has better hope, & believes the Major only postpones, for motives of business, or private affairs, the journey, & yet means to keep to his engagement.

M. d'A is at this time spending 2 days chez M. La Jard,[5]— the last Minister of war to poor Louis 16.—If he should return

[3] See iii, L. 203 n. 6.   [4] The letter is missing.

[5] Pierre-Auguste Lajard (1757–1837) was the eldest of the three sons of Angé-lique *née* Pelet (1731–1803) and Barthélemy Lajard (1721–80), 'président trésorier de France en la généralité de Montpellier, intendant des gabelles du Languedoc'. Having reached the rank of Adjutant-Général in the Army, Pierre-Auguste became Minister of War for a short time (16 June–24 July 1792, or in some accounts until 16 Aug.). Having fled in that year to England, he was living at present at Croydon. He was to return to France in 1799 and to become, under Napoleon, an officer in the Legion of Honour (1808) and a member of the Chamber of Deputies (1808–15).

before Mrs. Lock sends off the pacquet, I am sure he will add a line.

I have many things to say—& talk of—but they all get behind the present overbearing, engrossing disappointment, which will take no consolation, or occupation, except my dear Boy, who, fortunately, was out of the way when I first received it; for else he would have used the Letter very ill:—when I got that which announced that you were coming, (the 1 before the last, in which the Major himself wrote to James, & which James most kindly forwarded to me instantly, saying *We may now expect dear Susan in a few Days*—those words, from *him*, less easily elated than most of us, so transported me, that I appeared, to my poor Alex, in deep grief, from a powerful | emotion of surprise & joy, which forced its way down my cheeks: the little Creature, who was playing on the Sofa, set up a loud cry, & instantly, with a desperate impulse, ran to me, darted up his little hands, before I could imagine his design, & seized the Letter with such violence, that I must have torn to have prevented him: & then he flew with it to the Sofa, &, rumpling it up in his little hands, poked it under the Cushions, & then resolutely sat down upon it., I was too unhappy at that moment to oppose his little enterprize, & he sat still till my carresses, & evident re-establishment, brought him to my lap. However, when I put him down, & made up to the Sofa for my Letter, he began Crying again, & flying to his booty, put himself into such an agony, that I was fain to quiet it by waiting till I could take it unobserved. Yet he could not express himself better in words than by merely saying 'I don't ike ou to ead a Letter, mama!'— He had never happenned to see me in tears before, happy Boy!—& Oh happy Mother!——The little Soul has a thousand traits of Character that remind me of Norbury—both in what is desirable & what is fearful; for he is not only as sweet, but as impetuous—& already he has the same desire to hear me recount to him his own good & bad conduct at the end of the day that dear Norbury had when I visited Mickleham. Just now, when we took leave for the Night, he said 'And what was I to day, mama? = Good, my dear. — But what was I *to* dinner?—A little rude. = He then looks down, very conscious, but raises his brightened Eyes, to say 'And what *are* I now, Mama?'—*Quite* good, my love—' & then—O what pleasure to | his little heart!—He [Alex] is still extremely backward in his powers of speech, but retains his early faculty of making himself understood by looks & manner. He makes an even astonishing progress towards reading & if I dared suffer him to indulge his own propensity, he would apply from Morning to Night: but, far from urging, I am forced to repress him, as his little reflecting Countenance, & air of thought at every difficulty, make me fear letting his studies ever exceed what he takes for play.

— — What joy I had prepared him for on seeing Willy!— who I had assured him would be a new little papa, to take care of, as well as play with him — — — And his dear Aunt Phillips's ivorey Letters were his first instructors—& doubled my pleasure in the lessons, by making what had passed through her hands go from mine, & his Father's to the little darling urchin. — —

Charlotte is making a little Tour with Mr. Broome.[6]

You are remembered all round here, my dearest love, with extreme kindness, & the tender concern shewn for your safety during the rebellion by all who had known you at all, has been truly touching & unspeakably grateful to me. All Mickleham sincerely wishes your return there, & good old Mrs. Pollen & her sister Baker at dorking[7] send me messages of enquiry about your safety with almost every loaf.

Sunday, in my way from Mickleham Church, I stopt to speak to Mrs. Newton[8]—I was most sorry indeed to destroy the fair pleasure I had just raised! & she was sadly disappointed— she desires her best Love to good Susan—& pray remember me very kindly to that excellent creature, who is a comfort to all my thoughts.— | How anxious shall I now become about the N[orth] of I[reland]!—pray tell me the exact spot,[9]—where my tenderest solicitude, after Belcotton, will rest?—God bless the dear Boy!—my eldest son, —& Fanny my only Daughter!—

A *particular* friend of mine has something just now in project

[6] The rapid stages of a tour, beginning on 9 Aug. at Cobham and ending at Reigate, were recorded by Broome in verse, a copy of which (in CBFB's hand) is preserved in the Scrapbook (Berg) 'Fanny Burney and family. 1653–1890', p. 69: 'On the 9th after Dining we posted away / To refresh a few minutes at Cobham did stay.'

[7] For the Dorking bakers, see L. 265 n. 1.

[8] See L. 262 n. 1.

[9] Norbury was now at Fanet (see *FB & the Burneys*, pp. 289, 296, 301).

that she had given me leave to confide in you, with oaths of secresy, upon your arrival—but I dare not trust the secret to the post. If you can guess the person, do: though I must not *name* her, I may assent or dissent to your conjecture. Cherchez aux coins de la Lettre.[10]

⟶

——— Aug^{st} 29.

O my beloved sister this moment a newspaper tells me that a party of the French has landed—[11]

For the almighty's sake exert yourself *now* to come over immediately from that defenceless spot you inhabit—O Susan—think of the dreadful consequences that may await any delay —I write in an agony that makes all my former fears mere play—come, for god's sake!—my dear Mate is not returned from croydon—I shall send off this instant to Norbury park & beg it's immediate forwarding—

How I bless God our norbury was not already in the North! — — I *kneel* to the Major to suffer him to accompany you & Fanny, & Willy till this invasion is over—I must write to him myself—exert your utmost powers, my beloved soul, & let us hear a *line* at least at once—& till you sail—think of our horrour—

[*To Molesworth Phillips*]

Westhumble—Aug. 29—1798

Dear Major—send us off your wife & Children *all* I supplicate you—till the invasion is past.—no one can tell what may be its extent, nor what forces those already landed may enable, by manoeuvering, engineering, to land after them. The possession of a sea port is their's already. you have written to

---

[10] The initials 'F.d'A', appearing on the lower left corner of p. 8 of this letter, refer conjecturally to the plans for the production of 'Love and Fashion'. Cf. SBP's query of 8 Sept. (*FB & the Burneys*, pp. 284–5): 'and will not my Fanny explain her enigma to me when she answers this? I understand the initials in the corner, and long for an explanation—write between hooks [thus] my dearest. In all probability even that precaution will be unnecessary, but with it there is perfect security—'.
[11] This was the landing of about 1,000 French troops at Killala Bay in County Mayo on 22 Aug., a report of which FBA could have seen in an editorial in *The Times* (28 Aug. 1798).

Mr. Lock, to *James*, to *Charles*, & to *Me*, that you would send them,—but we knew the many difficulties that might occasion a change of plan, & yielded to the disappointment:—at present, however, the danger is incalculable—for this will give courage to all sort of yet disaffected to shew themselves, & it cannot be supposed you will be able to guard Belcotton at such a period, when all forces must be subject to marching orders from all quarters.—I beseech you not to be offended, dear Major, that once more I venture to entreat you will not scruple making a call upon the £100 in Mr. Maturin's hands, which we have never written for, in a constant hope it might be of service in any emergency towards hastening the Journey we are so anxious should take place. M. d'Arblay is at this moment absent, but I know we have only one mind in this petition. At a time of public calamity no one refuses aid, or I should not risk such a request. God bless you, Dear Major, I hope you will let Norbury also come till the ǀ invasion is over—he can find 1000 means to go back when it will be safe.

Yours ever F d'Arblay

292   West Humble, Journal
for [June–*pre* 22 November 1798]

To Mrs. Phillips

A.J.L. (Diary MSS. vi. 5108–[29], Berg), written up *post* 15 Dec. 1798
Originally seven double sheets 4to, of which the first double sheet and the first leaf of the second double sheet are missing. The five remaining double sheets are numbered 3, 4, 5, 6, 7   22 pp.

Edited by CFBt *with* FBA, *who annotated the 2nd ds.*, p. 3; *the 3rd ds.*, p. 1; *and the 4th ds.*, p. 1: West Hamble—1798; *the 5th ds.*, p. 1 (5122): West Hamble [*with an editorial link following a blank paste-over* (P5):] I am sure you must remember young Charles Moore the Lawyer: He is now a Counsellor & rising in reputation & fortune; *and the 7th ds.*, p. 1: West Hamble—1798

For CFBt's *work and that of the* Press, *see* Textual Notes.

[6 pages are missing]

... accomplishments. This, certainly, must make him[1] an over-bearing companion, were he married to any one but Charlotte;

292. [1] Ralph Broome (L. 256 n. 1), who had visited the d'Arblays *post* 14 August (L. 290).

Charlotte, however, has so profound an admiration for every talent he possesses & so implicit a credulity for every one he tells her he possesses, that she thinks herself the most blest of women that he has honoured her with his hand. And while this opinion lasts, they will be mutually happy, as a listner & admirer are all he requires. But I would to God it were as probable her part in this compact should be permanent as his!—to him she will always be submissive & respectful—& he will think her a model of wives: but she — — o the time will come, I fear, when she will sigh for the liberty she has lost, & repine at the adulatory price she must pay for kindness & peace!—

To me, however, he was entertaining & informing, as we talked of India, & he permitted me to ask what questions I pleased upon points & things of which I was glad to gather accounts from so able a traveller. M. d'Arblay, too natural to like a character of this factitious sort, could not endure him; but he had not my *desire* to see his best side; a desire which would make me tolerate greater arrogance, in order to find out what ever could balance it. Little Charlotte is clever & penetrating; but her dear Mother perceives not she is fast growing into a consciousness of her merits that wants repressing. Mr. Broome seems very fond of all the Children, & perfectly good humoured with them. I am very anxious about Charlotte, & by no means contented for her feelings, hereafter,—though I have no apprehension of her treatment, as I really believe Mr. Broome will always be kind to her in return for her unlimitted obedience.—But Charlotte is so good, & so affectionate,—I cannot be satisfied for her thus easily. |

Another family visit, which took place this summer, gave us pleasure of a far more easy nature, because unmixt with watchful anxiety: this was from Charles, & his Son, who, by an appointment for which he begged our consent, brought with him, also, Mr. Professor Young of Glasgow;[2] a man whose learning sits upon him far lighter than Mr. Broome's! O that it had been poor Charlotte's happy lot from *him* to have received

[2] John Young (*c.* 1750–1820), M.A. (1769), professor of Greek at Glasgow (1774), who had befriended CB Jr. in the years (?1778/9–81) when he studied at Aberdeen (*HFB*, pp. 72–6). See also R. S. Walker, 'Charles Burney's Theft of Books at Cambridge', *Transactions of the Cambridge Bibliographical Society*, iii. 4 (1962), 313–26. *A Criticism on the Elegy written in A Country Church Yard, being a continuation of Dr J[ohnso]n's criticism on the poems of Gray* was published in 1783.

the fascination that has thus caught her! Mr. Young has the *bonhommie* of M. de Lally; with as much native humour as he has acquired erudition. He has a face that looks all honesty & kindness, & manners gentle & humble. An enthusiasm for whatever he thinks excellent, whether in talents or character, in art or in nature; & is, all together, a man it seems impossible to know, even for a day, & not to love & wish well. This latter is probably the effect of his own cordial disposition to amity. He took to us, all *three*, so evidently, & so warmly, & was so smitten with our little dwelling, its situation, & simplicity, & so much struck with what he learnt & saw of M. d'Arblay's cultivating literally his own grounds, & literally being his own gardener, after finding, by conversation, what a use he had made of his earlier days in literary attainments, that he seemed as if he thought himself brought to a vision of the Golden Age—such was the appearance of his own sincere & upright mind in rejoicing to see happiness where there was palpably no luxury, no wealth.

It was a most agreeable surprise to me to find such a man in Mr. Professor Young, as I had expected a sharp, though amusing satirist, from his very comic, but sarcastic imitation of Dr. Johnson's Lives, in a criticism upon Gray's Elegy. This he sent me, many years ago, anonymously, with ¹ a note of extreme personal civility to myself, unsigned. Did you ever read? or do you remember it?—

Charles was all kind affection, & delighted at our approbation of his friend; for the professor has been such many years, & very essentially formerly; a circumstance Charles is now gratefully & warmly returning. It is an excellent part of Charles's Character that he never forgets any kind office he has received. He is now continually serving James Sansom,³ & *potently* & generously; & he gives time, attention, & kindness of every sort he can suggest to Mr. Pugh.⁴ Little Charles is a sweet Boy;⁵

---

³ James Sansom (d. 26 Jan. 1823), conjecturally a relative of the Burneys on the maternal (or Sleepe) side of the family who may have helped CB Jr. in 1777 when he was sent down from Cambridge and for a time barred from his father's house. In 1802 Sansom, man-of-all-work, was in the employ of CB Jr. at Greenwich. After CB Jr.'s death he became a pensioner of both JB and FBA.

⁴ The Revd. Matthew Pugh (*c.* 1739–17 Apr. 1810), 'near 50 years at St. James's, Westminster' (*GM* lxxxi. 496) and a friend of the young Burneys (*ED* i. 2, 77–82, 148).

⁵ Charles Parr Burney, now nearly 13 years old.

natural, unassuming, placid, sensible, & engaging. The Day was perfectly pleasant to us all, except my own Partner, who in the beginning of it had an head ache that confined him to his room; but who felt exactly as I did about Mr. Professor from the moment they met. I am sorry he lives in Scotland.

I learnt from them that Mr. Rogers,[6] Author of the Pleasures of Memory—that most sweet little poem—had ridden round the lanes about our domain to view it, & stood—or made his Horse stand,—at our Gate a considerable time to examine our *Camilla Cottage*, a name I am sorry to find Charles, or some one, had spread to him: & he honoured all with his good word. I should like to meet with him.

I grieved it was impossible to us to ask our dearest Esther & her family hither; but our bare walls & unpapered rooms I feared would give her the rheumatism almost from *fancy*, so delicate is her health. My Father came indeed—but for him I did what no one else would let me do,—but what he never discovered—gave him our own Bed & apartment: the only bed we have that has Curtains. Ah! my Susan! *You* have slept without them—& would to Heaven you *so* slept now! I have no fears, no scruples, no demurs for you!—but our Esther's health & delicacy are of a different sort, & she is used to every home comfort, & rarely well in the country.— |

Our beloved Father came to us in August for five Days, to our inexpressible delight: though the gaiety of our enjoyment was much lessened by his being seized with a little fit of the Gout, which, after the first day, prevented his strolling about, or more than quitting his room. Nor could he once see our dear Neighbours, though they called upon him here twice. He brought his present work, a poetical history of Astronomy, with him, & read it through-out to us. I had already heard the greatest part at Chelsea. I believe I have told you how much I like it, & how full of information & ingenuity I think it. Indeed it seems to me a work to do him great honour, as well as to be highly useful to the young in Astronomical knowledge & to ladies in general. *Women* I was going to say; but it is only as they are classed as *ladies* that this is a science likely to attract them. He was infinitely kind during his stay, to us, our boy, & our place. He brought Alex 6 little golden covered Books to

[6] See i, L. 24 n. 48.

begin his library; but he is grown now so extremely studious, that when not engaged with Company, or in discourse upon literary matters, it is evident he is impatient of lost time. Alex, therefore, had not the chance of occupying or amusing him he would have had some time since. This is easily accounted for by his way of life: Sally will not consult his taste, & he, of course, cannot think of conforming to her's:—there is therefore almost nothing but solitude for him at Chelsea—or a view of a species of dissention to which he has little been accustommed in his daughters. I have seen this with something beyond grief. He never applies to her even to Copy for him a NOTE, if either Marianne or Sophy[7] are at hand. This the good Girls, with wonder & regret, have told me ˡ themselves. Poor Sarah!—how much does she prepare for regret herself in what she loses of his confidence from wilfulness & selfishness?—

He had then been making sundry visits amongst his friends: we invited Sally to be with us during his absence, & give him the meeting: but she frankly gave me to understand she preferred remaining at Chelsea; where, I knew, she had the Girls very frequently, & James completely at her call, & the Coach at her orders.

M. Lajard spent nearly a week with M. d'Arblay. He was minister of War at the unhappy 10. of August, & his account of his endeavours to save the unhappy oppressed King on that fatal day, by dissuading him from going to the cruel Assembly, & to defend himself in his Palace, is truly afflictive.—His own escape after his failures was wonderful. He was concealed a fortnight in Paris. He is now tolerably easy, with regular œconomy, in his circumstances, receiving help privately through Hamburg from his Mother & Brother.[8] He is a steady upright, respectable Character, & *wins & wears* esteem. He had

---

7 EBB's daughters.

8 For Pierre-Auguste Lajard and his mother, see L. 291 n. 5. The brother here mentioned must be Pierre-Esprit-*César* (b. 24 May 1760 at Montpellier), a priest, who in the unfavourable days of the Revolution, gave up his frock and stipend. He had resided at various times at Paris, Lyons, Geneva, and England, but, by 1796, he had emigrated to Hamburg where, with a confrere from Montpellier, he engaged in a speculative traffic in gold ingots and French merchandise. His dossier (Archives Nationales) contains a number of depositions, phony residence certificates, attestations of a blameless life, and *inter alia* an offer of secret information in exchange for which he hoped to gain his *radiation*. By 1804 he was back in France but had not yet obtained the papers by which he could benefit from the general amnesty. He was still living in Paris in 1820.

a principal command, before he was raised to the ministry, in the National Guard under La Fayette, & with M. d'A.—

M. Bourdois,[9] also, spent a week here twice. He was born & bred at Joigny, & therefore is dear to M. d'Arblay by earliest juvenile intimacy, though the gradations of opinions in the Revolution had separated them: for he remained in France when M. d'A. would serve there no longer. He became aid de Camp to Dumouriez,[9] & is celebrated for his bravery at the battle of Jamappe. He is a very pleasant & obliging Character, & doatingly fond of little Alex from having adored his aunt, M[lle] d'Arblay,[10] & from knowing & loving & honouring all his family, | from his birth. And this you will a little guess is some thing of an avenue to a certain urchin's Madre. Besides I like to see any body who has seen Joigny. I was really quite sorry when he came again to take leave upon voyaging to the Continent. But before that time, he brought hither M. le Comte de Ricci,[11]—the officer whom M. d'Arblay immediately succeeded at Metz. & a *Gentleman* in manners, deportment & speech such as rarely is to be met with: elegantly polite & well bred serious even to sadness, & silent & reserved; yet seizing all attention by the peculiar interest of his manner. As soon as he entered our Book Room, he exclaimed 'Ah! de Narbonne!—' looking at our drawing—& this led me to speak of that valued person, with whom I found he had been always much connected. He corresponds with him still, & made me happy, in talking of his hard fate & difficulties, when he told me he had some money of his still in his hands, which he could call for at pleasure, but never demanded, though frequently reminded of the little deposit. But when I mentioned this to M. D'Arblay, he said he fancied it was only Money that M. de Ricci insisted upon appropriating as a loan for him; for that de Ricci,—who by a

---

[9] See iii, L. 245 n. 10; ii, L. 67 n. 7.   [10] See iii, L. 245 n. 8.

[11] Gabriel-Marie, comte de Riccé (1758–1832), maréchar de camp (13 Jan. 1792). He served with *l'armée du Centre* and later (20 July 1792) in *l'armée au Nord*. He emigrated to Holland *post* 10 Aug. 1792, where, according to Béatrice W. Jasinski, *Lettres Diverses*, ii. 534, n. 2, he had married 'à La Haye le 14 mars 1790 Magdalena-Sophia-Elisabeth-Juliana, comtesse van Rechteren, . . . née à la Haye en 1735 — donc plus âgée que Riccé de vingt-trois ans —, veuve de Nicolas Geelvinck, Herr van Stabroek, lequel était mort en 1787, lui laissant un riche héritage'. After her death (*c.* 1797) the comte married Henriette Louise Wilhelmine van Hompesch, countess of the Holy Roman Empire (born at the Hague 26 May 1774; died in Paris on 8 July 1809).

Resuming his service in the army in 1803, he was to become eventually préfect du departement du Loiret (d. at Buzançais on 23 Nov. 1832).

very rich marriage, & entering into a commercial business with his Wife's relations (Dutch people) is himself as rich as if not an Emigrant, is the most benevolent of human beings, & lives parsimoniously, in every respect, to devote all beyond common comforts to suffering Emigrants! His rich wife is dead, & he has married a Cousin of hers who was poor. M. d'A. says he knows of great & incredible actions he has done in assisting his particular friends. I never saw a man who looked more like a Chevalier of old times. He accompanied M. Bourdois here again when he came to take leave: & indeed they left us quite sad.— | He was going to take M. Bourdois to Hamburg, to put him into the house in which his money & power is lodged. M. Bourdois could stay here no longer; yet left England very reluctantly.

What few other visits we had were but Calls,—& from— Lady Burrel,[12] who came as soon as we were settled here; but whose visit I could not return till the following Summer,— when she came again, &, by her request through Miss Locke's, was let in, to our unfurnished Parlour. She was extremely polite & courteous, &, as our dear Friends like her, I imagine she may become pleasing: but I preferred her daughter Julia, who accompanied her, & whom I had twice met before with Mrs. Locke. She seems more natural.

Mr. Clay, the young Clergyman She has married since the death of Sir William, has visited M. d'Arblay repeatedly; but we have only *seen* him at Mr. Locke's. our house is too un-finished for any general admissions, except by appointment. He seems a little conceited, but good humoured, & talks rather too volubly, though by no means wanting in sense. I have met Lady Burrel twice since at Norbury park, but had the exertion to walk a second time to Dipden, her Mansion.

Mrs. Dickens[13] came to us also as soon as we were settled— but was not let in till her third call, when the naked Walls were more hospitable than continued negatives, but when, un-luckily, Mrs. & Miss Wall[14] made their visit, & I truly regretted I had not yet another time been *stern to my purpose* of shutting

[12] Lady Burrell lived at Deepdene. For her second marriage, see iii, L. 247 n. 23. Julia (c. 1782–24 Dec. 1856), Sir William's sixth child, was to marry 14 Apr. 1806 George Henry Crutchley, formerly Duffield (1778–1869).
[13] See iii, L. 241 n. 12.
[14] See iii, L. 203 n. 6.

out all visitors till we were fitted up for receiving them,—as her presence impeded a thousand questions I longed to ask as to Ireland—the dear lovely Norbury—& the *Major*.—Norbury, Mrs. & Miss Wall vied with each other in praising, | both for his person & manners. Dear Boy! how their description delighted me—& softened many feelings! — — I was glad to see any body that had seen them; & Mrs. & Miss Wall seem such excellent & solid characters I ought to have rejoiced independently of that consideration. I believe I did, too—

I excused myself very long from returning Mrs. Dickens' visit: I had almost an horrour of entering under her auspices a house owned by my most loved Susan—but it could not be ultimately avoided, & I have, at length, been compelled to see her do its honours — — I will not say one word of what passed in my mind on that occasion—I should write of nothing else, if I entered upon a subject of such deep regret & sadness.

Lady Rothes,[15] too, constant in every manifestation of regard, came hither the first week of our establishment—& came three times to denials,—when my gratitude forced open my doors. Her Daughter Lady Harriet was with her. She is a pretty & pleasing young woman, but I do not think she has as much understanding as her Mother. Sir Lucus came another morning, bringing my old friend—& ci-divant persecutor, Mr. Pepys.[16] They were admitted perforce, as I was just going into our Grounds with Alex, when they appeared at the Gate. Indeed I am always glad to see an old friend, for as such I should be very graceless not to reckon Mr. Pepys, whose tormenting tricks & watchings were all, I really believe, from a sincere wish to forward as well as devellop a transaction which he conceived would give me an happy establishment. His eldest son[17] was with them, & | seems a very unassuming & amiable young man. Alex was in high spirits, & amused them singularly. He had just taken vehemently to spelling, & every word he heard, of which he either knew or could guess the orthography, he instantly, in a little concise & steady manner, pronounced all the letters of, with a look of great, but very

---

[15] See i, L. 12 n. 13; iii, L. 209 n. 5.
[16] William Weller Pepys (i, L. 12 n. 11), who in former days evinced much interest (if not curiosity) in meetings between Fanny Burney and George Owen Cambridge (*HFB*, pp. 187–200; also i, L. 23, pp. 171–5.)
[17] William Weller Pepys (1778–1845), 2nd Bart. (1825).

grave satisfaction at his own performance, and a familiar nod at every word so conquered—as thus—

Mr Pepys—You are a fine Boy, indeed!

Alex. B, O, Y, Boy.—(every Letter articulated with strong, almost heroic emphasis.)

Mr P. And do you run about here in this pleasant place all day long?

Alex. D, A, Y, day.

Mr P. And can you read your Book, you sweet little fellow?

Alex. R, E, A, D, read. &c—&c—

He was in such good looks, that all this nonsense won nothing but admiration, & Mr. Pepys could attend to nothing else, & only charged me to *let him alone.* 'For god's sake don't make him study! cried Sir Lucas, also; he is so well disposed, that you must rather repress than advance him, or his health may pay the forfeit of his application.'

'O, leave him alone! cried Mr. Pepys,—take care only of his health & strength—never fear such a Boy as that wanting learning!'

I assured him we made no progress but by play, & for rewards, his Book never approaching him but for a recompense for good behaviour.

I was very sorry M. d'Arblay was not *visible,* as they were very pleasant & sociable, & seemed very earnest to be friendly in intercourse.

I forget if I have mentioned that Lady Rothes & Sir Lucas (the wife will come first here!) have bought Juniper *Hall*—not *Hole*, as, from its being lower, the residence Mr de Narbonne had was called. nor am I sure if they had not made the purchase before you left us—*for a year*!—!—!—When we returned our many visits, at length, we were let in by Lady Rothes, who was with only her Daughter, Lady Harriet, & who told us the Princess Amelia had just passed by, [|] with her suite, in her way to Worthing,[18] in Sussex, to try the sea air for a lameness in her Knee. I was so much vexed not to have been a little earlier, that I might have had the regale of a glance of her lovely countenance, that it quite spoilt my visit, by occupying me

[18] This was on 30 July. Thomas Keate's recommendation of the sands, the bathing, and the village of Worthing is printed in *Later Corr. Geo. III*, iii. 92–3, as are also the patient letters written by the Princess to her father (5/6 Aug.–13 Nov.) reporting such improvements as she could see in her health.

with regret. I have not yet told you a new instance of the sweet condescendsion of this lovely young Princess. In a Letter I had written upon the Queen's Birth Day, *at* Her Majesty, as usual, though directed to Miss Planta, I had given a pretty full & ridiculous account of my little Boy's passion for Her Royal Highness,—which lasted some months, during which he used to *look about* for her here, & wonder she did not come, & say 'Is Pincess Amela *don* to *darking*, to buy me a *take*?—' In the answer, Miss Planta says she had shewn my Letter to the Queen & the Princesses, & that it was most graciously received; & then adds 'Princess Amelia has ordered me to say that she is much pleased by being *preferred* by your dear Boy, & desires to be remembered to him very tenderly.—'

I am sure I need not tell you I answered this immediately, with warmest acknowledgements—nor that the Letter shall live for the little rogue, against he can comprehend its extreme condescendsion & goodness.[19]

Lady Templetown also made us 2—(or three, I believe) visits, shut out, from our original intent of exclusion till fitted up, even though she came with Mr. Lock. From Lady Rothes, we toiled on, through immense heat, first to Mrs. Dickens, who was out, next to Lady Templetown, who was denied, but had us called back. She had taken the house in which Mr. Benn used to reside at Leatherhead.[20] She was very ill, & it was very kind & flattering in her to admit us. I believe she likes M. d'Arblay very much. Her new married Daughter, Lady Hervey, was on a visit to Lady Bristol;[21] but her new Daughter in Law, the young Lady Templeton, was with her.[22] She was Lady Mary Montagu, daughter to the Present Earl of Sandwich, & a near relation to Lady Frances Burgoigne, at whose house she remembers meeting me, when she was a Child. She is now but

---

[19] The letter has not, however, survived. [20] See ii, L. 68 n. 44.

[21] For Elizabeth Albana Upton's marriage on 20 Feb., see L. 269 n. 11. Her mother-in-law was Elizabeth *née* Davers (1733–1800), who had married in 1752 Frederick Augustus Hervey, 4th Earl of Bristol (1779), the notorious Earl Bishop [L. 269 n. 11].

[22] Lady Mary Montagu (1774–1824), daughter of John Montagu (1742/3–1814), 5th Earl of Sandwich (1792), by his second marriage (1772) to Lady Mary Powlett (1753–79), had married in 1796 John Henry Upton (1771–1846), 2nd Baron Templetown (1785), cr. Viscount Templetown (1806).

The Earl's first wife, Elizabeth *née* Montagu (d. 1 July 1768), daughter of George Montagu (1716–1771), 2nd Earl of Halifax, was the niece of Lady Frances (*née* Montagu) Burgoyne (1710–88).

22, & seems a very good & well principled young woman, simple in her character & her tastes, devoted to the family of her lord, & of a most contented & generous temper. I rejoice for so great a happiness to Lady Templeton as such a fortunate connexion.

I was introduced to her, by Lady T.—& heard that the young lord was in Ireland. I had not seen him since he was at Eton, whence Major Price[23] had two or three times brought him to our Tea Table at Windsor.

Miss Caroline Upton[24] seems extremely pleasing, very sensible, & remarkably well bred. Miss Sophia, the youngest, appears to have many traits of genius & originality in her composition, but mixed with many more of caprice, fantasies, & airs. She sings delightfully, with a low Man's Voice, but a fine Italian expression, & a real feeling & enchantment in the act.—But I do not wish her the Mistress of future Norbury Park! though she most evidently sighs to become it, & almost sings herself into security—but the impression & the song cease at the same moment with William, who sees his power to be too general to be in any danger of yielding merely to its gratification. The gentler & sweeter Caroline is not, I believe,—less susceptible to his merit—but she has not the potent charm of song, & therefore attracts less notice, though, I think, she deserves, solidly, more. They are both extremely improved in person, & become very fine young women.

Fatigue joined to a kind reception led us to make a long visit ¹ at Lady Templetown's: & while we were there, Lady Henry FitzGerald arrived.[25] You know, I dare say, she was my old acquaintance Miss Boyle, Daughter to my ⟨presenting⟩ Friend Mrs. Walsingham? I had never seen her since she was a mere Girl; but she recollected me the moment she looked at me, & gave me her hand, & was extremely cordial in expressions of kindness at our meeting. She had purposed repeatedly coming to our Cottage, but Mrs. Lock, fearing it might be

²³ See *DL* iii. 227, 502–4; also i, L. 16 n. 12.
²⁴ See iii, L. 216 n. 16.
²⁵ See iii, L. 175 n. 3. FB had met Miss Boyle on 27 Dec. 1783 (*DL* ii. 239), when she was about 14 years old. Her mother Charlotte *née* Hanbury Williams (d. 1790), widow of the Hon. Robert Boyle *later* (1756) Boyle-Walsingham (d. 1779), FB had met at social gatherings in London in the years 1782–5 and was often a guest at her home in London and later at Thames Ditton (*DL* ii. 144–5, 180–1, etc.). Some of their correspondence is still extant (see *Catalogue*).

inconvenient to us, had deterred her. I was very glad to see the happiness & hilarity that beamed in her Eyes, & spoke in her voice & manner. She adores her husband, Lord Henry, who was her decided Choice, & with whom she has lived in uninterrupted harmony since their union. She has several little Children,[26] & brings them up, & nurses & teaches them all herself. She is one of the fondest of Mothers as well as of wives, & has behaved with a prudence in the affairs & severe trial of Lord Edward that has done her great honour, as it is attributed entirely to her happy influence & exertions that her own lord escaped the infection & infatuation of his Brother's principles & conduct: for he idolized lord Edward, & almost lost his senses at his premature death. She was in very deep mourning. The whole family resolve to wear black double the usual time.—

From thence we went to dear Norbury Park, where we dined & spent the Evening, with our usual delight in its unequalled society.

The two Lady Templetowns *returned our return* very soon—& Alex, again, was the Lyon to entertain them, for his orthographical performances, & their absurd abruptness, & undaunted intrusion, are really comic. He faces in full all the people to whom he is presented, & stands examining them with a look of reflecting earnestness, till they utter some little word that is familiar to him, & then he audibly & articulately spells it, without comment, or application; only Jumping round them, & round every Chair in the room, with delight at his success, & then returning to face the same, or some other person, till another word occurs which can again call forth his erudition. But though in this exhibition he is become so astonishingly bold & comically sturdy, the same terror & timidity rests with him of being seized, or even touched, by any but ourselves, & Amelia,—*the two Amelias* the rogue has pitched upon for such singular & single preference do not much disgrace his *elements of taste.* nor of ambition neither, you will say!—

The younger Lady Templetown seemed enchanted with the view of our simple dwelling, & all the more, in the romance of

---

[26] Cf. Thomas Moore, *The Life and Death of Lord Edward Fitzgerald,* ii. 93 ff.

Of Lord Henry's children, there were born at this time Henry William (1793–1839), Arthur John Hill (1795–1826), and William Lennox Lascelles (1797–1874).

early Youth, unhackneyed & unspoilt, for seeing it unfinished & unfurnished, & conceiving that we could be happy & gay in such a state. She ran up stairs, uninvited, & seemed longing to visit the kitchen, the bed Chambers, & the tool house,—the name of *a Cottage* had interested her, & to *know* people who inhabited one appeared to give her a romantic pleasure that, in her rank & situation, made her seem very amiable. She has one little Girl,[27] a few months old, whom she is extremely fond of, & I earnestly hope her present good disposition may be durable as it is respectable. But she is too young, & the World is too mischievous for dependence upon that, except where an early solidity of sense & judgement join the first feelings & propensities,—as in Amelia Locke. ⎮

Amongst the Norbury visitors of this summer were the *Hartsinks*[28]—now emigrated from Holland, & reduced from their splendid establishment, to so small a little dwelling, at Islington, that they called ours *a great estate* in its comparison! What lamentable changes has that eventful & dreadful Revolution brought to bear! I never hear but of ONE *good change*—it has caused which is that of *name* in a certain sister of yours.

We met them two or three times at Norbury Park, & they made me promise to admit them to see our Hermitage. Mr. Locke himself brought her in his phaeton. She seems softened by her misfortunes, yet still retains the strong marks, in her countenance, of the querulous unhappiness of her disposition, to which is now added that of her fate; though the latter she has borne very heroically, as it has cast an unkind & unfaithful husband, of whom she is very fond once more at her feet, all that remains for them being now her fortune, which, luckily, was still in the English funds. She enquired very civilly about you—so did Lady Templetown,—so,—or rather not *so*, but with warm interest & kindness does every body I see. And all the poor class about here remember my dearest Susan with

[27] Catherine Elizabeth, b. 5 Apr. 1798; and d. 14 July 1799.

[28] Jan Casper Hartsinck (i, L. 16 n. 10; iii, L. 203 n. 3) had been listed as a bankrupt in *The Times*, 20 Nov. 1797. Accounts of his financial difficulties, his lawsuits with his partners in business, the sale of his house at Hamburg, and his efforts to protect money advanced to him by the Prince of Orange are to be read in *Family Papers*, ed. Samuel H. Day (1911). His letters of 1798–9 are dated Islington but by the spring of 1802 (*post* 15 Mar. but *pre* 22 May), the Hartsincks, hounded by creditors in England, had removed to Paris.

gratitude, and are ready to cry when they speak to me of her as inhabiting so rebellious & dangerous a Country. Even beyond *my* expectations is the kindness of their remembrance—I am sure I need not say how it touches—gratifies me—

⟶

I am sure you must remember Charles Moore, the Lawyer,[29] —& his melancholy lamentations at the altered style of life of our friends, in being now so deeply engaged in assemblies & routes, that his family could not obtain one Evening from them during their town residence. I had always been pleased with your account of the respect he mixt with his regret in those complaints, & ¦ his verses upon the lovely Amelia when ⟨she⟩ had impressed me with a regard for him, by the idea of his admiration for that sweet Girl. It has since been confirmed to me by our Mrs. Locke, who has owned he has manifested the most marked yet hopeless passion for her almost incomparable Daughter. All this made me receive him with all the civility in my power, though nearly a personal stranger to him, when Mr. William Locke brought him to our Cottage. And the kind of sighing admiration with which he [walke]d round & about it, as if saying to himself how little may suffice ⟨when⟩ the WILL is unambitious!—much interested me in his favour.—He is now a Counsellor, & rising in reputation & fortune; but always faithful in melancholy fondness for the always grateful, but yet wholly untouched Amelia. William seems to love him, & brought him with pleasure, as to a scene he thought congenial to his taste. Alex was in high feather. The instant he saw them, walking steadily up to William, he pronounced 'L, O, C, K, Lock.' And, looking at his Companion, as he stept in after him, he added, with great gravity, & 'L, e, g, Leg.'

Charles Moore was inexpressibly amused with the little rogue, who, as they neither of them offered to seize him, continued his little ridiculous orthographical interruptions during their whole visit upon every word within his reach. Telling him how to spell his own name, Charles Moore, he charged him to

---

[29] Charles Moore (1770–1810), youngest son of Dr. John Moore (ii, L. 68 n. 41), had entered Lincoln's Inn on 7 Nov. 1788. In John Hughes, *New Law List* (1799) he appears as 'Special Pleader, Home circuit and Surry Sessions' with chambers at 1 Pump Court, Middle Temple. In *GM* lxxx (1810), pt. 2, 500, he is referred to as an 'auditor of public accounts'. See also Oman, pp. 62, 668 n.

remember it, adding 'I shall not forget *you*, I promise you, for I never saw such a little fellow ⏉ before!'

I was extremely surprised, about this time, to be told by the Maid a Gentleman & lady had called at the door, who sent in a card, & begged to know if I could admit them, & to see the names on the card were Mr. & Mrs. Barbauld:[30] I had never seen them more than twice; the first time, by their own desire, Mrs. Chapone carried me to meet them at Mr. Burroughs— the other time I think was at Mrs. Chapones.—You must be sure I could not hesitate to receive, & receive with thankfulness, this civility from the authoress of the most useful Books, next to Mrs. Trimmer's, that have been yet written for dear little Children, though this, with the World, is probably her very secondary merit, her many pretty poems, & particularly songs, being generally esteemed. But many more have written those as well, & not a few better; Children's Books she began the new Walk for, which has since been so well cultivated, to the great information, as well as utility, of *PARENTS!*

Mr. Barbauld is a dissenting minister. An author also, but I am unacquainted with his Works. They were in our little dining parlour—the only one that has any Chairs in it,—& began apologies for their visit: but I interrupted & finished them with my thanks. She is much altered, but not for the worse to me, though she is for herself, since the flight of her youth, which is evident, has taken also with it a great portion of an almost set smile, which had an air of determined complacence, & prepared acquiescence, that seemed to result from a dis-played humility & sweetness which never risked being off guard. I remember Mrs. Chapone's saying to me, after our interview, 'She is a very good Young woman, as well as replete with talents: but why must one always smile so? It makes my poor Jaws ⏉ ache to look at her.'

We talked, of course, of that excellent lady—& you will believe I did not quote her notions of smiling! The Burrows Family, she told me, was quite broken up,—old Mrs. Amy[31] alone remaining alive.—Her Brother, Dr. Aiken, with his family, were passing the summer at Dorking, on account of his

---

[30] For these visitors, see L. 280 n. 3.
[31] Amy Burrows (1730–1811) was a sister of the Revd. John Burrows (L. 280 n. 4).

ill health, the air of that town having been recommended for his complaints. The Barbaulds were come to spend some time with him, & would not be so near without renewing their acquaintance. They had been walking in Norbury Park, which they admired very much, & Mrs. Barbauld very elegantly said 'If there was such a public officer as a Legislator of Taste, Mr. Locke ought to be chosen for it.'

They enquired much about M. d'Arblay, who was working in his Garden, & would not be at the trouble of dressing to appear. They desired to see Alex,—& I produced him; & his orthographical feats were very well timed here, for as soon as Mrs. Barbauld said 'What is your name, you pretty Creature?' He sturdily answered 'B, O, Y, Boy.'

Almost all our discourse was upon the Irish rebellion, then breaking out. Mr. Barbauld is a very little, diminutive figure, but well bred & sensible.

I borrowed her poems, afterwards, of Mr. Daniel,[32] who chanced to have them, & have read them with much esteem of the piety & worth they exhibit, & real admiration of the last amongst them, which is an Epistle to Mr. Wilberforce in favour of the demolition of the slave trade[33]—in which her energy seems to spring from the real spirit of virtue, suffering at the luxurious depravity which can tolerate, in a free land, so unjust & cruel & abominable a trafic.

We returned their visit, together, in a few months, at Dr. Aikens lodgings ¦ at Dorking—where, as she permitted M. d'Arblay to speak French, they had a very animated discourse upon buildings, French & English, each supporting those of their own country with great spirit—but my Monsieur, *to own the truth of my private opinion*, having greatly the advantage, both in manner & argument. He was in spirits, & came forth with his best exertions. Dr. Aiken looks very sickly, but is said to be better. He has a good countenance, but a sort of speech that marks a kind of self satisfaction that sets those he converses with at no small distance. Mrs. Aiken seems vulgar, & out of the question. Miss Aiken, a Daughter, is a fat conceited Girl, who seems to think the World should be at the feet of a person coming from such a celebrated race.

[32] See iii, L. 179 n. 10; also L. 280, n. 5.
[33] *Epistle to William Wilberforce, Esq., on the rejection of the Bill for abolishing the Slave Trade* (1791).

Mrs. Barbauld & this niece accompanied us nearly all the way home, to lengthen the visit. They were to quit Dorking almost immediately.

The poor Mr. Daniel, whom you may remember as a very good & melancholy French Priest, visiting us at Bookham, Ventured over to France before the barbarous 4th of september, believing he might be restored to his friends: but he was seized, imprisoned many months, & then turned adrift into fresh exile, pennyless & hopeless. He returned so mournful, so depressed, that we have, perforce, made much more intimacy with him, from compassion for his undeserved sufferings. He lives at Mr. Swaine's,34 the apothecary, at Dorking, upon the little pittance he obtains from Government, & a few scholars to whom he teaches french. He is now much revived, & cheared with the hope of a new turn in affairs.

One new acquaintance we have found it impossible to avoid —the only house in West Hamble village which is not occupied by Farmers, or poor people, ⏐ is now inhabited by a large family from the City, of the name of Dickenson.35 They called here immediately upon our establishing ourselves in our Cottage. We were denied, & most unwilling to begin any new intercourse so near to us on uncertain grounds. But it was indispensable to return a first visit, & we were instantly admitted. You have been at the house, my dearest Susan, to see Me· de Broglio,36—it is now, they say, greatly improved. Mr. Dickenson, or Capt. Dickenson, as his name card says, is a very shy, but seems a sensible man, & his lady is excessively the reverse of *shy*, though

---

34 John (1736–1804), son of John Swayne (1704–73), 'Surgeon of Dorking'. As the parish registers show, this family of Swaynes originated in Ockley, where John Swaynes appeared as early as 1700. Successful apothecaries, the Swaynes later accumulated property in Dorking.

35 The family of Thomas Dickinson (c. 1754–1828) of Brambleberry, Plumstead, Kent, Lieutenant (25 Jan. 1778), Commander (5 Dec. 1796), R.N., and eventually (see the probate of his will 3 July 1828, P.C.C. Sutton 408) 'Superintendent of shipping in the Royal Arsenal at Woolwich'.

His wife was Frances de Brissac (c. 1761–1854), third daughter of Peter Abraham, late of the Liberty of Norton Folgate, Whitechapel (see the Admon., P.C.C. Jenner, Middx. July 1770). Peter Abraham de Brissac was buried, however, in Hackney, as were his (?)sister Frances (24 May 1759), his brother, or possibly his father, Amos James (5 Oct. 1758), and finally his widow Jane, who died on 21 Oct. 1809 at High-hill Ferry, Hackney, at the age of 80 (see also *GM* lxxix. 990; and her will P.C.C. Loveday 742, probated on 31 Oct. 1809).

The wills above, with that of Andrew Strahan (n. 37) name in all seven Dickinson children, three boys and four girls.

36 This was in 1792. For Madame de Broglie, see ii, Intro., xix.

by no means of his second qualification. She is open, chatty, fond of her Children, anxious to accomplish them, & extremely desirous to be upon cordial terms of good neighbourhood. She seems between 30 & 40, & very lively. She is of french origin, though born here, & of parents immediately english. But her Grandfather was a M. de Brissac. She has none of the nobleness of manners to bring such a name to the primitive ideas it has given us; but 8 Children, all affectionately fond of her, give her an interest, that, joined to her friendly disposition, & earnest desire of cultivating with us, have induced us to spend occasionally an Hour or two with her in an Evening, & to receive her & her family where they call here in a morning. We have excused ourselves, however, positively, though with great difficulty, from ever partaking of their table—even at Tea,—as it is out of our plan to enter into any intimacy of that sort without previous trial. The Children are some of them pleasing, & all of them civil & desirous to please.

A Gentleman, who seemed to belong to them, but whom we knew not, mean ⎮ while was yet more assiduous than themselves to make acquaintance here. He visited Mr. d'Arblay while working in his Garden, brought him News papers, Gazettes Extraordinary, political Letters with recent intelligence,— & exerted himself to be acceptable by intelligence as well as obligingness. M. d'Arblay, at length, one very bitterly cold Morning, thought it incumbent upon him to invite his anonymous Acquaintance into the house. He knew not how to name him, but, opening the door, where I was waiting Breakfast for him with Alex, he only pronounced my name. The Gentleman, smilingly entering, said 'I must announce mine myself, I believe—Mr. Straghan.—'[37]

And we then found it was the printer to the King, who is a Member of Parliament, son of the Andrew Straghan who was the friend of Dr. Johnson, and —— the principal printer of Camilla.[38]—Much recollection of the many messages of business which had passed between us, while unknown, during the Printing of that long work, made me smile also at his name—&

[37] Andrew Strahan (1750–1831), the printer (see *DNB*), M.P. (1796–1818), and the son not of Andrew but of William Strahan (1715–85), Dr. Johnson's friend. In a will probated 15 Sept. 1831 (P.C.C. Tebbs 542) Andrew Strahan left substantial legacies (some £16,000 in all) to the widow Dickinson and six of her children.
[38] For his printing of *Camilla* see iii, L. 168 n. 4.

we easily made acquaintance as I could readily conceive a very innocent curiosity on his side to see the Cottage which goes by the name of a work he brought into the World.—He has all the appearance of a very worthy, sensible, unpretending man, well bred & good natured. Long connected with the Dickensons, he seems to have an apartment at pleasure in their house, & to love their Children as if they were his own. He told us he had known Mrs. Dickenson from the time she was 7 years old.

Our first, & most excellent & regretted Neighbours, the Cookes,[39] continue to visit us whenever they have opportunity, & we made them two returns this Summer, in one of which we dined with them. Mrs. Cooke always makes ˡ my beloved Susan a principal part of our conversation.

Our Charlotte & her new husband, Mr. Broome, came to make us a second visit, & by appointment, breakfast with us, in the course of a little tour they made to Southampton. Miss Broome, his Daughter by an Indian lady, was of the party.[40] She is very silent & civil, & has very fine Eyes, & a look of modesty, though not of humility. I fancy her proud, but hope she is good, & will be sensible of the kindness with which Charlotte treats her. Mr. Broome was in great spirits—but I was—then—very miserable—the wretched transaction of J[ames] & S[arah] having just happened.[41]—

The last visit to us I have to record, is the second we had from my dearest Father—which he frankly made to fly—*for the first time*, he said from his home![42]—which the then situation of the affair of J[ames] & S[arah] had made wholly comfortless & dejecting to him!—God forgive them!—is all I can, or dare say— & preserve this most beloved & revered parent to forgive them too!—

It so chanced—very luckily for me in this instance,—that Lady Rothes & Lady Harriet Leslie were with me when he arrived. It saved the cruel, uncertain, difficult feelings of how to first meet, after such an event, & with all the consciousness of his avowed & acknowledged flight from the scene whence it had taken place. And those ladies had not quitted us five minutes,

---

[39] See iii, L. 122 n. 8.   [40] See L. 257 n. 11.

[41] This was the elopement of Sarah Harriet Burney with her half-brother James. FBA relates the story in full in Ll. 296, 297. See also *HFB*, pp. 281–5.

[42] SHB had departed on 2 Sept. and CB seems to have visited the d'Arblays during the latter part of September.

before Mrs. & Miss Cooke[43] came. They were enchanted to meet him, & his perfect harmony with them in political tenets made the circumstance pleasing to himself. When they were gone, we had our little dinner, which he had enriched with Fish from Chelsea, & during which came the lovely little Adrienne de Chavagnac,[44] with whom he fell | quite in love. This passed off all so well that we avoided any particular discussion the whole day. I will not here enter into what ensued when the avoidance was at an end, save to say he would speak of it but once—he desired to allude to it in no manner any more —He struggled only, he said, to forget it!—

Mr. Cooke visited him immediately—& we went to Bookham with him,—& to Norbury Park. And he dined at Sir Lucas pepys, & visited Lord Leslie[45] from our dwelling. We would fain have kept him on with us—but at the end of a few days business, & his renovated fortitude took him away—God send me the blessing of receiving him this next summer lightened from this heavy evil!

Mrs. Rishton was now settled at Chelsea—I have told you her dreadful Express[46]—our subsequent suspence—& misery— & final intelligence,—& the Letters which passed & re-passed. I draw a veil, therefore, over this mournful subject.—

I have no time to enter further upon Charles & Cecilia— except that they both came hither, to take leave, with marked distinction of regard, before they departed to prepare for Danemark[47]—The change for Naples you have heard from Mrs Locke. All my agony about your most beloved self you will easily spare my recapitulating. Our news at last—so welcome, so long desired, from M. de Narbonne you heard at the time.[48] And all our visits to our dear & ever cherished Friends at Norbury Park. I go always to the Pew where my

---

[43] See L. 263 n. 7. [44] See iii, L. 201 n. 5.

[45] George William Evelyn-Leslie (1768–1817), *styled* Lord Leslie (1773), 11th Earl of Rothes (1810), had married secondly on 21 Aug. 1798 Charlotte Julia Campbell (d. 1846).

[46] Maria Rishton's account of the elopement is printed L. 297 n. 5.

[47] Charles Locke (1769–1804) and his wife Cecilia Margaret *née* Ogilvy (iii, L. 177 n. 4), whose half-brother Lord Robert Stephen Fitzgerald (1765–1833) was the envoy extraordinary and minister plenipotentiary to Denmark from 7 July 1795 to 1 Aug. 1800. Charles was eventually appointed British Consul at Naples (see *Locks of Norbury*, chap. xiv). According to Oman, p. 164, the pay was small, however, 'and would hardly cover . . . living and entertainment expenses'.

[48] This is the A.L. (Berg) from the comte de Narbonne dated 28 Aug. 1798, *pmk* 15 SE 98 (see L. 294 n. 8).

Susan went when the Weather permits,—& never without offering up a prayer for her return.—I believe I may safely say *never*.

I intended a long article upon the Fair,[49]—but it is over so long I cannot write it—We took our Boy, for the first time. We met Lady Rothes & Sir Lucas & Lady Harriet on the road—they made us all three crowd into their Coach. Alex was loaded with Presents, which you must read to Willy, for the use of reminiscence. From dearest Mrs. Lock his first 6[d] Book. From Amelia, a Phaeton, & ninepins; from Augusta, a sword; from Miss Burrell a Cartouche Box; from his Father a sword Belt; from the young Lady Templetown, a capital Whip; from George, a Gun; from Miss Upton, sweetmeats; & from William, a noble Horse, as Tall as himself nearly!—Mama reserved her Gifts for less splendid occasions. The Duke of Clarence was at the Fair—& imagine my surprise that he immediately recollected me! & graciously bowed, & hoped I was well.! I was too much astonished to be ready with any answer I had seen him, indeed, not long before, with his sweet sister,[50] but I was then more dressed, & he knew who was with Her before he entered. We were caught in the Rain, & Lady Templetown's Carriage took Alex & me, with Mrs. Charles Locke & her two Babes, & a Nurse, to Norbury Park, where we all slept. Thus ends this year's Journal—save one more *Royal*,[51] though not *Court* Account—which I shall next prepare.

[49] The Leatherhead Fair opened on 10 October.
[50] Princess Augusta. See Court Journal (L. 255, pp. 24–5).
[51] This is L. 271, the Journal for *c.* 26 Feb.–10 Mar., which was written in late December, parts of it, certainly *post* 18 Dec. 1798.

To Mrs. Waddington

A.L.S. (Berg), 10 Sept. [17]98
Double sheet 4to   4 pp.   *pmks*   DARKING   11 SE 98   20 SE 98
wafer
Addressed: ⌜Mrs. Waddington / Lanover, / Abergavenny. ⌝
Readdressed: At the Revn^d G Waddingtons / Tuxford / Nottingham^shᴵ
Docketed in pencil, p. 4: W / —98

Septr 10.—98.
West Hamble, near *Dorking*, surry.
do not direct *Leatherhead*.

Your very interesting pacquet, my dear Marianne, gave me
great & sincere satisfaction. To know where & how to picture
you, when my thoughts rest upon you locally as well as mentally, is extremely grateful to me, & I feel all the kindness of
this conviction of your certainty of my true interest in ALL that
concerns you with peculiar pleasure, because it is in unison
with what I have always loved in you,—& not at all allied with
your little naughtiness & murmurings. You will make me very
happy by a speedy account that your Emily spared you any
terrour in the Measles, & is now quite well. How delighted
I should be to see you, my dearest Mary, with both your
Children, & my own capering between them! He is the most
animated little Rogue you can conceive. With your Emily
I should not dare trust him a minute; but I think, from your
character of my little namesake, I might persuade myself to
venture him with Her even from under my own Eyes. Your
contrast of the two sweet things is very amusing, & the justice
you do to both must make them equally contribute to your
happiness, as well as equally feel it reflected back on themselves.

I am much pleased with your traits of your lovely cousin,² &

---

293.   ¹ For the family visits of the Waddingtons, see the unabridged section o
Baroness Bunsen's Journal, ed. Maxwell Fraser, *NLWJ*, xi (1960), 285–309.
   ² This is Anne Dewes (1778–1861), daughter of Bernard Dewes (1743–1822) by
his first marriage (iii, L. 124 n. 8). In 1794 he had married secondly Judith Beres-
ford (d. 3 Dec. 1814, see *GM* lxxxiv, 612), the ill-humoured lady above.

your promise of more. I have not failed reviving her image at Norbury Park, of which all the Inhabitants have seen her with an ˡ admiration they still retain. I [am] really very sorry for [her] & Mr. B[ernard] D[ewes] as well as for [his be]autiful Daughter, in [this] very unpleasant connexion. It would be so easy in any wo[man] to mak[e him] happy, who strove, or wished to do it, that it is melanc[holy] to have such a domestic character thrown away—& I could point out hundreds, in a moment, who would so well have MERITED Mrs. D.'s loquacious ill-hum[our] that she might have exerted its whole force, so placed, wit[hout c]hagrining us with one p[art]icle of pity for it's receiver.

How you would smile were I to send you a plan of *our* House! I think the premises would stand, & very commodiously, alltogether in Mr. W[addington]'s Dressing Room. I except the Field, indeed, which is of near 5 acres,—almost as big as your poultry & Farm yard. Perhaps, however, you would rather *sigh* than smile, from your personal regret I should not be more sumptuously roofed: but if you entered the little dwelling, & saw its three owners—though as yet encircled but by bare Walls, you would soon feel reconciled to my lot.

Two of M. d'A's *ci devant Camarades*[3] came over here this morning to Breakfast with us—& you would have laughed at *their* laughter, who had lived with him in his former life, to hear him gravely declare ˡ that now—the height of his remnant ambition was to possess a COW!—When I see him thus meet his changed situation, what must his Compassion be, if the narrowness of hers, though it cannot but sometimes be productive of care, should ever cause her regret? But even the care has its pleasure, where its motives & its rewards are one.

I quite forget if I have told you that you were a Witch in your divination about my sister Charlotte?

Pray let me keep the very pretty fable & Drawings of my little Fanny, if you have any equivalents. Do you remember my having *your* first Drawing in water-colours?

You are so kind as to hope my beloved sister Phillips is restored to us—but no!—we have expected her for some Months—we expect her still—& with frequent promises from the Major; however, all affairs in that distracted Country are

---

[3] Probably Antoine Bourdois and Gabriel-Marie Riccé (L. 292 and n. 11).

so fluctuating, that one scheme & one scene makes another, & she still is there. And upon a spot wholly solitary & defenceless. Which keeps my Mind in perpetual anxiety. I hear that Fanny is become a very fine Girl,[4] though neither beautiful nor with any of Beauty's requisites, from fine features, or a fair skin: but she is of a pretty height, has a blooming complexion, fine Hair, the *embonpoint* so much now *in fashion*, & a look of innocence & goodness peculiarly engaging. Norbury, I also hear, continues to make admirers where ever he is seen. *He* is *really* beautiful, & bewitchingly attractive from his talents & manners. ❘

My dear Father, is, I thank Heaven, remarkably well, in Health & looks. He spent 5 Days with us last Month, which were truly dear to Me. Lady Templeton is come to spend the summer at Leatherhead, to be near Norbury Park. She & her Daughter in Law, who was Lady Mary Montagu,[5] made a point of seeing our Hermitage in its unfinished state, & were here last week. You may perhaps remember the young Lord at Eton? his lady is extremely pleasing, perfectly natural & unspoilt. Lady T[empleton]'s eldest Daughter is married to a Brother of the Lady Louisa Hervey you used so much to like; & he is said to be equally amiable. They have both left their strange Father out of their composition, & formed themselves from their deserving Mother,[6]—whom I have met at your revered Aunt's.—I am sure you have not forgotten Lady T[empletown] at the ancient Music, at least!—or the adventures that ensued upon your remaining behind her!—The *General*[7] is now attending Princess Amelia at Worthing. That Princess is become one of the most lovely & charming young Creatures you ever beheld.—You know, I conclude, Mr. Agnew has undertaken a circulating Library?[8] I hear from his good Wife

4 Fanny Phillips, now about 16.

5 Elizabeth Boughton Upton, Lady Templetown (iii, L. 216 n. 16), whose son John Henry Upton had married Lady Mary Montagu, daughter of the 5th Earl of Sandwich (L. 292 n. 22). Her daughter Elizabeth Albana Upton had recently married Frederick William Hervey (L. 269 n. 11). Lady Louisa Theodosia Hervey (d. 12 June 1821) was married in 1795 to Robert Banks Jenkinson (1770–1828), *styled* Lord Hawkesbury (1796), Baron Hawkesbury (1803), and 2nd Earl of Liverpool (1808). Jenkinson was M.P. (1790–1803), foreign secretary (1801–4, 1809), home secretary (1804–6, 1807–9), secretary of war and colonies (1809–12), prime minister (1812–27).

6 The Earl Bishop (i, L. 3 n. 122; iv, L. 269 n. 11) and his wife (L. 292 n. 21).

7 General Goldsworthy (i, L. 5 n. 10; and *HFB*, pp. 257–9).

8 See i, L. 9 n. 8.

occasionally, & always with pleasure. Tell me, again, of your handsome sister.⁹ And of the neice of Mr. W[addington] you mentioned at Bath.¹⁰ Adieu, my dear Friend,—

Ever yours invariably—
F. d'Arblay.

294   West Humble, 20 September 1798

To Mrs. Phillips

A.L. (Berg), 20 Sept. [17]98
Double and single sheet 4to   6 pp.   red seal
Addressed: Mrs. Phillips, / Belcotton, / Drogheda. / Ireland.

West Hamble, Septr 20.—98

I can only grieve now thus uselessly—& almost oppressively —to have broken in upon my beloved Susan's determined philosophy of acquiescence. I am, indeed, truly sorry to have added to her unavoidable evils those of conflicts for *my* sake, & *my* peace. I could not, certainly, mean to press your leaving *Norbury*, except while I concluded him to remain in Dublin. However, all places, I now begin to venture at flattering myself, may be safe now,—the defeat of the French party,¹ & the revealings of the iniquity of the Conspirators, must damp at once the spirit of Invasion, & the pretexts of Civil War.²—

⁹ See iii, L. 183 n. 4.
¹⁰ Of Benjamin Waddington's brothers and sisters (ten in all) several were at this time married with young families. See Maxwell Fraser, op. cit.

294. ¹ On 8 Sept. the French General Joseph Amable Humbert and the 800 French troops who had landed at Killala Bay on 22 Aug. surrendered to General Cornwallis, who in the double capacity of Commander-in-Chief and Lord Lieutenant or Viceroy of Ireland had arrived on 20 June (Fortescue, iv, pt. 1. 591–4; Oman, pp. 189–92).
² After the rebellions in Ireland were crushed in the summer of 1798 the Parliaments of both countries set up Commissions of Inquiry into the histories and actions of the several leading rebels, the extent of the conspiracies, etc., the progress and findings of which committees (as well as information emerging in the treason trials) FBA could have read from time to time in the newspapers. For example, *The Times* (27 Aug.) printed an abstract of 'the REPORT of the SECRET COMMITTEE of the IRISH HOUSE of COMMONS', which furnished an arresting *exposé* of the aims of the Society of United Irishmen, the extent of its membership, and the talents, audacity, and treason of its Chiefs. See also *AR* xl (1798), 'Appendix to the Chronicle', 159–70; and for the 'Report of the Committee of Secrecy of the British House of Commons', *AR* xli (1799), 'Appendix to the Chronicle', 150–82.

How black do those revealings bring out a young man for whose family we have so justly been interested, & whom I had really believed only guided by wrong-headed enthusiasm!— not by a dire & vengeful ambition, that could not be satisfied but by involving his whole Nation in bloody contention! —— How affecting is your last Letter,[3] my sweetest soul!—fear not I should think you urged by insensibility!—No, I understand better than I imitate you!—I cannot resign myself tranquilly to such a separation—but as my personal horrours & alarms are now passed, I will murmur less tumultuously.

My dear Father, however, is now planning a new scheme of establishment for himself—but he will write it you, he says,—or rather he has written it,— & his first wish, independent of all fears or doubts about Ireland, is to have you & Fanny his regular & settled inmates, to keep his house, & chear his bosom. I need not say what joy this would give me!—Charles would be happy to have Willy,—& this, as a *permanent*, not *temporary* plan, I must hope the Major will listen to. It certainly will not, like your being here on your own account, as before, be objection-able in point of œconomy, for as my dear Father *wants* you, both for aid & comfort, of course he would not permit you to come to him otherwise than as you were with him before your Marriage. *You would take no one's place* in presiding[4]—you would do nothing but good, & bring nothing but consolation. |

How extremely good Mrs. Cartland has been![5] how dis-interested & considerate! M. d'A. went immediately to Town, & immediately received the 92.10.0—& now, therefore, it

---

[3] This is the A.L. (Berg) of 8–11 [Sept.], *pmk* 17 SE 98, annotated in later years by FBA: 'Beautiful pious resignation to the severest human suffering from in-justice, unhappiness & malign tyranny'. The letter is printed in *FB & the Burneys*, pp. 281–5.

'Would to Heaven', SBP had written, 'my dearest Fanny cᵈ with any degree of composure resign herself to a destiny wᶜʰ it is vain to resist, & share with me an humble trust in Providence which shields me from such terrors as times like these might otherwise create. If I cease to struggle do not impute my seeming passiveness to an Insensibility that wᵈ be odious, but to a too certain conviction of the useless-ness of effort: & be not dissatisfied if under such circumstances yʳ poor Susan can derive some degree of support from the idea that her Duty, strictly speaking, is more compleatly fulfilled by relinquishing this journey with all its soothing & delicious temptations, than it cᵈ have been by accomplishing it thro' so many obstacles, & by a *compelled* acquiescence if any cᵈ have been obtained.'

[4] SHB had departed from Chelsea.

[5] Presumably it was Mrs. Cartland (iii, L. 215 n. 7) who received the Phillips family in July, when from possible dangers at Belcotton, they had moved for a short time to Dublin.

would more securely than ever perform its adopted purpose, should the journey—but I must not go back,—I must only conjure my beloved Susan to remember it is in safe & certain hands, whence it can be drawn from in a MOMENT,—if so blessed a moment for me should arrive as to induce you to claim it. (I am very much interested in the little hint of J[aney] P[aney] —I entreat its performance.[6] What a sweet Creature! how kind her kindness thus spread! pray tell her I have *longed* to send her *My* Love ever since I gathered her excellencies, & her appreciation of my Heart's dear Susan, & I have only been withheld from doubt if she knew how completely you had won me to her: but if she will encourage me by beginning, I shall be delighted to find myself permitted to try to make myself an interest in who has found so strait a way to My Heart, & who gives almost its sole *consolatory feeling* in your lengthened absence.) I want much to hear again of dear Mrs. Hill[7]—whether her husband is still detained from her by military duty, & where she & her Children now reside. I am very proud of her little Sir Hugh. I imagine Mrs. Barnewall still at Bath, but have not heard of her since Charlotte's excursion there. I hope the *little dear*, as Mr. Seward called Mr. Kirwan, is well again.

I know you will rejoice we have heard at last from M. de Narbonne—but so melancholy a Letter! so utterly triste et noir!—however, M. d'A. will probably copy you some part, & abridge the whole. It was extremely affecting to me—to us all. Mr. L[ocke] had begun to be really angry—a rare sensation for *HIM*! at so persevering a silence: & still he cannot, he told me last Night, be reconciled to it, till some explication arrives. M. d'A. has written a long supplication for some particulars, to which I have added my earnest entreaties. (He has *copiously* answered the queries about a lady of your acquaintance &

---

[6] Jane Brabazon had suggested that she might herself write to FBA (see SBP's letter of 8–11 [Sept.], op. cit.).

In accordance with directions given by SBP (in her letter of 8 Sept., see L. 291 n. 10), FBA enclosed the passage (above), ll. 6–15 '(I am very much . . . absence.)' in square brackets or 'hooks' as a warning to SBP to omit the matter when reading the letter aloud to her husband. The same warning is inserted ll. 30 ff. '(He has copiously . . . le temps)'.

[7] The inquiry here is for the girlhood friend of the Burneys, Elizabeth or 'Bessy', daughter of Richard Kirwan (iii, L. 216 n. 3), her husband Hugh Hill (ibid.), her sons Richard (b. 18 Nov. 1794), Edward Rowley (b. 29 Dec. 1795), Rowley Francis (b. 20 May 1797); and finally her elder sister Maria-Theresa, now Mrs. Barnewall (L. 275 n. 2), and Mr. Kirwan himself.

without much *retenu*.[8] I am curious to know how J[aney] P[aney] *now is* with le temps.)[9]

If I had not in waiting the hope of possible verbal communication, from the new arrangement at Chelsea, I would try to go on with my Court history[10]—but the | least prospect of speech makes penmanship a bore.—What a happy phlegm is that Mrs. Brabazon — — Certainly she will be immortal, if a period such as this finds her acting & going on just as calmly & commonly as a season of general repose.[11] But how it relieves me that J[aney] P[aney] is in your neighbourhood again. And how it soothes me that that neighbourhood is so good, so quiet, so loyal, &, above all, so sensible of My beloved Susan's presence & its worth![12] I quite love Susan, & more & more. She is a treasure to *us* as well as you. I want to hear more of Willy—& much more of Fanny; whether she now loses her infantine air & manner, & looks what so soon she must inevitably be, a young woman? Her *Form* is remembered with great eloge here,—& Amelia told me, lately, 'you can't imagine how singularly William himself always praises her figure & make.' Does she preserve her bloom? is she fairer, or tanned? does she discourse a little as a formed person, who feels entering into a new class? or keep her first playful & innocently endearing

---

[8] The letter in question, written from 'Tubingen . . . en Suabe' [Würtemberg], where the comte had been residing for more than a year, dated *ce* 28 *aoust* 1798, with a London *pmk* 15 SE 98, is extant in the Berg Collection. He is 'bien noir, bien triste' but he has not forgotten 'les plus respectables amis que j'aie au monde' though 'après plus de dix lettres perdues de part et d'autre, j'ai pu craindre de fatiguer même l'amitie'.

By 'a lady of your acquaintance' FBA seems to be referring in cautious parable to SBP herself, the only lady besides FBA mentioned in the letter:

Tout de suite après votre fils, mon ami, vous me permettrez bien de parler de celle qui sera à jamais ma plus tendre amie — quelle vie elle doit mener en irlande et quelle a du souffrir au milieu de toutes les horreurs qui ont desolé ce malheureux pays — ne perdez pas un instant, je vous conjure, pour me donner de ses nouvelles, de celles de ses enfants qui sont une véritable partie d'elle même ne se devouera t'elle jamais à vous, n'aura t'elle donc jamais un peu de bonheur, je suis bien sur qu'elle n'en cherchera, qu'elle ne peut en trouver qu'auprès de Norbury.

[9] In reply to this inquiry SBP in her letter (Berg) of 9 Oct. 1798 (printed in *FB & the Burneys*, pp. 290–2) related the circumstances of Jane Brabazon's engagement to the Revd. Robert Disney (*c.* 1769–1832), her plans for the future, and the Major's chagrin and spleen thereon.

[10] This is L. 269, eventually written *post* 18 Dec. 1798.

[11] Mrs. Wallop Brabazon (iii, L. 220 n. 4) of Rath House, who, 'wonderfully phlegmatic', had had her children inoculated for smallpox notwithstanding the unsettled state of the country and the menaces from marauding bands (SBP's letter of 8–11 [Sept.], op. cit.).

[12] See L. 291 n. 2.

juvenility of way & manner?[13] My kindest Love to her, *both ways*. Mrs. & Miss Walls account of Norbury was very bewitching, & just what I had hoped.[14] What was that story of his being expected at Lord Altamont's with his friend Domenic?[15]— Last Night at Norbury Park I heard that *Pichegru*[16] is really believed to be taken by the English! How I shall rejoice! People in general are all disposed to wish it, & to receive him well here. *Report* at this moment encircles Buonaparte with enraged *Turks*, who are to work the good for Christianity that Christians have failed working for it themselves, in overthrowing the Head of the Infidel Republic. But we fear to believe such propitious tydings to returning peace to Mankind.[17]—In a Letter I have this Morning received from our dear Padre, he says he sighs for an answer from Ireland that may comfortably form his new Establishment.—I heard from Esther last Week, to transmit extracts from your last to her, & she assures me she is now recovered from her terrible assault of pain. I have immediately *returned* her kind celerity, by extracts from my own last dear Letter: & sent them also to my dear Father.

our sweetest Friend will try to find time to speak of poor M. de Chavagnac, la princesse, M. De Lally, Adrienne—but I almost doubt her ability, she is so alternately engrossed by Mr. Charles & his departure, & by the approaching Fair. But *write*, she says, she *will*, & therefore this she will carry to Woodlands, whither she goes to-morrow, & thence forward it, with whatever, more or less, she can steal of time for adding.

---

[13] This query also SBP answered in her letter of 9 Oct., op. cit. (see *FB & the Burneys*, pp. 292–3).

[14] See L. 292, pp. 179–80.

[15] Norbury's friend Dominick Browne (1787–1860) was the son of Dominick Browne of Castle Macgarrett, County Mayo, and his wife Margaret (L. 288 n. 4), who was a first cousin of John Dennis Browne (1756–1809), 3rd Earl of Altamont (1780), cr. Marquess of Sligo (1800), cr. Baron of Monteagle of Westport (1806), to whose seat the boys had been invited for a summer visit.

In a letter of 9 Oct. 1798, op. cit., SBP explains how the Major, offended that arrangements for the journey had been communicated by Dominick's tutor (Gabriel Maturin) rather than by Mrs. Browne herself, declared without apology that 'Norbury sh^d not go—the consequence of this was a disappointment to the two boys, & that Mrs Browne was affronted'.

[16] See iii, L. 243 n. 1.

[17] Printed with some reservations by *The Times* (17 Sept.), but rejected as a 'senseless fable' by the *Morning Chronicle* (same day), was a report of General Bonaparte's having been 'surprized near *Cairo* by a numerous body of Tartars, who killed 8000 [French troops], and took 2000 prisoners; and that an army of *Mamelucks* had marched against the remainder of the Republican troops'.

The Denmark affair she will surely ׀ mention. It seems desirable in every way, save the possible length of absence from the poor Duchess, who is absorbed in total melancholy by the prospect of such a separation from the Child now living the most dear of all her Flock. He who is gone—the infatuated Ld. E[dward]—was *her* Idol—& the Idol of ALL his Brothers & Sisters. How he could unite such sweetly engaging domestic qualities, with so unfeeling, so vile, so sanguinary an ambition, is inconceivable! especially so early in life. The residence in Denmark of Cecilia's Brother, Lord Robert, as Ambassador,[18] is a powerful motive for preference of that *sejour* to any other. They will find friends at once, in a strange Country, who are at the head of their own Nation there, & little Children as playfellows for their babies, who are of the same age, & their immediate kindred. It is a very high appointment indeed for a beginning, & extremely flattering; & I really think will do more for the restoration of poor Cecilia *to herself* than any other circumstance. A complete new scene, new mode of life, & new necessity for exertion, joined to complete absence from every person & every thing that relates to her late bitter distress, may awaken a sort of new interest in her Being, that may shake off its heaviness of woe, & bring her forth once again to Hope & Joy. Her sufferings have been *terrible*, & threatened to fasten themselves in misery upon her character: but I found her already, last night, much *restored*, by compelled efforts of preparation, & even able to converse upon the new prospects without turning aside from what I ventured to offer of pleasure & amusement in them. She has promised M. d'A. a little view from Denmark, & Mr. Chas has promised to give it some danish figures in the actual habits of the Country.

I wish I could ease any of your solicitude about your old & most respectable friends amongst the Emigrés—but I never hear of them now! How often—how very often do I regret for *them*, also, my Susan's absence!—M. d'A. has trusted a few brief lines, unsigned & undated, to poor Ferdinand—but I doubt his ever receiving them, & the fear of involving him in mischief, as the correspondent of an Emigré, made those few so uninteresting &

[18] Lord Robert Stephen Fitzgerald (L. 292 n. 47), envoy extraordinary to Denmark (1795–1800), had married in 1792 Sophia Feilding (1773–1834) but of their four surviving children (as listed in Lodge) only Matilda (1793–1850) was born before this time.

dry it can scarcely matter whether he gets them or not—save that they contained an acknowledgement the good Uncle's Letter was received, & a request to make that known to him.

I was extremely provoked, when Mrs. & Miss Wall came, that I had just let in, | most unluckily, Mrs. Dickens,—who had been 3 times when I was not *visible*.[19] I had longed to talk so much—to *hear* so much, rather, of Ireland!—yet she had never seen you! —— But I should have been still more enquiring about my dear Norbury. Mrs. D. would outstay them.

Mrs. Bailey's house is still vacant,—but that, now, is wholly immaterial, as certainly you can only come over to my Father at present.—O how inexpressibly dear to me would it be to know *you* his Housekeeper & Companion! dear Soul!—what a solace to him! While I think of it—let me ask my Susan if she has any *choice* for this Fair ensuing, within her 7ˢ 6ᵈ—which is still in my possession? or shall I great *one* lot pretty considerable, or 2 or 3 or 4 small & joli?—

Our revered Mr. Lock just now came in, & hearing my employment, said in that voice of even pathetically penetrating power which you must so well remember 'Give my KINDEST Love to Her—'. He was in his Phaeton, but met here, by appointment, Mr. Chaˢ & Cecilia, Augusta & George. Cecilia is as interesting as ever—revived, though not re-cheared, & with looks of infinite sweetness & attraction. She thinks we shall not meet again before her departure, & took an almost melancholy leave of me, venturing her voice—painfully, to express a strong sense of the feeling she had heard I had had of her late misery. Her Eyes were swimming instantly, & I durst hardly answer her: but I was & am much touched for her. Unfortunately she quite adored this cruel Brother: & he clings still to the very heart-strings of all his family. She consulted me with regard to going to court: & I was happy to feel a *decided* opinion, so strong, from *certain* knowledge of similar situations, that I could not hesitate to pronounce upon the *necessity* of that measure, as Mr. Charles goes in a public capacity. She seemed languishing to avoid exhibiting herself, but did not contest what I urged,—on the contrary, she called Charles | to the

[19] See L. 292, pp. 179–80.

consultation, & when he, also, heard me, they mutually agreed to decide upon going. I was very glad of it, for I am sure they would else give very great offence.

Adieu, my ever dear & dearest Susanna!—the one hope now open by my dearest Father's petition will rest upon me with a little lightness till it is answered—& then—but I dare not anticipate *good*,—& will not evil. Heaven ever bless you, my most dear soul!

a visit just at Mid day from Mr. Daniel has prevented mon Ami from writing—his tender Love take from me—& the Letter of M. de N[arbonne] in the next pacquet.[20] My dear Child is well, & grows; but still thin.

295   [West Humble, –3 October 1798]

To Esther (Burney) Burney

A.L.S. (Berg), *n.d.*
Double sheet 4to   4 pp.   *pmks* DARKING   5 OC 98   wafer
Addressed: Mrs. Burney, / Beaumont Street, / Devonshire Place, / London.

I meant to have written a few lines to my dear Esther by our dear Father,—but could never afford a moment from him save for my little Rogue, who will be neglected for nothing mortal. But I wish to enquire if by Your means I can convey a Letter to James upon business.[1]

If this question should surprise you, as to *him*, I beg you not to divulge that I have asked it, for if a Letter by his own usual direction will reach him, he would be offended to know that I had doubted it. I am, however, painfully in the dark about

---

²⁰ See n. 8 above.

295. ¹ According to Maria Rishton (see letters of 9 Oct., 23 Oct., 30 Oct., and Nov. 1798, Eg. 3697, ff. 280–1b, 284–90b), the fugitives went first to Bristol, but returning to London, took lodgings at 37 Fetter Lane, using Tom's Coffee House, Russell Street, Covent Garden, as an address. They lived for a time near Kentish Town, doing their own marketing and cooking, but were next reported by EBB as living in a 'Groveling mean Style' in 'a dirty Lodging in a Suspicious House in Totenham Court Road'. The landlady's 'Daughter is a Common prostitute who brings home a different Visitor every Night—and they dare not both leave their Apartments together lest they shou'd be rob'd'. By January they were living in John Street, Fitzroy Square, the address that JB eventually gave to FBA (L. 304).

him. I have no certainty, but that he has parted from his wife; but whether by mutual consent, or by separate will, whether they are sometimes to meet, or are totally sundered—which of them is to have the house, or whether both are to go into Lodgings, &c—I am wholly uninformed. I am *extremely* sorry at the event, for reasons I am sure I need not tell you. But my Letter, you will easily believe, will not be to press their re-union, while I am so completely unqualified for judging why they part. It is about my own affairs I now wish to write,—though I should be most happy if—when opening an intercourse about myself, I could glide into it any thing conciliatory. What *her* faults in the business may be I know not;[2] but I must protest I never *saw* in her any thing to condemn, & I have seen many things that appeared to me perfectly right. My partiality, however, is all to James, & [|] therefore I cannot but conclude his *Heart* must have had provocation before his *conduct* could shew him thus warped & hardened against her. What most astonishes me is, that my Father himself does not know his direction!—He understands that *he*, not *she*, has quitted the house, upon which *there was a bill*,[3] he says, when he last was there, though whether for the *house*, or *lodgings* to be let, whether *both*, or only *one* was to quit, he had no information, & could not, therefore, give any.

My affair is simply to ask him to remember *our quarter day*, which approaches fast; & which we never know how to *pass unnoticed*. Charlotte used to receive *its dues* for us from Mr. Mathias, till she resided at Richmond: James then, kindly undertook the trouble—for what of kindness or trouble has he ever declined for his sisters!—Hard—hard will it go with me should any great blame be forced upon my mind against so excellent a Brother!—but indeed I am ill at ease about him—If you are *trusted* with his schemes, make me no answer concerning him, for I have no right to it in that case; if not, I think it very possible that by communicating with one-another, we may do some good.

Should you, all this time, know nothing at all of him or of this, I shall be truly sorry to have awakened an inquietude

---

[2] The Burneys always respected James's wife, *née* Sarah Payne, as 'desirous of doing right', though SBP in former times thought her cold by nature.

[3] A sign, rather, to let or sell.

I have no ˡ means to settle: but as I think it *impossible*, since the separation has been mentioned to me in a Letter from Mrs. Greenwich B[urney]—.⁴ I rather hazard these enquiries than remain longer silent.

I should be less moved by this transaction, from my knowledge of their frequent contention, & plans of parting, if I heard of James amongst the rest of you,—but I had written him, ere this intelligence reached me—ere it existed, indeed, a Letter so urgent upon proposed expedients about our darling Susan, that I have been really hurt as well as amazed he should make me no answer; & now, to know of such a change in his way of life, & neither to receive a word upon it from himself, nor to gather that he has ⟨not⟩ associated himself with any of his family since, seems so gloomy, & so extraordinary, that it really & even cruelly disturbs me.

My dear Father highly disapproves the measure—but talked as little as possible upon the subject; & it was my business to try to dissipate, not fix, ill-thoughts: I saw him often dejected, —but had recourse to books, reading, gardening, & Alex, & with very dear success, in generally cheering him. He was very sorry, & so am I, very truly, for poor Cousin James.⁵ There seems little hope, from your account, of his recovery. I fear he has thrown away his own life from want of foresight, first to its danger, & next to its value: for he would have thought it worth more than the pleasures for which he resigned it, had he seen they could not be held together. Dear Mr. Burney! May *his* temperance—constant, uniform, & universal, pay him in a longevity as precious to his family as to himself:—I say the same for his now *only* Brother. ˡ

I try, now, to compose my mind about our dearest of dearests —for I see no chance of her return till the M[ajor] comes himself. Indeed, she is so full of fears about Norbury, that I think her *wishes* bend not this way without him. The *North* of England,⁶ now the French have effected a Landing there, she holds to be no place of security—& I cannot wonder,—for I feel if my Alex were there I should be a stranger to a moment's rest. That Barbarian has fixed this spoke in the wheel of our

---

⁴ The letter is missing.

⁵ James Adolphus Burney (1753–98). The 'Worcester Journal' records his last illness and his burial at Bridgnorth on 29 Sept. 1798.

⁶ FBA surely meant to write Ireland.

entreaties,[7] to torture even her own desires into nothing but conflicting alternatives of distress each way. the lovely *Fanny should* be here, I really think—but who could take her from her Mother? & what were that sweet mother with neither of those charming children? Fanny, indeed, must now no longer be a child. My Mate is gone on a two days visit to an old friend at Croydon; a French *ci-divant* Baron, whom he loves very much,[8] & who was in the army with him. He took the opportunity of going as far as Ewell with our dear Father—who has indulged us with a week that we vainly tried to lengthen Our ever delicious neighbours are well, & we see them, *here*, very frequently: but we grow *worse & worse* Hermits for seeing any one else where. But we keep Greenwich in perspective, & *will* then get a peep at you, if we can get to Town by any means. We are quite unfixed, as to Time. My little man is well; I wish your Amelia could come & play with him this beautiful weather in our new forming Garden & Walks. Adieu, my dearest Esther— my kindest remembrances to dear M^r B[urney] & Marianne & Sophy. I hope Fanny continues well—in all ways? Mr. Lock called the instant my Father was gone with the glorious new news. Nelson for ever![9] What admirals we have! The Navy for ever! the true ANCHOR for England!—

ever—ever y^rs

F D'A.

Wednesday—Yours arrives as this must go—& I have only this scrap to thank you, & say how sorry I am for poor Cousin James:—I will speak about the Bonnets directly.[10]

[7] The effective threat that if the Phillips family were to return to England, Norbury at least could or must remain in Ireland (cf. SBP's letter of 8–11 [Sept.], op. cit.).

[8] Probably Pierre-Auguste Lajard (L. 291 n. 5).

[9] Official news of the battle of the Nile, fought on 1 Aug., did not reach the Admiralty until 2 Oct. (*The Times*, 2, 3 Oct.).

[10] For the bonnets, see L. 296, p. 210; and L. 325, p. 302.

Conjointly with M. d'Arblay
To Esther (Burney) Burney;
and Madame d'Arblay *to* Hannah Maria Burney

A.L.S. with PS. & A.L.S. (Berg), 22 Nov. [17]98
Double sheet 4to   4 pp.   *pmk*   24 NO 98   wafer
Addressed: Mrs. Burney / Beaumont Street, / Devonshire Place / London—

West Hamble,
Nov. 22ᵈ—98

I cannot wonder, my dearest Esther, you were willing to shirk taking the Pen in discussion, or narration relative to the subject upon which, I believe, we are so painfully of one opinion: Marianne's Letter shewed me the style in which the affair stood,[1] & was to be considered, & relieved me at least from suspence,—for it is written with the utmost clearness & candour. I will thank her myself before I close this sheet. You enquire if I have written to James!—You know I have been in a correspondence with him some time upon my *treasury* business, & that both of us wrote as if all were situated as usual; but when I found one more Letter only necessary on my part, I set aside that cold—but ordained—caution,—openly informed him I was acquainted with the step he had taken (avoiding, as bound to do, the smallest hint of its *manner*, or of our padre or Mrs. R[ishton]) & as openly acknowledged the grief & wonder it had caused me,—& how much I had sought to find means to stop its progress—but never knew his private & direct address till it appeared to be irreversible. I then only charged them always to remember that no difference of opinion & way of thinking could estrange them from my affection, which—most truly— I have begged *them* to try, should occasion arise to make it desirable or useful. To this he has answered most briefly— declining any longer to be my Agent, though I had *solicited* him, as a proof that I should invariably be at his service if called upon in return—says they are going into the Country[2]—but not

296. [1] The letters here mentioned are missing, though FBA copied some of them in her letter of 13–15 Dec. 1798 (L. 297, p. 218).
     [2] The 'fugitives' went for a time to Bristol.

whither—& only informs me his plan is to take Martin. But not one word ⏐ of how they are to live—how to employ their time—where they are to be, how I may direct,—nor one little wish of hearing from me, nor hint of any desire of intercourse,—though the whole tenour of my letter was inviting it! — — —

This has grieved me deeply,—but sadly, not angrily, as his Letter seems shy from consciousness, not unkindness—from awkwardness rather than coldness. Sally he never names, though I addressed them jointly in what I said of offers, & of regard; he only includes her by the word *our*, written over *my*, in speaking of his Country Plan,—& of kindest remembrances to M. d'A. I will not say I *fear* contrition has touched them,—for I love them too well not to *hope* it, since such is my opinion of their conduct that they have no way back to my esteem, nor to my notions of their deserving any future good, but by a sincere sorrow of the rash selfishness with which they have broken through all duties & ties to others for their own singular caprice & inclination.

Have you written to our beloved Susan about it? Or do you know if my poor Father, or James himself have? *I* am so tied, & the subject is so cruel, I wait till I hear from her that it has reached her before I touch upon it. I had hopes, till lately, matters might have been some what accommodated before the tale was told: but nothing of that style sooths my concern. Poor James!—his heart is not made to be callous long to the daring offence he has both given & influenced!—I am sure sooner or later it will make him very unhappy. May it but be in time to prevent a remorse that may embitter HIS old AGE!—God save him from that!—My Heart aches for him often,—for alienated as he now appears from *all* his connections & absorbed only in one partial affection, his Hour will come—an hour when he will wonder at his own madness. And She—poor Girl! What a lot has ⏐ she dealt herself! What has the life she has chosen that can repay her, when its novelty & *wilfulness* are past, for the life she relinquished?

This cruel subject is running away with all my paper, & I have not yet told you my rage against my leige lord & spouse for having sent you off 2 Franks without a line of my insertion. The Fact is, he met the opportunity at Mr. Lock's, when there one morning without me, as Miss Upton offered to carry his covers to Lord Hervey, then at Lady Templetown's house at Leatherhead;³—therefore,—though that I never thought proper to take into consideration, he could do no better.—He has begged you, also, to be his Creditor for 8ˢ as he knew not how to convey it, with White, the Taylor⁴ who was told to trouble you for payment. whether this was clear in the 2ᵈ frank is yet for us to learn; that in the *first* nothing was intelligible, I have plainly pointed out to him from your Letter— loving to make people feel agreeable to themselves.

I have been extremely disappointed with regard to Mᵉ du chastel⁵ for the sudden change of destination from Denmark to Naples, & the immense hurry of only *3 days* for all the preparations of a man & his Wife & 2 children for so long a voyage, put it out of Mʳˢ C. Lock's power to go any where herself, or see any body, or thing, but close relations & friends, & what was indispensably necessary. Mrs. Lock, however, our Mrs. Lock, promises me your recommendation & wish shall not quit her head till fulfilled, if the Bonnets continue to be made next spring, when she goes as usual to Town with her Girls, who both promise the same. However, I am *very* sorry for the present disappointment. I perfectly remember the truly interesting account you gave of this lady & her beautiful Daughter in your Ball Letter. |

We have deferred our Chelsea visit,—I have not here room to explain why; but that, with a *few more subjects*, may keep off ennui when we, at last meet. I am glad you have seen Charlotte—does she look happy? she wrote me word she *was* so, but it is long since,—& I have no sort of news about her of any recent date. I rejoice to hear Richard has accepted a Curacy:⁶ I hope it is pleasant to you? & that he is kept alive in the good Bishop's memory? Imagine Mr. & Mrs. L[ocke]'s mortification that their son has been detained ever since he left them at Portsmouth, waiting a change of Wind? They are believed, however, now to have sailed—& Mrs. L[ocke] is very anxious, & cruelly disturbed by all boisterous winds. They go the whole way by sea:

To what country place can J[ames] & S[arah] think of

---

³ See L. 292, p. 182. ⁴ See iii, L. 207 n. 4.

⁵ Madame du Chastel (d. *pre* 17 June 1799), an *émigrée*, the mother of two sons and a 'beautiful Daughter', of whom little is known. See further, L. 325, pp. 301-2.

⁶ For the curacy in question, see

retiring? & why this change from their London plan?—God bless you, my dearest Esther—& *yours*, to whom my love—& my mate's.—My boy is now a picture of Health as well as an *epitome* of all that is understood by spirits—nay, the very essence. So happily gay a little rogue I have scarcely ever seen.

adieu, dearest Etty—Ever & ever truly & affec^ly. y^rs

F. d'A.

Do you ever see Mrs. Chapone? My true respects to her if you can convey them. I have had a visit here from *Mr. Pepys.*— & the other day we let in Lady Burrel to our bare walls, after declining the honour repeatedly,—& she asked very particularly how Mr. Burney did, saying 'My Daughter (who was with her)[7] has the good fortune to be one of Mr. Burney's pupils.' Her Ladyship's house, (a vast Mansion) is the only building in sight from the front of our little Hermitage.[8] I hope Mr. B[urney] likes Miss Burrel, who seems very pleasing & modest.

[*By M. d'Arblay*]

Dear Mr Burney must know that the 2^d halves were sent the day following with the same direction. *N° 40.* I am affraid the Tailor (Mr White) has not called. for want of this true N° 43. my best love ^Γ⟨& compliments⟩^Π *to all*

⟶

[*From Madame d'Arblay to Hannah Maria Burney, written on the lower fold of* pp. 3–4.]

Miss Burney.

Will my dear Marianne excuse this most shabby scrap of thanks for her Letter?—*Letters*, I ought to say, only a blush ought to rise with the s at recollection of so long due a debt— which this morsel can only acknowledge, not repay. I heartily thank you for the unaffected openness of your narrative upon a VERY difficult & very embarrassing subject, & give you, my dear Girl, great credit for so palpably shewing your honest disapprobation, while still so warmly maintaining your JUST AFFECTION. I wish much to know if you have yet seen poor

---

7 See L. 292 n. 12.   8 Deepdene, discernible in the distance.

Sarah. I hope your Greenwich visit turned out well. If Mrs. G[reenwich]'s curiosity was not quite distressing, I am sure you must be happy with your uncle, from the pleasure he always meets & greets you with. ¹ I hope you have chearful Letters from dear Fanny, & comic & quaint stories & conceits from dear Sophy? & all the animals in dialogues from Cecilia? & a few (for all would be too many) of sparrow nests from Amelia? I was very sorry for your Uncle James' of Bridgenorth,⁹ & beg you to remember my kind love to your dear Blue¹⁰ when you write next. How Glad I should be if she should visit London while we are at Chelsea! The time for that is near, though not fixed. You will find your little cousin, & early admirer, turning out a most riotous Gentleman. Believe me, my dearest Marianne,

your ever faithful affectionate
F. d'A.

297   [West Humble,]–
13–15 December 1798

To Mrs. Phillips

A.L.S. (Berg),—13–15 Dec. [17]98, including copies of FBA's correspondence with JB
Two double sheets 4to   8 pp.   wafer
Addressed: Mrs. Phillips— / Belcotton, / Drogheda.
Docketed by SBP, p. 8: about brother James—

Decr 98.

My dearest—dearest Susan—that I could but see—& fold you to my Heart!——to know you thus every way suffering—& I knew how you must suffer—I am sunk with sadness you should have such accumulation—I well know this was a—
Your Letter just now received this Decr 13.—98¹
I began, I know not how nor what on a Copy of an extract sent me by our Esther—my own beloved Susan!—God Almighty enable you to preserve your precious precious health!—

⁹ See L. 295 n. 5.   ¹⁰ See i, Intro., p. lxxv.

297. ¹ This letter, evidently containing a comment on the elopement of JB and SHB, is missing.

all else; I must always hope, will come round to fairer times,—
but for *that* I tremble most of all,—& again & most fervently
conjure you to remember your solemn engagement to suffer my
immediate attendance should you be ill beyond a feverish
Cold—or nervous feverishness. *your* colds, indeed, once feverish,
are so soon inflammatory, that I think I wait too long, not to
insist on flying to you for them solely,—but as you feel Symptoms that announce a Cold as serious, or not, I do conjure you
to let me hear of them—not to *write*, with James's powders in
operation,—but to let my dear Fanny,—should the Major be
absent or engaged, or even Susan, whose care I wish you would
place it in,—for I think I might trust it.—It was truly kind,
truly characteristic of my own most dear to write so speedily
when aware of my inquietude.—The extract—how it touched
me! — — I have deferred the subject as long as possible—
I languished at least to put it off till we had *certainty*, however
unwished a one—& I thank God the suspensive state was
spared my tenderest Susan.— |

Let me, while I think of it, beg another *Letter to be torn off*
for either of our sisters—it is very satisfactory, & answers all
purposes.[2] our sweetly kind friend would never murmur at any
parts unshewn—but she would look anxious,—& her Speaking
Eyes would shew a disappointment her voice would never
utter. she so sweetly—sweetly receives our united confidence!—
so truly merits more than we can unite to offer her—Let me,
too, while I think of it, beg you not to be uneasy about the lost
sheet, save for the fear of whose hands it may fall into — as to
its contents, mon ami was so much interested about them, that
he had Copied them for himself: & he promises to Copy the
part you miss & send in this pacquet if possible; but certainly in
the next—I am, however, much disturbed whenever I think of
the terrible *ado* that will be made should such a narrative get
abroad. I often fancy it was lost in a stolen mail, & hope it was
destroyed. The other Letters which never arrived were of no
consequence that I can recollect except to ourselves. This was
the only one of a journal sort—&, indeed, had much dispirited
& frightened me from resuming that sort of style: but our

---

[2] A means of sending comments on the embarrassing event (above) that the
sisters wished to hide from Mrs. Locke, in whom were confided most of the concerns
of the d'Arblay and Phillips families.

inveterate absence brings me round. Sweet J[aney] P[aney]—
how I love her! & her anneau!—how kind to hint that the
climate mends!³ God keep it a little temperate! 'tis always the
best part of even *your* Letters that ever gives me that consolation. We hear no more of M. de N[arbonne] to our great
concern & surprise. We this moment have news Buonaparte is
Shot, with all his suite, for attempting the same rapacious
extortions in Egypt as in Italy & Switzerland.⁴ He was a scourge
to all Countries but his own,—& may his ashes bring the Peace
his restless Genius contributed always to distance! I will now
deliver myself up to the one subject. — — ⎮

ah—my dearest most darling Susan!—how completely have
we felt this blow alike!—& how sure was I we could not do
otherwise!—& all so tenderly you say of your sympathy for *me*
most truly I have experiencd dearest—dearest soul! for You!
—In the time of my first knowledge of the event, your name
never occurred to me but to wring my heart.—but let me,
nevertheless, hasten to try to relieve your precious mind from
what my own mind is relieved, 'horrible thoughts — ' I bless
God those, at least, have passed away,—& ever for a moment
to have been assailed by them makes all else *LIGHT*!—Can I say
more to point out to you the species of *acquiescence* to which I
have now made myself up? But I will write—since you think
I may—wholly & fully, only avoiding names, for fear of a
miscarriage of the Letter.—When first I heard the dreadful
tydings, every sort of horrour seized me,—as they were communicated by Mrs. R[ishton]—who sent me them *express*,⁵

³ A reference to the Major's ungoverned rages.
⁴ *The Times* (15 Dec.) published an erroneous report of a Council of War between
the French and the Egyptians at Cairo, at which meeting 'a gentleman from Tripoli,
who was present, drew a pistol and shot Buonaparte dead on the spot'. The native
officers then killed all the French officers, a proceeding followed by 'a general
massacre of the French'.
⁵ The alarm of [2 Sept. 1798] that Maria Rishton sent express by her servant
Thomas to FBA, 'the prop & Support of the Family in all Emergencies', is extant
in the Barrett Collection (Eg. 3697, f. 275):
My dear Fanny
   I don't know what to Say—or write but to you only dare I write—I have been
in town since Wednesday found Sally very low—and yesterday your dear
Father told me James and his wife were parted—to day after being out with Mʳˢ
Burney shopping on my return Molly told me Sally was gone up to town—with
James—but that never struck me and I was packing up some things when she
came into my room with a packet of letters directed to me inclosing two for your
Father one to Molly one to me the last I inclose mine—the one Molly has is to me
dreadful as it seems to say she does not mean to return.

& who evidently harboured them herself. She besought my instantly joining her, to help to tell the flight to our beloved Father — — in a state almost senseless, I shewed the Letter to my best friend—his freedom of all *idea* but of a *simple & selfish imprudence* recovered me. I considered it the same myself almost immediately—I determined *not* to go,—not to give the *eclat* of seeming to think my Father would require support,— not to let *him* himself suppose I imagined the evil of so deep a nature,—& I wrote to Mrs. R. by her express messenger,[6] to conjure her to be upon guard, & not cause surmizes irretrievable in their consequences, telling her I would hear their own account before I judged them, & beseeching her not to influence the opinion of my dearest Father by betraying any fears or thoughts beyond what the action necessarily & unavoidably created by its breach of *duty* & *decorum*:—I added, that I would not for the World, I unless summoned by my Father, present myself in the *deserted post*, that I had every claim upon my caution & kindness which repeated & never failing acts of brotherly affection could give him; & that I know he would never forgive a step that would seem to mark the event with terror, & stigmatize it with disgrace. I entreated her, however, to endeavour to discover their abode, & prevail with them to think better of the scheme. And I begged her to try to send Me their address,—for I flattered myself could I procure it that I had such things to represent as would have demolished their *desire* of secession.—Mrs. R. sent Me then a minute detail of the preceding circumstances:[7] I found J[ames] had left his wife & Children unmercifully, indecently, to pass all his time with S[arah]—that my F[ather] had been offended by his conduct, & angrily remonstrated—on its impropriety—& had received him with open repugnance,—not decreased, you will

Maria also transcribed the letter SHB had left for her: 'Dear Mrs R. Be so kind to give the inclosed to my Father on his return. And let me recommend to you to be so considerate as to let as little noise be made about our absence as possible.'

[6] FBA's express is missing.

[7] This is the letter of [3 Sept. 1798], Eg. 3697, ff. 276–7b, in which Mrs. Rishton gave the background of the elopement: JB's long-standing 'partiality' for his half-sister, his wife's allegation of an 'improper Attachment', his separation from her (for the third time), his request that he be allowed to board at Chelsea, and Dr. Burney's refusal. CB felt *dreadful* apprehensions about [their] uncommon Intimacy' —'Apprehensions which *shook* him with agony'. SHB, on her part, complained of her 'Father's Severity and Coldness towards her', his *bitter* raillery' and 'Harshness', and finally on Saturday 1 Sept. she penned her farewell notes ('I trust I am gone to be happy & comfortable—').

believe, by finding, through the frequency of his continued visits, that *he* was not their object. S. — in the course of this, considered only herself,—never felt for the wife, never thought of the Children, never cared for her Father & his sentiments:— & soon *quarrelled*, & very grossly, with Mrs. R. for *being sorry to hear J. & his wife were now parting*. Mrs. R. began to turn her mind into finding some other home, — — ! — — when THIS home, upon my F.'s refusing to let the self-divorced husband board with him by agreement, was left by S. in company with poor J.—!— *poor* indeed!—O Good God!—how fallen from that place where *we* had fixed him!—for, take the deed in its best Colours,—'tis *dark*—dark!—though not, I humbly hope— black!—

This statement of things determined me to assist him, if possible, to stop *calumny* from following *censure*: & I wrote a Letter far kinder towards him than, I own, I felt!—with the best representations I could devize, of imputing the step to his affronted honour, which defied scandal, & resented suspicion,— Since I found he had openly been attacked by his wife of an *improper connection*! Shocking! | & also, as Mrs. R. acknowledged, & *I*—alas! knew, such had been the accusation conceived & spread by one now no MORE[8]—Whom God pardon!—I there- fore *assisted* him with all my might, & in such a manner as he has truly merited from me all my life.—& my dear Partner said always 'Let us never forget it was he who gave us to each other[9]—'

⟶

Upon my F.'s return to town, he wrote to me—so much cooler than I expected that I was quite astonished, & greatly, indeed, comforted.[10] He approved my not coming, which, he said, would have been a step J. never would have forgiven, through its implications,—expressed a cold resentment of their conduct, & finished by a warm, animated, tender hope the place unkindly filled, unnaturally abandonned, might be filled

---

[8] Mrs. Burney's tale Maria and Stephen Allen had turned from with 'horror', 'tho I found', Maria reported (loc. cit.), that 'the Idea had taken strong hold of your Father—and agonized his Mind'.

[9] James, kindly taking CB's part, had given FB away on her wedding day (see ii, pp. 170, 176–7).

[10] CB's letters on this subject have doubtless been destroyed.

by one who would supply to him all the comfort of which he stood in need.—Ah—Judge if then we were anxious for news from Hibernia!—

⌒

I could not bring myself to write to you upon the subject, even when sure you could not escape its knowledge—for I knew not even where they were!—*That*, indeed, was an horrible time!—I thought them gone to America!—I knew the slander that must follow such a flight—I was *haunted*, as you say, by horrour & affliction—I dare not expatiate how—it would now be cruel—but my health is so strongly established, it did not suffer,—*believe me*—except by the *head*, & that, bursting & beating, was sometimes almost delirious—dreadful epoch! — — let me fly it, to the time we learnt they were actually in or near London.[11] All of which Esther has told you. I had sought earnestly, vehemently to get his direction,—but vainly!—I never obtained it, till the affair was *fixed*, by their knowing that my F. was determined to *leave them to themselves*. He most positively commanded me not to interfere,—not even to remonstrate— he has told me alas my dearest Susan—that he wishes never more to see or hear of them!—

Nevertheless, he has been so temperate, so astonishingly calm, that I do not despair that a reconciliation may be brought about by & bye—if *they* desire it—but that is not now the case!!!—Shame has made them callous to affection. |

In order to ascertain if his Letters followed him, I had my F.'s permission to address a common Letter to him as usual. I wrote only upon my *treasury* business. 2 or 3 Letters passed between us, merely on this subject,—written as if all were in its usual course. I suffered cruelly in so writing, but my F. exacted it—nevertheless, when, upon sending me Mr. M[athias]'s notes, he could hear from me only once more, I could not endure so to finish—& transgressed into something more natural, determining to own it to my F. & plead the impossibility he should suppose me ignorant of his situation. As I keep in my tablets[12] still what I wrote, I feel you will like to see it &

---

[11] At 21 John Street, Tottenham Court Road.   [12] See ii, L. 68 n. 7.

will therefore Copy it:[13] first premising that I was positively & peremtorily *bound* not to name my F. nor Mrs. R.—nor take any *Measures* whatever.

To—

Dear J[ames]—The notes have arrived safe, & we thank you heartily for your care & trouble. Let us continue to give it you upon this score, if only to keep in your claim a right to command & employ *us*, should occasion make it desirable to you. I had earnestly wished for your private direction some time ago, in hopes to bring about—some conciliatory measures—but I could not obtain it, till the step you have taken seems irretrievable. It has given me, I own,—the deepest affliction,—& most extreme astonishment—but,—if you have your own approbations—I here address you *both*— I shall endeavour to better reconcile myself to what my repining cannot prevent.—Would to God—more than ever! —our dearest Susan might be permitted to come over!— I will add nothing more, now, than that, however dissimilar may be our ways of thinking, my kindest wishes, &, if called upon, exertions, will, to both, be unchangeable.—

Thus much I ventured, in hopes of being authorised by them to act,—which would have taken place of my F.'s injunctions not to *interfere myself* however, my answer—but I will copy that also, certain I can give you nothing so satisfactory as his own words.

Dear Sister—I have sent the remaining part of the notes, which I hope you will receive in as quiet a manner as the former. It will not be in my power to continue your agent, as my being in town is only upon business, which will scarcely detain me beyond Christmas.

We are sensible of the kindness of your Letter. our plan is, as soon as I am ready to leave town, to take Martin into the country, & keep him with me.

our kindest Love to Mr. d'A[rblay]

yr ever affec^{te.} bro—

J. B—

---

13 The originals of the letters here copied are missing.

This seems casting off all intercourse—which I cannot attribute to unkindness but to consciousness, & distress how to speak of the transaction. I must own I wish them nothing to much as acute, bitter remorse. I see no other way left to restore them to any esteem. The step has been of such unexampled wilfulness of wrong, that I know not how it can be too severely punished,—yet I earnestly hope contrition will open their infatuated Eyes while it is yet possible to save them from endless self-reproach. My Letter will always be remembered by them, should that enlightened period arrive, as a mark that I am most willing to attempt acting for them—My F. bore the whole with a quietness of resentment truly unexpected, till they strove to engage Molly[14] in their own Service. This has irritated him cruelly—& since it I have positively been charged '*happen what may*' never to attempt an accommodation!—But I would not be withheld, if they were sensible of their ill conduct sufficiently to humble themselves before him in petitioning forgiveness. They know not his charge to me, however,—& yet, silently, but deliberately, decline my offered services. It is plain, therefore, they wish not for them,—nor for their effect!—They are both proud—&, where a resolution is taken, hard,—time only, therefore, will soften them, or accident: or finding some difficulty greater in returning to right, than persevering in evil!—for, if really left to themselves, it is probable they will soon wish to be | called to *others*! they are *perverse*,—& will soon cease to care so much for each other's society when they can have it so completely. What I have suffered as to J.— I will not enter upon —but a disappointment more severe, more terrible, in an upright Character I cannot conceive. *anger* & *disgust* were more prominent than *disappointment* or *grief* with respect to S.—but sorrow has been terrible for both!—but J. I thought so utterly incapable of leading another astray — — that I have even wished him *dead* ere such an action had sullied his fair character! —!—for a considerable time I was pursued, as if by tormenting demons, with his constant image, listening to my reproaches— & could not get rid of the idea that he was always at my side, hearing me: while the *other* — — I alternately execrated & pitied.—Thank Heaven, I am now tranquilised & restored—&, since I can do no good, I do as my dearest F. does himself—

14 CB's housekeeper, Molly More (ii, L. 68 n. 30).

strive with my utmost power to drive—force them from my thoughts. Copy this, my own Love!—'Tis all we can any of us do at present. They know they may command me, if they wish it— but their wish must be waited for. I shall long to know news of yr. Letter—In one from my dearest F. Yesterday,[15] he says— Dear—Dear Susey!—I know well how she will wish to come to me —especially now she knows how I have been abandonned!— —' *We* have made repeated offers of going: but he is willing to shew the *Post* unoccupied, both to the one who *quitted*,—& the one he wishes to fill it. But we shall go in a month for a few weeks. [*wafer*]—& Heaven bless my darling Sister

& most beloved Friend!

F. d A

Finished Dec[r] 15. 1798. |

[*continued on the margins of* pp. 1 *and* 3.]

My dear Boy is quite well—and very riotous. My Mate in perfect health.

How barbarous the Letter failure with dear Norbury![16] how like that of Boulogne! sweet soul! What a dreadful interval! Heaven guard you from such another! I conceive—*feel* it still for you—

I forget if I ever mentioned that Mrs. Newton[17] has been put upon the list of our angel Friends for a Yearly Fairing, (5[s]) upon Mrs. L[ocke] hearing it would be acceptable through the benevolent Braissant.[18]

I can send only this one sheet of Journal, not daring add a 4[th.] sheet to the pacquet.

don't wait to be able to write a long Letter, my most dear Soul, to let me know how you do—it will be *very cheap taken* as *comfort*, to have 3 lines now, of *truth*, good, or if bad to *know* it [xxxxx *3 words*]

Mon ami will copy the other for next time. Heaven bless You! I shall most impatiently wait news of yr. dear health. I leave much unanswered of your dear Letter—but thought you would prefer fullness on this subject.

[15] The letter is missing.
[16] Evidently a failure in correspondence between SBP and her son, which FBA may be comparing to the long delay in hearing from SBP at Boulogne, where she went for her health in 1784–5 (*HFB*, p. 187 n. 5).
[17] See iii, L. 237 n. 6.   [18] See ii, L. 68 n. 50.

298 [West Humble, 18 December 1798]

To Doctor Burney

A.L.S. (Barrett, Eg. 3690, ff. 96–7b), *n.d.*

Double sheet 4to (9·8×8″) 4 pp. less a cutting (0·8×7·9″), described in Textual Notes *pmks* DARKING 18 DE 98 18 DE 98 wafer

Addressed: Dr. Burney, / Chelsea College, / Middlesex.

Endorsed by CB: 1798

Edited by FBA, p. 1, *annotated and dated*: ✳· ✳· 18 Dec^r—98 (3) Alex' Birthday Princess Amelia.

p. 3, *annotated*: ✳·

Scribbling p. 4: Thieves

Edited also by CFBt, *see* Textual Notes.

Whether You call your Letter sprightly or not, my dearest Padre, to me it was both entertaining & interesting.[1] The astronomic work is so much my favourite that I am always eager to know its progress, whether in correction or fame: & I am delighted at such testimony as Herschel's.—To *instruct* Herschel in astronomy![2]—'pon Honour!—But I can easily conceive, he with all his depth of knowledge in the science, & his true genius for encreasing its sources to others, he might not be informed as you have informed him of the Biographical, nor, perhaps, chronological history of the art. I shall long for an account of the reading of the last Book;—I wish I could be by, to peep at him: *you* will not dare! But it would be comical to ME to peep at you *both*,—for though *you* can have no surprise in store, you are mistaken—pardon the phrase, dearest sir,—if you suppose you can read without blushing, the praise, however just, which with blushing will be heard. But as neither crime nor shame will produce the rosy tint, but merely modesty, & mixed up not with *pain*, but *pleasure*, I should infinitely enjoy a peep behind the Curtain at both.

298. [1] CB's letter of 10 Dec. 1798 (Berg), beginning 'You must not expect a spritely nor a long letter', was chiefly an account of Herschel's approval of his versified history of Astronomy and of the reception accorded his patriotic ballad on England's naval victories, which had been performed, at the Queen's request, at Covent Garden on 7 Nov. 1798 (Lonsdale, pp. 394–5).

[2] Herschel, having listened, on the occasion of a two-day visit at Chelsea, to five books of the history of Astronomy, had confessed that CB knew more of that subject than he did (*DL* v, 430).

I am very glad, after all, that you are spared a country visit.[3] The damps would frighten me for you—especially as West-humble is not in the right road! — — I doat on Lady Lucan's frank note:[4] & really I am much of her opinion. Mr. Locke but yesterday was observing that he never knew a Lord of the Admiralty[5] who had so many brilliant instances to blazon the sagacity of his projects, & wisdom of his researches into his own best means. *I* attribute it to his *modesty*: being free from pre-sumption, he *enquires*, & *listens*, & then decides. Most others decide first, & then, perforce, hear the unexamined reasons by which they have failed. I like the Censor change very much,[6] but not, I own, the other, which I do not | ᴦthink clear, though I clearly understand [it.] I am extremely pleased by the Parsons' anecdote,[7] & the King's demanding the song. &c.

I am much gratified at the thought of Herschel's portrait by Edward.—& much by your contradiction of the alarming reports about Lord Macartney.[8] I had a Letter from our sweetest Susan two Days ago.[9] she has been ill, but assures me she is quite well again. She is almost in anguish to be with you *now*. She has preserved fortitude & patience till this event, which has but just reached her—& I am thankful she never heard it in our long uncertainty of Their designs & abode. But she is wretched, longs to come to you, & never says she is not wholly forbid to hope—but does not explain how—yet

---

[3] The country visit is lost with the parts (some twelve lines) that FBA later obliterated.

[4] CB had copied a short congratulatory note sent by Lady Lucan (iii, L. 136 n. 8) on 'a most charming Song of yours' (i.e., the ballad above).

[5] First Lord of the Admiralty since 1794, Earl Spencer could rejoice in the battle of the first of June (1794), the battles of St. Vincent and Camperdown (see L. 255 n. 23), and now the victory of the Nile.

[6] CB had submitted for his daughter's approval changes he had made in the final stanza of his ballad: 'Inspir'd by the all nations / 'Gainst Gallia will rebel soon / T'avenge her depredations—' *was altered to* 'What surly Censor / But feels his heart grow lighter / From plans devis'd by Spencer / To make our prospects brighter.'

[7] Sir William Parsons (iii, L. 233 n. 6), professor of music and appointed in 1796 instructor to the Princess Royal (*DNB*), had reported the Queen's pleasure at CB's having sent her his ballad and her approval of 'the song itself'. 'Her Majesty employed him to write the Notes over every Stanza, that she might not have 2 places to look at, at once—but before he had done she sent to him for the printed Copy for the King to hear it.'

[8] *The Times* (7 Dec. 1798) had published an erroneous report 'of the Death of that highly respected and much esteemed Nobleman, Lord Macartney', a confusion arising, perhaps, from his resigning the governorship of the Cape of Good Hope in Nov. 1798.

[9] SBP's comment on the elopement of JB and SHB is missing.

acknowledges this is no season for a voyage, though *she* fears nor storms nor cold, that could convey her to *You*!—I do not wonder at your short '*No*'! to Molly's enquiry,[10]—& I will not touch upon the subject. I have not since heard any more, except from Charlotte[11] that they both dined with her about 3 weeks since; & she thinks their scheme does not wear a promise of happiness. How could it? — —

How proud will our Bookham vicar & his lady be of your remembrance,[12] should it be possible to put your kind idea in execution! I am very glad you hear from our dear Mr. Twining. How often do I think of his congratulatory letter on Capt. Phillips' marriage, where he said then in ⟨reference⟩ to the happy man—*happy* man, I say, for, with such a Companion, he must be that or a *MONSTER*![13] ah!—he is indeed just that!—the gentle Mr. Lock yesterday in speaking of his detaining her through all dangers in that wretched country, called his *whole conduct & whole composition* diabolical!—

But your cough, my most dear sir, how afflicting you should thus be worn & tormented, notwithstanding all your efforts & temperance. I long to add to your list of remedies but I know you will fly!—however, I cannot forbear saying that *your own flesh & blood* has found Nitre cool her lungs & give her immediate repose, after the most wearing night restlessness, beyond all other things she ever tried—1/4 of a spoonful to a Glass with a Glass of water—

I am sorry you made such a sluggard of *sposas*[14]—⊓

But now,—I have kept back to consign uninterruptedly the rest of my paper to a very high subject, concerning which you make enquiry.

As soon as I hear that Her Royal Highness the Princess

---

[10] These comments on Molly More and the runaways are also lost with the obliterations.

[11] CBFB's letter is missing though FBA's reply to it (L. 299) has survived.

[12] CB had signified his intentions of sending the Cookes a copy of the second edition of his ballad as soon as he could procure a frank.

[13] This was the Revd. Thomas Twining's letter of 14 Feb. 1782 to CB (BM Add. MS. 39929, ff. 293–4).

[14] CB's Sunday company were for the most part unmarried and FBA may be here referring to his facetious matchmaking:
'I had my sister [Becky, aged 80], Letty Brooks, Hetty, Mr Burney and Ned [Edward Francesco Burney] and little Amelia here yesterday . . . Marianne & Sophy—and invited Mr Pugh [aged 60, see L. 292 n. 4] to meet M'aunt—but he was shy—or in the pulpit—what a nice match w^d it be between him and Miss Becky!'

Amelia[15] was to sleep at Sir Lucas Pepys in her way to town,
I was crazy to arrange seeing her: I thought of applying to
Lady Rothes; but knew how many she must disoblige if she
made an exception, &, indeed, that she had no right to invite
any body to see any of the Royal family, as they only invite
people themselves, by established etiquette, every place they
inhabit becoming so far their own as to make all right of admission rest upon their own choice. After much deliberating,
I at length determined to take courage, & venture to ask permission of The Queen herself,—who, as well as His Majesty,
always deigned to encourage her Royal Highnesses gracious
disposition towards me. I wrote, you will be sure, in all humility,
but yet with great earnestness, representing how impossible it
was for me not to make an effort for the honour I so much
wished, when Her Royal Highness must rest *within sight* of our
little Hermittage. I addressed my Letter through Miss Planta,—
& imagine my extreme pleasure & gratitude, in receiving an
immediate answer, with *Her Majesty's leave for my visit.*[16] I was
quite penetrated by this condescendsion. I wrote then to Lady
Rothes, stating my credentials: in a very kind answer, she said
she had *intended asking me*: &, when I saw her, she said That Her
Royal Highness had made so many enquiries about our Cottage,
in the Journey, & about me, that she had thought she might be
authorised to venture at causing the meeting. The Queen's
own leave, however, rendered all clear; as well as most delightful to me. I begged Lady Rothes permission to bring my boy,
promising he should be kept back, unless demanded. She told
me her own 3 GrandDaughters, the Miss Leslies,[17] were to be
at her house in the same manner, *& that they & my boy might
flirt together* in an anti-room. I borrowed Mr. Locke's Carriage,
& was invited, by Lady Rothes, to her own Breakfast party.
I found with her Lady Albina Cumberland,[18] then Lady in
waiting upon the Princess, to whom she introduced me, &

---

[15] The Princess Amelia (see L. 292 n. 18), returning from Worthing on 30 Nov.
was to stop over at Juniper Hill. For FB's description of the Princess at age 3, see
DL ii. 403.

[16] The consent is extant in the copy that FBA included in L. 300, p. 229.

[17] The daughters of Lord Leslie by his first marriage (i, L. 23 n. 69): Henrietta
Anne (1790–1819), Amelia (1791–1817), and Mary (1793–1850).

[18] Lady Albinia Hobart (1759–1850), daughter of George Hobart (*c.* 1729–
1804), 3rd Earl of Buckinghamshire (1793). In 1784 she had married Richard
Cumberland (1760–94). According to the R.H.I., Windsor, she was Lady of the
Bedchamber to the younger Princesses from 24 July 1796 to 10 Oct. 1812.

General Goldsworthy & his sister, & Lady Rothes Daughter, Lady Harriet, & Mr. Keate.[19] Sir Lucas came to usher me in. The Princess breakfasted alone. I had some very pleasant chat with my old friends, the Goldsworthys, whom I was very glad to see. And, soon after, Lady Albina, who disappeared, returned, with the commands ¦ of the Princess that I should attend her—with my honoured little Rogue. I was most highly gratified indeed, &, at the same time, deeply touched by the interview. The sweet Princess—but just 15—was seated on a sofa, whence she could not rise but with the aid of her two physicians! yet looking most lovely, & with a sweetness of patience extremely affecting. She received me with all her wonted condescendsion —suffered me—invited me, rather, to embrace her, & kept me with her in soft & sweet discourse till Lady Albina whispered her it was time to admit Lady Rothes: who then entered, with Lady Harriet & the Miss Leslies. But, while we were yet quite alone, she said 'Now we are alone, my dear,—do tell me—let me ask you one question,—Are you writing any thing?—' She looked much disappointed when I answered in the nega- tive, & said 'But—is it true?—*upon your Honour?*—' & I was saved an answer which then grew embarrassing by the en- trances I have mentioned. Lady Rothes shewed Her R.H. your ballad, for, having thanked *you* for it through me in her hearing, I mentioned Her Majesty's graciousness in command- ing it at the Theatre. Lady Harriet then brought it in, & she read the words, to herself, but with evident pleasure. & gave it to General Goldsworthy, who had entered to bring her some papers. She was all indulgence to my Alex,—& again kissed him When she was removing, painfully lifted from her seat between Sir Lucas & Mr. Keate, she stopt to pay her Compli- ments & thanks to Lady Rothes with a dignity & self-command extremely striking: & then, turning her head towards me, said 'My dear Madame d'Arblay, I am very happy to have seen you again—' in a voice of softness I shall never forget. Nor will any who heard her. She is a sweet—sweet creature. & How in- finately good of the Queen—how gracious her permission!— She asked after Mons.r d'Arblay with the politest benevolence— shewed me a miniature picture[20] she had just received of *Miny*, as

[19] See i, L. 21 n. 20; iv, L. 292 n. 18.
[20] This miniature of Princess Mary (see also L. 300, p. 234) may have been that painted *c.* 1795 by Richard Cosway (Vitrine III. no. 148), according to Mr.

she calls princess Mary, & was all that imagination itself could paint — — — of beautiful kindness & condescendsion—that's not easy!—& *something beyond* for which I want a proper word.

Adieu, most dear Sir—ever your own
F. d'A.

My Mate's tender Respects—& true. |

[*continued on the margins of* p. 1]

The ⌐sweet P. A. charged me not to come to town till the Royal Family were there. But remember, most dear Sir, we wait your commands only, should you wish for us sooner.⌐

⌐Is there any truth in the report of News which reached Norbury Park yesterday ⟨of an attempt on⟩ Buonaparte? God grant it! We are inexpressibly enragé.⌐

299   West Humble, 28 December 1798

To Mrs. Broome

A.L.S. (Barrett, Eg. 3693, ff. 74–5b), 28 Dec. [17]98
Double sheet 4to   4 pp.   *pmks*   31 DE 98   31 DE 98   wafer
Addressed: Mrs. Broome, / Nº 12. Salisbury Place, / New Road, / Marybone
Endorsed by CBFB: Sister d'Arblay / Decʳ 1798

West Hamble,
Decʳ 28—98

You know what a vile unpunctual correspondent I am, my dearest Charlotte—so instead of talking of that, let me begin with thanking you most cordially for the happy feelings you give me for your dear self in what you say of your own situation. I am truly—truly rejoiced you are able to bestow them. *No one*, I am very sure, *no one* could more fervently desire them. And so give my love & compliments to Mr. Broome & tell him.

Kindly, too, I thank you for your most affectionate willingness to be again troubled with my commissions. I accept the offer frankly, & with the pleasure I always feel in owing any thing to my kind Charlotte—though not with pleasure *unmixt*, God knows, at this moment, from the reason which occasions my

Graham Reynolds, Keeper of the Department of Prints, Drawings and Paintings, the Victoria & Albert Museum.

changing my *creditors*.¹ If, therefore, any time from the *10ᵗʰ* of next month, you can see Mr. Mathias for my receipt, I shall be much ˡ obliged. I am wholly of your opinion that *'this parting & pairing off'* does not promise happiness to either Goers, or Stayers;—it has been a precipitate measure, &—but I will not enter upon a subject so painful to me as what forces my blame upon those I always wish & seek to love & defend.

Various causes have deferred our purposed visit to Chelsea & Greenwich & Salisbury Place:² they are too long & entangled for a Letter, but I will explain them all when we meet. How kind you & Mr. B[roome] have been in your prescriptions for my Mate: but he has no courage to attack mercury, however qualified, or *quantified*. He is, besides, except a cold that he has caught within these 2 days, in very perfect health. So is my little Man, & enchanted when I talk to him of his *destined* visit to his 3 Cousins. He has conceived a respect for Clement, since he has heard of his man's attire, that would much please the little Scholar had I leisure to recount ˡ particulars. How extremely—how elegantly pretty is the acrostic on my dear little Charlotte! And I think it as well as hope it *literally*, not *poetically* true. I really never saw an Acrostic in which the initial limits were so free from forcing false praise, or omitting true. You will be sure of my joy at the Chelsea intercourse.³ And I am very glad all goes so well upon the Children's affairs with Mr. B.'s new arrangements, as well as that Miss Morton continues so high in your esteem & regard.⁴ I think that, indeed, an essential part of your happiness, because connected with the accomplishing your tenderest duties. Your Godson is completely prosperous, in all ways, at this period, & just 4 years old,—an epoch which he regards as the height of human bliss & ambition, since its arrival was kept by a Goose & plumb cake: & he very gravely, & very fondly, said 'I hope my Papa will be 4 years old, too, now!' He enquires after every body's age, now, & hears with pity, if not contempt, any number of years either more or less

299. ¹ The flight of JB and SHB.

² CBFB's address (above).

³ According to an account of a Sunday dinner at Chelsea on 23 Oct. (Maria Rishton to FBA, 3–[25] Oct., Eg. 3697, ff. 284–5b), CB had by that time brought himself to receive Broome at Chelsea: 'all went off very well tho' Broome is an *Odious tedious* Companion and will never suit the Dʳ.'

⁴ CBFB's account of the new arrangements is not extant, but Elizabeth Morton (iii, L. 212 n. 4), the governess, was to be retained.

than 4. He is excessively impatient for his manly apparel, & thinks rather meanly of me for ⟨not⟩ exhibiting in it. 'When shall you be big enough, mama, he says, to wear breeches & spatterdashes?' | Such accoutrement, indeed, so exclusively fulfils all his ideas of what is desirable, that when Mlle de Chavagnac, a young lady of 3 years old now at Norbury park, sent him a little Paper of Plumbs, & I asked what he would send her in return, he answered 'I will send her some breeches & spatterdashes—when I have got some.—'

I have most melancholy Letters from Ireland, where our beloved sister has been very unwell—*ill*, rather, but assures me she is recovered. God preserve her!—& God bless my dearest Charlotte—in her so far happier lot—long & long—most affectionately,

> & ever faithfully
> hers is
> F d'A.

M. d'A.'s most kind remembrances. Distribute for us both Love & warm wishes. I am much pleased you are so near Beaumont Street. All Miss [Cam]bridge's Letters lament your depar[ture fro]m Richmond.

300   [West Humble, December 1798]

To Mrs. Phillips

A.J. unfinished (Diary MSS. vi. 5134–42, Berg) for December 1798, including copies of FBA's correspondence with Miss Planta and Lady Rothes
One double sheet (9·4 × 7·6″) and a double and a single sheet (9·8 × 7·8″) numbered respectively 1, 2, 3   9 pp.
Edited by FBA, p. 5 (5138), *top margin, annotated*: Finale of 98
p. 9 (5142), *top margin, annotated*: Finale—98
Edited also by CFBt *and the* Press, *see* Textual Notes.

Finale of 1798

And now, my beloved Susan, I will sketch—from the memorandums I always keep when absent from you—my last Court history of this year.

The Princess Amelia, who had been extremely ill since my last Royal admittance, of some complaint in her knee which caused spasms the most dreadfully painful, was now returning from her sea bathing at Worthing, & I heard, from all around the Neighbourhood, that Her Royal Highness was to rest & stop one night at Juniper Hall, whither she was to be attended by Mr. Keate the surgeon, and by sir Lucas Pepys, who was her physician at Worthing.[1]

I could not hear of her approaching so near our habitation, & sleeping within sight of us, & be contented without an effort to see her; yet I would not distress Lady Rothes by an application she would not know how either to refuse or grant, from the established etiquette of bringing no one into the presence of their Royal Highnesses but by the Queen's permission. So infinitely sweet, however, that young Love of a Princess always is to me, that I gathered courage to address a petition to Her Majesty herself,—through the medium of Miss Planta—for leave to pay my homage.—I will Copy my Answer, sent by return of Post.[2]

My dear Friend,

I have infinite pleasure in acquainting you that The Queen has ordered me to say that you have Her leave to see dear Princess Amelia, provided Sir Lucas Pepys & Mr. Keate permit it.

&c &c &c |

With so complete & honourable a credential, which I received most gratefully, I now scrupled not to address a few lines to Lady Rothes, telling her my authority, to prevent any embarrassment, for entreating her leave to pay my devoirs to the young Princess on Saturday Morning.[3] The Friday I imagined she would arrive too fatigued to be seen. I intimated also my wish to bring my Boy,—not to be presented unless demanded, but to be put into some Closet where he might be at hand in case of that honour. The sweet Princesse's excessive graciousness to him gave me courage for this request. Lady Rothes sent me this answer—[4]

300. [1] The Princess, having gone to Worthing 30 July, was to return to London on 1 Dec. See also L. 292 n. 18. Lady Rothes lived at Juniper Hill, however, not Juniper Hall.
  [2] The original is missing.   [3] Saturday morning 1 Dec.
  [4] The original, later dated by FBA '28 Nov.—98', is preserved in the Scrapbook (Berg), 'Fanny d'Arblay and friends. England. 1759–1799', p. 50.

Dear Madam,

Your Note prevented mine. I had written to you to say that I thought you & your Son would like to see my Royal Visitor. She leaves Juniper on Saturday at twelve. As I know Her Royal Highness will be happy to see you & yours, I think you had better come by Ten, if you please, & Breakfast here. My little Girls must be presented: they, too, will be in waiting, & your Boy may flirt with them.

Ever yours, dear Madam
Sincerely,
Rothes.

This kind Note made me perfectly comfortable; though I was surprised she had ventured to intend summoning me without a licence. But she told me, afterwards, she had been informed, | by Sir Lucas, that the Princess had enquired so much of how near I was to Juniper Hall, & whether she could see my house from the road, that he had judged such a measure would please her. How gratifying! The *little Girls* Lady Rothes meant are her Grand Children, the Daughters of Lord Leslie by his marriage with Miss Pelham.[5]

It was the First of December—but a beautifully clear & fine day. I borrowed Mr. Locke's Carriage. We were shewn into a small Parlour, by a whispering Man out of Livery, who seemed so impressed with Royal AWE, that not only he could hardly be heard speak, but hardly be thought to have anything heavier to drag about than a paper Machine for his body, so lightly on tip toe he skimmed the floor. Her Royal Highness, he said, was at Breakfast in her own Drawing Room, & had yet admitted only her own Attendants.

Sir Lucas came to us immediately, & ushered us to the Breakfast Parlour, giving me the most chearing accounts of the recovery of the Princess. Here I was received by Lady Rothes, who presented me to Lady Albinia Cumberland, widow of Cumberland, the Author's, only son, & one of the Ladies of the Princesses.[6] I found her a peculiarly pleasing woman, in voice, manner, look, & behaviour. |

This introduction over, I had the pleasure to shake hands with Miss Goldsworthy,[7] whom I was very glad to see, & who

---

[5] Lady Rothes's grandchildren, aged 8, 7, and 5 (L. 298 n. 17).
[6] See L. 298 n. 18. [7] See i, L. 5 n. 10; see also *HFB*, pp. 256–9.

was very cordial & kind,—but who is become, alas! so dreadfully deaf, there is no conversing with her but by talking for a whole house to hear every word! With this infirmity, however, she is still in her first youth & brightness, compared with her Brother—who, though I knew him of the party, is so dreadfully altered, that I with difficulty could venture to speak to him by the name of General Goldsworthy.[7] He has had 3 or 4 more strokes of apoplexy since I saw him, & has lost his front teeth, & his mouth is drawn a little awry. When I thought of lovely Marianne Port — & her unaccountable desire to belong to him—how I rejoiced she was saved a trial for which I believe her fortitude so unequal as that so great a change in him would have caused her! She still, however, in all her Letters, speaks of him with a tone of regret that assures me she writes his name with a Sigh! 'Tis a strange infatuation—but infatuations in the purlieus of Cupid are endless.—

I fancy he had a strong consciousness of his alteration, for he seemed embarrassed & shy, & only bowed to me, at first, without speaking. ⎸ But I wore that off afterwards, by chatting over old stories with him. Mr. Keate the surgeon[8] was also there,—but silent & formal; Lady Harriet Leslie alone was added. She is very modest & quiet, & brought up not to speak unaddressed. Lady Rothes was absorbed in anxious cares about her Royal Guest; Sir Lucas was happy in the honour his house received, but too much occupied by it for general conversation. Lady Albina seemed only observant of the last new Comers,—Mr. Keate was ill at his ease & stiff;—& the General quite silent. I, on the contrary, was so charmed with having permission to wait upon the sweet Princess, that I was highly in spirits, & attacked poor deaf Miss Goldsworthy, & relieved the general distance & reserve by pouring into her Ear my enquiries about her Royal Highness, & messages of humble thanks to the Queen for the graciousness of granting my petition. My Boy was silent & still,—but looked well, & was much admired.

The Princess Breakfasted alone, attended by Mrs. Cheveley.[9] When this general Breakfast was over, Lady Albinia retired. But in a very few minutes she returned—&, to my infinite

---

[8] See L. 292 n. 18.   [9] See L. 255 n. 1.

delight, though surprise, said 'Her Royal Highness desires to see Madame d'Arblay, & her little Boy.'

My surprise, you will believe, was only that I was summoned ⎮ before Lady Rothes had been admitted; not that she would see me—& certainly I did not feel the surprise singly! I saw it general—& could only hope that her dear impatience to see me first would create no ill will, in consideration of my being known to her from the time she was 3 years old.[10] That my Child was called too, before the little Miss Leslies were admitted, they must attribute to the same cause, & love her for being so natural in so high a station.

The dear Princess was seated on a sofa, in a French Grey riding Dress, with pink lapels, her beautiful & richly flowing & shining fair locks unornamented. Her Breakfast was still before her, & Mrs. Cheveley, in waiting. Lady Albina announced me—& she received me with the brightest smile, calling me up to her, & stopping my profound reverence—by pouting out her sweet ruby lips for me to kiss. I am sure I cannot wonder if Lady Albina was astonished at this affectionate condescendsion, for it was totally unexpected, & gratefully touching, to myself.

She desired me to come & sit by her; but ashamed of so much indulgence, I seemed not to hear her, & drew a Chair at a little distance. 'No, no, she cried, nodding, come here—come & sit by me here, my dear Madame d'Arblay—' I had then only to say 'twas my duty to obey her, & I seated myself on her Sofa. Lady Albinia, whom she motioned to sit, took an opposite Chair, & Mrs. Cheveley, after we had spoken a few words together, retired. ⎮

Her attention now was bestowed upon my Alex,—who required not quite so much solicitation to take his part of the Sofa. He came jumping & skipping up to Her Royal Highness, with such gay & merry antics, that it was impossible not to be diverted with so sudden a change from his composed & quiet behaviour in the other room. He seemed enchanted to see her again, & I was only alarmed lest he should skip upon her poor knee in his carressing agility. She was all smiles & sweetness with him, though I feared his spirits might be overpowering,

[10] Since July 1786, when FB first went to Court as Keeper of the Robes (*DL* ii. 403).

after her long confinement & illness. But she would not suffer me to talk of taking him away,—& when I told her how comically he had been smitten with her, & talked of her even after our return to West Hamble, she was much amused, & gave him whatever remained of her Breakfast that she thought likely to please him. I even ventured to repeat to her his speech —which I believe I wrote to you, of 'Princess Amelia gave me such a SOFT Kiss! like *Amene's!*' She laughed, & bowing forward her head, while she held out her graceful hand & arm, sweetly said 'I'll give him another! Come, Alexander!'—The little Rogue very readily obeyed, & immediately returned the 'SOFT KISS' he received. |

I bid him in vain, however, repeat Ariel's 'Come unto these yellow Sands—'[11] which he can say very prettily,—he began, & the Princess, who knew it, prompted him to go on; but a fit of shame came suddenly across him—or of capriciousness—& he would not continue.

She asked with the kindest condescension after M. d'Arblay, & said ' I do think I saw him in Norbury Park, (She had driven through the low park, of which Mr. Locke had sent the key to her attendants, in her first journey to Worthing) sitting under a Tree.—Did I?—I hope I did!—'

I was sorry to answer no,—& Alex, listening, called out 'Papa lives at West Humble!' as if to *correct* her idea of seeing him in Norbury Park! Lady Albina took much notice of the little Man, & endeavoured to allure him to embrace & play with her: but he flew her, & would only come to the Princess, or jump & caper from one end of the Room to the other.

Lady Albinia soon after left the Room: & the Princess, then, turning hastily & eagerly to me, said 'Now we are alone,—do let me ask you one question, Madame d'Arblay,—Are you— are you—(looking with strong expression to discover her answer) writing any thing?' |

I could not help laughing, but replied in the negative.

'Upon your Honour?' she cried, earnestly,—And looking disappointed! This was too hard an interrogatory for evasion— & I was forced to say—the truth,—That I was about nothing I had yet fixed if or not I should ever finish, but that I was rarely without some project.—This seemed to satisfy, & to

[11] *The Tempest*, I. ii. 375–87.

please her; & she smiled, & nodded, with a look that said O, then, something will yet come out!—

I told her of my having seen the Duke of Clarence at Leatherhead Fair—'What, William?' she cried, surprised. This unaffected, natural way of naming her Brothers & Sisters is infinitely pleasing—She took a Miniature from her pocket, & said 'I must shew you *Miney's* picture,—'¹² meaning Princess Mary, whom she still calls *Miney*, because it was the name she gave her when unable to pronounce Mary. A time she knew I well remembered. It was a very sweet miniature, & extremely like her Royal Highness. 'Ah! what happiness, I cried, your Royal Highness will feel—& give—upon returning to their Majesties & their Royal Highnesses!—after such an absence, & such sufferings!—' 'O!—Yes!—I shall be so glad! she cried,

[*The next page, p. 10, is blank. The conclusion of the journal is missing, cf. L. 314 n. 1.*]

301   West Humble, 4 January [1799]

To Doctor Burney

A.L. (rejected Diary MSS. 5152-[3], Berg), 4 Jan.
Originally a double sheet 4to, of which FBA later discarded the second leaf 2 pp.
Edited by FBA, p. 1 (5152), *annotated and dated*: ⁖ -99   (I) West Hamble Life of *Gay*   Frugality perhaps unexampled in real Life
Edited also by CFBt *and the* Press, *see* Textual Notes.

West Hamble,
Janʸ 4ᵗʰ

The sweet kindness of this invitation, my dearest—dearest Father, would have nearly made us set off as rapidly to your loved arms as if you had said you wanted us *instantly for YOUR-SELF*, had you not dropped that the two dear Girls were coming to you again. But as that is the case, & to read such a long load of schottff, we will only prepare to succeed them. As to our-

¹² Cf. L. 298 n. 20.

selves, we have no frights, never having even heard of the robbery, but this moment in your Letter.[1] So sequestered are our lives, that we only by accident know of any thing that goes forward. We think ourselves, too, quite safe, from our notorious paucity of possession. We never keep money in the house; we pay our bill quarterly, as soon as we receive it; & only keep current cash for immediate necessaries. And we have no plate—(*except some dessert spoons & salt-sellers*) which makes the greatest temptation to robbers. M. d'A. is seen working all day without a Servant or Gardener, & our style of life, & ⌐ our income are pretty publicly known. What, therefore, is there to attract such Gentry? Do not be uneasy for us, dearest Sir,— M. d'A., nevertheless, will get a blunderbuss, or *some such thing*, in consequence of your information. He is now nursing a very severe cold, caught by working ⌐with extreme imprudence in the cold of the Evening at⌐ covering plants on Christmas Eve! ⌐He has kept his room since then, though most reluctantly, till within the half hour that he has ⟨walked⟩ out again.⌐ I am sure he would be much safer in Chelsea! for the sight of his Garden, when he cannot work in it, is a constant suffering to him.

⌐It was the Fugitives, my most dear Padre, not the E[xpense] that led us to postpone our visit, for I thought, *till now*, there was something rather reserved in your desire of our coming, & that you thought, like me, they had better be removed to their destination, wherever that might be, before our arrival. But the words of welcome in this morning's⌐[2]

[*the second leaf is missing*]

301. [1] On reading in the *True Briton* (3 Jan. 1799) of the 'daring & premeditated' robbery on Friday last of 'the beautiful Mansion' called Lonesome, near Dorking, CB had seized his pen 'in a fright' to urge the d'Arblays to come to Chelsea. 'Five Horsemen [had been] seen early on Saturday morning, near the spot, returning with great speed towards London.'

[2] 'Don't write but *come*', CB had written in his letter (Berg) of 3 Jan. 'You never can be more welcome, or minister more comfort to me than now' and these were the words (see L. 304, p. 243) that persuaded the d'Arblays to make an immediate visit to Chelsea.

Conjointly with M. d'Arblay
  and Charles Burney
To Esther (Burney) Burney

A.L.S. & A.L.S. & PS. signed (Berg), Feb. 1799 [*dated in hand of* CB Jr:]
Greenwich, Feb. 1799
    Double sheet 4to 4 pp. *pmks* P.P.U. Greenwich 18 FE 99 wafer
    Addressed: Mrs. Burney, / Beaumont Street, / Devonshire Place.

Greenwich

Feb, 1799

What!—a *Letter* to thank for too?¹—& how sweet a one—
My dear & most kind sister how many thanks had I mentally
written before!—& lately as we have left you, with what joy
would we *bonnement* accept your invitation for tomorrow were it
possible!—for to be with *YOU*, & *yours*, is not the way to get
tired of so being. However, the *decency* of the thing put aside in
regard to our short sejour here, we are not *movable* from my still
encreesed cold. My hoarseness now would do to frighten the
Dragon of Wantley.² M. d'A. thank Heaven is not worse, nor
Alex, — — but I was fain to nurse till half past two this fore-
noon.

Pray say all that you can suggest of Acknowledgements to
M. & Mᵉ de Sᵗ Marie³ for their polite & kind invitation. Your
sample on Wednesday redoubles my natural *goust* for such
chosen individuals of the most amiable—unhappy—& injured
people breathing. I wish you had seen that sweet Mᵉ du chattel⁴
—I wish not to *see*, but to *know* her now, & that it were possible
it could be intimately. I thank You a thousand times for pre-
vailing with her to come, & you must thank her in *my* name as

302. ¹ The d'Arblay family after a visit to Chelsea (*c.* 5–31 Jan.) had visited Esther
for ten days (1–10 Feb.) or (8–18 Feb.) and were now with Charles at Greenwich.
See Ll. 303, 304.
    ² See the ballad in Percy's *Reliques* (1823), iv. 200:'. . . For from his nose a smoke
arose, / And with it burning snivel; / Which he cast off, when he did cough. . . .'
    ³ Among the *émigrés* to whom EBB introduced the d'Arblays was Jean-Jacques-
René, marquis de Sainte-Marie (b. 1730), seigneur d'Agneaux, who had married
in 1774 Louise-Françoise de Pestalozzy. *AN* (1860), p. 221, lists three sons, one of
whom was guillotined, but no daughters.
    ⁴ Spelled variously du Chattel, Du Chatel (see L. 296, n. 5).

well as your own for suffering me to engross her. What sweet things she said of my dearest Etty!—I shall write them all to our Susan, who will doubly enjoy them, from delight that such a character has fallen into the way of your consolation. If you can write to that most beloved while we stay here, send me a pacquet by the penny post. However thick, it will depart as soon as I hear from her again, which I I hope will be very soon. —How gratifying to me is your kindness to my little Boy! Indeed the dear Child was taken *with a love of you* in yourself & your dear Mate & Children. *'I want 'em ALL*, as he expressively said, *I Want 'em ALL together*. So do I!—& had I but accommodations in my dear Hermitage, what exquisite delight should I have in embracing you there! — — you have promised, however, to try an *august/2/*, or *July/1/* repose there[5]—& then, if you *had* Curtains—you could undraw them—& if you *had* tapestried rooms, wish them bare walls—thus we shall be perfect from our very imperfections. And my kind—affectionate Marianne promises to sleep by your side, as Fanny did by our Susan's.—But Mr Burney—we must give him another sofa bed in M. d'A.'s little dressing room; for We shall all be discontented if that dear & excellent soul does not bring you. our lonely, though beautiful walks, will only tantalize you without him, so much you will feel how he would like such rambles. And dear Sophy we must hope for in the next *batch*. Amelia *ought* to come in the first,—but we have only one crib!—& she is too big even for that. what can we do? for she must by no means be left out. Perhaps make two parties, & have her with you & Mr. B[urney] & Marianne & Sophy together next. Settle the *how* as you can, my dearest Hetty, but settle it so that the two warm months may be sure to bring us the gratification which I none of our deficiencies shall rob us of enjoying. yet they are such as make me blush in the midst of my solicitation. But you well know *where* there is *NO* deficiency, & there alone must look for your comfort & feel your welcome—in our Hearts.

I am sure my Boy may be included—we dare not now talk of any of you in his hearing, for we have no way to keep of *rudeness* but by *forgetfulness*, therefore we divert his thoughts into other channels. How you can speak with regret that our visit is over, wretches as we were with our obstinate colds all the time,

5 EBB was to make a visit to West Humble in August (see L. 329, p. 317).

is '*a surprising* — ' never ready for breakfast—& lolloping & sniveling all day long! the dear kind Girls relinquishing their warm room for the attics with so good a grace, though in the midst of the snow & frost!—I don't know what to say to you all —so I shall beg M. d'A. to finish.—

God bless you, my dearest Esther—give my kindest Love & thanks to my dear Mr. Burney, & my dear Girls, & take them most cordially & truly from your ever affectionate

F. d'A.

I hardly know how to end for all I have done—& am called off—poor Mrs. B[urney] is far from well—Charles all warmth & cordiality. Little Charles an excellent Boy.

[*By M. d'Arblay*]

Je vous dirai moi, en francais qu'en depit des taxes de Mr Pitt qui ne se doute pas du tort qu'il fait aux marchands de papier[6] avec le quel je comptois couvrir partie de nos murailles, vous serez parfaitement dans notre chaumiere avec quelques matelats mis à coté les uns des autres, et vos repas pris sur l'herbe et à l'ombre dans le bois qui couvre notre habitation. J'espère que nos poules ne nous laisseront pas manquer d'oeufs; et pour ma part je me charge de vous fournir bon nombre d'aspèrges et d'artichoux. Vous voyez que d'après tout cela, il n'est pas douteux que la reception qui vous | attend sera des plus brillantes — Voulez vous bien, chere soeur, vous charger auprès de Madame la Marquise de Ste Marie de nos remercie-mens et du regret sincere que nous eprouvons egalement d'avoir manqué l'occasion de faire connaissance avec elle et d'entendre Mademoiselle sa fille dont le talent prodigieux pour son Âge n'est connu de Mad^e d'Ar—que par ce que vous et moi lui en avons dit. Quelle sourire de jouissances pour sa charmante mère que l'admiration que ce talent excite generalement surtout quand elle se dit qu'il est l'unique fruit de ses soins, et qu'elle voit sa fille être la seule que semble ignorer à quel point le succès les a couronnès. Voulez vous bien aussi presenter mes respects à Monsieur de Ste Marie.

Adieu, ma trés aimable soeur, mille et mille tendres compli-mens à mes nice nieces & their Father — Ne m'oubliez pas je vous prie quand vous verrez la famille Du Chatel[7] — et Faites

6 See iii, L. 173 n. 4; and *AR* xxxvi (1794), 211-12.   7 See L. 296 n. 5.

agreer mes hommages à l'Excellente mère ainsi que mes complimens aux enfans etc the same to Mr Caquery[8] & my respectful admiration to *Miss frye* & her sister[9]

Y. d'Ar — —

[*By Charles Burney*]

Pray send me, if known, Mr Burnside's[10] address.

CB

303   West Humble, [8] March [1799]

To Doctor Burney

A.L., incomplete, the first leaf only (Berg), Mar.

Originally a double sheet 4to, of which FBA later discarded the second leaf   2 pp.

Edited by FBA, p. 1, *annotated and dated*: ※ 9^*th* 99   (2) after a dear Chelsea ⌜& Greenwich⌝ visit.

west Hamble, March
Friday—

It would have made me blush to have received your Letter before I wrote, my kindest Padre, had I deferred writing but from cruel causes—You know we flew Greenwich from the Measles—& the 2d. day after our return,[1] my alex was taken extremely ill—we concluded the infection had seized him, & prepared ourselves for the Malady—but though an eruption appeared, its symptoms were of a different sort, & held us some

---

[8] Cf. L. 310, p. 266. He probably belonged to the large Royalist family of the DeCacquerays, many of whom fought in the army of the princes or the *émigré* regiments. See Henri Jougla de Morenas, *Grand Armorial de France* (6 vols., 1934), ii. 303.

[9] Sarah (*c.* 1775–1844) and Mary (d. 22 Jan. 1806) were daughters of John Ravel Frye (d. 26 June 1799) of Wimpole Street and his wife Sarah *née* Pott (d. *pre* 1803), the eldest daughter of the surgeon Percival Pott (1714–88). See *DNB*. Mary, described by SBP (Journals of April 1789, Eg. 3692, ff. 14–15) as 'one of Mr. Burney's best pupils', was to marry in 1803 Henry Charles Lichfield (*c.* 1756–1822), 'Soliciter to his Majesty's Treasury' and a Bencher of the Inner Temple (see *GM* xcii. 380).

[10] Robert Burnside (1759–1826), M.A. (Aberdeen, 1780), was one of CB Jr.'s early friends and correspondents (see *Catalogue* and *DNB*).

303. [1] *c.* 27 February.

days in constant suspence, when his fever encreased so alarmingly, that it was literally impossible to count his rapid pulse—& his skin burnt like fire—with a total disgust even to the sight of a Cake or bon bon—Ill he was indeed!—we then sent for Mr. Ansel from Dorking,[2] who said he had no Measles, but the Chicken Pox,—the fever, | however, was so violent & so far beyond what so trifling a disorder generally gives, that Mr. Ansel & ourselves conclude a Worm Fever—to which you may remember his hereditary right—was at the same time operating. Since then he has had the Nettle rash,—but began, 4 days ago, to amend, & with a speed equal, nearly, to his seizure,—for already his appetite is more than returned, & his strength, which had frightfully failed him, comes back hourly. He is not yet well enough to quit his room, but we think he will be able as soon as soon as the the 2d. winter yields to milder weather. He has still a Cough that requires regimen & great care, for his week's fasting, has emaciated him till Mr. Lock is fatter! I bless God every moment to see him as he is! A Child's illness is so fearful!—][3]

304   West Humble, 12 March 1799

To Mrs. Phillips

A.L. (Berg), 12 Mar. 1799, including copies of FBA's correspondence with JB
Three double sheets 4to   12 pp.   numbered 2 and 3
Addressed: Mrs. Phillips, / Belcotton, / Drogheda.
Annotated by SBP, p. 12: about brother James & S.
Docketed by FBA, pp. 5, *and* 9: March —99.

West Hamble—*dear* West Hamble
March 12. 1799.

The first Pen I take after a lingering & most anxious Nursing my two Alexanders ever since the 2ᵈ Day of our return to our peaceful abode is to speak to & open my Heart to my dearest loved of loved sisters—I am truly grieved our Mrs. Locke sent

2 See i, L. 6 n. 4.
3 The text in square brackets FBA probably copied from the top of the second leaf, which in her editorial capacity she discarded.

off a pacquet during my inability—had I known such was her determination, I would have written two words at all hazards: & 2 days after it was gone, came this pacquet from our Esther— truly provoking!—yet I have not dared hint at the chagrin it occasioned me, as the sweet Creature who did it was impelled by the tenderest motive to my Susan, the fear of her uneasiness at the lengthened silence. I must press her, however, this time, to relinquish our general discretion with Mr. Windham, & hasten off a second pacquet this Week.—I must set aside all general Journal, this Hettina Letter taking so much room—&, indeed, my thoughts being too much occupied by one subject for the power of recollecting & combining any other till that one is spent,—for sad as it is, I well know my Susan is more interested about it than about any other in the world—so, till my two irreproachables were ill, was I!—but that, & some events I have to relate, have much blunted now the exquisite sort of sensation & pain it gave me a few weeks since, when it absorbed almost all my faculties as well as comforts. — —

But first—ere this swallowing Gulph takes the rest of my paper, let me answer my dearest Susan's Letter—Letters,[1] rather, for my last from Chelsea was so hurried I know not what it either mentioned or omitted.—Ah my loved Susan!— I find you have been repeatedly ill—I gather it more through Esther than by yourself—How I dread the shatter to your delicate frame of reiterated attacks, however lightly you state them!—God almighty preserve & support you, my most loved soul!—I fear distressing you by my own repetitions upon this theme—yet I never can ꞁ hear of your illness, & forbear re- urging our agreement, & reminding you how wretched I should be if I did not build upon your strict adherence to it. Say something again upon this, when you write, I beseech. I always want new assurances from knowing your dangerous manner of thinking too lightly of your bodily evils.

And now take our warmest thanks for your kind promise that if any thing within *Your 100* would be convenient to forward the

304. [1] Besides a letter (Berg) of 5–12 Jan. (printed in *FB & the Burneys*, pp. 293– 301), there survives of SBP's letters of the early months of this year only a cutting (3·1 × 7·8″), written in March, which, being primarily a comment on JB & SBP, may be one of the '*cuttings*' recommended by FBA as a private means of communi- cation on that subject (see Ll. 297, p. 213; 329, p. 316). A second 'cutting' in which the Major had apparently expressed sympathy for CB is missing.

blessing of your return, we shall have the preference. on this we build—& *next Month* conceive hopes our wishes may be gratified—for surely APRIL is SPRING? What you tell me of the Major's just indignation at a late event, & his kind disposition towards my dear injured Father gave me great satisfaction—& opens a prospect the MOST sweet to me of any I can view. May you but be able to clear—& to realise it, my own Susan!—How anxiously will this idea rest upon me till your next!—

I know not if I have ever told you—what a million of times I have thought over, your cruel—useless anguish at the barbarous post mistake[2] upon dear Norbury's quitting you? but I have felt for few things more, the precarious state of all Ireland at the time considered, & the species of conjectures & fears so impossible to name—or to avoid. Always say what you have time for of that dear lovely Boy—& my ever dear Fanny,—The last account of *Willy* is charming.[3] His *naiveté* & good humour & honesty & fun all amused us extremely. And nobody relates Children's prattle so well as my Susan. You will remember, too, how much you have interested me for J[aney] P[aney] & let me hear if you are easy about her at Naas.[4] I fear for all Ireland while the Union is suspended, — is Drogheda still quite tranquil? And do you know any thing of Mrs. Hill?[5]—But nothing quite so much, & so constantly excites my solicitude as to know how the climate agrees with you. Your late accounts, in defiance of your illness, are rather chearing. May they continue so!—Your kind wishes of seeing & watching my alex in his gradations to boyhood are very touching to me—you must be very quick now—for next summer I am menaced with his leaving off his Lady-like attire.—How beautiful is Norbury's discrination ˡ of the beauty of our Mrs. Locke & Amelia, & the wisdom & goodness of Mr. Locke & our Father! 'tis just the very boy of Protocol.[6]—*C'est tout dire.*

---

[2] Constantly alluded to in Irish correspondence of these years were the worries and vexations accessory to robberies and delays of the post (e.g., *FB & the Burneys*, pp. 296; and SBP to FBA, 28 Apr. 1799, Berg).

[3] In her letter of 5–12 Jan., op. cit., SBP had given 'some traits of this little person—who is an original—& if his Papa did not spoil him wᵈ be—not *all* I cᵈ wish—but a great deal nearer it—'. And there follow several pages of direct conversation bringing very much to life not only the child but his father and the allegiances and relationships within the family.

[4] Naas, about twenty miles from Dublin, was the scene of a violent outbreak on 23–4 May, see W. H. Maxwell, *History of the Irish Rebellion in 1798*...(1845), pp. 71–3.

[5] See iii, L. 216 n. 3.   [6] Norbury's imaginary island (i, L. 23 n.2).

These dearest Letters will swallow all my time if I suffer this new side to look any longer into them—I will now, therefore, go at once into a history which I will mix with no other—to what other, indeed, can it belong?—

I believe I have told you that my extreme repugnance to see these poor fugitives—to meet *J*—upon such new terms as seeing him in mere compassion—& duty!—occasioned our deferring our Chelsea visit to the last moment the delay was possible. Indeed, I wished them, also, to see how far were all the family from alert to take Sally's place,—& to let the continued vacancy prompt some effort to return.—But, at length, my dearest Father plumply wrote word We could never come at a time when we could administer him more comfort![7]—these words—& a Chaise for us & our goods were seen & ordered in the same minute. Yet my best ami was far from recovered from a desperate cold, caught, as usual, by Gardening imprudence. I shall omit all for another opportunity & relation that belongs to aught else but poor James & Sarah. M. d'A. & I were both of opinion we could not be in town, & not offer to see them,— though I felt half dead with the very idea of meeting his Eyes— &, unavoidably, finding my own sink under them, & my hand, that used so heartily to come forth for the mutual grasp, find itself inevitably passive & all but shrinking from his touch!— The first impulse of the kind heart of M. d'A. was to call upon James himself,—but upon deliberation he relinquished it, as it really appeared to me a respect publicly due to my Father that we should not visit them from his HOUSE, unless we could either obtain his sanction, or see in themselves some disposition to being received by Him again. I frequently started the subject, at first,—but found it would not bear discussion. It not only caused immediate change of countenance, but a mixture of gloom & agitation rested on his spirits the rest of the day, | & I always found that his night afterwards had suffered from it. If I persevered, in the hopes of leading to something satisfactory, he cut me short himself, with much displeased emotion, saying 'For God's sake don't let us talk upon this subject!— ' It appeared forcibly to me, by all I could gather, that though he gave no injunction, he expected, even involuntarily, that we

---

7 This was CB's invitation of 3 Jan. 1799 (see L. 301 n. 2).

could not visit those who fled him while under his roof. And this, afterwards, I brought to proof. We settled, therefore, to propose seeing them at Hetty's, where we hoped a Young party, & a little Music, might take off from the terror of the first interview—for indeed it was upon my spirits with mingled horrour & fright—horrour for my own changed feelings—& fright lest by betraying them I should offend the very persons I forced myself to see merely *not* to offend—for from Their sight —happiness & pleasure are flown for ME!—& only by a view or belief of their contrition can return — — And then—& I feel, even now, my love of my still always dear James would soon bring back all my blighted affection. — —

When we saw, & consulted with Hetty, she most kindly & considerately proposed, before I could ask her, this very meeting under her roof. So, afterwards, did good Charlotte, both completely conceiving that, in the present state of things, we could not with propriety see them elsewhere. To visit them at their own lodgings, unpressed, uninvited by themselves, would have been sanctioning their conduct—not only in their flight from our Father, but the subsequent & most unnatural insensibility with which they have forborn to palliate that measure by any conciliatory attempts to be restored to any intercourse with their Family—a family they have deserted & disgraced!— This passed with | Hetty the day or two after our arrival at Chelsea: & the day following the arrangement, I received, sent round from West Hamble, a Letter from James himself. I will Copy it.[8]

Jany 16. 1799

Dear Sister,

The enclosed receipt for the legacy should be signed by Mr. d'Arblay & yourself. Mr. Gleadhill[9] has wanted it, as there is a limitted time so be so good to send it soon. Within the receipt is your quarterly receipt from Mr. Mathias's office. They think the Money will be payable some time next week. I tried, but could not procure a frank. I hope you will escape for double postage. My kindest love to Mr d'Arblay. Martin is with me, & desires his love to Alexander the little,

---

[8] JB's letter is not otherwise extant.
[9] Richard Gleadhill (d. Aug. 1807), an attorney, of 11 Lothbury and New Grove, Mile End (*Holden's Triennial Directory 1805–7*). The legacy is not elsewhere mentioned.

& Alexander the great—but for fear of mistakes he tells me
to say not of Macedon.

Your ever affec^{te.} Brother
J^s Burney

Please to direct to me N° 21.
John Street near Fitzroy Square.

This little note gave me real pleasure, for I thought it shewed
a desire to renew the intercourse which his declining to be even
my agent with Mr. Mathias, though he continued in town,
seemed completely to break. My whole wish & sole remaining
hope for him was to be authorised by himself to bring about a
sufficient reconciliation to enable them both to see my dear
Father again: & if once they visited at Chelsea, no part of the
family need hesitate as to the propriety of seeing them even
upon their own terms & own grounds. Nor should *I*, even if it
were *refused* them—all that to ME is so unconquerably repugnant is that it *rests with themselves*—or at least they have reason
to believe so, since they have made no offer, & received no
rebuff whatever. |

I wrote therefore immediately the following answer—which
I first put upon my tablets,[10] from the difficulty I now find to
express myself to him, & have kept there purposely to Copy for
You, well knowing the interest you will take in all that passes
between us at this period.

Dear James,

As I am now at Chelsea, I meant to have transacted for
this quarter my treasury business myself; but as your
voluntarily undertaking it once more seems to imply a desire
to put a period to an estrangement which a late event has
cruelly caused—I accept your kind assistance as usual, &
send back the receipt, & beg you to have the goodness to
enclose me the Notes, cut in halves, in two penny post
Letters—or perhaps you will call & leave them for me in
Beaumont Street.—This last circumstance disposes me to
believe you would not be sorry to see me again: Suppose we
meet at Hetty's? She has kindly proposed inviting you both
for that purpose some Evening to Tea. We shall spend a few
days at Mr. Burney's when our visit is over here, which will
last till the return of Mrs. Rishton from Hampshire. I will let
you know the time when I know it myself.

[10] For the erasable tablets, see ii, L. 68 n. 7.

Your Letter has but just followed me from West Hamble. I will send the paper to Mr. Gleadhill as soon as I can get it signed by 2 witnesses. I was very glad to see Martin on Sunday, who behaved perfectly well. M. d'A. sends his kind love.

⸺

Whether I signed or finished it more, I forget but certainly if any thing was added it was merely the *yours* &c— |

To this I received, a few days after, this answer.

Dear Fanny,

Your Letter has puzzled me a good deal, I should not have sent the receipt from Mr. Mathias's office, if I had known you were in town, or that you were soon expected. Mr. Gleadhill had applied to me several times for the legacy receipt, the last time I saw him very pressingly, which determined me to delay it no more, & having to send you one receipt by post, I thought it a matter of convenience to let the other accompany it.

The receipt you have sent I have left with Coutts people,[11] put to my own account. They, without further trouble, will get the money as it becomes payable at the office—. And I have placed to your account at Coutts 25£. which will be paid to yourself, or to your draft, whenever you call or send. Let me beg you to enclose Mr. Gleadhill immediately the Legacy receipt, by the penny post, as I am very apprehensive that, by the delay, there will be expence incurred at the Stamp office. Mr. Gleadhill's direction is Lothbury.

your ever affec^{te} brother

J. B.

⸺

You will easily believe I was much struck at having no sort of notice taken of my proposal of a meeting, or my touch upon the alacrity with which I seized his first offer of serving me, as a renewal of intercourse. It would be fruitless now to mention the various conjectures to which this gave birth: but as he seemed uneasy about the receipt, I sent it directly, with a few hasty words, telling him I had done so, & nothing else, save beginning | Dear James, & ending yrs ever ⸺ ⸺

---

[11] The bankers.

We could now only resolve to wait till our Chelsea visit ended before we took any other measures; but, mean time, to prevent any offence on my own part, I begged of Hetty & her Girls, should they happen to meet them, that they would mention my having expressed a desire of our spending an Evening alltogether as soon as I was able: & I told the same to Charlotte.

Soon after, Marianne & Sophy called upon them,—& were detained, almost by force, to dinner. They both told me they could never lift their Eyes up when speaking to Sally!—& feared she would see how little they could bear to look at her!— But Marianne said 'Mr. & Mrs. d'A. are coming soon to be with us, & then you'll come & meet them, won't you?—' Sally looked down, then, with a sort of smile they could not comprehend. Marianne added 'You will be glad to see Mrs d'Arblay at our house, sha'n't you?—'—But she neither raised her head, nor answered, except by this same smile.—!!! —When I heard it—I would, I cried, it had been a tear!—that better would have suited the sort of consciousness that might belong to her, & *must* belong, were she sensible of her situation.

Charlotte told me she, also, soon after, called upon them—for the first time: & said Marianne's speech to James. James made no answer—She concluded he would *be so glad I would see him*, she told me, that she imagined he had not heard her, & repeated 'You & Sally will come to meet them, at our house, won't you, for we expect them soon for some days.' 'O—you do?—' was all he said; &, much affronted, she determined not to ask them any more. |

These accounts, you will be sure, amazed & perplexed me.— But I must pass on from comments to facts. We left Chelsea after Dinner one Thursday,[12] & arrived to a very late Tea in Beaumont Street. I begged the invitation to be made immediately, & Hetty consented, & Marianne wrote to Sally— saying that we were but an hour come to the house & that her Mama, with her kind love, invited her & dear uncle J[ames] to dine with us the next day. She added many apologies that her Mama had not yet called, which she hoped Sally would excuse, from her colds, & the severe weather. Then put in *our* love to both, & finished.—To this note—so far more civil, as well as

[12] Apparently on Thursday 1 Feb.

kind, than Sally had any right ever more to expect while thus a willing fugitive from her Father & home, came an answer to this effect—

Dear Marianne.

My Brother James cannot come. He sends love to all. I have such a pain in my face (—. & then an account of a swelled gum, & bad weather, which made her fear a fall without an arm..

This was *all*. No *reason*, no *excuse* whatever from James!

& no *love*, no message whatever from herself! nor a word of regret from either, nor a hint of hoping any other meeting? — —

We stayed 10 days at Mr. Burney's—& heard of them no more, nor ever saw them!—That they had conscious feelings to make a meeting unpleasant, I could conceive, & easily enough pardon—but in a manner such as this to relinquish it!—!— However, Hetty's Letter finishes the history.[13] She has been so kind as to send it me open to forward, & you will see, there— *It is James* | *who complains*! it is *he* who is entitled to display resentment!—alas—poor James! Were it as easy to make friends, as to break with them, his behaviour would be less unwise, though not less unkind. — — But to you, my Susan, to you I need not expatiate upon what it has cost me to see ALL THE BROTHER thus concentred to ONE point, exclusive of all other that I so long believed unchangeably dear to him! He expects to be thought of as heretofore, & not only to escape reproach, or censure for his conduct, but to see it treated with respect & applause! — — What I imagine, & all I can imagine to account for his behaviour to myself, is—that he fears I shall remonstrate against his proceedings, & propose a reconciliation to which he is too proud to submit, or which he fears might end in SUBVERTING his plan. And that, to avoid this danger, he affects a resentment it is, I think, UTTERLY impossible he can feel—for to have written still more kindly than I have done, he must, knowing my turn of mind, have concluded me false, not friendly, hypocritical, not lenient.—

Tell me your opinion, my own Susan, & let me have one Letter directed to Hetty at our house, which shall be wholly for myself, as a mere bit to cut off cannot contain a satisfactory

[13] EBB's letter is missing, as is also SBP's to JB.

view of a subject so deeply close to us, & which cannot be touched upon in our Letters of *every other trust!*—And let me know if your ¹ own sweet touching lines to him—which I cried over—have had any answer. You ask what has passed upon this subject with our beloved friends—for a long while I said nothing, save that I was ill—for indeed *that* was impossible not to say, so absent & disturbed & dejected I irresistibly appeared: but when I recovered, & saw the affair, in its terrible manner, settled,—I said, alone, & in a hurrying way, to our tender friend,—I know you have felt by your Eyes—for my late uneasiness—but it is over now—& was only occasioned by my not seeing with the same Eyes as a person I dearly love—' I then briefly stated that J[ames] had parted from his wife, & S[arah] was gone to keep his house: without a hint *how*, or ought else of circumstance, save that I much blamed *her* preferring that house to my dear Father's—& J[ames]'s leading to such a preference. This much was forced from me, by necessity, from the excessive sadness they had most tenderly sympathised in, & from making known how it happenned that you were invited over to keep my Father's house.—That dear Father!—while I was with him, & pressing to be summoned whenever wanted, he said — — If Susan could come—that indeed would be a comfort to me—for *I* should be a comfort to *her!* I cannot take You from your husband & boy—I would not take Hetty from her good Mr. Burney—but Susan—*our* comfort would be *reciprocal!*—She & her good Fanny might make me as happy as I could make them — '

The *Spring* idea so delighted him!—Mrs. R[ishton] goes the beginning of May—& then fixes elsewhere, & returns no more.¹⁴ —I had many anecdotes from *her* which I have no room for on this subject of regret — — ¹

At N[orbury] P[ark] the exquisite delight of any prospect that would bring *you* to Chelsea, makes all previous incidents appear trifling, & therefore they drop the little they have heard, enquire no more, & only join in my prayers for my poor Father's wishes being heard. I must now only briefly add, that my Alex has been very ill since our return, but is recovered, &

---

¹⁴ Maria Rishton had now made plans to settle permanently at Bury St. Edmunds (see also L. 314), though she seems not to have left Chelsea until the autumn of 1800 (see her letter to FBA, 21 July [1800], Eg. 3697, ff. 300–1b; also L. 334, p. 329).

only waits soft weather to go abroad, & his naughty papa just ditto, with rheumatic torture, from his garden—but he is now well again, & promises much future discretion. He has just got a charming Letter from M. de N[arbonne]—& will Copy it for next | ⟨pacquet⟩ if possible. at least your own share.[15] God bless you, my dearest of Loves! & God send you to my dear Father!—my Mate—all flannel & wraps, sends tenderst Love

305　　　　　　　　　　West Humble, 13 March 1799

Conjointly with M. d'Arblay
To Sarah (Rose) Burney

A.L.S. and PS. (Osborn), 13 Mar. [17]99
Double sheet small 4to　4 pp.　*pmks*　DARKING　15 MR 99　wafer
Addressed: Mrs. Burney, / at Dr. Charles Burney's, / Greenwich, / Kent.

West Hamble,
March 13. 99

I have received such true pleasure from your Letter of this morning, my dear Rosette, that I will not go to rest to night till I have thanked you for it. Far enough am I from *condoling*,—compleatly & cordially I *congratulate* you on this dignified attack.[1] I have not a doubt but its effects will be salutary, & render the rest of your life a general blessing, when so often, & so calamitously, you have lamented it, for yourself, as a bur-then. Indeed your own Letter, written so immediately after it, convinces me of the happy change it will produce And I rejoice with all my heart that the cruelly agitated state in which I left you has found a vent that promises so durable & consolatory a termination of your long sufferings. |

15 This was the comte de Narbonne's letter (Berg), written at Tübingen, Würtemberg, on 1 Feb. 1799 and bearing the London *pmk* 7 MR 99. Fuller than usual, it contained a detailed recipe for the preparation of *choucroute*; expressed anxiety for the outcome at Naples and the safety of his wife, daughter, and mother; inquired about a commercial treaty that he had thought concluded between England and St. Domingo; rejoiced that the troubles in Ireland had been quelled and that for SBP he has only now to fear the oppressions of 'son farouche mari'. 'Mon ami donnez moi bien en detail des nouvelles de sa position mon dieu que je voudrais la savoir reunie a vous, dût elle prendre ma chambre dans un petit palais enchanté.'

305. 1 See L. 274 n. 1.

I should have repeated my enquiries ere this, had I not gathered your amendment from your purpose of going to the assembly;—which I now, however, take for granted was impossible.—We have been but dismal here, since our return— my Alex was taken very ill the second day; we concluded he was sickening of the Measles, & treated him accordingly; but the eruption had another appearance, & he had a very high fever; we sent for medical assistance from Dorking, & found he had the Chicken pox,—this was succeeded by the nettle rash, & both have been accompanied by a worm fever, & a perpetual Cough. He is now, I thank God, nearly recovered, but is thinner than I ever saw a Child of his Age, & has still very bad Nights, [|] & his naughty Papa, by beginning too early, & staying out too late, in his Garden, laid himself compleatly up with the rheumatism before his son was half well. The double nursing & total confinement have not, you will believe, much added to my own health, however, M. d'A. is now considerably better, though wrapt in a night Cap & flannels, & still obliged to keep his room. As soon as milder weather shines upon us, I think the air will recruit & re-establish us all. I truly rejoice your house is already restored to its prosperous state.

I am sure I need not say the pleasure with which I read what you have written of my dear Brother. Perhaps no one knows better than me how truly he deserves your affection, for with all the confidence which you will forgive his placing in me, since you give me the same yourself, I have never [|] heard him name you without the most unabating pity for your sufferings, & invariable tenderness for your person. Pray give him my kind love, & take for both that of M. d'Arblay.—I am always much gratified when that last named Gentleman is seen long & well enough to be appreciated.—My dear child's first exercise, after a fever that took from him all the use of his limbs, was drawing about your noble waggon.

My—our love to dear & amiable Carlino, & best Comp^{ts} to Mrs. Bicknell, & believe me, my dear Rosette, ever yours

F d'A.

[By M. d'Arblay]

My love to all with a [thous]and thanks for the *welcomest* News papers—I mea[n to read] every one—

To Doctor Burney

A.L.S. (Berg), 14 Mar. [17]99
Double sheet 4to   4 pp.   *pmks*   16 MR 99   16 MR 99   wafer
Addressed: Dr. Burney, / Chelsea College, / Middlesex.
Endorsed by CB: 1799
   Edited by FBA, p. 1, *annotated and date retraced*: ⁙ —99   (3) Illnesses. Dr. Johnson's Literary Club. The Obriens.—

West Humble,
March 14.—99.

What a terrible time we have passed since we left You, my dearest Father! we seem to have gone about only to cause trouble, & excite pity, & to turn every place we have encumbered into an hospital!—Your dwelling, already so called, was the Temple of Hygiea to us compared with every other habitation we annoyed. Thank Heaven, however, my Mate is now restored to ease, & my Boy has recovered his strength & appetite. But the first is still in a Night Cap & flannels—& the other has restless nights, & is thin enough for a caricature of a French baby fed upon soupe maigre.[1] We wait fine weather for air & exercise in our field, & from that expect full re-establishment. I have been only attacked by a Cough & Cold, which were violent enough to demand total abstinence from animal food, —& which still forbid my *usual excess*: but I have been exceedingly harrassed with anxiety, & shall not feel freed from it till my little Man's own better repose brings back mine:

I am quite afraid to hear how *Your* Cough is, my dearest Padre, upon this 3ᵈ return of Winter. It has snowed all to day, ǀ & the night does not look as if to-morrow meant to make any apology. I should not wonder if it should provoke Hetty to send to Lord Kinyon[2] for his opinion upon its legality,—for I remember her proposing to do so by Lord Mansfield, formerly, upon a season of similar churlishness.

---

306. [1] An obvious reference, often repeated, to Hogarth's *Roast Beef of Old England*.
   [2] Lloyd Kenyon (1732–1802), cr. Bart. (1784), cr. Lord Kenyon, Baron of Gredington (1788). In 1788 he succeeded Lord Mansfield (i, L. 24 n. 51) as Lord Chief Justice.

ꞤWell, but—Mr. Lock called yesterday, to shew me a Letter from Major Phillips in which he tells him that he encloses a draft long due, that his law suit[3] is to be heard by the Lord-Chancellor next week & that as soon as it is adjusted, &c it shall be possible, after it, *Susan shall come to England* but it is so worded there is no understanding whether he means *as soon as he can accompany her*, or *as soon as he can fit her out*. You know his vague, unsatisfactory style. But he apologizes to Mrs. Lock for *apparent breach of promise* in not bringing her back at the end of the first year, & says the delay was unavoidable. The rest of the Letter is upon politics, stating the utter impossibility at present of the union, &c. We hardly know if then to gather comfort from his Letter or not, his answer is so diffuse, but certainly we gather his affairs must be in better train, by the enclosed draft. Ⅰ Mr. Lock, himself, immediately wrote to express his satisfaction at the promise, & the earnest wish that his family can soon return— God send her amongst us, sweet soul!—I have had no Letter from her since that I read with you at Chelsea, but Mrs. Lock has had one of a much later date, & so I find has Esther.Ꞥ

I am very glad at the revival of the club, & the nomination not only of *Mr. Canning*, but of a man of Letters not *M.P.* besides, *Mr. Marsden*;[4] for in a *Literary club*, honoured by having been instituted by Dr. Johnson, Learning, Letters, & talents should have the lead, & Rank, power, & Riches emulate one another to support them.—The play adventure amused me much.[5] I should have marvelled, indeed, if the young democratic lord had found you at once open-hearted & handed: yet I always wish party spirit sufficiently kept under to let the general commerce of the world go on uninfluenced by it, if

[3] This seems to have been the long-standing suit in Chancery, Molesworth Phillips *v.* his mother's relatives, George Eccleston, John Darcy, and William Eccleston, the elder, of Drumshallon (see a bill entered on 28 June 1785, Chancery Bill Book, Rolls Office, Dublin). The editor is much indebted to Professor Edward A. Bloom, who kindly searched for the entry in the records.

[4] The allusions following are lost with CB's letter, which must have referred, however, to the meeting of the Literary Club on 26 Feb. 1799, when both William Marsden (iii, L. 199 n. 20), an orientalist, who on 3 Mar. 1795 was 'induced to accept the post of second secretary of the admiralty' (see *DNB*), and George Canning were elected. Canning had previously been blackballed at least once, possibly twice. See CB to FBA, 4 June 1798 (Osborn).

[5] 'The play adventure' is lost with CB's letter as is also his visit to Burlington House.

only that the wrong side, Not being exclusively confined to the wrong side, may have a chance, by the mixture, of being brought over to the right Side. ⌈The account of the Play meriting little attention indeed⌉—I am much pleased at your independent establishment of *conviviality* at Burlington House. & was much interested by your account of the obvious—& not very *fache* at their *taste in reading* — — but quite confounded by the abominable conduct of Lady Frances Quin![6]—I remember seeing ┃ her at Weymouth, with 3 Children!—much respected, & well behaved! I remember, too, her taking a prodigiously sudden fancy to me, when quite a Girl, at Mrs. Sheeles's boarding school,[7] & chatting & playing with me by every opportunity during one day:—&, on the next, when I had been dejected by some hints of the illness of my dear Mother, her much amazing me, by bluffly saying 'lord, how dull you are to day! you were very agreeable yesterday,—but if I'd known you'd have grown so stupid, I should have left you to yourself.'—Lady Lucy,[8] Mr. digby's wife afterwards, was the reverse in kindness & consideration: she called me her *Child*, & took the office of *School Mother* upon her for me. She was much older than Lady Frances—& I am sure I thought much wiser.

I shall long to know how *Cecely* bears continuation—[9] ⌈My fondest love to the dear Girls, if you I hope, will write again. My Mate's kind re^gd—

Dearest & most dear Sir.

your F. d'A

As I cannot write to Hetty till next week, may I entreat that Will. may call on her, & say that Alex is better, & that her Letter is gone to Ireland? pray excuse this, dear Sir.⌉

[6] Frances Muriel Fox-Strangways (1755–1814), who married in 1777 Valentine-Richard Quin (1752–1824), cr. Bart. (1781), Baron Adare (1800), Viscount Mount-Earl (1816), Earl of Dunraven and Mount-Earl (1822). At Weymouth in 1789 FB could have seen the three eldest children Elizabeth (1779–95), Windham-Henry (1782–1850), and Lady Harriet (1784–1831).

[7] In the 1760s CB taught the young ladies in Mrs. Sheeles's (or Shields's) Boarding School on Queen Square and there he had boarded his own children (FB, SEB, and CB Jr., then aged 10, 7, and 4) during their mother's last illness in 1762. Mrs. Shields may have been the wife of the John Shields who emerges in the Holborn Rate Books for the years 1752–63.

[8] See i, L. 21 n. 8.

[9] CB had been re-reading *Cecilia* (5 vols., 1782), see his letter of 3 [Jan.] 1799 (Berg).

To Hester Maria Thrale
later Viscountess Keith

L. copy in hand of M. d'A (West Humble Letter Book, pp. 135–6, Osborn), 20 March 1799

Westhamble, Dorking
March. 20. 1799.

To. Miss Thrale

I thought myself quite unfortunate in being a second time in town before your residence there. You have promised to let me hear from you *when settled anywhere*—but no account arrives, & as your servant told me you would be in Cumberland street in March, I must send off a little flapper, with an intimation that I begin to think it very long since I have heard of your health & proceedings—for indeed, my dear friend, there are passages in your last letter[1] that often recur to me with an inquietude that will always accompany any doubts of your happiness. Your description of Cecilia & her sposo[2] is such as to make one sigh at the means of enjoyment which so wantonly are thrown away. For if, with all his weakness & faults, she still likes him she must through *him* be happy, or not be happy at all. But for *you*— I think associating with them, beyond what systerly humanity & real duty demand, would be madness. You require—& always, I thought, required some spirited associates to animate your existence into pleasure, for with every power of aiding & abetting gaiety & enjoyment, I never remember in you those species of independent spirits that could find food in themselves for hilarity and happiness. With such a couple, therefore, as you paint, however you might escape the infection of peeveeshness, & secure as you must be from that of folly, you would soon sink into secret but wearing depression, or only be saved from it by a general loss of apathy. I must wish you gayer Inmates.—And your Sisters, my dear Susan & Sophy, certainly are such,— lively pleasing, amiable, & obliging; [but I] suspect them to be so completely wedded to each other as to leave less place for their very deserving elder sister than will satisfy her feelings, or

307. [1] Cf. L. 287, which is almost a duplicate of this letter.
[2] See iii, L. 217 n. 2.

fill up the vacuity with which the human heart always aches, in reflecting characters, when unconvinced that its affections give & receive equal pleasure: |

That something presses heavily on your mind, though you religiously strive to chace it, is clear—& indeed, to go on 'from year to year in constant doubt & uncertainty', is enough to wear down your spirits & exhaust all force of exertion. Is it *inevitable*? or would Dʳ Johnson, if alive & knowing your situation, only say to you as he did to Mʳˢ Reynolds[3] 'Ponder no more, Renny,—whatever you do do it, but ponder no more! —' Perhaps your decision hangs upon some event yet in the womb of time: you are then compelled to endure your present uncertainty; but if it depends upon yourself alone — — permit me to give you a counsel which you may consider, whether or not you adopt: Resolve to relinquish the affair on which the doubt is impending at once, & positively; & Act as if it were out of your power to do otherwise.

Your peace, perhaps, then may insensibly, return, which during any suspence must continue always broken — — but if on the contrary it does not return, if the negative state you avow changes into positive unhapiness—reverse the decree!— Try yourself in this manner, rather than waste your valuable life in hesitation. I think I know you will pardon the liberty I here take,—at least when I assure you I shall take perfectly in good part receiving no answer whatever to the whole of what I offer on this subject. You must be sure it can only spring from a sincere interest in your happiness, joined to no small opinion of your understanding & candour. A great deal presents itself to my imagination,—but as my surmizes may all be fantastic and unreal, I will here bid them to be quiet.

[2] Sir Joshua's sister Frances Reynolds (1729–1807).

To Mrs. Broome
and Ralph Broome, Sr.

A.L.S. (Berg), 21 Mar. [17]99
Double sheet 4to   4 pp.   *pmks* DARKING   MR 99   2⟨   ⟩   MR 99
wafer
Addressed: Ralph Mrs. Broome / Nº 12. Salisbury Place, / New Road.
Endorsed by CBFB: Sister d'Arblay / March 1799
Numerical calculations, p. 4

West Hamble,
March 21ˢ⟨ᵗ⟩—99

If Chance has not kindly stood my friend in finding some
means of acquainting you, Dear Sir, & Dearest Charlotte, how
I have been situated since my return to our Hermitage, what a
totally graceless, as well as peculiarly ungrateful Wretch must
I have appeared, not to have sent my congratulations upon the
subject, & thanks for the manner of your joint communication![1]—In Charlotte's gentle Judgement I know, indeed,
I may trust; her long knowledge of my faithful affection would
withstand a thousand cloudy appearances, confident that Time
must clear up what accident or misfortune alone could cause:
but what is my claim for such forbearance, such lenity, such
partiality from Mr. Broome? None! none!—unless this dear &
happy flitch cannot be obtained but by their sliding so precisely
into one another's opinions as mutually to relinquish all
separate powers of discrimination or decision.

Not once, indeed, have I had my Pen in hand, since hither │ I
came, but from implacable necessity—for two days after our
landing on this quiet coast, Alex was taken extremely ill—& has
continued so far from re-established, that this very afternoon is
the first I have dared venture him out in the open air. I will
spare you the details of his complaints, or my terrors; this last
matter of fact will point out to you that I have never one

308. ¹ The 'joint communication', preserved in the Scrapbook (Berg), 'Fanny
Burney and family. 1653–1890', pp. 64–5, consists of verses written by the Broomes
on the first anniversary of their marriage (1 Mar.) attesting to a 'durable Increase'
of 'Affection' and laying claim to the flitch of bacon annually awarded at Dunmow,
Essex. Broome's Address 'To Mʳˢ D'Arblay' included the tribute: 'You only did
your Sister's Choice approve / And saw how Reason might unite with Love. . . .'

moment been absent from him, night or day, nor had my Mind sufficiently disengaged for writing—reading—or conversing even when he slept. The particulars our sister Burney will give, if you wish for them, as a pacquet of consequence obliged me to write her a few lines during his almost worst state: but I charged her not to spread them, as I was too much oppressed, both with fear & fatigue, to answer any Letters, however kind, of enquiry. And which of my dear Sisters or who amongst my friends, would have forborne making some for a little Creature of such peculiar comfort & ˡ so exquisitely a blessing to his parents? Here I do not apprehend Mr. Broome—I feel sure of his kind participation, for his evident benevolence to Children is with me his first trait for securing my dear Charlotte's happiness.— the Joy I take in it, & the gratitude I feel for the flattering propensity he shews to ascribe to me any share of it are all I can offer in return for this exceeding kind Address, which I shall hoard among the few memorials equally gratifying to my pride & welcome to my affection.

M. d'Arblay has again had a violent rheumatic attack—from his old bad Garden courses—& is still a figure miserably venerable from his wraps & fleecy attire. But what ungenial weather have we had! Mr. Broome would have found equal difficulty, had he visited us, to satisfy either his Farmer's or his Beauty's Eye. I am charmed with my Sister Burney's account of the expected success of Mr. B[urney] with her unfeeling Debtor.[2] We are deeply anxious & disturbed about Ireland— the Major has ˡ again written something like a promise for our Susan's restoration[3]—but not of a very satisfactory nature. His pertinacity is truly lamentable, the wretched & dangerous state of that devoted Country considered.—Do you hear or see any thing of the Recluse Man & Maiden?[4]

Adieu, Dear Sir, & Dearest Charlotte—

My kindest love to the dear & amiable Children, & Compts —to Miss Broome,[5]—& to Miss Morton.[6] M. d'A. joins me in every kind & warm wish that can be formed for the continuance of your mutual happiness, & mutual sensibility to your united lots.

F. d'A.

[2] See also L. 310 n. 6; L. 346, p. 365.   [3] See L. 306, p. 253.
[4] JB and SHB.   [5] See L. 257 n. 11.   [6] See iii, L. 212 n. 4.

To Mrs. Waddington

A.L.S. (Berg), 23 Mar. [17]99
Double sheet 4to   4 pp.   *pmks*   ABERGAVEN[NY]   26 MR 99   wafer
Addressed: Mrs. Waddington / ⌐Lanover Court / Abergavenny ⌐
Readdressed: post Office / Bath
Docketed in pencil, p. 4: W

West Hamble, Dorking,
March 23d—99

Your last Letter, so interesting, so open, so entertaining,
merited twenty answers, my dear Marianne,—though it has not
yet been even acknowledged. I am really sorry, & have long
regretted that day after day has disappointed my intentions—
not so much of clearing my debt,—I am not so proud with one
I love so sincerely—but of giving me new claim to fresh intelligence. That wish alone now ever draws forth my pen,
beyond certain duties, & indispensable necessities, for a general
repugnance to Letter-writing grows so fast, & so irresistibly
upon me, that if my affections did not goad me with continual
reproaches, I believe I should not write 3 Letters in a Year.—
I hardly know, now, whether to begin with some account of
myself, or to talk in answer—but the latter wish prevails, &
therefore behold me with you in York, completely entering into
all the emotions you so expressively describe at the renewal of
your old intercourse with your excellent Friends, who were
prized by dearest Mrs. Delany, & whose names & characters
are familiar to me, though Mr. F. Montagu[1] is the only one of
them I ever saw—& not him since the early part of the trial of
Mr. Hastings. It's concluding period I did not attend, for I was
already settled in a Country residence from whence nothing of
a public nature has ever drawn me.—Have you seen the
account of Mr. Hastings in Mr. Seward's last Biographiana?[2]

---

309. [1] Frederick Montagu (1733–1800), M.A. (1757), M.P. (1759–90). See also
Delany, *passim*.
   [2] William Seward had included in his *Biographiana* (2 vols., 1799), ii. 610–28, a
Memoir of Warren Hastings by 'the strenuous and grateful friend of that distinguished person', namely Major John Scott (1747–1819), later Scott-Waring (*DNB*;
also *DL* iii. 423, 427). Seward's intention to honour Hastings is indicated in his

I know your opinion of that work in general to be tolerably unfavourable, & certainly this is not an article to retrieve its credit with you,—but remark, it is only published, not written by Mr. Seward ¹ &, indeed, a narrative less adequate to its purpose of celebrating an oppressed Man I have seldom read: the language is dry, the events are told sleepily that ought to be recorded with enthusiasm, & the character is drawn up so vaguely & diffusely, that it leaves no fixed impression even of the writer's own sentiment of it.

I never wonder that meeting with those you have not seen since *april—88* should affect you—otherwise, Mrs. Cholm-[ley]³—was not amongst those with whom you had been sufficiently intimate for any tender attachment; & her own manners are reserved, even with those with whom she is much connected, though her character is perfectly deserving esteem & regard. However, I well conceive it was less herself than the reminiscences she awakened which so forcibly touched you. The orphan Miss Phipps must be always, while young, an object of interest. What a loss has she not sustained in the endearments of a mother who would have adored her! I spent a few days with Mrs. Cholm[ley] & Mr Sm[elt] at Kew previous to their resigning that habitation, since my own resignation from the Queen's House, & though seriously, they passed very pleasingly.⁴

Do you think I did not smile at the anecdotes you have picked up of my dearest Friends' sons? I wish I could hear more of them. Mʳ Wᵐ was here yesterday, on a visit to my *Alexander* (you ask his Name, & to that tremendous Warrior's he joins *Charles Louis*, from his two godfathers.⁵—This little Being is honoured with the peculiar favour of Mr. Wᵐ, who supplies him with Horses according to his growth, & looks at him with

Introduction, p. viii: 'One Living Character only is introduced, that of the Saviour of the extensive and important dominions of INDIA for that country which has alone ungratefully refused to acknowledge the obligation.' Included as well (ii. 609) is Dr. Johnson's laudatory letter of Jan. 1781 to Hastings. FBA was to contribute the second paragraph to CB's review of *Biographiana*, *Monthly Review*, xxix (1799), 294.

³ Anne Jesse, the daughter of Leonard Smelt, became the third wife of Nathaniel Cholmley (i, L. 12 n. 18; L. 3 n. 83). Her stepdaughter Anne Elizabeth Cholmley (1769–88) had married in 1787 Constantine John Phipps (1744–92), 2nd Baron Mulgrave (i, L. 13 n. 10), but had died in childbirth in 1788. The orphan, Anne Elizabeth Cholmley Phipps, was now nearly 11 years old.

⁴ For this visit, see i, L. 12, p. 94.

⁵ Louis, comte de Narbonne-Lara (i, L. 33 n. 36) and CB, Jr. (see iii, L. 179 n. 2).

PLATE II

William Locke Sr., of Norbury Park, and his daughter Amelia
From a sketch by Sir Thomas Lawrence

a tender goodness to make one regret he | loses any more of his youth without entitling himself to the full enjoyment of the paternal feelings evidently in his nature. My dear Boy had been very ill—& he had kindly partaken his family's concern for him, & could not, he said, be satisfied of his recovery without seeing him. The little Soul has kept his room a month with alternate attacks of Fevers, Chicken pox, Nettle rash, & worms —alltogether resulting, we imagine, from heated blood through a total change of hours & air & exercise during 6 weeks which we have spent from home. I must defer telling how & where till my next, as I have not done with your own progress yet. You have more, you say, to tell me of Mr. Rawlins[on—][6] let me hear it, pray. He mistook in thinking [that] lovely Amelia Lock had her portrait at the Exhibi[tio]n. Lawrence has painted it, slightly, but it has only appeared in his own Apartment, & at Norbury Park. The last news that has been received of Mr. Cha[s] L[ocke] was from Minorca,[7] where he had just learnt the misfortunes & flight of the King of Naples; he was preparing to go to Palermo. His really lovely wife (though no complete Beauty) & his two infant Children accompany him. The eldest, 2 years old, has had a very dangerous fever, & is reduced to a skeleton; the youngest, whom her Mother nurses at her breast, is very flourishing; but poor Mrs. Charles herself has suffered very seriously & frightfully by terrible falls, from the violence of various tempests in which she could not keep her feet, & from one of which she received such a blow on the head as to remain some time senseless,—yet | her youngest baby, who was in her arms, she held unhurt! How wonderful & how beautiful is the power of maternal care!—Your pleasure in meeting with the F[anshawe]s[8] must rather have sprung from former intimacy than former fondness, for though you met, erst, very often, I recollect that you were far from admiring them. Do you remember the piano forte parties? &c—I believe they are good souls, though, & if constant & affectionate, I can never wonder they should now have gained a weight with you which innumerable

---

[6] Unidentified.

[7] The letter of which FBA gives the contents was dated 24 Jan. 1799 and addressed to Mr. Locke. It is printed in the *Locks of Norbury*, pp. 152–3. Ferdinand IV (1751–1825), when the French advanced toward Naples, had fled to Palermo on 21 Dec. 1798.

[8] Catherine Maria Fanshawe (1765–1834), the authoress (*DNB*), and her sisters Penelope (1764–1833) and Elizabeth Christiana (1778–1856).

former favourites of brighter parts must have lost from wanting those solid qualities. *Pray* let me have at least two sheets of Bath adventures; & very particular accounts how your dear Children go on; you have made me well acquainted with their several merits, & I only wish I could present my little urchin to them. An excellent, though new friend of ours, the wife of our Bookham vicar, Mrs. Cooke,[9] is now at Bath: & if you can set aside the prejudice her appearance & solemnity of manner may give rise to, you will find her a cultivated, well bred woman, as well as scrupulously honourable, & warmly zealous for those she loves. I should like you should talk to her, that I might hear of you from her. Her Daughter[10] is sensible, but stiff & cold, & by no means equally amiable in her disposition *now*, though I think improving, & opening into something better. Do, for my sake & gratification, make up to them. 'Tis so long since I have seen even a face that has seen yours!—But Mrs. Agnew writes me word[11] she hears you look extremely well. God bless you, my dearest Marianne. My dearest Sister is still in Ireland—alas! —— all Mr. Lock's family remember you with constant & affectionate regard.

Ever yours

F. d'A

310 West Humble, 24 March 1799

Conjointly with M. d'Arblay
To Esther (Burney) Burney

A.L.S. & A.N. (Berg), 24 Mar. [17]99
Double sheet 4to   4 pp.   on p. 1, 12 lines, and on p. 2, 22 lines of cross-writing   *pmks* D[ARKING] 26 MR 99 wafer
Addressed: Mrs. Burney, / Beaumont Street, / Devonshire Place, / London.

West Hamble,
March 24. 99.

You have entirely misunderstood me, my dear Etty—& lest the obscurity of my phrase, or some omission, or whatever other

---

[9] See iii, L. 122 n. 8.
[11] The letter is missing.

[10] See L. 263 n. 7.

blunder, that has caused the mistake, should urge you to any painful effort, I must hasten a few lines to assure you I never had the most distant intention of Your shewing my Letter to James—far from it—could I *help* him, I would stop short of NOTHING to do it,—but to *hurt* him nothing could induce me; to lose him *you*—the only one of his tribe he seems now to see, I should think barbarous. I have only written what he has forced from me, in consequence of his injustice, & which I could only have withheld from writing, after *his* complaints, by an indifference to censure such as he has possessed himself—but which I believe to be as far from his real character as from mine. No, my dearest Esther, while they will *let* you shew them your countenance, for God's sake give it them. If the time ever should come when I may gather, however distantly, that they revive to any species of sensibility of having thus wantonly thrown me away from them,—they shall find me ready immediately—instantly—& I heartily to return to them. —— ——

Both my Alex.'s are considerably better. The elder has resumed his Gardening,—without yet suffering, & the younger has, at last, gone forth into our domain. To day he took his last *Macdonald Lozenge*,[1] but with no appearance of worms, though with much general benefit.

I am quite grieved by what you say of that charming Mᵉ du Chattel[2]—I have hardly ever seen a more interesting, engaging person, or one whose sadness so irresistibly saddens. What will become of her beautiful Daughter? That, & her sons, alone, I believe, by what dropt from her most pathetically to me, will make Death wear any appearance of horrour to her. What would not one give it were possible to relieve her mind upon this subject!—

I am sure you sigh, like me, for news from Ireland —— —— this general Martial Law[3] has something very terrific in it, though I

310. [1] In *The Times* (11 Mar. 1799), 'CHING'S WORM-DESTROYING LOZENGES' had been advertised as being 'used and recommended by . . . the Lord Chief Baron [Sir Archibald Macdonald, 1747–1826]'.

[2] See L. 296 n. 5.

[3] *The Times* (26, 27 Feb.; 11, 16, 19 Mar. 1799) printed news of the introduction, amendment, and passage of what came to be known as 'the Attorney General's Bill to *legalize* Martial Law'. 'The object of it was to give to the Lord Lieutenant a

doubt not its necessity. I shall long, now, to know who is commanding officer of the district of Belcotton,—for ǀ he will now be all powerful. I wish he may be an acquaintance of the Major's,—but I wish far more Susan was known to him—like your Mᵉ du Chattel, if she were but *seen* by him, I should be so sure of his interest in her favour that my mind would be more at ease. You gave me great pleasure by saying our dear Father was in good spirits. I often think that—but for the shock of the manner of the business, he is relieved by a certain separation, for there was so little of filial attention of obliging-ness, that I believe his mind was severely, though secretly worked & wounded & offended every day, if not every hour. I am quite glad you spare your dear girls to him. Do you see Mrs. J[ames] B[urney]? remember me to her kindly when you meet, & thank her for her Note, which I had no time to answer. I have written to Mrs. Chapone,⁴ & told her *You* would explain to her how we were situated, with continual illnesses,—snow, &c—&c, so as to be prevented paying her our respects from your house, which I had willingly promised to do. I am very anxious to hear some news of poor Mr. Mulso⁵—she wrote me word, while I was still at Chelsea, she had lost all hope—but as I have never seen his death announced, nor ǀ heard of it, I hope he is recovering. I am sincerely & affectionately attached to that admirable woman, whose life is in strict conformity to the purity of her writings, & who is as liberal in her sentiments as she is well informed in her intellects. We have some hopes of seeing Carlos here to spend the day with us to-morrow.—How I wish we could all drive our Chaises thus kindly to one another's doors! It will be a feast to us to have him at Camilla Cottage, which he worked so zealously towards erecting. our sweet friends are well up the Hill. Mr. Lock & Amelia were here yesterday. We have not yet been able to *get* to them, but are promised for Tuesday, if Alex. keeps well. The little rogue

power of issuing orders for the summary punishment of offenders by Military Law; and also for preventing the Civil Power from interfering with the decisions of Courts Martial.' As a means of quelling rebellion, still found to be prevalent, the bill enabled 'Courts Martial . . . to try in a summary manner, and punish with death, or otherwise, persons *suspected* of aiding, assisting, and abetting Rebellion, or injuring the persons or properties of his Majesty's loyal subjects in furtherance of such Rebellion, as well as those found acting in Rebellion'.

⁴ This correspondence is missing.

⁵ Mrs. Chapone's brother Thomas Mulso (*c.* 1721–99), author of *Callistus; or the Man of Fashion* and *Sophronius; or, the Country Gentleman,* had died on 7 Feb.

has had a visit expressly to himself from Mr. William, who is as partial to him as his kind Aunt Burney. He often drives his coaches & Horses to Beaumont Street, & then says 'now go to Beaumont Street House—& let's see Cousin Amelia, & Aunt Burney, & big Cousin Marianne, & Sophy, & uncle Mr. Burney, & live all together again.—' This is a very favourite idea with him. I intended but 3 explanatory lines but chattery with my dearest Esther has urged me on insensibly. We always rejoice, both, for a great many reasons, at the weeks we spent with you, though we blush at our infirmities in that period.— M. d'A. often declares *if only to know Mr. Burney* 'twould have been well worth while. He has taken to him cordially. God bless you, my dear soul.

Ever & most affectionately yours
F. d'A.

Love to Charlotte when you meet
We laughed at the ⟨Worsop⟩ account.[6] Mr d'A. joins quite in all your wickedness, for which he has a good taste. ∣

[concluded on the margin of p. 1 *and in cross-writing on* p. 2]

Kindest Love to Mr. Burney & my dear Girls when they return—We are always sorry we missed Fanny. ∣

We are so provided & promised about soap & Candles, that I am quite sorry we can enter into no new engagemt. but if *you* can trust us, we shall gladly shew our poor good will towards M^{le} De la Landelle[7] as to sugar—& take 12 more at the same price, & 12 cheaper common, for pies, &c I can beg Charlotte to settle the balance with you from our next Mathias acc^t wh^{ch} she will be so kind as to receive. &, as we are in no haste for these articles, they need not be forwarded till you wish to send by the same conveyance another pacquet for our dearest Exile, which I shall be able to let her have enclosed in mine, in about a fortnight — ∣

[By M. d'Arblay, cross-written on p. 1]

I am extreemly sorry of what you say about my poor friend Reuchin's family.[8] Pray when you see him be so kind to tell him how much I grieve for him. I hope he has more care of

---

[6] A sum owing to C. R. Burney for music lessons. See further L. 346, p. 365.
[7] See iii, L. 215 n. 14.   [8] Unidentified.

himself. When I saw him he was in very bad health. — — He has indeed my best wishes—Pray remember me to M^rs De Cackerey.⁹ Tell also to M^rs Du Chatel she must have more care of herself if it were but for the sake of others. for if we have seen her only once feel so keenly her sorrows, what must be the feelings of her friends!—A petition more — — which is to present in the manner the best to be welcomed my respect to the two amiable Sisters¹⁰ I fell in love with. Our relationship preventing such a thing with Dear M[arianne] & S[ophy] they must know that I mean only their two English friends. Adieu Dear sister.

311   West Humble, 1 April 1799

To Esther (Burney) Burney

A.L.S. (Berg), 1 Apr. [17]99
Double sheet 4to   4 pp.   *pmks*   P.P.U.   2 AP 99   wafer
Addressed: Mrs. Burney, / Beaumont Street, / Devonshire Place, / London.
Endorsed by EBB: answered April 3ᵈ.

West Hamble,
April 1ˢᵗ—99

I quite regret that your Letter did not come to me on one of our post Days, my ever dearest Esther, that I might instantly have told you how much I at once feel for, & admire your purposed plan. It's success I am not afraid to say I am sure will be all you can desire. I would wager with any one that *next year* you will have more offers of pupils than you will think necessary, from circumstances of ease & health, to accept. *This year* is too far advanced for more than a sprinkling, as people's plans are already arranged, in general, either for Masters fixed upon before, or for none. But it cannot be that your willingness to give forth your talents shall be known, & not be seized upon eagerly, as soon as *the times* will permit: for *the times* make a deduction from every calculation, whether of pleasure or business. Do not be anxious upon this score, my dear sister, nor

⁹ For the *émigré* families DeCacqueray and du Chastel, see L. 302 n. 7; L. 296, n. 5; and L. 325, pp. 301–2.
¹⁰ The Frye sisters (L. 302 n. 8).

judge there is any backwardness of pupils, because not immediately ready. I will boldly say, I have not a single doubt
but that, in a short time, instead of having to apply, you will be
applied to—&, in a little space further *solicited*. Your *Health* &
strength are all you must watch & care about.

I never in my life saw a more appropriate, more interesting, ।
or more truly respectable Letter[1] than that to sweet Mrs. Lock.
I am sure she & her family all think the same. Amelia is really
delighted with the idea of renewing her musical studies, which
these vile times had stopt; & she has naturally such a soul for
every thing, that I think you will have great pleasure in improving her, & even flatter myself she will be able to catch
much of your own expression, her propensities are so much in
the right, or same, line. She most sweetly said to me, in speaking of her pleasure in the scheme 'I am sure if it were only to
pass an hour with Mrs. Burney, without any music, it would be
a great delight to me.'

Yet I frankly confess I am sorry, my dear Hetty, you had not
given me some intimation of your purpose yourself, however
hastily, before it reached me by 3 other channels—Mrs. Lock,
Miss Cambridge, & Mrs. Chapone: for it caused me inexpressible perplexity & inquietude, at hearing from the 2 latter of
your plan, without knowing what it was, & from the former of a
Letter upon peculiar affairs, which she did not explain, till she
found I was already, through the latter, in solicitude for information. It is true, I am helpless to assist it, — — but which of
these or of *any* others, out of Ireland, will so tenderly, nay
fondly be interested in it? & M. d'A. not only approves, but
highly admires । you for it—& seriously says he thinks, in a
while, *you will ruin all the Masters in London.*—But I am letting this
swallow my paper, when a subject so home to my feelings is still
untouched,—your dear Girls.—

I know our dearest Father fondly encourages a belief he is
reserving himself an asylum for our Susan, & a companion he
so sighs for;—he is else so affectionate to your dear Girls, I
think he would not *hesitate* in begging to have Marianne to live
with him—& Sophy to frequently spend such time as you
could spare her for:—but that darling Exile's coming at all is
still so uncertain—& coming to *remain* so unlikely, that I

311. [1] The letters herein mentioned are missing.

cannot bear he should lose such a successor merely from a false hope that will make him more than ever regret her.—Will you, my dearest Esther, suffer me, *wholly from myself*, to entrust my Father with your plan about Sophy? I can easily see *YOU* cannot, lest it should seem like making the proposal; but *I* can so do it as merely to express my anxiety at his losing such a solace during such a heartless uncertainty,—&c.—& say you were delicate of entering upon that, or any subject that mig⟨ht⟩ pain his kind & paternal Heart with a view of the necessity of your submitting to such a privation. I would word it very truly as I think you would most like. I have been tempted to write to him without applying to you for leave: but your charge is so solemn of secresy that I dare not. Yet I really do not even think it will be right to take any measures for this scheme without letting him know in time. Should he miss our Susan—what an added chagrin!—should she come, as you well say, all would give way joyfully, & the dear Girl be no loser by having first spent some time with her Grandfather. You may depend, however, upon my saying not a word from *YOU*, nor a syllable like a *proposal* from myself. I know the discomfort of such arrangements if not wholly voluntary. But I *wish* it with all my Heart, NEXT to my darling Susan,—& hope, therefore, you will entrust [|] me with discretionary powers, which I will use by the Golden Rule of doing only as I would be done by.

Your B—anecdote it is not possible to be angry at, 'tis so contemptible. What a sordid Wretch!—I am very sorry I missed dear Fanny,[2]—My kindest Love to her & her dear sisters. Truly they all three have it. I am sorry, too, for *your* sake, to say the Locks never go but for a Month to town—though they generally stretch it to 6 weeks. But I shall now less scruple exacting your promise for West Humble, as I hope you will be able to give Amelia, here, a little more time. By here, I mean up the Hill—for we, alas, have no Instrument —which, if we have always regretted, how much more shall We when we possess you & dear Mr. Burney!—Give him our joint & most sincere love.

I have had the most touching, yet most beautifully well written & charming Letter from poor Mrs. Chapone I almost

---

[2] Fanny Burney, usually at her post of governess at Lord Percy's (iii, L. 142 n. 3).

ever read.³ I cannot refrain from thanking her for it, though it will be scarcely fair. But if you see her again, tell her, with my truest respects, & most affectionate sympathy, 'tis impossible to resist. she says she much honours your purpose of aiding Mr. B[urney] in paying Mr. P[itt]'s unmerciful taxes.⁴—Poor James! If *ill*, what can be his spirits or comfort?—Will Sally stand a sick in an only companion? I should wish you to say, without further comment, when you see him 'I've had a Letter from F[anny] & she bids me say she is extremely sorry to hear you are not well, which I had written her word.' It will be a little opening, if he chuses to make use of it. I die for news from Ireland. Not a syllable since your last!—Miss Cam[bridge] says she was very sorry she was hurried away from you. A Relation of Mrs. G[eorge] C[ambridge]'s was just dead.⁵ she would have let almost nobody else, she says, in: But she took it kind, she adds, you entrusted her with your pla[n] [*tear*] ⟨ ⟩ if *at* Richmond you expect any business? or [*tear*] *from* it? Have J[ames] & S[arah] been with you since? God bless you, dearest Etty—Prosper—& preserve you! prays yours ever

F. d'A. ǀ

What will bring dear Cecilia to you?

I heard from my dear Carlos you were all well on Sunday at the Bishop's.⁶

I have an opportunity to send this for the penny post— ǀ

³ This is the undated letter (Eg. 3698, f. 123), printed *DL* v. 432–4, in which Mrs. Chapone tells of the death of her favourite niece, Jane Jeffreyes, in childbirth. See also L. 313 n. 1.

⁴ See L. 312 n. 2.

⁵ Cornelia Van Mierop (*c.* 1769–1858), who had married on 13 Jan. 1795 the Revd. George Cambridge (i, L. 8 n. 7; L. 11 nn. 3, 4, 5). Her sister Martha Kuyck had died at Twickenham 8 Mar. 1799 (*GM* lxix, 259; and will P.C.C. Howe 404, probated 10 May 1799).

⁶ Brownlow North (i, L. 3 n. 10), Bishop of Winchester.

To Charles Burney

A.L. (The Hyde Collection), 3 Apr.
Single sheet 4to   *pmks*   LEATHER / HEAD   4 AP ⟨99⟩   4 AP 99
wafer
Addressed: D⟨r⟩ Charles Burney, / Greenwich, / Kent.
Docketed in pencil, p. 1: 469

Wednesday April 3ᵈ

I have just received your Monday's Letter, my dear
Carlos. I should be glad not to send the Books before I give one
brief revise to my own revisings, which I can do in a week. But
if that cannot be spared, a word shall carry them to you on the
very day I receive it.

As to the Table—I see so many advertised, that we really
think it had better not be shewn at present. The Broker will
never take it for this year's sale so late, full as I see him of such
articles: & it is better not to remain in *his* garret till another, but
in that of the carpenter himself.¹ However, you are left to your
own ultimate discretion. This is but *an int.*

God bless you & yours. Kindest Loves.

The income Tax² is so much heavier upon our *revenue* than we
expected, that this final arrangement, with P[ayne] & C[adell]
will be most welcome—& the *2ᵈ Ed.* still more so, even independent of that capital consideration. But I hope not 4000
again for *one!*³ Tis such a disadvantage to the reputation of a
Book, because never imagined by the public.

312. ¹ CB Jr., in a letter now missing, had evidently asked FBA to send a copy of
her comedy 'Love and Fashion' (L. 266 n. 7), which, as events were to show, he was
to offer to Thomas Harris (*c.* 1738–1820), manager of Covent Garden.
² This was the first income tax. The bill was ordered on 4 Dec. 1798 (*Parl. Hist.*
xxxiv. 26) and was given royal assent on 21 Mar. 1799 (*CJ* 54: 386). It was gradu-
ated, those with an income between £60 and £65 paying 0·83 per cent. Those with
£200 or more paid 10 per cent. The d'Arblays would have had to pay 0·9 per cent
or about one pound.
³ These remarks refer to plans for printing a second edition of *Camilla*, see L. 314
n. 5.

West Humble, 4 April 1799

To Mrs. Chapone

L. incomplete copy in hand of M. d'A (West Humble Letter Book, pp. 133–5, Osborn), 4 Apr. 1799
Edited by CFBt
Also L.S., incomplete copy in hand of CFBt (Diary MSS. viii. 5154–6, Berg), taken from the above copy
Double sheet 4to   3 pp.

Westhumble April 4. 1799.

To Mᵗˢ Chapone,

It was from your own affecting account, my dear Madam, that I learnt your irreparable loss though a letter by the same post from my syster B[urney]—contained the melancholy intelligence. I will not attempt to say with what extreme concern I have felt it. Your 'darling niece' though I must now be glad I had never seen, I had always fancied I had known from the lively idea you had enabled me in common with all others— to form of what she ought to be. If this second terrible trial,[1] & the manner in which you have supported it, had not shewn me my mistake, I should have feared from the agonised expression of your countenance—which I cannot forget—in our last mournful interviews, that the cup was already full!—But it is not for nothing you have been gifted,—nor that so early you were led to pray 'The ill you might not shun, to bear.'[2] Misfortunes of this accumulate—I had nearly said desolating nature always of late years, sharpen to me the horrours of that part of the F[rench] R[evolution] which to lessen the dread of Guilt gives Death to eternal Sleep—What alleviation can there be for sufferers who have imbibed such doctrine? I want to disperse amongst them an animated translation of the false

---

313. [1] The death of Mrs. Chapone's niece Jane (*c.* 1760–99), the elder daughter of the Revd. John Mulso (*c.* 1721–91), prebendary of Winchester Cathedral (1770). Having married in 1798 the Revd. Benjamin Jeffreyes (*c.* 1748–1800), Fellow of Winchester College (1784), Jane died on 12 Mar. 1799, after giving birth to a dead child. See John Cole, *Memoirs of Mrs. Chapone* . . . , pp. 36, 54, 63; and a tablet in Winchester College Cloisters.

Thomas Mulso had died on 7 Feb. (L. 310 n. 5).

[2] The line is quoted from Mrs. Chapone's poem 'To Health', *Works* (1807), iv. 154.

principles beautiful conviction & final consolations of Fidelia.[3]
For since in this nether *Sphere* with all our best hopes alive of
Times to come,

> *Even virtue Sighs while poor Affection mourns*
> *The blasted comforts of the desart heart.*[4]

What must sorrow be where Calamity sees no opening to
future light? & where Friends when separated, can mark no
haven for a future reunion. but where all terminates for ever
in the poor visible Grave, against which all our conceptions &
perceptions so entirely revolt that I, for one, can never divest
the idea of annihilation from Despair? Hope — — —

I read with much more pleasure than surprise what you say of
Mʳ Pepys.[5] I should have been disappointed indeed had he
proved a *Summer-Friend*. Yet I have found many more such, I
confess, than I *had dreamed of in my poor philosophy* since my
retirement from the broad Circle of life has drawn aside a veil
which, till then, had made profession wear the same semblance
as Friendship. But few, I believe, escape some of these lessons,
which are not however more mortifying in the expectations
they destroy, than gratifying in those they confirm. You will be
sure, dear Madam, but I hope not angrily, of one Honour I am
here venturing to give myself — — — Mʳ D. entreats you
to accept his Sincerest Respects — —

[3] The 'Story of Fidelia' was narrated by Mrs. Chapone in three papers (nos. 77,
78, 79) of the *Adventurer* (1753–4).
[4] These lines, which FBA in her editorial capacity attributed to Elizabeth
Carter, occur in verses 'To Mrs. Vesey / 1766', *Poems on Several Occasions* (3rd edn.,
1776), pp. 94–7.
[5] In a letter of *pre* 1 Apr. (Eg. 3698, f. 123) Mrs. Chapone had referred to W. W.
Pepys as 'that excellent man . . . whose worthy heart you do not half know, &
whom compassion has improved from a delightful companion & intimate old
acquaintance to the most tender, attentive, and affᵉᶜ son to me'.

West Humble, 14 April 1799

To Mrs. Phillips

A.L. (rejected Diary MSS. [5153a–b]–5154–[4c], Berg), 14 Apr. [17]99
Three single sheets 4to, the first single sheet being a leaf from an old
letter already bearing a wafer 6 pp.
Addressed, p. 2: Mrs. Phillips, / Belcotton, / Drogheda
Addressed, p. 6: Mrs. Phillips.
Edited by CFBt *and the* Press, *see* Textual Notes.

This First.

⟨———⟩

April 14.—99—

My dearest Soul—

I send one hasty fresh sheet—
one Copy by my Mate of what you missed of Court Journal,[1]
& the remaining sheet of the same account—long since written,
but waiting opportunity—& M. de N.'s Letter.[2]

My kindest Love to my dear Fanny—& to Willy—& kind
remembrances to your good Susan.

I rejoice you hear good news [of] Norbury.

My dear pet is not yet re-established—but he is better. He
sleeps very irregularly, & *certainly* has worms,—& this next
week he is to be terribly disciplined, once more, to try to expel
them.

My last accounts of all our family speak them well.—
Charlotte assures me she is happy.

The enclosed to Norbury Charles of Greenwich[3] wrote
for his Cousin while we were there, but I had not room in the
last pacquet. That for Fanny I also brought then, but could not
insert.

What I enclose from any of them, I do under *my* hand—not
to seem encroaching on our privilege.

Is it not cruelly vexatious that we should have spent 6 weeks[4]
from our home in the winter, & our dearest Friends spend

---

314. [1] Possibly the missing close of L. 300,'my last Court History of this year' [1798].
  [2] The comte de Narbonne's letter of 1 Feb. 1799 (L. 304 n. 15).
  [3] Charles Parr Burney, now about 14 years old.
  [4] From *post* 4 Jan.–*c.* 28 Feb. (Ll. 303, 304).

another 6 weeks [*wafer*] in Spring? We could not contrive it otherwise, but it is [*wafer*] truly provoking. Heaven bless my best beloved Susan—ever! ever! bless but as I love her!— |

West Humble—
April 14. 99—

I could write a whole Letter my own beloved Susan in merely speaking of yours—but I have not a moment for more than my thanks, and a general word or two, to prevent any suspence I can obviate. I am now just applied to, at last, for my preparations for a 2ᵈ Edition of Camilla:⁵ & I am engaged almost day & night in a revision. You will believe how entirely, when I tell you it has confined me from making a visit to Norbury Park, though this is the last week before the London Journey, which for 6 will separate us. But the Work is so long, & the people, waiting to the last moment for the application, are now in such haste, that I am obliged to relinquish every thing for proceeding with the business. And it would be unjust not to say I am extremely pleased with the necessity, though not its urgency; for the times are so changed since the publication, that the Publishers, who thought they should print the work again in 5 Months, have been silent about it till these last 10 days: & say the sale of all books has had a stagnation that has only been forced by Politicks. And I had really begun to fear a 2ᵈ Edition would never have | been demanded—which was the more alarming, as our account for advertisements, extra—Books, proposals, &c—&c has never been settled, & was to be deducted from the last payment of the Copyright, which is not due till the 2ᵈ Edition is printed. Besides the *honour & glory*—which I own, poor as we are, goes yet further in our anxiety, mutually, than even the more substantial pen.

This will not be uninteresting to my Susan, to whom whatever can concern us in these *high* particulars will always, I know, be nearly as important as to ourselves.

Yet another subject rises ever uppermost,—& I must hasten to say that NOTHING more has passed since I last wrote. I heard

---

⁵ The second edition of *Camilla* was not to appear until 1802, having been advertised by Cadell & Davies in *The Times* (6 Feb.) of that year. For samplings of FBA's revisions, see Edward A. and Lillian D. Bloom in their edition of *Camilla* (1972).

from Hetty that James was not well, & talked of the Country again—& I sent him a message, by her, that I was sorry to hear of his indisposition. I did this, because I would let him see it shall always depend upon *himself* to be what he will with me—but I have had no answer. W.iether she gave the message, & received none, or forgot it herself, I know not. He is too much in the wrong, every way, to come round himself, I know well,—And I shall miss no opportunity [|] of always trying to convince him I can separate his late action from my general affection, & by that means preserve it. But if he would exact from me—from Us, rather, an approvance of his conduct,—ALL MUST END between us! —he can never have it. But his own regard will, I hope, with a little reflection, make him contented more rationally. I think what you inserted about Sally was qu[ite] inevitable.[6] Poor wretched Girl!—she is more detestable in this business, because younger, & therefore more unpardonable for total unfeelingness; but she is less culpable in—by far!—for James *HAS* principles, & knows he has led her, as well as himself, into a defiance of all right.—But—as my dearest Father says in a Letter to me, *ALL THIS* is nothing compared with our deprivation of Susan![7]—'*This*, says he, is a subject to shrink from with resentment & disgust—*that* to cling to the very heart strings!—' And till *June* now must we put off Spring?—I am shocked & terrified about the Law Appeal[8]—alas—if on that hangs our hopes, mine are cruelly feeble!—Does the Major know Mrs. Rishton leaves Chelsea entirely in May?[9] My Father's ardent hopes of *you* keep him from any attempt at an establishment, but he cannot live without some female society & care—but he cannot bear [|] to form any plan, or even think of any, while an opening remains of hope. It is impossible to describe the earnestness of his wishes for your arrival. It makes him quite turn away from every other idea. Yet I hope he will take one of our dear nieces till your arrival. I mean to propose it. I am always uneasy in thinking of him without *one of us*, though he has solemnly pledged me his word he will never be ill

---

[6] Such insertions on small cuttings of paper meant for FBA's eyes alone were commonly lost, though one at least survives (L. 304 n. 1).

[7] CB's comments on JB and SHB seem to have been systematically destroyed, though the second part of the quotation evidently relates to SBP.

[8] See L. 306 n. 3.

[9] Maria was not to leave Chelsea, however, until Sept. 1799 (L. 334, p. 329).

without sending for me immediately.—You will have heard our dear & excellent Esther's most worthy plan of aid to her family.[10] I am sure it will prosper, & every where do her honour. The *same events I had to relate,* which helped the *illnesses* to blunt my so lately excruciating feelings about J[ames] were not *personal,* my love—they were accounts given me, in town, by Mrs. R[ishton] & by Molly[11] of the parties—accounts so subversive of good opinion & respect, that it was impossible in hearing them not to find all softer feelings, whether of kindness or of grief, diminished, by augmentation of offence. A million & million of thanks for what you say of your *Health & promise,* my own dear & if possible dearer than ever—*innocent*—*estimable* Sister. Heaven bless you!—

You can always, *thus,* send me *letters through esther* safely.

I am delighted with what you say of Hetty's kind Letter.

3¹5   West Humble, 20 April 1799

To Mrs. Waddington

A.L. (Berg), 20 Apr. [17]99
Double sheet small 4to   3 pp.   *pmks*   [DA]RKING   22 AP 99   wafer
Addressed: Mrs. Waddington, / Nº 3. / Great Pulteney Street, / Bath
Docketed in pencil, p. 4: W

West Hamble, Dorking—
April 20*th* 99

My ever dear Marianne—It is HERE I must hope to see you— in my own little Hermittage—I could not till now be sure if I should not be called to Town.

Do not disappoint me—& let me know the Day,—not for any preparations—I have no power to shew you my affection *outwardly*—but that no ill chance may make me out on one of our long strolls, or very few visits. Norbury Park, is, unluckily, empty,—its dear Inhabitants are in Town for 6 weeks. They are at Nº 10 Manchester Square. I can Answer for the pleasure they will ALL experience in seeing you. Shall I negociate a

---

[10] The plan to offer music lessons (see L. 311, p. 267).
[11] CB's servant Mary More (ii. L. 68 n. 30).

meeting? or would you rather write? or risk a chance call? The *latter* has very little to hope, they will be so full of engagements.

M. d'A wishes much to kiss your Hands—& how I shall love to see you kiss the Cheeks of my little Boy!—He is tormented dreadfully with Worms—otherwise all health, & *always* all spirits. Can you possibly bring me your dear Children? I long to embrace them. Dearest Marianne, do not let this be a dream. — — You will smile at our bare walls, | & unfurnished Dwelling—& *more* than simple way of life—but it will not be with *pity*, when you see how well it agrees with us. Should you see again any of the *Elect* who remember me, such as the 3 you have mentioned, Mrs. H. More, Mrs. Holroyd, & Miss H. Bowdler,[1] pray tell them I never forget the pleasure I have owed to them, & am always eager to hear of them & their welfare. My Father has just promised me Miss H. More's new work, which I am told is excellent.[2]

I met General Goldsworthy at Lady Rothes,[3] in my neigh-bourhood, when he was there in attendance upon the Princess Amelia, in Her R. H.'s way from Worthing to Town—& we talked much of old times—& of one he called *his old friend*. Can you guess who so sage an antique lady might be? He said He should be at Bath this season — — so, *I* said, would be also that ancient dame—& he seemed much to enjoy the idea of a *rencounter*. Who is the *Mr. G.*[4] you mention being at Bath? |

My dear Child is taking Ching's Lozenges.[5]

I hope you will meet with my good friend Mrs. Cooke.[6] Remember my caution of not judging from *exteriors*!

God bless you, my dear Friend—I shall *depend upon seeing you*.

Alas—like Me—you will be ready to cry at sight of the Chimney piece of your beloved aunt D[elany][7]—the paper, in our absence during the dreadful weather, got damp, & all the beautiful ornaments of her elegant hand are dropt off—little more than the outline remains unimpaired!—I am sure I need not to *YOU* say how this has grieved me.

315. [1] See ii, L. 42 n. 4; i, L. 3 nn. 128, 87.
[2] Hannah More had recently published *Strictures on the Modern System of Female Education* (2 vols., 1799). It was advertised on 16 Apr. in the *Morning Chronicle* as 'This day published'. [3] See Ll. 298 and 300.
[4] Conjecturally, the James Greene, Esq. (*c.* 1760–1814), M.P. for Arundel (1796–1802), who had subscribed to *Camilla*.
[5] See L. 310 n. 1.
[6] See iii, L. 122 n. 8. [7] See L. 260 n. 10; also iii, Ll. 144, 191.

Pray be as early, & to stay as late as possible.

I can venture to offer *YOU* our bread & Cheese fare—& M. d'A. opens his Heart with mine to all my friends. But— ormé! we have no Bed I could venture to propose to any one but a *Sister*, as you will see—& see with wonder that I have even proposed it at all—

316   West Humble, 22 April 1799

To Mrs. Broome

A.L.S. (Berg), 22 Apr. [17]99
Double sheet 4to   4 pp.   *pmks*   DAR[KING]   23 AP 99   23 AP 1799 wafer
Addressed: Mrs. Broome, / Nº 12. Salisb⟨ur⟩y Place, / New Road, Marybone.
Endorsed by CBFB: Sister d'Arblay / april 1799

West Humble,
April 22ᵈ—99

You are very good, my dearest Charlotte, & Mr. Broome's adroit ingenuity had full success;[1] but I dare not attempt to imitate it, lest, if I fail, you should not own it: & these double Letters, merely upon my own business, I have always franked to whatever person I have addressed their troublesome contents. I shall entreat you to be so kind as to let us have 6 notes of £2—& 11 of one. making £23, enclosed in a Letter to be sent to Mr. Lock's Nº 10. Manchester Square. Mrs. Lock will convey it me safely next *Friday*, with a pacquet she is so good as to make up for me of other commissions, which will come with the Weekly Cart which travels from Norbury Park to Town during her residence there.

The remaining £2 I entreat you to keep back for paying some sugar commissions Esther has undertaken for me. M. d'A. also has a debt of 16 with either James or Mrs. B[urney] he is not sure which, for some *plated spoons*. Be so kind as to enquire of which ever you see first, & to pay it from the £2.—with our best thanks.

316. [1] Part of CBFB's letter of *pmk* 20 AP 99, to which this is the reply, survives (Berg). Mr. Broome's 'adroit ingenuity' is lost with a part torn away, but he seems to have offered revisions for *Camilla*.

I heard with great amazement your anecdote of the Female Recluse.[2] It was my first intelligence of it. I am extremely glad it has taken place. How is it that she was alone? Can James make his mind easy at a *voluntary* banishment from a Parent now 71?—I tremble to think what may be his compunction hereafter if his Heart does not soften ere long. If I had seen him I ¹ should have run all risks in representing to him what his own *future* feelings may be, as well as the danger of such an example to be cited or remembered by his own Children in after times. But probably he suspected what I should attempt, & therefore avoided me. How do they now seem? *Can* they be happy, thus wilfully casting off their nearest & most unoffending, (at least) Friends & Relations? They were a constant draw back to all my enjoyment while we were last in Town, from the continual struggle between censure & pity, for their ill conduct & their certain repentance, which they kept alive in my mind. I am heartily glad, however, that Sally, at length, has taken this one right step. That they should speak of indifferent things only cannot surprize me: what else could they talk of, unless his appeased resentment led him to wish to call her back? or her own contrition had urged her to solicit being again received? I have been in the dark about all family events for some time, because my nursery employment was scarcely over before another bantling demanded all my cares.[3] I only now begin to hope to breathe—not to *breathe* yet!—for my Boy is even at this time under a course of Ching's medicines, for the second time.[4] The little animals that infest his little body, & devour all that should nourish it, are of the smallest kind, & the most difficult, I fear, to conquer. He is better—but neither sleeps well, yet, nor *unthins*. *Fattens* is out of all sight or pretension. ¹

I beg Mr. Broome to accept my sincere thanks for his corrections; unfortunately, I was forced to send off my amended (not prepared!) Copy two days ago; but I hope & believe I shall be able to convey without errour his emendations.[5] Mr. Twining

² The extant part of CBFB's letter gives an account of 'the *sequesterd persons*' (JB and SHB), their indifferent lodgings, the notes that had passed between 'the female recluse' and 'her Padre', and finally her 'morning Visit at Chelsea'. 'I hear she was much agitated, that she stay'd abᵗ half an hour, & that they talked only of indifferent things—'. See also L. 326, pp. 305–7.

³ *Camilla*.   ⁴ See L. 310 n. 1.

⁵ Cf. L. 314, p. 274. The 'Copy' may have been the printed pages of a first edition of *Camilla*. Extant, in any case, until the twentieth century but burned in all probability at Camilla Lacey in 1919 was a copy of *Camilla* 'in 5 vols very roughly

has had the goodness to send me some corrections for every volume, & to read it all through, a second time, pen in hand for that purpose.[6] This has not only facilitated my labour, but done for me a work I could not, with any labour, *so* have done for myself. I have not patience for the species of *improvement general* & RADICAL Mr. Broome supposes me engaged in,—nor am I sure it would have been *kindly taken* by so many subscribers, had I made sufficient alteration to have sunk the first Edition in value, so soon after publication. I have dealt more in *omissions* than *changes*,—except simply what were verbal, as far as I was struck with what was faulty, or as I have been aided by Mr. Twining. I will shew his admirable Notes some day to Mr. Broome as a mark of my opinion of his own. I am not at all surprised Mr. Broome found Camilla yet more incorrect than Cecilia, for I had not a moment to revise it, & three volumes were *printing* while the *fifth* was *composing*.[7] You will always oblige me, my dear sister, by Copying for me any hints, observations, or corrections of Mr. Broome's upon any *schtoff* that falls from my pen. |

Carlos, & his wife, gave us one day about a fortnight ago,— each in good health & spirits. I have had no *newer news* than I gave You in my last of our Susan—our post was not to blame this time; the Letter was written for a conveyance to town by Mr. Lock, which changed its day. The Notes need not be out as they come through such safe means.

Adieu, dearest Charlotte. My kind Love, & M. d'Arblay's in its company, to your little namesake, & Marianne, & Clement, —& our Compliments to Miss Broome & Miss Morton.

ever & ever most affectionately yours
F. d'A.

M. d'A. is much obliged by Mr. Broome's Horticultural wishes for him. Nothing, after his tiny fire-side, comes so home to him at this period.

---

bound in stiff paper, with notes and alterations by F.B.' (see the correspondence of May 1911 between Ann Julia Wauchope and Leverton Harris. BM Eg. 3707, ff. 271–9). Some such work sheets as these may have been sent to Cadell and Davies.
   [6] Mr. Twining's first set of corrections are extant (Berg). See iii, L. 226 n. 12.
   [7] See iii, Ll. 192, 193.

I should be extremely glad also, of one Box of certain little Ballets recommended by Miss Cambridge. If directed to me, Mrs. L[ocke] will forward them any time for a Month to come.

& try to recollect, dearest Charlotte, our little account, that we may again start Clear.

317   [West Humble, *pre* 25 April 1799]

To Doctor Burney

L. copy in hand of M. d'A (Berg) of part of a letter now missing

A fragment of used paper, single sheet 4to (9·7 × 7·9″) with lower right corner (3 × 3·1″) cut out and missing. The *verso* has a sketch in the hand of FBA for a fictional character Mr. Medito ('A character in retired life . . . human nature!—')

I heard with great happiness of your good looks & spirits at the Bishop's from Charles.[1] Hetty has since sent me a similar account. I honour her determination to aid the good & well-fare of her Family. the teaching season being now so short, that however full M^r B[urney] can with difficulty bring his affairs round without fear, if not distress. I grieve at the project of any fresh separation in the family, but cannot wonder, the times considered; & certainly the good fortune of Fanny, well as it is merited by that deserving Girl, may lead dear Sophy to submit to a similar fate with less repining. You will be so kind, my dearest F[ather] as not to mention it to either of them, unless they have already begun the subject, for H[etty] writes to me upon it in confidence, & does not say whether or not she has yet apprised them of her design *positively*.[2] That she has long had *the idea*, they well know,—but I fear by what I can gather, poor Sophy has the same repugnance to the scheme that so long made

317. [1] Probably at the town house of Brownlow North, Bishop of Winchester (i, L. 3 n. 10).

[2] The plan to give music lessons (L. 311, pp. 266–7), of which in a footnote to the copy of this 'scratchment' that FBA included in her letter (L. 318) she says CB was apprised. It becomes clear (in L. 318) that the indirect purpose of this letter was to suggest to CB that he might take his granddaughter Sophia Elizabeth Burney (1777–1856) under his roof and so relieve the financial burdens in Beaumont Street.

F[anny] unhappy.[3] May she but—should it prove inevitable, find a second Lady B[everley] to console her!—M[arianne] is not thought of for such a measure, first, I believe, because she has some expectations from aunt Bl[ue][4] & 2^{ly} because M^r B[urney] &. my S[ister] think they may keep one of their companions at home without imprudence. Besides, Marianne has never prepared for such a stroke, & poor S[ophy] has had it hovering over her some years. I own I feel depressed at its necessity— & especially at the extreme incertainty about our beloved Suz[anne] makes me think it a resource the less for my dear F[ather], whom the good Girls tenderly love. However, H[etty] says she has no intention of fixing *this* business till the Autumn, for she thinks S[ophy] now looks delicate, & hopes to recruit her health as well as improve her in music, &c—by that time & |

[In a letter of 25 April to EBB (L. 318) FBA gave a summary of the missing conclusion of this letter]

Then followed more of hopelessness of our darling Exile, with a paragraph from herself that she could only have a *glimpse* of expectation of a *visit*, not a *residence*, without the Major.

3^{18} West Humble, 25 April 1799

To Esther (Burney) Burney

A.L.S. (Berg), 25 Apr. 1799
Double sheet small 4to   4 pp.   wafer
Addressed: Mrs. Burney, / Beaumont Street, / Devonshire Place.

West Hamble, April 25th 99
My dearest Esther,

I have had a long Letter from my Father—without one word of answer to the chief subject, purport, & spirit of mine:[1]—

[3] In 1795 EBB's daughter Frances had been happily placed as governess with the family of Algernon Percy (1750–1830), 1st Earl of Beverley (1790). See iii, L. 142 n. 3; L. 182 n. 5.
[4] Charles Rousseau's sister Elizabeth Warren Burney (i, Intro., p. lxxv).

318. [1] CB's letter is missing, but of FBA's veiled plea for EBB's daughter Sophia Elizabeth Burney (L. 317) he evidently took no notice.

but as he writes in perfect good humour, I am certain he is not offended at what amounted to no more than an *intimation*,—& I am inclined to think he is meditating something he will perform wholly himself, & wholly himself make known. He must *carefully* have avoided the subject, as he names you—names the dear Girls,—& replies to every thing else I mentioned in my Letter. This, to me, augurs *well*,—I trust I shall not be disappointed: for I think he would *undoubtedly* have spoken upon the subject in a general way, had he not some purpose of doing it in a particular one. He is to be at your *Great Concert for Great Folks*, he says, on Monday. As I thought you would wish to know *exactly* what I said, I have retained a *scratchment of the same*, taken from the original (not *written as a Copy*) & will now give it you word for word, as it may be useful in case of a conference on the subject.—

[*Here* FBA *included a copy of the excerpt* (L. 317) *of her letter to* CB *with a short summary of the remainder of that letter* (see p. 281–2).]

All this was so much the principal purpose of my Letter, that it cannot by *accident* have been passed over. My dear Father loves to be let alone—& he will act, I doubt not, by some plan of his own. I have had *some reason* for all I have said beyond what you pointed out that I think you would not disapprove were we to commune upon it together; but I cannot detail longer, from uncertainty what may strike you. You will see, however, that if it is a plan he thinks unfeasible, nothing has been said to make his inaction mortifying. I did not dare *propose*—but I think I must have set his own ideas at work in proposing. |

I know you must be now so exceedingly occupied, that I shall not dream of any answer, unless something occurs upon this subject with our dear Father—& then I shall be very anxious for a few lines. our sweet Mrs. Lock's last Letter to me says 'I have the delight of seeing dear Mrs. Burney's gentle Form sitting by my Amelia at this moment.—'

My poor Alex is still Chingified.[2]

Will you, my dear sister, order us 1 doz p^d of the same sugar as the last of Me de Grouvelle,[3] & another dozen of the

---

[2] See L. 310 n. 1.   [3] Unidentified.

cheapest she sells? And if she can send them to Mr. Lock's, Mrs. Lock will have them forwarded to us by her weekly cart. I have commissioned Charlotte to pay for them, if you will be so kind as to let her have the account—which she will balance from what she transacts for us wth Mr Mathias.

God bless you, & prosper you, my dearest Esther! our united Loves to Mr. B[urney] & Marianne & Sophy & Amelia. ever

most affectionately yours
F. d'A.

M. d'A. will not budge one inch from his prophesy about the Masters.—

[Postscript added apparently by Marianne Burney or another of Esther's daughters]

if Mrs Hawkins & [o]ur d^r Cecilia are still with you[4] [b]est love to both.—

319   West Humble, 2 May 1799

To Mrs. Locke

L. imperfect copy in hand of CFBt (Diary MSS. viii. 5156–8, Berg), 2 May 1799
Double sheet 4to   3 pp.
Edited at the Press.

To Mrs Lock.   Westhamble
                                            May 2^d 1799

Poor Mr Seward!—I am indeed exceedingly concerned— nay, grieved for his loss to us[1]—to *us* I trust I may say, for I believe he was so substantially good a Creature, that he has left no fear or regret merely for himself. He fully expected his end was quickly approaching. I saw him at my Father's at Chelsea, and he spent almost a whole morning with me in chatting of

---

[4] Cf. CB's letter (Eg. 3690, ff. 98–9b) of 8 Apr.: 'The Hawkins's are at Hetty's with Cecilia, who though not so pretty as she was, is a nice and clever little girl' (iii, L. 132 n. 5).

319. [1] William Seward (i, L. 1 n. 9; iv, L. 309 n. 2) had died on 24 Apr. 1799. Cf. CB's letter (Eg. 3691, ff. 198–9b) of 8 Apr.: 'Poor Seward! is very dangerously ill with water on his Chest; a kind of dropsy . . . to w^ch *tapping* will do him no good!'

other times, as he called it,—for we travelled back to Streatham, Dr Johnson, and the Thrales. But he told me he knew his disease incurable;—indeed he had passed a quarter of an hour in recovering breath, in a room with the servants, before he let me know he had mounted the College stairs. My Father was not at home. He had thought himself *immediately dying,* he said, 4 days before, by ¹ certain sensations that he believed to be fatal; but he mentioned it with cheerfulness—and though active in trying all means to lengthen life, declared himself perfectly calm in suspecting they would fail. To give one a proof, he said he had been anxious to serve Mr Wesley,² the Methodist Musician, and he had recommended him to the patronage of the Hammersleys³—& begged my Father to meet him there to Dinner, but as this was arranged, he was seized himself with a dangerous attack, which he believed to be mortal. And during this belief, 'willing to have the business go on,' said he, laughing, 'and not miss me, I wrote a letter to a young lady, to tell her all I wished to be done upon the occasion to serve Wesley & to shew him to advantage;—I gave every direction I should have given in person, in a complete persuasion at the moment, I should never hold a pen in my hand again.'

This letter, I found, was to Miss Hammersley.

I had afterwards the pleasure of introducing M: d'Arblay to him—and it seemed a gratification to him to make the acquaintance. I knew he ¹ had been *'curious'* to see him, & he wrote my Father word afterwards he had been much *pleased.*⁴

My Father says he sat with him an hour the Saturday⁵ before he died, & though he thought him very ill, he was so little aware his end was so rapidly approaching that, like my dearest Friend, he laments his loss as if by sudden death.

---

² Probably Samuel Wesley (1766–1837).

³ The family of the banker Thomas Hammersley, whose burial 30 Oct. 1812 is recorded in the register of St. James's, Piccadilly. Of a firm of bankers, 76 Pall Mall (*London Bankers,* p. 77), he lived at this time at 'Brompton-park house'.

Miss Hammersley would have been his eldest daughter Anne (*c.* 1773–1841), who was to marry on 7 Oct. 1805, at St. James's Church, the Revd. William Ward (*c.* 1762–1838), D.D. (1826), Rector of Great Horkesley (1817–38), Bishop of Sodor and Man (1828). The cultivated interests and philanthropy of the families is described by Edith Caroline Wilson, *An Island Bishop (1762–1838)* (1931).

⁴ Seward's letter, dated Dean Street, Thursday, is preserved in the Scrapbook (Berg), 'Fanny Burney and family. 1653–1890', p. 11: 'Md^e d'Arblay look'd very well. . . . M. d'Arblay I had now the pleasure to see . . . & was very much pleas'd with him.'

⁵ On Saturday 20 Apr.

I was sorry too, to see in the newspapers the expulsion of M[r] Barry from the Royal Academy.[6] I suppose it is from some furious harangue. His passions have no restraint, though I think extremely well of his Heart as well as of his Understanding.

320   West Humble, 8 May 1799

Conjointly with M. d'Arblay
To Mrs. Phillips

A.L. & A.N. (Berg), 8 May 1799, including copies of letters from FBA and SHB
Double sheet 4to   4 pp.   wafer
Addressed: Mrs. Phillips, / Belcotton, / Drogheda.

West Hamble,
May 8th 1799

Your dear Letter, my most dear Susan, has sadly lowered my hopes—far as they were from being sanguine! I begin to fear it is but—in its consequence,—unkindness to dwell so much upon our wishes,—it seems but to keep alive a never ending struggle, & oppose all your efforts to resignation!—Sometimes I plan a total abstinence from the subject, & to wait for its renewal by the Major himself,—but I never can adhere to that plan,—my hopes, my *violent* wishes will not be repressed—not demolished, at least,—& they break out in fresh entreaties & urgencies, whether I will or not! — — — — I have hinted to our dear Father, in a Letter which will accompany this to Manchester Square,[1] the *half year* since you have seen his hand. I am sure he will be as much amazed as shocked. He fears tormenting you, by pressing upon the subject always next his heart,—& he hates to write so unnaturally as to avoid it. This he has told me. But *any* manner, would be preferable to *none*, I know well, for I can judge my beloved Susan by myself.

[6] This news FBA may have gleaned from *The Times* (26 Apr.): 'MR. BARRY, Royal Academician, and Professor of Painting to the Royal Academy, has been expelled from that institution by the President and Council.'

320. [1] No. 10, where the Lockes were staying for the London season.

The *why* — — *why—why—*I feel very sympathetically as to our dear Esther. There is no choice, however, now, between giving up all but bare subsistence, or earning pleasure & comforts to add to it. The world is through-out upon one of these two plans. *You*—& *I*—should prefer the former, with retirement, & dear though limitted society; but Esther, if of the same opinion, is in another circle; she must live in London, & therefore wishes to live there with some elegance & enjoyment. And the step she has taken is nothing less than *necessary*, in times so extremely severe.[2] But I am more concerned at her thinking it indispensable—& I believe justly—to place Sophy in the same situation as Fanny: for Sophy, poor dear Girl, is equally repugnant to the measure, though she will submit, from the happiness which so unexpectedly has resulted to Fanny, with a better grace. *My* wish, like yours, is that she should be taken home by our dear Father till your arrival. I have done what I could to promote such a scheme. She could then return instantly to her home, & she would be *improved in Music*, & in *French*, & my Father might *help* & *dignify* the plan, by having her under his roof, & introducing her a little amongst his friends: such as visit him at home, I mean. But he makes no answer, as yet, to what I have ventured upon this subject.[3]

I wish you would always begin upon a *mutilated* sheet, my Susan—when any family subjects of profound secresy—such as of J[ame]s to discuss. It is so comfortable to read what has no restraint: & alas!—when can we name them naturally & openly at once? I have a new anecdote to surprise you with—& I know your deep interest upon this subject too well to defer a moment any communication I can forward.

Imagine my astonishment to receive the following Letter by the post.[4]

[*from Sarah Harriet Burney*]   20. April, 99.

Before you can have taken any step in the business I wrote to you about this Morning, again I trouble you, my dearest sister, (& implore your forgiveness for this apparent capriciousness,) to forget every word you have read. I sat down passionately & hastily, unawares of the resentment—such a step was likely to create in my Brother's Mind. He will do

---

[2] See L. 311, pp. 266–7.   [3] In L. 317.
[4] The originals of the letters herein copied are missing.

nothing towards ¹ preventing the effect of my first Letter himself—but he seems so much incensed at it, that I have not the courage to persevere in my plan.

You will hate me for thus trifling with you,—but rather endeavour—O my dearest sister, to forgive, & pity me.— Friday Night.

I am sure I need not tell you the various sensations with which I read this extraordinary Letter. I had received no preparatory one; & M. d'A. is so wicked as to insist none ever was written, & that the reference was merely an excuse for writing.—But, this idea is checked by the, then, so *unnecessary* complaint of James's sombre rage, & the call upon Me for pity in her helpless dependance upon his tyranny!—for such seems the tenor of the Letter.⁵ I am, however, extremely, & to my Heart rejoiced she has written, & shewn me, what I always concluded, that she never doubted the sincerity of my regard, nor of my eagerness to come forward to prove it,—though, while all went [well] or while she thought it right it should seem to go well, she c[ared not] to accept my invitation to a meeting, without even saying she was *sorry*, or thanking me for wishing it, circumstanced as she stood, & certain as they both were of the dreadful grief & indignation their conduct had caused me.—But my pacquet is so enormous, I must repress all commentary to copy my answer,—which was written immediately.

21. April—99—

With the greatest amazement I have just received a few lines, referring to a Letter that has never reached me, & containing allusions to a plan which I cannot comprehend. Pray endeavour to trace if your Letter was put into the post. I shall make all the enquiries I can about it at Dorking. Write speedily, my dear Sally, with a firm reliance that I will either do, or omit to do, whatever you may wish that you think can conduce either to serve or console you,—if either should in the smallest degree be in my power. My original disturbance is again renewed,—though not, indeed, so bitterly as ¹ while you seemed both *WHOLLY to forget* you had a sister at West Hamble.

⁵ For idealized portraits of JB, see the character of Somerset in SHB's *Clarentine* (3 vols., 1796), i, 93–4; ii. 104, 261, etc.

I have so little room, now, that I must instantly write you the answer, certain you would be extremely perplexed & chagrined to wait for it till next pacquet.

[*from Sarah Harriet Burney*]   23^d April—99—

The Letter, my dearest sister, concerning which you naturally express such surprise, fortunately never was delivered at the office; which I did not discover till after the second was put in. I have since destroyed it, & am extremely concerned to have given you so much unnecessary uneasiness, as well as most sincerely grateful for the kindness with which you assure me of your readiness to serve or advise me. The firm dependance I have upon this is a very great comfort & pleasure to me, & will encourage me, should any occasion present itself sooner to apply to you than to any other human being.

My Brother desires his kind love, & will write before he leaves town, which, with little Martin, we now mean to do very soon. Accept my repeated excuses for the perplexity I occasioned you, & *believe me*, my dearest sister, your ever most grateful

S. H. B.

No Letter, however, from James is yet arrived, *May 8.*—but I hope to receive one, & to be again upon terms of affection & *intercoursing*,—though, alas, no more of faith or approbation. But I am sure my dearest Susan will be glad this has passed, strange as it is. *I* am, & easier & happier beyond all description. God bless & preserve my own beloved—best beloved Susan! This immense pacquet i⟨s to sh⟩ew you I do not correct Camilla, & have done with the revis[ion.[6] Be]st tenderest love to Fanny—& Norbury, who I hope is now with you, or [*wafer*] & dear little Willy—& the Major—if at hand—. Alex is well— His padre means to write fo[r *wafer*]

Mrs. Newton & her family are well.

Remember me to Susan.

[*By M. d'Arblay, p. 3*]

Je remets au prochain paquet à vous ecrire, ma chere petite Soeur. Aujourdhui, je vous dirai seulement que vous m'avez

---

[6] On 20 April (see L. 316, pp. 279–80).

accusé trés injustement d'une indiscretion dont j'aurais pu être très capable. le boisterous weather est de mon invention. il y avait *tout bonnement* le mot propre. j'ai simplement et de mon autorité privée fait usage de l'image, en employant le style figuré —j'embrasse vous Fanny Willy Norbury *con permissione &* amore —

321   West Humble, 13 May 1799

To Mrs. Locke

L. copy in hand of M. d'A (West Humble Letter Book, pp. 68–9, 90–91–92, Osborn), 13 May 1799

To Mʳˢ Locke Nº 10 Manchester Square

May 13—1799.

I write before due time to tell my dearest friend how much I am pleased at her new project.[1] I am sure it will turn out delightfully. The dear King will see my Fredy with real pleasure, from old remembrances, & take an interest in her daughters, & the Children of a most beloved person of whom he almost constantly speaks to me when I am honoured with his notice: & the Queen will be really gratified by the measure. My adorable Princess Augusta will employ her intelligent Eyes in reading all your characters,—to my infinte future satisfaction— & Princess Elizabeth will be graciousness personified. The others will probably not to be present. All of them, I believe I may venture to say—will think of Whestamble—though the discourse at Court is so very concise that they will not name it.

I conclude my dearest Friend will be presented by Lady Templetown[2]—It is always most desirable, I know by the many presentations of which I have heard the history all round, to have the ceremony performed by a friend, than merely left to the common course of the lady in waiting; & my Fredy has

---

321 [1] In view of Charles Locke's appointment (L. 292 n. 47) as British Consul at Naples, the Lockes decided to attend the drawing-room on the occasion of the King's birthday (4 June), the most splendid and brilliant that has been witnessed for many years (*The Times*, 5 June).
  [2] See L. 269 n. 11.

such a circle of acquaintance who would emulously whish to come forward upon such an occasion, that if, unhappily Lady Templetown should be indisposed, she can be at no loss, save from abundance of choice. But ⏐ in that case,—let me use my valued privilege of sincerity with the Friend dearest my heart, in suggesting that she will elect some one rather from being in favour with the Queen, than only from personal preference. Much of the pleasure of this business depends upon this attention—& all those who would willingly act as Lady Cottorels,³ are not in this predicament. Lady T[empletown] herself stands not where she *has* stood—but her known long friendship would make her election expected & therefore approved.

I shall long to have my dear Augusta & Amelia look their best. My kindest love to them, & as they have been talked of a good deal (to my *undoubted* knowledge) tell them I supplicate they will give up a Ball or an Opera or two, a night or two before, that they may carry a little natural bloom, where so little is seen, & where none other is respected, however generally exhibited. They all feel what Mʳ Locke, I recollect, once admirably expressed upon this subject 'How one should admire rouge—if one could forget the motive that put it on!' So that my sweet Amelia need not be afraid of being pale,—but still, I would rather she should spare a little racketing, & be otherwise.

One of the 3 opportunities in the course of every year which I seize upon to bring myself to the remembrance of Her Majesty, occurs next Sunday, on her *real* birth day⁴—is there any thing my dearly beloved friend would ⏐ like I should say upon this occasion? I had intended, on first hearing the scheme, to gently intimate that its idea was *fixed*, though long & always *wished*, by the late events relative to Mʳ Charles. For that will seem natural, & account to the conjecturing & discerning Queen both why it is done now, & why it was not done sooner. *The House* will with Her go for nothing, since the *Court* is stationary. If my dearest Friend does not object to this,—nor our Oracle—I think I can so word it as to be satisfactory—For what have I to do but give way to my knowledge of what her lovely maternal character might stimulate? — — I would not,

---

³ A generic term derived from the office of Clement Cottrell-Dormer (1686–1758), knighted (1710), master of the king's ceremonies (1711–58).
⁴ On 19 May 1799.

however, upon second thoughts follow my first idea of doing this at once, lest it should oppose any design or view of which I am ignorant. Officiousness is so mischievous, that I am resolved plainly to beg a hint of a *yes* or a *no*, or of any thing whatever, if any thing there is my dearest Friend can conjure up to employ me in so much to my taste. I only regret my letter does not go *after* the presentation, so sure I am I should then have a charge to expatiate upon all your sensibilities to the graciousness I am convinced will be displayed. However, on the *4ᵗʰ of June*, I shall write again—& then!

O how I am grieved at the impossibility Mʳ Locke should accompany | & support you! I hope Mʳ William will exert himself though I am a little afraid the horrour to a *dressed coat* will still stand in the way. I may venture to tell you now, that the Queen told me she had been informed, upon your marriage, that *Mʳ Locke had declared he never would let you go to Court, lest you should be corrupted*—! I need not say how I answered this. I think it was Lord Dalaval⁵ reported it, but am not entirely sure, though she named some one at the time. Mʳ Locke's inability to stand in the circle, was fully however, known by the interviews in my apartment, before the Queen made me this communication,—acknowledging how much at the period she believed it, it had offended her. Her message enchants, but without at all surprising me. They will be quite *glad*, I am sure of it, to see my dearest Friend—& they have long desired to see my dear Augusta & Amelia. Charge the dear girls not to have their Feathers so long or so forward, as to *brush the royal cheeks* as they rise! a circumstance she has mentioned to me with some displeasure, to have happened. I know they will *look*, for they will *feel pleased*, however frightened,—& the Queen has often told me, that indispensable as she holds modesty for young Ladies, & respect & deference—*She never* | *feels much gratified when they look so scared as if they came to Her for a punishment.* How *Perfect* will my Fredy be in all she most approves! Her own tact & exquisite nature will be her sureties. I could not forbear writing all this; I am so much interested in the approaching event. Heaven bless my ever dearest Friend—& Her's!

⁵ John Hussey Delaval (1728–1808), cr. Bart. (1761), M.P. for Berwick about twenty years in all, cr. Baron Delaval [I] (1783), [GB] 1786.

To James Burney

A.L. draft (Berg), *n.d.*
Single page 4to written on p. 3 of A.L.S. JB to FBA, 12 May 1799, ds.
2 pp. 4to, *pmks* Tottenham / Court Road 13 MA 99 wafer
Addressed: M^rs D'Arblay / West Humble / near Dorking / Surry.
Endorsed by FBA: 12 May—1799
Edited by FBA, p. 1, *annotated*:+Al.—O [*all out*]

I thank you most sincerely for your Letter,[1] which indeed
I could not read with dry Eyes—for I thought I had lost you—
but I see, my dear James, I have found you again—Again
I know you, my dear Brother, in your candour as well as your
affection. I should be truly grieved at the moment of receiving
this mark of your unchanged regard to give you any painful
sensations; but it is impossible for me not to say you have never
had '*cause of complaint*—' never! And you would even now be
very sorry to know the sufferings you have occasioned me.—
But I will not oppose your call for oblivion by useless retrospection,—except in applying to your justice to suppose, for
only one instant, the transaction reversed. Would you not have
been apt to exclaim 'What! does she not think me worth one
conciliatory word, either upon her motives, or her designs, in
taking so extraordinary a step? Has she so little care for my good
opinion? so little thought for my anxiety?

Here ends all I will ever say upon this subject, unless called
to it again by yourself—if, therefore, it will amuse you to
suppose me taking a similar dance from my Family & Home
with Richard[2]—smile as you may, but be just in thinking how it
might strike you, unexplained.

The kindness with which M. d'Ar. is attached to you, my
dear James, is as invariable as it is strong; & he would even
separately have proved it, which he daily wished to do during
our absence from home, if indispensable reasons had not made

---

322. [1] JB's original letter of 12 May, to which this is the reply, is extant (Berg), as is
also the copy of it that FBA included in her letter of 29 June 1799 to SBP (L. 326,
p. 305).
[2] FBA's half-brother, Richard Thomas, now 31, was 16 years her junior. His
sister, now 26, was 23 years younger than JB, her half-brother.

it requisite we should act in concert. He sends you his kindest love—Take mine with it, my dear James, with my inalterable warm wishes for your health & welfare. My heart yearns to speak to you of my Father,—but I fear offending you by unasked counsel. Yet I often think with regret, nay alarm of the uneasy feelings you may be hoarding up for future days—& this hint I must give you—if you think any thing gained by *delay*, you are much mistaken! quite the contrary! All is hardened by it.—Pardon this hint—& pray let me hear from you as soon as possible after you are arrived at your place of destination,—& never may I again be at a loss how to direct to you!—I shall be very anxious to know that your health is re-established.

323   [West Humble, 26 May 1799]

To Mrs. Phillips

A.L. (rejected Diary MSS. 5760–[3], Berg), *n.d.*
Double sheet large 4to   4 pp.   red wafer
Addressed: Mrs. Phillips, / Belcotton— / Drogheda.
Edited by FBA, p. 1 (5760), *annotated and dated*: West Hamble, May 26.—99
Edited by CFBt *and the* Press.

I have just heard that our dearest Mrs. Locke will send a pacquet to my most loved Susan on Tuesday,—for which I shall seize time to write a sheet with all speed, which must be sent by a conveyance that offers for Arnold[1] this Evening, to be forwarded with a basket of Flowers for Manchester Square. I find my enormous pacquet is not yet received,[2] & therefore am not tempted to regret having no more journal ready, as I dare not risk two following on insecure premises, lest their contents should suddenly appear in some Irish magazine.—Mrs.

323. [1] Edward Arnold (*c.* 1738–1816), described in the parish records (Mickleham) as 'Bailiff to Mr. Lock' and mentioned in a codicil (1806) of his will (P.C.C. Collingwood 554), probated 3 Nov. 1810, for £125. The 5th or 6th Edward, he was descended from one of the oldest families in Mickleham, there being sixty-eight Arnolds baptized between 1549 and 1635. See Samuel Woods, *Mickleham Records* (1900).
[2] That containing L. 320 and other enclosures.

Locke has kindly sent me my Susan's *May 10^(th)*[3]—& I thank
God *this* time I have escaped the horrour of the fear of Invasion,
by the immediate assertions I received, with the first news that
reached us of the sail[g] of the Brest Fleet, that it was making
towards the mediterranean.[4] But ever, my dearest love, write as
quickly as you can, upon any alarm, as it is not one time in a
thousand that I am spared every sort of horrid fear which
suspence & dread can give me. I know well your invariable
fortitude, as far as regards your mere self,—but I cannot adopt
it for You—so don't expect it!—But I am much disappointed
Norbury is not with you; I had built, from a passage in your
last, upon his being now arrived at Belcotton. I must share
your reliance upon Mr. Maturin,[5] who will surely never let him
travel alone, if any disturbance is to be apprehended.—My
Susan will know, by the great pacquet, that I have done with
Camilla.—How kind to give us all the comfort you can as to the
Climate! Indeed it is literally ǀ all that softens the sad feelings
hanging on all else. I *dare not* give way to hope about the L.
suit[6]—dare not subject myself to what I should feel upon a
disappointment if I listened to hope.—I can only hope in
Providence—which I thankfully feel assured will yet unite us—
yet give us the exquisite—unspeakable delight of again meeting! — — — I told our dearest Father you pined, though
never re-pined at his long silence—for just as you had told me
you had not heard from him for *half a year*, came a Letter
from him, in which he tenderly bewails your lengthened
absence, & adds—nor have I even seen her hand since Christmas.—I told him of the pacquet Mrs. Lock was preparing; &
I hear from her he has made use of it.[7]

We are quite *solaced* you are to see Mrs. Disney,[8]—do try to
present something to her from me, in such a way as may be
received favourably,—though I am half vexed to be made love

[3] Possibly extant in the Locke Papers.
[4] *The Times* (3, 8, 10, 11, 14, 18 May), speculating on the destination of the Brest
Fleet, which had sailed on 26 Apr., had as late as 14 May considered Northern
Ireland a distinct possibility. Only on 22 May were they able to report themselves
'in possession of something in the shape of positive information'. The Fleet had
been sighted 'off the *Tagus*, steering to the South East', with the intention, it was
thought, to join the Spanish forces at Cadiz.
[5] Henry Maturin (iii, L. 215 n. 7).
[6] See L. 306 n. 3.
[7] Possibly CB's letter of [25 May 1799] (Eg. 3960, ff. 100–1b).
[8] *Née* Jane Brabazon (iii, L. 222 n. 20).

her & esteem her & like her so entirely, now I no longer see her
the support & constant comfort I had pictured her. I have not
your generosity—yet I am truly glad she is happy—but I
wanted her to be *happy* WITH *you*—not *away*—We cannot learn
with certainty where *Mesdames* now are; the news papers are
contradictory, but all concur that they have left Sicily.[9] How
earnestly I wish their route may be where M. de Narbonne
may have the exquisite & long-sighed for pleasure—bliss,
rather, of seeing them! They could not, I feel sure, behold—
without feeling all their tenderness revive. But what I conclude
still separates them, is M[e.] La Com[sse] & her *beau*,[10] who are
with them, & whose own tale, self-told, has probably been of a
nature to banish *him* who could not be heard without banishing
them.

‎

I am always extremely glad when I hear of Mrs. Hill. I imagine Mrs. Barnewall[11] is still at Bath. As you mention a Letter
of James May 2[d]—I hope it is such a one as to give some conso-
lation to you—You will receive some, I know, to hear his long |
promised Letter to me is at length arrived, & is all that can be

[9] The daughters of Louis XV, Marie-Adélaïde de France (1732–1800) and
Victoire-Louise-Marie-Thérèse de France (1733–99), half-sisters of the comte de
Narbonne-Lara (ii, Intro., p. xiv). The sisters and their retinues, having been
forced by the advances of the Republican armies to leave Rome, had taken refuge
at Caserta (24 Dec. 1797) under the protection of the Queen of Naples, who,
however, abandoned them in her flight of 22 Dec. 1798 to Sicily. The sisters then
crossed Italy in the unusually cold December of that year, and from Manfrédonia
embarked in such ships as were procurable for Trieste, where Madame Victoire
died of cancer on 7 June 1799. The harrowing tale of their distresses (a garbled
account of which FBA may have seen in *The Times*, 19 Feb.) is supplied by the
comte de Chastellux (below), *Relation du voyage de Mesdames, tantes du Roi . . .* (1816);
by the comtesse de Narbonne-Lara (below), a paper 'Discours de Réception'
presented by M. le Bon Lombard de Buffières and printed in *Annales de l'Académie de
Maçon* (*Société des arts, sciences, belles-lettres et d'agriculture*), 2nd series, vii (Maçon,
1890); and by Casimir Stryieński (below).
[10] According to Casimir Stryieński, *Mesdames de France* (2nd edn., 1911), p. 272,
Mme la duchesse de Narbonne-Lara (ii, Intro., p. xiv), dame d'honneur de Madame
Adélaïde, 'ayant plus de quarante ans de services', wielded an influence over her
mistress much resented by the rival suite, namely: Henri-Georges-César, comte de
Chastellux (1746–1814), maréchal de camp (1788), chevalier d'honneur de Madame
Victoire; his wife (m. 1773), Angélique-Victoire de Durfort (1752–1816), dame
d'honneur de Madame Victoire; and Mme la comtesse Louis de Narbonne-Lara,
dame d'honneur de Madame Victoire.
It may have been in conflicts between the suites and their rival purposes that the
comte de Narbonne's character was reviewed and his interests damaged.
[11] Formerly Elizabeth and Marie-Theresa Kirwan (iii, L. 216 n. 3; L. 275 n. 2).

conciliatory & conceding. I hope to Copy it for you, as I know you will like to see his own words, in my next pacquet. I have not now time for this must go as quick as possible, no opportunity of sending occurring for to-morrow. But I will not ever hold back intelligence upon this subject which with you, as with me, keeps I know its first place of importance. M. d'A is a little afraid he did not begin what he copied of the schotffe at the right place. Pray say. He has taken the amazing trouble & toil of copying the whole, from the pleasure the interview gave him! though he may always re-hear it *DE VIVE VOIX*! Alex. makes no great progress in embonpoint, but his appetite mends, & his strength is surprising, his slight make viewed & considered. I wish you could see Adrienne[12]—'tis one of the most winning Children I ever beheld. not to quite love her is impossible. She is gentle, yet arch, sensible, yet simple, & so fat & babyish, that she is delightful; while, though not really handsome, she has Eyes of so touching an expression, & a voice so melodiously sweet, that you must only once look at her, & once hear her, & take her to your arms & heart. She is all that can reward,—nay *amply* reward the even exquisite goodness of Mrs. Locke, who now doats upon her. Poor M. de Chavagnac! what a treasure & a blessing is yet in reserve for him should his unhappy life be spared for the meeting! I have seen nothing I should so much like to consider as the future partner of my Alex. —our dearest Father enjoys excellent health & *public* spirits—& I believe *banishes* all he can that depresses in *private*. Resentment is a powerful diminisher of sorrow, in diminishing the feelings that first excited it, of wounded esteem, & disappointed expectations. I wish I could tell your good Susan news of her sister,[13] but I have not heard of her within a month; She was then quite well. I shall endeavour next Sunday to see her, in my way from Church.—How can you ever name Mr. Windham, my dearest Susan! except to rejoice he causes me the peace of mind I feel in sending you pacquets. But *we* have *only* you to *buy* hearing from—*You* have *all else* but us!—& I often think of that with pain, & always *try* to get something besides my own inserted within my Cover. If you knew—& saw *how* we *buy news*

---

[12] Adrienne de Chavagnac, now 4 years old, daughter of Louis-Vigile, comte de Chavagnac (iii, L. 201 n. 5; L. 215 n. 12).

[13] Mrs. Newton (iii, L. 237 n. 6; iv, L. 262 n. 1).

of you!—if you *could* see—not ME alone—but US—when a Letter from you arrives—you would say indeed this is *very cheap pay* for delight so extreme!—I expect now to hear before this arrives—but remember, my best beloved Susanna, if the Brest Fleet make any circuit, & turn, at last, for Ireland—for god's sake endeavour to cope with every difficulty in coming to us quick—quick—quick! & *write* instantly, & often, however briefly, I conjure you. This is from no real suspicion of such an event, but merely because we all know the first wish of the French is to land in Ireland, & therefore that if it should be possible, it will be done. But I suspect them now seeking to recover Buonaparte, all their Generals having failed them.[14] Is Mrs. Wall[15] returned to Ireland? We have never heard of her since her little short visit. We had no means to return it at *Epsom*. Pray say so, with all sort of regrets, if you write. I esteem & like both Mother & Daughter & should be glad to hear the amiable son is happy. Heaven bless my beloved Susan! & *Her's.* ever! ever! |

How charming are the traits & accounts you give Amelie of the poor around You! & how it consoles me You are in such a vicinity![16]

324   West Humble, 30 May 1799

To Esther (Burney) Burney

A.L.S. (Berg), 30 May [17]99
Double sheet small 4to   4 pp.   wafer
Addressed: Mrs. Burney, / Beaumont Street, / Devonshire Place.

West Hamble—May 30. 99

I am extremely pleased with my Cloak, my dearest Esther, & return you my best thanks for its *accomplishment*. I entreat you to let me know what besides acknowledgements I owe you for this kind trouble.

We are so exceedingly touched by your most penetrating

---

[14] For instance, the defeats of Jourdan at Stockach (25 Mar.); of Schérer at Magnano (5 Apr.); and of Moreau at Cassano (28 Apr.).
[15] For the Wall family, see iii, L. 203 n. 6; L. 222 n. 4.
[16] Possibly extant in the Angerstein Papers.

accounts & traits of the respectable & charming M̄ᵉ du Chattel,[1] that we almost repine at our inability to shew better than by words what we feel for her. Your descriptions & my remembrance never meet with dry Eyes,— a more affecting sight than that of her interesting figure & countenance, joined to hearing her soft sad accents, I cannot well conceive. That she seems to hang upon you for some consolation will be to YOU a consolation by & bye, though now it is a pain; for she can only do it because she sees your tender sympathy, & knows she looks at one who feels for her. what you have done *besides* feeling & comforting touched *us* as much as it could *her*.—How do I wish it were not utterly impossible to us to come a little forward upon such an occasion! But—to go on, from quarter to quarter, is ALL we can contrive—so many more are our expences than we prepared far when our little building so deeply diminished our little revenue. The Income Tax,[2] which we have not yet paid, we have not yet, also, discovered from what of our comforts we must deduct.—Public affairs, however, are now so very flourishing, we indulge a hope the Peace will yet come that may take off this heavy draw back to subsistence.—

Fully, my dear soul, I enter into your unabated anxiety to see your dear Girls in some security of honourable provision: & your statement was not wanted to deter me from so false a calculation as I must have made to have supposed your little acquisitions could serve to portion them.—I well understand, that if they suffice to replace what you have so hardly been compelled to draw out, & to give you the relaxation you so much require & deserve with less difficulty to dear Mr. Burney, they do *wonders*—but we must not expect from them *MIRACLES*. That you may have all you chuse, ⟨or⟩ have time to undertake, I never doubted,[3] & M. d'Arblay only begs you will conduct yourself with *caution* before those who will feel, if not rue your sway—for you know his fears.—But you make me uneasy in talking of umbrellas—my dearest Etty, if you risk colds, you will undo all your prosperity. Besides, I have always thought the general mischief to dress, in dirtied shoes, in washwomen's Bills for *Bas* & peticoats, & in ruined ribbons & Hats, much

---

324. [1] See L. 296 n. 5; L. 325, pp. 301–2).   [2] See L. 312 n. 2.
[3] In his letter of 8 Apr. (op. cit.) CB remarked that 'M̄ᵗ B. has more scholars th⟨an⟩ he can teach, & Hetty herself has 3 or 4'.

more expensive than Coach or Chair Hire, though not so immediately paid. As to our dear Father, I am glad you judge with me he must be *left alone*. I am certain he would chuse one of your dear Girls *after* Susan—but She has not only his first wish, & first thought, but she has a claim, by what has passed, that, in fact, *binds* him, & since the odious M[ajor] still says she *shall* come, our padre is not even *at liberty* to form any other but transient engagements. This, I doubt not, keeps him silent. He fears the M.'s seizing the notion of his having a resource at hand, & will not take any measure not even conditionally, that may risk his losing that dearest daughter & sister. Heaven knows how much her taking that tender filial place is the wish of us all!—*Yours* I well know it to be as fervently as his or mine—*C'est tout dire*—but I am firmly persuaded he will keep the vacancy while he has any hope the M. will keep his *given promise* —but if—alas—it fails, that you will have the kindest & most cordial request to give him what NEXT to that treasure he will most desire, one of your dear Girls. This is my sincere opinion.

Miss Cambridge laments extremely her ill success at Richmond, but says she has written to you herself. I flatter myself you will now be able to go to your rural retreat there, for fresh air, *without* business,—by your intention to renew your lessonings next year. Surely you ˈ will well have earned air & quiet unmolested. Miss C. laments, also, not being able to help giving herself so *agreable a neighbour*.—How I rejoice dear Marianne has had such success for poor Mlle du Chattel![4] I know how it will gladden her kind heart. Poor little Amelia! I long to hear she & Sophy are better. Good Aunt Rebecca must be greatly enlivened by their society. My kindest love when you see, or write to her. I should have liked extremely to have seen dear little Cecilia. M. d'Arblay sends you both his cordial love, & many thanks for your most kind offer of lodging him if called to London. I congratulate you on having had the *happy* benevolence of recommending M^e de Ste Marie[5] so many scholars. I know how *doing* good *gives* it to my dear Etty. It is for that reason I do not fear for your health in this new employment. I know to assist your excellent partner in the arduous task of helping his family will lighten your spirits, & that your

---

⁴ See also L. 325, p. 302.   ⁵ See L. 302 n. 3.

spirits & health are much connected. only, do not spare the
expence of the moment, to incur that of a much longer period.
No fresh news from Ireland. God bless you, my dear sister,—
Distribute our Loves—& take them tenderly—

F. d'A—

Our little Man won't grow fat—but he grows tall. My love
to James & Sarah when you next see th[em if] they are not yet
gone. I have told you [of his] Letters, & of mine?— |

And is it, then, *fixed* that Richard resigns the curacy offered
by Mr. Poulter?[7]—How sorry—sorry I am!

325 West Humble, 17 June 1799

To Esther (Burney) Burney

A.L. (Berg), 17 June [17]99
Double sheet 4to   4 pp.   wafer
Addressed: Mrs. Burney, / Beaumont Street, / Devonshire Place.

West Hamble,
June 17. 99

I can hardly tell you, my dearest Esther, how much I have
been affected by your most touching account of M[e] duchastel,
whose death I had never heard of, & whose life I had, vainly,
hoped would yet have been spared for days of some recompense
to so much sorrow. But such a finish! after sufferings so un-
merited & so extraordinary!—she was certainly one of the most
interesting Creatures I ever conversed with, & your history of
her, in all its parts, & in every way you have ever named her,
makes me sure she was one of the most estimable. But that her
little debts—little, I doubt not, as well as inevitable,—should
have involved danger even to her poor remains[1]—is so shocking,

---

[7] See L. 296, p. 210. The Revd. Edmund Poulter, *formerly* Sayer (c. 1756–1832),
was at this time rector of Meonstoke, Hants. He had married Ann Bannister
(c. 1753–1839), a sister of Henrietta Maria *née* Bannister, the wife of Brownlow
North, Bishop of Winchester (formerly of Worcester) (i, L. 3 n. 10). This couple
had evidently come to share the Bannister-North kindness for the Burneys.

325. [1] As in the case of J. C. Bach's death in 1782 (Papendiek, i. 151), there was
the fear that creditors might seize the corpse and sell it. For the fear also of resur-
rection men, see *AR* xix (1776), 'Chronicle', 128–9, 'Projects', 119–20.

so afflicting, one is almost obliged—being helpless to do good—
to fly from the subject. Yet it will pursue—& it haunted me all
night, & woke with me the next morning—You can bear it a
little the better, (though you will feel it much the *longer* from
the intimate knowledge you had of the tender sufferer) for
having done, alltogether, so much good to her.—for that is a
balm indeed to sorrow & pity. That amiable M. Cousadin[2]
you have taught me highly to respect & like. I beg to hear
from time to time how the poor Mlle duchastel & her Brothers
go on,—I am very sure you will never be long uninformed of
their proceedings yourself—It must ever be tenderly interesting
to me to hear of the fate of her Children. Her own name it is
long since you have let me | read with dry Eyes.—& M. d'A.
has been almost unhappy in his inability to shew his concern &
feeling & respect for so sweet a Character.

I am very sorry to plague you about altering the Bonnet—
which I think highly elegant,—but CANNOT wear.—It is
impossible for you to conceive my horrour of exhibiting my full
face in such a tiny, delicate, finical Machine, that seems made
for a fairy form & *Nymphic* Countenance. I live in such complete
retirement, that the Fashions do not break in upon me enough
by degrees to make me have courage, or inclination to adopt
them while yet new. I must entreat some alteration that may
render it sufficiently *passée* for such a rustic Hermit as myself to
wear it without blushing. As soon as you, who live in the *midst
of things*, can exclaim, 'I would not wear it for the World!' it
will just suit me. Remember, it is only the *littleness* I object to;
the materials otherwise are so simple, as well as so very pretty &
elegant, that I like them extremely. I only beg a *brim*, or en-
largement, or some thing to shade the Phiz. When you come to
our Cot, you will better conceive than by any description the
sort of style that will be in unison with such a Recluse as its
mistress. The time you mention for giving us that real happiness,
my dearest Esther, will perfectly | suit, & most cordially delight
us. We have *no choice* as to time, but what belongs to fine warm
weather, on account of our slender accommodations. Indeed,
for your very delicate frame I should chuse July or August, were
we even better fitted up, the very air being genial or adverse
according to its heat or cold. we only beg a fixed time, not to

---

² Unidentified.

clash with the very few other attempts we dare make at the indulgence of seeing those we love: as those two Months are the only ones we can venture to name. I am quite delighted you will go to Norbury Park in the same excursion. It obviates much remorse in bringing you to our little Cell. You have *completely* conquered the sweetest of my Friends this last Spring, & she was *nearly gone* long before. But now she has seen so much of you, she says—& this Hour only she has quitted the room in which I write it—she finds you one of the most pleasing & amiable & ENGAGING Creatures she has ever met with— '*Charming*! she added, with emphasis, she is *charming*!—' The Miss Lockes came to us yesterday Evening, & made use of much the same sort of language—Amelia declaring the few Hours she had had with you Hours of real delight to her, though hopeless to make them of much profit from the total want of time for study & practice. |

Will our dear Girls like to come before, or after? Pray ask & arrange that. If you & Mr. Burney can bear, in a *very* tiny room, some crib contrivance for Amelia, we should be enchanted to see her, & to give to our Alex the delight of shewing her our *copse*— in which they are not too tall to *lose one another*, & *meet unawares*. Think of this, my dear sister. Should she by any chance not be invited to Norbury, we can keep her in safety & comfort & pleasure with us during your separate excursion.

I shall be extremely glad, my dear Etty, if you can be kind enough to make out our debts to you, *sugars*, *Bonnet*, *Rice*, *Currants*, *cloak*, &c on a scrap to give to dearest Mrs. Lock, or send to her before sunday next, & she will be so kind as to discharge the same. It very much behoves our very small income to be *out of arrears*, that we may always know on what we have to depend. We shall soon entreat you to settle for us with our dear Aunt Beckey. I think it VERY long since I have heard from our beloved Susanna—God bless her—& *her* & *my* dearest Esther!—kindest Love to Mr. Burney—& to the dear Girls if returned. A little Cold keeps me from Norbury Park, I have not therefore seen Mr. Locke, kept at home also by the same reason. My Gardener's kindest Love. you have charmed him by fixing on his best *Pea season* for coming—if—as last year, the Birds do not marr it. |

[*concluded on top margin of* p. 1]

I am truly sorry Edward is not better. our kind Love & best wishes to him. The *Sea-scheme* is very promising, & very kind. I am afraid to torment him by repeating invitations hither— but if *before* or *after* you, he could & would come, our air is very good, & his welcome would be most cordial. pray say to him.

326   West Humble, 29 June 1799

To Mrs. Phillips

A.L. (Berg), 29 June [17]99 including copies of FBA's correspondence with JB
Double sheet & single sheet 4to   6 pp.   red seal
Addressed: Mrs. Phillips, / Belcotton, / Drogheda. [*franked? but cover missing*]

This First.
The rest at any time:

West Hamble,
June 29th—99

We have now all round heard from my darling Susan since we have written—& though I am only easy just after hearing, I languish immediately to have her again in debt, that the time may the quicker revolve to bring fresh news.—Never, sure, were Letters so beloved that give such sadness!—but the Anchor[1]— the faithless Anchor—always removed & removed!—from Winter to spring, from spring to summer—& *now*, to what point? May any of us write to enquire?—in *any* way?—For Heaven's sake say if there would be any chance,—my F[ather]— would do *any* thing,—that he should be *doubted* in his earnest wish—his *first* desire, is too irritating—Tell me, my most loved Susan, if there is any measure that could be taken to facilitate at least this *visit*—for I am now subdued into feeling I should hardly breathe for excess of joy in the *real* prospect of seeing— embracing you—only for an Hour: — — — I will say no more, but wait your answer to this question.—Every hope now seems to hang upon it. But—for Heaven's sake, my Susan, do not let the Year wane away without any *trial*, if any trial may again be made.

326. [1] The Major's promise to return with his family to England.

Have a *whole quire of mutilated paper* at once, my dearest,—'tis
the best way: only carefully avoid any Written marks at the
cutting—& if you draw a line, it will be safer not to cut till it
arrives. 'Tis the only way to be comfortable, with this blasting
secret business[2] which still demands concealment, & still preys
on both our minds, though far less corrosively than at first: &
upon all other minds it seems, by much occupation & little
time for reflection or recollection, dying away as if it had never
been.—But I will now Copy poor James's Letter,[3] which I know
you will read with nearly the same emotion I did myself — —
indeed the only emotion of a *soft* kind I have had since this
transaction. All else has been bitter indeed!—

Dear Sister,

I am greatly concerned that any misapprehension should
have so much separated us. I thought I had cause of complaint,—yet your first Letter from Chelsea was so cordial
& kind, that I ought not to have taken, much less to have
given offence. One cause of my now writing is a business
I wish to have cleared up: though, without such occasion,
I should not have left London without writing to beg an
oblivion of all misunderstandings, before my departure. The
business part is concerning the £25 at X^{mas} which I placed
at Coutts for you. I wish to know if you have yet drawn for it,
as, if you have, there is some mistake in my account which
must be enquired into. I will beg you to write me word. If
you have not received it, perhaps you would like to have it
sent by the post, which I can do.

I do not so little understand your disposition as not to feel
certain that, with or without atoning by apology, any advance I shall make will be kindly received. I am, indeed,
sorry that my *hastiness*—let me call it—prevented our meeting when you were in town. We are now endeavouring to
get away as soon as we can, which I hope will be in the course
of the Week. Sally desires to be affectionately remembered,
& Martin his love to Alexander. |

I remain your ever affc^{te} Brother
James Burney.

May 12.—99.

[2] The elopement of JB and SHB.
[3] The original of JB's letter, dated 12 May 1799, 21 John Street, Tottenham
Court Road, with a draft of FBA's reply (L. 322) is extant (Berg).

I know you will be more glad of a copy of my answer than of any comments I can make,—though I could write many,—but one remark I must not omit,—you find the Letter he had scouted to Esther is now praised—he had been at a loss how to avoid me, in his consciousness, & said what first occurred to him,—but on re-reading, probably found there was no possibility of dwelling upon what he had suggested. The 2^d Letter it is impossible should either have pleased or pained him,—it was but of three words. Therefore it seems as if he now meant to cast the blame of the business upon M. d'Arblay!—!—that he had not visited him separately!—Poor dear James!—conscious & proud, he knows not how to gloss over a conduct that his own justice & native integrity must place, at times, where we place it! How I felt for him, however, in thus humbling himself to apology & kindness my answer, I hope, will shew. — — —

[*here* FBA *copied her reply*, L. 322]

Remembrances to Martin in all our names finished my Letter. |

At the other side of the same sheet, I wrote to Sally, whose 2^d Letter I had not answered. I wrote as kindly as I knew how, desiring to hear how she went on, how she employed herself, how she was settled, & every particular she could write that would remind me of her former confidence, with strong expressions of satisfaction in her promise to apply to me without reserve if I could ever in any manner be of the least utility or comfort to her. I have kept no copy of this,[4] but you will easily imagine what else might accompany a Letter written expressly to shew her I was always open to her returning to a more natural conduct. I mentioned, too, my particular satisfaction that she had taken so right a step as to have been at Chelsea.[5]

What James thinks of my Letter I have not yet learnt; but I really felt it a duty to give him that hint about our dear & injured Father,—who, I know, is more & more incensed, not less, upon this unhappy subject. I doubt, indeed, now, if any

---

[4] The original is also missing.   [5] The visit of *pre* 20 Apr. (L. 316 and n. 2)

application for reconciliation would be received; but it ought, nevertheless, to be made, & would a little *internally* soften the irritation of his revered bosom, whether it led to pardon or not. Sally's desire of admission was resisted some time—though, originally, it had been *proposed* by himself. But he was disgusted doubly by her delay of accepting his lenient offer. He received her with the most petrifying coldness & sternness. Who can wonder? She burst into tears,—& they were both long silent. They then spoke only of common topics,—& in a very short time, he said he must prepare for an engagement ˡ & she retreated. What a wretched interview!—Yet I am glad it passed. *My* account is confidential from our dearest Padre himself,—& you will allude to it only to me, as far as only from me you gather any thing. You may be sure of the use I make of the openning for occasional intercession that his communications give—but I can only intercede for his *pity* of their infatuation!—not for his *relenting*, since James gives no such power to me, nor even to himself[. H]ow deep—how indelibl[e a] blot in all his fairest character! how dangerous, how dreadful a precedent if he disagrees hereafter with Martin!—And he *will*, I have no doubt. The little Salina[6] you ask after is a very fine Child indeed, with a sweet & open Countenance,—*how* her Father can thus desert her is truly astonishing, as well as wrong, for he had purposed educating & rearing her to be the consolation of his life. Alas he will find, too late, in forfeiting his claim, now, to her gratitude, he will risk it to her affection hereafter. Mrs. Rishton goes to *Pow*[7] at present, & afterwards takes a house of her own at Bury. I will get another pacquet immediately ready to succeed this, when I hear of its safety, even if before I receive my own *dearest mede* for such a quantity of scrawl. Heaven bless my ever ever dearest Susan! ever! ever!

My kindest Love to *all three* branches I hope I may say,—but to *two* certainly. I think the story of *Alex*[8] may be ventured to be read to the trio, *ONCE,*—with proper cautions, & will much amuse them. I say *once*, that they may not get it by heart. I shall be so glad to enable you [to] procure my dear Fanny a little amusement—& Norbury [whe]n he arrives. You must judge if

---

[6] Sarah Burney (iii, L. 217 n. 14), now 2½ years old.
[7] See L. 289 n. 5.
[8] Probably AA's adventures at Court (L. 270, pp. 91–101).

Willy is sage enough to [be] yet trusted in a matter of discretion. Heaven bless my dear love—Always Love to the Major &c

No fresh news from M. de N[arbonne][9]—we cannot tell where he retired during the storm all around him. we must hope soon to hear.

I am charmed you have your sweet Janey Paney[10] So near you. I must always call her by that name which first made me so much love her. If she were always near you, I could be more resigned, from the high idea I conceive of her sweetness & worth.

This first. The rest at leisure—

327   West Humble, 22 July 1799

To Mrs. Broome

A.L.S. (Berg), 22 July [17]99
Double sheet 4to (9·2 × 7·4″), the first leaf of which was cut down to 5″, evidently before the letter was written 4 pp. *pmks* PAID / 21 JUL 99 24 JY 99
 Addressed: Mrs. Broome, / Nº 12. / Salisbury Place / New Road / Midlesex
 Endorsed by CBFB: all These from my / Sister Fanny

West Humble—July 22. 99

My dearest Charlottenberg[1]—you are a most excellent Charlottenberg—& a woman of business indeed. My Mate is very sorry he could not get a moment to call upon you,—nor even upon my Father; he merely went to Town for the bank,

---

[9] The comte de Narbonne, lately at Tübingen (L. 294 n. 8, L. 304 n. 15) seems to have moved to Eisenach (Émile Dard, *Un Confident de l'Empereur; le Comte de Narbonne 1775–1813* (1943), p. 141). Würtemberg was not overrun by the French until 1800, but the d'Arblays could have foretold the future from reports of the 'skirmishes' taking place between the 'advanced posts' and the French (see *The Times*, 30 Apr., etc.). See also the appeal (27 May 1799) of the Princess Royal (i.e. the Duchess of Würtemberg) to her father for help (*Later Corr. Geo. III*, iii. 215–17; also Stuart, *Dtrs. Geo. III*, p. 42).

[10] Jane *née* Brabazon, now Disney (iii, L. 222 n. 20).

327. [1] The nickname given to Charlotte by Mr. Crisp of Chessington Hall.

& — — for the agreeable recreation of mixing one little taste of pleasure with his business, he visited a Dentist, & made him a present of a capital tooth. This was his sole relaxation.

I return the receipt, & entreat my dear Agent to procure the £25,—& pay it to Coutts, in the Strand, in the name *Alexandre Gabriel pieuchard d'Arblay* Esqr,—His sufferings from a sudden tooth ache prevented his abiding in town to ǀ receive & place it himself.

When you have been able to do this, be so kind as to let me have a line *thereupon*, as we shall not venture to give a draft till certain it will be *honoured*.

———

My dearest Friends, Mr. & Mrs. Locke, were very happy you were at home, & VISIBLE, when they called. And they were glad to see Mr. Broome, & your little ones.

All you say of James chagrins me very much[2]—I must always hope for a more favourable aspect—family dissentions are so dreadful, & so few things can offer consolation for them, that I had always hoped *our house* would have escaped ǀ them. And— till very lately, no family Harmony has been more completely uniform & happy. With regard to myself, I have no virtue in saying I bear no resentment for their strangeness when I was in town,[3] as far as it was personal: for they have both written me conceding & very affectionate Letters,[4] by which I gather— what, however, they do not avow, that they only feared an interview, lest I should have attempted some remonstrance or persuasion against their conduct. And even if they repent it, they are characters that must act for themselves. They will not submit to be advised, even by those whose advice, like mine, they might reject without offence. And perhaps the less, because our *opinions* are probably the same, though their rash natures, in an untimely moment, urged this scheme. James, I am convinced, never can approve what he has done. He has too much native sense of right; & I greatly fear he will suffer very severely from his reflexions by too long delaying to let his *better*-self—which I aver to be a VERY GOOD one—conquer

---

[2] CBFB's letter has probably been destroyed.   [3] In Jan.–Feb. 1799.
Copies of which are printed in Ll. 320 and 326.

his worser—as Hamlet has it. Poor Sally I pity too, heartily—however wrong she has been, she is young,[5] & has so many sad years before her for regret, that no blame or resentment I can think her punishment light.—

I have not heard from our dearest exemplary Susan a great while. I am never easy when she is silent—yet all in Ireland seems now smoothing & tranquilising. I have lost all hope of seeing her till the Peace—ah—when will *that* come?—Is Mr. Broome amongst the sanguine of the present moment? The people around us here talk of nothing but approaching negociations. You say nothing of giving us a day?—so I sha'n't be of the *despair-party*, but hope you are *catholicking* the thing over, as Mr. Greville's old Tenant says for *calculating*[6] We expect Esther & Mr. Burney to our little *trap beds*,—they think the Country air will make them amends for all inconveniences. I shall be very anxious for dry weather for them—in our *curtainless* & paperless apartment. My Father will come also, as usual, but to him, as usual, we make over our own room, &c. And he is too near sighted & unsuspicious to find it out. The Darking stage always stops were your Horse rested when you Breakfasted here. But I dare not propose such a lodging to Mr. Broome—though I made so little scruple with you. But if you can give us a Day—I trust you will. Remember us kindly to Mr. B[roome] & the dear ones—Alex is well. The *vital air* agrees with him wondrously.

ever, dearest Charlotta, your most affect^{ly}

F. d'A. I

P.S. Be so good—my dear Agent, as to pay only £20 into Mr. Coutts' hands to our account, & to give the odd 5 to our sister Burney to bring to us when she comes, which we expect will be soon. The *Bas* fitted admirably.

---

[5] SHB was nearly 27 years old, however.

[6] Presumably some former tenant of Wilbury House, Wiltshire. Fulke Greville (i, L. 1 n. 10) was CB's early patron (*Memoirs*, i. 27–36; *HFB*, pp. 2–4).

To Doctor Burney

A.L. (Diary MSS. vi. 5168–[71], Berg), 25 July [17]99
Double sheet 4to   4 pp.   *pmks*   29   29 JUL 99   red wafer
Addressed: Dr. Burney, / Chelsea College, / Middlesex.
Endorsed by CB: M*rs* Darblay / 1799
    Edited by FBA, p. 1 (5168), *annotated*: ✳ ✳ (4) Graciousness of The Queen
upon my Marriage Answer to charming Narratives.
    Edited also by CFBt *and the* Press.
    Also L., incomplete copy in hand of M. d'A (West Humble Letter Book
pp. 116–20, Osborn)

West Hamble,
July 25th—99

'Fore George, a more excellent Song than t'other![1]

Why my dearest Padre, was ever any body gifted with such
powers, & endowed with such materials for using them before?
Your subjects rise & rise—till *subjects*, in fact, are no longer in
question. I *do* not wonder you felt melted by the King's goodness—I am sure I did in its perusal:—And the Queen—my
ever gracious—ever most condescending Royal Mistress!—her
naming me so immediately went to my heart. Her speeches
about me to Mrs. Locke in the Drawing Room[2]—her interest
in my welfare, her deigning to say *she had never been amongst
those who had blamed my marriage*,—though she lost by it my
occasional attendances—& her remarking '*I looked the picture of
happiness*'—had warmed me to the most fervent gratitude, &
the more, because her saying she had never been *amongst those*
who had blamed me shews there were people who had not
failed to do me ill offices in her hearing—though probably,
& I firmly believe, without any personal enmity, as I am

328. [1] An adaptation of Cassio's comments (*Othello*, 11. iii). The substitution "Fore
George' for "Fore God' occurs familiarly in a contemporary catch or round. The
combined phrases FBA here utilizes in a comparison of CB's letters (Berg) of 18 and
22 July. In the latter, printed *DL* v. 437–42, CB had given an account of a visit to
Herschel at Slough and of their attendance on the evening of 21 July on the
Terrace at Windsor, where 'in the midst of a crowd of the 1st people in the Kingdom for rank & office' CB had been greeted so graciously by the King and the
Queen as to be 'afterwards looked at as a sight'.
    [2] On 4 June. Mrs. Locke's recording of this conversation, if made in writing,
may be extant in the Locke papers.

unconscious of having any owed me; but merely from a cruel malice with which many seize every opportunity, almost involuntarily, to do Mischief—& most especially to undermine at Court any one presumed to be in any favour. And still further, I thought her words conveyed a confirmation of what her conduct towards me *in my new capacity* always led me to conjecture—namely, that my guardian star had ordained it so that the real character & principles of my honoured & honourable Mate had, by some happy chance, reached the royal Ear before the news of our union. The dear King's graciousness to M. d'A. upon the Terrace, when the Commander in Chief—just then returned from the Continent, was by his side,[3] made it impossible not to suggest this—& now, the Queen's again naming me so *in public* puts it—in my conception—beyond doubt. My kindest Father will be glad, I am sure, to have ADDED to the great delight of his recital a strength to a notion I so much love to cherish.

The account of the Terrace is quite enlivening. I am very glad the Weather was so good. It was particularly kind of it, for I am sure it has been very *unjulyish* since.—How sweet what the King said of my dearest Father's writing![4] You see how consistent & constant is his opinion. But still more I love his benevolent solicitude lest your method of *making time* should injure your health. Think of that, dear *Master Brooke*![5]—Your *creepings* are surely the effect of over labour of the brain, & intense application.

I want excessively to hear how the Herschel Book went off[6]—whether there was much to change;—as I think it impossible there should not be some modes peculiar to every man's own conceptions of his own studies that no other can hit without consulting him & whether the *sum total* seemed to give the last & living Hero of the poem the satisfaction it ought to do. Pray let me hear about this as soon as you can, dearest Sir,—but pray only make notes of any alterations,—& let the alterations

[3] This was on 7 July 1796. See '*Windsoriana*', iii, L. 199, p. 191, and n. 15.

[4] The King had questioned CB about his literary pursuits on the same evening (21 July) in the 'music-room in the Castle, next the Terrace' (*DL* v. 441). On CB's confessing that he took time from his sleep to write, 'the considerate good King' had remarked, 'you'll hurt your health'.

[5] Cf. *The Merry Wives of Windsor*, iii. v.

[6] Book xii of CB's versified history of astronomy was to be entitled 'HERSCHEL' (*DL* v. 439).

themselves wait to be accomplished in our quiet retreat, at the given period of our indulgence, which I presume to continue for the end of August, as you do not again touch the subject.

I am very anxious, meanwhile, for your trying the Hot well— & that before you go to Dover[7]—for I think it impossible— unnaturaly—you should resist Mrs. Crewe; who, next to your immediate family, seems most truly & affectionately to know how to value possessing you.

The visit to the P[ss] of W[ales] is charming.[8] I am charmed she now lives so chearfully & pleasantly. She seemed confined not merely as a recluse, but a Culprit, till quite lately; & now — — *your* visit has just been succeeded by Mr. Pitt's![9]—How can the pr[ince] be so much his own enemy! in politics as well as happiness!—for all the World, *nearly*, take her part,—& all the world *wholly* agree she has been the injured person, though some few think she has wanted retenue & discretion in her resentment, the public nature of her connexion considered, which does not warrant the expectance of the same pure fidelity a chosen wife might look for.

I love Miss Crewe for following her mother's footsteps, in consulting you[10]—& Miss Hayman seems a lively & amiable character.[11]—I am vastly gratified by the mistake-dinner at the

[7] For the visit to Walmer Castle, where Pitt and his war ministers were assembled on the occasion of the embarkation of the 'Secret Expedition' to Holland (Fortescue, iv. 641–5; Oman, pp. 200–36), see L. 332, pp. 324–5; L. 334, pp. 331–2; L. 337, pp. 339–40.

[8] At a 'delightful *dejeuner*' at Mrs. Crewe's villa in Hampstead in late June, CB had met the Princess of Wales ('—her face is extremely pretty—& her vivacity, & gracious good-humour to all around her, delightful—Of what parts the P. of W. must be made to say that "his flesh creeps wth disgust & horror . . .", I know not'), and the Princess, charmed in her turn, had invited CB to Montagu House, Blackheath, near Shooter's Hill, for a concert of music on the evening of Friday 12 July. 'My reception was the most gracious possible—H.R.H. treated me like an old acquaintance—showed me a kind of Green-House or conservatory w[ch] she had added to her Parlour with great taste & judg[mt] to keep rude starers at a distance. . . .' See CB's letters of 2 July 1799 (Barrett, Eg. 3690, f. 104-b) and 18 July (op. cit.).

[9] Pitt attended a 'grand entertainment' held by the Princess of Wales at Montagu House on 21 July (*The Times*, 22 July).

[10] When Mrs. Crewe was out of town, Miss Crewe had consulted CB on the difficulties involved in accepting an invitation received from the Princess of Wales (CB's letter of 18 July, op. cit.).

[11] As 'confidential companion' and Keeper of the Privy Purse (1802–20) to Caroline, Princess of Wales, Anne Hayman (1753–1847) had lately (see CB to FBA, 8 Apr. 1799, Eg. 3690, ff. 98–9b) employed Mrs. Crewe to explore the possibility of CB's attending the Princess once a week at Montagu House, Blackheath, as in the past he had attended the Thrales at Streatham (*HFB*, p. 70). Later, having at Mrs. Crewe's *déjeuner* (n. 9) made a conquest of Miss Hayman (as well as the Princess),

D[uke] of Portland's. Nothing could be more lucky. And the two military men you sat between will make *my* military man's mouth water, when he hears the recital.[12] He is gone on a little visit to M. de Lajard[13] at Croydon. I expect him back to night. And, indeed, *require* him, notwithstanding my little Alex. For much as I love *retirement*, & country Life, I love not *solitude*, nor seclusion.—It is therefore I always feel anxious when my dear Padre has not some one actually under his roof, besides his excellent Molly[14]—for though I build upon her grateful care, I want him always to have some little seduction from his studies. —⌐I grieve but without surprise—at the impression made ┐ on your mind by poor J[ames] & S[arah]—*poor* indeed, to have made such a one But earnestly as I should rejoice to soften it, & to serve them, your feelings are so much the dearer to me, that I certainly will take no measures against your consent, nor do anything contrary to your wishes. You will not, I am sure, forbid my occasionally naming them, & letting you know how they go on, & when I am informed myself, which shall always be when it may, as I think you alone have any right to hold out from their concessions which to me, knowing the pride of their characters, is affecting, & which once combined in the daring disposition shown by their flight I had ceased to expect. Heaven help & pardon them.—

I had heard of your good looks again from an Eye witness of last Sunday—Mr. Pepys, who came hither with Lady Rothes, & Sir Lucas. They much rejoice in your joining their Evening parties, which they did not much surprise me by saying you

---

CB had been invited to make her 'a morning visit in the *round Tower* (part of the pr[ss] of Wales's palace)'. This '*back-stair*' visit, subsequently arranged in a series of letters for 13 July, proved 'out of the question', however, when an invitation arrived from the Princess herself for Friday 12 July (CB's letters of 8 Apr., 18 and 22 July, op. cit.).

[12] Having, by mistaking the date, missed dining at Burlington House, along with Mrs. Crewe, on Wednesday 10 July, CB, despising 'leading strings', presented himself 'at his Grace's door' the following night and being shown upstairs 'to a larger and more stately room than that I had dined in there before', found among a distinguished military and naval company Henry Joseph Swinburne (1772–1801), Captain in the 82nd Regiment, 'an intelligent & amiable young Man', and William Bentinck (1764–1813), Count (H.R.E.), R.N., Captain (1783), later to be gazetted Rear-Admiral of the Blue (1805), of the White (1808), and Vice-Admiral of the Blue (1810), 'a fine figure & manly Character', whose father CB had known in Norfolk. Seated between these two at dinner, CB had, besides general conversation, 'information sotto voce' on many particulars, 'curious, instructive, and interesting'.

[13] See L. 291 n. 5.

[14] See L. 297 n. 14.

greatly enlivened.—Your Miss Perry's very sweet *Girls*,[15] & our two dear Girls, Fanny & Sophy, gave me much pleasure by their visit, & their desire of being easily pleased. If you accept the Bishop of Salisbury's invitation, I beg you to remember me to Mrs. Douglas,[16] whom I saw continually at Windsor, where she was almost *anxiously* obliging to me. My respects also to the Bishop, who gave me his Portrait angelically. We expect dear Etty & her excellent sposa next *Tuesday*. They will certainly return you your Reviews.

Send more—if they, & for one carriage, may not as well stay till you fetch it? What you have said in vol. 24 is deeply interesting.[17] What hopes are now alive about France! I shall hope!—

Heaven guard my dearest Father—ever & ever most
dutifully & affectionately
Your F. d'A.

I have but one letter from Ireland this great while. But [*wafer*] had all these last months shows any.

Mr. Lock's longer & long [*wafer*] promise.

[*wafer*] is it known if Bartolozzi will remain in England?[18]

---

[15] While waiting for Dr. Herschel's return to his home at Slough on 20 July, CB had met two guests already there, Maria (1781–1849) and Sarah Matilda (1782–1852), the eldest daughters of Caleb Hillier Parry (1755–1822), M.D. (1778), of Bath, and sisters of Sir William Edward Parry (1790–1855), the Arctic explorer. 'More natural, obliging, charming girls' CB had seldom seen, '& more-over, very pretty' (*DL* v. 438). Talented in music, they had all played and sung as they waited for their host. The eldest was to marry in 1805 Thomas Garnier (1776–1873), sometime Dean of Winchester (*DNB*).

[16] See i, L. 23 n. 47.

[17] Almost certainly CB's review (see Nangle, p. 210) of Seward's *Supplement to the Anecdotes of some distinguished Persons* . . . (1797), the *Monthly Review*, xxiv (1798), to which CB appended a footnote in praise of William Locke as a critic and patron of the arts.

[18] It was not until 2 Nov. 1802 that Francesco Bartolozzi (i, L. 35 n. 2) left England to take charge of the National Academy in Lisbon (*DNB*).

To Mrs. Phillips

A.L. (Berg), 28 July [17]99
Single sheet 4to   2 pp.

West Hamble—July 28—99—

I have just received your dear Letter of the 18th my beloved Susan,[1] & I will *EXPEDITE* a pacquet with all the speed I can.— helas—'tis *so* only—by relations such as I can make, I ought to write!—all else—all most close to me—all I could write upon with the speed of thought, from having it ever uppermost— I ought to fly — — — I can only aggravate — — never soothe —the little *cuttings* were as safe as they are interesting— continue that mode, my dearest, for such themes as we can only breathe to each other.[2] The hopeless state of hope for me—for Etty—our padre—my Mate—our sweet friends—I will try not to touch upon—your desire to soften *our* regrets is too penetrat- ing—with what bitter feelings I should write if I checked not my unavailing pen — — — This time I will have done—& only pray for the firmness of your precious philosophy & resignation. & that they may not be tried as *long* as they are tried *severely*!—

I truly rejoice my Alex's court adventures amused you— I shall be very glad my dear little trio should be diverted with them. I know how they are pre-disposed upon such a subject, & with such an object. I am a good deal disappointed at only 5 meetings with J[aney] P[aney][3]—that sweet feeling Creature, who knows so well how to appreciate a wasting violet—no! not *wasting*, I hope, neither, though now was*ted* most indisputably. — — But you don't mention your health—& though I must hope from that, I cannot forbear still more fearing—yet I must try to suppose it accident. We have had one day of our [dear]est

329. [1] SBP's letter (Berg) of 18 July, *pmks* 22 JY 99   22 JUL 99, acknowledges FBA's letter of 26 May (L. 323) but is chiefly an extended commentary, in her former style, on FBA's Court Journal (L. 270), with a detailed review of Alexander's precarious conduct and adventures there ('I c^d not throughout the whole account prevent a feeling of some pain for his beloved Mother, whose anxious apprehen- sions I could thoroughly comprehend, & sympathise in.').

[2] These cuttings have disappeared. For one of an earlier date which has sur- vived, see L. 304 n. 1.

[3] Jane Disney (iii, L. 222 n. 20).

Father—of which more hereafter—but I must now say, I thought, ⎮ all things considered, it was best to read him one of the *slips*—it was more satisfactory than leaving him to his conjectures, & it was far far more touching, tender, & impressive than any thing I could have related partially. He was very much affected by every word—but indiscribably shocked at the most remote idea of any *extension* of displeasure, or wrong,— any *possibility* of blame beyond the *principal*⁴—& charged me to find means to tell Mrs. Le blanc that he desired her to be as sure of his *justice*—as of his *pity*—& as confident of his tenderest love as of his existence.—& he wishes to hear as if no such thing was in being—he conceives well the impossibility of such a subject's being treated between you & also its uselessness. Therefore tell that dearest person to write when she can as an *alien* in regard to that business.

I shall now devote every minute to a narrative pacquet & get it ready for sending off while our Esther is here—she comes in two days,⁵ & I shall delight in making her write with me from our Cottage, melancholy as to us both will be the distance to which we address our Letters—

330   West Humble, 10 August 1799

To Sarah (Rose) Burney

A.L.S. (Osborn), 10 Aug. [17]99
Double sheet 4to   4 pp.   *pmks*   LEATHER / HEAD   10 AUG 99
10 AU 99   wafer
Addressed: Mrs. Burney, / Dr. Charles Burneys, / Greenwich / Kent
Docketed in pencil, p. 4: Fn d'Arb / 65—

West Humble, near *Dorking*,
Aug^st 10.—99—

If you measure my concern for your happiness & welfare & feelings, my dear Rosette, by the punctuality of my answers to

⁴ As may be seen from CB's letter (Osborn) of 19 Oct. 1799, his account books (Berg), and later letters to CB Jr., the 'demon of a Maj¹', who had seldom managed to pay the interest (£80 per annum) owing CB on the mortgage of £2,000 lent in 1795, was now, with his 'profligate procrastinations', over £100 in arrears; and SBP had long feared that her father's displeasure might be extended to her.
⁵ EBB was expected on Tuesday 30 July.

your Letters, you must do me the utmost injustice. But I trust I have too fully, & too frequently explained my real &—alas— encreasing repugnance to Letter writing to have now any doubt left on that subject, or any thing new to add. Indeed it is but the simple truth that I am sincerely grieved for your uneasiness about your beloved sister & her amiable Daughter.[1] I must hope all will terminate well, but I can never wonder at the anxiety which hangs upon the suspence.

Your last Letter lost 3 days by being directed near *Leatherhead*, where we have no longer any ǀ communication, instead of *DORKING*, whence we receive Letters 4 times a week—& even when it arrived, I could not immediately answer, as we had an engagement impending for meeting the Count Lally de Tolendal at Norbury Park, which left me in Doubt what time I should be at liberty to name, & I would not write till I could speak positively. you are very good to think of trying a *night* with such accommodation as you have seen—pray bring *Flannel night Caps*—for our *camp Bed* is very airy. Yet I cannot propose the *Inn*, as at Bookham, because it is nearly a mile distant. I must only hope for good weather. If you know how to bring such a thing with you, you will delight us—& the corn Merchants & Hay makers to boot.

Monday the 15th we shall expect you, & offer up our prayers for a kinder sun to welcome you than we have seen ǀ these 2 Months. I shall fear a little for your health, I own, in the experiment of our *Camp equipage*,—but you know how *rural* it is, & will surely not venture if you do not feel yourself equal to the risk. My sister & Mr. Burney have escaped evil from it, but my sister is grown quite stout in comparison of her former self. Yet, at the last, she frightened me a little with something approaching to rheumatism in the head. I hope to God it is gone off. How I wish Charles could come! a fellow Camp Bed to your own we could fit up, & I should not have the apprehensions for *him* that I have for his more delicate *rib*. How I should rejoice if he would give us a surprise so agreeable!—*Sunday* perhaps could alone suit him—but our *Cook*, such as she is, is that day to be from Home. We would all turn cooks, however, sooner than

---

330. [1] Anne Rose (d. 26 May 1808) had married on 17 Aug. 1780 Edward Smith Foss (*c.* 1756–1830), a solicitor. Their daughter Isabella (b. 1782), presumably now ill, died on 1 Nov. 1799, aged 17 years 18 days (see A.L.S. Berg, from CB Jr. to M. d'A, 8 Nov. 1799).

lose any day he could spare. But you give us no hope of him—
& therefore I name *Monday*, when the brave old dame will be
at her usual post. You know its magnificence, so I make no
apology. M. d'A. is at Norbury ǀ park, or I should have
messages to add of tender import—My Alex the younger shall
speak for himself, & recite Tom Thumb to you. I dare not ask
for my dear little Charles, as we have no hope when the school
opens of seeing him. But my kind Love to him—& my best
Comp^ts to Mrs. Bicknell.

Adieu, my dear Rosette—
yours ever—
F. d'A.

331   [West Humble,] 14 August 1799

To Mrs. Phillips

A.L. (Diary MSS. vi. 5172–[3], Berg), 14 Aug. [17]99
Double sheet 4to 4 pp. A strip (1·7 × 7·6″), cut from the top of the
second leaf, is now replaced wafer
Addressed: Mrs. Phillips, / Belcotton / Drogheda—
Heavily edited by CFBt, *as see* Textual Notes.
Edited also by the Press.

August 14th—99

 I know that my most beloved Susan—my dearest dearest
Susan did not mean I should see her true account of her
precious health—but it arrived at Westhumble while Esther
was there—& it has been engraven on my Heart in saddest
characters ever since—The degree in which it makes me—
I had almost said wretched—would be cruel to dwell upon—
but had the Letter finished as it began—I must have surely
applied for a passport—without which there is now no visiting
Ireland. In case, my sweet Soul!—you are relapsed,—or do not
continue improving—tell me if there is any way I can manage to
make a surprise give no shock of *horrour* where I have no expectation of giving *pleasure*? I would not offend—nor add to my
beloved's hard tasks, God knows!—Should I write *there*, in that
case, for *leave*? or what do?—At all events, and if the recovery

continues, give me a hint or two, I entreat. I consult no one here—I must do such a deed by *storm*,—I am sure of consent to every thing that my happiness & peace demand from the only one who can lawfully controll me—& that is enough.—

My pacquet I had ready—so I will send it—but Esther wished me to wait for her writing—& this morning I have a Letter from her to say she has sent her Letter by post. This vexes me, for I have delayed mine solely for her, & now delayed it for nothing but ˡ the cruel mortification of keeping up my own anxious—anxious suspence. — — I know my tenderest Susan will not let it last beyond what is inevitable. A few lines—from my dear *Fanny*, if her head is bad, or there is any impediment, I shall be most thankful for. I shall count the days till I hear very ill—very ill at ease— —

The dear pacquet our Esther brought had given me great pleasure. The Letter for Mrs. Growcott[1] has been carried to her by *old Betty*,[2] who lived near her, & whom you may remember at Bookham, where she succeeded Sophy Arnold.[3] This old Betty is now our Cook, (*&c*) again. she says Sally[4] is extremely well married, to a steward of her lord's, & they are set up in some business together. Poor Hester is still very feeble & helpless. Any Letter to any of the family I can always send with ease, as Betty often goes past their door in her visits to her Father. And I shall convey any Letters from theirs *enclosed in mine*. I have made the same offer to good Mrs. Newton for my good Susan, to whom I beg to be *particularly* remembered, with my most earnest entreaties she will watch my Heart's beloved— ˡ I will return the interesting little notes of your Fanny next time. & Mrs. Hill's Letter.—I finish off this now in the *horrid* haste of expecting the Lady Diamonded all over,[5] self-invited, to pass the *day & night* with me!—

I cannot recollect what I have last written or copied for you about J[ames] or S[ally]—pray tell me, as I am in doubt if my last dispatches have been forwarded to you or not.

My Alex is extremely occupied with his Chimney sweeper—

331. [1] Recorded in the Dorking parish registers are the burials of William Grow-cutt (19 Sept. 1808), at the age of 78, and of his wife Ann (8 Jan. 1818), aged 81. Their daughter Hester was baptized on 17 Oct. 1779.

[2] Elizabeth Parker, mother of Betty (iii, L. 237 n. 4).

[3] See L. 323 n. 1.

[4] Sarah Growcutt, baptized 6 Aug. 1770.

[5] Norbury's description of his aunt 'Rosette', CB Jr.'s wife.

whom he regards with all his most reflecting looks of curiosity. *I* shall keep him—he comes from my Susan—& I never had a play thing at Alex's age I so much loved as any thing endorsed by her, now—

God bless—preserve you, my dear—dear invaluable Susan! my most beloved Sister!—& speed me a little line—& don't wait, I beseech, leisure for a long Letter—nor give yourself its fatigue.

The sweetly kind Amelia has given me one of her dear locks— She is all made up of sympathy &—hereditary goodness—

God almighty [g]rant I may hear better news of my Susan!—

Where poor M. de N[arbonne] has been driven we know not[6] —one of the French princesses is dead—but not p^sse Adelaide— we have just heard that M. de N. is now in actual correspondence with Louis XVIII—I am *very* glad, though excessivly astonished how it has been brought about. When we hear particulars, you shall have them—The Diamond is just arrived.—

332   West Humble, 28 August 1799

To Mrs. Phillips

A.L.S. (Berg), 28 Aug. 1799
Double sheet 4to 4 pp. wafer
Addressed in pencil: Mrs. Phillips
Mutilated by CFBt, *parts of it used as paste-overs in the construction of the composite 14, 28 Aug. 1799* (Diary MSS. vi. 5172–[3b]), *see* Textual Notes.

West Hamble,
Aug^st 28th—1799

The news with which this pacquet will turn, my most beloved Susan, will occupy & interest you out of all thought for yourself—for any one, indeed, but our sweet Amelia, & her dearest Parents—yet as *my* prevalent thought is—& will be, till I hear, YOU,—I at least rejoice that this news must force an instant Letter, in which I supplicate for a *true* statement of your dear—dear health, which is ever uppermost in my mind, & inviting a thousand fears, that I strive in vain to dissipate.

[6] See L. 323 n. 9; L. 326 n. 9.

O that the Major would spare you here to celebrate this event![1] what a true joy would it be to your faithful Amelia,— what a blessing make her marriage to us all!—That it may prove so to her beloved Parents is my most earnest prayer—I can hardly tell in what manner to write you my own sensations upon it. I know you would be as difficult as myself how to be contented for Amelia—but if I am not in personal extacey—I feel all the reflected satisfaction of seeing her family all happy, & she herself completely so. 'Tis in fact unreasonable to feel any latent regrets where all the principals feel none. yet — — if I must '*to be sincere*,' 'tis certain *I* had not so chosen for Amelia! —though, as Protestants can buy no indulgencies, & her Father & William are therefore unattainable,—& as the only other person that, in my Heart, I have ever thought deserving her (our own Padre excepted) was too old (for I cannot weigh his being too *poor*) to propose I her waiting till he could form her an establishment[2]—why it is but unjust, I allow, not to be more fully satisfied with Things as they CAN be—& ARE. So I must try to do better. The real contentment of her inestimable Parents must buy mine. Her *own*—which is still, nay, much higher, must make the purchase of yours, & of every one's. The Father in Law, Mr. Angerstein,[3] has made the opening of the business the most noble that is possible. Applied to only when Amelia & *Her* Friends had already consented, he gave his sanction with a generous warmth & cordiality truly delightful. I think I am sorry it was not for himself! — He seems to have so much Heart, & sincere benevolence.—Perhaps the son may inherit it all—perhaps what seems to me insipid coldness, may be shyness—& I may hereafter be more *independantly* contented. I must hope so. With what joy will I then give the joy of hearing it to my dearest Susan!—who I know will be uncomfortable that I am not more enchanted,—But it is difficult to be enchanted for this lovely Girl, who seems to merit more than this World allows beyond once or twice in an age to be united.

I am very little acquainted with him—hardly more than by sight. Let me not therefore prejudice you. I cannot write on

332. [1] The marriage of Amelia Locke (1776–1848) to John Angerstein (*c.* 1774–1858), which was to take place at Woodlands by special licence on 2 Oct.
  [2] Unidentified.   [3] See L. 334 n. 4.

this interesting subject but sincerely to my Susan,—but as she knows my *many peculiars* in my ways of thinking, it is but just to say I may perhaps be the ONLY person not completely satisfied. Should he prove perfectly amiable, my scruples will easily be vanquished—but I had wanted—for HER—the most brilliant parts with the most exquisite feelings. — — Just before I began this, the incomparable Pair came to tell me they would immediately send you a pacquet— | & that dear Amelia had already written to you. How I love her for that! so hurried—so taken up—so many calls—so *full* within—to leave all for taking her own pen to my Susan is truly sweet, & marks her fervant & tender affection beyond any other mark that could have been found, for her mother's hand & mine together my Susan would have accepted in her name, during these first days of emotion & business. But nothing could have *compensated*—we could only have *palliated* my Susan's loss of her own writing. I have now no time for getting ready any journal,—nor dare I, indeed, risk a 2ᵈ Mˢ. of that species while a first is unacknowledged. But I will be quite prepared for the next opportunity with such further little circumstances as may constitute a sort of narrative for my dearest's leisure. I have given no particulars relative to this MOST interesting transaction, because I conclude the Letters from Norbury Park will convey them all—except my own private opinion—which you must only *privately* answer, in the slips. I thought that, like myself, you would rather hear the plain truth, be it what it may, than any vague flourishes.—

[Whether] the plain truth may be such as I may like to hear when, at length, I receive it from Belcotton!—Give it me, at all | the events. Let me know the *real* state of your health & feelings—& ask no more about our chances—I will no longer torment you with that subject—I have only to regret I have so often [*line cut out*] tender concern for disappointed hopes that have a constant bitterness behind them.—Let me not fail to give you the great Joy of hearing that Mr. & Mrs. Locke BOTH assured me, just now, they were more & more contented with this affair, & that all their House were more & more rejoiced it had happenned.

I shall take this opportunity to enclose you a Letter from Charlotte, which I have had through our Etty, to send when I could, & one from Sophy to Fanny which has been forwarded

me through Miss Cambridge. I keep Mrs. Hill's Letter to shew
Charlotte when I am able, as I know it will much gratify her.[4]
And I shall keep also sweet J[aney] P[aney]'s till next time, as I
wish our Mrs. L. & our Amene to see them, & have had no
quiet reading moments with them since they have been in my
possession. My Mate sends you his tenderest Love. My Alex is
well & blyth, & in great fashion for a new accomplishment he
has acquired—invented, rather, of which I shall scribble details
here after. People here are very sanguine that Ireland is quiet—
& will remain so,—& that the combined Fleets[5] can never
reach it. How are your own politics upon that point? *Mine*
will take their colour, be it what it may. [*line cut out*] our dear
Father is visiting about, from Mr. Coxe's[6] to Mrs. Crewe,—
with whom he is now at Dover, where Mr. Crewe has some
command.[7] We are all in extreme disturbance here about the
Secret expeditions. Nothing authentic is arrived from the first
armament—& the 2[d] is all prepared for sailing.[8] Two of Lady
Templetown's sons are gone, Greville[9] & Arthur.[10] Lady
Rothes younger son is going, John Leslie.[11] Mr. Boucherette[12]

---

[4] These letters have not survived.

[5] The combined fleets of France and Spain, moored at Cadiz for ten days, had
set sail on 21 July, steering north-west (*The Times*, 1, 6, 9 Aug. 1799). On 14 Aug.
The Times reported that the fleet, 'consisting of 62 sail of ships' had been 'seen off
Cape Finisterre on the 4th inst.' and concluded 'If this account be correct, Lord
KEITH cannot be far a-stern of them; and we may yet indulge the hope of another
proud day for England.'   [6] See i, L. 32 n. 1; iii, L. 242 n. 6.

[7] John Crewe (i, L. 24 n. 29; iv, L. 266 n. 4), Lieutenant (1790), after a shifting
career with several regiments and the militia, was gazetted Lt.-Col. of the 9th
Regiment (24 Aug. 1799). He later attained what seemed to be the nominal ranks of
Major-General (25 Apr. 1808), Lt.-Gen. (4 June 1813), and General (22 July 1830).
Cf. *Barthomley*, p. 323.

[8] These were embarkations of troops for the calamitous attempt to restore
Holland to the Stadtholder (Fortescue, iv, pt. 2, 639–710). Sir Ralph Abercromby
had embarked with 120,000 men on 13 Aug., arriving at the Helder on the 27th.
A second division under the Duke of York was to set out on 8 Sept.

[9] Fulke Greville Upton, *later* Howard (1773–1846), who had joined the 1st Foot
Guards (28 Apr. 1793), held the ranks of Lieutenant and Captain (as of 15 Oct.
1794).

[10] Arthur Percy Upton (1777–1855) of the Coldstream Guards (28 Apr. 1793),
Lieutenant and Captain (2 Dec. 1795), was, in this campaign, A.D.C. to Abercromby (cf. L. 413, pp. 489–90). Transferring to the 1st Foot Guards (1807), he was
to serve on the staff of the Duke of Wellington in the Peninsular War, eventually
attaining the rank of Lt.-Gen. (1837).

[11] The Hon. John Leslie (1759–1824) of the 1st Foot Guards (1781) had attained
by 1796 the army rank of Colonel (3 May), Lt.-Gen. (1808). A Captain in his
regiment at this time, he was to become its Lt.-Col. (1813). He was the son of David
Leslie (1722–1802), Earl of Leven and Melville, *not* the son of the Countess of
Rothes and her first husband (i, L. 12 n. 13).

[12] See iii, L. 150 n. 14.

has a Brother in Law gone, Captain Barnes.[13] Both officers &
men are gathered from all quarters. Heaven grant them speedy
safety, & ultimate PEACE! God bless my own dearest Susan &
strengthen—& *restore* her!

Amen! Amen

F D A.

We are going directly to Norbury park, not to defer sending
off this important dispatch.

333   [West Humble,]
–14 September [1799]

To Esther (Burney) Burney

A.L. (the first leaf, Berg; the second, Barrett Eg. 3690, f. 119-b),—14
Sept.
    Two single sheets 4to   4 pp.   *pmks*   DARKING   16 SP 99   18 SP 99
18 SEP 99   High St. M ⟨   ⟩ / U. P. P.
    Addressed: Mrs. Burney at / ⌈Beaumont Street / Devonshire place
London⌉
    Re-addressed: Mrs Lea's^I / Richmond / Surry
    Endorsed by EBB: 1799 / Answered
    Edited by CFBt.

Sepr 14

In the expectation of a visit from dear Charlotte I must
prepare a few lines to my dearest Esther. I can never bear to
pass an opportunity, however little alert I may be in making
one. And first of all I must tell you this beautiful September
mingles a world of spleen with its gay chearing to my composition, from the grudge which its immediate predecessor has
left upon my mind for being so foul when I so sighed to see it
fair. It rained, too, all the time my excellent Friends Miss
Cambridge & Miss Baker were here. I don't know what the
Elements mean by fixing every particle they can gather together
of inhospitality & blustering rudeness just around our little
dwelling.—as if they thought Hermits had nothing to do with

---

[13] Michael Barne (1759–1837) had joined the 7th Light Dragoons in 1778,
becoming their Lt.-Col. (1799), which regiment served in this expedition under the
Duke of York. He had married on 2 Oct. 1798 Mary Boucherett (*c.* 1764–1858),
sister of Ayscoghe Boucherett (iii, L. 150 n. 14; L. 152 n. 5). The Boucheretts,
often at Norbury Park, are described in SBP's Journal of 10 July 1789 (Eg. 3692,
f. 51b).

the rights of Friendship, nor the happiness of social kindness, & so took upon them to storm our Cell every time we seemed to forget being Anchorets, & set about appearing to Live like folks of this World. Every one of them seemed bent upon doing its worst. The Water was always at hand—& at head, too,—to deluge us, if we presumed to brave the atmosphere from without our Hut,—the Earth was always at foot—& up to the ancle, too—to repress, & sully [|] us, if we ventured to court one view beyond the precincts of our proper Windows,—& the Air broke forth into the most passionate acts of violence, even to buffetting us with our own Coats & Garments, if we dared but to open a sash for a peep at a prospect only a few miles distant— but the most provoking of all were the tricks played us by Fire —which, not contented with denying us its *natural* heat, from the customary rays of the Summer's Sun, made us ashamed to apply for *artificial* heat, because, forsooth, the Month was yclept August!

I was sure you would be extremely gratified by sweet Mrs. Locke's eagerness to be herself the narrator of the approaching nuptials,—& so you would had you witnessed the lovely Amelia's pleasure in finding you upon her Mother's select list for that purpose. I took upon me to assure them both I was quite sure the news was not received till it was answered—& indeed they had no doubt of that. They are now all at Woodlands,[2] Mr. Angerstein's seat, which is but 6 miles from Town, & therefore Mrs. Locke goes thence to make her preparations, which will be infinitely elegant & handsome. The young man is Heir to a very large fortune, & seems, most happily, to have every disposition for spending it generously & benevolently. I am sure if She guides the helm such will be its direction, for she is All her exquisite Parents could themselves wish for sweetness of sympathy in every human distress.

Sept^r· 14—

This Letter was begun upon news from Charlotte I might expect her this Week—but stopt upon a second Letter to

---

333 [1] EBB had probably taken lodgings with the widow Lea, an enterprising business woman, *née* Anne Croom (*c.* 1761–1836), who had married on 21 Dec. 1791 Aaron Lea (*c.* 1766–98).

[2] See Cyril Fry 'The Angerstein's of Woodlands', *Trans . . . . Greenwich . . . Antiquarian Soc.* vii (1966), 86–105.

postpone the expectation—I had therefore meant to cast it aside till the day before their arrival—but—a Letter of far deeper interest is just come from Ireland[3]—in which our truest darling charges me to write *for her*, to assure you of her amendment, & entreat you to be no longer uneasy, & to excuse her not writing at present, as,—during her Letter to me, —Norbury was arrived at Belcotton. I am truly glad. He will be, I am sure, as the sweet soul says, Her best physician. God grant her assurances may but be as true as they are kind! I never doubt her veracity but about her own health. In all things else it is gospel. The M[ajor] has written me a few lines that would have made me the happiest of human beings, could I say the same of *him*! for he positively promises that the first 50£ he can command shall restore Susan to her friends—Ah— if that were all — — but my terror is lest he only wants again to play upon our feelings by exciting our hopes.[4] I know not how to dare build again internally upon his professions. Indeed I try to suppress, not encourage hopes, so severely I have suffered from repeated & grievous disappointments. We shall probably none of us hear from her again till her dear little Doctor is torn from her arms—nor even then till she has recovered the first sadness in which his absence involves her. Unless, indeed, she receives Mrs. Locke's Letter upon sweet Amelia—& then she will write instantly to Norbury Park.

I thank you, my dearest Esther, for your very lively account of your visit at Mrs. ord's, & Lord Chartley,[5] &c—& I beg you, if you again meet Miss Ellerker, to give her my acknowledgements for her kind remembrance. *Harriet* Ellerker I think can hardly recollect me; but the eldest sister ᐯ has drunk tea with me at Kew Palace, while I had apartments there.[5] I am always glad to hear any thing softening to austerity of a person I have loved & honoured so much as Mrs. Ord. A near relation of one of her most intimate friends, Miss Burgoigne (eldest sister of Mr.

[3] Of this letter there survives only an enclosure (Berg), a cutting (2·9 × 8″), dated 4 Oct., and meant for FBA's sole perusal. The slip gave guidance on how to offer passage or travel money to the Major in a way he might accept.

[4] This letter is missing. FBA refers to the disappointment of August 1798 when Phillips had assured JB that he was bringing his family to England (L. 289, pp. 161–2; L. 291, pp. 167–8).

[5] Elizabeth (1751–1831) and Harriet Mainwaring Ellerker (1759–1842) and their brother-in-law Baron Ferrers of Chartley (L. 337 n. 16). See also iii, L. 126 n. 7.

Montagu B.)[6] is now at Dorking, & comes to our Hermitage frequently. She was Lady Mary Montagu, & is now married to Lord Templetown, & a most unassuming, kind, sensible & domestic character, & very interesting from her extreme affliction at the loss of a little Baby, her first & only Child.[7] She will, however, soon be again a mother, & I hope with better success. Her young lord is just gone to Ireland, upon urgent business, & she will remain here not only till his return, but till she is brought to bed, & has innoculated her Child—such is her terror of carrying a second Infant to Town, where she lately lost her first in consequence of its catching the small pox. Lord Templetown was looking about him here, before his Irish journey, for a spot to build upon, he is so enchanted with the Country around us, & she is so anxious to live a retired Country life with a little family.—You will be happy to hear that Miss Amelia Locke is to have a Town House[8]—though no country one, for she & Mr. A[ngerstein] are to divide their Summer between their two Father's, at Norbury Park & Woodlands. I had a Letter yesterday from my dear Father, still at Dover, at Mrs. Crewe's.[9] God bless you, my dearest Esther, Our joint kind loves to dear Mr. B[urney]—&c—Alex is quite well just now—& in highest Spirits & merriment—he often wants Amelia— |

[*written at the top of* p. 10]

I know you will be curious about *some*thing—so I will not omit to mention that *noth*ing whatsoever is yet done, & we are come to no determination whether *any* thing ever *will* be done.[10] Love to dear Aunt Becky I beg.

[6] Frances Burgoyne (i, L. 3 n. 5) was the eldest daughter and Montagu Burgoyne (1750–1836), the second son of Sir Roger Burgoyne (*c.* 1710–80), 6th Bart. (1716) and his wife *née* Lady Frances Montagu (1710–88).

[7] Lady Templetown's (L. 292 n. 22) only child, Catherine Elizabeth (b. 5 Apr. 1798), had died 19 July 1799. The child she was expecting, Henry Montagu Upton, was to be born 11 Nov. 1799.

[8] In Great Cumberland Place.

[9] For CB's letter (Osborn), dated Dover, 9 Sept. 1799, see L. 337 and n. 1.

[10] Probably the production of 'Love and Fashion'.

To Mrs. Phillips

A.L. (Berg),—19 Sept. [17]99
Double sheet 4to   4 pp.   wafer
Addressed: Mrs. Phillips, / Belcotton / Drogheda / Ireland
Edited by FBA.

Yes, my sweetest Susan, I *am* comforted[1]—the best medicine
I think now administered to you—I figure to myself what
resuscitation would be to me the sight of Alex after a ten
Month's absence.—Far more than your utmost assertions THIS
comforts me,—it comes home to my credence in a way for
which words have no passage. Dear loved & lovely Boy!
doubly dear to me for his happy influence over a health so
precious to me.—

The Major's words, however,—in the previous Letter—gave
me a start of joy that was almost—from the acute fears which
even at the instant accompanied it, convulsive—I must write
to him once more—I think I am now authorised—& my Mate
& I will make a little joint address. Perhaps, meanwhile, the
petition of the lovely Bride elect, Amelia, may have *worked our
work* without further solicitation. Would to Heaven such a hope
might be confirmed! — — How touching is every word you say
of Norbury's arrival—appearance—character—& behaviour!—
I am delighted at Mr. Maturin's even encreased regard &
contentment—& at the dear Boy's for his Tutor. That last
speaks every thing for his improvements & his conduct at once.
If to come over separated you from that sweet little fellow,
I should be less urgent; but it does not—or does it for so short
a period!—since you are so little together though within the
same shore, that it seems there almost more tantalizing to be
parted from him than here.

Mrs. Rishton ⎸ has now finally left Chelsea;[2] yet our dear
Padre resolutely forbears & postpones all establishment for

334. [1] This letter, with its description of Norbury Phillips, is missing.
    [2] Maria Rishton had probably gone on a tour with Mrs. Allen (L. 289 n. 5)
before settling at Bury St. Edmunds.

a companion & house-keeper, while the most remote hope remains in view of his Susan—whose presence & cares & society he covets unceasingly. I know he means, else, to make some arrangement; nor is it fitting he should be without a female of his family to attend him, as well as to bask in the sunshine of his kindness. But heavy would be the Hour to him in which he should be reduced to appoint any in his most beloved Susan's place!

⸺⸺⸻

I wrote directly to our Esther, whose anxiety I knew to be great. Our padre we have spared all hint of your illness. And he has been visiting Mr. Coxe & Mrs. Crewe, & is in high health & spirits, thank Heaven.—But I cannot, still, make out what I have last Copied to you of my correspondence with the Recluses. And to *Copy* is too wearisome for risking its being useless. Let me know how the last Letter begins that I have sent you, & then I shall be able to go on without difficulty or doubt.

⸺⸺⸻

The question you ask as to what Etty heard I cannot refuse to answer—yet shall be glad to know is safe—you will find the species in a parenthesis.[3] I would tell you all about the sweet Amelia, but that I know not what Mrs. Locke may tell herself— I am well aware no subject will be more interesting. We talk & think of it for-ever. The favoured Mortal[4] appears to be amiable & benevolent, by such accounts as are transmitted, & well disposed to be all I his beauteous Partner shall desire. I doubt not but, with all her gentleness, her influence will be entire & uncontrolled, not only over her Mate, but all his house, for the worthy Father adores her,—looks at her with looks of love, & studies her wishes with enthusiastic ardour to have them all gratified. Dear sweet girl! may she but know

---

[3] Information about the play 'Love and Fashion' was evidently to be conveyed within a 'Safe' or cutting and within parenthesis.

[4] John Angerstein (*c.* 1773–1858), M.P. (1796–1802, 1835–7), son of John Julius (i, L. 16 n. 9), underwriter and philanthropist, whose spacious house, 100 Pall Mall (with thirty-eight of the pictures with which the rooms were filled), was later (*c.* 1824) taken over as a National Gallery. The house is described by J. M. Scott, *The Book of Pall Mall* (1965).

enough of felicity to escape regret at leaving such a Home & such Parents!—I cannot but tremble for her, whatever appear her prospects, even to herself. Nobody has so much to relinquish —none so little to gain by any change.

I continue to keep hints in my pocket Book for a general Giornale for my beloved Susan, & so I shall till we meet, while I can send pacquets free, if they produce amusement to her— I have none other to offer her, & this, which lets her know all our proceedings, shews her also who of our mutual friends or acquaintance are *living & looking*, &, in some degree, what they are doing,—at least as far as I now know myself. Ah—could we, indeed, as you say, finish this Century together!—Can my dearest Susan give me any hopes *herself*? Be sure of my strictest observance of your injunctions—God forbid I should add to your—I must not say *what*—by any tremors at the idea or fear of ⟨imprudence⟩ or precipitance on *my* part—only remember *your* part of the agreement, & then depend upon mine that *you* shall be my sole signal for motion. What tears all you write about it brought into my Eyes!—& shook my whole frame!— it's well, my dearest Susan!—I am forced to abstain free & full expressions of all that passes within!—I shall resolutely hold as much back as possible.

with regard to M. de N[arbonne] we have heard nothing more[5]—it was from M. de la tour du pin[6] we heard of the correspondence with Louis XVIII. We are anxious for personal intelligence of his actual residence & safety & plans. How he must have been persecuted from spot to spot! ⏐ And much grieved, I am sure, for the death of M^e. la tante,[7] though it is not his own peculiar *princesse*. The public are now in great solicitude at a report of a great Battle in Holland,[8] which is not official, & which, consequently, is feared to be bad. Lady Templetown has 2 sons there—Greville & Arthur.[9] Lady Rothes has one, the Hon. John Leslie[9]—2 of the Fullers are

[5] See L. 326 n. 9.
[6] Frédéric-Séraphin, comte de la Tour-du-Pin-Gouvernet (1759–1837), baron (1808), marquis (1817). See also iii, L. 237 n. 9.
[7] Madame Victoire (see L. 323 n. 9).
[8] This was the engagement of the 10th (Fortescue, iv, pt. 2, 664), in which General Abercromby was victorious.
[9] See L. 332 nn. 9, 10, 11.

gone from the Rookery.[10] Colonel FitzGerald, aid de Camp to the Duke of York, from Mickleham—where he resides, when not on military duty, with his Mother & Father in Law, Colonel & Mrs. Milner.[11] General Burrard[12] had left his Wife & Children at Dorking—And Ensign Nixon[13] has left his near Guildford, who were at Bookham when he went on the last expedition, to Ostend.[14] Thus we are surrounded by anxious friends of the forces, for whom it is impossible not to feel a lively interest, added to the quick general sensation which so important an armament excites. More of terror than hope prevails, from our frequent failures on the continent. O that PEACE could by any means—permanent of promise—be but obtained!—

Adieu, my ever dearest Susan—& one injunction more let me solemnly add: if you *ever*, at *any* time, perceive an opening by which ANY sort of Letter or means might have a chance of accelerating a Meeting—remember the BLESSING you will confer by such a hint—& for God's sake let no cruel scruple

[10] The two youngest sons of Richard Fuller (*c.* 1713–82), the banker, Cornhill, who had bought the Rookery from Daniel Malthus in 1768.
Joseph (d. 16 Oct. 1841), an Ensign in the Coldstream Guards (1 Aug. 1792), Lieutenant and Captain (22 Jan. 1794), continued in the army with the ranks of Captain and Lt.-Col. (18 June 1801), becoming finally Colonel of the 75th Regiment (1832) and General (1838). He was knighted in 1826.
His younger brother William (d. 1815), Cornet with the 10th Light Dragoons (9 Mar. 1791), Lieutenant (Feb. 1793), Captain (20 June 1794), was commissioned a Major (26 Sept. 1799). Lt.-Col. (1 Jan. 1805) and Lt.-Col. of the 1st Dragoon Guards (Aug. 1805). He was killed at Waterloo.
[11] George Milner (1760–1836), Ensign 3rd Foot Guards (1776), Captain (25 Apr. 1792), eventually became their Lt.-Col. (1806). He had obtained the army rank of Colonel (3 May 1796), with later promotions Major-General (1 Jan. 1801), General (1819).
In 1786 he had married Charlotte *née* Colombier (*c.* 1752–1844). Her son by a former marriage was James Fitzgerald (d. 17 July 1802), A.D.C. to the Duke of York, see *GM* lxxii (1802), 693. He had obtained a commission as Ensign in the 3rd Foot Guards (25 Apr. 1792), had the rank Lieutenant and Captain (19 Mar. 1794) and was gazetted Major (4 Sept. 1799) and Lt.-Col. (29 Dec. 1801).
[12] Harry Burrard (1755–1813), M.P. (1780–1802), cr. Bart. (1807), had married on 20 Feb. 1789 Hannah Darby (d. 1833). Born before this time were five sons and a daughter: Paul Harry (1790), John Thomas (1792), Charles (1793), William (1794), Edward (1797), and Laura (1796). See Debrett's *Baronetage* and the parish records of Dorking. At this time Burrard was third Major of the 1st Foot Guards; and, with the army rank of Major-General, he was in command of the 2nd Brigade of Abercromby's forces.
[13] John Lyons Nixon (*fl.* 1795–1819), a Cornet with the 7th Light Dragoons (3 June 1795), apparently transferred to the Coldstream Guards with the rank of Lieutenant and Captain (12 Aug. 1799), eventually attaining the rank of Lt.-Col. (1811) with the 4th West Indian Regiment.
The Bookham parish registers record the baptism of his daughter (9 Jan. 1799).
[14] Possibly with the Guards, who were unworthily chosen (Fortescue, iv, pt. 1, 587–9), to participate in a 'paltry' plan of destroying a canal between Ostend and Bruges in May 1798.

keep you from instantly communicating it—We should think ourselves immediately *rich*, my darling Susan! if by a little more œconomy we could contribute to what is our FIRST wish upon earth—Embracing You again!—our, I say, for if I except *only* his Uncle, I am sure my Mate has no other superior. Think of this—& Heaven bless you, ever! & preserve you! — — our joint kindest Loves—especially to your dear little Guest, sweet Norbury. & Fanny & William.

Sept. 19.—99. Just going to be sent to Woodlands.

335   West Humble, 25 September 1799

To Doctor Burney

A.L., incomplete, extant in four cuttings pasted to A.L.S. FBA to CB, 1 Oct. 1799 (Diary MSS. vi. 5180–[3], Berg), 25 Sept. 1799

Conjecturally a double sheet 4to (9·7×8″), 4 pp., the first leaf of which was cut up and pasted as described in the Textual Notes; the second leaf is missing *rectos* and *versos* of two fragments.

Edited by FBA, p. 1 *annotated*: ❖ M^{rs} [*cut*] Hopes of Susan[’s] return— *Edited also by* CFBt.

West Humble,
Septr 25—99

What a Crowning to your Honours, my dearest Padre,[1] is this [*cut*] such a succession of distinctions can

[*a segment of the leaf is cut away*]

think, was written—at least never of ME was [written. I should] ⌐instantly have scribbled my thanks for your great indulgence in giving me such a regale,[2]—but that I have doubted how to direct from the uncertainty you express of whether you should remain longer at Dover, or run to Chelsea—*un*certainty on *your* side I should have set down for *certainty* on Mrs. Crewe's, but for the cruel weather, which has been all against her. I have therefore been hoping to gather some news through Esther,

335. [1] The recognition accorded to CB in 1799 made that year, in Lonsdale's opinion (p. 394), the happiest of his life.

[2] CB's letter of 9 Sept. 1799 (Osborn) is printed in *Memoirs*, iii. 272–7.

Charles, or Charlotte, where you might be—but none arrived—
& the objections [*line cut away*] the letter's unimaginable⌐

[*a segment of the leaf is cut away*]

I must, ⌐first,⌐ however, mention, that my Mate & I can ill
brook this shabby hint of shirking—that he still rears young
peas, & houses beautiful Carnations for you,—& that I had
determined to wait only for the first fair Day to put in my
rightful Claim. This very one ¦ upon which I write is the *First* in
which we have escaped Rain for a fortnight: & now, therefore,
we may surely hope for a fine autumn. What, then, says my
dearest Father?—I [*cut*]

[*a segment of the leaf is cut away*]

[Will] he not think of us?—*Who* can he think of to *quite* so much
delight with his sight?—In *England* no one!—In *Ireland* I own
there is one to whom it must be yet MORE precious, because so
cruelly long witheld — — Ireland, my dearest Padre, leads to
the immediate subject of this Letter.—Whether gayly or sadly
to usher what I have to say I know not,—but *your* sensations,
like mine, will I am sure be mixt. The Major has now written to
Mr. Lock that he is anxious to have Susan return to England!

[*4 obliterated lines, partially cut away*]

[She is *in an*] *ill state of health,* he says, & he thinks it necessary
she should try *another atmosphere*—Would to God without this
last alarming clause I could have related this offer of her
return! [*cut*] [to hope her return to us—sweet—Sweetest soul!—]
must be our first wish—How blest will be the ⟨Moment⟩

To Esther (Burney) Burney

A.L.S. (Berg), 28 Sept. [17]99
Double sheet 4to   4 pp.   *pmks* DARKING   30 SEP 99   wafer
Addressed: Mrs. Burney, / Beaumont Street, / Devonshire Place / London—
Endorsed by EBB: Answered. Sep. 30th / 1799
Scribbling, p. 4: Paper / Cambridge

West Hamble, Septr 28th
99.

I can hardly settle with myself, my dearest Etty, whether to communicate with joy or affright what I have to write to you— that again the Major promises to let us have our beloved Susan —The *joy* speaks for itself,—but the *affright* hangs upon his acknowledging her ill state of health is the reason he deems it necessary to let her try a change of air. Besides which, the barbarous uncertainty of his performing his promise is a dreadful drawback to full content. 'Tis to Mr. Locke he has written his intention, & therefore it seems far the most *probable*, at least, of any hope hitherto given. Heaven grant it may at length be fulfilled! Here, I should hope, she might be restored—attended, fondled, soothed as she would be, by those whose tenderest affections are hers, & are returned by her own, there is every reason to trust we might re-establish her. All my prayer, therefore, is that SHE MAY COME!—The Letter was upon business otherwise, & says not one word of any of the Children, whether Fanny & Willy were to accompany her, nor whether he should do so or not himself. |

I have written of this to our dear Father, but, as to you, without congratulation or condolance. I think *you* will—like me —be too much alarmed for very high hopes—yet I do really now believe the Major must be serious. Mr. Locke himself has *no doubt*. *She*, he says, knows not of his writing. It cannot, therefore, be now only to play upon *her*. He does not mention if Norbury is still with her or not. Mrs. Lock & her sweet Amelia see nothing *but* the fair side of this, & expect her with unmixt delight. But her Letter to you[1]—the picture she there drew of

336. [1] The letter that EBB received at West Humble in the week of 30 July. Cf. L. 331, pp. 319–20.

her declining health & weakness, never has wholly been from my mind since, & therefore the motive assigned by the Major breeds poignant anxiety—though no longer *despondence,*—for if indeed we may be blest by her return, I think it *impossible* we should not revive her.

In a period such as this, a line from her will be invaluable. Let us, my dearest Esther, mutually send intelligence of any she may write, during this suspence. The last time her hand reached my Eyes, was in a Letter to Amelia, of congratulation, written in instant answer to her receiving the news. Norbury then was with her, for he finished it. I was lent it for one day, but do not recollect its date. The date of the Major's is Sept. 15. It is an exceedingly proper & well written Letter, & speaks of Her health as a subject to which all other things should give way. What a comfort to us all, in this uncertainty, is her possessing that faithful Susan! she will so well nurse & attend her on her journey! — — — How do I wish I could take that office! — — —

He has not desired that any of us should be acquainted with this—nor yet enjoined any silence. We cannot settle whether to write or not, with any satisfaction to ourselves. So often have I addressed the Major ineffectually, that I even fear to do it might *thawrt* rather than advance my wishes!—Yet, luckily, I had sent him a few lines, in answer to those I mentioned to you in my last, which I think *may* be productive of good. With what *excess* of impatience shall we wait for the sight of her loved hand! — — —

Adieu, my dearest Esther—I have once or twice thought to spare you this anxious interval—but determined finally *to do as I would be done by*, which is, to hear *all the truth* where this precious object is in question, & then judge it—& *bear* it as I can.

My mate's & my kind Love to Mr. Burney—& your Girls— What a cruel wet season! It blights all my hopes at present of seeing again my dear Father.—The marriage will take place next Week.[2] Pray write a few lines to the Bride when you hear or read it is over. You are a great favourite, & I know they will give her pleasure.

Ever & ever yours,

F. d'A.

[2] On 2 Oct. 1799.

My Alex is well, & to be *manified*[3] on the *wedding Day*, by way of making us a little festival on the occasion, for his rapture in the expectation is at least equal to a Bridegroom's joy.

337   West Humble, 1 October 1799

To Doctor Burney

A.L.S. (Diary MSS. vi. 5180–[3], Berg), 1 Oct. [17]99
Double sheet 4to   4 pp.   *pmks*   3 OCT   3 OCT 99
Addressed: Dr. Burney, / Chelsea College, / Middlesex
Endorsed by CB: Mrs Darblay 1799
Edited by FBA, p. 1 (5180) *annotated*: ⁖ ⁖ (6)   Susanna, Walmer castle
Mrs. Genl Milner.
Edited also by CFBt *and the* Press.

West Humble, Octr 1. 99

What a sumptuous feast have you given me, my kindest Father! It was our whole Morning's regale, so slowly we could bear to read, for fear of too soon ending it.[1] I wish some kind friend or other would always be giving you a Letter to enclose for me, & that you would always forget so to do, that ALWAYS you might be stimulated to make amends by preparing a parcel for the Coach! But—like you, I must speak first of our dear Susanna. ⌐I am much pleased & strengthened in all my hopes, by finding the Major had already intimated to you his design of settling ere long in England again. I have told you of his firm lines to me, also, upon that same promise. And this seems to shew a plan of some premeditation, which the dear Soul's illness may only have hastened. M. d'Arblay concurs with you,

---

[3] To appear in trousers rather than petticoats.

337. [1] Late in August (Lonsdale, p. 398) CB had joined Mrs. Crewe, who, to share in the excitement of the moment and to bid farewell to her son, had taken a house at Dover quite within reach of Walmer Castle, where Pitt and his ministers (Dundas, Canning, and others) had assembled for the occasion of the embarkation of the Duke of York (8 Sept.) on the 'Secret Expedition' to Holland (see Fortescue, iv, pt. 2, 639–709; Oman, pp. 200–36; *Later Corr. Geo. III*, iii, Ll. 2027–30).

CB's letter of 9 Sept., op. cit., reflects his delight in the brilliant company and his impression of the events, though the printed version, *Memoirs*, iii. 272–7, includes errors, alterations, and additions introduced by FBA in her editorial capacity of some thirty years later. CB's letter of 15 Sept., printed in *Memoirs*, iii. 278–80, is missing. FBA here comments on both letters.

that it will be most political to leave the affair of the promise to Mr. Lock wholly unnoticed till he makes it otherwise known & more directly to our family.⊓ I grow more & more sanguine, as I put circumstances together; but shall never be easy nor assured till I hear she has actually touched English ground. O what a sound of joy! ⌐At all events, with such hopes before us, I rejoice my dearest Father's judgement & foresight guided him to hold completely back about any other female companion. Mine were more desperate & I had uneasily wished one of the dear Girls under your roof, now even yet, & even if they come, I dare not build upon your having Susan & her good Girl completely,—I greatly fear the Major means to *come in a body* & settle here himself—But there is no guessing *where*, nor *how* —&⊓ | therefore, if we get her but to this side the Channel, the blessing is, *comparatively*, so great, that I shall feel truly thankful to Heaven.

How you have made me fall in love with your ladies, Susan Ryder,[2] & Jane Dundas,[3] & the whole family of Greys![4] I am enchanted with your reception & intimacy amongst such sweet mannered & minded people as you describe. But Mr. Pitt! ——— I am really in Alt when I see you presenting him your Letter from Dr. Herschal.[5] Solemn, yet heart warming is your account

[2] Among those at Dover, according to CB's letter of 9 Sept., were the Hon. Dudley Ryder (1762–1847), M.P. (1784–1803), paymaster-general (1791–1800), and his wife Lady Susan (1772–1838), daughter of Granville Leveson Gower (1721–1803), 1st Marquis of Stafford (1786). She, 'a Sweet Creature—handsome, accomplished, & perfectly well-bred. . . . Sings & plays well in a true taste.'

[3] There, also, were Henry Dundas (1742–1811), M.P. (1774–1802), Treasurer of the Navy, and his wife Lady Jane (1766–1829), daughter of John Hope (1704–1781), 2nd Earl of Hopetoun (1742). She, 'another charming creature, and one of my flirtations'.

[4] On Monday 2 Sept. Mrs. Crewe and her party had dined with General Charles Grey (1729–1807), Commander of the Southern District (1798–9), whose headquarters were at Barham Court near Canterbury. Placed on the right of the General's lady, i.e. Elizabeth *née* Grey (*c.* 1744–1822), CB was charmed despite her being the mother of the 'furious parliamentary democrat' (i, L. 24 n. 46). Engaging, also, were her daughter Hannah Althea (1785–1832) and her mother (Elizabeth *née* Ogle), now 85, but 'a great and scientific reader'. 'What a distinguished race!' FBA later interpolated in her editorial capacity. CB only wished they could keep their eldest in order.

[5] In a letter of 15 Sept. CB told of a telescope that Pitt had had 'constructed under the superintendence of Herschel' and of how Canning, handing him a book of instructions, had asked him to assemble it. In some dismay and very much doubting his competence, CB had applied to Herschel, whose obliging reply, he was able to produce for Pitt, 'who read it with great attention, and, I doubt not, intelligence'.

of the Embarkation.[6] God send us more good news of its result!
like you, we are sadly alarmed by the *Second* affair, after being
so elated by the *first*.[7] Yet the taking the Dutch Fleet must
always remain a *national* amends for almost any loss. Mrs.
Milner, of Mickleham,[8] who has a son, by a former husband,
now Colonel FitzGerald, & aid de Camp to the Duke of York
(& probably of the staff you met at Walmer Castle) has sent me,
lately, a message to desire we *should acquaintance*. It came
through Lady Rothes, & consequently I expressed proper
acknowledgements. two Days ago she came to make her first
visit. Her present husband, who is also a Colonel, called at the
same time on M. d'Arblay, with whom he had made a *speaking
acquaintance* while we were building our Cottage. We found
them very agreeable people, well bred, well cultivated, &
pleasing. The Colonel is serious, she is lively, but they seem
happy in each other. I am the more disposed to think well of
them, because not only the Duke—but the *Duchess* of York
twice breakfasted with them, in journeying from ¦ Brighthelmstone. This has put them in *high fashion* in this neighbourhood.
She tells Me she is the *worst of visitors*—& I assured her that
having heard that character of her was one of my first inducements to venture at her acquaintance, not only from the flattery
of her selection, but from the sympathy I felt in that defect.
They walked *all round our Grounds,*—the *wood, Copse,—meadow*—
Eat one of our Apples, just gathered from our virgin orchard,
& found all M. d'Arblay's flowers of the first fragrance.—
Could they fail being pleasant people?—Pray wish well to
Colonel FitzGerald for their sake. I was happy not to see his name
amongst the Killed & Wounded—nor that of the Hon. *John
Leslie*, Lady Rothes' son,[9]—nor those of *Greville* nor *Arthur
Upton*,[9] Lady Templetown's sons: nor Mr. Nixon,[10] late of
Bookham, nor General Burrard,[10] now of Dorking—what an
anxious period, through Relations or connexions, independent
of general humanity, does this Expedition make! Heaven

---

[6] For the military 'in high spirits and glee' and the cannonades from the battle-
ments, see *Memoirs*, iii. 277. The picture of the Duke of York 'composed, princely,
and noble', was FBA's addition to CB's account of the royal embarkation.

[7] The Dutch fleet had surrendered on 30 Aug. 'without the firing of a shot', but
news must have reached England by now of the hopeless disasters suffered by
Abercromby's untrained militiamen in the dikes and dunes of the Helder (Fortescue, op. cit.).

[8] See L. 334 n. 11.   [9] See L. 332 nn. 9, 10, & 11.   [10] See L. 334 nn. 13, 12.

prosper it! What is Mr. J. Crewe called? *Captain?* I[11] hope it is not he who is named amongst the wounded?[11]—You make me wild to hear the Emperor's Hymn & Tuvarrow's March.[12] Their popularity at Dover & Walmer Castle were most seasonable & delightful. They quite set my Heart a beating with pleasure & exultation for my dearest Father, only in hearing of them. But *YOU*, forsooth, to preside over the Bottle! Ha! Ha!—Mr. Pitt, however, could not risk his intellects, so he chose well for preserving them.[13] The Mrs. Lloyd's story is amusing, though almost incredible.[14] The Houses of Parliament & Bench of Bishops, for Dancers, made me laugh heartily. Brave M[r] Pitt & M[r] Canning.[15]

⌐But I feel a little disappointed & let down at the word of the Richmond ¹ visit. I cannot but think *any terms* upon which Edward could visit Italy, for what of statues, Temples, busts, buildings, are still remaining, would answer, by making him known, & teaching his Employers to respect what is due to his talents, which then would have a far wider field to display themselves. As to *their* patronage, it is so beneath him, that I think any change would be both preferable & honourable, & there can be no fear but he would get as good employment & pay as he has from *them* at any earning I am often really grieved at his present obscurity, & its hopelessness. You don't mention that he was of the party, on the Monday Assembly at Lady Leicester's[16] — — Even were he ever so ill-paid, the

[11] Lt.-Col. of the 9th Regiment (L. 332 n. 7). Crewe appears in the list of the wounded in *AR* xli (1799), 'Appendix to the Chronicle', 107. It was perhaps in this action that he lost the sight of an eye (*Barthomley*, p. 323).

[12] Haydn's 'Hymn to the Austrian Emperor' ('*Gott, erhalte den Kaiser*') CB had translated into English, and then versified it to fit the tune (Lonsdale, p. 395). 'Suwarrow's March', inspired by the spectacular marches of the Russian field marshal, was one of CB's musical compositions (see Scholes, ii. 351, 298–9).

Lady Susan Ryder (n. 2) and Miss Crewe had sung the hymn, CB accompanying them and joining in the chorus, after which he played his march and Pitt, who, though neither knowing nor caring 'one farthing for flutes and fiddles', listened attentively (*Memoirs*, iii. 274–5).

[13] In John Crewe's absence, the honour was voted to CB (*Memoirs*, iii. 279).

[14] Rachel Lloyd (*c.* 1720–1803), Maid of Honour to Augusta, Princess of Wales, and later (19 Oct. 1764) Housekeeper of Kensington Palace (R.H.I., Windsor). Having failed to recognize Sheridan, she made to his face invidious remarks about his patriotic melodrama *Pizarro* (first presented 24 May 1799), impugning as well his loyalty to king and country.

[15] On Miss Crewe's lament that the embarkation of young men would ruin the balls, Pitt had pledged 'partners plenty—both Houses of Parliament!' and Canning had offered 'the whole Bench of Bishops!'

[16] Charlotte Mainwaring Ellerker (1754–1802), who had married in 1777 George Townshend (1753–1811), Baron Ferrers of Chartley (1770), cr. Earl of the

honour of the family would be engaged to Patronize him ever afterwards. I have heard you say, an artist should *pay himself* to see Italy, and Italy, wasted as it is, is still the first spot in the world, for a Painter. — — But the worst for me & mine is this wet season, that will not so settle as to make me dare talk of West Hamble—& that is a mortification & disappointment I feel more than I think it right to worry you with bearing.— So adieu with thanks, not grumblings, my dearest Padre—for if any *Letters* could make me amends for absence[17] those would be such as you send to your

ever grateful & affect^e

& dutiful   F. d'A

My Chevalier is much gratified with all that *you* say & that the *King* says of Sir Sidney Smith,[18] for he thinks you may go back 200 years to find an exploit equal to his at Acre. His kindest Respects.⊓ |

Tomorrow the lovely Amelia will be married—And your youngest Grandson will put on a Man's attire! Q^y who will be happiest to-morrow, John Angerstein—or Alexis d'Arblay?

---

338   West Humble, 12 October [1799]

To Mrs. Phillips
and Molesworth Phillips

A.L.S. (Berg), 12 Oct.
Double sheet 4to   *pmks*   DARKING   18 OC 99   wafer
Addressed: Mrs. Phillips, / at Major Phillips, / Belcotton, / Drogheda.
IRELAND / To be forwarded immediately.
Docketed, p. 1: 1799

West Hamble

Octr 12th

My dear — — darling Susan must not wonder at a Letter by the common post—I can wait no conveyance—I can lose no

County of Leicester (1784), 2nd Marquis Townshend (1807). Her sisters Elizabeth and Harriett (iii, L. 126 n. 7; and iv, L. 333 n. 5) lived in Richmond.

[17] In a letter of 9 Sept., CB had expressed his 'dread' of 'the idea of September'. This remark was revised in FBA's version to read 'I dread letting the autumn creep on at a distance from my own chimney corner'.

[18] CB's remarks about Admiral Sir William Sidney Smith (1764–1840), famous for the defence of Acre (Mar.–May 1799, see *DNB*), are lost, presumably with missing parts of his letters (above).

time—I have just seen Mrs. Lock—& she tells me that Mr. Lock has had a Letter—while he was at Woodlands—from the Major, in which he talks of your coming over to try a change of air for your health, which is in a dangerous state — — O my Susan!—may you be set out before this arrives!—But if not—for the sake of your whole family induce the Major to make you begin the journey instantly.—

I must be sincere with you, my dear love, not to alarm or surprise you—I have been so greatly shocked & frightened, that M. d'Arblay promises *I shall set out for Belcotton* immediately, to nurse & attend you, if it is still inconvenient to the Major to let you come & try your native air, or if he thinks it too late in the Season.

In that case, I shall trust to the Major's hospitality & politeness—or, if your house is too small to admit me, take a lodging at Drogheda. Thence I shall not fear a rugged walk, to sit by you, & look at you, & watch till you are well enough to make the journey.

only—by return of post, let me have one line, to say *where* we may meet, whether in England or Ireland. I can give you no other choice. I must *COME*—& *IMMEDIATELY*—if I do not hear you are setting out directly.

The winter is so quick advancing, that I shall be very glad to have one of us en route without delay. M. d'Arblay, on that account, says he shall hurry me off with the utmost expedition, unless you are actually setting out.

Meanwhile, I shall make every preparation in my power to be ready, when your answer arrives, for hastening to you.—except I find you are coming hither without loss of time. In that case, I will try to repress my alarm, & wait for you.

But you must not trifle with me, my dearest Susan—you must not, indeed!—if I have a vague, unsatisfactory answer, *I SHALL SET OUT* & run all risks at once.

If, indeed, you can come here—if the Major thinks the air of your native land may be beneficial, as I understand he has said to Mr. Lock, a thousand times I shall prefer the meeting here—for my poor Father is sick—tired—offended, almost, by your procrastinations, & cannot pass the winter without a female of the family for his Evening Companion,—though he is particularly well & busy & in spirits all day. But I dread his taking one of our dear nieces, who may find Chelsea dull, & then rather dispirit than enliven his solitude—though they are excellent Girls, & — — were *YOU* out of the question, I should think they might be his greatest comforts. But his Heart *yearns* for you—he told me he never would dispose of his spare room while he could have any Expectation of seeing you, ⎮ for he wants the solid consolation & conversation you can give, & thinks, with Fanny, *you* might find employment at Chelsea to wile away the hours of his engagements, & chear him at their conclusion. He almost *PINES* to have you—& that makes me pray Heaven our meeting may rather be at Chelsea than at Belcotton.

In a Letter I yesterday received from Charles,[1] he says he will fetch you all himself from the sea side, if you will let him know where & when you land: & take Willy to himself & his school with the greatest pleasure. He is affectionate, & *stable*, & flourishing in his affairs.

⌒

your last Letter is just come, my sweetest Susan—you give me no comfort as to your health—& my project is *deeply fixed* to see you, at all rates.

We in vain beg the Major to consider—for this most earnest wish of my *LIFE—our* purse *yours*, he takes no notice of our petition,—yet we feel satisfied this is no period, after such misfortunes to his Country, & such a Law suit,[2] for travelling expences—*YOU* must not be so cruel to us, my Susan—& in the full belief you will not, we shall act. M. d'Arblay is NOW setting off for London, to Sell out £50 & put them into the hands of Messrs Coutts, payable to *you*—or *your* order. Consider this, therefore, as *DONE*—for DONE it will be in a few HOURS. I shall not put you to the post of a Letter to tell you so—you will be as *sure* you may draw *the instant this comes to hand* as if the note was enclosed in it. The money *MUST* go to the Voyage—all that is to fix is whether it be for *MINE* or *YOURS*. Heaven bless & preserve you! My darling! my Heart's dearest Susan— ⎮

338. [1] The letter is missing, but CB Jr. was to carry out this plan.
   [2] See L. 306 n. 3.

[*To Major Phillips*]

My dear Major—I hate to torment you with what I know you dislike, *Letters*—but I am now so uneasy about our Susan I can no longer defer ocular proof of her state of health—if you think the season too far advanced for her delicate frame to travel to Chelsea, do not let her set out, for God's sake—I will come to you—& lodge at Drogheda, if you are crowded. If you think, as when you wrote to Mr. Lock, her native air may do her good, let her not lose a moment. & do not refuse to let *her*, at least, draw on Coutts for her journey. We do not dare, in *your* Name, without your leave, to place money—but we take that liberty with *her*, & without waiting her consent, that no more posts may be lost, in case you really think she may yet travel. The money will be at Coutts in her name before this Letter reaches the sea side. She need not, therefore, wait a moment for Drawing for it—but I must depend upon *YOU* to settle whether it is too late in the year for her safety. If so, I build upon your old & first kindness, my dear Major, to receive me—for come I must—so well I know her Constitution, that I think I could nurse her better than anybody. Decide for us *quickly*, dear Major—lest we miss on the road. My Father will have an eternal obligation to you for sparing her, if it can be done without danger. He is hurt by the delay, because he counts *72*!—but he will be yours ever more if you speed her to him, & if you think it *prudent* to let her travel.

God bless you, dear Major.
F. d'A.

[*To Mrs. Phillips, written on the margins of* p. 1]

P.S. Amelia was married the 2ᵈ. Mr. & Mrs. Lo[cke] & family only came home for the Fair, the 10ᵗʰ—& I have seen them but a moment. Mr. Lock, I find, says he depends *positively* upon seeing you, & is much pleased the Major wrote to him about it. He, indeed, is persuaded, he says, from the Major's Letter to him, you must ere this be set out. May he prove right! How happy should we be if the whole party were to come, & Englishize again the Major, & dear Norbury—& Willy & ⟨Fanny.⟩

We have just made acquaintance with the happiest Mother

in England—*Capt. FitzGerald's*[3]—so highly mentioned by the D[uke] of Y[ork] & sent over to be promoted upon the last great victory & taking of Alcmaer. The uptons both safe—& young Les⟨lie⟩ & General Burrard[4]—All is most prosperous & glorious in the Expedition—thank Heaven—

I have seen Mrs. Newton twice lately—tell your good Susan, with my best wishes—she is well, & has got two nurse children.

339   West Humble, 15 October 1799

To Doctor Burney

A.L.S. (Berg), 15 Oct. [17]99
Double sheet large 4to   4 pp.   *pmks*   17 OCT 99   17 OC 99   wafer
Addressed: Dr. Burney, / Chelsea College, / Middlesex.
Endorsed by CB: Mrs Darblay / 1799
Edited by FBA, p. 1, *annotated*: ⁜ (7) dreadful First avowal of the dangerous state of SUSANNA ELIZABETH PHILLIPS! & her wish to return to our BOSOMS!

Oct. 15.—99
West Humble.

on Saturday, my dearest Sir, I had a Letter from our beloved Susan,[1] in which she speaks of her health in terms so afflicting that I think we must now all once·more make a desperate effort to rescue her from her captivity, or tremble at the risk of her passing another Winter in such a situation — — The cruel Major can never have even told her your earnest & affecting demand of her return—for, while she owns all her courage subdued, & all her fortitude at an end, from *something*—she explains not what—*which has happened*, & that her prayer now day & night is once more to visit England—Her Father—Sisters

---

[3] FBA had evidently seen in *The Times* (8 Oct.) a report of the engagement of 2 Oct.: Capt. FITZGERALD [L. 334 n. 11] . . . arrived at Mr. DUNDAS's Office with the Official Correspondence' on the 'ENTIRE DEFEAT OF THE FRENCH AND BATAVIAN ARMIES . . . AND THE CAPTURE OF THE TOWN OF ALKMAAR.' Four days later (6 Oct.) the Duke of York lost control of his troops, and Alkmaar was recaptured by the French (Fortescue, iv, pt. 2, pp. 696–7; *The Times*, 15 Oct. 1799).

[4] L. 332 nn. 9, 10, 11; and L. 334 n. 12.

339. [1] Only a cutting (2·9×8″) remains of this letter, which FBA says (L. 340) was begun 28 Sept. and concluded 4 Oct.

—Brothers—Friends—She drops a hint that she doubts if that *ever* can be if this winter begins with her at Belcotton—

Whether the *something* is relative to any new discovery or barbarity or misdemeanour of the M— or alludes only to her growing consciousness of encreasing feebleness & bodily suffering, she leaves in the dark—& only says it is ǀ not possible for her to unravel the mystery *NOW*—nor at a distance.—But she never before expressed such a yearning to return—a yearning that seems as if Life & Death hung upon its taking or not taking place.—

We begin to suspect the M. now holds back from bringing her because he has incapacitated himself from paying you & Mr. Lock your interest[2]—for I take it for granted the *beginning of October* has elapsed like the beginning of so many other Months—ah—dearest Sir!—could you, all unjust & abominable as it seems—consent to tell this Geoaler you will wave the payment yet a month or two longer,—*in consideration of the expences of the journey back to England of his sick wife—though no other consideration could make you submit voluntarily to the extreme inconvenience & difficulty which must be the result of such a sacrifice.*— Forgive, Dearest Sir, this idea—which I only communicate from knowing the preservation of this inestimable soul is the thing nearest & dearest to you—And I have a horrour of her being suffered to remain there ǀ another winter that is so very great, that M. d'A. has consented to my writing word to the M. himself That if he cannot let Susan come over, I shall make a voyage to Ireland to see & to nurse her. This we think may accelerate his resolution—& if it fails—I shall never be easy again without fulfilling it. Mrs. Lock had so affecting a Letter from her this Morning, of her weak state, & the urgent *cries of Nature* to return to her home—Father—& Friends—that she has written her a private Letter, under cover to her good maid Susan, to tell her that £50 shall immediately be placed at a Banker's, payable to *her* drawing, in the whole or part, instantly. —& supplicated her to use every effort to return before the winter sets in, & try not only the *paternal roof*, & *fraternal love*, but the friendly & congenial air of Norbury Park, which once before restored her, when in all appearance upon the point of a consumption.

2 See iii, L. 226 n. 8.

Charles, too, who was here on Sunday, will write about Willy—& I am sure kindly, though he did not tell me how.

The sweet Soul, after saying 'for a year past I have languished to be able to re-visit my dear Father, & try to Soothe & chear *him*—' adds a question, whether I think your spirits equal to taking her *now*, when she ¹ is so reduced & sickly as to want soothing & chearing herself?—

I have ventured to answer I was SURE nothing on Earth could conduce so much to the consolation of your days as to receive HER in whatever way she was able to come to you. ⌐But I suspect by this the M. has ⟨never⟩ shown her your recent correspondence!—she knows nothing of his writing to Mr. Locke! nothing of his writing to Charles!—but she tells me now⌐ She will no longer resist any measures we can combine to take for forwarding her escaping passing this Winter at Belcotton. I am sure she must have some reasons very forcible. Sometimes I think she may have found a danger she has never yet apprehended from *rebels*—that some party has arisen near them or some pikes been dug up—She mentions that *Mr. Wall*,³ her old mickleham friend, has just been forced, by a discovery of this sort, to fly his lone house, though his Wife has only lain in 4 days!—The M. certainly means to come over also, though whether to stay or return does not appear. Otherwise, I am so uneasy, I should long to set out at once to try to bring her. But I feared doing it unexpectedly. Mrs. Locke's sweet act of friendship is my best hope. Heaven bless & preserve my most dear Father! & grant me the joy unspeakable of once more feeling his loved arms encircle at once his Susan & his

F. d'A—

Charles generously insists upon taking the whole expense of Her Journey from her landing. He has written so to the M.

³ Charles William Wall (iii, L. 222 n. 4), whose second daughter Elizabeth Lucy may have been born at this time.

To Esther (Burney) Burney

A.L.S. (Berg), 15–18 Oct. [17]99
Double sheet large 4to   4 pp.   *pmks*   DAR[KING]   21 OCT 99   wafer
Addressed: Mrs. Burney, / Beaumont Street, / Devonshire Place / London
Endorsed by EBB: 1799
Scratches in ink, p. 4.

Octr 15—99
West Hamble

You have seen but too clearly, my dearest Esther—& your
worst prognostics are confirmed!—The sweet soul knew nothing
of the Letter to Mr. Lock—& in answer to mine upon that
subject, asks what of hope can be annexed to such mystery?—
yet says the M[ajor] never fails asserting *they are coming to
England!*—But the most melancholy of all is her health! she now
speaks to me of it as she has done before to you, & seems too
ill for any attempt at disguise, nay, owns her courage to be
totally subdued, & no wish to remain but a return to her Native
Home & Friends — — — — This most affecting Letter—which I
received on Saturday—& which was begun Sept. 28, & finished
Oct. 4.—I have answered in a way you will hear, I am sure,
with pleasure, though mixed with sensations of a combatting
nature—my terror for her very preservation was so great, that
M. d'A. consented to my writing word that if the M. could not
let her set out immediately—or did not think her well enough—
I should forthwith make a journey to Ireland—& see & nurse
her myself.—And this most religiously I mean to do, if he is still
obdurate. My wretchedness at the thoughts of her consuming
away to a lingering death in *that* prison with *that* geoler ¹ conquers
every obstacle of cowardice & of expence that oppose my voyage.
I should never be happy again not to make this *attempt* to save
her, since my most generous Mate sees her worth & her danger
with my own Eyes, & thinks NO risk & NO cost too great for
flying to her rescue.

In my Letter to the M. I have put my plan & my fears
wholly upon *his own* statement of her dangerous state to Mr.
Lock. What *she* says I dare never refer to—

oct. 18. 99

Some interruptions, my dearest Esther, kept this from the post on *Baker's Day*—& M. d'A.'s return, & informing me he had acquainted you with all we knew, had made me give up any present intention of writing: but I have now something I must communicate, as I know it will delight you for our dearest beloved, & renew better hopes—Mr. Lock—in his sweet wife's name & writing, has transmitted 150 to his own Banker, to be drawn for by our Susan, for paying any debts that may prevent her setting out, as well as her journey: & Mrs. Lock has written the most touchingly sweet & eloquent Letter I ever read, *imploring* her to have no false delicacy at such a period,. where the happiness & peace of so many depend upon her generous acceptance of an assistance their whole Souls offer her, & which to refuse would be unworthy the kindness of her gentle Heart, which would be half broken by being refused *herself* if the situation were reversed. It is impossible to me to forbear writing you this, my dearest Esther, though I have only this moment written it to our dear Father—but your meetings are uncertain—& the pleasure it has revived in my saddened & terrified heart makes ˥ me hope you will receive it as comfort & hope to your own. The Bride, too, has written to the M. a most soothing Letter of entreaty. Miss Lock has added a few lines. &, to complete all, Mrs. Lock has condescended to write him a *personal* invitation to Norbury Park—though I believe no object exists so baleful to her Eyes! What a generous noble friendship is this!—

I thank you for the sweet Letter you have sent me by M. d'A —How much more forcible must be her desire to come over since it was written! it is dated the 24. Sept. & she there seems desirous I should not know her weak state, lest I should aggravate it by my fears—yet in her last to me, finished Oct. 4, she says so much more! says she doubts if she shall EVER come, unless it is immediately!—that her spirits sink—her courage is subdued—& she consents to ANY measures I can adopt or arrange to hasten her return! Something unexplained hangs upon her earnestness—& it is something she says she *cannot* explain—whether it regards her health—or any new discovery of ill conduct in the M.—or any reason to believe rebellion rising in her neighbourhood—there is no fixing—but I suppose it one of these 3 things. She even lets me see, now, her *wish* I should go to her, if the M. is still obdurate, though hitherto, when I have proposed it, she has *conjured* me not to have such a thought, lest it should render him outrageous. Something therefore of deep moment must have happened. Heaven grant it may *not* be about health, all other things being more retrievable.

Mrs. Lock has had a Letter since—dated Oct. 9. & written with the first great earnestness she has ever suffered herself to express then ¹ to return to us—O England! England! she says— my Father—my 'Sisters—my friends!—shall I ever see you more?—I think I shall die of the joy—yet I feel as if I could not OUTLIVE a disappointment!' What touching words!—charles has been very kind & liberal—he has written to the M. he will be at the whole expence of her Journey from Belcotton to Greenwich, if he will let her come. This on Sunday—when the Lock affair had not happened. And that, as a point of delicacy, you will only discuss when alone with my F[ather] & Mr. B[urney]. It is not *my* business to spread it—but I could not resist to you three. I am sure my Susan would not *wish* me. How she will be melted—yet soothed & gratified by such exertions!

M. d'A. says you will be so kind as to procure & enclose me Mr. Mathias's receipt. We are not in haste, so don't do it till you go that way. Many thanks for the paper. If I have a Journey to Ireland to make, you must pray I may not buy it for nothing!—What a stimulus would it be to me to require it for *her*! if she inspirits me by recovering! but, if unhappy, no MUSE is so mute as Mine. Alex was enchanted with his Letter from Amelia. Pray kiss her for it, & thank her. When he can write, he will answer it with joy. He comes to me now with every bit of paper he can find, & gravely says 'If you please, ma'am, here's a Letter.' But when his papa announced what he brought him, his next exclamation to that of pleasure was 'And haven't you brought me a Letter from Aunt Burney?' So you see you keep your place with him. What a bewitching description our Susan has drawn of Norbury! He had always every promise of extraordinary talents: but the Music is all but incredible.

My Mate's kindest Love to you & dear Mr. B[urney]—You will distribute it from both to your fireside. I am happy to hear

Richard is so much better—pray tell him so, with my most affectionate wishes for his complete recovery. God bless you, my dearest Esther—& may ONE of us have speedily better news to write of our sweetest sufferer!

ever & ever yours most
truly & affectionately
F. d'A [

when you write, mention how the Ellerker intercourse goes on—& if any hopes of Edward.[2]

341   West Humble, 18 October 1799

To Doctor Burney

A.L.S. (Berg), 18 Oct. [17]99
Double sheet large 4to   4 pp.   *pmks*   19 OCT 99   19 OC 99   wafer
Addressed: Dr. Burney / Chelsea College, / Middlesex
Endorsed by CB: Mrs Darblay / 1799
Edited by FBA, p. 1, *annotated and the year 99 retraced*: ✳ ✳ 99 (8) Terror
Terror—Terror for the sweetest of the sweet Susanna Elizabeth Phillips
M^r & Mrs. Lock's exquisite Friendship
Annotated, p. 4, in an unknown editorial hand: Suppressed

West Hamble.
Octr 18. 99

Nothing but my full conviction that all our loves & all our anxieties for the return of this beloved Soul put together can but *equal* yours, my most dear Sir, could have prevailed upon me, even in the anguish of my first fright, to have proposed such a sacrifice on your part—but I know well what her life is to you— & I knew you had been kept in ignorance of her lingering ill state of health till very lately—& therefore I permitted impulse to guide my pen, in pointing out that measure, though with the strongest possible sense of its abomination, injustice, & even attrocity—save to gain so great an end—an end to pay us for

340. [1] For patronage or employment for her cousin and brother-in-law Edward, the artist (i. lxxv), EBB had been placing hopes on the Ellerker sisters and their in-law the Earl of the County of Leicester (L. 333 n. 5; L. 337, pp. 340–1, and n. 16).

all that all round can do—for we have taken our own part to our fullest ability—& what *you* would think beyond it—in our efforts, long before this application: though, as yet, he has declined our offers. But, I thank God, my most dear Father, things are now in a rather better train—in so much, that I think your proposing to be the victim to this cruel scourge may be dispenced with—for Yesterday Evening Mrs. Lock acquainted me, That dear Mr. Lock—considering by her last Letter, that her return was of some high necessity, & yet | that the journey expences might not be *all* that made it impracticable, as there might be debts of a nature to demand immediate payment before they could leave their neighbourhood—has added £100 to the £50,—& placed it at his own Banker's, Martin's,[1] in *her* name, for her sole use & disposal; & Mrs. Lock has written her another Letter under cover to the good Maid, to 'implore her not to break her heart by any false delicacy about making use of the Money, but to let it bring her strait to Norbury Park, there to be nursed for Chelsea.—'—

What exquisite goodness! what true friendship!—I should have written it to my dearest Father this Morning, if I had *not* heard from him, as it makes me far less anxious about his making such an offer to the Major. Nor is this all—Mrs. Lock has forced herself to write a very kind Letter to the M[ajor] himself—though she almost abhors him—to beg him to be speedy, & even to *invite* him to bring her himself—And this, with their present sentiments of him, is more heroic than all the rest. The sweet Bride has written to him also, joining the most lively entreaties to every species of courtesie. Nothing now seems left to be done—if all | these efforts fail, he has only meant to make us all, as you say, bid for who shall bid highest—& yet retain his pledge of our patience & affection. In that case, all that is left will be my actual voyage. For I cannot suffer any difficulties or hazards to let her pass a Winter she *acknowledges* herself to dread without seeing & solacing her, if I may not bring her over. But I do not *now* think things so desperate—I fully expect [an] invitation to *himself* will soften his pride, & flatter his vanity, & induce him to come with her. Mrs. Lock has even said he will ensure the *gratitude* of all her Family by speedily arriving with her. For Mr. Lock says—If we would

341. [1] Martin and Co., 68 Lombard Street. See *London Bankers*, pp. 108–12.

sooth this Tyger, we must tame him by keeping from him our opinion of his savageness: he may then keep it under—otherwise it will burst into its native rage, & destroy the prey it has unfortunately within its grasp. So I think, now, dearest sir, we may rest.—

I wrote my last in my Mate's absence—but our *Baker's* day did not take it on the date it began with. He is returned, after sleeping one Night at Croydon, with M. La Jard.[2] He tells me he passed a charming Hour with You—but shocks me for the idea of the sacrifice I had suggested, by letting me know you have now no Carriage, & that the Sum is £100.[3] I did not imagine it so much. God forbid it should become necessary | to do any thing about it! But I know what my Susan is to my dearest Father—& therefore, if nothing else will do, must still wish this done, from a certainty *every* sacrifice would be more supportable to him than her loss. Her staying another Winter would be nothing, after all that has passed, but for her own words—That she does not think she shall now outlive it *there!*— What reasons she must have to use such words! Her last Letter —in which they are—is dated Oct. 9. It is to Mrs. Lock.

Depend upon hearing instantly—& faithfully—my dearest— dearest Father, when I get an Answer to my *Menaced* Journey[4] —or when Mr. or Mrs. Lock obtain any—or Charles.—I feel sure this Letter will a little tranquilise you for waiting, because it does me,—& I know how our Hearts meet to enfold her. The Season is very forbidding—but it is SHE who presses it—& she says she cannot explain *why*. That, therefore, must be left to her powers & discretion: we have only to forward letting her judgment have the decision. Your Letter luckily arrived on Baker's Day, & as I think & hope the contents of this will afford you some comfort, I shall send this off express. My Mate sends you a thousand Respects, & wishes he could oftener beat up your quarters for such Hours. He is sorry I had written to you about new forbearance—I should be sorry too, were it for any

---

[2] See L. 291 n. 5.

[3] FBA had suggested that CB sacrifice the annual interest (£80) that Phillips owed on the mortgage of £2000 (i, Intro., p. lxxi). CB's letter of Thursday [17 Oct.] is missing but in his letter of Saturday 19 Oct. he hastens to add 'I wᵈ pay any debt if it was incurred for the purpose of bring͛ *her*, Fanny, Willy, & her good Susan, over immediately'.

[4] See L. 338, p. 342.

thing but your own Susan—& she is more precious than all things! Heaven bless my dearest Padre, ever & ever! & aye!

F. d'A. |

My dear Boy is quite well—God grant I may not be forced from the little careless rogue at this period!

My dear Father's Letter this moment read.

342   West Humble, 26 October [1799]

To Doctor Burney

A.L. (Berg), 26 Oct.
Originally a double sheet large 4to, of which FBA later discarded the second leaf 2 pp.
Edited by FBA, p. 1, *annotated and dated*: ∻ ∻ 1799 (9) Promised Return!
CONTINUED EXPECTATION & HOPE & DREAD

West Hamble, Oct. 26.

God be praised, my dearest Father, I have just got a double Letter, half from our precious Susan, half from the Major, with a positive engagement to come to England in about a Month![1] — — alas—she owns she is *now* not well enough to travel!— but that she is preparing warm cloathing, & nursing to obtain strength for a voyage on which her revival & very life seem to depend, so deeply now is it become her wish. She had just received my Letter,[2] offering to fetch her, & begging to nurse her—with my protestation to the Major that come to her I must, if she were not well enough, or his affairs not conveniently circumstanced, for her coming hither. But though she does not oppose this proposal with her former earnestness—for I have made it repeatedly—She says '*ENGLAND* is the place where we must meet'—& | adds—'it is only some strange fatality can now prevent my being there in about a month—not earlier—but November is as good a season as the present, & often milder.'

342. [1] SBP's part of the letter, a single sheet 4to, dated Sunday 20 Oct. 1799, survives (Berg) with a copy (Armagh) and is printed in *FB & the Burneys*, p. 302. FBA has made a faithful paraphrase or quotation of the contents, in part, here, in part in L. 343.
 [2] FBA's letter of 12 Oct. (L. 338).

She assures me she is amending, though slowly, & that her complaints are not dangerous now, though they might become so from the fatigue of a long journey, if undertaken before they are removed. She does not say what they are. Nor explain her late hints. ⌐But the Letter was written openly to be seen by the Major.⌐ She says—'I beg you to say to our loved Father the things you will feel & know I wish to have said, till I can write to him myself.' & commissions me also to write of this approaching event as fixed to Esther & Charles &c & Norbury Park:— 'for my nervous complaints, she says, render writing difficult to me—& sometimes scarcely possible.'

This is almost the whole of her short Letter. ⌐The Major writes with a brave good humour, & says he will accept our offered pittance for the journey, should it be wanted, certain he can soon re-place it in that case, but he is⌐ |

[*second leaf is missing*][3]

[*marginal writing*, pp. 1 *and* 2]

My Letter to Susan & the Major has been answered *within* a fortnight!—

My Alex is well—& I need not say the grateful joy of Heart with which I look forward to being spared leaving him—which was quite torture to my apprehensions, from his extreme heedlessness. |

I forgot to tell you, dear Sir, the Major says he hopes This will be the last year of his poverty.—

[3] The second leaf, bearing the Major's part of the letter, has been cut away. See however, L. 343, pp. 356–7.

To Esther (Burney) Burney

A.L. (Berg), 27 Oct.
Double sheet 4to   4 pp.   *pmks*   DARKING   PAID   29 OCT ⟨ ⟩
wafer
Addressed: Mrs. Burney / Beaumont Street, / Devonshire Place, / London.
Endorsed by EBB: 1799

West Hamble, Oct. 27.

I have had my answer most astonishingly soon, my dearest
Esther, from our dearly beloved, & from the Major himself[1]
I have written it to our Father, but will again, also, to you, as I
have some things to add that are personal between us, as well as
to enclose the receipt you are so good as to transact with Mr.
Mathias.

The *coming* they both speak of as *fixed*, in a manner that leaves
no room to doubt. it is sincerely meant on his side, as well as
wished on her's,—but alas—the draw back to the happiness of
this reliance is her acknowledging herself now too ill to make
the journey—but she assures me her complaints are not
dangerous, though they might become so, she says, by the
fatigue of a long journey, undertaken before her strength is
recovered. She declines my coming over—but not *vehemently*, as
heretofore; therefore, if her journey, finally is prevented, either
by her own weakness or the M.'s caprices, I am sure, by her
manner, she wishes me to put my scheme in execution. But—
by some of the few expressions of her short mention of her state
of health, I am led to concur—reluctantly—in your idea—
for she says 'though my complaints are not dangerous, they are
such as, in travelling, would ⌐ be painful & inconvenient.—'—
Yet, alarming as this will be, Mrs. Lock, to whom I communicated your notion, says it is perhaps less so than her general
weakness & feverish habits, & *nameless* complaints, *without* such
a cause.—& that, if we get her but once amongst us, all may
be nursed off, & do well. Heaven send it so! — — — she
charges me to write to you for her, & to let the *purport* of her
Letter be sufficient answer, at present, for a very kind one she

343. ¹ See L. 342 nn. 1, 3.

has just received from you. Her's to me is all written under the Eye of the M. for she begins by saying 'He will write himself.' This accounts for no explanations of many circumstances,—though it is very consoling she should write so positively of her return with his immediate knowledge. My Letter has probably determined, & forced his *owning* his determination—for she says 'I am not only nursing to strengthen for the journey, but preparing warm clothing. And November is often a milder month than October.' These words are truly satisfactory.

The M.'s Letter is in high good humour—he seems really moved by M. d'A.'s exertions, & speaks with very unusual kindness of our joint Letter. He will come to see her safe amongst us, he says, & then — — will you break your Heart?— *RETURN* ˡ to Ireland. — — — Huzza!—Huzza! — we shall light up Bonfires on that blessed day — — —

I have just got a Letter from James,[2] in which he informs me he has written himself to the M. to propose meeting Susan upon her Landing., whenever it may be, & conducting her safe to her journey's end—or, if he cannot cross the Channel with her, to cross it himself, & fetch her completely. This gives me infinite pleasure. It shews his Heart still in the right place—wrong as has been his head. And it will soothe our ⟨dea⟩re⟨s⟩t Susan, who has so long been used to consider herself as his first favourite, & has seemed, of late nearly set aside by him. His services will not be wanted, as the M. will come & stay amongst us, he says, for *a few laughs*, before he goes back: but James knows not that, & therefore his offer is as kind, & will as such be received, as if it were accepted. I am really very glad of this—*so* glad to feel pleased again with a Brother I have so esteemed as well as loved till this last act—last act but *ONE* I will now say, & let my thoughts rest upon the last of all—his tender affection to our Susan. ˡ

When you have got the draft on Drummond,[3] my dearest Esther, will you be so kind as to change it into *two TENS* & *one FIVE* & to enclose us one of the tens in your next Letter, & keep the other & the five till some other occasion?

God bless you, my dearest Etty—our kind Love to Mr.

---

[2] JB's letter is missing.
[3] Robert Drummond (*c.* 1729–1804) of the firm Robert Drummond and Co. See *London Bankers* and *GM* lxxiv (1804), 95.

B[urney]—& to your Girls & Richard—I hope you are all well. I could not s⟨ave⟩ the post Yesterday—You know how we are situated. Susan says *writing* is now always difficult, & sometimes SCARCELY POSSIBLE to her — — So that her Letters must all in some degree be circular. Heaven bless you—

344   [West Humble, *pre* 19 November]

To Mrs. Phillips

A.L.S. (Barrett, Eg. 3690, ff. 182–3b), *n.d.*
Double sheet 4to   4 pp.   wafer
Addressed: Mrs. Phillips, / Belcotton, / Drogheda.
Docketed: C. 21
Also docketed: F RAPER [*to whom perhaps this letter belonged or to whom it was lent. It may not have reached Belcotton before Susan left*]

My Heart is too full for expression, my best—dearest beloved Susan—with the hopes thus permitted of seeing you—& the terrors of your health—Would to God I could aid you in the journey! — — I *supplicate* you not to make it—in spite of all our dearest wishes encircling it—if you feel your strength doubtful— Let me, in that case, come over to you, my dearest soul—you know how little I want of accommodation—& What could I want & be with you? — — It will only be reversing the 50— which bring us to meet at Belcotton instead of West Humble. Remember it is unalterably fixed at Coutts till we meet, & as much longer as to entirely suit the fullest convenience of the Major—whose little Letter to us has obliged us inexpressibly[1] James writes me word he has offered to fetch you, if the Major cannot come. I am much pleased at this, & am sure it will be soothing to you, though it is far better the Major should bring you himself, he knows the roads, &c so well by heart.—I want to write to my dear ⎸ Fanny, & tell her how I shall rejoice to see her again—but that your illness checks all feelings but impatience. Your Letters now shall be circular, my Susanna— when you write to ONE of the family, it shall serve all. You are so much occupied—or so much in want of rest—that you must

344. [1] See L. 342 n. 3.

write very little—a few lines alternately to ALL, twice a week
till we meet or once if that is too much. I shall write no more but
scraps—

Esther begs you to let Fanny be spard to her on your arrival,
if you are well enough, for a few weeks—*I* shuld make the same
request, but fear she ought not to be parted from you—we are
all vying with one another to make arrangements who shall
accommodate you most ¦ & be[s]t—but *I* wish you ALL to go
first—in a body to Norbury Park, where you can best be
nursd, from a thousand reasons, & where the Major will find
most comfort for as many. Mrs. L in a little note says—'Our
precious Sister will best console my L—for his Daughter—'
What can she say after that?—William there may see Noses to
his mind[2]—& if difficult already, make himself 10 times more
so with every *ungrecian* one he sees. They all expect Fanny there,
too, at first. So Chelsea must come next—& *next*— —the *longest*
sejour, I hope!—

I wish to God I knew enough of your complaints to send
anything good for them! There is a *mephitic water*, recommended
by Miss Cambridge, that for the Gravel is reckoned a specific—
It has done wonders, to her own immediate knowledge—can—
& may we send you a vial?—It is of like efficacy in the rheumatism—I could wish—earnestly—to understand your case—
I dread the proposing any thing—pressing even the travelling!
& will only add HERE—or THERE—meet we must! Heaven bless
you, ¦ my own sweetest dear Sister!—Heaven bless—& restore
you,

prays—continually—your

F. d'A.

My Mate greets—loves—expects you *sans cesse*—My Boy puts
you into his all his *orisons*. & yesterday he came to me, & said
'I have been asking God, mama, in the Garden, to send Aunt
Phillips over back to us.'

Remember you are only to scrawl over one page to any body
now,—direct it how you will, it shall travel to the whole circle
of your anxious Friends. The Major will be very generally
popular for bringing you over at this time, as it is universally
expected the Brest Fleet is now watching a moment to sail to

---

[2] Subject to paint.

Ireland, with troops.[3] But yet—let your *health* decide the coming or staying! I beseech—

345   West Humble, 19 November 1799

To Esther (Burney) Burney

A.L.S. (Berg), 19 Nov. [17]99
Double sheet 4to   4 pp.   *pmks*   DARKING   21 NOV 99   wafer
Addressed: Mrs. Burney, / Beaumont street, / Devonshire place London.

turn over cautiously

Nov. 19. 99.
West Hamble

My dearest Etty,

'Tis my turn now to have the dear commission of spreading news from our beloved Susanna. I have this Day a Letter, dated *Nov. 11th*, with an assurance she is greatly mended,[1] & un-remitting in hopes & preparations & Nursings for her journey: but she still names no Day for its commencement, but repeats she shall remain some time at Dublin, where she hopes much benefit from the skill & kindness of Mr. Keirnan,[2] who will have charge of her. she again gives her direction at Mrs. Cartland's,[3] but does not press for any Letter, & would have none of a private nature, I believe, ventured; as all her motions are precarious. Her eagerness to arrive seems augmenting every moment— 'O my God! she cries, to be once again in England—with you all—will pay me for all I have suffered—will *over*-pay me!—' What affecting words! & what do they not convey both of what she has gone through, & of her tender love for us?—Dearest Soul! I now indeed look forward with a beating Heart to a

---

[3] On 25 Oct. at least eight vessels actually sailed from Brest, and the rest of the Fleet was reported 'ready for sea'. General opinion was that they were 'destined for Ireland' where they 'might even with a small force be productive of infinite trouble and mischief' (*Morning Chronicle*, 1 Nov. 1799).

345. [1] This letter is missing.

[2] Phillips's brother-in-law, an apothecary, who lived on Henry Street, Dublin (iii, L. 215 n. 2).

[3] See iii, L. 215 n. 7.

speedy meeting. Her chief anxiety seems lest the Major should perceive, on his arrival, the disgust he has excited in us, & the chief purport of her Letter is to beseech us all to repress such feelings, & all apparent resentment, that he may *leave her behind in peace & amity.* She dreads some new outrage from his vindictive temper, should he receive any mortification; & when I write, which will be very soon, I shall venture to promise | for us all the utmost forbearance. She wishes only to be directed to at Mrs. Cartland's, hoping to be there before an answer could reach Belcotton: but not advising or pressing writing at all at present. However, as I can do it gratis, I shall say nothing that might not be published at Charing Cross, & then I am sure it will be a great comfort to her to hear me individualize every one of her family for health & welfare. She commissions me to distribute her *bulletin.* She has missed *2* Letters from me—& one had begged her own directions about our meeting. I shall write for them again, & tell her again your most hospitable invitation, which it will be *her's* to accept or postpone for us, though *our's* to give Our cordial thanks, in either case.

I have written to our dear Padre—& shall to Charles. This is all I have to glean for you from my short Letter. When you write next, pray enclose another $\frac{1}{2}$ of a *ten* & the fellow, the next time of writing.

Now to other matters.

Your extreme contempt, Mrs. Hetty, of my dealings with low tradespeople[4] shall not dishearten me from continuing them; shall I give you a dialogue, which past previous to the delivery of the goods, & will put you into a little hot water, for a punishment for your haughtiness? Yes, I will; but *read it alone.*—so here turn to t'other side in a spare room. |

Scene St. James's Street

Enter Agent & Upholsterer,[5] *meeting.*

Ag. I was just going to beat up your quarters.

---

[4] That is, with theatrical managers and producers of plays, for with respect to the comedy 'Love and Fashion' FBA had by this time received the heartening message from CB Jr., dated 30 Oct. 1799, and preserved in the Scrapbook (Berg), 'Fanny Burney and family. 1653–1890': 'Huzza! Huzza! Huzza. Mr. H[arris] admires the Fable—& will bring it into use, in the month of March!—

'H[arris] is surprised, that you never turned your thoughts to this kind of writing before; as you appear to have really a genius for it!— —There now!'

[5] Obviously CB Jr. and Thomas Harris (c. 1738–1820), manager of Covent Garden Theatre.

Up. I am glad to save you the trouble.

Ag. I want to speak to you upon a little business. A Lady—
a relation of Mine—has written a play—Will you act it?

Up. A Lady?—Is it your sister?—

Ag. Suppose it is—Will you Act it?

Up. If I see nothing that seems positively against its succeed-
ing, certainly. But — — You must let me have it.

Ag. When you please.

Up. Immediately.

Ag. It is at her hermitage. I will send for it.

Ug. Do, & directly. But — — have you read it?

Ag. I — — I don't — — know!

Up. pho,—what do you think of it?

Ag. I — — don't know.—

Up. Pho,—that's worse still!

Ag. I am no judge.

Up. pshaw—

Ag. Besides—a lady—my sister—how can I speak?

Up. Well, that's true. Let me have it in two days.

Ag. All she urges is secresy. She is bent upon making the
attempt unknown.

Up. And why?—A *good* play *will* succeed,—& sometimes a
bad one—but if there be a circumstance, as here, that will
strongly prepare the public in its favour,—why should we
lose that circumstance?

Ag. I will speak to her about that: but be very secret mean-
while, | especially if you decline it, as it is then her intention to
try the other house,—& it *must* not be blown upon.

The result of this dialogue, was sending the Goods forthwith,
as soon as fair Copied, to the Upholsterer, but with reiterated
charges to secresy, from a firm persuasion the chances are better
without than *with* expectation.

Therefore, if you meet Agent, be upon your guard, as *he* will
make confidents if he knows *I* have, & otherwise is perfectly
compliant.—what sweet weather is this, if our beloved may
avail herself of it! she seems to have only her health to combat,
no more caprices in the M[ajor] who is now all *gentle attention!*—

adieu, my dearest Esther—& give my kind love to Mr.
B[urney] & to Richard & Marianne & amelia & Sophy—I am
very sorry indeed poor Richard does not amend—pray men-

tion him particularly when you write. I hope Edward is quite re-established. We shall now surely meet soon, my dear Hetty, either here or with you, for a general embrace around our dearest restored Exile, according to her decision.

God [bless] you—ever yours truly
& affec^ly
F. d'A.

346   [West Humble,] 28 November 1799

To Esther (Burney) Burney

A.L.S. (Berg), 28 Nov. 1799
Double sheet small 4to   4 pp.   *pmks* [DA]RKIN[G]   30 NOV 99
wafer
Addressed: Mrs. Burney / Beaumont St / Devonshire place / London
Endorsed by EBB: Answered Decr 3.

Nov. 28th—1799

I had just, my dear Hetty, received a Letter material for you as your Letter itself arrived[1]—Yesterday, while we were breakfasting at Norbury Park, came one from our beloved Susan to Mrs. Lock—which she desires me to *circularise*. She is only at Belcotton—but the M[ajor] is at Dublin—whence he has written to me himself—taking lodgings for her to rest there on her journey, & see Mr. Kiernan,[2] & preparing for the voyage, in regard to the packet, &c. This is some little beginning, & will appease, I hope, your immediate uneasiness at the delay. I try to make it quiet mine, which was growing very violent. She thinks she may now undertake the journey but has had several drawbacks, & suffered inexpressibly from her apprehensions of a relapse, & being unable to come. But—God be praised, they seem now past. she enters upon no particulars— & says she cannot at a distance. I am sure there is some *local* complaint of a cruel nature?—sweet soul!—Let her but arrive, however, & I shall have nothing but hope. She has given, however, a positive answer to the Norbury invitation— declining it entirely at present, to settle herself instantly with

346. ^1 This letter is missing, as are most of EBB's letters.
       ^2 See L. 345 n. 2; and iii, L. 215 n. 2.

our dear Father,—We shall thankfully, therefore, my dearest Esther, accept your kind offer, & embrace her from your House—not *at* it, alas—for I c⟨a⟩n gather by her style she thinks not of any removal till much amended, she owns she expects to be dreadfully fatigued— | Her next Letter, she says, will be to you, from whom '*She has received a very sweet one*' I shall be very anxious to know if it will come from Belcotton again, where she talks of yet remaining a week (dating Nov. 19.) or— from Dublin! I am sure you will let me know—& then send t'other half of the Gentleman who came very perfectly, his imperfect state considered, this Morning.[3]—Mrs. Lock bid me give her love to you. she has been much pleased with your Letters—& execution of her requests. &c. Mrs. Angerstein is still in Lincolnshire. She tells me I have a neighbour here,—a Lady of Dorking, who desired her to enquire if we were fixed to make us acquaintance, or would receive her for one, & who is quite an enthusiastic admirer of my eldest sister—so upon this, I gave a gracious assent—It is a very respectable lady, I know, though she has so odd a taste. Her name is Holford.[4] When you are with me in more human weathers you must go to her. It is a sweet walk to Dorking in *a proper Season*—I dare not name any *Month*,—only *knowing*, for certain, that *August* must be out of the | question. I have just written to our pappy— & want to get ready fo[r] t⟨o⟩-morrow's Baker—I shall write also to Charles & James. The latter did not come—& M. d'A. went a mile to meet him, as we were, unluckily, at Norbury Park when his Letter arrived. He complains of his Chest—but writes in good humour, & with his old kindness. Tell me something of him—his spirits—his Health—plans, &c—He says he had much he meant to consult me about but does not intimate of what nature. If I know him at all, he has done nothing this last twelve month—with so much internal satisfaction as he felt from a step so much in his good old way as that he took for Susan[5]—*took*, as far as good will & real intention may pass for action. And with me they are coin of equal currency. I am truly glad at thus *finding him* again.

[3] A reference to money, cut in half for safe remittance through the post (see L. 343, p. 357; L. 345, p. 361).

[4] Possibly Elizabeth *née* Streater (*c.* 1774–1858), the wife of John Carteret Halford (1753–1837) of Vineyard House, Richmond.

[5] See L. 343, p. 357.

I left dear Mrs. Lock yesterday fabricating a note to Mrs Windham[6] in favour of poor old M. de la Landelle.[7] I hope— & cannot doubt but it will be successful. How rejoiced I am about Worksop![8] Dear Mr. Burney! how indignant I felt at his thrown away toils!—Richards amendment gives me sincere pleasure. My Love to him I beg— | I imagine you will have your Letter from our Susan in a very few Days—& therefore, not to torment you too often, I will wait till then for the 2ᵈ half. My Alex [is] again reviving from his last worm attack— & now regularly taking a doze of Bark as soon as he gets out of his Bathing Tub every Morning. He is *thinned* again—by discipline for those odious animals—but *all alive* always. His spouting fit is over for the present. I believe he thought it a *peticoat* accomplishment, for he has relinquished it since he has assumed the manly attire. adieu dea Etty—Our best Love to Mr. B[urney]—& marianne & Sophy & Amelia—& whenever you can, to Fanny & Cecilia. Charlotte writes me word she thinks Mr. B[roome] will remain all the Winter at Brighton— The MS. was returned about 10 Days ago, without a word.[9]—! *agreable* enough! & ⟨pritha⟩! *keep counsel.* I was very philosophic —⟨more so⟩ than my Companion — — —

Once more, God bless you.

F. d'A.

[6] Cecilia *née* Forrest (1750–1824), who had married on 10 July 1798 William Windham, the statesman.

[7] See iii, L. 215 n. 14.

[8] A town 26 miles north of Nottingham—the site of one of the Duke of Norfolk's residences. Cf. L. 310, p. 265, a reference to an account (for music lessons) at that time (March 1799) unpaid.

[9] The manuscript of 'Love and Fashion'. CB Jr.'s letter of 30 Oct., op. cit., contained some suggestions for revision.

To Doctor Burney

A.L.S. (Barrett, Eg. 3690, ff. 105–6b), 28 Nov. [17]99
Double sheet 4to   4 pp.   *pmks*   DARKING   30 NO 99   30 NOV 99
wafer
Addressed: Dr. Burney, / Chelsea College, / Middlesex.
Endorsed by CB: M^{rs} D,arblay / 1799 / D ⟨ ⟩ y
Edited by FBA, p. 1, *annotated, the year retraced*: ⋇ 99 (10)
Hope more alive of the return of the most angelic of human Sufferers.—
Buonaparte—character of him conceived in 1799—just what F:d'A thought
up to 1815.

West Hamble,
Nov. 28—99

At length, my dearest Father, in thanking you for your kind
& charming Letter,[1] I have to report something *like* progress in
the name of our most beloved Susanna. Two Letters, of the
same date, *Novr 19th* are just arrived from Ireland,—one written
by the sweet soul herself, & directed to Mrs. Lock, which she
desires may be *circular*, & the other from the Major, & directed
to me. She is still at Belcotton, but announces that the Major
had actually, at length, left it for Dublin, to make preparations
for the voyage, as well as for her sojourn there. She thinks herself now equal to the undertaking, though she feels she must
travel slowly & cautiously. She gives a definitive answer, in the
softest & most grateful terms, to Mrs. Lock's earnest desire to
see her immediately at Norbury Park, & there to nurse her till
her recovery,—she says she could resist it for one thing only—
but that one thing has intervened—her dearest Father's OWN
desire to receive her in all her feebleness, & shaken state, &
nurse her himself—This, she says, has been such balm to her,
that she feels as if to see him again—& meet his commiserating
Eyes—& be under his roof & his care, would make him *give her
a second life*!—Nothing can be so touching, my dearest Padre, as
her expressions upon this subject. I regret I have not the Letter,
that I might copy them all.

Mr. & Mrs. Lock, you are sure, are too just & kind to enter

347. ¹ That of 19 Nov. 1799 (Osborn), excerpts from which FBA printed in *Memoirs*,
iii. 280–2. The letters of 19 Nov. from Ireland are missing.

any protest against such a determination. They will resist her, indeed, in nothing—not even in a request which puts their friendship to the severest | ⌐trial, that of inviting the M[ajor] *without her* [the las]t thing that, I believe, entered into their own calculations as possible to support. But they immediately declared they would do it, & with a readiness, in the midst of their disappointment in not having *her*, that I know not how enough to admire. We happenned to be at Norbury Park when the Letter arrived, at Breakfast. We had slept there. She charges me to express the extreme thankfulness of her good Susan for your naming her, & not expecting to have attendance—she expects to be dreadfully fatigued, & was peculiarly gratified to have her aid, as she has nursed her through all her illness,—& as there are new complaints belonging to it which she never explains, & which she cannot, she says, enter upon. Poor dear, dear Soul! we well know what she suffers when she permits herself to speak of complaints.⌐

—O when once she has but mounted your stairs, my dearest Father, what Heaven will break in upon my mind!—now sadly clouded still with a conviction of her whole frame being shattered—your air, thank God, now for a double sake, is good, —&, once mounted, I shall scarcely have a fear for her. But I know not how to let hope quite predominate till then.

⌐The Major's Letter was written also the 19— & is dated Dublin. He says he has just secured Susan a Lodging, at a quiet House, & in a good situation, for resting & consulting Mr. Kiernan. & he is seeking too a Vessel in which she can sail with the best accommodation. He writes in good humour, &, Susan says, now he has received civilities from us all round, seems cordially disposed to us⌐ all — — |

The dear soul says that her next Letter will be to Esther, ⌐from whom she has just heard.⌐ That kind & ever hospitable person invites us to her House, to take, thence, an embrace of our restored treasure. It is quite irresistable after *such* a parting —so long, & so cruelly circumstanced. ⌐We shall see you, therefore, dearest Sir, as arranged, very soon, our stay, for many reasons, must now be short, but it will be truly delicious.⌐ I have indeed no words to say the joy I shall experience to see her once again—& see her under your protection!—what a delightful account you have given me of the Abbè Delille! I had

367

much wished you to see him, & am charmed with your description of him,[2] notwithstanding your intimation of his being
so far from an adonis. How I should enjoy such a meeting! & to
hear him repeat such verses!—& how I rejoice that this first
poet, (I believe) now breathing, is what you tell me in principles,
morals, religion!—natural, too, good humoured, & civil!—
How I wish you may cultivate with him!—What you give of
his debate with M. de Calonne concerning the abominable
Sieyes[3] (for abominable I hold him to be) is very interesting &
entertaining. M. d'A. no longer thinks this new revolution
likely to be more lasting than its predecessors, now Buonaparte
has taken the same violent & tyrannic measures which, eventually, lost them.—I think him so vindictive, & such a man of
blood, that his reign will be severe, &, consequently, short: but
what may be effected while it lasts is curious, agitating, &
alarming. Do you gather anything of what Ducos is?[4] We are
quite ignorant—But any man who would be otherwise than an
adulating tool to Buonaparte will ⟨not partake any longer in
the State.⟩[π] |

I have been reading lately his own—i.e. Berthier's, account
of the expedition into Syria[5]—& the cold barbarity with which
he relates his wanton vengeance on those who opposed his
progress, even when conquered, & flying, by demolishing their
Harvests, poisoning their water, & burning their habitations,
has made me shudder till his name is almost a terrour to me.—
And now, to see him act with precisely the same arbitrary injustice which made his predecessors so unpopular, shews him as

---

[2] At the breakfast described (op. cit.) CB had met the poet Jacques Delille and
heard him repeat from memory fragments of some of 'his best works'. 'I like his
declamation as much as the substance & texture of his poetry—He is a fair reasoner,
wth excellent principles, moral, Religious, & truly philosophical.'

[3] The poet (above) and the statesman Charles-Alexandre de Calonne (1734–
1802) had entered into 'a debate on the character' of Emmanuel-Joseph, comte
Sieyès (1748–1836), formerly (1788) Vicar-General of Chartres, the unfrocked
priest and wily statesman elected in this year to the Directory. CB gave the two
character-readings at length (*Memoirs*, iii. 281–2).

[4] Pierre-Roger Ducos (1754–1816), a magistrate of mediocre abilities, who, as a
member of the National Convention had voted for the execution of Louis XVI.
After the *coup d'état* of 18 June 1799 he was appointed a Director and on 9 Nov.
a Consul, in which office he was to serve as 'a buffer', it was thought, between the
Abbé Sieyès and Bonaparte. 'Every body looks on the Consul *Ducos*, as *Dummy* at
3 handed whist', CB had replied in his letter (Osborn) of 1 Dec.

[5] Possibly *General Buonaparte's Narration of the Siege of St. Jean d'Acre*; *General
Berthier's Details of the Syrian Expedition*; *and Sir Sidney Smith's Letters from on board the
Tiger*, published earlier that month (see *Morning Chronicle*, 11 Nov.).

shallow as he is cruel, & confines his talents, with all their splendour, to the art of war—& there I believe them to be indeed transcendant.—But they won't suffice to make him a civil Dictator: & if he means to Keep his power, he must always be at the head of an army. I had some little hope, for a short time, he might have some better scheme in view than his own aggrandizment. But I see no prospect of that sort now. ⌜Pray have you Goldoni's life?[6] Mr. Lock desires me to say he has a head of *Galileo* which he shall be most happy to ⟨commit⟩ to any use you can make of it, if you wish for it—but none whatsoever of Kepler.[7] I must hope you will yet ferret one out. I am very glad you keep *that* [wor]k always going on. It deserves all your time. How Susan will love to hear it! — — My Chevalier's best Respects. My Boy is better again—blyther he cannot be.

> adieu, most dear sir—ever your most dutiful
> & affect^e   F. d'A.⌝

348   West Humble, 10 December 1799

To Mrs. Phillips

A.L. (Diary MSS. vi. 5184–[7], Berg), 10 Dec. [17]99
Double sheet 4to   4 pp.
Edited by CFBt *and the* Press.

> West Humble
> Decr. 10. 99

O My Susan—my Heart's dear Sister!—with what bitter bursts of sorrow have I read this last account — — with us— with yourself—your children—all—you have *trifled*, in respect to health, though in all things else you are honour & veracity personified—but nothing had prepared me to think you in such

---

[6] CB, in his letter (Osborn) of 19 Nov.—⟨1st⟩ Dec., replied: 'No—I have no life of Goldoni—'. Later, however, FBA seems to have procured a copy of *Mémoires de M. Goldoni pour servir á l'histoire de sa vie et á celle de son théâtre* (3 vols., 1787). For her comments on the work, see L. 420, pp. 504–5.

[7] Obviously for illustrations for CB's versified history of astronomy (L. 376, p. 417).

a state as I now find you[1] — —!— — Would to God I could get to you! — — If Mr. Kiernan thinks you had best pass the winter in Dublin, *stay*—& let me come to you—venture nothing against his opinion, for Mercy's sake—Fears for your health take place of all impatience to expedite your return— only go not back to Belcotton — — where you cannot be under his direction, & are away from the physician he thinks of so highly.[2] I shall write immediately to Charles about the Carriage—I am SURE of his answer before hand—so must *YOU* be— act, therefore, with regard to the carriage, as if already it were arranged. But I am well aware it must not set out till you are well enough to *nearly* fix your I day of sailing. I say *nearly*, for we must always allow for accidents. I shall write to our dear Father—& Etty—& James—& send to Norbury Park—but I shall wait till to-morrow, not to infect them with what I am infected. How I love that charming Augusta![3]—tell her so— I am almost tempted to write to her—& to Mrs. Disney[4]—& to Mr. Kiernan — — I expect every body to love & be kind to my Susan—yet I love & cherish them for it as if it were my wonder—

I had so hoped to write no more to Ireland!—alas—what a downfall to my joy that the journey was commenced! yet—the sleeping on the road had given me a shock that prepared Me— at the time of reading it—for all that follows—but M. d'A. & Mrs. Locke had re-assured me, by their great satisfaction the journey *was* commenced—so had Hetty — — But now— I rather *fear* its continuance—& CONJURE you not to press it against the judgment I of Mr. Kiernan—whom you make me quite revere for his courage & exertions. Remember, my dearest

---

348. [1] This was the folio letter (Berg) of 4 Dec. 1799, *pmk* 7 DE 99, that SBP managed to write from lodgings No. 22 Henry Street, Dublin. It was printed in part in *FB & the Burneys*, pp. 303–5, and annotated by FBA: 'The last Letter written immediately to myself from Ireland by my adored sister Susanna—one ONLY was added fr^m Park Gate!'

The seriousness of SBP's illness was now evident enough in the necessity found to stop for a night in a journey of about forty miles from Belcotton to Dublin, in the invalid-diet, the repeated visits of the physician Dr. Purcell (below), and in the anxiety of Mr. Kiernan, who at first 'pronounced that he w^d not let [her] stir for a *month*'.

[2] John Purcell (?1740–1806), M.D. (Leyden, 1759), Assistant Lecturer in Anatomy at Trinity College (1772), and an Honorary Fellow of the Royal College of Physicians and Surgeons, Dublin (1806). He had married 29 Sept. 1774 Eleanor Fitzgerald (*fl.* 1757–92), the sister of Phillips's friend John (i, L. 24 n. 15).

[3] Augusta Kiernan (iii, L. 215 n. 2), now about 17 years old. 'I really half long', SBP had remarked (op. cit.), 'that Augusta were my *Child*—if she were, I w^d be contented with the portion of love she shews me—'.   [4] See iii, L. 222 n. 20.

soul, the Winter will not last for-ever—the *expence* must be out of all question—Oh my Susan! how *rich* you make us ALL feel, when *your* health—or regaining your sight, comes in play with any *pecuniary* diffi[culty]; you will never, I trust, be so un-generous so unkind as to hesitate on *this* score—seeing how our souls are *all one*, our purses *all one* on this subject. We are ready to contest nothing but pre-eminence of exertion. I fear already— you have almost destroyed yourself in silence! — — o my Susan! — — that I could come to you! But all must depend on Mr. Kiernan's decision. If you *can* come to US with perfect safety, however slowly, I shall not dare add to your embarrass-ment of persons & package. Else—Charles's Carriage—O what a temptation to air it for you all the way!—Take no more large paper, that you may write with less fatigue, &, if possible, *oftener*—to *any one* will suffice *for all.* | And don't be disheartened by *receiving* no answers—for as you can have no uneasiness about US, & we can write *only* about your health, we shall be unwilling to send on, when we lose our conveyance—& this will be when you leave Dublin. Till then, as long as you are unable to fix *your* journey—or *mine*—we shall write in answer to all intelligence we receive, direct or indirect. My Father is *enchanted* you will go to *HIM* immediately, & take your Home at once—he shall embrace you *3 fold* for that, he says—he so longs to establish you!—& shall be so truly glad to see dear Fanny by your side & your *worthy Susan* (his own words) but he means to write no more—unless you lengthen your stay with any certainty. Let your HEALTH *alone* guide you now, I supplicate!— You have left it so long the *last* thing, that we shall lose ALL if you make it not the *first*! give me some assurance of your amendment in this point, in pity, my Susan, for I am quite shaken with terror.

God almighty bless you, my love!—remember how much of peace & happiness hang on your real care of yourself!—My Mate is truly yours—my Boy longs for you—Love to the Major— Fanny—Norbury Willy—& make all the excellent Kiernans accept my something more than Compliments my sincere regard — & *kiss me Augusta*.

The more I think of your travelling, thus weak & ill—& ignorant as I am of your real state—which tortures me with painful & continually changing conjectures—the more I am alarmed—If frost sets in, it will kill you, you cannot bear the sharp cold—if high winds, I shall fear the sea—& then, *sea-sickness*—indeed, I almost *dread* your setting out—all are so kind—considerate—skilful in the Keirnan Family. I could not be uneasy, however mournfully disappointed, if you pass the severe season there, & come over with the first mild weather, & *recruited health*—I am relieved—*so* relieved you are no longer out of reach of help!—God bless—bless & preserve you, my most dear & loved Sister! ᶦ

We will attend religiously to every hint & forbear accordingly—

349   West Humble, 14 December 1799

Conjointly with M. d'Arblay

To Charles Burney

A.L.S. & A.N.S. (Osborn), 14 Dec. [17]99
Single sheet small 4to (8·1 × 6·3″), of which the upper half of 2nd leaf is cut away   *pmks*
16 DE 99   16 DE 99
Addressed: Dr. Charles Burney / Greenwic[h] / K[ent]
Docketed in pencil, p. 1: 1799
Editorial marking in pencil, p. 3:—writing of A' D'Arblay Husband of Fanny

West Hamble
Dec. 14. 99—

I read your Letter with Tears of pleasure,ᶦ my dearest Charles—& cannot help writing to tell you so, though I have nothing else to say that might not wait. What a joy will it be to that beloved sufferer to find you had so generously & kindly anticipated her request! This, indeed, will make me—make us all amends for her remaining so long—so well I know the tenderness & care she will experience under your immediate direction. I like the plan beyond any other—to have her with only her excellent maid will make the journey so quiet, it will

349. ᶦ CB tells that it was Charles's plan to travel with his son Charles Parr (now about 14 years old) by the Chester Mail Coach to Parkgate and bring Susan back to Chelsea in 'a proper travelling Chaise'. See CB's letter (Osborn) to FBA, 24 Dec.

half recover her. To separate her from the ungovernable *spirits* of the Major will be a real mercy, in her delicate & even terrifying state. God bless you, my dear Charles, *No* holy days will leave such *lasting* pleasure upon the Tablets of your Memory as these!—these which you devote to so kind—so brotherly—so generous a purpose,—a purpose which may not only *serve*—though ⎮ that might be sufficient recompense for you—a sister so dear—but Save her—for I really think she can travel in no other way without a danger it would nearly be suicide for her to run — — & to have her return to Belcotton — — would nearly break all our Hearts. God bless you, my dear Charles! again & again I cry!—

I am truly concerned your poor Rosette is so indifferent. Pray give her my kind love, & best wishes. I imagine it is the death of her amiable & favourite Niece[2] that sits so heavily upon her health & heart. I am very sorry too for poor Mrs. Bicknell, who so greatly requires—& I think I may say deserves health & strength—from the excellent & chearful use she makes of them. Pray remember me to her kindly, & assure her of my concern & regard. M. d'A loves & honours you for this feeling exertion nearly as much as I do—we are both ever & ever more

yours, Dearest Charles.

F d'A. ⎮

[*By M. d'Arblay*]

What a Kind kind of Brother you are, my dear Charles! Indeed I am almost angry with myself not to have it in my power to love you more than I do, when I find you every day more and more to be loved. What a princely reward you shall receive in bringing back that suffering angel! Those if not merry Holydays will be so endearing for an Heart like yours. As to the purse I think you never will have it more empty than the heart. Amen!

my love at Home et Peace abroad

A

---

[2] Isabella Foss. See L. 330 n. 1.

To Ralph Broome, Sr.

L. copy in hand of M. d'A (West Humble Letter Book, pp. 120–1, Osborn), 27 Dec. [17]99

To Ralph Broom Esqr in answer to a letter of his dated December 1779.[1]

Westhumble Decr 27.—99.

Dear Sir!

I am much flattered by the entire concurrence of our opinions upon a point so important as that of the education & disposal of my syster's Children. I heartily wish I had known it when she was with us, as I should not then have scrupled enforcing my sentiments: but we avoided all serious discussion of the subject, since, though she declared she acted wholly by her own inclination, I concluded that and your suggestions to be one equally from her sense of conjugal duty, & her warm attachment. If therefore, she ever takes a single step which does not shew both, I am convinced it can be only from misunderstanding your wishes. But, I fancy, judging by your own quickness, you have thought it sufficient to have her to devine them— a mode rarely adopted without involving mutual errour, for while both parties, intentionally are gratifying each other, both eventually, may be thwarting. I infer this from believing it impossible my sister could form such a plan, except, either to obey or oblige you: the first, her open & voluntary declarations here assured me was not the case — — the second, I would not touch upon, because it is the last motive I | could blame, or would contest. Imagine then my surprise at your letter of this morning. Surely, if your meaning had been as clearly comprehended by Charlotte, whose first desire is your ease & satisfaction, she could not pursue a measure that must be painful to her feelings nor risk the wonder if not censure, her separation from her Children may excite. There can be no doubt but she concludes her undivided attention will be the offering the most

350. [1] Ralph Broome's correspondence with the Burneys has been destroyed, this copy by M. d'A surviving only by chance in the West Humble Letter Book (above). The date 1779 is an error in copying.

welcome she can made you; but if her tenderness for you has
misled her, & your own notions of her maternal claims make
you willing to relinquish the whole for the half—Write to her,
explicitely, to stop or reverse her proceedings, & take in payment the security of the most affectionate gratitude from her
very sweet Girls—Charlotte, in particular, young as she is, will
feel such a mark of your generous kindness as a call upon her
most earnest endeavours to manifest her sense of it. With
Marianne I am too little acquainted, to be so undouutedly
responsible for her, but I believe her nature of that kind &
gentle sort that will follow, almost implicitly whithersoever
her sister may lead. And the greatful happiness, of such innocent minds will be a very genuine source of pleasure to one who
—like you—give so much more time to sober reflection than to
the World's bustle. I declined entering upon this affair with my
dear sister, from an apprehension my opinions were different
from those which have every right to her highest consideration,
& even now, that I have the satisfaction to find they coincide,
I shall not name your letter to her, unless it should be mentioned
by herself, as I think this a business which ought to be arranged
entirely & directly between yourselves.

We hope, when our next excursion takes place, you will be
returned to town yourself.

I am, dear Sir &c — — —

351   West Humble, 31 December 1799

To Charles Burney

A.L. (Boston Public Library, MSS. ACC. 16), 31 Dec. [17]99
Double sheet 4to   4 pp.   *pmks* EPSOM JAN 1800   wafer
Addressed: Dr. Charles Burney / White Lion / Chester.
Annotated by dealers(?) *or* BPL(?), p. 1: Josiah H. Benton Fd. / Apr. 11,
1939 / EE / c

West Hamble,
Dec. 31.—99

Whatever are your crosses & disappointments,[1] my dearest
Charles, certainly you were never entitled to such excellent

351. [1] CB Jr. had arrived at the White Lion, Chester, on 26 Dec., and on the 27th

375

clear, serene, salubrious & gay spirits as at this juncture. The heavier the snow, the worse the roads, the colder the Frost, the more perverse all accidents, — — the greater become your claims for that sweet peace of mind which passes all adversity.— Yet gladly, most gladly should I have seen you divested of nearly half these rights!—for I feel to my very Heart the adverse winds—the inclement season—& the precarious tenure of your last attempt for accelerating a meeting.—Dear *Itty Panny*'s Letter—meant to save you alarm, yet exciting such distressing perplexity, much as it vexed me for you, & your subsequent dilemma, yet enchanted me by containing such undoubted testimony of the arrival of her beloved Mother upon English shores—O that an event so long—so ardently desired, should thus be checquered! for I am terrified more than I will tell you that that dearest sufferer [1] has not been able to write even to our Padre[2]—but perhaps ere this is received her dear Hand may have gladdened his longing Eyes—He writes to me,[3] not knowing you could find time, & transcribes most of your Letter. My dear Charles, were it only for the kind feelings with which it has filled his Heart, your toils & their concomitants would be paid! so warmly he is delighted with this fraternal exertion. Disinterestedly, & totally for her sake — — who so

he wrote three letters, one to Rosette (missing), one to FBA (Osborn), and one to CB (Barrett, Eg. 3700A, ff. 22–3b). These letters reached London on 30 Dec.

Having heard on the 26th from a passenger 'who came in the Mail from Holyhead' that the Major, Susan, and the children had been on the same yacht with him but that they had sailed on to Parkgate, Charles went to Parkgate, but could glean no news of the landing.

Receiving on the morning of the 27th a letter from Fanny Phillips ('Itty Panny') reporting that the yacht was windbound in Holyhead, he was about to set out for Holyhead, not without misgivings, however, as the wind was due East and his 'Hibernian Niece' had added that her mother would go to the Inn in Parkgate if she could get there.

[2] The Phillipses had landed, however, not at Holyhead but at Parkgate on Monday 30 Dec. 'between 3 & 4', and that evening SBP was able to write a short joint note (Berg) to FBA and the Lockes and a note (Barrett, Eg. 3700A, ff. 54–5b) to CB:

Oh my beloved Father—once more I tread on English Ground, once more I breathe the blessed air you breathe—I am greatly fatigued by an uncommonly long passage which yet I have borne better than I could have expected— . . . I have not seen or heard of dear Charles, but little doubt I shall soon have the joy of seeing him—You dearest Sir will communicate my arrival to our dearest Esther from whom it will travel to all most interested—We are in good lodgings not a room being to be had at the Inn where Lord & L[y] Altamont are wth their Suite—the good fire revives me—Heaven bless preserve & restore me to you dearest Sir—

y[r] S.E.P.

[3] This is CB's letter (Osborn), 29 Dec. 1799.

well merits it!—as you have done it, never was any private action more popular—all my admirable Friends at Norbury Park are *charmed* by it—Mr. Locke speaks of it with the most benevolent pleasure—Mr. William said It was truly praiseworthy, though singularly deserved—& *Mrs*. Locke desired me to express to you, in her immediate name, the great *JOY* it was to them all to conceive their beloved Friend would be under such tender care from the moment of her touching again her native Land. Of Mrs. Crewe you will hear from our dear Father.—I will certainly write ' immediately to your poor Rosette, of whom your account grieves me sincerely:[4] I earnestly hope you will find her better on your return. I conclude you had not an instant to see about the *Furniture* I mentioned to you.[5] I shall now wish you to arrange my meeting with the upholsterer upon my going to Town to embrace my dearest sister. Esther makes us promise to inhabit her House for that purpose, as soon as the dear soul arrives: but I shall beg my Susan to fix her *own time*, in case she may have any reasons to having it quicker or slower. My Mind will be so in Heaven when I know her safe at Chelsea, that I can readily be guided by her own wishes for haste or delay. Tell her this—with the tenderest Love of my Heart. I can stay a *very* short time now,—as I have a plan, *you know*, for a longer excursion in a month or two. you *comprendez*?—& perhaps can settle my route with her yourself. She knows nothing of my Table[4]—I feared the post. but if it will give *you* any pleasure to speak of it to her, when *totally* alone, I cannot deny it you. In that case, confab. together as to my first short London visit. I can see ' the Upholsterer, Mr. H[arris] from or at Beaumont Street, without any revelations. But various domestic circumstances will make it necessary I should be the *shortest* time possible from Home at present. I shall not attempt Greenwich till my *serious visit*—when perhaps this beloved soul may be well enough to meet one there, as well as receive me at Chelsea. Arrange it for me between your two dear noddles as best seems suited to both: but try to see H[arris] & state what I wrote last, in case he has no more to say, or wants more previous consideration what to urge. How kind it was of you

---

[4] CB Jr. had left Rosette 'deplorably low, & ill'.—'Do', he had asked FBA (op. cit.), 'write to her; as I do this post to her & to honoured Papa.—'
[5] 'Love and Fashion' and a meeting planned with Mr. Harris L. 312 n. 1).

to write from Chester! I was almost ill with inquietude for news—& ill enough at ease shall I be till I hear she is actually with you & better! God bless you, dearest Charles! ever

My Mate's kindest kindest Love—our Boy is well—our best Love to your dear Charles, whose enthusiasm in your Journies delights me. How pleased will Fanny [&] Willy be to meet their Cousin & travel on with him !

Alex—hearing us talk much of our delight in your kind expedition for aunt Phillips, just now very gravely says 'I think my God Papa is almost as good as my common papa that lives here!'

---

352   West Humble, 1 January [1800]

To Sarah Rose Burney

A.L.S. (Osborn), 1 Jan.
Double sheet 4to 4 pp. *pmks* DARKING JA 1800 wafer
Addressed: Mrs. Burney, / Greenwich, / Kent.

West Hamble
1ˢᵗ Janʸ—A happy new Year to you!

My dear Rosette,

In a few lines I have just had from my dear Brother,[1] filling me with alarm & uneasiness for my poor sister, I have the added concern of learning that he left you very ill & very low, when he undertook his most kind & exemplary fraternal expedition. What is it that now so cruelly disorders you, my dear Rosette? Is it the wound you cannot heal from the loss of your Isabella?[2] or is the attack bilious? or is the gout preparing a new assault? In the latter case, I have always heard that your so much lamented Father[3] suffered almost intolerably from an unconquerable depression previous to a fit: & so did my honoured Friend Mr. Crisp,[4] who always declared the pain itself less insupportable than its preceding sensations. Pray let me hear—

---

352. [1] See L. 351 n. 1.   [2] Rosette's niece, Isabella Foss (L. 330 n. 1).
[3] Dr. William Rose of Chiswick (i, L. 7 n. 17).
[4] Samuel Crisp (ii, L. 96 n. 3).

unless writing is irksome or fatiguing to you,—what it is ⎟ Charles
alludes to—for he writes in too much haste for explanation, &
I only gather that he is in much anxiety about you. I shall not
mention what he tells me of my dear sister, for he says he has
written to you himself.—but the thought of her being wind
bound in such weather—& the fear of her missing him, by
being brought round in the yatcht, while he is traversing the
Welsh mountains to join her, give me the most dreadful
inquietude. I could hardly have believed it possible an event
I have so devoutly wished & prayed for could have happened
in a manner to so checquer my joy, & sadden my expectations.
Her situation has long been the draw back to my own happiness
—& not even her so near approach can now appease the ⎟ terrors
I have imbibed for her health—the wretched apprehensions lest
she should be restored to us too late for its re-establishment!
— — God almighty forbid!—

We mean to go to see her as soon as ever she herself dictates
the moment—for at first, she will have so much joyful emotion
to experience, that she seems to express a desire we should not
come immediately. Our stay, from domestic reasons, will be
too short to allow us to get to Greenwich, but if you are well
enough, we hope to do that early in the spring—when, I trust,
we shall not be quite such moping Invalids as when we last
tried your hospitality.⁵ This time we are *bespoke* by my sister
Burney, & have been only waiting the poor sufferer's arrival to
fulfil our engagements.

I could not wonder at your account of poor Mr. & Mrs.
Foss,⁶ whom I never think of without very sincere commiseration. pray remember my Compliments to them when you meet
or write. ⎟ I am heartily glad your good & sensible & observing
Charles accompanies his Father in this his good work. I wish
he had a sister for whom he might imitate it. — — not—not,
indeed, a sister to want such an exertion—but a Brother, if
affectionate, will always find occasions to shew kindness. That
M. d'Arblay sends you his best wishes—I need not tell you. —
—Remember us both kindly to Mrs. Bicknell, who I am very
sorry to hear has been much indisposed, though I know not
how. My Alex has lost his spirit of spouting, but is particularly
well just now. So is his mother, & hardened by going out daily

⁵ In Feb. 1799 (L. 302).   ⁶ Rosette's sister and brother-in-law (L. 330 n. 1).

in defiance of all this severe weather—which I feel, however, in every pore for my dear sick Traveller!—Adieu, my dear Rosette.—

> yours ever most sincerely
> F d'A.

353   West Humble, ⟨7⟩ January 1800

To Doctor Burney

A.L. (rejected Diary MSS. 5188–[91], Berg), ⟨7⟩ Jan. 1800, including extracts and paraphrases from A.L.S. (Barrett Eg. 3698, ff. 78–9b) CB Jr. & Molesworth Phillips to FBA, 2 Jan. 1800

Double sheet 4to 4 pp. *pmks* LEATHER HEAD 8 JA 1800 8 JAN 1800 wafer

Addressed: Dr. Burney / Chelsea College / Midlesex

Endorsed by CB: Mrs Darblay / 1800

Edited by FBA, p. 1 (5188), *annotated, dated, and the year 1800 retraced and underlined*: ❊ ❋ [*incorrectly*] 1801. Jany 1800 (1) F.d'A's Last Letter when ye Life was lent & Earthly Hope permitted relative to my Heart's darling Susanna—

Edited also by CFBt *and the* Press.

> Jany Jan^y ⟨7⟩

My dearest Padre

Excess of anxiety & alarming suspence have kept me from making any reply to your two very kind Letters of information.[1] —always, as you truly say, better than nau thing,—though so comfortless in all but *her* reaching an English harbour, that I thought it better not to commune with my dearest Father, while I had the deep apprehensions which then agitated me—Now— this moment—I have sent over to Dorking, & received thence a Letter from dear Charles, beginning

> Park Gate, Jany 2^d 1800[2]

I at length write under the same roof with our dear dear Susan—My Journey through the North of Wales, Ninety

---

353. [1] For one of these letters, that of Tuesday 24 Dec. 1799 (Osborn), see L. 349 n. 1. At this time CB was apprised only of CB Jr.'s departure on 24 Dec. ('his fraternal love is truly exemplary & heroic'). He was also told that the Major, to bring his family over, had accepted of 'a Nobleman's yacht'.

[2] The original is extant (Barrett, Eg. 3698, ff. 78–9b).

Miles in, & 90 Miles out, proved ᴵ of none effect³ — — — — —
our poor Susan is sadly reduced & enfeebled—& cannot
travel yet — —

He then most kindly adds he will take the Major a little tour
to Liverpool, Manchester, &c to give her time to rest; from her
excessive fatigue, & recover a little strength, without making
the efforts for speed which their remaining by her side might
excite. How truly considerate!

He will write his next Letter, he says, to You, dearest sir.⁴—
And I feel sure you will let it circulate to our Hermitage. This
you will kindly send on to dear Esther—I wrote to Beaumont
St. yesterday, deferring our journey till we have the beloved
Susan's. own directions. But she has yet sent me none—

She was extremely agitated by the meeting charles—& all
the more severely, no doubt, for his cruel expedition *of a Week*

³ In a letter to CB of 1 Jan. 1800 (Barrett, Eg. 3700A, ff. 24–5b) CB Jr. went into
some detail on his futile travels of 28–31 Dec. 'in the Snow, & Ice, in December—
over Welch Mountains' to Holyhead and back. On his return on Tuesday night
(31 Dec.) he had sent over an express to Parkgate and on Wednesday morning
1 Jan. he received a reply from Fanny Phillips saying that her mother was in
lodgings there. CB Jr. was later (8 Jan.) to tell his father that when he first saw 'the
sweetly patient Invalide' he thought 'she could not live two days' (Eg. 3700A,
ff. 28–9b).

⁴ His next letter to CB, that of 6 Jan. (Eg. 3700A, ff. 26–7b), was an announcement of Susan's death:
My dearest Father,
I want alas! that consolation, which I would willingly give.—Our poor dear,
dear Susan!—In order to keep her as quiet, as possible, on Friday, I went over to
Liverpool with the Major, & the 3 Children; Fanny, Willy & Charles—On our
return, last night, I found the dear Patient feeble;—but up,—& apparently
better. She was truly rejoiced to see me return; & much delighted at my having
executed some commissions for her, as she termed it so cheaply & nicely—I left
her about ten.—
She passed a sad Night.—The complaint in her Bowels, which had torn her to
pieces for several weeks; and had reduced her to a shadow, raged violently.
This Morning, while we were at breakfast the Maid, Susan, came & called out
the Major, & Fanny, with a face of alarm,—& with tears.—They went upstairs—
but returned in about ten Minutes;—& thought the fright produced more by
Susan's fears, than real danger.—Fanny at least ⟨did⟩. The Major was silent on
the subject; ⟨bu⟩t, (as he afterwards told me,) took Fanny out soon after, on
pretence of buying shoes; but in reality to prepare her, for what he dreaded.—
Susan the Maid called me up, a few Minutes, after they went.—I staid an hour
by the poor Soul's bed; but she knew me not:—she saw me not—she spoke to me
not.—
Phillips & Fanny soon returned;—and about twenty minutes before two,—
[*Charles was evidently unable to conclude the letter, but in a postscript tells of the Major's
proposing to send Fanny to CB and of his own plans to bring Willy and the maid Susan to
Greenwich.*]
The Major was to write to Mr. Locke, 'who will unfold this sad tale to our dear
Fanny'. 'What a bitter, lamentable and shocking disappointment to us all!— / In
much affliction, ever yours, / CB.'

for nothing but Cold & expence!—& disappointme[nt!] The M[ajor] concludes the Letter & has the courage to say 'We *are all very merry & comfortable* here—under one roof—

Charles says he is sure poor sweet Susey will recruit much the more easily for the tranquility she will enjoy during their excursion. I don't doubt but the sweet Soul has been much worse for her shock about Charles's useless sufferings—

⌜I must send off this immediately for the Post in haste—⌝

God bless my dearest dear Padre We are quite well—& build upon embracing you soon So happily!—

I write in enormous haste ⌜this now being *Baker's day*⌝—

354   [West Humble, 9 January 1800]

To Doctor Burney

A.N. (Diary MSS. vi. 5192, Berg), *n.d.*
Single sheet 4to 1 p.
Edited by FBA, p. 1, *annotated and dated*: ✣ 9th Jany 18 1800. 1800—9th. Jany

These were the last written lines of the last period—unsuspected as such!—of my perfect Happiness on Earth——for they were stopt on the Road by News that my Heart's adored Sister, Susanna Elizabeth Phillips, had ceased to breathe!—The tenderest of Husbands—the most feeling of human Beings for his soul-attached Wife, had only reached Norbury Park, on his way to a believed MEETING with that ANGEL, when the fatal blow was struck &——he came back to West Hamble—to the dreadful task of revealing the irreparable loss to which his own goodness, sweetness, Patience, & Heart pierced sympathy could alone have made supported!—

Added, line 6: Amen!— / F d'A
Edited also by CFBt *and the* Press.

My most dear Padre

My Mate will say all say—so I can only offer up my earnest prayers I may soon be allowed the blessing—the only one I sigh for!—of embracing my dearest Susan in your arms & under your roof!—

To Doctor Burney

A.L. (rejected Diary MSS. 5194, Berg), 9
Single sheet 4to   1 p.
Edited by FBA, p. 1, *annotated and dated*: ✻ 9. Jany 1800   (2.) Just after the fatal news of Death had reached West Hamble—from Park Gate![1]
Written in the agony of Letters from Cheshire announcing that all was over!—& while preparing to visit at least her loved Remains!—& to attend them to their last Home!———But the Design was rendered abortive by our finding—on arriving in London—that the Roads to Cheshire were so broken up by Deep Snow, as to make travelling post impossible[2]—&—alas—the Funeral had already taken place——
Edited also by CFBt *and the* Press.

O my dearest Father—the dreadful account I have just received determines us to set off directly for Park Gate—
We have just sent for a Chaise—
Heaven preserve my most beloved Father!
9*th*

355. [1] Molesworth Phillips's letter (Eg. 3700A, ff. 237–8b) to Mr. Locke, dated 6 Jan. with a London *pmk* 8 JAN 1800, would have reached Norbury Park on Thursday morning 9 Jan.:
> My dear Sir
> Death has released our poor friend from great suffering
> have the goodness to communicate this intelligence to
> M^rs D'Arblay in what manner you may think most propper
> you were one of the last she spoke of.
> > yours much obliged
> > M. Phillips

Burial was to take place on Friday 10 Jan., as CB Jr.'s letter of 8 Jan. (op. cit.) stated, and as the editor was to verify (summer of 1960) in the entry in the parish registers of St. Mary and St. Helen, Neston: 'Anno Domini 1800 / January / . . . Mrs Susannah Elizabeth Phillips wife of Major Phillips dau of Dr Burney of Chelsea bur 10.' Later in that summer the Vicar, the Revd. George Basil Hempton, found the grave and such interest did the sad story incite that the parishioners have now replaced the crumbling and defaced stone with a new one. See also Mary Ryan, 'A Stone for Susanna', *Cheshire Life*, xxx, no. 12 (Dec. 1964), 84–5.

The original stone had been engraved simply 'In memory of Mrs. Susannah Phillips, wife of Major Molesworth Phillips, and daughter of Dr. Charles Burney. [*The rest was illegible*].' CB's memorial poem (*Memoirs*, iii. 296), though reduced. on Phillips's request for an epitaph (L. 375 n. 7), from twenty-two lines (Osborn) to ten had evidently proved too long for the purpose.

[2] Following this desolating event, the d'Arblays went to Chelsea, where they remained about a month before visiting CB Jr. at Greenwich for another month. They returned to West Humble on 2 Mar.

356   [Chelsea College, *post* 9 January 1800]

Conjointly with M. d'Arblay

To Charles Burney

A.L. & A.L.S. (Osborn), *n.d.*
Double sheet 8vo   4 pp.
Addressed: Dr Charles Burney / Greenwich

O my Charles—how can I write—or see—or stay away
from you! — —*you* are the object upon earth the only one I
envy! O my dear Charles—how heavenly is your consolation
compared to mine! — — I can find none but in my friends—
You have it in Her Memory—

but I write in my dear Father's name to beg you will instantly let him have poor Fanny, should you go to Greenwich
with her before we can reach you by the steps we are trying—

He & I—who must try now to be to her Father & Mother—
will receive her from your hands as our best hope of comfort &
spur to exertion—You ∣ my dearest dearest Charles are 100000
times dearer to me than ever—all that we gathered that is
not distracting in this calamity is owing to you—your generosity kindness—affection— —

My Angel—that saint & Martyr now at length at rest—told
me once—after a menacing of a stroke like this—she had made
it her sole request that her Daughter might be sent to me, &
committed to my care & guidance — — This is a sacred remembrance & I will adopt the dear Child to the utter most of my
poor power—but ∣ it can only be mentally & affectionately, for
my dearest Father says he will never part with her, & promises
himself all he can gain of future happiness in her attachment &
in making her happy himself. *You*, my dearest Charles, must
always be close to her heart & her gratitude—the sweet orphan
shall have all the soothing & the good we can unite to bestow
upon her—My dear sympathizing Husband as much as any—

It will be somewhat less dreadful to us to see her before she
is in mourning without—we have yet avoided that shock here
—we see only one another—& poor Hetty—But my dear
Father feels tenderly your kind motive—& thanks you from his

Heart. My best hope for him is in this dear Girl, whom he passionately longs to take to his bosom. His fortitude is edifying.

God bless you—dearest, excellent Charles— [1]

[*By M. d'Arblay*]

Thursday last[1] we received the dreadful blow in a letter of the Major. At night we were in Charring Cross, but very luckily we could not find any place in the Mails, all full till the Sunday. We were, besides, assured that even with four Horses we would not reach Park-gate, on account of the bad road, before Saturday. At last, our dear Fanny, was obliged to relinquish her last hope to follow with you the departed Saint, & at midnight we arrived here Chelsea. May your sister and all of us sustain with fortitude such irreparable loss. Pray, my dearest friend, come as soon, as possible. I hear with the greatest pleasure dear M^r[^{s}] Burney is better—I hope Mrs Bick^{ll} & her son will soon be so

God bless you, my dear & ever more dear friend! that is the most ardent prayer of your afflicted   A. d'A.

357   [Chelsea College, *post* 9] January 1800

To Mrs. Locke

L. copy in hand of CFBt (Diary MSS. viii. 5196–8, Berg), Jan. 1800
Double sheet 4to   3 pp.
Edited by the Press.

Jany 1800

'*As a Guardian Angel!*'—yes my dearest Fredy, as such in every interval of despondence I have looked up to the Sky to see her— but my Eyes cannot pierce through the thick atmosphere—& I can only represent her to me seated on a Chair of sickness— her soft hand held partly out to me as I approach her, her softer Eyes so greeting me as never welcome was expressed before— —& a smile — — of heavenly expression speaking the tender

356. [1] On Thursday 9 January.

gladness of her grateful soul that God at length should grant our reunion.—From our earliest moments—my Fredy—when no misfortune happened to our dear Family, *we wanted nothing but each other*.—joyfully as others were received by us, loved by us, all that was necessary to our happiness was fulfilled by our simple junction. This I remember with my first remembrance— nor do I recollect a single instance of being affected beyond a minute by any outward disappointment if its result was leaving us together. She was the soul of my soul—& tis wonderful to me my dearest Fredy that the first ¹ shock did not join them immediately by the flight of mine—but that over—that dreadful— harrowing—never to be forgotten moment of horrour that made me wish to be mad—over—the ties that after that first endearing period have shared with her my Heart come to my aid— Yet I was long incredulous—& still sometimes I think it is not— & that she will come—& I paint her by my side—by my Father's —in every room of these apartments destined to have checquered the woes of her life with rays of comfort, joy, and affection.— O my Fredy not selfish is the affliction that repines her earthly course of sorrow was allowed no shade!—that at the instant soft peace & consolation awaited her she should breathe her last!—You would understand all the hardship of resignation for me were you to read the joyful opening of her letter on her landing to my poor Father,¹ and her prayer at the end to be restored to him!

O my Fredy—could you indeed think of ME—be alarmed for ME on that dreadful day?—I can hardly make that enter my comprehension—but I thank you from my soul, for that is beyond any love I had thought possible—even from your tender heart. —— ¹

Tell me you all keep well and forgive me my distraction— I write so fast I fear you can hardly read—but you will see I am conversing with you—and that will shew you how I turn to you for the comfort of your tenderness—yes—you have all a loss indeed!—

357. ¹ SBP's letter of 30 Dec. (L. 351 n. 2).

To Esther (Burney) Burney

A.L. (Berg), *n.d.*
Double sheet 8vo   3 pp.   wafer
Addressed: Mrs. Burney
Endorsed by EBB: Jan.—12—1800

I begin now to long to see you my dearest Hetty—for now I have got the better of my terrible disposition to an impossibility to shed a tear—which forced me into screams for some vent to the weighty oppression upon my soul—*you*—who loved her likest to my own love *YOU* methinks I would live & die with—My dear Father bears the stroke wonderfully[1]—considering she was certainly the thing dearest to him upon Earth—I have not half his fortitude—though I have so much stronger ties to consolation in the most sympathising of all hearts & my darling Boy—But so unexpected! — — —

I am glad you will come to morrow,[2] my dearest Hetty—O how SHE loved you!—Angel! angel!—Prepare yourself for fortitude to meet her little ⏐ Willy & most faithful maid—we hope to have them to-morrow—I have hope only alive in seeing her Fanny, & mentally adopting her, as the sweet soul once told me was her wish should I survive her—

I have most sacred remembrances of that desire, & would even take her to share our poor little mite & our sous, but that our dear Father says he never will part with her—God grant she may inherit those qualities which may make her divine mother return to our recollection as we watch her conduct!

---

358. [1] According to EBB, however, CB's 'shock was terrible'. See her letter (Berg) as well as CB's (Osborn), both to CB Jr., of the same date (9 Jan. 1800): 'There was nothing in the chain of human calamity that c⁴ afflic me more than the contents of your letter of yesterday! . . . What a loss to us all! but to me irreparable! The first wish of my heart was to enjoy during the short time I have a title to expect remain among the living, to enjoy her sweet temper, tender heart, sound judgment, exquisite taste, integrity, & acquirements!'

[2] On (?) Monday 13 Jan. (see also L. 359). As may be seen from FBA's paraphrase, CB Jr.'s letter of 8 Jan. (op. cit.), *postmarked* in London 11 JA 1800, had now arrived with the information that Willy and 'the good and faithful Susan' were to take the stagecoach to London, while Charles himself, travelling by chaise with his son and Fanny Phillips, meant to go on to Greenwich, where Fanny could have the help of Rosette and Mrs. Bicknell in outfitting in black. According to CB's 'Memoirs' (Berg), he arrived on Thursday, 16 Jan., bringing 'Fanny and . . . Willy to Chelsea, Motherless!'

Charles does not talk of coming hither till Wednesday or Thursday—good dear Charles!—he is the only being on Earth I envy!—O so to have seen her!— | even in those last moments[3]—how would it soothe remaining life—*now* to *me* — — *then* to *Her*! whose love—whose too tender love for us has lost her!—for she studied only our peace, not her own danger—

I write on my hand—& can hardly be legible—but you will feel all you cannot read, & make it out—Heaven protect you, my very dear sister—alas—my *dearEST* & enable you to preserve your precious health, which I tremble for sometimes—but—we must think of HER fortitude, & follow her—when we can—for that may we be purified almighty God!—This is my constant prayer! adieu, my Hetty—Love me all the more for knowing how SHE our angel loved us both

359   Chelsea College, 13 January [1800]

To Mrs. Locke

L.S. imperfect copy in hand of CFBt (Diary MSS. viii. 5200–[3], Berg), 13 Jan.
Double sheet 4to   4 pp.
Edited by the Press.

TO Mrs LOCKE

Chelsea Jany 13

Yes my dearest Friend I do indeed look up to the sky for her —but it is cloudy & thick—& I never can see Her! — — yet I can only go on by seeking Her—& fancying there will be a break that will shew Her—Her image is forever before me—her angelic look!— —her heart penetrating smile, her eyes beaming benignity—This day, this Hour it is a Week since her sweet breath perfumed this cloudy atmosphere—I have been obliged

---

[3] CB Jr.'s letter (above) has the conclusion of the scene that he was unable to complete on 6 Jan. (op. cit.): 'Our poor Susan went off, as she had lived, without a murmur! I felt, indeed, the last tremor of her pulse!—' And he had followed, as later letters were to add, 'a solitary mourner' to her grave.

to keep aloof from my poor Father till it past over—We are waiting her Fanny, Willy & the excellent Nurse How do I wish I could take them all—yet that is not true for I am more content my dear Father should have my poor little girl to whom I believe and trust she will prove a consolation. He looks forward to her as such and expects her impatiently. He bears up with a fortitude the most astonishing, I thank God! I have begun a letter to poor Norbury but am not yet able to get on with it. I know how kind you would be to my poor Child— I thought your generous hearts would feel my trust in your goodness ¦ as a solace not a weight.

O had this stroke been inflicted at Belcotton—how differently could I have resigned myself to it! But now—on the very eve of restoration to all she most prized—her own beloved mind unconscious of her body's danger—only at 10 oclock on Sunday night planning her restoration with Charles—& before two the next day—[1]

The will of God be obeyed and yielded to!—but heavy is the hand of affliction with which He has visited us — — Saint & Angel! — — she has been lost by being all Soul prematurely— —the fear of giving alarm to us prevented her taking it herself— & she saw not her danger—she saw herself already in all our arms—She has fallen the sacrifice to an excess of disinterested tenderness for those she loved—no—not *she*—we are the sacrifice.—if *SHE* is not happy! — — She was all ready—all prepared—the suddenness therefore of the change to herself conveys no shock —and when I think and dwell upon her perfections I feel that could I but have seen her once under this roof—once in her Fathers arms—and have closed her loved eyes myself, I should ¦ not have dared murmur—nor even grieve— my Brother Charles—the only Being on Earth I envy—was with her nearly to the last instant[2]—I am most thankful for that. He has behaved like Her Brother—he is now travelling slowly back with both the dear children & the faithful maid — — How my heart yearns to find my dear Fanny resembling my departed Angel! Poor Charles—though he has written to *all* else—sends

---

359. [1] FBA seemed to have CB Jr.'s letter of 6 and 8 Jan. (op. cit.) by heart. In his letter of 8 Jan. he had told of his last conference with SBP and of travel plans fatally blasted on Monday 6 January.

[2] See L. 358 n. 3; and also the letter below.

word he has not courage to write to me[3]—alas he knew she was the Soul of my Soul from my first remembrance in life!

gratefully—thankfully—in the midst of my anguish I look upon the kindest the most indulgent, the sweetest of minds that is tied to me by every tie the most sacred & beloved in this calamitous period—and it was *SHE* first made me love him—and it was Her M[r] Lock gave me his hand at the Altar—an event that now almost saves my intellects.

To her *Death*—she who was so fit to die—and whose life had so little—till now—to be wished—I could have composed myself ever since I knew her sufferings—had not the close to them seemed *so* promised and approaching — — But the Catastrophe I has been so timed as to make resignation nearly impossible—I must pray to God for new lights! pray for me, my Fredy!—my dear Amelia— —

360

[43 Beaumont Street,[1] 25 January 1800]

M. d'Arblay
To Madame d'Arblay

A.L. (Berg), *n.d.*
Single sheet 4to, of which the lower part has been cut away, leaving a remnant (5·8 × 6·2″) 2 pp.
Edited by FBA, p. 1, *top margin, numbered*: 20

London—Samedy *matin*

Je t'ai mandé hier, ma chere amie, que Charle devait diner ici aujourdhui. Nous parlerons de l'affaire que tu me recommandes.[2] [xxxxx ½ *line*] Je suivrai en cela ton instruction, mais

---

[3] On 8 Jan. CB Jr. had begun a letter ('I have been afraid to write to my dear d'Arblays. . . . Ten times have I taken up my pen, but in vain.—'). This letter (Berg), completed only on 11 Jan., was *postmarked* in London on 13 JA, but addressed via Dorking to West Humble, must have been long in reaching FBA.

360. [1] With Fanny Phillips's arrival at Chelsea there was no accommodation for M. d'A (see L. 412), who then went to EBB's home, Beaumont Street, Devonshire Place.

[2] 'L'affaire' was some embarrassment with the account at Coutts's or the difficulty M. d'A found in making himself understood there. Cf. his letter (Osborn) to CB Jr., *pmk* 21 JA 1800.

en rechignant, car entre nous soit dit, je ne connais rien au monde comme notre cher *Home* Ce n'est pas assurement que j'aye à me plaindre, au contraire. Jamais on n'a été mieux reçu: mais outre que tu n'es pas ici ni le cher petit Alex, je n'y vois point notre book room et ne trouve nulle part la comfortabilité que nous savons si bien apprecier et mettre en pratique. |

[xxxxx *12¼ lines. What can be read of this obliterated text seems to concern further business affairs with Charles.*]

361   [Chelsea College, *c.* 1 February 1800]

To M. d'Arblay

A.L. incomplete (Berg), *n.d.*
Single sheet small 4to the bottom of which was sliced away leaving a remnant (7·3×6·5″) 2 pp.
Edited by FBA, p. 1, *annotated and dated*: 1800 (17) Soon after the lamented & irreparable loss of my angelic Susanna. I was then at Chelsea college with my dear afflicted Father, & my true PARTNER in all was at Mr. Burney's.

Je suis bien fachée que vous ne vous portez pas bien, mon bon ami—donnez moi de meilleurs nouvelles si'l est possible— & si vous ne pouvez pas venir me voir—Je suis comme vous m'avez quitté—morne—mais resignée de plus en plus—& tout-ce que j'entens, & tout-ce que vois—me confirment que jamais Elle ne nous auroit été accordée que pour mourir!—O take & keep & bless her precious Spirit, almighty God!—

I have a most kind & excellent Letter from Mrs. Chapone[1]— & the most beautiful one I ever saw is come from Mrs. Disney to Fanny[1]—such a testimony to The ANGEL's worth—& such consolation to stop murmurs of her departure, as have been very beneficial. [*line cut away*] | our Alex is well, & all else— The Queen has deigned to desire to see me—yesterday morning I had the summons[2]—which shook, yet made me very grateful indeed for so unexpected a proof of Her gracious

361. [1] Mrs. Chapone's letter of sympathy, dated 20 Jan. 1800, is extant (Eg. 3698, f. 124). That of Jane (Brabazon) Disney is missing.
[2] The summons is missing but the audience was to take place on Wednesday 5 Feb. (L. 363).

benevolence,—may I not say kindness—? but I was very unwell after you left me & had much fever all that Night, & yesterday through-out.—I have taken a medicine, & am now better. I was incapable to appear then—utterly.—I have just received a few lines this morning from dearest Mrs. Lock that she is better, too.³ I am uneasy about my poor Charlotte—if

[*a line cut away*]

362

[43 Beaumont Street,¹
3 February 1800]

To Charles Burney

A.L. (Osborn), *n.d.*
Double sheet small 4to   2 pp. with mounting tape along spine   *pmks*
High Sᵗ Mbne U.P.P.   3 FE 1800   FE   wafer
Addressed: Dʳ C Burney / Greenwich / *Kent*

Nothing could be better than your Letter, my dear Carlos, nor can any thing be kinder than your Kindness—I have sent the first to the P.P. & will accept the second in the shape of your Coach & self on Thursday.² To-morrow morning³ I have the high honour of a Royal audience—for which I am truly unfit, in all things but the most grateful sense of the goodness & graciousness which accords it me. M. d'A. is at Chelsea, but left me free leave to comply with any propositions I might receive from you.

My dear Father was here just now, quite appeased in the expectation of *secresy*, but dying to see a paragraph disclaiming *authority* for what has been declared⁴—He sends his love ᐟ to

---

³ Mrs. Locke's letters, returned at a later time to the family, are not available. Mrs. Angerstein's sympathetic letter, dated [7 Feb. 1800], extant (Barrett, Eg. 3698, ff. 68–9b), is a reply to a letter written by FBA and apparently delivered by M. d'A himself, 'with sweet details' of AA's 'tenderness & almost *inspired* little efforts' at consoling his mother.

362. ¹ M. d'A and FBA had evidently exchanged accommodations (see L. 360 n. 1).

² CB Jr. must have offered to come with his coach on Thursday 6 Feb. to take the d'Arblays to Greenwich, where they were to remain for about a month.

³ Not 'To-morrow' but the day after, that is, Wednesday 5 Feb., see L. 363.

⁴ *The Morning Chronicle* (29 Jan. 1800) had made the announcement: 'Madame d'Arblay, *ci-devant* Miss Burney, has a Comedy forthcoming at Covent-Garden

you, & says Susan has a Brother at Epsom,[5] whither she proposes carrying Willy, if you have no place yet at Greenwich,
& approve the idea. He says that Willy has such complete
ascendance, at present, over Susan, that if they were in a lodging
at Chelsea, he is sure he would run out, & be for-ever at the
College, where my Father's fears of the infection are insur-
mountable obstacles to such visits—you will not wonder—

Let a P.P. Letter answer this part of mine to my Father himself, as I shall not be at Chelsea before I see you.

God bless you—pray say for me all I ought to say for myself
to Rosette—I am much incapable of doing it—

363   Greenwich, [7] February 1800

To Mrs. Locke

> L.S. copy in hand of CFBt (Diary MSS. viii. 5204–[5], Berg), Feb. 1800
> Double sheet 4to   2 pp.
> *Edited by the* Press.

To Mrs Locke.

Greenwich Friday Feb^y
1800

Here we are my beloved Friend—we came yesterday[1]—all
places to me are now less awful than my own so dear habitation

My royal interview took place on Wednesday—I was five
hours with the Royal Family—3 of them alone with the Queen
whose graciousness & *kind* goodness I cannot express. And each
of the Princesses saw me with a sort of concern & interest I can
never forget. I did tolerably well—though not quite as steadily
as I expected—but with my own Princess Augusta I lost all

Theatre.' Charlotte Barrett, in commenting on CB's 'panic' at the plans, states
(*DL* v. 459–60) that 'Mr. Harris highly approved the piece, and early in the spring
[of 1800 had] put it in rehearsal'. Despite FBA's and CB's objections, the gossip
columns continued to comment on the play; e.g. *The Times*, 29 Mar. 1800, reported
that 'Madame DARBLAY, late Miss Barry [*sic*], has turned her attention to the
Stage, and gives us hopes of a Comedy' (see also L. 345 n. 4).

⁵ William Adams, whose baptism on 11 Sept. 1771 as well as the baptisms of his
children (1798–1802), are recorded in the parish registers of Epsom.

363. ¹ On Thursday 6 February.

command of myself—she is still wrapt up & just recovering from a fever herself—and she spoke to me in a tone—a voice so commiserating—I could not stand it—I was forced to stop short in my approach, & hide my face with my Muff—she came up to me immediately—put her arm upon my shoulder, & kissed me—I shall ¹ never forget it — — How much more than thousands of words did a condescension so tender tell me her kind feelings!—*she* is one of the few beings in this world that can be—in the words of Mr de Narbonne, 'all that is *douce* & all that is *spirituelle*,'—his words upon my lost darling!—

It is impossible more of comfort or gratification could be given than I received from them all.—

364   [Greenwich, 10] February 1800

To Doctor Burney

L., copy in hand of M.d'A (Rejected Diary MSS. 5228–[9], Berg), 11 Feb. 1800
Single sheet 4to   2 pp.
Edited by CFBt *and the* Press.

Monday feb 11—1800

I hasten to tell you, dearest Sir, Mʳ H[arris] has at length, listened to our petitions, & has returned me my poor ill fated¹— —wholly relinquishing all claim to & for this season. He has promised also to do his utmost, as far as his influence extends to keep the news papers totally silent in future. We demand therefore no contradicting paragraph as the report must needs die when the *reality* no more exists. Nobody has believed it from the beginning on account of the premature moment when it was advertised This release gives me present repose which indeed I much wanted—for to combat your—to me—unaccountable but most afflicting displeasure, in the midst of my own panics & disturbance, would have been ample punishment to me, had I been guilty of a crime in doing what I have

---

364. ¹ FBA's comedy 'Love and Fashion', see Ll. 345 n. 4, 362 n. 4. CB, remembering no doubt the humiliation attendant on the production of *Edwy and Elgiva* on 21 Mar. 1795 (iii, L. 161 nn. 1, 2), was opposed to a second theatrical venture.

all my life been urged to, & all my life intended, writing a Comedy.[2] Your goodness, your kindness, your regard for my fame, I know have caused both your trepidation, which doomed me to *certain* failure; & your displeasure that I ran, what you thought, a wanton risk. But it is *not* wanton, my dearest Father. My imagination is not at my own controll, or I would always have continued in the walk you approved. The combinations for another long work did not occur to me. Incidents & effects for a Dramma did. I thought the field more than open—inviting to me. The chance held out golden dreams. The risk could be only our own for—permit me to say, appear when it will, you will find nothing in the principles, the moral, or the language that will make you blush for me. *A failure*, upon those points only, can bring DISGRACE—upon mere control or want of dramatic powers, it can only cause *disappointment*.

I hope, therefore, my dearest Father, in thinking this over, you will cease to nourish such terrors & disgust at an essay so natural, & rather say to yourself with an internal smile, 'After all—'tis but *like Father like Child*—for to what walk do I confine myself?—She took my example in writing—She takes it in ranging—Why, then, after all, should I lock her up in one paddock, well as she has fed there, if she says she finds nothing more to nibble—while *I* find all the Earth unequal to my ambition, & mount the skies to content it? Come on then, poor Fan—The World has acknowledged you my offspring—& I will *disencourage*[3] you no more. Leap the pales of your paddock—let us pursue our career—& while you frisk from novel to Comedy, I, quitting Music & Prose, will try a race with Poetry & the Stars.

I am sure, my dear Father, will not infer, from this appeal, I mean to parallel our Works—no one more truly measures their own inferiority, which with respect to yours has always been my pride;—I only mean to shew, that if my Muse loves a little variety—She has an hereditary claim to try it.

F. B.

[2] After the publication of *Evelina* in 1778 FB had been encouraged by Mrs. Thrale, Arthur Murphy, Sheridan, and others to try her hand at comedy, but her first comedy 'The Witlings' had been prudently suppressed by CB and Mr. Crisp because of its daring satire on the blue-stockings (see *HFB*, pp. 95, 132–8; *DL* i. 255–63). Her best comedy 'A Busy Day' she was yet to write.

[3] A term borrowed from Mrs. Anne (see *DL*, v, 437; and v, L. 543 n. 2).

To James Burney

A.L. excerpt, copy in hand of FBA (⅓ p. in West Humble Letter Book, p. 122, Osborn), 11 Feb. 1800

Also L. excerpt, copy of above letter in hand of M. d'A, appearing on p. 2 of his copy of a letter, FBA to CB, Monday ⟨ ⟩, 1800 (rejected Diary MSS. 5228–9, Berg) Single sheet 4to greenish 2 pp.; *annotated by* CFBt, p. 1: *To Doctor Burney*; *editorial markings*: MAD^e D'ARBLAY; *editorial signature in pencil*, p. 2: F. B

To Captain B. Feb 11—1800

Shall a blow like this strike us—& shall we not write to each other?—Comfort we cannot give, the blow is deadly—irreparable—it strikes at the root of happiness—O my dear James, who can replace her? Where shall we look for her like? Her head—her heart—which was dearest?—and at what a moment have we lost her!—just as she seemed restored—just as I thought I almost felt her in my arms!—and without the least preparation—without the most remote suspicion of any *present* danger—though the state of her health has long made me restless

To Esther (Burney) Burney

A.L.S. (Berg), *n.d.*
Double sheet 8vo 4 pp. black seal
Addressed: Mrs. Burney / Beaumont Street / Devonshire place / London
Endorsed by EBB: 1801
Docketed in pencil: 1800

My kindest Esther will I know be glad to hear my mind is at rest on *one* subject which has disturbed it—though not, indeed, deeply,—what, of a mere worldly nature, just now can? But Mr. H[arris] has listened at length to my earnest solicitation, & returned my MS. & suffers it total postponement to another year. This has somewhat helped my harrassed repose, for the idea of bringing out a Comedy at this period—though its whole materials & business had been all arranged so long before it, was always dreadful to me. The aid it is *possible* it might have brought to other matters I relinquish without murmuring, to be spared so jarring a [|] shake to all within.

How are you, my dear soul? Better, I must hope. I repeat passages of Mrs. Disney's incomparable Letter[1] continually & they contribute greatly to tranquilize me,—by their picture of the *lasting sufferings* to which she thought our angel while on Earth destined—& she knew her—& her story—& her expectations—& her miseries *3 years* later, in many instances, than we did—I take one of her sentences on this subject, or on that of Her Great reward, for a sort of text every Morning, which I try to make serve me to discourse upon with my own soul—or my beloved Participator—for the rest of the day. I have found [|] nothing yet so useful to me. They are *all* kind & considerate here, & I am much to myself & my Child—This is absolutely necessary to me—for exertion extended beyond certain limits sinks me to nearly my first state.—no—not *first*. — — That is past—dreadfully past—for-ever!—The Letter you have forwarded from sweet Mrs. Lock[2] finishes with 'remember me most kindly to my dearest Mrs. Burney.'

I had not yet written I had left you. My poor Boy is under discipline, but in unalterable spirits.

God bless you—& preserve your health, my dearest Esther—my love to dear Mr. Burney—& to your dear Girls & Richard —truly—tenderly yours, my dearest Hetty

F. d'A.

Willy & Susan [Adams] are going on very well at a lodging—Willy will soon be well again, it is thought. Clement[3] is loved by all.

M. d'A's. kindest Love to you—& all yours—

366. [1] The missing letter to Fanny Phillips (L. 361 n. 1).   [2] Cf. L. 361 n. 3.
[3] Clement Robert Francis (i. lxxiii).

To Mrs. Waddington

A.L. (rejected Diary MSS. 5206–[7], Berg), *n.d.*
Double sheet 4to   2 pp.   *pmks*   P.P.P. Deptford Br   ⟨ ⟩   black wafer
Addressed: Mrs ⌈Waddington / Lanover / Abergavenny⌉
Docketed in pencil, p. 1: Feb. or / March / 1800
[*In ink*]: 1800
Edited by CFBt *and the* Press, *see* Textual Notes.

I know not how to write to you—yet think it cruel to your kindness to be forever silent—I have had a loss that almost rent my Heart in twain—though I have a Husband I adore—a Child I idolize—a Father—Sisters & Brothers past expression dear to me—& Friends loved so as words cannot speak—but She that is gone I thought just restored—she had reached our shores—she had written me—& what a Letter![1]—what exquisite sweetness of unparrellelled tender joy in our approaching re-union — — — I thought her—I almost felt her again in my arms — — — —

May the Almighty—who had fitted as well as taken her to himself but teach my sorrow to yield to Her joy!—And may her pure soul join that to which ALMOST alone on Earth I could compare it—of your revered Aunt Delany! — — And when I my own Hour comes—ah my dear Marianne—what a blessed idea—& hope that then I may be purified to join them—to join *THEM*—& be joined by the loved surviving groupe—Thoughts such as these are the only soothers of agony—

I hope you are recovering—tell me so if you can—I have not your direction—I must send this to Lanover—We are now at Greenwich with my Brother Dr. Charles—I spent a Month with my Father[2]—& am most thankful that his fortitude makes me now leave him without fear for his health—My sweet Fanny Phillips is established to live with him. God bless you, my dear Marianne

---

367. [1] This is SBP's letter (Berg) written from Parkgate on Monday night 30 Dec. [1799] *pmk* 2 JAN 1800: 'My own Fanny . . . must from none but myself hear of my late landing in beloved old England— . . . we arrived between 3 & 4 this afternoon I am greatly fatigued & ready to drop asleep. . . .'
[2] From midnight 9 Jan. to *c.* 2 Feb.

Your confidential Letter came safe to West Hamble—& I earnestly hope you are now recovered—& your Children quite well.

F. D'A.

368   West Humble, 4 March 1800

To Doctor Burney

A.L.S. (Berg), 4 Mar. 1800
Double sheet 4to   4 pp.   *pmks*   DARKING   7 MR 1800   7 MAR 1800 wafer
Addressed: Dr. Burney, / Chelsea College, / Middlesex
Endorsed by CB: rec^d 7th Mar. / 1800
Edited by FBA, p. 1, *editorial annotation*: al. O [*all out?*]

West Hamble   March 4.
1800

I feel very anxious, Dearest sir, to know if your cold proved as slight as I hoped, & if it is now quite conquered. Not the *Cough*—that, I am too sure, will not yield to frost & snow! but the additional cold & feverishness. We got home safe, & our Alex is perfectly well, &, I hope, will want no more *Ching*[1] at present. M. d'A. carried the Goldoni's[2] to Mr. Lock the next morning, who desires his kindest compliments & thanks for them.

The Letter which I venture to enclose,[3] my dearest Father, you must not be angry with me for sending. You have brought me up in the love of peace making, for I never saw you omit a conciliating office that fell in your way. I have long seen, & more than once hinted to you, that I was sure James heartily repented the rash—wild—& unjustifiable step he has taken. His regret for not being *employed* re-doubles mine, as it would not only have saved him from this wrong measure, but because I feel convinced, from the general probity of his character, he

---

368. [1] See L. 310 n. 1.   [2] Volumes of Carlo Goldoni's plays.
[3] A letter from JB.

would *well* & *heartily* have acted, & fought, (if called upon) when once engaged in the service. And he is so excellent an officer, he would now, probably, have been an Admiral. Even yet, perhaps, your interest & influence (could you feel that security & reliance in his given honour that I do, so as to act for him warmly) might draw him from obscurity & penury, to be of service to his Country, &, with his admirable professional talents, of use & honour [|] to his Family. But of this I am sure he has no hope, after so deeply & cruelly offending you—yet is convinced application by any other means would be vain, since he can have no other guarantee for his sincerity. Mr. Windham has said something to this purpose. Nor, indeed, am I sure, in the present shattered state of his health & spirits, if he continues the wish, though I know he nourishes the regret, in the hopeless, but self-devoted obscurity to which he now seems destined. I believe his heart has long been as unhappy as it can well hold—& now he no longer disguises it. He is dreadfully punished—

I do not presume to make this representation with the expectation of an answer—I know you too much—& too justly irritated: all I dare hope is that the knowledge of his contrition, his evident unhappiness & ill health, & his avowal that the *wish nearest his heart* is your forgiveness, may silently, though not immediately, work their way in your kind & generous mind to soften a little the too justly incurred bitterness of your thoughts against him. And this for *your* sake as well as his—for it had long been a mournful reflection to me that one of my dearest Father's Children should seem hardened against his displeasure. *Seem* I say, for I never thought that though Sally alone *applied* for pardon, Sally alone covetted it. She knew her youth offered superior palliation, & thence felt superior courage [|]   James, I have a notion,—from the time his Eyes were opened to what he had done, thought it as desperate for pardon as for remedy, & doomed himself to fight off as he could the gloomy penitence that took possession of him. But the late calamity & forever irreparable loss on Earth to You & us all, has made him every way wretched in thinking of you, & miserable to express some sense of his deep concern for your grief—& for his offence. I am told that when he was in town he looked extremely Meagre & ill, & was very low-spirited as to his opinion of his own health.

As his complaint is a tightness upon his Chest, I imagine he fixed upon Bristol in hopes the Water there might relieve it.

Forgive this address, my dear Father, by considering for which of your own Brothers or Sisters you could have refused a similar one. I dare hope for no present reply—& shall therefore write again, as ususal, without one, in a short time, or as soon as any thing occurs.

⁓

Three hundred Labourers, & poor Men, assembled yesterday in Dorking, declaring they would work no more, while bread was at such a price,[4] unless their wages were again raised. They made their application at Lord Leslie's,—who must have ¦ been much distressed how to act. This we heard from our little maiden, who went thither on an errand. The result has not reached us. They declare they cannot keep their families from starving. It will be dreadfully difficult what to decide.

I must tell you the history of our Garden when I write next— M. d'A. says it is a most rueful one, & full of disasters. He desires his most affectionate Respects. I entreat my kindest Love to my dear Fanny, & that she will write to me soon. I have run away with her commission money—but I am sure my sister will trust her till Easter.

Adieu, dearest Sir, ever your most dutiful &

affectionate daughter   F. d A.

---

⁴ 'A wet, late, and scanty harvest', 'the waste of war', and the closure of continental ports from which grain could be imported had caused by February acute shortages of wheat, 'enormous' increases in the price of bread, and bread riots all over the realm. A Parliamentary committee was set up by the House of Commons to investigate the causes of the shortage (amounting among the poor, almost to famine) and to suggest remedies, see *AR* xlii (1800), 129–37; and the realistic picture presented by Arthur Young, *The Question of Scarcity plainly stated* . . . (1800). The very poor had to depend on the charity of the gentry and on such doles as they could force from local magistrates (cf. L. 371, p. 407; and L. 375 n. 5).

Conjointly with M. d'Arblay

To Charles Burney

A.L. and A.L. (Osborn), 4 March 1800
Double sheet 8vo   4 pp.   *pmks*   DARKING   7 MR 1800   ⟨7⟩ MAR
1800
Addressed: Dr Charles Burney / Greenwich / Kent
Docketed in pencil, p. 4: 6—2 / 75—
Scribbling in ink: old news / papers—

West Humble
Dorking
March 4
1800

We were very sorry, my dear Charles, to leave town before
you arrived—but we stayed till past 3 in the hope of a peep—

How kind of you, my dearest Carlos, to wish me again in
your observatory, mournful as were my visits there!—I had
feared they could only have been depressing to your own
spirits, which I grieved to hurt, when the bustle of necessary &
laudable occupation, joined to stronger nerves, had recovered
them. I thank you, however, the more, for the true affection I
feel in such kindness.

A very particular circumstance will call me to town, for a
day or two only, the first week in April—The princess Amelia
has desired to see your little Godson—should it happen I should
be able to fix | a time for this Honour which her very sweet
Royal Highness does the little *dabble* when you should be at
liberty to shake hands with me, though but for a moment, it
would sincerely gratify me. I shall at least let you know the
period, to try my chance. M. d'A. as my stay will be so short,
will not leave his rose trees & cabbages.

I have not yet begun *Sir Hugh*[1]—my house has much necessary employment for me first, so I must defer *the Classics* till
more at leisure. I find, however, USEFUL employment the best
tranquiliser, & however my heart still aches—I have less of the
violent emotions which | have hitherto torn me—but I must

369. [1] Possibly more revisions of *Camilla* (cf. L. 314 n. 5).

fly this subject—Pray give my kindest thanks to Rosette with my love, & tell her I often felt her quiet forbearance & feeling consideration in leaving me so much to myself—It was wise as well as kind—for any more exertion would but have more shattered me.

God bless you, dearest Charles—

How much we were provoked at missing you on Sunday!— our *three* loves to your dear & deserving young Representative—my best wishes, with best Compliments to Mrs. Bicknell whose gentle interest in what was passing within me I often saw in her Eyes—I hope she is now better.

Fanny has heard at last from poor Norbury who writes just as I expected from his tender love— |

[*By M. d'Arblay*]

my best loves to all the dear inhabitants of Greenwich School I entreat Charles the 2ᵈ to take care of a cane I left: I am very much attached to it, because it is a present of Wᵐ Locke.

As to Charles the 1ˢᵗ I thank him for the precious augmentation, of my Library, which however is not yet considerable enough not to make me long after the daily comfortable reading of news Papers with which I hope to be

gratefully ⟨Alex⟩ |

370   West Humble, [10]–11 March 1800

Conjointly with M. d'Arblay

To Esther (Burney) Burney

A.L.S. & PS. (rejected Diary MSS. 5208–[11], Berg), 11 Mar. 1800
Double sheet 4to 4 pp. (8·7 × 7·4″), from which the upper fold, a segment (2 to 2·3 × 7·4″), has been removed from the top of 2nd leaf
pmks DARKING 14 MAR 1800 wafer
Addressed: Mrs. Burney / Beaumont Street / Devonshire Street. / London
Endorsed by EBB *in pencil*: answered March 17 Fanny P—'s Money
Edited by CFBt *and the* Press.

West Hamble,
March 11ᵗʰ 1800

If you knew not the cruel state of my mind, my dearest Esther, you must think me the most graceless of human beings

never to have written—never to have thanked you for your
excessive kindness, nor dear Mr. Burney for his great hospitality, nor your dear Girls for their affectionate attentions — —
but I have found my sadness so extreme—so depressing to all
exertion—so mischievous to all the purposes of social-chearful
life, that I have thought it right to refuse seeing even Mr. &
Mrs. Locke—with all my love, my reverence my fondness for
them, lest I should re-infect them with a grief so uncontrollable
—& by shutting myself up, with only my sympathising partner
& supporter, & our mutual little Darling—I have quieted my
nerves, though not raised my spirits,—& I am sure my tender
sister will be glad to hear even that, & that my convulsive
emotions, at least, are nearly over.—I have given my | self
wholly up to house arrangements, & œconomical examina-
tions & affairs,—& to renewing my lessons with my little Love—
who grows more & more carressingly endearing to us daily, in
defiance of his almost unequalled spirits. And, indeed, I did not
wish to write till I had broken the hard spell which seemed to | ob-
struct returning consolation by making me so grievously dread
a meeting with those dear pitying & truly sympathising friends
that sought it—for I feared it might make you think me *wilful*
in despondence—I have waited, therefore, till I could tell you
that shock is past. On saturday[1]—the day before yesterday,
Mrs. Locke came to me—M. d'Arblay fetched her, without my
concurrence, or even suspicion, & they settled together to force
me to the interview, since my courage never rose to consent
to it. I will not tell you how it passed—I need not—our own
was so like it!—in bitter—bitter grief!—And yesterday she came
again—& Mr. Locke also—That, indeed, was a severe trial!—
I am thankful it is past—upon my knees alone I could let him
come up to me—I would fain have spared *him* what was a relief
to *me*—I could not command myself—the thought of all SHE—
our angel owed him—& of her tender exquisite veneration for
him, overpowered all my feeble resistance, & I was compelled to let my sorrow—my gratitude—& my anguish take
their own way. I flatter myself, however, he was not hurt,
though deeply touched—for he could not be surprised. He
knows how reciprocally we had all but adored him from our
first acquaintance, & he seemed to scarcely know |

370. [1] On 8 Mar. 1800

my reverence & affection for him are—if possible—augmented.
To day they were both coming again—when the snow prevented them, & brought me only a most sweet billet from our
dear Mrs. Locke. These little circumstances will, I know, give
some satisfaction to my dearest Esther, who will see the deepest
draw backs to my revival over, & turned, now, into sources of
comfort—for such every interview after the first must prove.
Norbury Park, however, I have not yet had fortitude to enter—
but I soon shall—I trust—&, that sad effort over—nothing will
remain but to acccommodate myself as I can to our afflicting
deprivation, & recover my chearfulness here by an humble—
but O my dearest Hetty! an extatic hope of our re-union hereafter! With this sweet thought—that THERE we may join Her—
& *there* finally meet each other—let me drop this loved subject—
which has carried me far beyond what I purposed, & left me
little room for much I meant to add. *Chiefly,*—your health, my
dear soul, I wish to have a true account of,—& next—your *mind*
—I know your resignation, from generous thoughts of HER,
added to virtuous & indispensable ⌐ [resignation to the Will of
God.]²

so earnestly I *wish!*—Tell me something of your proceedings,
when you are able to write—whom & what you see, as well as
what you feel—all is interesting to me, as connected with you
& your life.

I have had a very kind Letter from poor James, who seems
to me every way unhappy, though he does not call himself so.
How I pity him!—M. d'Arblay sends you his kindest Love, &
begs you to distribute it copiously around you, but chiefly to
our late worthy & dear Host. We hope Richard continues
amending in health,—& that you often see my dear Father
God bless you, my dearest Esther ever most faithfully & truly
affectionately yours

F. d'A.

[*By M. d'Arblay*]

A thousand tender thanks from Dʳ Okborne to the dear
inhabitants of *Bioumont* Street—Could they be so good as to

---

² The phrase in square brackets was copied by CFBt presumably from the segment that she had cut out and discarded.

send to Mʳ John Angerstei⟨n⟩ a Map of Westphaly left by him³
in the bureau of *his* chamber? Mʳˢ Anger[stein] would have the
kindness to bring it when she comes.

371   West Humble, 22 March 1800

To Doctor Burney

A.L.S. (Diary MSS. vi. 5216–[17], Berg), 22 Mar. 1800
Originally a double sheet 4to, of which FBA later discarded the second
leaf 2 pp
Edited by FBA, p. 1 (5216), *annotated in larger hand than usual and date
retraced*: ⁙ 22ᵈ *1800* (3)
M. d'Arblays losses & Misadventures in his Garden after its neglect from
our absence & fatal Calamity—
Edited also by CFBt *and the* Press.

West Hamble
March 22ᵈ *1800*

Day after Day I have meant to write to my dearest Father—
but I have been unwell ever since our return, & that has not
added to my being sprightly. I have not once crossed the
threshold since I re-entered the house, till to day, when Mr. &
Mrs. Locke almost insisted upon taking me an airing. I am glad
of it, for it has done me good, & broken a kind of spell that
made me unwilling to stir. M. d'Arblay has worked most
laboriously in his garden; but his misfortunes there, during our
absence,¹ might *melt a Heart of stone.*—The Horses of our next
neighbouring Farmer broke through our Hedges, & have made
a kind of bog of our Meadow, by scampering in it during the
wet; the sheep followed, who have eaten up ALL our Greens—
every sprout & Cabbage & Lettuce, destined for the Winter—
while the Horses dug up our Turnips & carrots, & the swine,
pursuing such examples, have trod down all the young plants,
besides devouring whatever the others left of vegetables! our
potatoes, left—from our abrupt departure, in the Ground, are
all rotten or frost-bitten—& utterly spoilt; & not a single

---

³ By Md'A, characterizing himself as the pedant in *Camilla*.
371. ¹ Of about two months following 9 Jan.

thing has our ⌐ whole Ground produced us since we came home. A few dried Carrots, which remain from the in-doors collection, are all we have to temper our viands. What think you of this for people who make it a rule to owe a third of their sustenance to the Garden? Poor Mr d'A.'s renewal of toil to supply future times is exemplary to behold, after such discouragement. But he works as if nothing had failed, such is his patience as well as industry.

My Alex, I am sure you will be kindly glad to hear, is entirely well—& looks so blooming no Rose can be fresher. I am encouraging back his *spouting* propensity, to fit him for his royal interview with the sweet & gay young Princess who has demanded him, who will, I know, be inexpressibly diverted with his speeches & gestures. We must present ourselves before Easter, as the Court then adjourns to Windsor for 10 days.[2] My Gardener will not again leave his Grounds to the four footed marauders, —& our stay, therefore, will be the *very* shortest we can possibly make it: for though we love retirement, we do not like solitude. I long for some further account of you, dearest Sir, & how you bear the mixture of business & Company, of *fag & frolic*, as Charlotte used to phrase it.— ⌐

our assemblage of poor here at Dorking, by hundreds, about the price of bread, forced the [ma]gistrates to allow to each man 1ˢ a week while it continues so high!—[3]

[the second leaf missing]

[2] Before 13 Apr. The audience was later arranged to take place on Thursday morning 10 Apr. (L. 374). Besides lyrics from *The Tempest* (L. 300, p. 233), Alex's repertory would seem at this time to have included parts of *Tom Thumb* (Ha! dogs! Arrest my friend before my face!), 'The spacious firmament on high' (Addison), and Shenstone's *A Pastoral Ballad*. See L. copy (Berg), FBA to Mrs. Locke, Nov. 1824.

[3] For the bread-riot, see L. 368 n. 4.

To Mrs. Broome

A.L. (rejected Diary MSS. 5212–[15], Berg), 22 Mar. 1800
Double sheet 4to   4 pp.   wafer
Addressed: Mr⟨s.⟩ Broome, / Brighthelmstone.
Endorsed by CBFB: Sister d'Arblay / March 22ᵈ 1800 / ansᵈ in april.
Edited by CFBt *and the* Press.

West Hamble
March 22ᵈ 1800

It seems very long since I have had any communication with my dearest Charlotte—yet would still, I fear, be longer, were I left to the natural bent of my present feelings—which are more than ever averse to writing. The constant Journal—the never omitted memorandums of all that concerned me, which you know to have been kept up ever since I held a pen in my hand, during every absence from my earliest—darling confident— now suddenly broken off, & dissolved, has made the very action of writing laborious—painful—almost anguish to me — —

Time will wear this away—time—& more submissive reflexions upon the change that to HER must be as much happier as to me it is more wretched—wretched, ⏐ from the excess of my affection to that departed Angel in defiance of such remaining blessings as scarcely any one ever enjoyed before, & as no one can more sensibly value.—*But* — — I had them all *with* HER!— I could not, however, resist the opportunity now offered of enquiring after your health, my dear Charlotte—& your Children's, & Mr. Broome's. And I hope you will be able—& willing—to send me a good account of all. Nor would I refuse myself the pleasure of introducing you & Mrs. Cooke[1] to each other again. I flatter myself you will cultivate her acquaintance, & reap from it the real advantages it may bestow. I have found her a most sincere & excellent friend, active, zealous, kind & honourable. Such a character will make you prize her society, & she is disposed to wish for yours with real warmth; & she is strongly ⏐ prejudiced in favour of Mr. Broome, not only, as all the World is, by his simkins' Letters, but by having heard him

372. ¹ Cassandra Cooke, wife of the Revd. Samuel (iii, L. 122 n. 8).

highly mentioned by Mr. Hastings, with whom she has been long acquainted, & whom she admires almost of all men breathing the most. I am not sure if the good Mr. Cooke will be of her party, or only occasionally join it—but you must *look your best* at him, for, you know, he fell in love with you at Bookham. I often—nay constantly, regret we could not remove these valuable neighbours with ourselves to West Hamble. There is no telling how how melancholy was the whole of our absence from hence,—& I have been so unwell & dejected since our return, I have not, as yet, had spirit even to go to Norbury Park—though its truly sympathising & dear Master & Mistress come to me here frequently. Mr d'Arblay resumes his Gardening, but with depression & disappointment—our Alex is our life & support—& grows more companionable & dear every moment — ¹ & the state of my Mind seems to make an impression upon him that—though unconscious how or why—softens & tames him, & leads him to be most touchingly tender & carressing. We left your charming Boy² well, happy, & in high character with all his Masters. I had not spirits to desire to see dear Charlotte & Marianne—pray give my kindest Love to both, & say my sight could have given them no pleasure, or I would have exerted myself to meet them. But I know their Hearts are affectionate, & would rather have been wounded than gratified by my altered appearance. The things were, I hope, returned safe, that you kindly lent me? I was forced to commit them to sister Burney's maid. Thanks for your admirable Lozenges, & Medicines. Both have been very serviceable to me. Tell me your Holyday arrangements,—& all else that interests you & can bear writing—for no grief—however deep—can lessen for you the true interest & warm wishes of your ever affectionate & faithful

F. d'A.

M. d'A. sends you his love. Give both our best comp^ts to Mr. Broome, & don't omit to tell me of his health when you write, & how you occupy your time at Brighton.³—

² Clement Robert Francis, now 8 years old and a pupil at CB Jr.'s school at Greenwich.
³ See a Journal (92 pp.) kept by the young Charlotte Francis (Barrett, Eg. 3706A).

To Esther (Burney) Burney

A.L.S. (rejected Diary MSS. 5218–[21], Berg), 26 Mar. 1800
Double sheet 4to   4 pp.   p. 4 [5221] *already inscribed*: West Hamble
pmks DARKING   28 MAR 1800   wafer
    Addressed: Mrs. Burney, / Beaumont Street, / Devonshire Street, / London
    Endorsed by EBB: March 1800 / answered / April 7.—
    Edited by FBA, CFBt, *and the* Press.

West Hamble
26. March 1800

Your kind—tender Letter, was very balsamic to me, my
dearest Esther—& the tears I shed over it were less bitter than
my general tears—*much* less—for I *rejoiced* at *your* frame of
mind,—rejoiced most sincerely that my dearest Esther has
reasoned & soothed the grief of her heart into such a submission
to the will of God.—To HIS will my dear Hetty will not doubt
I bow down—but I have not had the power to submit to it
chearfully, nor to regard it otherwise than as a Chastisement!—
alas may it's severity at least prove expiatory, if the dreadful
torture with which I have been afflicted has thus fastened upon
me for my own sins!—I know you too partial to think I have any
to call forth such a punishment—nor have I thought I had
myself—yet perhaps I may now suffer for having weighed &
considered them too lightly. Her Death—I humbly trust—has
only been ordained for her happiness—it is the unconquerable
heaviness of my sorrow that alone can fall upon me.

Yet this thought occurs but with my writing it—for I am not
a seeker of severe decrees—I view Religion with only | chearful
ideas—I see God only in his mercy—& I have no horrible
apprehensions of having incurred the divine displeasure—
Heaven be praised my thoughts all rise into hopes upon the
subject of my ultimate account—though many & many are the
faults & imperfections which may merit the chastening hand of
affliction. SHE—sweet saint!—prayed that her hard exile might
prove expiatory — — I must pray that this soul-harrowing loss
may prove so to me! — — My dearest Hetty—I wish you
could hear Mr. Locke talk upon this subject—hear the sweetly

consolatory—nay enlivening—nay joyful ideas he forms &
encourages upon a Death such as her's,—a mere earthly dis-
appearance of excellence so untainted.—I wish I could give
you his discourse,—but I cannot recall it with justice even to
myself. I have lost my power of retaining & retailing—& my
recollections & ideas all run—I know not how—incoherently
against one another. Did I tell you my plan of collecting *Texts*
for every morning?[1]—I am convinced it will be a means to
better still my disordered mind & spirits into tranquility than
any other I can adopt— | but I have not yet had time for it.
I devote all that my dear Companion spends in his garden to
House affairs & lessoning my Alex—& when M. d'A. is within,
he reads to me while I work or converses—which does me more
good. The almost endless, though nameless matters of domestic
œconomy, in a small dwelling & household. & income such as
ours, have given me occupation best adapted to my present
powers, because demanding no other attention than what is
obvious Small, however, as my progress to content is,—I make
some—& my worst efforts are all over save ONE!—visiting the
spot we had destined for her bower![2]—& that I will do very
soon—but am forced to rest & recruit between every piercing
exertion—I have already been out 4 airings with dearest Mr.
& Mrs. Lock — — & they were attended with a thousand
circumstances to [make] them—at first, deep tragedies—but the
last—of this morning—I found I bore far better—& I saw my
beloved Mr. Lock more satisfied about me. Mrs. Lock had a
cold, & could not come—& my Alex was indulged with taking
her place—Yesterday afternoon I did what I know my dearest
Esther will be glad to hear—I went—at last—to Norbury Park

373. [1] This practice FBA followed in later years, as may be seen in her Notebooks.
   [2] M. d'A commemorated the visit, which was perhaps not made until May, by
occasional verses (Berg), taking the form of an address or prayer to SBP:
   Modele, des Vertus qu'on admire et qu'on aime,
      Du plus terrible des fleaux
   Triste proie ici bas, c'est au Sein de Dieu même
      Qu'enfin tu goutes le repos!
   Vois tu dans mon humble hermitage
   Comme tout est changé, comme ta pauvre sœur
   A perdu (te perdant) santé, moyens, courage?
   Je te dois ma compagne; acheve ton ouvrage:
      Ange du Ciel!—modere sa douleur!
The verses were annotated by FBA: 'May 1800 / Written for my perusal on my first
mournful visit to the spot my beloved Husband had destined for my darling
Susanna's own—May I merit his tender prayer by accepting his consolation!'

—I will not tell you how terrible my re-entrance was to the house—the spot—where I saw her last![3]—it almost brought back my ¦ first torture—but I am thankful it is over—& I hope now to reap again all the tender sweetness of their exquisite friendship & goodness. The family happened to all dine at Lady Burrels,[4] except Mr. & Mrs. Lock—which made me take the opportunity.—yet—such as I am—I feel I am better here than elsewhere—& fit only for home till time softens my feelings—I am therefore truly concerned at the command[5] which must so soon force me hence—though so to shew my bantling would have been my pride & happiness a short time since!— M. d'A. will not accompany us—for prudential reasons, as our excursion will not *require* him, & shall be the briefest I can make it. I am quite sorry I forgot to mention to you my carrying off dear Fanny P[hillip]'s 3 G[s]—I named it to my Father, & imagined it would travel to you immediately I have had a very kind Letter from poor James, who speaks ill of his health, & whom I think far from happy—poor fellow![6]—how I pity him! —I will tell Miss Baker[7] when I write your message, &c—I had written a few lines to Miss C[ambridge][7] by the post that brought your Letter. Tell me a little of your goings on,— business—& engagements when you are able to write—It will do me nothing but good to be brought into the World by *you*, & by the interest I take in all that *must* carry YOU into it—& pray give for us both the kindest remembrances to Mr. B[urney] & all your family. I sincerely hope poor Richard is better again. Alex is delightfully well, & frequently talks of you all, & desires to go again to *the London House*. adieu—my dearest Esther— Heaven preserve—& bless you!

F. d'A.

[3] It was in the Hall of Norbury Park on 7 Oct. 1796 that FBA had seen her sister for the last time (iii, L. 203, p. 201) and from 'the gallery Window' above that she watched her chaise disappearing in the distance. 'I could only go to your deserted room—& only pray for your safety & restoration.'

[4] At Deepdene. See iii, L. 247 n. 23.

[5] At the command of Princess Amelia (see L. 374).

[6] Cf. L. 370, p. 405 and L. 368 n. 3.

[7] Sarah Baker (i, L. 10 n. 6) and Charlotte Cambridge (i, L. 1 n. 6) of Richmond.

To Charles Burney

A.L. (Osborn), 7 Apr. 1800
Double sheet 8vo　1 p.　*pmks*　9 AP 1800　9 AP 1800　wafer
Addressed: Dr. Charles Burney / Greenwich / Kent
Postdated in pencil, p. 1: 1800

april 7. 1800
west Humble

My dearest Charles,

Wednesday I arrive at Chelsea,[1] to carry my Boy to Her R[oyal] H[ighness] the P[rincess] A[melia] early on Thursday Morning—.

good Friday I shall pass with our Father—& Saturday return to my Hermit & Hermitage—

If you can contrive to let me see you for a moment, it will be a real revival to me, dearest Charles.

My our kind Love to Rosette & Charles the Junr—

& always remember us to Mrs. Bicknel—with whom Mrs. Angerstein was *extremely* pleased—which gave me great pleasure in rebound—but no surprise.

To Doctor Burney

A.L.S. (Diary MSS. vi. 5222–[5], Berg), 27 Apr. 1800
Double sheet 4to　4 pp.　*pmks*　DARKING　1 MY 1800　1 May 1800
wafer
Addressed: Dr. Burney, / Chelsea College, / Middlesex.
Endorsed by CB: 1800
Edited by FBA, p. 1 (5222), *annotated*: ✶ ✶ (4) Retirement the Nurse & Harbinger of Grief—
Edited also by CFBt *and the* Press, *see* Textual Notes.

West Hamble, *April* 27th
1800

My dearest Sir,

I was quite rejoiced in the good account I received of you yesterday through my dear Fanny & which I have daily planned

394. [1] On Wednesday 9 April.

soliciting from yourself, but daily failed doing. My Pen & I have quarrelled—or, rather, we sulk, for we have not had sufficient commerce even to disagree. Except for unavoidable memorandums of household matters, I have never touched it since my return home.[1]—But for the generous kind—& almost incomparable companion whose continual & unwearied study is my happiness, I know not into what sort of a lethargy my mind might fall. My dear Boy, too, with my domestic Concerns, give me constant employment, unstrung as I am, past all description, for mental exertions. Retirement is a woeful encourager of Dejection! & the last receipt I would prescribe for recovering the wounds of disappointment. The bustle of the World is, indeed, at such times, repugnant to the feelings, but I believe it very necessary for fitting us to live in it. I pitied my dearest Father at first for being compelled to rush into it,[2] but I now rejoice such was his situation as to make it inevitable; for I find by my own sad experience how ǀ ill retreat agrees with shaken health & repining spirits—for though I do my best, & am with two persons dearer to me than my life, I have so much time for retrospection & regret, & so much opportunity for nourishing grief, that not all my sense of its uselessness can conquer its ascendance. A rural spot & existence such as ours, nearly secluded from all commerce with the World, is perhaps —where the mind is at ease, the love of the Country predominant, & the internal arrangement happy, the most blessed this Earth can bestow—such, till now, we, at least, have found it. — — but for the visits of Affliction it is the most dangerous that can be imagined. Busy scenes, & varied occupations, are certainly the best friends to sorrow—they force the thoughts to other subjects, & the mental Eye to other views, till, insensibly, the accommodation comes on to Life as it *is*, which removes from our constant meditation the vainly tormenting phantoms of Life such as we would have it. Very unfortunately for a juncture such as this, Mr. Lock's family—our only sympathising friends & cheering society—After spending a fortnight at Blackheath, all went to Town for 6 weeks. For

375. [1] Presumably on 12 Apr. (L. 374).

[2] CB related in his 'Memoirs' (Berg) that it was long before he went into society. 'I was so much afflicted and out of spirits at the unfair loss of this beloved daughter, that I hardly accepted of any invitations to dinners, assemblies or concerts for near 3 months. I neither went to the Club or Theatres.'

common Acquaintance I ¹ am unfit, & if I were not, the roads all around us are impassable for Lady visiting on foot—so that we are wholly & literally *des Recluses*. My Alex, however, improves in all that I can teach, & my Gardener is laboriously recovering from his winter misfortunes. He is now raising a Hillock by the Gate for a view of Norbury Park from our Grounds,³ & he has planted Potatoes upon almost every spot where they can grow. The dreadful price of provisions makes this our first attention.⁴ The poor people about us complain they are nearly starved, & the Children of the Journeymen of the Tradesmen at Darking come to our door to beg half pence for a little Bread! What the occasion of such universal dearth can be we can form no notion, & have no information; the price of *Bread* we can conceive from the bad Harvest,—but Meat—Butter—& *shoes!*—nay, all sort of nourriture or cloathing, seem to rise in the same proportion, & without any adequate cause.⁵ The imputed one of the War does not appear to me sufficient, though the draw back from all, by the Income Tax⁶ is severely an underminer of comfort. What is become of the Campaign? are both parties incapacitated from beginning? or is each waiting a happy moment to strike some definitive stroke?—we are strangely in the dark about all that is going on, & unless you ¹ will have the compassion to write us some News, we may be kept so till Mr. Locke returns. The kind visit of poor Charles was most grievously ill paid by bad Weather & a fierce attack of his old pain—& he left us the next day quite comfortless at such a termination of his generous kindness. I have heard, however, he is since better, & we hope to see him in a fairer season. Your golden Pippin Tree has 3 blossoms upon it this spring, for the first time—& M. d'A. hopes you will not again out-stay his peas.

I beg my kindest Love to Fanny—I will write to her by the

³ Constance Hill, *Juniper Hall* (1904), pp. 241–2, says that in her day the mound was still there.

⁴ The parliamentary committees (L. 368 n. 4) had strongly recommended substitutes (for bread) such as potatoes.

⁵ Elizabeth Lady Holland, on 11 June 1800, wrote: 'Bread is 17½*d*. the quartern loaf, butcher's meat from one shilling to 14*d*. pr. lb, poultry enormously dear; and every other article of consumption in proportion', see *The Journal of Elizabeth Lady Holland (1791–1811)*, ed. the Earl of Ilchester (2 vols., 1908), ii. 102. Cf. ii, L. 95 n. 5, where the 1791 price of meat is 6–7*d*. per pound. See also the annual average prices of corn in *AR*, 'Appendix to the Chronicle', p. 149.

⁶ See L. 312 n. 2.

next Cart that carries Greens & Flowers to Mr. Lock. I hardly know how to entreat you to write me a few lines yourself, my dearest Padre, so full I know is your time,—yet *nothing* ever so lightens my heart & chears my spirits, in all seasons, as your admirable accounts when you can indulge me with them—so that, if it were possible—it would be of great service, as well as delight to me.[7] I wish much to know a little of where you go, whom you see, & *what you think*, of these times, & whether we are to fight again, or try who can hold out longest without fighting,—& if Suwarrow[8] is alive only in your march, or meriting such another, & if the archduke *Charles*[9] is as worthy as ever of a Christian name so dear & so respected as that he claims is to the Heart of my dearest Padre's ever most dutiful

& affect^e

F. d'A.

M.d'A's tender respects, & my bold Boy's plump Love. | I would keep this for Mr. Lo[cke]'s cart, but that I am not yet certain of its day of passage.

376   West Humble, [9 May 1800]

To Frances Phillips, *later* Raper

A.L. (The Hyde Collection), *n.d.*
Single sheet 4to   2 pp.   *pmks* ⟨ ⟩ 9 MY 1800   wafer
Addressed: Miss Phillips / at Dr. Burney's / Chelsea College / Middlesex
Endorsed: June 1800

West Humble.

What a dear Girl you are, my Fanny—what a dear good Girl to give me such returns for my scanty earnings!—I am

---

7 If CB was able to comply, his letter is missing, his next extant letter being that of 27 May 1800 (Berg) concerning Phillips's request for an epitaph for Susan.

8 In spite of strenuous, if not spectacular marches and efforts, General Count Suvarov (1729–1800), the Russian field marshal, disappointed of the help he had expected from his allies, had been defeated by Massena on 26 Sept. 1799. He returned to Russia and died in disgrace on 18 May 1800, his series of brilliant victories for the moment forgotten in favour of the great defeat.

9 Archduke Charles of Austria (1771–1847). FBA, doubtless recalling his victories in the field (including that of 29 Mar. 1799 over Jourdan), had probably also read his circular letter (*The Times*, 30 Dec. 1799), in which 'The HOUSE of AUSTRIA disclaims the reproach and the insinuation of listening to a SEPARATE PEACE'.

regaled my love, by what regales you, & far from blaming your dissipation, as you call it, I rejoice you have such innocent recreations, as best support your spirits, & encourage your exertions to keep up your dearest Grandpapa's.

[Hav]e *Music, reading, & Italian,* take their turn,—for I know you will lament missing such opportunities if neglected now. You are very good to tell me of your *workmanship,* & beginning stores. I am charmed you are to go to De Montfort[1] with sweet Mrs. Angerstein. Pray indulge me with a full account of your dinner, party, & the performance—such Letters from you are truly interesting to me—& every word relative to that loved Family is next dearest to me after our own. Dear Norbury! how right is his spirit, & how tender at the same time is his Heart! How I love him!—& how I love his love of my dearest Fanny!— I grieve I cannot write to him thus, by free conveyance. Pray tell him nothing else stops my more speedy answers. Give my best Love & duty to my dearest Father—& remember me most kindly to my Sister & M[r.] B[urney] & all your cousins & Mrs. Sandford & Mrs. Rishton when you see them. God bless you— |

I will not attempt to say what I feel about Harriet[2]—can *she* be good who so little feels goodness?—I own I doubt—I trust Augusta's[2] *Heart* will guide her judgement, & better direct a truer Piety—a piety to love *good works,* & reverence *good workers—*

The head of Galileo[3] which Mr. Locke presents to my dear Father will accompany this, & be ready for the first time you call again or send.

376. [1] Joanna Baillie (1762–1851) published *De Monfort* in the first volume of her *Plays on the Passions* (1798). First performed at Drury Lane on Tuesday 29 Apr. 1800, it ran until 9 May.
[2] Fanny Phillips's cousins Harriet and Augusta Kiernan (iii, L. 215 n. 2).
[3] Cf. L. 347 n. 7.

377   [West Humble,] 20 May [1800]

From M. d'Arblay
To Madame d'Arblay

A.N.[1] (Berg), 20 May

Double sheet 12mo ($3\frac{1}{4} \times 4''$) written on the *recto* of the first page 1 p.
The double sheet is sewn into a marbled paper cover ($3\frac{1}{2} \times 4''$) with two other double sheets, one of which is partly torn away.

What do you speak of a mind at a loss to express it self, you who are so well gifted with all what can deck thoughts by words—Try to understand what I mean and cannot write. What you told me just now of our darling seems to me a very endearing consolation for your too much though so justly afflicted soul. Don't forget that our beloved sister wished above all to see you happy. Her everlasting love is the same, and your happiness is yet her impérissable wish. Why will you not gratify it! — —

378   [West Humble, 20 May 1800]

To M. d'Arblay

A.N. (Berg), *n.d.*

Two double sheets 12mo ($3\frac{1}{4} \times 4''$) written on the *verso* of the first page of the first ds. and the *recto* and *verso* of the first page of the second ds. of the booklet described above. 3 pp.

Hélas—Je fais de mon mieux—et faire davantage me paroitrois l'oublier—du moins, me passer d'Elle—selon le jugement sur les morts du Docteur Johnson. qu'on peut se passer de tout le

---

377. [1] This note was treated as a *thème* and like those in ii, Appendix, 188–205, corrected by Madame d'Arblay as follows:

p. 1, l. 3: what can   *corrected to* that can
     l. 10: all to   *corrected to* all things to
     l. 12: her impérissable *corrected to* her never ending

Monde.[1] Il me semble, je l'avoue, que cela n'est que juste, qu'autre fois j'ai crue severe—mais—ce n'est pas de mon propre experience à moi que je le dis! Oh non—d'Elle je ne me passerai jamais—d'Elle—de vous—de mon Petit— |

Ecrivez moi, par reponse, les noms de chacun de vos Parens, commençant par le plus prochain, M. vôtre oncle Bazile—après cela son frere, ou ses freres, me donnant un petit page sur chacun, afin de me faire me ressouvenir du moins de leurs noms, et leurs degrés de parenté, & de vôtre opinion de leurs caracteres.[2] |

Eh bien, mon maître, vous ne me repondez pas? Dites moi, je vous prie, quelque chose de vôtre maison, et de tout ceux qui peuvent encore être en vie—parlez moi de cet aimable M. Bazille, nommez moi la rue où il demeure, contez moi tout ce qu'il peut lui concerne—Je m'interresse à tout—& vous me parlerai de Mᵉ vôtre tante après, et fort au longue.[3] |

378. [1] See *Life*, iii, 136–7.
[2] A suggested topic for a series of *thèmes*, such as are printed in ii, Appendix, 188–205.
[3] FBA's own text was corrected by M. d'A as follows:

11.	Il me semble . . . severe	*to* Ce jugement qui m'avait jusqu'a present paru severe j'avoue que je ne le crois que juste.
1.	de mon propre . . . dis	*to* mon experience qui me le fait dire.
11.	d'Elle—de vous—de mon Petit—	*to* d'Elle—ni de vous—ni de mon Petit—
11.	me ressouvenir . . . parenté	*to* du moins ressouvenir de leurs noms, et de leurs degrés de parentés
1.	tout ceux	*to* tous ceux
1.	ce qu'il peut lui concerne	*to* ce qui peut le concerner
1.	vous me parlerai	*to* vous me parlerez
1.	fort au longue.	*to* fort au long.

[West Humble, 13 June 1800]

To Esther (Burney) Burney

A.L. (Berg), *n.d.*
Double sheet 4to 3 pp. *pmks* LEATHERHEAD 13 JUN 1800
wafer
Addressed: Mrs. Burney, / Beaumont Street / Devonshire Street / Portland
Place / London
Endorsed by EBB: *sic* / June 14th *1800* / June 14. 1800

M. d'Arblay charges me, my dearest Esther, to write some
little explanation of the Note in which, by sudden impulse, he
enclosed the Letter to you which I had prepared for the Post.[1]
M. Bourdois is the only Friend he has ever seen in England who
was Born in his own Town, Joigny; he has known him all his life,
& not only has that early attachment of first youth alive, but
loves him also though the medium of a Brother who was amongst
his very peculiar Favourites. Me Bourdois, the Mother of this
gentleman, still resides at Joigny,[2] where the beloved maternal
uncle of M. d'Arblay lives:[3]—it is therefore very strongly the
wish M. d'A. that this Friend should be well received by *MY*
Friends, & conceive a favourable idea of the connexions he has
formed with his English Wife—not merely for the pleasure M.
Bourdois may himself receive, but for that which it may be in
his power, whenever a Peace carries him back to his own
Country, to give to his truly revered uncle. For this reason, he
trusts, you will pardon his entreating you to make a new
acquaintance, which he would not idly intrude upon you.

He by no means, however, wishes you to make a concert, or
great party for him—that would not answer his intentions,
which are simply to let him see, in a friendly manner, yourself
& your family, without form, or shew, or ceremony, but with
kindness & intimacy, & to put him upon that list of Callers who
are admitted, for a little chatting visit, at such times as they
happen to present themselves when you are not particularly
engaged or busy. This, he says, will infinitely more gratify M.
Bourdois than any set party. Various *revolutionary* fatigues &

379. [1] M. d'A's note is missing.
[2] See L. 381 n. 1.
[3] Jean-Baptiste Bazille (iii, L. 231 n. 3).

struggles & misfortunes & contentions, make him now only earnest for quiet society, not public amusement. M. d'Arblay bids me also add he hopes Richard will come forward also upon this occasion—though his chief dependence is upon Marianne, for as she has the most leisure, he has the less scruple, he says, in charging her to *faire l'aimable* the most liberally.

I have the less reluctance in executing this commission, because M. Bourdois is a man whom you will all find will gain upon you by acquaintance. He is one of the most obliging, | generous, feeling, & sweet-tempered creatures, with an exceeding good understanding & much cultivation, that you well can know.

God bless you, my dearest Esther—I am getting rather, I think, better—SLOWLY! SLOWLY! — — I hope soon to hear from you in answer to my last.

Kind Love to Mr. Burney — — & —

NB. all this is necessarily public, as Mr dA makes his recommendation to you all—but I must add, privately, There are some Family reasons, which I cannot explain till we meet, that make me as anxious as Mr d'Arblay himself that this Gentleman should *like Beaumont street.*

380   [West Humble, *post* 18 June 1800]

To David Ritchie

A.L.S., draft (Barrett, Eg. 3698, f. 229), *n.d.*, written on p. 3 of an A.L.S. double sheet 4to, from Da⟨vid?⟩ Ritchie, *dated*: 18 June 1800 3 pp. *pmk* 18 JU .800 wafer *addressed*: Madame De Arblay / Bookham / near Leatherhead / Surry

Edited by FBA, p. 1, *annotated*: D. Ritchie's Project. And Reply. p. 4, *Docketed*: H—11b

The answer.

Sir,

I am much obliged to the good opinion & kind intention which have induced you to desire to include me in your plan;[1]

380. [1] In a letter of 18 June (Barrett, Eg. 3698, ff. 228–9b) David Ritchie (1763–1844), minister of Kilmarnock (1800), ordained by the Presbytery of Edinburgh (1797), D.D. (1813), had invited FBA to contribute as the Muse Euterpe to a periodical work he planned to call 'The Piety of the Universe' or 'The perfection of the Deity displayed in the External World'.

but as I neither feel abilities nor courage to enter such lists, I can only beg you to accept my thanks, & to believe me, with every good wish for the success of your laudable project,

Sir,

Your obed[t] servt.

F d Arblay.

381   [West Humble, *c*. 20 June 1800]

To Esther (Burney) Burney

A.L. (Berg), *n.d.*
Single sheet folio   2 pp. with a wafer tear on upper right margin   *pmks*
DARKING ⟨21⟩ JUN 1800 wafer
Addressed: Mrs. Burney / Beaumont Street, / Devonshire Street / Portland Place— / London
Endorsed by EBB: June 1800   [*in pencil*:] Letter 1st
Also copy in hand of M.d'A (West Humble Letter Book, pp. 125–7, Osborne)

A friend of M. d'A.'s—a son of a physician,[1] of a very respectable family, whose eldest Brother is now also a physician of the first eminence & distinction & fortune in Paris, was going, just before the Revolution, to be married to a young person immensely rich—but the revolution broke off the match, & he entered the army—&, after various events, he became, like so many mo[re] a poor Emigrant in England; where he resided in a Country town fo[r] some years, devoting his hours to *STUDY* & *GARDENING* alternately, & waiting, in utter privacy & retirement, the hopes of some change in his situation, which was *ALL BUT* destitute, yet supported with the utmost fortitude & patience & good humour. In this interval, he passed, occasion-

381 [1] Edmé-Joachim Bourdois (b. 1721), sieur de la Motte, docteur en médecine at Joigny, had married on 20 Feb. 1747 Edmée (1727–*pre* 27 Sept. 1800), daughter of Edmé Moreau, notaire et tabellion du comte de Joigny. They had three sons and a daughter: Edme-Joachim Bourdois de la Motte (1754–1837), chevalier (1812), a physician in Paris; M. d'A's friend Lambert Antoine Bourdois de Bréviande (1761–1806), see iii, L. 245 n. 10; Joseph-Marie Bourdois de Paroy (1765–*post* Sept. 1800), mort en émigration, garde du Roi dans la compagnie de Luxembourg; and Edmée-Flore Bourdois (b. 1759), who had married a M. Goudot de Vermond (d. 1785), officier d'Infanterie. Most of the information above was kindly supplied by Mlle Vanneroy of the Municipal Library of Joigny as excerpted from 'Notes concernant la Famille Bourdois prises par Perille-Courcelles, Avocat à Joigny de 1820 à 1830 . . . continuée par Mr. Piochard de la Brulerie'.

ally, a few days with us, & always appeared to me so amiable, that when, about a year & half ago, he came to take leave, upon a new plan formed with the Count de Ricci,[2] from which he hoped to ameliorate his affairs by commerce, I was really quite sorry to part with him, & M. d'A. was extremely dejected. But he was tired of inactive waiting, & we wondered not at his resolution.—We were long in ignorance of his fate—but at length, very lately, were most agreeably surprised by his sight & his history—he had succeeded in his enterprise, & was returned to England entirely at ease, & in full expectation of securing, before the end of August, all his new fortune in the Bank of England.—'Now, then, quoth I M. B[ourdois]—you must *marry*—you are just the man to be happy in domestic life.' 'I assure you, ma'am, he answered, domestic life has long been all I have covetted: I may truly say ever since I saw how happy it has made M. d'Arblay—ever since I was first at Bookham, I have thought This is the life which would now suit me best.—' —And, lest this should not be flattering enough, he soon added That he thought, also, his best chance for attaining it, would be with an *English* woman.—'We must look about for you, then, cried I,—but *money*—I suppose there must be, of course, *Money*?' 'Why, answered he, if I met with a woman of irreproachable conduct, & amiable manners & character, whom I could love, & persuade to have the goodness to love *me* — — I think I have enough for *two*.'

Soon after this, M. d'A. came to me with a look of great vivacity, & said 'I have been finding out a Wife for Bourdois!' 'And who?'—'Marianne.' I laughed—as nearly as I *now* laugh!—& felt incredulous, but yet declared nothing could more delight me, if he thought that really & truly M. B[ourdois] was serious in saying he required no fortune.—M. d'A. assured me he had sounded him, & found that he was quite sincere, & highly disposed to listen to any hint or advice upon this subject he could receive through our means; that he had been so much struck with our happiness, as long to wish to tread in the same paths, though *Fortune NOW* had so far superiorly favoured him, that it would not be with the same rigid œconomy. I was quite enchanted, I own, at this idea—for in many particulars I

2 See L. 292 and n. 11.

thought the two persons alike, & in all, that there are no differences that could interfere with happiness to both. Finding this my opinion, my dear zealous Mate went & spoke out to M. B.—though, you are sure, all *en badinant*—however, M. B. seriously declared he had such firm reliance on the Friendship & Feeling of M. d'A. & on the opinion, &c, of his Wife, that I he liked the idea of all things,—& they settled between them that the acquaintance should immediately be made. M. B. said he would not ACT, even if all answered his [wi]shes, till his affairs were completely arranged, so as to obviate any uneasiness to *her* [*tear*] friends, in case she should be favourable: but he thought he could do nothing so [we]ll as to see her, & converse with her, & find how their humours tallied, & see if [*tear*] he had, first, a *desire*, & next, a *chance* of obtaining her esteem & approbation. [I be]gged M. d'A. to assure him, I was *certain* she would not give her hand without her heart, as she was a particularly honourable character—&c & a thousand other things, similar, passed—& though *to me* M. B. never spoke of the idea, to M. d'A. when they were alone, he spoke of nothing else! My room now is too short for more detail—but to tell you that his intentions, should they *mutually* like each other, are the most generous imaginable—such as have drawn tears into my Eyes, & a most fervant wish for the event into my heart. M. d'A. has had a private Letter from him in consequence of every meeting,[3] & he writes the most open & undisguised acknowledgements that, thus far, she answers all his expectations & all his wishes, & that he is *almost in despair* at the threat of a breach in the opening prospect, from her plan of going for some months to a distant Country. Now, my dearest Esther, thus the matter now stands. I have *no* authority to make you this confidence, which must be sacred; but I could not hear of the Worcester Journey,[4] at so critical period, without thinking it my real duty to let *you* into the secret, that you may judge if, or not, it would be best to postpone her leaving London, till she sees whether a visit of 3 months may not change into an eligible establishment for her whole life, with a worthy, cultivated, generous, & most kind hearted Man, who would make, I feel no doubt, one of the most amiable husbands in the World to a woman who could deserve

---

[3] These letters are missing.
[4] Marianne's usual summer visits to her aunts (see i, p. Intro., p. lxxv).

& return his affection. Think it over, my dearest sister, & write
to me fully & confidentially. There are so few men of this dis-
interested nature now in the World, that it is well worth consideration. He writes, too, in highest terms of you, Mr. B[urney]
Fanny P[hillips] & Richard. He is *warmly* disposed to the whole
family—*certainly* I shall invite M[arianne] again—nothing but
my sadness has prevented me.—& that has made me think it
kinder to *her* to defer the invitation. I will *now* have YOU direct
the time for it. I have no right to give you leave to consult ANY
ONE about this affair as it *now* stands—we must *only* consult with
each other—M. B. loves my alex—as if he were his own son—
Can you wonder I am interested for him? *him*—& a D[aughte]r
of my dearest sister?—& that D[aughte]r my own first natural
favourite?[5] nevertheless but for this W[orcester] scheme, I
should not have thought myself justified in giving even YOU this
intimation; but have let the matter take its own Course. As it is,
should all prove abortive, I must depend upon your burying
this Confidence in your own breast. I have said I believe *her*
affections wholly disengaged: I never examined her, but the
general appearance has a sort of gay ease, that announces
internal freedom. If I am mistaken upon this important point,
I am sure you will *now* give me a hint for *his* sake, to drop the
idea.

382   West Humble, 20 June 1800

To Sarah (Rose) Burney

A.L. (in the possession of F. W. Hilles), 20 June 1800
Double sheet 8vo   3 pp.   *pmks*   DARKING   21 JU 1800   21 JU 1800
on p. 4 *of which Mrs. Burney scribbled a draft reply.*
Addressed: Mrs. Burney, / Dr. Burney's / Greenwich / Kent

20. June. 1800
West Hamble Dorking.
Alas, my dear Rosette, from ME have you been expecting
comfort & chear?—To feel for your sufferings, & sincerely wish
you happy & well, I can still do as well as ever, & as warmly;

5 FBA's first (or eldest) niece. Cf. *ED* ii. 164, n. 2; 171–9.

but to keep up any correspondence, to write a single Letter, except of necessary business, or some peculiar occasion, —— this is no time for such an application to me! I have lost, at present, all energy & courage for Letter writing—it makes me melancholy only to take up a pen—it revives & redoubles my affliction to be forced to use it. Time only can soften off these sad feelings, but while they remain thus bitterly, I could only add to your gloom, not diminish it, by ¹ complying with your request.

I am truly sorry for poor Mr. & Mrs. Foss—how greatly are they to be pitied!—¹

To your plans I say nothing, as you cannot reflect, without being sure of my opinion: but you must be certain of always finding such a poor welcome as we are able to give you at Westhamble, when our single little Chamber is at liberty—at present, M. d'Arblay has engaged a Gentleman to come & Garden with him, whom we expect every day, & we have only that one room.² Though, indeed, while you are still so unrecovered from the illness you mention, & which I grieve to hear of, I ¹ think it would be great imprude⟨nce⟩ to come to a place so out of reach of all medical help. I know not of any physician in all the neighbourhood, nor even at any distant town: & I should be ill at ease to have you removed from Dr. Millman³ to a house so ill adapted for sickness as ours.

I have heard nothing of my poor Brother since the rash you spoke of preceding his journey to Harrowgate, except from Fanny Phillips that he did not look at all well. I am very sorry—& must hope for better times to All!—

Adieu, my dear Rosette—M. d'A. desires his Love & Comp^{ts} My dear child is well, & our sole joy. I shall be heartily glad to hear your health is restored—your spirits will then be restored also, I trust.

---

382. ¹ L. 330 n. 1.

² Rosette's confused resentment at what she considered a rebuff may be reflected in the incoherent scribble on p. 4 of FBA's letter:

To ask *favors* my *Dear* Madam *merely* to have them *refus'd*—is *the* | ⟨that cant⟩ | & unnecessary—to see *you* my *best* & *Dearest* frd woud indeed be a *Comfort* Home I cannot *live* long if I am further *oppos'd* I can do no more & only beg to die in peace no matter how soon *Ask* any *thing* my *Belov'd & honoured Mother* I most *solemnly* promise you *I* will answer in the affirmative.

³ Francis Milman (1746–1821), M.D. (1776), President of the Royal College of Physicians (1811–12), etc. (see *DNB*).

To Esther (Burney) Burney

A.L. (Berg), *n.d.*
Double sheet large 4to   4 pp.   *pmks*   EPSOM   ⟨2⟩ JUL 1800   wafer
Addressed: Mrs. Burney / Beaumont Street / Portland Place, / London—/ If
not there, to be / forwarded to Richmond directly.
Endorsed by EBB: Answered / July 6th / 1800 / Mrs. d'Arblay /

I hardly know how to write to you, my dearest Esther, I am
so compleatly perplexed—in all things but my wishes—what
to say of my *VISION*, as you will call it, though prophetic of
reality I must still hope it. A cruel circumstance has just happened, which not only *undoubtedly retards* all operations, but,
eventually, *may* wholly *impede* them. The Agent of M. B[our-
dois] is just dead,—died, I think, upon his passage, but of that
I am [not] so clear, as that his death has involved M. B. in
business & alarm,—business that calls for nearly every moment
of his time in Town, & alarm lest his affairs should so be prejudiced as to force him back to America to set them right. He
came to us with this mortifying event on Saturday,—& left us
on Tuesday yesterday, at 5 in the Morning: or rather, left our
village, where we procured him a Bed, since here we have but
one Room. This so excessively disappointed me, that I have
scarcely known how to write to you, from not being able,
myself, though upon the spot, & in the fullest confidence of M. B.
to decide what is best, at present, to do;—stop the acquaintance, till his affairs are arranged, from the fear it may end in
nothing,—or encourage it through-out its difficulties & uncertainties, from the hope it may end to our satisfaction &
happiness.—It will be full 6 weeks before he can judge how he
may be situated.

Mean while, I have at least the pleasure—if it prove not a
melancholy one—to assure my dearest Hetty that his good
opinion of Marianne goes on augmenting, that he is pleased
with all he sees of her, & that her own behaviour & demeanour
are perfectly what I could wish them—unaffected, chearful,
& sensible. You may believe, thus precariously circumstanced,
I am studious to avoid giving her the smallest hint of what I
have written to you, yet 'tis impossible she should not see that

427

M. B. though never exceeding the gallantry of almost every French gentleman, watches her with a very flattering air of approbation as well as attention—but I delight to see that it excites in her neither coquetry nor prudery,—yet as much of pleasure as I desire, for any thing marking *partiality* would, now, make me uneasy—though, should all go well, I should not only wish, but think it indispensable to their mutual happiness.

This, however, will not be difficult to raise, should the vision realize: he is so very deserving, so truly amiable, open hearted, kind, & worthy, that her Heart need only indulge its best feelings to find itself attached to him. *You*, I am sure, will be so sincerely. I heartily wish you could have heard the conversation he had with M. d'A. on the subject, & one which followed with myself. To M. d'A, he made known his purpose to fulfill some duties which he has prescribed himself for *others*, before he suffers himself to make his own settlement—he has a Mother & a sister[1] whom he loves tenderly, & he determines to secure them each some sort of annuity from his fortune, as the first use he will make of it, after merely securing his ¦ own independance: this Mother & sister he fears to be quite ruined by the effects of the Revolution, though they are both still in France, which they have never quitted. This Sister, till this new plan occurred, he meant to make mistress of his house when the Peace allows his joining her. she is an extremely amiable woman, & a widow without Children. Nor is this all his pious generosity suggests to take place of self-consideration: a particular friend, to whom he owed his own late success, in its commencement, is now utterly ruined himself, by the breaking of the House, in Hamburg, to which he belonged;[2]—this excellent man, M. B., will not rest till he can find some means to help to re-instate him. These 3 he holds as sacred duties—& when they are fulfilled—what a prize—should all go well—will be the Man who has such a Heart for our Marianne!—I am more interested than ever in desiring the union, though some what more fearful than ever of success. In a very long conference I had with him on Monday,[3] he spoke the most gratifying & flattering things of M[arianne] that could be heard, & lamented

---

383. [1] For Bourdois's family, see L. 381 n. 1. For his widowed sister Madame de Vermond see v, L. 527.

[2] The comte de Ricci (L. 292 n. 11).   [3] On Monday 30 June.

his inability to give immediate way to that sort of distinction of manner to her that might draw her out to discourse seriously, let him dive into her sentiments, & lead to what he earnestly desires, a *mutual* attachment.—But he will take no Measures to endeavour to engage her affections, or give her any idea of what passes between him, M. d'A. & me, till *sure* there could be no after draw-back from accident or pecuniary disappointment. So implicit, said he, is my reliance on the friendship & honour of M. d'A. & upon your &c—&c—&c— / (unwriteable) / that, I protest, if settled in my affairs, I should ⎮ think myself secure of felicity to take, from your joint hands, a wife blindfolded!— but when, to such a conviction of what must be her worth & character, I join a person, appearance, & manner that so com- pleatly meet my taste, & promise me happiness—I think I may venture to affirm that I shall not a moment hesitate in endeav- ouring to make myself acceptable to her, by engaging her regard, if my expectations are answered of realizing what I think necessary to the joint comfort of our lives.' Such is the now state of matters, my dearest Esther—he will be here again next week for a few days, & then give himself wholly to business that will prevent his return for some time. What can we arrange? To prevent *her* suspicion, it may perhaps be best to let the Worcester journey take place immediately after she leaves us—& *I hope* best that it should last but 6 weeks instead of 3 or 4 Months. It is a delicate business: but my great point will be gained, of their seeing each other so intimately, before that long separation, as to *fix him*—I will trust, to be always hers, if his affairs second his generous nature. If not, we must submit—& try only to remember that, after a peace, he means to settle in France—*that*, I told him, was the *only* objection there could be on OUR side, that *I* could form—as want of Fortune might be on *his*. To the last he would not listen—to the first, he said in *our* family, at least, a French husband must be seen to have power to make an English wife happy—& the example would not, he hoped, be set in vain. Pray write openly—I shall take care to receive my Letters alone till I hear from you, that M[arianne] may not even see your hand, to avoid wonder &c Heaven bless you, my dearest Etty—

[*marginal writing*, p. 1]

When you write to M[arianne] take no notice of this Letter, as I do not mention writing to her.

[*in pencil*]

Not a Syllable relative to our private communications concerning M[arianne], S[ophy], & F[anny] shall transpire— Depend upon that in any conversation with M[arianne]—

384   [West Humble, mid-July 1800]

To Esther (Burney) Burney

A.L. (Berg), *n.d.*
Double sheet 4to   4 pp.   wafer
Addressed: Mrs. Burney, / Beaumont Street, / Portland Place—
Docketed in pencil, p. 1: mid July 1800

With so very important an interest to discuss, it seems almost shocking, my dearest Esther, that I have not written sooner; but if I could give you the history of my Mind, as well as of my time, you would not wonder—but I must leave both untold, to come at once to the business of our mutual thoughts—for yours, I am sure, though you are so distant from the scene of action, will as constantly have taken that bent as mine while I have been upon the spot.

Our dear Marianne will have related to you the unexpected event of last night. Nothing could have been more sudden—or less designed by M[r] B[ourdois] himself till a very short time before it took place. But, pleased more & more with Marianne, & more & more seriously persuaded he was in the right road to happiness, he felt uneasy in letting her depart for such a length of absence, in utter ignorance of the impression she had made, as well as without power to divine whether or not she felt any interest in what might be his opinion of her. He consulted me, in the same open & unreserved manner he has done through the whole affair, if I thought he had better, or not, hint to her his sentiments & his situation. I was truly & completely at a loss what to advise,—I could not think of him as I do, & not wish the advancement of the intercourse,—yet was fully sensible of the justice & propriety [|] of his obstacles to any declaration, while unable himself to answer for his own future conduct. I will not enter upon all the pros & cons of this conflict—they were really very embarrassing, though the pleasure with which I saw our wishes so amply fulfilled in the real regard conceived for our dear Girl by so deserving a character, made it impossible for me to make the distress very serious—except when the chance of such an attachment's being thwarted by untoward circumstances made me *fear* its becoming reciprocal.—But I hope Marianne will remember better than I am now able to recount all I endeavoured to explain to her of the truly honourable & truly kind feelings which kept up the struggle in the bosom of Mr B. till a sudden opportunity of being alone with her finished them, by a declaration to herself of the incertitude of his situation, & the perplexity & distress with which it combatted the desire he felt every moment encreasing of avowing to her frankly his esteem & regard.

Things being brought thus forward, my dearest Esther, I am rejoiced, now, that Marianne is going so soon to Worcester, since it would be really wrong to let what seems to me their mutual propensity to one another augment by continual intercourse, while any doubt hangs upon the powers of Mr B. to follow his now *decided* inclination. Marianne will tell you all I myself know upon this subject, in which, as we cannot act, a more minute knowledge would be useless, & therefore I forbear seeking it. she will tell you, too, all I know of his expectations & hopes in respect to his affairs, & of the manner in which they were [|] changed into such prosperity as to give him a *certain* independance & competence for himself—& the most rational & probable belief in *acquiring* one that, without imprudence, he may share with another. But this waits TIME for *proof* — — & therefore their present separation I now look upon as a *fortunate* circumstance, in keeping back any further engagement, mental or verbal, till they know what may be their destiny. And this, upon cool deliberation, is his own opinion—especially as, had she remained with you or us, he would *undoubtedly* have postponed informing her of his sentiments till he could solicit a full knowledge of her own, & yours & Mr. Burney's consent. Indeed, were it now not to take place, he would very seriously reproach himself for what would, then, make him seem acting with dangerous & unnecessary precipitation. This same reasoning, upon further consideration, also, appears to point out that they had better not correspond. When he first mentioned it to me, the pleasure which I thought it would produce—to *both* —& my own peculiar alacrity of wishing to shew Mr. B. my entire reliance in his honour & discretion, which I believe to be even *exemplary*, made me hastily give an affirmative voice to the idea—but it will not bear reflection, because I do not see how she can answer him, without involving herself in a positive engagement—which he is the first to even *desire* she should think herself free from, though he now holds himself bound if his hopes are accomplished at the expected arrival of certain Vessels; &c—He, too,—how could he write?—to treat only of his affairs, places the delay in the light of some *merchandise*, & would be indelicate on her part, & seem ungenerous towards him: & to write of his hopes & feelings would be just as premature as to speak of them. It will surely, therefore, be best, & clearest, & wisest, to have no correspondence till his doubts are removed. He is sensible of this now himself, & was awakened to discuss & decide against it, by her own evidently appearing startled at the proposal. I am very glad she did, as it sustains up to the end the good sense, modesty, & propriety which have marked her conduct during the whole *unconscious probation*, & which have confirmed his esteem, & deserved it. |

I know well that nothing will more gratify my kindest Hetty than to hear that the mingled anxiety & pleasure of the whole of this transaction, with what I think must ultimately conclude in the permanent & very rare happiness of our dear Marianne with so dear a friend of my own most invaluable Life's Partner, has shaken me from my deep sorrows, frequently *really*, & always *apparently* relieved me from their weight. I now, however, feel an absolute necessity of a little perfect rest—rest & recollection—for this has been a great effort upon my spirits, & they *harrassed*, though certainly *lightened*. I express myself ill—but you will conceive me—

Tell my dear Marianne how truly satisfied & pleased she left me—I know she will not be indifferent to that—I would send her my *warmest joy* but for the perverse *if's* that check it— M. d'A. however, will not hear of them—but we had all better keep them in mind till they terminate: Mr. B. had earnestly

wished yourself & Mr. Burney alone to be acquainted with the
state of the business—but I have been representing to him *all
about* dear good Blue,[1] her claims & her discretion & her fondness, & he is even happy to yield to them. God bless you, my
dearest Esther: & may Heaven grant this solace to your long
maternal cares!

pray settle with M. d'A. when we may have the hope of your
coming, my dearest Etty & Mr. B[urney] & Amelia—

385   [West Humble,] 17 July 1800

To M. d'Arblay

A.L. (Berg), 17 July 1800
Double sheet 8vo   4 pp.   *pmks*   DARKING   18 JUL 1800   wafer
Addressed: Alex. d'Arblay Esqr, / at Antoine Bourdois Esqr, / N° 85—
corner of Clarges Street, / Piccadilly, / London
Edited by FBA, p. 1, *annotated*: (18)

July 17. 1800

I am going to answer to-morrow Morning's Letter—

Oui, mon ami, I am bien sage,—I have reflected upon my
dear—too dear—but most sad purpose, of devoting your
absence to my cherished papers—& the idea of your repugnance
& remonstrance conquers my wish—I have not touched—I will
not even look at them.—

Yesterday I cut Roses half the day—& gave the rest to our
best beloved—whose lessons have been neglected, till he is
grown so wanton & playful I am an hour in gaining his attention to a syllable. But he is very good—very sweet—very dear—
He was terribly afflicted when he found you were gone, &
retired to cry under the Bow Window. I called to him to come
up stairs, & comfort *me*,—he dried his Eyes instantly, flew to
my arms, & said 'Yes, Mama, we'll both be one another's
companions as long as we live! but why don't Papa be our
companion too? Did Bourdois want to take him ᐟ to Mr.
Smallwood's?'[1]

384. [1] Marianne's maiden aunt Elizabeth Warren Burney (see i, Intro. p. lxxv).
385. [1] Richard Peter Smallwood (d. 1815) of Green Farm, Mickleham (see Land
Tax Assessments, 1780–1815 and the Court Roll of the Manor of West Humble).

I found he had no idea you were gone or going further, & let the matter pass, & played with him; but soon after he broke forth into an exclamation 'What a kind Boude to give Papa a ride in his Chaise!'

But when we were called to dinner, he was quite angry with Nanny for having laid the Cloth, & raising his voice to a tone of deepest authority, most emphatically said 'Nanny, you must never bring the dinner till Papa & Boude come back! Never! as long as you live!'

I was forced now to confess the truth, which he heard with great chagrin. But he was made infinitely happy in the Evening —our dearest Mr. Locke came upon Jenny, whilst I was Rose-Cutting in the Garden,—& Mrs. Locke walking by his side— I must defer telling their intelligen[ce] till we meet, except that Miss J[ennings][2] wil[l be] at Norb[ury] P[ark] *this day*—they came into our little Parlour for about half an Hour—& then I walked back with Mrs. Lock, & our happiest of little Men was carried before Mr. Lock, upon Jenny, the whole way,—& esquired me home afterwards. Imagine his joy & transport. It is arranged between Mrs. L[ocke] & Me that you are to make a private visit, *incog.* to William, to wish him joy, before the affair is announced publicly, or the Lady is seen. You will not mention it *any* where in its present state—Heaven bless you— I make a very forlorn Widow—but I have remembered your Cucumbers & your carnations, & expect a world of commendation upon your return—Will you disappoint me?

My best thanks to my sister for a most kind & comfortable Letter—& best Love to Marianne—& best Compts. to *good kind Boude*—but *best of all* come home yourself to your two fondest poor Athanases—besides—the chickens don't heed us a straw—they certainly saw you set off for London, for they eat Peas & bean[s by the] Peck, & scoff poor Alex & me, let us shout & contest the point how we can.

P.S. Pray don't let this scrawl drop or be thrown about—or out of your own hands.

---

[2] Elizabeth Catherine Jennings (*c.* 1781–1846), daughter of Henry Constantine Jennings *later* Nowell (1731–1819), virtuoso and collector (*DNB*), and his second wife (1777) Elizabeth Catherine *née* Newell (*c.* 1761–1831). The marriage of Miss Jennings and William Locke II (1767–1847) was to take place in Marylebone church on 4 Aug. 1800. See further, L. 387 n. 1.

To M. d'Arblay

A.L. (Berg), 18 July 1800
Double sheet 8vo   4 pp.   *pmks*   DARKING   JUL ⟨180⟩o
Addressed: M. d'Arblay at M. Bourdois, / Nº 85. / Corner of Clarges Street /
Piccadilly / London
Edited by FBA, p. 1, *annotated*: (19)

July 18th 1800.
West Hamble.

Vôtre chere Lettre[1] ne m'a pas fait beaucoup de mal ce matin—I read it—à nôtre maniere—to our little darling, & with great applause. He had a quarrel while dressing this morning, that will not make you very angry with him:—He had run away from being combed, till I was forced to make him stand in a corner: Nanny pressed him to come out & submit. 'Yank!' he answered—'What's that, my dear?' 'That means I won't come.' 'O, very well, sir; then I'll go about my business.' 'Adducee, Nanny!' 'What's that, sir?' 'That's I *will* come.' 'Come, then, my dear.' 'No, Nanny, yank!—'

She burst into a fit of laughter, upon which, sturdily walking up to her, with a voice of great displeasure, he said 'Don't laugh, Nanny! You must not laugh!'

'Must not I laugh, sir?'

'No, Nanny, never!'

'O la!—what for?'

'*NEVER*, I tell you, Nanny, never as long as you live—when Papa's gone away!

'I don't laugh because your Papa's gone away, my dear, I only—'

'I don't say you do, Nanny; but it *looks* as if you did,—& I don't like you should laugh at *any* thing when Papa's gone away, because it *LOOKS* as if you were ill-natured, whether you are so or not *in real*.'

And then he gravely added 'You must go & tell Betty she must not laugh neither, never as long as she lives, till Papa comes back.'

386. [1] This letter is missing.

'Why then, my dear, you must not say that nonsence.' 'What nonsence?'

'Why that yank, & Adducee—'

'What do you call that nonsence for, Nanny, | when you don't know nonsence from French?'

Nothing will, I trust, defer your return to-morrow. The Norbury family all go to Woodlands on Monday, if the Bride elect & her Mother[2] go to Berkshire or Twickenham, as is expected. I have seen some Letters which announce William to be perfectly happy. I am truly rejoiced that, the resolution taken, he is satisfied with his decision. Amelia comes to Norbury P[ark] to day, for *presentation* upon the occasion. No one else is to be admitted during this first introductory visit, nor till the business is arranged finally: but Mrs. L[ocke] is sure William will be much pleased by a private congratulatory *shake hands* from you in his own Apartment.

You give me infinite pleasure by your intimation of approbation of my dear Marianne's conduct. She is really in a trying situation. I have a Letter that is all I can wish from my dear sister, who enters into the *Worcester* & *correspondence* affairs very cordially & comfortably, & is excessively gratified by our friend's *empressement* in speaking so early   Marianne, she says, seems quite happy. |

⌐I have just written to my dear Father. Pray don't forget White,[3] Taylor, Milk nor the *cheese*. Remember me in the best way you can to *dear good Boude*,   our Boy says 'To be sure he will come back with papa, because I asked him *to come & live with us always, & he's too kind to disappoint us, because he's promised us another Visiting soon & he's broke his promise once already, Because, I suppose he forgot it.* adieu now Alex Papa.¬

² See L. 385 n. 2.   ³ See iii, L. 207 n. 4.

[West Humble, 26 July 1800]

To Esther (Burney) Burney

A.L. (Berg), *n.d.*
Double sheet large 4to   4 pp.   *pmks*   DARKING   26 JUL 1800   wafer
Addressed: Mrs. Burney / Beaumont Street / Devonshire Street / Portland
Place / London
Endorsed by EBB: ⌜1799⌝ [*corrected in pencil:*] July 26 / 1800

My dearest Esther,

I fear lest this beautiful season should be lost by further delay
of your intended kind visit—I beg you therefore to settle about
coming as soon as you conveniently can: I have written the
same to our dear Father, but can procure no satisfactory answer
—& the hope of it has kept me silent to you, as, of course, We
intreated him to name his own time. May I beg you, my dear
Hetty, to attack him yourself? to tell him when you can come,
& know if that time will be likely to clash with his own design.
There is no other person—NOW! !—! I should make you second
to,—but second *here* long—LONG may you remain! Will you be
kind enough to write me the result of what you can do after
applying to this dear personage? And then let your coming be
as speedy as to follow your intimation?

Billing & cooing are much in fashion—Mr. William Lock is
going to be married—to a very beautiful young Woman, Miss
Jennings, whose Portrait you must have seen at the Exhibition.[1]
We were presented to one another a few days ago, in the family
assemblage at Norbury Park,—but the whole party is just now
at Woodlands—I am eager they should return before your
arrival—& would therefore, as their stay is | uncertain, rather
prefer your waiting till that took place, but for my dread of a
change of weather. Decide, however, wholly for yourself—au
pluriel—as our dear *Father's* time & convenience is the only
thing serious with *us*—& all seasons will Welcome you alike
to our roof—though I wish it alas—*more*, not less of added
attraction than last year—Last year—when here—you received
that melancholy account of Her fading health[2] — — — alas—

---

387 [1] Sir Thomas Lawrence's portrait of Elizabeth Jennings (L. 385 n. 2) shown
at the spring exhibition 1799 of the Royal Academy of Arts. The *Morning Chronicle*
(29 Apr. 1799) referred to the painting as 'the prettiest female figure in the rooms'.
  [2] Cf. the opening of FBA's letter of 14 Aug. 1799 (L. 331).

that afterwards she so assiduously sought to counter act its effect! — — — its *natural* effect, of calling me over to her! — — — poor Norbury, in a Letter I have lately received from him,[3] expressly says, that he knew she would not avow her dangerous & suffering state to us, because sure, if she did, I should go to her—& sure my reception would be cruel! — — — sweet Angel! ever considering only how to spare *others*! considering it till she died the victim of her tender disinterestedness!—

I have had this morning a Letter from Marianne,[4] written in the most rational & unaffected manner possible—she plainly shews she is determined to hold her suspence with spirit, & hear its result with courage, whatever it may be—but it is also so very clear she feels the merit of M. B[ourdois] & is charmed by his avowed partiality, that I shall quite afflict myself that the affair has gone so near to her affections, should it fail. I have also a Letter from M. B.[5] lamenting in warmest terms his own uncertainties, & declaring himself wholly & forever devoted to her, should they end as he wishes, & should she shew no repugnance to receiving his homage. He professes himself, alone, in the mean time, *bound,—her* free.—Have the kindness, my dearest Hetty, to say this to her, *from me*, when you write, & to beg she will accept that, at present, at least, for an answer from myself. It is all I could say, were I to write—& writing I put aside, but for absolutely necessary occasions, as one of the evils I most shrink from. I have been forced to entreat M. d'A. in the same manner to answer for me to M. B.—who not only is tormented with his *inevitable* difficulties, but with fears that Marianne is indifferent to their conclusion—not from personal

---

[3] This letter, postmarked RAMELTON 1 JUL 1800, preserved in the Scrapbook (Berg): 'Fanny Burney and family. 1653–1890', p. 58, is quite plain on the subject: 'my dear mama often told me during her last illness that she did not mention her real situation to her friends as she saw very plainly that you would have come over to her which she did not wish as she had it not in her power to assure you of so kind a reception from every side as from her dear self . . . if Bellcotton & Mickleham had always exhibited such domestic happiness, & such tranquillity as I often figure to my self you enjoy at Westhumble what a pleasure it would have been to her during her long absence from her nearest relations & friends, to have seen some of them in Ireland.'

[4] This 'thank-you' letter, dated Worcester 22 July 1800, *pmk* 24 JY, is extant (Barrett, Eg. 3698, ff. 5–6b). It gives an account of Marianne's return to London with 'Rolla' (M. d'A) and Bourdois, her departure on Friday (18 July) for Worcester, and her reception by her aunts, who had walked a mile and a half to meet the mail coach. 'M^{rs} S[andford] has brought to Wor^r a brilliant account of the beauty of dear little Alex "*God bless him*"!'

[5] This letter is missing.

dislike to him—which he would have retired from as a man of sense, uncomplaining, but from a coldness of character. These are doubts into which I do not enter, for they ought not as yet to be discussed—& for that reason I decline *writing* him my sentiments—but I think her manifestly touched by his willing preference, & extremely sensible of his worth, & very happy in the prospect it opens to her of such a Mate—a protector—& an establishment for the rest of her Life. Indeed, if I did *not* believe this, much & affectionately as I love her, I love *him* too much, esteem & regard him too sincerely, | & *owe* too much to his extraordinary friendship & opinion of us both, to *wish*—much less promote—the union. It would be acting ill by both. However, I shall be glad when all that remains is to call her forth! I feel well assured of her *consoling propensities*, though I *would* not have them prematurely exercised.

God bless you, my dearest Hetty—& pray try to understand my embarrassed writing—& do you & dear Mr. B[urney] & Amelia fix entirely your *own* time for coming, & only write it to us, after consulting our dearest Padre—

---

388   West Humble, 28 July 1800

To Esther (Burney) Burney

A.L. (Berg), 28 July 1800
Double sheet small 4to 4 pp. *pmks* DARKING 30 JUL 1800
31 JY 1800 T.P.P. / U. wafer
 Addressed: ⌐Mrs. Burney / Beaumont street / Devonshire place / London—¬
 Re-addressed: Mrs. Burney / Mrs Lees[1] / Kew road / Richmond Surry

West Hamble,
July 28—1800

Monday[2] will perfectly do for us, my dearest Esther—but we are disappointed quite about little dear Amelia—though I dare not combat your serious objections of the pecuniary sort in bringing her, for we grieve at your own—& for so short a time—though that, also, I dare not combat. I am ill at tilting just now,

---

388. [1] See L. 333 n. 1.   [2] Monday 4 Aug.

—& scarcely know if you would not think me more generous to acquit even yourself & Mr. Burney of your promise. This, however, I cannot do, unless you tell me, *bonnement,* you should be indebted to me for such a sacrifice. I think, however, you will yourself be more comfortable for coming & talking over the innumerable things we can discuss, de vive voix, relative to our hopes & fears for dear Marianne—I have the matter & its success most seriously at Heart, & cannot tell you how deeply I shall be disappointed if the fates should prove adverse especially now, that you seem to see & feel M. B[ourdois]'s worth as we do.—& that he writes us word how much he likes my dear sister. |

We have so little—so much less than ever, at this moment, to offer you in our Cottage, that I feel a little discomforted by what you say of your reluctance to quit Richmond—My dearest Esther, give it up without scruple, if you really desire it —I can never take ill your feeling for yourself, & doing what is most comfortable to you, the great expence of the two Journies considered, & the shortness of time you destine to us: & your *previous* arrangement not to exceed it convinces me you are in earnest to be back within the week. The sweet FAMILY up the Hill are still at Woodlands, & will be all wholly engaged with the Bride elect, & bridal preparations, till after the Ceremony, which I imagine will take place in a few weeks.[3] This is much against us.—& *FOR* us, there is nothing but a solitary, though most affectionate welcome.

My desire to see you, & my fears lest I drag you | hither, with expence & inconvenience & hurry, merely from a kind apprehension of hurting me by declining to come, struggle with each other, so that I hardly know how to write—I wish I could see into you a moment! Do, however, as nearly as you can, exactly what you will *best like to do,* & believe me, my dear Hetty, that will best gratify me. our *wish* for you, I am sure you cannot doubt, the tenderness of mine, nor the warmth of Mr d'Arblay's—there is nobody—but my Father—I shall so love to embrace:—therefore, my dear Soul, understand me better than I explain myself, for I write to save the post—& I have lost all knack of being clear in a hurry.

May we beg you to settle our mids^r little business with my

---

[3] The marriage was to take place on 4 Aug.

dear Aunt Beckey?[4] M.d'A. forgot it when in Town, though he entirely meant it in setting out. We will thankfully return it when you come—& pray give her my kindest Love—& assure her I should not fail coming to Richmond, if the times were more propitious for such excursions. But they are niggardly times, & we must only pray for better.

Your pious regard to the gluttony of your litigious friend entertained me much—I think no account can be better ballanced.[5] Poor Susan Adams yesterday spent the Day with me. I am quite mortified at her unsettled state & the misconceptions that have occasioned it. And how *very* vexatious the again rejected curacy of poor Richard,[6] & the ill health & weakness that thus stop his beginning promotion!—

Adieu, my dearest Esther—If you are able to come without serious derangement, I am sure you will—if *not*, tell me so honestly—but if you don't write, We shall expect you to Tea on Monday, & dear Mr. Burney, to whom our kindest Love—& en attendant We shall Welcome the postman's absence.

I am beginning enquiries every where again for poor Susan Adams—a *nurse* place she would like best—& if possible within occasional ⟨re⟩ach of Willy—I have, therefore, caused application to be ⟨mad⟩e to Miss Angerstein at Blackheath—Love to worthy Letty [Brookes][7] M. d'A.'s *true love* to you—Alex will expect Amelia God bless you, dearest Etty—

---

[4] Doubtless the charitable donation scrupulously paid by the Burneys to elderly and indigent relatives.

[5] The anecdote is lost with EBB's letter.

[6] For a curacy previously rejected, see L. 324 and n. 7.

[7] See iii, L. 150 n. 6.

To Doctor Burney

A.L.S. (Berg), 31 July 1800
Double sheet 4to   4 pp.   *pmks*   DARKING   1 AU 1800   1 AUG 1800
wafer
Addressed: Dr. Burney / Chelsea College, / Middlesex
Endorsed by CB: 1800
Edited by FBA, p. 1, *annotated and dated*: ⁎ (5) Invite to West Hamble.
marriage of William Locke & Miss Jenyns. ⟨Wildly happy⟩ Alex.
Edited also by CFBt.

West Hamble,
July 31. *1800*

We shall delight to see you, my most dear Padre, & our dearly
loved Fanny—who shall have her *whisp*[1] without ceremony, &
she is young & healthy & gay enough to sleep well any how,
with a kind welcome & old friends.—But how can you talk of
only one night for yourself, in the first indulgence? If indeed
your engagements make that requisite, at least remember what
a Debtor you go away, & make l'amende honorable at your
return, when you fetch you dear little plump Potatoe.

The *Match broke loose* the very day after I wrote it privately:
but I am most thankful to find & observe all rises upon examination, & that the prospect is much brighter than I had conceived from my sight of its opening. The lady, indeed, has a
most distinguished lot—may she deserve it! If she should not,
Lady Rothes & I agreed, the other Day, She will have a *World
of Enemies*. For William is universally loved & admired &
esteemed—& the sweet family with which she is immediately
to live, is perhaps the first in the Kingdom for every amiable &
attractive domestic virtue. To be Daughter to Mr. & Mrs.
Locke—to be Sister to Amelia—& the chosen Wife of William
—if she has a sense of her happiness, what, on this earth, will
be incomplete?—

I met at Church last Sunday Mr. & Mrs. Pepys, & all their
fine family of tall Children[2]—& Lady Rothes persuaded me to
accompany them all to Juniper Hall, with my Alex, where

---

389. [1] A dialectal word (Southern Irish) for a wisp (a small bundle of straw or
hay) to serve in CB's term for a bed for his Irish grand-daughter Fanny Phillips.

we stayed the whole ǀ Morning, & met Sir Frederic & Lady Evelyn,[3] & your admirer Lord Leslie,[4] & my Boy was mighty popular, though most entirely at his ease, & as much *sans* façon as a Young Prince of Wales. But the little Wretch looked so brightly well, & wildly gay, that his freaks & fancies only engendered mirth, & Mr. Pepys, who has now seen him three following years, is as partial to him, apparently, as, apparently, he for so many years has been to his Mother. M. d'A. & I were invited to be introduced to the Bride elect while she was at Norbury Park. She seems very natural, free from vanity or airs, extremely good natured, & unconscious of the celebrity of her beauty,—which, however, I own I think has been exaggerated. Amelia has much more perfect beauty; but I hope she is very amiable, & will know how to bless her happy stars,—& merit them. All the Locks, but William, are now at Woodlands, & he is with his Belle at Miss Berry's.[5] ǀ

I shall entreat a line to tell us your Day, when you can fix it, that our *Whisps* may be ready. *Panny* must add one reproach more to her list, if you have not time to write. Pray bring Prog to leave here for work upon your return—&—if you can spare them, 2 Vols. of Goldoni,[6] to change for the two at Norbury Park.

My Chevalier Jardinier sends you his best Love & Respects, & a thousand thanks for your kind purpose: his Peas & Beans are burnt up for want of Rain, his Goose berries & Currants have been devoured by our Cock & Hens, his Cherris & Raspberries have been pecked by the Birds — — but he has reared some of the finest double Carnations you ever smelt. So bring the least stomach, & the best nose possible. Adieu, Dearest Sir,—⌐I dare not enter upon the subject [that] ⟨is the⟩ bane of our lives—more & more abominable[7]

⟨ever, &⟩ ever
F. d'A—! —! —¬

---

[3] Frederic Evelyn (*c.* 1734–1812), 3rd Bart. (1767), and his lady, Mary *née* Turton (*c.* 1746–1817). Their seat was at Wotton, Surrey.

[4] See L. 332 n. 11.

[5] Probably at Little Strawberry Hill, Twickenham, the house left by Horace Walpole to Mary Berry (1763–1852), the authoress (*DNB*), and her sister Agnes (1764–1852).

[6] Copies of Carlo Goldoni's plays that FBA had been sharing with the Lockes since March (see also L. 368).

[7] A reference to Molesworth Phillips's impending visit to England (see L. 394 and n. 4).

To Doctor Burney

A.L.S. (rejected Diary MSS. 5230–[3], Berg), 13 Sept. 1800
Double sheet 4to   4 pp.   wafer
Addressed: Dr. Burney / Chelsea College.
Endorsed by CB: F. d.'Arblay
Edited by FBA, p. 1, *annotated*: ⁂ (6) projected Marriage of Marianne
Burney with M. Bourdois.
Edited also by CFBt *and the* Press, *see* Textual Notes.

Septr 13th *1800*
West Humble—

With what solid & heartfelt satisfaction do I now take up my
Pen to participate—as I trust—in the joy of my dearest Father
at the happy opening prospects of our dear Girl Marianne!—
A Native of Joigny, M. Bourdois has been known to M. d'Arblay
from his birth—there is nothing, therefore, to fear of future
drawback, or discovery, in a Character established during its
whole life in amiability & worth. We longed to open a little to
you upon the subject when you were here, but were deterred
by some difficulties still existing in the powers of M. Bourdois
to make his proposals; & I felt, too, that Esther would scarcely
have forgiven my depriving her of the pleasure of being the
first to announce to you an event of such infinite importance to
her. I do indeed firmly believe she will find in this Gentleman
a kind & useful Friend to herself & all her family during his
whole life; nor will even his living Abroad, which, at the Peace
he means to do, impede his active services, should occasion
call them forth, for he purposes making frequent visits ǀ to
England, which he loves very much, & he will keep up a constant intercourse with this Country. That he was not *born* here,
seems the ONLY OBJECTION, against a million of *inducements*: &
how few marriages are made here without one drawback!—
Besides which, *the English Boys*, as Sir Hugh says, *are one or other
the backwardest about coming forward, in the point of matrimony*;[1]—
so that I cannot wonder the alltogether of this offer should
appear so unexceptionable. M. Bourdois' situation in life,
pecuniarily, is far above any of Marianne's expectations, &

390. [1] Cf. *Camilla*, ii, bk. iii, chap. 2.

while his Mind is highly cultivated, & passionately fond of
literature, his disposition is of the most domestic & gentle cast,
& in the highest degree generous & open. To this I must add
he has an activity of mind & character peculiarly adapted to
contribute to the happiness of Marianne, whose nature is rather
helpless, though her understanding is clear & good. I hardly
know any two people that I think may meet in this greatest of
Lotteries with more rational promise of doing well. I Marianne
is amiable, pleasing, lively, & sensible—she is deeply penetrated
with her fair lot in engaging such a good & truly disinterested
Partner, & she cannot but rejoice, also, in the happiness
accrueing to her anxiety-worn Mother in seeing one, at least,
of her five Daughters thus Amply provided for. *This* is the
consideration that *I* have felt, almost equally with my tender
interest in the welfare of Marianne, & my affectionate esteem
for a friend of M. d'Arblay who loves him/M. d'A,/as a Brother,
& honours him as a Parent: for impossible it is that one man
can think more highly of another than M. Bourdois does of
M. d'Arblay.

This subject has swallowed all my paper—& I can only add
to it our tenderest thanks for your kind though so disappoint-
ingly short visit, & our earnest hopes you will next year make it
longer.

I had a Letter yesterday from Charlotte confirming her
recovery, though confessing herself in a very weak state, & much
reduced. Mr. Broome writes verses to press us to Brighthelmstone[2]—but we are home poultry, & love not to take wing. I

Adieu, most dear Sir; M. d'A. is truly yours—& our little
wild Boy wants you ⌐*to do* for him⌐ very much again. Lady
Rothes & Sir Lucas charge me with compliments, & Mr.
William Lock came to return your Bridal visit just half an
Hour after your departure from West Hamble. The Miss
Berrys,[3] he says, were quite sorry they missed you both here & at
Norbury Park.

Ever & ever yours, Dearest Sir, most dutifully

& affectionately
F. d'Arblay.

[2] The letter and verses are missing.   [3] L. 389 n. 5.

445

Conjointly with M. d'Arblay

To Esther (Burney) Burney

A.L.S. & PS. (Berg), 13 Sept. 1800
Double sheet 4to   4 pp.   *pmks*   DARKING   15 SEP 1800   wafer
Addressed: Mrs. Burney, / Beaumont Street, / Devonshire Street / London
Endorsed by EBB: answered / Sep. 20ᵗʰ

West Hamble, Septʳ 13ᵗʰ
1800

To wish JOY[1]—to write congratulations to my dearest Esther
—*What* a JOY to *Me!*—True, true, NONE like *us* can partake in
your happiness—for none other can so completely know the
value of its source. A tender & active Friend, my dearest Hetty,
will be given to YOU, & your whole House, as well as the kindest
Husband to our dear & fortunate Marianne, whom I do indeed
felicitate with my whole Heart, & shall henceforth regard as
amongst the happy chosen few of this mortal state.

You are truly kind, my dearest Etty, not to even glance a
reproach at my silence to your very interesting Letters[2]—I can
fully exculpate it, *NOW*,—but I was then of the *sworn privy
Counsel*, personally consulted in every step that was meditated,
a partaker in every doubt & difficulty, & bound in honour to
leave the Principal to Act without any interruption or communication or anticipation or interference whatever. To *YOU*,
yet more deeply interested in his proceedings than myself,
(though *you* alone can be so,) |I could not bear to write
evasively—nor yet answer to myself a *second* breach of my
bond in precipitating your knowledge of his intentions: nor
would you have been the happier for my communications, for
they must have varied endlessly, & only kept your anxiety still
more keenly alive, till the very period when he ended it himself. nevertheless, it has often hung painfully upon my Mind,
& when the doubts have preponderated, I have been more
frightened than I will now tell you—*your* disappointment, & my

391. ¹ On the return of Antoine Bourdois, obviously, and his engagement to
Marianne Burney.
² The letters are missing.

dear Marianne's—joined to my best Friend's & my own,—I am sure they would have weighed heavily—HEAVILY upon me, & for a long—long time. But now there is nothing more to fear— the die is finally cast, & by next December, at furthest, I trust our final congratulations will go round. It *may* be in October!— but most glad I am he would not wait to know the exact time before he decided publicly upon his ultimate determination. It will be still late in October before he can know more himself, unless some unexpected good fortune intervenes. But all this you will hear more clearly from himself—or perhaps have already heard. |

That Marianne was at Abberley[3] Mr B[ourdois] knew well— & took his measures accordingly,—but I will not enter into details which you may, now, perhaps, have learnt at full length. —you may imagine how warm a Letter M. d'Arblay—the more than confidant of his excellent Friend & Town'sman, has written upon this final narrative. But he would not address him at Worcester, as we conclude him returned. To-morrow's Post will bring us a certainty. I am quite concerned, in the midst of my satisfaction, at your ill account of yourself—for Heaven's sake take *peculiar* care to get rid of your complaint as quickly as possible. I cannot wonder at your agitation, but let it now subside into gentle & chearful serenity. If ever Mother had reason for a tranquil trust in a Child's welfare, you have it now. The *only objection*, you know, *she* likes the better!—I shall write to our dearest Father immediately. *He* won't like that objection quite so well—but he can find no other, &—where is the *English* man who will not leave him *one*?—As to poor Charlotte, she has been very really & very seriously ill, in so much as to write me a Letter of the most alarming kind as to her danger— But it is now past, & I have this very Morning a long Epistle from her written in good spirits, & announcing recovery of all but strength & flesh—& an invite to us to Brighton from Mr. Broome almost *vehement* in earnestness. |

I am very sorry poor James looks so ill—pray let me have his direction when you write next, that I may write to him. I have a little pacquet of Letters for you, which I found in the Bag

---

[3] Abberley (about twelve miles from Worcester) was the parish in which Richard Allen Burney (Marianne's brother) had since 1797 spent his 'Oxford vacations' (iii, L. 229 n. 7).

left me here by my most beloved lamented![4]—& another for our dear Father. I have found none of my own yet—but imagine them in a parcel left at Norbury Park, which I have not yet had the force to ask for & examine. shall I keep yours till we meet? or send them in a parcel by some safe opportunity? it is but a small quantity.

Joy to dear Mr. Burney! Joy to Richard!—M. d'A. will write to wish it you All with his own Pen. Heaven grant it unalloyed as I *expect* as well as *wish* it, & blessed will be to my ever dear Hetty the Day that consigns her dear Girl to so tender, so worthy, so generous a Protector for Life!—

Amen—Amen!

F. d'A.

[*By M. d'Arblay*]

Dear Sister, Brother, & Nephew.

I give you joy with all my heart. *She* will be happy. *He* will be happy; and *We* all must be happy in their happiness.

God bless you and give you comfort till the final conclusion of the highly interesting business.

Amen!

[*By Madame d'Arblay*]

Sunday Afternoon

I come this moment from visiting Mrs. Lock in her Bed, with a furious Cold—I have promised to excuse her not writing, & give hers & Mr.'s Lock's tenderest congratulations. They are quite delighted. & extremely pleased with your Letter.

---

[4] Evidently letters left by SBP before she went to Ireland.

To Esther (Burney) Burney

A.L. (Berg), 21 Sept. 1800
Double sheet 4to   4 pp.   *pmks*   DARKING   22 SEP 1800   wafer
Addressed: Mrs. Burney, / Beaumont Street, / Devonshire Place / London.
To be forwarded to / Richmond

West Hamble,
21ʳˢᵗ Septʳ 1800.

It is impossible for me not to give ease to your maternal feelings, my dearest Esther, though your call upon me has a good deal perturbed me—but I must trust, & solemnly exact, that what I say upon this subject must be to *yourself* alone— *yourself*, whose happiness in the approaching event is so dear, so even balsamic to me! My dearest Esther! your Letter of this Morning, your truly MOTHERLY JOY, & expressions of fond security & contentment, have filled me with a pleasure I cannot describe, & my Heart, just now, beats to no other tune. —How then, can I suffer any alloy to the purity of your satisfaction which I have means to remove?—Impossible! I must rely on your strictest discretion, & openly reveal to you, That I know M. Bourdois determined upon *making a settlement* upon our dear Girl, if he loved, & found himself loved by her upon mutual experiment, before he ever saw her. This he declared to my best Friend,—who whispered it to me,—& this made me use the terms I have used in naming his intentions & their generosity, & the consequent motives to satisfaction from ALL the family, should the Union take place.

Upon this assurance, my *dearest* Sister—(alas) let your mind rest. | The pleasure you would have in communicating it to our friends will not be lost, but must be delayed. Marianne, knowing that not one of her family have ever had any previous arrangement made for unhappy contingencies, except Mrs. Broome, will not think upon the subject,—& I would not for the World my intelligence should reach her. M. Bourdois has his own plans,—& has trusted them, in *this* point, only to M. d'Arblay,—he has also, like all generous & feeling characters, his susceptibilities—leave him therefore to himself, I entreat, &

let him take his own time, & his own way, to publish his designs; I know I should cruelly mortify & disappoint his measures, by anticipating them. Relieved, therefore, from every apprehension that could annoy your own perfect joy, guard for MY sake, the secret I entrust to you, & only to all others say you have no doubt, from his tenderness & honour & goodness, he will take care the woman he marries shall never be distressed by accepting him.

NB These have been his own words to M. d'Arblay, who, warmly as he has acted, would not have felt such eager Zeal ⏐ had not this generous Creature given him such early assurances of his right—nay, noble way of thinking.—Yes, my dearest Esther—your dear Girl will be placed in comfortable indepen- dance as to fortune, should she be the Survivor—though I have not the smallest doubt but that her happiness will be such in his life, as to make this circumstance more material to her friends than to herself., — —

Poor M. Bourdois is just now extremely wretched—he finds he has lost for ever a Mother[1] he most tenderly loved, & hears at the same time, that she had suffered dreadfully from the effects of the cruel Revolution—which he execrates in every three lines of his Letter, during the Reigns of Terror—& now, that he could solace & aid her, she is no more!—He has sent M. d'Arblay the Letter containing the sad tydings, which is a truly affecting one, from his only & most loved sister, herself reduced to great distress, & an account that even his Elder Brother is absolutely ruined! the Brother he thought in such prosperity! His younger Brother, also, now in the Austrian army, writes him word that having been in Engagements almost innumerable, he has acquired—he hopes, some glory—though point d'Argent!—This extraordinary Friend of ours will be the relief, the resource, the existence, almost, of all his House! And, had not his feeling Heart, so fortunately for *himself*, I trust, as well as Us, been captivated by our Marianne already, I question if he would not have devoted himself & fortune wholly to his ruined race! Now, however, he has other calls, which already he holds equally sacred,—& nobly, I doubt not, he will fulfil all. ⏐ This unhappy news, however, even in *decency*, as well as from grief & affection, must postpone the celebration. We have

392. [1] For the Bourdois family, see L. 381 n. 1.

entreated him to arrange his affairs for making our Cottage his head quarters, & only to go backwards & forwards upon business. With his Heart's friend, his Books, & our Alex, who he almost idolizes, his spirits will revive better in this quiet retreat than any where else—within 118 Miles—

Upon further thoughts, I must consent to your whispering, with every caution, my private intelligence to dear Mr. Burney, *your* Husband, *Her* Father, & *my* sincerely esteemed Friend.— AND to our own dear Padre—whose solicitude may else be hurtful to his satisfaction, & whose invincible prudence & almost unrivalled sense of Honour will completely secure me from fearing my unauthorised confidence may do the mischief of occasioning any disappointment to the internal plans of one who so well merits being left to follow them.—I think it is quite right the Wedding Garments should be arranged at Worcester,—there is more time there for thought & management, & it will be an occupation to delight away the period of *waiting*,—not *Suspence*, for Suspence is WHOLLY ended. How very fortunate M. B[ourdois] took his Worcester Journey just as he did! *now* he could not, nor for some time—but their open correspondence will contribute to restore *him*, as well as keep *her* Gay & pleasant & occupied. How much I rejoice his dear *SISTER* still lives! M. d'Arblay says he is sure, so amiable she is, & so uncommonly sweet-tempered, that Marianne will love her as a sister of her own. With what pleasure I think of the *WEDDING DAY* of my dear Hetty![2] May her Daughter's but prove as productive of lasting comfort & affection! I can wish no more:—& the excellent Mr. Burney's brightening prospects for future times fill me with extremest satisfaction. Heaven bless you, my dearest Esther.

I am almost afraid of your Carte blanche, my Esther—M. B[ourdois] will only be grieved if you are too liberal—*really* grieved. Let her buy nothing but White, for I am sure M. B[ourdois] will not wait till his Mourning shall be over.

---

2 In 1770. See *ED* i. 102.

393   [West Humble, 3 October 1800]

To Mrs. Waddington

A.L. (Berg), *n.d.*
Double sheet 4to   4 pp.   *pmks* DARKING 3 OCT 1800   wafer
Addressed: Mrs. Waddington, / Lanover House, / Abergavenny— /
Monmouth
Docketed in ink, p. 1: October 3ᵈ 1800
Scribbling in ink, p. 4.

Have you been hurt by my long silence, my dear Marianne?
I have been a little hurt by yours,—mine, I think, must be
understood,—your's I must at least hope has not been from
illness,—I would rather suppose, & find it displeasure, which
will give me much less pain, for it must soon wear away—
Soon, indeed, when I tell you—if you have not conjectured it—
the laborious weight of oppressive—eternal regret which has
made me, from a bad correspondent, cease to be any correspondent at all. I have wholly left off all Letter writing—since
that fatal 9ᵗʰ of January[1]—except from Business, or the anxiety
raised by the concomitant silence of those I love. This last
motive now again draws forth my pen,—&, once again drawn
forth, I must hope it will never more so long lay dormant.

I will not again enter upon the fatal—sacred subject—I am
well aware how it is ecchoed by my friends that where a misfortune is irreparable, Grief is unavailing, & should be checked
—but alas—that the misfortune is irreparable—that the grief is
unavailing—O therefore it is I find them so hard to bear!—Yet
never, I believe, where the Heart has so been torn by an abrupt
separation from the Friend of its first feelings & fondness, have
ties so exquisitely dear remained to soften the direful blow; nor
should I, while supported ⌐ by such loved objects, thus deeply,
or thus long have mourned, but that circumstances of aggra-
vation the most bitter & calamitous made the sudden—unprepared deprivation nearly shake Reason from her seat.

I am mixing, however, now, much as usual with the World.
That *as usual*, as you know, is what others would call total
seclusion; but I only mean to tell you that I have resumed my

393. [1] The day on which FBA received the news of SBP's death (L. 355).

customary habits, my intercourse with my friends, & my former way of life—though not, alas, with my former too—too visionary hopes of PERFECT HAPPINESS!—Gratefully, however, let me own, all *but* perfect it yet is, since I feel that I would not exchange the little spot on which I live with its Builder & its Heir for any situation or possession, not So occupied, the World has to offer. Repining, therefore, you see, is what I have as little right as inclination to, & THANKFUL I am for my lot—all mingled as it will now for ever be with deepest disappointment & regret. ——

But your Emily,[2] my dear Friend—is she wholly recovered?— I have wished a thousand times to write about *her*, when I have sought & wished only to hold back from writing about myself. Pray let me know how she is, & what her complaints proved. My Boy, you will be glad I am sure to hear is now in flourishing health,—always very thin, but strong, gay, & active, & blessed with All that can make him to *us* a blessing.—I need not, after saying that, be very minute in describing him—You will soon paint to yourself his quickness, his intelligence, his gaiety, his tenderness, & his ever varying Countenance, & interesting little Figure. How I wish he could meet your Emily! Your dear & excellent Fanny[2] would be quite a matron to him, though, while she reprimanded his naughtinesses, she would irresistibly be amused by them. I should have been glad to have seen your Children's pictures even at the time you offered them,—but not at the purchase of making a new acquaintance! I could scarcely hear—when I received that offer, to see my nearest friends—Now, however, I am resigned—[p]hilosophized—or blunted into a being more *resembling* wh[a]t I was, externally, & if a similar opportunity should occur, I should conquer my general averseness to new faces, if only on such a condition I could see a sight which, now, would be really very dear to me. Your account of Mr. Greene,[3] too, is very prepossessing: I know you to be difficult—I might perhaps say fastidious—& I doubt not but he is very amiable, or uncommonly agreeable, by the rank in which you place him. I am glad to tell you—if you have not heard it, that Miss Fielding, Matilda,[4] is entirely recovered,

[2] Emilia was now 6 years old; Frances, 9.
[3] See L. 315 n. 4; and v, *passim*.
[4] Matilda Feilding (1775-1849), daughter of Commodore Charles Feilding (d. 11 Jan. 1783) and his wife (1772) Sophia *née* Finch (*fl.* 1746-1815), daughter

—& can walk, dance, or Jump, as well as ever! This is such a cure, so unexpected from the length of her attack, & so deserved by the extreme & exemplary patience with which she sustained it, that it has given me pleasure & surprise to hear it. The beauty of Lady Robert, I am told, is *wholly* vanished! it is most extraordinary, at so early a period in her life,—but, what is [|] yet more extraordinary, considering that for her beauty she was married, is, that her Husband loves her more than ever. These circumstances you may depend upon, as they were told me only last Week by his sister, Lady Lucy Fitzgerald,[5] who called here while at Norbury Park, & who is a very sensible, pleasing, & highly bred woman. You will have been interested, I doubt not, in the marriage of Mr. William Lock,—we all were deeply. There is reason to hope it will prove very happy; his Bride is of a beauty quite celebrated, & of a disposition the sweetest, most complying, gentle, & yet gay, that can be conceived. You will be kind enough to rejoice for me at a marriage which will, ere long, take place in my own family—the eldest Daugher, Marianne, of my sister Burney, with M. Bourdois, a most intimate friend, & townsman, of M. d'Arblay, &, happily, possessed of all that, in MY friends opinions, M. d'Arblay wanted, a very good fortune. May they but be as happy WITH as WE have been WITHOUT it! I can wish them no better. our Norbury friends always enquire very kindly about you. *Amelia* will soon be a Mother, & is in extacy at the expectation, though more constantly suffering than any one but your poor self I ever knew. Pray tell me you are now *quite* re-established—your approach to that *quite* was very grateful to [me.] Poor Mr. Smelt is gone[6]—& Mrs Montagu[7] & Mr. Digby![8]—I *KNEW* Genl Goldsworthy intended visiting you[9]—God bless you, dearest *Mary*—

of Lady Charlotte (Fermor) Finch (iii, L. 175 n. 5). Matilda's sister Sophia Charlotte (1773–1834) had married in 1792 Lord Robert Stephen Fitzgerald (1765–1833) the diplomat.

[5] See iii, L. 175 n. 3.

[6] Leonard Smelt (i, L. 12 n. 18) had died on 2 Sept. 1800.

[7] Elizabeth Montagu (i, L. 3 n. 82) had died on 30 August. See her obituary *AR* xlii (1800), 'Chronicle', 31.

[8] The Hon. Stephen Digby (i, L. 21 n. 8), 30 June.

[9] See i, L. 5 n. 10.

[West Humble, *pre* 30 October 1800]

To Esther (Burney) Burney

A.L.S. (Berg), *n.d.*
Double sheet 4to 4 pp. wafer
Addressed: Mrs. Burney, / Beaumont Street
Docketed by EBB, p. 1: Octr 1800

When I received your first Letter, my dearest Esther, I was too unwell to enter into any engagement, though unable to bring myself to write a negative to your kind urgency while uncertain if I might not sufficiently recover to write an affirmative. But this is not the case,—I continue under a necessity of observing a pretty rigid regimen in Medicine, & my little Boy, too, is under a rather severe discipline, in the course of Ching-ing.[1] We must not bring you Invalides [on] so joyful an occasion,[2]—my Heart will be truly with you,—in wishes, in gratulation, almost in *ex*ultation at your happiness,—my dearest *Maria's*[3] happiness,—& the happiness of a Friend I esteem & regard with the sincerest interest—Of this you must ALL be sure,—if there could be a doubt, it would so much hurt me, that I should break through every barrier to remove it—But what must I have been all this time, if ANY interest beyond your own THREE can go beyond OURS in this transaction? I may be judged by something less perishable than words,—& to that something I securely commit your sentence. |

Thus far, my dearest Hetty, is public—& you will accordingly promulgate—but now—for your private Ear—I must be more diffuse & more confidential, with condition that *Maria* alone should have the rest whispered to her—O my dearest Hetty— I have been terribly shattered again by the communication of my poor Fanny P[hillips][4]—that dreadful bane to all the pure &

394. [1] See L. 310 n. 1.
[2] The marriage of Marianne Burney and Antoine Bourdois, which was to take place on 30 October.
[3] It was discovered (see the 'Worcester Journal' of this year) that in the baptismal registers Anna Maria's name had, by mistake, been spelled with an 'H' and that her 'Christian name was therefore, according to Law—*Hannah* Maria'. At this time Marianne chose the name *Maria* and is known henceforth as 'Maria Bourdois'.
[4] Fanny Phillips's letter is missing, but in a letter (Berg) of 27 October 1800 CB expressed his alarm that Phillips was 'coming over, is now I believe in England'.

perfect hope of my Heart she thinks now *certainly* in England —
— she has been some time expecting him, & that expectation
has kept me cruelly harrassed between my reluctance to withstand your most kind invitation, & my dread of some acci-
dental rencontre—but *NOW*, that she seems to *know*, though only
by some implication of circumstance, that he is actually in
England,—all hesitation ends—& YOU, who Are so intimately
acquainted with the state of my Mind—my opinions, & my
feelings upon this fatal subject, will be the last to wish to see me
exposed to even a possibility of a meeting that my Nerves could
so ill bear. I am SURE, my tender Esther, I am SURE of the
sympathy with which you will more than allow ˡ of my retreat,
you will even *desire* it, with such apprehensions hanging upon
my journey. Could I find a Balloon to convey me to your
house, & back again on that same morning, I would mount it—
for I have no fear of his venturing to shew his baleful visage on
such an occasion—but it is the previous day—& days that I
shrink from—especially as my dearest Father invites me to be at
Chelsea, where he has a natural claim to shew himself.

Nevertheless—should his apparition *certainly* vanish before
that period, *undoubtedly* fleet over to those shores to which it
belongs—I would yet come, & witness as well as partake in your
Joy & my dear Maria's felicity—If so happy an incident should
take place, I shall therefore *SUDDENLY RECOVER* — — pray
remember that, & let all else be solely buried in your own bosom,
& that of the Bride elect,—for to HER the whole of this is so
important & interesting, that I would wish her to be completely
au fait—but that Wretch whom I fervently pray Heaven my
Eyes may never be blighted with seeing more—is of a character
so vengeful, that I would rather my non-appearance should be
placed to illness—even at Chelsea & certainly with your other
dear Girls, &c—&c— ˡ

I hope nothing new will occur to alarm our dear Padre about
F[anny] P[hillips] but I feel a little frightened for poor R[ichar]d
who I think will difficultly keep heart-whole.—Adieu, my
dearest Esther—my kind love to Mr. Burney, & distribute it
about to your whole House—& extend it to James—And say to
Maria that whether my person is here, or in Beaumont Street,

The Major had revealed the purpose of his visit to no one, and CB's apprehension
over losing Fanny increased daily (see CB to Mrs. Crewe, 13 and 26 Nov., Berg).

my Heart will most truly be with HER—YOU—& M. Bourdois
on that Morning which promises—I firmly believe, Happiness,
prosperity, honour, & good of every sort to the rest of her life.

ever ever affect^{ly} y^{rs}

F. d'A—

I am quite pleased Molly is coming to be our neighbour—[5]
how kind of you to spare her!—what a *very* pleasant thing for
our new Housekeeper! All our Norburyites are enchanted at
this connexion, & for *YOU* as much as if you were the Bride
yourself. *Dear* Mrs. Burney! Mrs. Lock frequently exclaims,
what a happiness this must be to her! what a relief to a thousand
cares & anxieties!—& Mr. Lock helps M. d'A. to seek a habitation for them—

Alex says—'If Cousin Marianne is to be changed into Cousin
Maria Bood, I suppose Aunt Burney is to be Aunt Burney Bood,
—& Cousin Amelia will be Cousin Amelia Bood.—'

---

395   London, 14 [November] 1800

M. d'Arblay

To Madame d'Arblay

A.L. (Berg), 14 [*misdated*] Oct. 1800
Single sheet 4to, of which the lower part has been cut away leaving a
remnant (8·1 to 8·4 × 7·8″)   1 p.
Edited by FBA, p. 1, *top margin, numbered*: ⌜N° 21⌝   21

Piccadily. Octobre[1] 14. 1800 — —

Mon depart est decidé,[2] ma chere amie: mais j'ai besoin d'un
compagnon et ce compagnon c'est toi. Tu as trois jours, peut
être même quatre, pour faire tes preparatifs;[3] sans en faire part

---

[5] At Sand Place, Dorking (see L. 399 n. 1), which Bourdois was to rent.

395. [1] Written in error for *Novembre*.

[2] On Monday 17 Nov. M. d'A was to set out for Holland, where, in a country at
peace with France, he could make claim for property confiscated by his emigration
of 1792.

[3] M. d'A returned to West Humble on Sunday 16 Nov. to arrange a *'joint
departure'* but for the reasons explained in the letter to CB Jr. (L. 397), FBA
decided to remain with Alex at West Humble.

à qui que ce soit au monde. Ce ne sera qu'au moment même de quitter Londre que tu communiqueras ma resolution à ceux qu'il est indispensable d'en informer. La paix peut se faire longtems encore desirer, et la position de nos affaires ne me permet point de remettre à une epoque plus eloignée le soin de rassembler s'il se peut les foibles debris de ma petite fortune. [xxxxx *5¼ lines*] En Hollande ma famille pourra me faire passer des secours sans se compromettre.[4] Je suis sûr, au moins, de pouvoir de là, lui expedier sa procuration qu'elle me demande, et cet objet très important ne peut souffrir un plus long retard. J'ai dejà même beaucoup compromis nos interêts dans l'espoir de la paix qui n'arrive point.

[xxxxx *8 lines*][5] |

396   West Humble, 17 November 1800

To Doctor Burney

A.L. (Diary MSS. vi. 5234–[7], Berg), 17 Nov. 1800
Double sheet 4to   4 pp.   *pmks* DARKING   18 NOV 1800
18 NO 1800   red wafer
Addressed: Dr. Burney, / Chelsea College, / Middlesex
Endorsed by CB: Voyage en Hollande / 9ᵇʳᵉ 1800.
Edited by FBA, p. 1 (5234), *annotated*: ⁑· West Hamble Nov. 17. 1800 (7)
M. d'Arblay gone to the Hague to send off a procuration on to France.
Edited also by CFBt *and the* Press.

West Hamble,
Nov 17. 1800

I think it very long not to hear at least *of* you, my dearest Padre—⌐& I do entreat you will delegate [*blot*] [our] Fanny to send me news of your health. I have not answered her last Letter. I shall not like to risk a Letter to her, till I know she is sure of receiving it as heretofore—& I have no intelligence or knowledge as to whether she is yet restored to her⌐ tranquil & happy security.—[1] alas ⌐*mine*⌐ has been broken in upon by

---

[4] These circumstances FBA explains at length in her letters to CB and to CB Jr. (Ll. 396, 397).
[5] M. d'A's small hand when heavily inked over by FBA has proved impossible to read, but L. 396 probably paraphrases the obliterated sections.

396. [1] Veiled reference to the expected arrival of Molesworth Phillips. See L. 394 n. 4.

severe conflicts since I wrote to my dearest Father last—which I would not communicate while yet pending, but must now briefly narrate.

My Partner—the truest of Partners—has been erazed from the List of Emigrants nearly a year[2]—& in that period has been much pressed—& much blamed by his remaining Friends in France, by every opportunity through which they could send to him, for not immediately returning, & seeing if any thing could be yet saved from the Wreck of his own & family's fortune: but he held steady to his original purpose, never to re-visit his own Country till it was at Peace with This—till a Letter came from his beloved Uncle himself,[3] conveyed to him through Hambro', which shook all the firmness of his resolution, & has kept him, since its receipt, in a state of fermentation, from doubts & difficulties & opposing wishes & interests, that has much affected his health as well as tranquility—all, however, NOW, is at least decided—for a few days since—he received a Letter from M. Lajard,[3] who is returned to Paris, with information from his uncle's eldest son,[4] that some of his small property is yet unsold, to about the amount of £1000—& can still be saved from sequestration, if he will immediately go over & claim it—or, if that is impossible, if he will send his *procuration* to his Uncle, from some Country *not at War with* France—[5]

This ended all his internal contest—& he is gone—this very

2 An 'Extrait des Registres du Secrétariat de la Légation française en Batavie' confirms that on 8 Frimaire an IX [29 Nov. 1800], before the Minister Plenipotentiary of the French Republic in Batavia, signatory of the document, M. d'A had sworn an oath of allegiance to the laws of the Republic and had deposited in the archives at Batavia a copy of the decree of the Consuls of 1 Floréal an VIII [21 Apr. 1800] that had ordered his name stricken from the list of *émigrés* (Archives départementales de l'Yonne à Auxerre, item Q 534).

3 Jean-Baptiste Bazille (iii, L. 231 n. 3), whose letter is missing as is also that of Pierre-August Lajard (L. 291 n. 5).

4 Jean-Baptiste-Gabriel-Édme Bazille (1767–1804).

5 M. d'A gave power of attorney to Bazille before the Minister Plenipotentiary of the French Republic at The Hague. The date of this procuration, however, is not clearly established: Ll. 400 and 402 indicate that M. d'A did not sail for Holland until *c.* 24 Nov.; yet a document of the sub-prefect at Joigny, dated 11 Ventôse, l'an 9e [2 Mar. 1801] refers to the 'procuration par lui donnée le 10 Brumaire Der [2 Nov. 1800]'. This same document declared M. d'A 'réintégré dans la libre possession et jouissance de tous ceux de ses biens meubles et immeubles non vendus'. It also authorized the 'receveur des domaines' to give Bazille all title-deeds and rents due M. d'A since 21 April 1800, the day his name had been removed from the list of *émigrés*; but this official, unfortunately, declared only that he had received no rents for properties belonging to M. d'A which proved, he stated, 'qu'ils ont tous été vendus' (Archives départementales de l'Yonne à Auxerre, item Q 534; see also v, L. 461).

Morning, to Town, to procure a passport, & a passage, in some vessel bound to Holland.—

So unused are we to part—never yet for a week having been separated during the 8 years of our union—that our first ¹ idea was going together—& taking our Alex—& certain I am nothing would do me such material & mental good as so complete a change of scene: but the great expence of the voyage & Journey, & the inclement season for our little Boy, at length finally settled us to pray only for a speedy meeting. But I did not give it up till late last Night—& am far from quite reconciled to relinquishing it even now. — —

He has no intention to go to France—or he would make an effort to pass by Calais—which would delightfully shorten the passage—but he merely means to remain at the Hague while he sends over his *procuration*, & learns how soon he may hope to reap its fruits. — —

I can write upon nothing else just now, my dearest Father—the misfortune of this call at such a boisterous—dangerous season will oppress & alarm me, in defiance of all I can oppose of hope—yet the measure is so reasonable, so natural, I could no longer try to combat it. I shall write immediately an explanatory Letter upon the affair *for* the Queen.

Adieu, dearest dear Sir — —

If any news of him reaches Me before his return—I will not enjoy it 5 minutes previous to communicating it to my dear Father. ¹

He hopes at all events to be able to embrace you, & beg your benediction before he departs—which nothing but the very unlikely chance of meeting a vessel just sailing for Holland immediately can prevent.

Alex is well—& O what a support to me!

⌐Mr. William Lock—who called here with his handsome Wife, while I was writing this, charged me to present you his particular & affectionate Respects. The rest of the family is at Woodlands, where Mrs. Angerstein is very happy in nursing her Son & Heir.¬⁶

⁶ John Julius Angerstein III, born on 9 Nov. 1800.

West Humble, 18 November 1800

To Charles Burney

A.L.S. (John Comyn, grangerized *Diary*, vi. 21), 18 Nov. 1800
Double sheet 4to 4 pp. *pmks* DARKING 19 Nov 1800 NO
green wafer mended
Addressed: Dr. Charles Burney, / Greenwich, / Kent.
Post-dated by FBA, p. 1: 18 Nov. 1800 / West Hamble

My dearest Carluci—

M. d'Arblay has just left Westhamble—to set sail for the Continent—

I know I need say nothing to excite your interest in such a step—I will only briefly narrate its cause.

It is now nearly a year since he has been erased from the list of Emigrants—& consequently at liberty to revisit his Country & native Friends—but he had early determined against ever taking that measure while France was at war with England.— A few days since, however, he received a Letter to inform him some little part of his property was yet unsold—& might be re-claimed, now he was erased, if he went over immediately or sent his *procuration* to his nearest surviving Relation, from some country *not at War with France*—but it must be *signed—sealed—*& *witnessed* in such country, or his friends would be personally endangered for even receiving it. The sum in question does not quite amount to £1000—but that—for us—is a capital object— & therefore he unhesitatingly resolved to go to Holland instantly. He went to Town to make enquiries concerning passport ˡ & passage—& returned on Sunday[1] to arrange *our joint* departure —for I could not consent not to share his fate through-out be it what it might—but—after innumerable discussions & cruel conflicts—we finally fixed he should go alone, from fears of the sea in two voyages at such a season for our Alex—& from drawbacks to the *OBJECT* which carries him, in the added expense—the more than doubled expense of our all going.—He left me Monday—yesterday morning—meaning to go to Chelsea—*You*—Mr Lock at Woodlands—Beaumont Street— &c—but he heard immediately of a vessel new going to sail—

---

397. ˡ On 16 Nov.

& this morning I have a few hasty lines from him, charging me to explain his situation to you all,[2] for that the suddeness of the sailing gave him barely time to exchange money for dutch currency, & prepare some warm covering—particularly a *peruke* —for the cold voyage—

I am not very gay, my dear Charles—nor shall I feel a peaceful moment until I have news from *abroad*. |

But I am amazed—& rather frightened—you have not given me the word *Safe* for my parcel[3]—I should be vexed indescribably if it is not arrived, as I have laboured very seriously in its preparation, & inserted all the amendments, verbal, of Mr. Twining, & all the Reviews, besides whatever I could devise to Abridge & ameliorate the whole. It has taken me a great deal of time, as will, I trust, be visible in its amend- ment. Hurry alone, I hope, has kept back the *Safe* I begged.

I have a beautiful drawing of Mr. William Lock which, if they thought it worth engraving *well*, I would send you—but not else. It is the parting of Camilla from her Father when she goes to Mrs. Berlinton, in the 5th volume.[4]—& he has given to the two figures, Mr. Tyrold & Camilla, a strong resemblance to Mr. Lock & Amelia, though not a *portrait* of them, or designed likeness. |

I know how vexed my beloved Traveller will be he could not get to you—*particularly* vexed, as *particularly* he loves you— warmly—*fondly*—The kind & good M. Bourdois accompanied him to town to help about passport &c—& is with him yet, probably, at Gravesend—to which place he was to go this Morning. *Maria* is quite well—she was here just now, blooming & lively. My Alex is very prosperous—& says, when we conn Latin—'Mama, I think the *accusative case* is the kindest—for that says amo magistratum, I *love* the Master.' So I, too, am for the accusative case, for I *love* the Master (of Greenwich School) with all my Heart & soul. Witness F: d'Arblay.

Love to Carlos—& best Comp[ts] to Mrs. Bicknel.

---

[2] This note is missing.

[3] Revisions for *Camilla*. See L. 314, p. 274; iii, L. 226 n. 12; L. 204 n. 3; and L. 211 nn. 1, 2. It is the original printing, however, that is to be reprinted in 1972.

As may be seen in a letter of 4 Nov. 1835 (Houghton) to Richard Bentley, FBA occasionally employed herself for most of her life in revising *Camilla*. Some of the late revisions, made on the backs of letters bearing *pmks* 1831 to 26 Apr. 1836, are extant in the Berg Collection (220 sheets and scraps acccompanying *Camilla*).

[4] No such illustrated edition has yet been located.

I have never had any Letter from P[ayne] or C[adell] & Davies.

398 [West Humble, 27 November 1800]

To Charles Burney

A.L. (Berg), *n.d.*
Double sheet 4to   3 pp.   *pmks*   DARKING   ⟨2⟩7   NO 1800
2 ⟨7⟩ NOV ⟨1800⟩   wafer
Addressed: Dr. Charles Burney, / Greenwich— / Kent

Would to God I *could* send my kind Charles as comforting a Letter!—but my beloved husband set sail on Saturday afternoon for Rotterdam[1]—& the violent storm that arose on Sunday Night, & lasted all yesterday, *here*, has put my nerves into a tremor from which nothing can recover them but news of his safety, for which I am hourly praying, but dare not hope to receive some times as there is no intercourse with Holland but by neutral ships, & clandestine measures.

How kindly you have managed all!—I will write about placing the money another time—you will guard it *en attendant* at your Banker's—our sister Esther is now just come hither from the good & dear Bourdois's[2]—& I must only have her to thank you again & again for your exertions & skill—but I don't quite understand what the 110 *Copies* can mean[3]—we have hardly so many *acquaintance*—However, all is so unexpectedly ameliorated, it may be best, perhaps, to make no investigation —Heaven bless you ever! You shall have a line the very Hour I hear good news of Arrival— |

Love to Mrs. Burny & Carlos
& Compli[men]ts to Mrs Bicknel — —

398. [1] On 22 November.
      [2] At Sand Place, Dorking.
      [3] This proposal is lost with CB Jr.'s letter as are the banking transactions above.

[Sand Place,[1] Dorking,
11 December 1800]

To Charles Burney

A.L. (Berg), *n.d.*
Double sheet 4to   *pmks*   DARKING   11 DEC 1⟨8⟩00   11 DE 1800
wafer
Addressed: Dr. Charles Burney, / Greenwich / Kent

My dearest Charles,

I have just received the glad—glad tydings that my dearest
of Friends is safe in Holland — — He landed at *Dort*, I know not
when,—nor care—He writes instantly, & without detail—but
he says he is perfectly *Well* as well as *Safe*—

I thank God! — —

I am sure you will be happy for me—The dear Bourdois
seized the moment of happiness—they were with me this
morning—to coax me, with your Godson, to their house, to
spend the day. I now write thence, & am charged with their
kindest Loves—

pray dispense mine to Rosetta & Carlos—

& best Comp[ts], to Mrs. Bicknel—I feel sure they will all
rejoice for me—

399. [1] Though the house at 'Sand Place' was set 'on a high sand bank', it took its
name, originally Sondes's Place, from a family of Sondes who migrated to Surrey
in the fifteenth century. See H. E. Maldon, *A History of the County of Surrey* (3 vols.,
1967), iii, 144; and John Timbs, *A Picturesque Promenade Round Dorking, in Surrey*
(1823). According to the Land Tax Assessments, the owner at this time was the
Right Hon. Lord Grimston (1748–1809) and the 'Occupier', Hugh Bisshopp
(ii, L. n. 1), nephew of the Hon. Mrs. Bateman (1727–1802), benefactress of EBB
and her family (i, L. 11 n. 9; v, L. 517 n. 5).

To Doctor Burney

A.L.S. (Diary MSS. vi. 5240–[1], Berg), 16 Dec. 1800
Double sheet small 4to 2 pp. *pmks* DARKING 17 DE 1800 17 DEC 1800 wafer
Addressed: Dr. Burney, / Chelsea College, / Middlesex
Endorsed by CB: 1800
Edited by FBA p. 1, *annotated and dated*: ※ 16th Dec. 1800 (9) M. d'Arblay's return to England
Edited also by CFBt *and the* Press.

He is returned—My dearest Father—already!—My joy & surprise are so great I seem in a dream—I have just this moment a Letter from him, written at *Gravesend*![1]—

What he has been able to arrange as to his affairs, I know not —& just now cannot care, so great is my thankfulness for his safety & return. He waits in the River for his passport—& will, when he obtains it, hasten—I need not say—to WestHamble—This blessed news my dearest Father will I am sure be glad to receive—I am sure, too, of the joy of my dear affectionate Fanny.—

He will be here, I hope, to keep his Son's 6th Birth day, on Thursday.[2] He is well, he says, but *horribly fatigued.* | Heaven bless & preserve you, dearest Sir,

Your own dutiful & affectionate
F. d'A.

16th Decr 1800.
West Hamble.

⌈He was out from ⟨London⟩ to Gravesend one day short of 3 weeks—& that he must almost have lived at sea—in that period, though he does not name the length of either of his voyages.

I hope to God, my dearest Father, I hope to God you will as soon be relieved from the horrible fléau that persecutes you. Esther gives me hopes.⌉

400. [1] M. d'A's letter is missing. Cf. a letter (Berg) from Antoine Bourdois, 16 Dec. 1800.
[2] On Thursday 18 December.

West Humble, 16 December 1800

To Esther (Burney) Burney

A.L.S. (Berg), 16 Dec. 1800
Double sheet small 4to   4 pp.   *pmks*   DARKING   17 DEC 1800
wafer
Addressed: Mrs. Burney, / Beaumont Street, / Portland Place, / London—

> West Hamble
> 16—Dec—1800.

Think of my joy—my surprise—my gratitude to Heaven—
my dearest Esther—that my terrors & anxieties are wholly
ended—that I have just received news my beloved Husband is
returned!—I know how you will feel this for me—so kindly
you partook in my sadness & fears—I thank you for your very
kind Letter—it was just adapted to my sensations when I
received it, & its sympathy was very balsamic—Alas my mind
has been so woe-worn—& woe-prepared, this separation was a
trial almost beyond me—but it's so speedy—& so fortunate—so
BLESSED let me say termination, revives—renovates me—&
severe As has been the experiment, it is very probable ! its
effect—like that of many violent medicines, may be salubrious.
—I hope, however, it will be the only one of the kind I shall
ever swallow!— — —

I had very little More to write than I told you, my dear soul
—I only knew My voyager landed at *Dort*, instead of *Rotterdam*,
—but I knew that was of small consequence, as it is not many
Hours distance in travelling. What he has been able to effect
I know not, as he enters into no details. But I fancy, by his so
sudden return, he merely made out his *procuration*, got it
properly witnessed & authenticated, & came back in the first
Vessel he could find. ! what *time* he landed I did not tell, for I
do not know. I had merely entreated to hear of his safety, &
that was all he mentioned. I shall hope to have him here for
his son's Birth day—our Alex will be 6 year's old next Thursday.
He is now at Gravesend, waiting his passport,[1] which he has sent
for from Town. Your Maria & her good sposo are both quite

---

[1] Aliens disembarking at coastal ports required special passports to enable them
to travel inland.

well—I saw him yesterday morning for a couple of Hours, but the Weather was impracticable for a female. I fear We shall soon lose their *vicinity*.

Horribly, he says, he is fatigued!—poor soul—he must have been upon the Sea almost the whole of his absence. I have written to our dear Father—How I grieve & *revolt* at his being thus persecuted by the Heartless Insulter![2] — — — pray ¹ let dear Charlotte—& James—& Sally know my happiness—*My happiness* will be words precious I know to all my family!— I shall write to Charles, with whom I have business also. But were *I* out of the Question—out of the World—*this* news would be welcome to you all, I feel sure. And dear good aunt Beckey! I knew not she had any share of my anxiety, or would sooner have named her—give her now my joy with my kindest Love. All this at your leisure, however, for no one can so soon expect it. I long to hear your Face is better, my poor soul—& am truly sorry for its attack. pray try *Camphorated spirits*, a few drops in a spoonful of water, every Morning. with me 'tis a *specific*.—

God bless you, my dearest Esther. Alex sends his Love & says he shall *fetch his Wife* [as soon a]s he is six year's old—Love to Mr. B[urney] & Richard & amelia ever & ever yours

F. d'A.

402   [West Humble,] 16 December 1800

To Charles Burney

A.L. (McGill), 16 Dec. 1800
Double sheet 8vo (4×6·5")   4 pp.   *pmks*   DARKING   17 DEC 1800
17 DE 1800   green wafer
Addressed: Dr. Charles Burney, / Greenwich, / Kent.
Docketed in pencil, p. 1: FB
            p. 3: Madame d'Arblay.
            p. 4: 6" 1.

I know the postage will be *cheap* that shall tell my dearest Carlos my best of all friends—dear & excellent as are my others—is returned!—to my unspeakable joy & gratitude &

401. ² The letter to CB, conjecturally including references to the 'Heartless Insulter' (?Phillips), was probably destroyed.

surprise, I have this Morning a letter dated *Gravesend*! The weight it has taken off my soul almost revives it to—once more —pleasure, as well as thankfulness & satisfaction. I know Rosette & Carluc—& Mrs. Bicknel will rejoice—but few on Earth perhaps more cordially—if *as*—as my dearest Charles.—

I will write about the *monish* when ⏐ I have seen him—I hope he will arrive to keep his son's 6ᵗʰ Birthday, the 18ᵗʰ. He is detained now for his passport, which must be sent him from London—his letter was begun on board the vessel on *Friday*, & finished on Sunday—he was out from Gravesend one day short of 3 weeks in all. What he has been able to do, I have yet no account. Probably merely to forward a properly witnessed & ⏐ authenticated *procuration*.

> Heaven bless you—
> my Boy is perfectly well.

16. Decʳ 1800. ⏐
1000 Thanks for the papers—
    3 missing following last week—
      all else right—

403   West Humble, [16 January 1801]

To M. d'Arblay

A.L., mutilated (rejected Diary MSS. 5242–[3], Berg), *n.d.*
Conjecturally in the original, a single sheet 4to (*c.* 8 × 6·4″)   1 p.
Edited by FBA *and also by* CFBt, *who took two cuttings from this letter and three from a letter of 23 Feb. 1801, which five cuttings were pasted to a blank sheet to form a composite, bearing* FBA's *editorial dating* 16 Jan. 1801. *Edited at the* Press, *see* Textual Notes.

> West Hamble—Dorking
> Surry

How tormenting that this ancle attack should thus unreasonably add to your harrass & hurries!—I count the hours till you can return & rest it—*else*, you know, I should let them pass on without solicitude!!—our little delight is just as you left him, all that is prosperous & chearing, in body & mind: but he insists upon it he loves ME more than I do him, because he cannot coax me to say I love him more than I do YOU—& he uses every little tender reproach he can suggest to persuade me I am very unkind not to place him FIRST. Dear little soul! he is high enough, God knows!—I am infinitely anxious to see your Letters—& understand if your uncle's is consolatory, & if M. de Narbonne knows yet the dread & irreparable blow our happiness has everlastingly received on EARTH — — *FIRST*—best & dearest source of all that remains to me—*First*, even before this calamity—I shall welcome you to-morrow!—My kindest Love to dear Maria & Boud—& I hope you will see none other after reading this |

404   West Humble, 18 February 1801

To Mrs. Waddington

A.L.S. (rejected Diary MSS. 5244-[7], Berg), 18 Feb. 1801
Double sheet 4to 4 pp. *pmks* DARKING 19 Feb 1801 wafer
Addressed: ⌈Mrs. Waddington / Lanover House,⌉ near / ⌈Abergavenny— / Monmouth.⌉
Edited by CFBt *and the* Press.

West Hamble, *Dorking, Surry*.
not *Leatherhead*
18. Feby 1801.

Will you not be tempted to cast away my Letter angrily, & even unread?—My tardy Letter, so ill, by its slouth, expressing either what I feel or what you deserve? My dear Marianne!— The Cause is now, indeed, gone which heretofore has made me —to all but Her I have lost—a most unequal & irregular Correspondent, even where warmly I have loved, & sincerely wished a constant intercourse:—but though GONE—forever!— from my sight, it lives in my memory—my mind—my eternal regret—& Letter writing—beyond even any other species of writing, will probably be the last to which I shall be able to return, without a pang that makes it amongst my cruellest exertions.

You will hardly think, while I avow this, how very wide is the difference I experience from Letter-*reading*—yet, if you had seen me when perusing both your last, you would comprehend & believe it. They were touching to me, my dear Mary, from their confidence,—their tone of other days, & the gentle kindness which forbore reproach at my silence. It is so only I can be tamed from the wild sorrow which has ravaged all my habits, as well as happiness—it is so only my dear Mrs. Lock herself has brought me round to have pleasure again in her tender & indulgent friendship.—for at first, my two other selfs, with whom I live, were all I could bear to see, all I could even wish to support. The blow, my dear Friend—was so dreadfully tragical—the contrast of reality & expectation—the suddenness of horrour, taking such abrupt place of Hope that seemed, at that moment certainty — — |

I am glad I have been obliged to turn over, for it shall turn me from this fatal theme—& I will answer your interesting Letters:—And with your Emily I must begin—for of her I most frequently think—I will ingenuously own to you I am the more anxious for her, because many traits you have occasionally given me of her Character & disposition strongly resemble what I could recount of my Alex—& if He had such disordered health,—I can imagine my sufferings, & easily, therefore, bring yours home to me. If you are able to give me any better account of her, you will truly rejoice me. Your descriptions make her so fascinating a little being, that I wonder not you are so wrapt up in her—though I see, with equal pleasure & approbation, that the worth & goodness of her amiable & deserving Sister have their full weight in balancing your maternal affections.[1]— Your Louisa,[2] too,—is she recovered? *mentally*, as well as corperally? I am quite indignant at your sketch of the injurious delusions which have blighted her fair hopes & rosy health. Pray tell me some thing of her in detail—I must be much interested for one who has been to you, as you say 'entirely what you wanted'—by which I hope you have in her a faithful, sympathising, confidential & tender friend.—But poor—poor Mrs. Granville!—there my concern comes home indeed! how

404. [1] Cf. L. 393 n. 2.
[2] Louisa Port (1778–1817), who, much against the wishes of her family, was to marry in 1803 the Revd. Brownlow Villiers Layard (1779–1861).

irreparable, indelible a blow! an only, & so beloved a Child![3]—
How little I thought, my poor friend, that YOU, also were
destined to exclaim 'O God! what a year was the last!—' Pray
let me know if Mrs. Granville is able at all to revive. I pity
sincerely her poor husband, too,—What a complete break up
of all their possible happiness!— |

About your own health I am very solicitous—your account
of it is far beyond ⟨un⟩satisfactory—My dearest Mary—keep
your Mind as equal & your Spirits as calm as your utmost
strength of exertion can effect. I wish I knew whether this
Letter would find you at once at your home, or again trying
Clifton, for—your little darling—I feel checked when I write
Letters that may travel from post to post, & be possibly lost.
I have much I could say, though I am sluggish in saying it—
The poor voisin—I cannot but wish to know if the stroke were
from mental causes.—Tell me. I was sure you would be affected
by the death of Gen¹ Goldsworthy.[4] Your long & mutual
friendship—& the countless & singular circumstances that hung
upon it, made him always an interesting object to you. I have
had no account, as yet, of Miss Goldsworthy,[5] or of any particulars: but his life has long been in the most precarious state, &
perpetual expectation of its sudden failure has kept all his
friends in constant alarm. I met him at Lady Rothes, in this
neighbourhood, when the Princess Amelia passed a night there
in her way from Worthing,[6] & he was so changed, & so conscious,
that he scarsely spoke one word during the breakfast, at which
I joined them: but afterwards, when we happened to be next
each other, he resumed his usual gay tone & sprightly chat, &
we talked together of old times, & of *you*, with much frankness &
spirit. It was the only meeting I ever had with him since I retired
from the royal household. I am sure Miss Goldsworthy will be
deeply afflicted.—I must not close my Letter without speaking
of Norbury Park—My dear & revered Mr. Lock—is, thank
Heaven! quite well. We see him almost | daily—for so kind &
indulgent to our fondness of his sight he is, that he scarcely ever

---

³ John Granville (1779–1800), only surviving child of the Revd. John Dewes
later Granville (1744–1826) and his wife Harriet Joan *née* de la Bere (d. 1825), had
died on 8 July. See Maxwell Fraser (op. cit.), pp. 285–309.
⁴ General Goldsworthy (i, L. 5 n. 10) died on 4 Jan. 1801. For GMAPW's
girlhood infatuation, see L. 300, p. 230; and *HFB*, pp. 256–9.
⁵ See i, L. 16 n. 2.   ⁶ See L. 300 and n. 1

takes an outing, without gratifying us with a call. I can compare him, for every excellence, only with your venerated aunt Delany—& for every similar perfection, I can compare them both only with the ANGEL I have last lost.—Some few others I could name with similar qualities—& gratefully let me say to you amongst those with whom I am most closely connected: but trials such as HERS they have been spared—& therefore I cannot pronounce upon them as equally purified.—Mrs. Angerstein is a Mother such as *you*, all wrapt up in her baby,[7] watching & following & adoring it, as you did yours at Luston. Mrs. W. Lock[8] proves a very estimable woman, with great goodness of heart, & uncommon sweetness of temper. But you are rightly informed, that lovely as she is in face & person, she has not that expressive beauty which is so marked in the fine features & countenance of her husband.—I must not omit to tell you my health is again restored, nor that my spirits are tolerably calmed, All that could soften so dread a stroke by tenderest sympathy in one whose Existence is My Existence has mercifully been granted me—& my Boy makes sorrow & sadness fly at his gay approach—yet Time only can really heal a wound that has lacerated all my first, dearest natural feelings—through aggravations of calamity that make the fatal event but a part of the anguish which my poor Sainted Sister's sufferings inflicted. adieu, my dear Marianne—& may you be enabled to send more [enliven]ing accounts of yourself & your family

to your ever affect[e]

F d'A.

[7] See L. 396 n. 6.   [8] See L. 385 n. 2; L. 387 n. 1.

To M. d'Arblay

A.L. mutilated (Berg), 23 Feb. ⟨1801⟩

Originally a double sheet 4to (*c.* 8·3 × 6·4″), from which CFBt took three cuttings for the Pasteup (rejected Diary MSS. 5242–[3], Berg), dated 16 Jan. 1801. The top of the double sheet is extant, and, still joined at the spine, there remains of the first leaf a segment (2·6 × 6·4″) and of the second leaf a segment (1·7 × 6·4″). The three cuttings used as Pasteovers are also extant, but missing are two segments (*c.* 1·1 × 6·4″) and (*c.* 2·3 × 6·4″) that in the cutting would have been released from the bottoms of the first and second leaves respectively. 4 pp.

Addressed: A. d'Arblay Esqr, / at A Bourdois Esqr, / N° 1. Clarges Street, / Piccadilly / London.   *pmk*   DARKIN[G]   wafer

Edited by FBA, p. 1, *annotated and the date* 1801 *retraced*: 1801 (18/2)

Mutilated by CFBt, *see* Textual Notes.

West Hamble,
Feb. 23^d ⟨1801⟩

How kind to write me so much—when so little would content me!—Every line is a little recruit to me—& I look forward to to-morrow as a blank the most complete.

But—My dearest *Chevalier*, let me talk to you of your *Chevalier-born* son—

We were reading together yesterday *Princess Fair Star, & Prince Cherry*[1]—& in the midst of an adventure, he suddenly stopt short, & exclaimed: 'O Mama! what a mistake the author has made!—I think he has wrote quite nonsense! for he says Fientosa does all the wicked things the naughty Queen orders her—& just before, he had said Fientosa was the Queen's Maid of Honour!—'

What say you? Will you not own your boy?—

[*the bottom of the page is cut away.*]

⌐*condescendsion*, I would still prefer a lengthened separation *at once*, to your return upon the same errand, or any delay of a determination through your absence. I merely seek an end, be it what it may.⌐ How I wish I had petitioned for a line by the

---

405. [1] 'La Princesse Belle-Étoile et le Prince Chéri' by Marie Catherine La Mothe, comtesse d'Aulnoy (*c.* 1650–1705). A translation 'The Story of the Princess Fair-Star and Prince Chery' was included in *A Collection of Novels and Tales of the Fairies. Written by that Celebrated Wit of France, Countess D'Anois* (London, 3 vols., 1728).

Coach to-morrow! the Day is so long—the Evening so lingering, in my present state of mind, when I have nothing upon which to build either hope or conjecture as to your return — — ! — I have again taken to Me de Sevigné—I find nothing like her for attraction at this period—nothing resembling her, on *paper*, for sensibility, taste, & *Esprit*.—

[*the bottom of the page has been cut away*]

⌐How sorry I am for my poor Sister Burney's retu[rn] of pain! I hope you have told her I will write the mom[ent] we have fixed our plan—& that our visits to our fath[er] will be considerably more pleasant by delaying, if poss[ible] till April our excursion. We have hitherto always been ill & confined in dreary & cold-catching weather [*cut*] when for an hour I am sure we shall both enjoy, & be more enjoyed, later in the year, & then your *planting* with what again ⟨groweth⟩ at our dear Bookham is [*cut*] high beauty the morning. I give you no commissions & ⟨so⟩ you must suggest, what you know so well for me— as from me [to] our Friends. For other commissions I am too uncer[tain] of ⟨ones⟩ taken here to ⟨know⟩ what to wish: but *Biscuits* & cu⟨rran⟩ts—*Soap Candles* ⟨*Mustard*⟩ Sugar Treacle ⟨   ⟩ & *Flour Rice* as you [think] best. &c.⌐

⌐[We] shall long for ⟨Fri⟩days' *Post* or *Coach*!—

'Tell Papy I beg him to come directly, for we're never quite happy without our dear P. because we love him so much we can't help wanting him every *minute*, not only every day, but every *moment*!' cries Alex, while I write. And adds [*line sliced*] he must do something I bid him when⌐

[*bottom of page cut away*]

To Charles Parr Burney

A.N. (McGill), *n.d.*
Originally a single sheet 4to, part of which seems to have been cut away, leaving this remnant (5·2 × 6·1″)   2 pp.   *pmks*   D[ARKING]   4 MR 1801 MAR 180[1]   green wafer
   Addressed in the hand of M. d'A: Dr Charles ⟨P⟩ [*leaf cut*] / Greenwich / K [*leaf cut*]
   Docketed on address panel: M^{rs.} D'Arblay

Mr. Charles Burney

I write to my dear Charles, in the confidence of his kindness, to assist a *female Usher* with some hints how to use Ash's Grammar[1] for a Pupil in preparation—whether it is to be learnt *by heart* throughout, beginning with the introduction—or with the Grammatical Institutes. In short, to try to recollect how he began himself, that I may endeavour to spur on his little Cousin to emulate his career. I would not trouble your dear-toil-worn Father with an enquiry you can so well answer; I I know how gladly you would assist him in far greater matters— & I do not apply to your Mama, because my little manly urchin will pay greater regard to the advice of a male than a lady, having already said to me—'I am better than you, mama, for *wisery*, for all I'm only your son, because I'm a Male, & you're only a Female, you know, Mama.'

God bless you,
my dear Boy.

406. [1] John Ash (*c.* 1724–79), LL.D. (1774). His *Grammatical Institutes; or, an easy introduction to Dr. Lowth's English Grammar* (1763) had run to at least fifteen editions by 1796.

To Esther (Burney) Burney

A.L. (Berg), 17 Mar. 1801
Double sheet 4to   4 pp.   *pmks*   DARKING   18 MAR 1801   wafer
Addressed: Mrs. Burney, / Beaumont Street, / Portland Place, / London.
Endorsed by EBB: answered / march. 23 1801
Scribbling, p. 4: Beaum^t St— / N° 21—Brown / Botanical painter

West Hamble, 17th Mars,
1801

You may indeed believe me, my dearest Esther, wretched Correspondant as I am, I should long since have written—have thanked you for your very kind Letters & invitation, & have better *shewn* the interest I never fail to *feel* in your current, as well as essential affairs, but that I have expected, from Day to Day, these three months past, to be able to fix the time of our excursion from home—but at this very moment, I find myself as ignorant as ever, & therefore I can no longer refrain from renewing the only method of intercourse still in my power.— I won't say *if YOU are* not tired out by my silence & irregularity —I know how you can allow for these sins of omission, which, though I have not the shamelessness to justify in themselves, you will always find, the long run, compatible with the sincerest truth of affection—though, I am grieved to be forced to own how much it is wanting in *apparent* kindness. Don't judge me by it, however, my dearest Esther—& the less, as—alas—I cannot promise to Mend!—for I can only write, now, from an anxiety to *hear*, or the fear of being thought unkind. Even formerly— in my *ci-divant* Days, when Letter writing was a delight to me, I was | always a most unpunctual Correspondant—upon what basis, then can I now build hope of reformation?—I am to blame, indeed, to have entered upon the hopeless—*graceless* subject,—& I think, in future, I shall cast myself upon your mercy, & *cut it* wholly: trusting that, through all my pen irregularity, you will see my affection's faithfulness for I can solemnly say to myself—which is taking the only earthly Judge, I cannot recollect one instant of my life in which my Heart has not warmly loved you.

Another large pacquet of your Letters to our loved lost Angel is just fallen into my hands. I have found them in an immense parcel brought me by Mrs. Lock, which She had left sealed up at Norbury Park—& which Mrs. Lock, in the tenderness of her heart, has only brought since she thought me better able to look it over, which has been since the return of my first friend from Holland.[1] But I have only opened it within a few Days,—waiting my own best courage for the purpose—I find the greatest, *far* greatest part all to be returned to Mrs. Lock, as it consists of her own Letters, from the beginning of the friendship formed with that adorable family, to within the 2 last years of our angel's residence amongst us. Those of the 2 last, I found the Letters of in the great Chest at your house, & in the Bag left in mine. A few, also, I find of James's, & of Charlotte's—but very few. A copious one of our dear Father—, which, like yours & Mrs. Lock's, are tied up & endorsed, every one, with *month* & *year*, & a general cover to all, of *examined*—by which I conclude they were all such as the dear soul *meant* to keep, not put by either in haste, or for future sorting & selecting. All, however, put together, are nothing to my own immense pacquets,[2]—My God! what volumes have I written to her!—yet nothing weighs so heavily on my remembrance & regret as that I writ not more! — — —

I shall bring all these with me to town.

I can hardly tell you how disappointed I felt by hearing of the return of your tooth ache, through M. d'A. after your welcome intelligence that you were *cured*. Pray let me know, if possible, that it was a transient *visit* only. There is a subject I have little *gusto* to entering upon, & yet would not have you think me wilfully holding back from. Think a little, to your own self, & you will guess it, & then add this much further: That even yet I know not what is purposed as to *time*, or even whether at *any* it will be heard of!—My Agent is *dead silent*, & my own wishes & desires about it are nearly in the same insensible state. This keeps me patient in an ignorance that—15 months ago, would have kept me on the rack. All I have myself interfered with, is a renewed insistance on *incog*, if any trial is made.

407. [1] M. d'A. had returned *c.* 16 Dec. 1800 (L. 400).

[2] In normal practice the letters written by these correspondents to SBP would have been returned at her death to the writers; for what is known to survive, however, and for the correspondence of FBA and SBP, see *Catalogue*.

For that I am indeed inexpressibly earnest.[3] Uncertain as we are, you must not think of us till we are actually set out. | Our plan is to *begin* with Chelsea—& then suit your convenience, at the *time*, for being second, 3^d or 4th—We are all unwell— M. d'A. returned with the most malignant sort of Cold I ever saw—which my poor little Love caught first, & then myself—& it hangs upon us all still, so as to make it very little desirable to us to quit home just at present. How much I have been occupied & distressed & afflicted about the excellent King, you may easily imagine, & how excessively I rejoice in his blessed recovery.[4] Your account of R[ichard] & F[anny] P[hillips] disturbs me a good deal.[5] I fear the *opposition* has been too vehement, & rather aggravated the matter? *reasoning* soon appears *persecution*, where followed up by strict measures, to so young a Girl. Tell me what you think of this management? my only hope is from her mixing with others, & seeing more of the world, & having something more eligible & prudent fall in her way—but I own I feel for R[ichard].—who is little likely to meet any thing so lovely & attractive equally well inclined to him, in his present secluded life. I am really MUCH concerned at the whole. I have infinite satisfaction in all I gather of *Maria* & M. Bourdois—who seem as happy as our wishes anticipated them. My kindest Love when you see them & to dear Blue— but first & foremost to dear Mr. B[urney]. Alex. sends his Love to Amelia, & hopes she will make him *a good Daughter*. Our dearest fr^{ds} up the Hill come down *daily* to see us—but my Cold has made me shy—lest I sh^d infect them. I was much surprised yesterday by a visit from a Lady who w^d not be denied—& proved to be my old fr^d Miss Thrale[6]—God bless you, dearest Esther—ever—

[3] The revival of plans for the production of 'Love and Fashion' (see L. 364).

[4] The King was recuperating from a second 'major' attack of the illness now convincingly diagnosed as porphyria (see *Porphyria—a Royal Malady*, being articles published in or commissioned by the *British Medical Journal*, 1968, pp. 10 and 13). Initially diagnosed as a 'severe cold', the King's illness, as well as public alarm, became serious enough to warrant daily medical bulletins from 22 Feb. until 11 Mar. when the last report indicated that 'the King's health requires only time to be perfectly re-established' (*The Times*, 22 Feb.–11 Mar. 1801).

[5] Cf. L. 394, p. 456.

[6] 'Queeney' Thrale (i, L. 11 n. 4).

To James Burney

A.L.S. (PML, Autog. Cor. bound), *n.d.*
Single sheet small 4to 2 pp. *pmks* DARKING 18 MAR 1801 wafer
Addressed in the hand of ?M. d'A: Capt ⌜⟨Burnei⟩⌝ Burney / N° 9 Charles
Street / Soho Square / *London*

I am quite gratified, my dear James, to find you so perfectly
reasonable in your expectations. I dread nothing so much as the
disappointments arising, almost constantly, from too sanguine
hopes. Lord St. Vincent[1] must necessarily have claims from
Those who have served immediately under him, that he is
bound in Honour & Justice to satisfy first. That you *will* have
your turn, as soon as it is possible with propriety in regard to his
own essential engagements, I have not a doubt—but I own I
dare not myself expect it for some months. My chief wish is to
have you employed during the Summer: you have been so long
unused to sea hardships, that I should be much concerned to
have you resume them in winter, without a warmer seasoning.
Even should Lord St. Vincent go out, so powerful a recommendation he would be bound to give of you, that I look upon your
being employed, & properly & honourably, certain every way.
And much as I have wished you a ship under Lord Spencer, it is
still an added pleasure to be promoted by a *professional* 1st L^d

408. [1] John Jervis (1735–1823), cr. Earl of St. Vincent (1797), and cr. (27 Apr.
1801) Viscount St. Vincent, had been appointed on 19 Feb. Lord High Admiral
(1801–4) in Addington's newly formed ministry.
   In an earlier part of his long career on the sea the Admiral had apparently
come across JB (as see CB's remarks on the matter, i, L. 17 n. 11) and, placing
some hopes on favourable recollections, JB had evidently addressed him in his new
office. Though this correspondence has not been found, a later recommendation
(29 Dec. 1806) by the Earl is extant in the Pierpont Morgan Library: 'Sir / Whenever I am referrd to, I shall be ready to bear testimony to your ability, as a Circum
Navigator, and ingenuity, as an author, upon Subjects of discovery, Characters,
which have plac's you very high, in the estimation of / Sir / Your very obedient /
Humble Servant / St Vincent.'
   JB's efforts of this year are also shown in his letter of 6 Jan. 1801 (PRO ADM,
vol. 1526, No. 530) to the Secretary of the Admiralty Board [Sir Evan Nepean]:
'Sir / I beg leave to renew my application to the Lords Commissioners of the
Admiralty for employment, & have the honour to remain Sir / Your most obedient
/ humble servant / James Burney.'
   Despite CB's view of the matters, disobedience to orders was perhaps the real
cause of James's being set ashore.

of the Amiralty.[2] Such must be best judges whom they bring forward. I saw an article in the papers, of L^d St. Vincent's purposing to employ the old officers before he made new ones,[3] that I thought | very àprôpos, & read with great satisfaction. Where is it Ld. St. V. had *known* you? Sally mentions his recollecting you. It is very pleasant indeed to be advanced because *recollected* by an officer so high in the service as Ld. St. V. I have again ventured to touch upon a certain subject to our F[ather] but had *no* answer—save a most kind & warm invitation—through Fanny Phillips which shews him not offended. We shall not be very long, certainly, before we make our round: but we are all quite unwell, from a most inveterate & invincible Cold which M. d'A. brought from Town, & has made us a present of, that we may all cough in chorus. We wish to stay to be entirely cured before we risk that air again. Alex s^d to little Nanny t'other Day 'Nanny, there's a Man in the Garden that's a *Head older* than papa What's the reason of that?'— 'I don't know, indeed, Sir, there's no reason for such a thing as that.' 'Yes, but there is, Nanny, for Uncle James told me there was a reason for every thing, so what's the reason of that?' You see he has not forgotten you. My love to Sally, & to Martin

Ever yours
my dear Brother
F. d'A.

 [2] With the change of ministries, Earl Spencer (i, L. 3 n. 123), First Lord of the Admiralty since 1794, was succeeded by the Earl of St. Vincent (above).
 [3] According to *The Times* (6 Mar. 1801), the Earl of St. Vincent 'refused every application that has been made to him for promotion by young Captains, or others newly appointed; having declared his intention of giving the preference to all those persons of whom he has an opinion, who have been the longest on the Half-pay List.'

Conjointly with M. d'Arblay
To James Burney
and Sarah Harriet Burney

A.L.S. & A.L.S. (PML, Autog. Cor. bound), 29 Mar. 1801
Double sheet 4to   3 pp.   *pmks*   DARKING   30 MAR 1801 wafer
Addressed: Capt James Burney / *N^o* 9 Charles Street / Soho Square /
London

[*By* M. *d'Arblay*]

West humble 29th March, 1801

Dear James,
Your sister rejoices at your not being ordered yet to tread the
watery steps of the unfortunate Invincible:[1] As to me, I think
that such a terrible catastrophe is the best insurance for at least
twenty years, that Pilots will be more careful to do their duty.
Thus as soon as Earl St Vincent will be pleased to be as good as
his word, I will in spite of all sisterly fears and anxieties dring
a bumper of *Small* beer to the health of his Lordship.
A thousand thousand thanks my dear James for your kind
offer to pass at ⟨Mr Wimburn⟩,[2] which I think would be productive of good consequences.
Please to pay at Mssr Coutts on my account the Mickleham
50 pounds, and nothing more, because after a little *consultation*
between us about that business we have agreed that it was to be
So.

My love to Sally and Martin
Your's for ever
A. d'Arblay ｜

409. [1] H.M.S. *Invincible*, of 74 guns, one of the oldest ships in the navy, sailing
from Yarmouth on 16 Mar. with a full complement of men and bound for the
Baltic, struck 'the sand-ridge called Hammond's Knole, within five leagues of
Yarmouth', and sliding off some twenty-four hours later, sank to the bottom (*The
Times*, 20 Mar.), losing 400 of her 600 men. The Great Fleet of the Baltic had sailed
on 12 Mar. and Nelson's second great victory, the Battle of Copenhagen, was
fought on 2 April.
[2] Possibly the surgeon and apothecary Richard Wimburn (d. 13 Dec. 1801) of
Jermyn-street (*GM* lxxi[2]. 1157).

[*By Madame d'Arblay*]

I could not but be thankful you escaped the command of the *Invincible*, indeed, my dear James.

As to the £50—interest upon it, or re-payment as to stocks, are wholly out of the Question. It was lent HER—that beloved Angel, to facilitate her return—& though by him accepted & used—in part, as I have found by her own writing, for debts of his previous to their setting out, yet so far its purpose was answered, as that of drawing her from the detestable spot where her Death Bell was rung,—& therefore let the principal alone be paid, as was meant in the loan.

Adieu, my dear James—I have little doubt but we shall catch a glimpse of you before you sail, for I have no idea Ld St. V[incent] can name you to a Vessel till he has served his immediate claimants, & I have, as yet, seen but 2 names of his own nominati[ng]

yours ever affectly

F d'A. |

Our colds, my dear Sally, are still lurking & oppressive, though on the wane: but I think we shall not miss joining our Cheer to the general huzza that must hail our Brother's nomination.—What hard conditions of Peace are these of poor Mrs. R[ishton]![3] We shall not, I hope, in our new ministry, be so severe! I am really shocked & grieved. Is not Stephen much hurt? But how can *Maria* have effected Such a transaction? & how has *Richard* escaped it? I cannot comprehend this, but am very glad for Stephen. You will find our poor Alex terribly thin, by long discipline, for the Cold first, & now for worms: we wish to recruit him before we venture him to town. Adieu, my dear Sally—

ever faithfully yours

F d A

I always hear with sincere satisfaction of your Chelsea visits— & wish you to omit none that can conveniently be made—

---

3 To comply with some new terms exacted by Rishton as the price of separation, Maria had evidently made some disposition of, or stopped inroads into, the Allen money, but the documents available throw no further light on the matter.

The Revd. Stephen Allen was Maria's brother; Richard Thomas Burney, her half-brother. See i, Intro., lxxiii–lxxiv.

To Mrs. Waddington

A.L.S. (Berg), 4 Apr. 1801
Double sheet 4to (9·1 × 7·3″), from the first leaf of which two cuttings were
taken for Pasteovers, leaving a segment 4·8″ still attached to its conjugate
leaf   4 pp.
Addressed: Mrs. Waddington, / Lanover House, / Abergavenny.
Edited by CFBt *and the* Press.

West Hamble, Dorking, Surry.
April 4ᵗʰ 1801.—

Well may You, at least, my dear Marianne, join in the
opinion you quote of Mᵉ de Genlis, that the life of every Woman
is a Romance![1] How singular are your accounts! to *me* how
interesting—& to *any* body how entertaining! yet I fear to hear
the END of the present episode,—though you are much mistaken
if you fancy you have ever given me the beginning. In truth,
I should be glad to go a little backward in the narration, that I
might have a clearer comprehension of what is yet to ensue.
You have awakened an anxiety for the chief OBJECT of this part
of the Romance, which I beg you to satisfy. The blanks, indeed,
I fill up—but whether rightly or falsely how can I tell? — —
Let me not, however, risk omitting to mention that Mrs. Locke
is much pleased with the little Cutting,[2] & with your sending it
to her, & desires her kindest acknowledgements & remembrances; & she told me, yesterday, *That William said the female
figure was really clever.* — — I, too, am much gratified by the
little view from my namesake, & beg you to thank & kiss her
for me; but did she herself write the accompanying note? *vrai?*
vraiment? That your Emily is better, gives me a very serious
satisfaction, for I think your peace of mind, & powers of happiness, enwrapped [*part of a line missing*] about my Alex—[*a line
missing*] ⌉ who is, that Heaven only knows if either of us could
support without him an existence which he every Day—every

---

410. ¹ The theme of *Les Mères rivales* (4 vols., 1800).
    ² Mrs. Waddington, taught the art of paper-cutting by her great-aunt Mrs.
Delany (cf. iii, p. 165), taught it in turn to her children. A collection (Berg) of
figures of children, etc., executed in silhouette on white paper and cut out, is probably the work of the young Waddingtons.

Hour—& every minute contributes to enliven and charm. I am sorry you cannot see him—& the more, as there is little chance he should continue long such as he now is, externally—& the little Rogue does not excite much horrour in stranger beholders[3] —how should he in *your* Eyes, which would view him with pleasure as mine, be he what he might?—He would be very glad to see your young designer, & talks of her, from what I have shewn him of her works, with an interest & familiarity that often amuses me. 'Mama, he says, tell Fanny Waddington to *cut me out* some more pretty pictures;—but think of a little girl making a fable, Mama!—Tell her to *make me* another: how clever of her, to *make me* fables!—Tell her she may come & see me, Mama—& I'll lend her my bricks to build houses,—when I've shewn her how, that she mayn't do some mischief, out of a mistake'—&c he intends, very soon, he says, to marry—&, not long since, with the gravest simplicity, he went up to Mr. William Locke, who was here with his fair Bride, & said 'How did you get that wife, *William*? because I want to get such a one —& I don't know which is the way.' And he is now actually employed in fixing sticks & stones, at convenient distances, upon a spot, very near our own, where he means to raise a suitable structure for his residence, after his nuptials.—You will not think he has suffered much time to be wasted before he has begun deliberating upon his conjugal establishments.

[Here two lines have been cut away.] [1]

short excursion the end of last year—dreadful year!—to Holland?—We hope its effects will prove prosperous, but nothing yet is ascertained.—& perhaps may not be till the Peace—Peace! shall we ever have it?—

Mrs. Charles Lock, from continual ill health in the Italian climate, has been driven to return home, & Mr. Charles to beg leave of absence from his *consulship* to conduct her & her two babes[4]—with a *3ᵈ* expected—Indeed, since this permission has been requested, the affairs of Naples have taken such a turn,[5]

³ For some outside testimony, see L. 387 n. 4.

⁴ Charles Locke, however, came alone on a brief mission to England, as his wife, expecting a third child, 'could not face the fatigue of the long overland journey'. Returning to Naples in June, he and his entire family left for England only at the end of August (*Locks of Norbury*, chap. xix).

⁵ Owing to the delay in communications from foreign ports, FBA had probably only now read in the newspapers (e.g., *The Times*, 25 Mar. 1801) that on 18 Feb. an Armistice had been signed between the French Republic and His Majesty

that it may merely have saved them either a forced retention, or a flight. They are supposed to be now fast approaching our shores, & the late stormy weather has caused much inquietude for them.

Mrs. Angerstein's Baby has, unfortunately, no maternal resemblance—but it is a very fine Child, though I know not how to forgive it for its ushering itself into life with so little taste. She began nursing it herself, most successfully, & with delight unspeakable; but she has not been able to go on with the delicious task, for the Child & herself have both been sufferers from internal complaints, & it has been, most reluctantly on her side, weaned at 3 months old. Mr. & Mrs. W^m stroll about the Country, arm in arm, & are quite happy, & seem trying which shall look handsomest: though for exquisite expression the advantage is wholly his: but her Countenance has a cast of ingenuousness, & speaks a native, inartificial character, ⟨m⟩arks so genuine & so rare, as to be very engaging, & ⏐ create every hope of permanent good to the connexion.

How I have marvelled at your *latter* History of Mr. & Mrs. Granville![6] Tell me more of your Louisa[6]—And where is the lady you were attaching yourself to a year or two ago with a promise of much esteem & regard? Did she fail your expectations? or have you lost sight of her from necessary separations? Adieu, dearest Mary—

ever most truly yours
F d'A

Have you seen Mrs. Piozzi's Retrospection?[7] Miss Thrale has promised to send it me. She, (Miss T.) surprised me with a very friendly & kind visit last week—though I had been—alas— a year & 3 Months without answering her last Letter!—When will *you* so end a silence?—We have still postponed our annual visit to our friend—& stil⟨l⟩ [lack] spirit & energy to make it— though deep in promises, & determined to [*corner torn away*]

the King of the Two Sicilies. The ports of Naples and Sicily were then closed to English vessels and commerce and Englishmen in Naples hastened to apply for passports to return home.

⁶ See L. 404 nn. 2, 3, and Maxwell Fraser, op. cit., pp. 285–309.

⁷ *Retrospection; or a Review of the Most Striking and Important Events, Characters, Situations, and Their Consequences, which the last Eighteen Hundred Years Have Presented to the View of Mankind* (2 vols., 1801).

To Charles Burney

A.L. (Berg), *n.d.*
Single sheet 8vo   1 p.   *pmks*   Jews R. Chelsea / P.P.U. / 25 ⟨ ⟩ 1801
To be Delivered / by 10. o'Clock / on Sund. Morn.   wafer
Addressed: Dr. Charles Burney, / Greenwich, / Kent—

My dearest Carlos,
    I have been all this week in hopes of seeing you, first on *Monday*,[1] next on *Wednesday*—I now write in our joint names to propose our little visit to Greenwich, for as early in next week as will suit you & my dear Rosette. We can stay but 3 Days, as we are hurried in our return home, & have Beaumont Street, & clarges, to fulfil afterwards, & M. d'A. is in an agony to be again at his Garden in this fine weather.
    God bless you,—My kind Love to Rosette & Carlino, & best Comp^ts. to Mrs. Bicknell. M. d'A & Alex. desire Loves If this season is not perfectly convenient, don't scruple a postponement, dearest Charles—

To Charles Burney
and Sarah (Rose) Burney

A.L.S. (Osborn), 27 Apr.
Double sheet 8vo   2 pp.   *pmks*   Jews R Chelsea U.P.P.   27 ⟨AP⟩ 1801
wafer
Addressed: Mrs. Burney, / Greenwich, / Kent.

Chelsea College,
April 27th
My dear Charles & Rosette,
    Every thing turns out so unluckily for our meeting, this time, that we must defer it to our next excursion.

411. [1] That is, on Monday 20 April.

We could not go first to Esther, as Blue¹ is there for another Week *certain*, &, if not hurried, probably for more.

I made a positive previous agreement to be at Chelsea but a Week, which concludes this day, as there is no accommodation here for M. d'A.—& we are now become such a Darby & Joan, that, except by the compulsion of business, we do not arrange our minds to a longer separation.

We shall remove therefore at once to Clarges street,² where we meant to go next Week—*after* you & Esther:—&, as M. d'A[rblay] has punctiliously promised himself to return to his own self-appointment to our Cottage, we must only send you our benediction, & hope, since the Mice cannot travel to the Mountain, the Mountain, in the course of the summer, will travel, to the Mice.

adieu, my dear Charles & Rosette—ever yrs.

F. d'A ¹

I could not answer by your Messenger [*tear*]   we were at the Bᵖ of Winchester's³ till [*tear*]

413   West Humble, 20 May 1801

To Doctor Burney

A.L.S. (Berg), 20 May 1801
Double sheet 4to   4 pp.   *pmks* DARKING   21 MAY 1801   21 MY 1801   wafer
Addressed: Dr. Burney, / Chelsea College / Middlesex—
Endorsed by CB: Battle gained in Egypt / 1801
Edited by FBA, p. 1, *annotated*: My Charlotta Barrett—al. O [*all out?*]

West Hamble, May 20.
1801.

We have been so much occupied since our return, my dearest Sir, that I was quite amazed this morning to recollect that a fortnight had elapsed since I had the blessing of your Sight, & yet that I had not put in my petition for the best solace in

412. ¹ Elizabeth Warren Burney (i, Intro., p. lxxv).
     ² To visit Antoine Bourdois and Maria (see L. 414, p. 492 and n. 4).
     ³ See L. 414, p. 493.

losing it, your writing. But *first*, our little rioter has much alarmed me, by a Cough which seized him with some menace of its being the Whooping sort, which at this time is in the town of Dorking; & though I should be relieved from continual apprehensions by his actually having, & *surviving* that cruel disease, I yet am unable to wish it him, in his present thin habit of body. However, as he was feverish, I gave him James's Powders, for 10 days, as an alterative, & without confining him; &, as it has *entirely cured* him, I now find it was merely a bad Cold—*Secondly*, I had all my house & household matters to fresh arrange, which is no little business, in this retired dwelling, where we take in stores for nearly a year at a time, from the difficulty of procuring any thing briefly, & as wanted. *Thirdly*, we are becoming grand, & papering two of our rooms, & our tiny Hall;—Fourthly — — but *if I should tell you till to-morrow*, plain matter of fact is so dull, that the more home I brought the motives of my tardiness, the less they would answer in excusing me, for the less could my dear Father retain such a parcel of stupid schtotff. |

But a piece of good public news makes my heart always jump to your bosom—and I cannot rest till I have tried to shake a pen with you upon it. I am the more rejoiced, too, in this ratification of the glorious battle of the 21st of March, because Mr. Chas. Locke was its first courier.[1] How will Buonaparte make out This, also, to be a defeat on our side? But the loss of Gen[l] Abercrombie is a severe draw back to joy—How eloquent, how noble the eloge of him given by his successor![2] Mr. d'Arblay says they are just the words that should be engraven on his

413. [1] On 1 May 1801 *The Times* reported that 'Mr. CHARLES LOCKE, the British Consul at Naples . . . has brought . . . very important intelligence . . . of a decisive engagement having taken place in Egypt between the English and French armies, in which a complete victory had been gained by the former. . . .' This was the Battle of Alexandria.

[2] Sir Ralph Abercrombie (1734–1801) had died on 28 Mar. of a wound received during the defeat of the French at Alexandria on the 21st (Fortescue, iv, pt. ii. 834–47). He was succeeded by Major-General John Hely-Hutchinson (1757–1832), now promoted to Lt.-Gen. and Commander-in-Chief in Egypt (May 1801), cr. Baron Hutchinson of Alexandria and Knocklofty (1801), K.B. (1801), 2nd Earl of Donoughmore (1825).

Hutchinson's praise of the coolness, perspicuity, and courage of his commander-in-chief may be read in a letter to the Hon. Henry Dundas, dated 'Head-Quarters, Camp, four miles from Alexandria, April 5, 1801' and reprinted in *The Times* (16 May) from the *London Gazette Extraordinary* of the preceding day: '. . . it is some consolation to those who tenderly loved him, that, as his life was honourable, so was be death glorious. His memory will be recorded in the annals of his country—will his sacred to every British soldier, and embalmed in the recollection of a grateful posterity.'

National Monument.—I have been inexpressibly delighted & consoled by the speech of Mr. Addington relative to the dear King.[3] I hope you call to felicitate Mrs. Goodenough[4] that her Brother has had the happiness of dispensing joy thus to all of any worth or heart in the united empire.

We expect the good & dear Bourdois's in our neighbourhood the end of this Week. They will spend some previous days at a friend of Mr. B[ourdois]'s whence they are to see Epsom Races. —I have received a very *morne* letter from poor Charlotte—who fears you have been addressed in a very strange epistle, but which she did not see, only she doubts it was improper, because it was written, she says, 'in one of his PAROXYSMS of FRETFULNESS — ! —' ǀ Poor thing!—I am truly concerned to find that she expects very soon a Month's confinement—for herself![5]—It is possible, indeed, a babe may be a cement to more harmony & affection—but should it be otherwise, what a new care, new danger, & new trial for her weak nerves will not this prove! I knew nothing of her situation till just now; but she tells me that her little charlotte, to whom she has communicated it, has behaved incomparably upon the occasion, generously rejoicing in the idea of a new little relation, promising it the most sisterly tenderness, & soothing her poor feeble Mother with a kindness & address truly charming. That is surely a very super- ior little Girl, & is born with very high sentiments of what is right & good. Mr. Br[oome] was at Bath, when this Letter was written, whither he was gone for his health, which Charlotte says has suffered incessantly these last two years, from bile & suppressed gout, which render him fractious & gloomy — ! — & she begs I would entreat you to attribute solely to these causes, any thing he may have said of a complaining or unkind nature in his Letter. Poor infatuated thing!—What a life of quiet enjoyment has she thrown away, thus thanklessly! — — Lady Templetown & all her family are now on a visit at Norbury Park. L^y T. is in great anxiety about one of her sons, Arthur, who is in the Guards, & may be soon chosen for

[3] Insistent questioning by the opposition in the House of Commons on 14 and 15 May as to whether His Majesty had actually held Council with his ministers led finally to Addington's defensive outburst (see *The Times*, 16 May).

[4] Anne Addington (d. 1806) had married in 1770 William Goodenough (c. 1743–70), B.Med. (1767).

[5] This child, born *pre* 6 July (see L. 417), was baptized Ralph Broome on 5 Sept. 1801.

Egypt, though an aid de Camp to the Duke of ' York[6], whom he attended to Holland. A Letter is just arrived from General Moore, written by himself, with the happy tydings that his wound is certainly curing fast, & never was dangerous. It is in the leg, however, & as yet wholly disables him from service.[7] I want much to hear something of Gen[l] Hutchinson, & what hopes may be entertained of his being equal to so great a command, at so critical a period. I have heard him highly spoken of *at court*, for his conduct in Ireland during the rebellion,[8] but it was in anecdotes that denoted his urbanity of character, in protecting females, or relieving distress & terror; but I must hope he has judgement & bravery in a peculiar degree, as well as kindness & Gentleman-like qualities, by his belonging to such an officer as Gen[l] Abercrombie, who I conceive to have chosen & named his own Staff. Let me entreat my dearest Father to let me have a few lines, at least, ere long—just of his health, & his goings on;—I hope my dear Fanny is quite well, & —— *is it prudent?*—for, *begar, I like it that Girl!*—'[9] My kind Love to her. Adieu, Dearest dear Sir, ever & ever your truly dutiful &

affectionate F d'A

M. d'A.'s best of Loves & resp[ects.]

---

[6] For Upton's services in 1799, see L. 332 n. 10. He was A.D.C. in 1794, however, to the Duke of York. Cf. *AR*, 97 (1855), 244.

[7] John Moore (1761–1809), Major-General (1798), K.B. (1804), Lt.-Gen. (1805), had been severely wounded in the leg during the battle of 21 Mar. at Alexandria and did not resume his command until 29 June at Cairo (Fortescue, iv, pt. ii. 832–41, 852, 855).

[8] On hearing that the French had landed at Killala on 22 Aug. 1798, Major-General Hutchinson, then in command of the province of Connaught, had made the necessary dispositions to receive the enemy at Castlebar. Now in Egypt, Hutchinson had survived an abortive attempt by some of his officers to relieve him of the chief command and was marching toward Cairo where he would defeat the French on 22 June (Fortescue, iv, pt. i. 592, pt. ii. 849–56).

[9] Probably Fanny Phillips, though the words quoted are those of Fanny *Burney's* employer Lord Beverley (iii, L. 142 n. 3; and L. 242 n. 16).

To Mrs. Broome

A.L.S. (rejected Diary MSS. 5248–[51], Berg), *n.d.*
Double sheet 4to 4 pp. *pmks* DARKING 23 MY 180⟨1⟩
red wafer
Addressed: Mrs. Broome, / Brighthelmstone, / Sussex—
Endorsed by CBFB: Sister d'arblay / May 1801 / ansᵈ / June—1801.
Edited by FBA, CFBt *and the* Press.

May I not congratulate my dearest Charlotte on a prospect of
so endearing a nature? I know she will not want fortitude for its
preceding trials—but I know, also, she has only to reflect on
the lovely loves she has already made her own, to have every
mortal reason for hope she may raise & rear a Fourth Comfort
& Joy for her future existence.[1] This must be my own expectation, & what I must court & indulge, to parry off the anxiety
of all belonging to the previous suffering—& I must entreat my
dearest Charlotte to cherish all that can give her most courage
& lead to most enjoyment. Your dear little namesake, that
charming Girl, whose character has already pourtrayed such
strong-marked worth & genius, will be the tenderest sister, I am
sure, to the new relation you will bestow upon us, & I wish her
to be with you from the period of its birth, that her affections
may be caught by its first helpless, yet interesting infancy. How
do I wish it were possible I could nurse you myself, but alas—
who could nurse & watch my Alex, who wants both Nursing &
watching as much, nearly, as the little stranger will: for his
constitution is yet unfixed, & his character is wilder than the
wind; & M. d'A.'s coming to the Sea Coast, unless ⎮ with a
passport to depart to another Country, is utterly impossible.[2]
The attempt for such a licence has been made, & proved
abortive, even for French priests: how then can there be any
hope for a French general officer? As to my quitting him—that
only could be if you were ill—or in any distress—or had any

---

414. [1] For Charlotte's three children, now aged, 14, 11, and 8, see i, Intro., lxxii–
lxxiii. Ralph 'Dolph' was to be born *pre* 6 July (L. 417) and baptized 5 Sept. 1801.
  [2] As a precaution against intelligence of English operations being transmitted to
the French, the Duke of Portland's office had issued 'positive orders . . . to arrest or
send away every Alien who shall be found to reside within ten miles of the coast'
(*The Times*, 15 Sept. 1800).

peculiar wish for me, that a short time could fulfil: for we are so indispensably knit together, & our hermitage so completely demands us both, that death only will, I trust, ever separate us. The *retirement* of this Cottage suits our mutual taste & inclination, while we inhabit it in concert; but it's solitude would be too much for either of us, were we parted. We reciprocally feel we could not live in it alone: This will answer my kind Charlotte's propositions ⟨upon this⟩ subject, for which I cordially thank her, though [time m]ust shew them impracticable. But yet—if you wish me to come to you, from any important feelings of your own, make no sc⟨ru⟩ple to say so & to sum[mon] me, for M. d'A. would as little be able to refu⟨se⟩ me to your desire, for a short time, or nearly as little, as I should be able to refuse myself.

With respect to my own health, it is again re-established, & my spirits begin to resume some appearance of their former state—some appearance, I say—for fundamentally they can never—NEVER be the same!—O no!—the *perfect* happiness on which they were built has received a mortal stab—which, however its wound may be healed, by my husband—my child— my Father, my sisters—Brothers—& dear Friends all, will leave a scar—a sore—a piercing pain for the rest of my earthly career. But—without this blow—when I look *around* me, & see the lot of others, I am compelled to say, I should have been TOO HAPPY!—for THIS world, too happy!—since now, even NOW— I see not with whom I would change!—

our excursion has certainly been very serviceable to me. We were absent little more than 10 days[3]—but we spent them amongst our Friends, & ⟨public⟩ places, & the exertion has been salutary, for I have returned far more able to employ myself, nay, *enjoy* myself, in my own loved home, than when I left it. We were one week at Chelsea—where we found my dear Father quite well, & Fanny P[hillips] a charming, lively, innocent, & most endearing companion to him. The rest of our short time we spent at Mr. Bourdois,[4]—*Blue* happened to be at Esther's, till we left town, & Charles was so full of engagements, he could not have been *within*, unless w[e co]uld have gone the following week; but we did not think Alex well, & were in extreme haste to return to our Hermitage.—In that period, we

---

[3] From *c.* 21 Apr. until *c.* 6 May.   [4] At Clarges Street (see L. 412).

spent a day with my sister Burney,—saw James, Mrs. J. Burney, (not [to]gether!) Sarah, Martin, littl*est* Sally—Fanny B[urney] Sophy, Richard, | *BLUE*—Charles & his son—dined with our lov⟨ely⟩ young friend Mrs. *Amelia* Angerstein—with my old friends Miss Thrales. & with the Bishop of Winchester. & Miss Norths:[5] & I got a short interview of Mrs. Boscawen, Lady Bankes, Miss Goldsworthy, Miss Gomme, Mrs. Hammond, Mrs. Hagget, Miss Grants[6]—& *spit cards* at many others—We went also to one opera, one Play—& one Concert, at Solomon's, & to the Exhibition.[7] All this, with our unavoidable Shopping, w[ith much] hurrying, & I scarcely felt to recover my breath, till I had been returned to my quiet home some da[ys.] If Mr. Broome is come from Bath, I beg my Comp^ts. And pray give my best & ki⟨n⟩dest remembrances to Mr. & Mrs. Cooke.[8] I *anxiously* hope you see those excellent people often—I never cease to regret my own distance from them. Pray tell them so. You have promised me to say how the Bath waters agree with Mr. Br[oome] don't f⟨orge⟩t I beg—& wri⟨t⟩e without much *trouble*, for ⌐'I now have no quiet hours of time—nor enough—& it is ⟨mixed pleasure⟩—¬much thought & wit would be thrown away—give me therefore only plain matter of Fact, & true affection such as is yours ever from your

faithful F. d'A.

I shall reall⟨y⟩ be very anxious for frequent news of you, my dearest Charlotte—do not forget that!

[5] Brownlow North (i, L. 3 n. 10), whose daughters Louisa (d. 16 Dec. 1820), Lucy (1775–1850), and Elizabeth (1776–1845) were unmarried at this time.
[6] These friends of FBA are identified or mentioned respectively in i, L. 12 n. 10; iii, L. 136 n. 9; i, L. 16 n. 2; L. 7 n. 5; L. 21 nn. 17, 18, and 16. Lady Banks *née* Dorothea Weston-Hugessen (1758–1828) had married in 1779 Sir Joseph (1743–1820), cr. Baronet (1781).
[7] Salomon's Concert, the last of the season, was performed on 23 Apr., and the Exhibition of the Royal Academy was opened to the public on the 29th.
[8] See iii, L. 122 n. 8.

415   [43 Beaumont Street, 6 June 1801]

To M. d'Arblay

A.L. (Barrett, Eg. 3693, ff. 229–30b), *n.d.*
Double sheet 4to   3 pp.   *pmk* 6 ⟨J⟩U .801   wafer
Addressed: A. d'Arblay Esqr, / at A. Bourdois's Esqr— / Sand Place, /
Dorking / Surry.
Edited by FBA, p. 1, *annotated and incorrectly dated*: June—1798—*London.*
(16) Written during a few days absence from my best Friend—
Docketed in pencil: N° 3

Pleasure is seated in London—Joy, Mirth, Variety,[1]—but
Happiness—O it has taken its seat, its root, at West Hamble!
—The more I am away, the stronger I feel that there, & there
alone, to *ME*, is its abode. And those who have no West Hamble,
know it not—Hope, & disappointment,—vain Glory, & repin-
ings,—high exultation, & desponding Mortification—make
their rotation with such endless velocity in this great Capital,
that peace of Mind, even spirits, chearful temper, & Heart-felt
Contentment, are driven away by the turbulence—to repose
themselves in our quiet retirement, which never yet seemed
quite so preferable to all other habitations as I feel it at this
moment; for all I have seen, all around & about me, is made up
of passing pleasure, & lurking inquietude.

I have nothing personal to complain of—but this is the
state in which I have found *The World*—& most thankfully to
God shall I return to-morrow. to | my thrice dear Cottage, &
Him, the Friend of my Heart, for whose sake I so prize it. I can
enter into no accounts now, as I write in Beaumont St. where
I am come to pass the day, by appointment to meet Charles,
who will be here at 3 o'clock, & has procured a Family Box
for the whole party to see Mrs. Jordan to night,[2] after which my
Father will send for Fanny P. & me to Chelsea—& to-morrow

---

415. [1] FBA had come to town for her annual audience at the Queen's House (see
L. 416), though after SBP's death she wrote no more Court Journals. 'It has rarely
happened,' reported *The Times* (5 June) on the occasion of the King's birthday on
4 June, 'that the Court has been more full or splendid. . . . Amidst the general
felicity, it seemed to occur to every bosom . . . from how many dangers it had
pleased Providence to rescue the Empire, by prolonging the life, and restoring the
health of the King!' For the King's illness, see L. 407 n. 4.
    [2] On 6 June, at Drury Lane Theatre, Mrs. Jordan (L. 255 n. 49) played in
Garrick's *The Country Girl* (see *The Times*, 6 June).

— — but I cannot fix my hour. I am sorry to have come out before the post arrived, lest you should have written me any directions: should there be any for to-day, they will be too late.

My Father took me on Wednesday to Le Texier's,[3] where I was much amused. I have been forced so frequently to desert poor Alex, that I believe the charm of his enchantment at the excursion is pretty well broken, & he will be nearly as glad to return as myself. My *Hour* being uncertain, don't think of leaving our dear Bood's till Evening—nor, if M. Talon[4] keeps to his appointment, till *Night*. I shall know the reason, & not suffer myself to be disappointed.

All from hence send you & your *Hosts* milles amours.

James promises to hasten the Chairs, which he says are well finished, & fitted him very comfortably.

416   West Humble, 12 June 1801

To Mrs. Broome

A.L.S. (Barrett, Eg. 3693, ff. 76–7b), 12 June 1801
Double sheet 4to 4 pp. *pmks* DARKING ⟨ ⟩ JUN 1801 wafer
Addressed: Mrs. Broome, / Brighthelmstone, / Sussex
Endorsed by CBFB: Sister d'arblay / June 1801. / Ans^d by Mrs Cooke

West Hamble,
12th June—1801

It is a truly great blessing to me, my dearest Charlotte, at this interesting period, to know my excellent Friend Mrs. Cooke is so near you. She has kindly promised to write to me the instant you have the happiness of giving life & light to your little Babe—& I know I may depend upon her friendship for the utmost consideration of my anxiety, in a detailed & a repeated account. She assures me you are in even remarkable

---

[3] 'En sa maison, Lisle Street', Leicester Fields, A. A. Le Texier (1737–1814), formerly of Lyons, but in London since 1775, gave the highly successful readings described by his contemporaries (e.g., Madame du Deffand (Walpole, vi, 32). On 3 June FBA and CB would have heard *Le mariage de Julia* (see *The Times*, 3 June).

[4] Conjecturally, Antoine-Omer Talon (1760–1811), lawyer, parliamentarian, and Royalist, whose travels, including visits to America, somewhat parallel those of Bourdois. See M. L. E. Moreau de Saint-Méry, *Voyage aux Etats-Unis de l'Amérique, 1793–1798*, ed. Stewart L. Mims (1913), pp. 102, 223, 396.

good looks, & in good spirits.¹ I am most thankful to hear it—& delighted that your dear Children are all coming to you. I rely much upon Charlotte. I entreat you to give her my kindest Love, & tell her I much regret losing sight of her so long—though—alas—I fled her when last under the same roof with her²—young as she is, she has both feeling & understanding sufficient to comprehend the dreadful sensations that made it ⏌ even right I should avoid her.—*Me* she could not console—I was, then, inconsolable—& her I might deeply have affected. I am now more quiet, & nearly resigned—I look forward to future meetings, & consider that, meantime, I see no one so happy here as myself—for all else seem seeking, regularly, something they cannot find.

I have been just writing to my dear Father—& as my mind is very full of my dear Charlotte, & her situation at this moment, & as I know how bad a Correspondent you are, I nearly made you the complete Subject of my Letter,³ & said for you all I thought you would most wish me to say.

I went to Town last week for a few days, on occasion of the birth day—& had the Joy of seeing once more The good King, almost recovered, & The ⏌ long suffering Queen & Princesses, & congratulating them on so auspicious an event. I saw all our own family, & all are well: my Father & his young Companion remarkably so. I heard an exceeding good account of dear Clement from his uncle Charles, & I find, as usual, every body loving & admiring the dear & deserving boy. When does Charlotte leave school? Will poor Marianne be contented without her? our sister Burney is very thin, but well. *Maria* & M. Bourdois are very happy, & within a very attainable walk of us.⁴ Alex is much grown, & just as gay & active & riotous as ever, but, if possible, yet thinner. We can never fatten him: but he sleeps well at present, eats well, & chats well, therefore there is no cause for inquietude, I thank God.

Mrs. Cooke seems to expect your confinement sooner⏌ than you do yourself. You have good help, I doubt not, of all sorts, but pray let me know if it is to your liking? How I wish, now, you had our faithful Susan Adams!—but probably you will

416. ¹ This letter is missing.
² Presumably during FBA's visit of 6 Feb.–2 Mar. 1800 to CB Jr. at Greenwich.
³ This letter is missing, but cf. L. 413.
⁴ At Sand Place, Dorking. See L. 399 n. 1.

have a wet nurse? yet to suckle the little Soul yourself might be very healthy, as well as delightful. you don't tell me a word of this ⏐ pray mention *all such things* when you write next.

I hope Mr. Broome is returned, or will return, quite recovered from Bath. Pray give our comp^ts to him—& to Miss Broome— & believe me ever & ever my dearest Charlotte

most affectionately most faithfully yours—

F d'A.

My most affect^e remembranc[es] to Mr. & Mrs. Cooke—with a thousand thanks for the note & kind promise of the latter

417   West Humble, 6 July 1801

To Charlotte Francis *later* Barrett

A.L.S., facsimile (NPG, grangerized *DL* v. part iv, pp. 464–5) FBA to Charlotte Francis with a page in the hand of FBA as if from Alexander then 6 years old

Apparently in the original, a double sheet 4to   3 pp.   *pmks* DARK-ING   8 JUL 1801   wafer

Addressed: Miss Francis, / at Ralph Broome's Esqr, / Brighton, / Sussex

West Hamble, July 6
1801

Joy to You, my dear Charlotte—joy to dear Marianne, & Clement—& to Mr. Broome—& to your dear Mama a thousand times Joy. Tell her I am delighted with the truly satisfactory account you have been enabled to send me of her safety, & her spirits, & her fine little man: & tell yourself, my dear Charlotte, that your Letter, & its writer, are very dear to me. You could never have given so gratifying, or so convincing a proof of your warm affection for your fond & deserving Mother, as by so kind a reception of your/our/new little Relation. I expected it from you, my dear Girl;—but I do not love you the less because my pleasure is without surprise. My Alexander is so charmed with your message, he insists on dictating his own Answer. M. d'Arblay sends you his kind Love—my kind*EST* to my dear sister, & our united Compt^s &

congratulations to Mr. Broome. — — I have frequently wished to say something ¦ to you of that dreadful night when—though under the same roof with you, I fled your sight—as well as of the subsequent period, when I avoided you, though so near as Chelsea¹—but I will not, at this happier epoch, awaken your sympathy for that never—never to be forgotten calamity—you could not, I trust, doubt my affection, though I fear you must have been hurt by my avoidance; which, however, proceeded wholly from my unwillingness to wound your warm, youthful feelings, unavailingly, with a view of my terrible affliction. — —

God bless you, my dear Charlotte—

ever your very affectionate
Aunt & Friend
F. d Arblay.

I shall write immediately to our dear Miss Cambridge. ¦

[*from Alexander d'Arblay in hand of* FBA]

My dear Cousin Charlotte,

You say you intend to write a little Book for me: *I* intend to write a little Book for you; to be called The history of little Tom, the Beggar Boy; to which will be added The Tub. Walker's merits; which will be a very pretty little comedy. The first scene is thus acted to you.

Scene The First.

There was a poor little Boy, who was an Orphan, for he was born without a papa & mama; & he had no money of his own. So he had a Friend, & his Friend came & told him, that he would give him a little Tub, & that if he would go with his Tub, & go into the Field, & get upon his Tub, & ride round it, that he should have a shilling a Day.

The end of this — & —
Scene 2ᵈ must be differed to another opportunity.

417. ¹ For the first evasion see L. 416 n. 2; the second would have been during FBA's visit to Chelsea, 9–12 Apr. 1800.

To Esther (Burney) Burney

A.L.S. (Berg), 13 Aug. 1801
Double sheet small 4to (7·9 × 6·5″), from which a segment (2·2 × 6·5″)
was cut from bottom of the second leaf 4 pp. wafer
Addressed: Mrs. Burney, / Beaumont Street, / Portland Place.
Endorsed by EBB: August 1801

13. august
1801.
West Hamble.

My dearest Esther,

The receipt arrived safe & sound—& will forthwith be
returned for its value by M. Bourdois.

You could not take a better manner for making that Gentleman sensible of your kindness towards him, than by addressing
it to one who is so deeply interested in it, & so anxious for its
constant continuance. I am quite vexed in the fear that bad
weather will prevent my carrying him & reading him a page
that will give him such sincere pleasure. I shall put it, however,
in good hands, for he shall not lose it: especially as the Letter
happens to contain no one word of a peculiar cast, or which you
would or could care for being published.[1]

My dear Father was already gone—for how long we know
not. He left us yesterday between 4 & 5 in the morning, quite
well, thank God, & promising better behaviour on his return.
I am truly sorry for the account you give of poor Richard,—I
earnestly wish him to at Last *try* the Country air: & to Richmond
he could go nearly by Water all the way. Indeed he ought to
lose no time in any attempt that may better him. It was very
kind of you to so immediately transact our *treasury* business.
I was very sorry you had the plague of going twice—& in such
sultry weather—Thanks, dearest soul. I enclose a few lines to
our dear Aunt Beckey, for you to take whenever you go.
Nothing worth postage, or in haste. I am glad Miss Harriet
Wainwright[2] is so sentimental a Husband seeker with a

418. [1] EBB's letter is missing.
[2] Harriet Wainwright (*c.* 1760–20 Nov. 1843), vocalist and composer, whose
opera *Comála. A Dramatic Poem from Ossian* (dedicated to the Marquis of Wellesley
and printed in 1803) had been performed at the Antient Music in Hanover Square

previous resolution only to *marry for Love*, how fortunate to meet with the dear Object who could inspire it just where others go only to *Marry for Money*!

This morning's rain, which stops my going to | see dear Cecilia,[3] really vexes me. Mr. & Mrs. Locke were very sincerely concerned at missing you. They returned late on Monday Evening. I wish I could have had a quiet week of the sweet Cecy to myself. I am sure we should have been good friends, for I see she can be made happy without sport & company, much as her vivacity makes her enjoy them when they come in her way. Norbury[4] pleased me much by saying, this morning, when we were talking of her, & praising her, 'And she loves her Mother so much—I like her the more for that.' — — Do you not trace a sweet hereditary *feel* in those words? But how amazingly |

[*four or five lines cut away*]

when she was ill, & he knew of it. I hope she is now recovered. Be so good as to give my love to her when you see her, & tell her I was very sorry—& am very glad—&c—

[*four or five lines cut away*]

Yours ever & aye—

F. d 'A.

on 26 Jan. 1792. In 1796 she went to India, composed in 1799 the *Seringapatam Chorus*, recovered her singing voice, and married *c.* 1800 John Stewart (d. 12 Jan. 1807), Lt.-Col. of the 52nd Regiment and A.D.C. to Wellesley. Tipped into the British Museum's copy of the *Chorus* is a printed slip recording Dr. Burney's opinion of the work as 'so ingenious and so new, that it reminds me of no other chorus. . . . Great meditation and experience were necessary to carry on so unwieldly a score without confusion; and I know of no female contrapuntist in Europe, Asia, Africa, or America, who could surpass, if equal, the merit of the composition.' In an autobiographical sketch prefixed to her *Critical Remarks on the Art of Singing* . . . (1836) Mrs. Stewart tells of her early career in London, where she made Pacchierotti the model of her style. She had the 'good fortune' also, she relates, 'to get acquainted with Doctor Burney, and his musical and highly talented family. The Doctor, who was particularly partial to Pacchierotti, extended his partiality also to me, from my being so correct a copy of the great original.'

    [3] EBB's daughter Cecilia (iii, l. 132 n. 5), evidently visiting at Sand Place.
    [4] Norbury Phillips, who, with his sister Fanny, was spending a month in West Humble (L. 421).

To Doctor Burney

A.L. (Diary MSS. vi. 5252–[5], Berg), Sept. 1801
Double sheet 4to   4 pp.
Addressed: Dr. Burney, / Chelsea College
Edited by FBA, p. 1 (5252), *annotated and dated*: ⁜ ⁑ 1ˢᵗ [Septʳ 1801](2)
Disappointed visit. West Humble Drawing Room. M. de Lally—his character.
Edited also by CFBt *and the* Press, *see* Textual Notes.

West Hamble
Septʳ 1801

My dearest—kindest—cruellest Father!—that so long & so interesting, & so clear a Letter should give me so great a disappointment![1]—& that Fish so admirable should want its best sauce!—indeed I cannot help a little repining, though when I think of damps & rheumatisms, I am frightened out of murmuring: for in this lone Cottage I would not have you indisposed for the Universe. But 'tis very *provocas*—yet I have so much to be thankful for, & so thankful I feel for that much, that I am ashamed of seeming discontented—so I don't know *what for to do* ! — — And the Carpet!—how kind a thought!—Goodness me! as Lady Hales[2] used to say, I don't know what *for to do* more & more!—But a Carpet we have—though not yet spread, as the Chimney is unfinished—& room incomplete. Charles bought us the *Tapis*—so that, in fact, we have yet bought *nothing* for our best room—& meant,—for our own share—to buy a *Table* — — & if my dearest dear Father *Will* be so *good* & so *naughty* at once, as to crown our *salle d'Audience* with a Gift we shall prize beyond all others, we can think only of a Table—Not a dining one, but a sort of Table for a little work & ⎮ a few Books, *en gala*—without which, a room looks always forlorn. I need not say how we shall love it;—& I must not say how we shall blush at it—& I cannot say how we feel obliged at it—for the room will then be complete in Love offerings. Mr. Lock finished glazing, or polishing, his

---

419. ¹ CB's letter is missing.
² Mary *née* Hayward (Coussmaker), Lady Hales (i, L. 23 n. 54), an old friend of the Burneys (*ED* ii. 184 n. 1).

Impression border for the Chimney on Saturday. It will be, I fear, his last work of that sort, his Eyes, which are very *long-*sighted, now beginning to fail & weaken at *near* objects. *but* dedommagement for early blindness is in later years—when all the short-sighted become objects of envy of those to whom, in juvenile years, they are objects of pity—or sport.

⌐I feel much pleased Griff[3] has written amicably, & I am edified by your kind & literal purpose of supplying him still with articles of importance & your recent. *That* is the high style! & I have quite your good opinion, on good & ill, *at bottom*, of Griff, & I am every way glad no war is to be declared. As to *public* war or peace, none here have any idea of your hint as to October parliamenting, but conclude it merely for supplies.⌐[4] We have spent the greatest part of last week in visits at Norbury Park, to meet M. de Lally, whom I am very sorry you missed. He is delightful in the Country—full of resources, of gaiety, of intelligence, of good humour; & mingling powers of instruction & entertainment. He has read us several fragments of works of his own, admirable in eloquence, Sense & feeling—chiefly parts of Tragedies—& all referring to subjects next his heart, & clearest in his head—namely, The French Revolution & its calamities, & filial reverence & enthusiasm for injured Parents. His Heart & Memory never seem for a moment to lose the impression made on them by the ill usage & hard fate of his Father,[5] & he meets no similar subjects in

[3] Ralph Griffiths (1720–1803), founder and publisher of the *Monthly Review*, to which for many years (1785–1802) CB had contributed (see Lonsdale, pp. 408–10, 500). CB had now proposed to conclude this work in favour of contributions to Abraham Rees's *Cyclopaedia; or, Universal Dictionary of Arts, Sciences, and Literature* (39 vols., 1802–19; 6 vols. of plates, 1820). Griffiths's wounded feelings at the ungracious remarks with which CB had terminated a connection of so many years are reflected, howbeit affectionately, in his letter (Berg) of 31 Aug. (partly printed by Lonsdale, *supra*).

[4] On the contrary, though no reduction in taxes could be expected, the King, on the opening of Parliament on 29 Oct., spoke of peace rather than war, stating that preliminaries of peace had been ratified with the French Republic (*AR* xliii. 1801, 'State Papers', 210–11). The debates following led to the Peace of Amiens (25 Mar. 1802).

[5] Thomas Arthur, comte de Lally, baron de Tolendal (1702–66), *maréchal de camp* (1748), who, defeated in India in 1761, was sent to England as a prisoner of war. Accused in France of treachery, he returned, was imprisoned for two years, sentenced on 6 May 1766 and three days later, beheaded.

Lally's defence of his father, for example, *Discours du Cte de Lally-Tolendal dans l'interrogatoire qu'il a prêté au Parlement de Dijon, en qualité de curateur à la mémoire du Cte de Lally, son père, le 16 août 1783* (Dijon, 1783) and *Mémoires et plaidoyers présentés au Conseil d'Etat pour la mémoire du général Thomas-Arthur, comte de Lally* (Rouen, 1779) finally resulted in the annulment of the judgement that had led to his death.

history, without an impulsive desire to draw them into dramatic effect, & in such a manner as to give vent to his own retrospective indignation & sorrow.[6] Like ⎮ Hamlet, he seems, in all his serious & solitary moments, walking about the world in constant meditation upon the sufferings & the wrongs of his Father: but as, though his feelings are as tender, his nature is not as melancholy he banishes these reveries when he mixes with society, & is as gay & social as if a stranger to every care. He is a truly amiable, as well as Superior Man, & I heartily wish my dearest Father had met him *here*. I am quite sure you would both, afterwards, have sought to meet elsewhere.

⌐As to Lady Rothes,[7] I shall really be afraid to *abord* her. Mr. & Mrs. Lock are much disappointed, & Mr. & Mrs. Lock *will* be, for they had *'put in their oar'* so warmly. I was forced to promise to speak a good word for them. Well! I must tell them, as you do me, not to be *bumptious*! I join with you completely in form as to the £200—& in ⟨requite⟩ to him, all received to be excusable ⟨on⟩ loan. He *has* written but I have seen none of the Letters & believe the Ireland return still unfixed, for Norbury—Adieu most dear Sir. M. d'Arblay is penetrated with your kindness & your notings 1000 thanks for the work— which I shall send p^r Fanny the refunding—I shall long for news of how your history on academie goes & the further work unfinished for Encyp.[8] Heaven then bless my dearest Father

prays ever most dutiful & Affect^e

F. d'A.⌐

Alex's Love & Duty & his most oracu[lar] [*wafer*] word to *do for* him [*wafer*]

---

6 For instance, his tragedy *Le Comte de Strafford* (Londres, 1785). Cf. *Essai sur la vie de T. Wentworth, comte de Strafford, principal ministre d'Angleterre et lord lieutenant d'Irlande, sous le règne de Charles I, ainsi que sur l'histoire générale d'Angleterre, d'Ecosse et d'Irlande, à cette époque* (Londres, 1795).

7 For Lady Rothes, see i, L. 12 n. 13. The purpose of the solicitation is lost with CB's letter, but may concern plans for William Phillips. Cf. L. 422, p. 509.

8 See CB's leather-bound notebook (Osborn), of some 96 pages, entitled 'Memoranda for Musical Articles to be furnished to a new edition of the Cyclopaedia of Chambers commenced July 17th 1801' in which the first entry begins: *'Accademie royale de Musique* was the title given at Paris to the establishment of the opera. . . .' Other contributions are described by Lonsdale, pp. 411–23.

To Doctor Burney

A.L. mutilated (Osborn), 6 Sept. 1801
Double sheet 4to (8·8 × 7·2″), from which a segment (3·7 × 7·2″) was cut
from the lower part of the second leaf 4 pp. *pmks* DARKING SP 1801
Addressed: [*in part cut away*] Burney, / Chelsea College, / Middlesex.
Edited by FBA, p. 1, *annotated and the date retraced*: ⸪ ⸪ 6 Sept. 1801 (1)
Goldoni / Miss Berrys, / Horace Walpole

West Hamble.
6ʰ Septʳ 1801

Magnificent, my dearest Padre, quite magnificent will be the
two noble Card Tables. I remember them perfectly, & am
much obliged to Molly for so kindly recollecting them. They
will do a thousand times better than any Tavolina, which,
therefore, would be wholly superfluous, & if my beloved
Father can spare them, I know not *any* furniture I should like so
well. We have two exact places for them—as *na*-tral as if they
were alive, in the two sides of our *fine* room. And if you will but
come & use them — — not at *whist*, though!—What a pleasure
to us to see how handsome we shall grow—like Admiral
Saunders,[1]—by & bye. I won't talk of being ashamed, & all
that, because I am so much more pleased than *honteuse*, that
the words don't present themselves: & the more as, I think, no
room looks really comfortable, or even quite furnished, without
two Tables—one to keep the Wall, & take upon itself the dignity
of a little tidyness, the other to stand here—there—& every
where, & hold litters, & *make the agreeable.*—I felt such a terrible
disposition to murmur when I wrote last, that I believe I quite
forgot to thank for the Goldoni,[2] which, as usual, afforded me
much *quaint* amusement. The minutie of the ceremonials, not
only of entrances & exits, but of sitting or standing, bowing &
courtsying, eating & drinking, & all species of little personalities
left by all other writers (ie, at least of England or of France) to

420. [1] Sir Charles Saunders (*c.* 1713–75), Vice-Admiral of the Blue and Commander of the Fleet in the St. Lawrence (1759), K.B. (1761), M.P. (1750–75), and
First Lord of the Admiralty (1766), Admiral (1770).
[2] For *Mémoires de M. Goldoni*, see L. 347 n. 6; and for Goldoni's plays, Ll. 368,
and 389.

conjecture, or to being taken for granted, seem to give a good deal of insight to the detail of manners & customs, & such as nothing else, short of a residence in Italy, *could* offer. His Moral, too, is always good, & his design is studiously virtuous. He is bold against vice, though a warm advocate for respect to official power, & all established etiquettes of rank & subordination. I should imagine him to have been as useful a member of the community as ever existed, for he seems regularly to have kept in view the General Good in the conduct of his pieces, as well as the business of his own art, in displaying character, or passion, for exciting merriment, or illustrating some practical Duty by examples. *HERE*, his pieces—what I have read of them at least,—would not succeed, from their simplicity, the singleness of their story, & quantity of dialogue with scarcity of event. But a man with his talents, could have fashioned his materials for us, or for any nation in which he had chanced to reside.

Last week, ˡ we had a long & very social visit from the two Miss Berrys & their Father,[3] brought to us by Mr. & Mrs. William Lock. They were very lively, very cordial, & very agreeable: & renewed our former acquaintance with an earnestness of cultivating it in future, that were flattering in the highest degree: pressing to see us both at Twickenham & in Town, & obviating all *maternal* objections, by assurances they had a Bed just fitted for Alex. They enquired much after you, & were very pleasant. I could not but recollect Lord Orford's quaint Speech when he first presented us to each other—which was at Lady Hesketh's: 'There!' said he, having formally named us, 'now I've put you togethe[r] you can't help getting on—but I'm glad I've been the Pimp!'![4] — — I should have written more quite immediately, but Fanny informed me you were going to Richmond on Monday, ˡ ⸢& that there were hopes of you being there detained a few days. I would not be so unkind to Esther, & your numerous friends around her rural

[3] Robert Berry (d. 19 May 1817, 'at an advanced age', *GM* lxxxvii^{1}. 570); his daughters Mary and Agnes (L. 389 n. 5); and Elizabeth Catherine (Jennings) Locke (L. 385 n. 2).

[4] FB had a visiting acquaintance with Lady Hesketh (i, L. 24 n. 5; and *DL* v. 108) but there seems to be no record other than this of her meeting the Berrys there.

abode, as to surmise you can venture thither, on the contrary, I think in this beautiful weather the excursion may be really salutary, as well as pleasant. I only regret for myself, not envy others. I entreat the *below* may be given to Fanny ⟨to answer⟩ & cut off.⌐

⌐My most dear Father's most affectionate & dutiful &

grateful   F. d'A

M.d'A's rheumatism is past ⟨once again⟩ & he is jolly & gay.⌐ | We expect Charles, &c, on Sunday

421   West Humble, 19 September 1801

To Mrs. Broome

A.L.S. (Berg), 19 Sept. 1801
Double sheet 4to   4 pp.   *pmks* DARKING   21 SEP 1801   wafer
Addressed: Mrs. Broome, / Brighton, / Sussex.
Endorsed by CBFB: Sister d'arblay / Septʳ 1801 / ansᵈ Septʳ ⟨28ᵗʰ⟩

West Hamble
Sept. 19. 1801.

My dearest Charlotte,

It would have given me so very much pleasure to have settled Susan Adams[1] with YOU, that I have been quite unwilling to send a negative, though I have had little hope of power to send any thing more comfortable. She has been engaged, through Mrs. Locke, some months to nurse the new born Child of the Primate of Ireland;[2] but as I have had some private intelligence, from her sister at Mickleham, that she had not been quite contented with her prospects, having discovered she was to be carried for 3 or 4 years to Ireland, I determined not to rest till I procured some certain, & more immediate, as well as recent, information of her plans & state of mind:—This morning I have obtained what I have waited for,—but not what I have wished: she has settled her mind now to the

---

421. [1] Formerly SBP's maid (iii, L. 216 n. 11).

  [2] Louisa Stuart (1801–23; see *AR* lxv. 205), youngest daughter of the Hon. William Stuart (1755–1822), Archbishop of Armagh and Primate of Ireland (1800), and his wife Sophia Margaret *née* Penn (*c.* 1765–1847).

consequences, & is fixed to remain with Mrs. Stuart, her new mistress. Fanny Phillips, who is now on a little visit to Esther at Richmond, has met with her ˡ There, & heard her resolution from herself. I regret it very much, as I know the benefit to my dear Charlotte's health that might accrue from the ease of mind she would feel in trusting her little boy to so faithful & careful & tender a deputy. It is truly unlucky. I do not personally know any one I can recommend to you at present; nor does Mrs. Locke, to whom I have applied for help: but I had a Letter, a year or two ago, from *Arline*,[3] the good slave of Mrs. Scwellenberg, begging I would try to get a place of a *dry* nurse for her sister, a married woman, forced by her husband's misfortunes, to go to service. If this woman resembles Arline, she would be a treasure, for Arline is one of the best & trustiest Creatures living. Should you like I should enquire! Have you any objection to a German by birth? they have been here so long as to be perfectly at ease in their english. The Sister, however, I have never seen, though from the circumstances I mention, I have tried to serve her. I shall take no ˡ step, however, without your direction, but I think so highly of Arline, that, if you have nothing better & more evidently promising before you, I think you might safely try her Sister. In case you say you will, send me terms to offer, to shorten the business. *She* does not expect very high wages, Arline says, but is anxious for kind usage. I have no one else to mention—& shall be very solicitous to know you provided, & satisfied. Pray do your utmost to *forbear* over straining your unsettled health, & fatiguing your weakened frame: remember your health is the health of your little Boy; he can only flourish, at present, by your flourishing. I am extremely glad his pappy is so happy in him, & that you have such rational, as well as pleasant hopes, of his salubrious efficacy. I am delighted, & deeply interested, in your account of my dear Charlottina, her nursery, her Godmothership, & her intended tutoring. Tell her just so Amelia Lock acted by her youngest Brother, between whom & herself there is just the same difference of Age as between your dear Girl & little Ralpho.[4] My Alex is ˡ charmed by her answer, & *periodical*

---

[3] Arline (*fl.* 1787–1801) had been described by FBA in 1787 as 'a poor humble thing, that would not venture to jest, I believe, with the kitchen-maid' (*DL* iii. 269).

[4] FBA, however, was mistaken in her calculations. Young Charlotte, born 17

promise, & exclaims often 'How good. natured Cousin Charlotte must be!—only I think her Tragedy's very like a comedy.' And he repeats some of D⟨iddles⟩ speaches, particularly the request of *Tongue-holding*, & the *hint* to good Frost, in Support of his opinion, & says 'As this makes me laugh, may be, if Cousin Charlotte writes me a Comedy, to my surprise, it will make me melancholy!'—Poor Fanny & Norbury P[hillips] spent a month with us—my Father, a Week—*Maria*, no longer Marianne,[5] dined here yesterday, with her good Sposo, her Brother Richard & sister Fanny, now both on a visit to her. Mr. Bourdois is all kindness & hospitality to all her family. We mean to spend a day with the worthy Cooke's[6] next week. They are well, & invariable in kind remembrance of you. When you see again my dear Friend M[rs] Baker,[7] pray give her my kind Love. I need not ask you to give it to your dear Children— especially Charlotte—nor my best Comp[ts] to Mr. Broome. We expect Charles & his Family to spend the day here to-morrow. I am far better, in all ways—& probably as well now as ever I am likely to be again—Most happy in my dear home—yet full of eternal regret for my lost treasure. Heaven bless my dearest Charlotte

ever & aye hers
F. d'A.

M. d'A.'s kind Love. |

I know nothing of the ingredients of Ching's Medicine—but it demands great care. Mr. *Lowdal*[8] recommends *Tin powders*,[9] a heaped sixpence at a dose, as safer, & better for the stomach.

I am very glad my dear Charlottina remembers Bookham with pleasure—I wish she could try West-Hamble.

Dec. 1786, was 14 at the birth of her brother Ralph in the summer of 1801 (L. 413 n. 5); Amelia Locke, born 8 Feb. 1776, was only 9 when her brother Frederick was born on 23 May 1785.

⁵ See L. 394 n. 3.   ⁶ At Bookham (iii, L. 122 n. 8).
⁷ See i, L. 10 n. 6.   ⁸ George Lowdall (iii, L. 231 n. 1).
⁹ Powders of tin (*stanni pulvis*) were used during the eighteenth century as an anthelmintic.

To Doctor Burney

A.L. (rejected Diary MSS. 5256–[7], Berg), *n.d.*
Originally a double sheet 4to, of which FBA later discarded the second
leaf   2 pp.
Edited by FBA, p. 1 (5256), *annotated and dated*: ⁂ Sep^t 21—1801   (3)
Receipt of Tables, & account of the Drawing Room Furnished by Friends—
(Dr. B.   Dr Chas   Miss Thrales   Miss Cambridge   Mrs. Geo. Cambridge
Mrs. Broome   Charlotta & Marian Francis   Mr. & Mrs. Lock.   Miss Baker
Edited also by CFBt *and the* Press, *see* Textual Notes.

Sep^t 21. 1801

The Tables are this minute arrived, my dearest Father,
looking so handsome, & so respectable, we hardly know our
little room again. Most fortunately, they will just be here to
greet Charles & Co, who are coming for the Day—& would
not, else, have found where withal to lay a hat or newspaper.
They precisely suit Carlos's Carpet, & I rejoice to make them
so soon shake feet together. They are arrived quite safe, & free
from flaw or injury. And, lo & behold, into the bargain, here
comes a Letter from Miss Cambridge, informing me she is to
bring *Mrs. George*[1] next Friday, which same Mrs. George is to
bring her painted Curtain for our Bow Window! So was ever the
like!— *It's well you spoke in time*! I hope you think! for now there's
nothing left to be done. Our friends must all be like so many
Alexanders the Great, when they visit our best apartment,—sit
down, & weep that there are no more deficiencies to conquer!—

⌐Fanny P. writes me word the Col.[2] declines, upon mature
consideration, the Cadetship for William[3] she bids me ⌐ ask
for a *Writer's* place— I shall surely mention the request to Mr.
Lock—but I am by no means sure Mr. Angerstein has it
equally under his patronage. The doubt seems, however, to
hang upon grounds equally worthy deliberation, namely the
natural *courage* of poor William, which is thought not promising for any military line. Esther grieves me in her Letter

---

422. [1] Charlotte Owen Cambridge and her sister-in-law Cornelia (L. 311 n. 5),
wife of the Revd. George Owen Cambridge (i, L. 1 n. 6; L. 8 n. 7) of Twickenham.
   [2] Molesworth Phillips was promoted in rank from Major to Lt.-Col. on 1 Jan.
1798.
   [3] John William Phillips, born 12 Sept. 1801, was now ten years old.

(which I received yesterday Morning,) by saying my dearest Father did not accompany her to Richmond from fear of the rheumatism. *Fear*, only, I hope? as *privately*, I ever hope business, & the old accusation, *glad of a twinge or two*—& that you are *pretty well*, when the excuses were all made & the Books & papers properly orkbornized.[4] — — I was very glad to hear from Fanny that she had first paid poor faithful simple Susan Adams the money due £30—& five over. This magnificent interest pleases me much, though I own I attribute it far less to her claims & her worth, than to her actual settlement in the family of the Primate of Ireland.[5] I wish much to know if the account of the Qua[rter] was exact, & if my dearest Father is once more paid—Is there any truth in the report that[¶]

[*the second leaf is missing*].

[4] A verb derived from the name of the pedant (Orkborne) in *Camilla*.
[5] See iii, L. 216 n. 11; and iv, L. 421 nn. 1, 2.

INDEX

to Volumes iii and iv

Members of the British nobility are listed under family names with cross-references to titles.

Members of the French and European nobility are listed under the name and title by which they are best known, with cross-references to other names or titles.

Women are listed under their married names, with cross-references to maiden names and earlier married names.

In listing members of family groups, the alphabet is normally disregarded in order to clarify family relationships.

Index

Turns again to novel writing. Determines to publish *Camilla* by subscription, iii.

1796: Publishes in July the novel *Camilla*, a five-volume work dedicated by permission to Queen Charlotte, iii. 158. The kindness of the Queen in granting permission and an audience in which she deigned to receive her presentation copy from the author's hands, as did the King his, were heartfelt triumphs described at length in a series of Journals, 'Windsoriana', iii. 172–96, addressed to her father and well calculated to dispel his initial fears of the disastrous results, public and private, likely to accrue from her marriage to a Frenchman, a Constitutionalist, and a Roman Catholic.

In October bids a sad farewell to her sister Susanna Phillips, who, resigning her Mickleham home, had perforce to accompany her husband to his farmlands in Belcotton, County Louth, Ireland, iii. 201.

1797: Takes the risk of the age in having her son inoculated with smallpox, iii. 282–5, 288–91.

Removes in the autumn from 'The Hermitage', Great Bookham, to Camilla Cottage, West Humble, a cottage designed and in part built by d'Arblay himself on some acres of ground lent him by William Locke of Norbury Park. The period following, the d'Arblays later designated as the happiest of their married life.

Out of concern for her sister Susanna, isolated in Belcotton, and from her own need to communicate with her, begins a series of Journal-Letters, Court Journals, and the like, which were franked in thick packets to Ireland.

1798: Writes at length on the first serious disruptions within the Burney family, the marriage of Charlotte Francis, much against the advice of her father and

brother James, to Ralph Broome; and the elopement of James himself with his half-sister Sarah, iv. 116–25; 191–300 *passim.*

Writes the comedy 'Love and Fashion', a justification, on the model of *As You Like It*, of life in the country and a marriage for love, iv. 65. Has her brother Charles arrange for its production, iv. 270.

Follows the course of the rebellion of '98 in Ireland, with active worries for the safety of the Phillips family.

1799: Troubled increasingly over the situation and the health of Mrs. Phillips at Belcotton, offers to travel there to nurse her, offers a home at Camilla Cottage, offers travel-fare, adopts every means in her power to expedite the journey home, iv. 212–378 *passim.* Hears in November and December that by slow stages the journey was begun and that Susanna had landed with her family at Parkgate, iv. 380–1.

1800: Hears with violent and convulsive grief that Susanna had died at Parkgate, iv. 383. Finds at Charing Cross that because of the January snows no coach could reach Cheshire in time for the funeral, iv. 383. Remains with members of the Burney family at Chelsea, London, and Greenwich for six weeks, iv. 384–99. Recovers slowly at West Humble, affirming repeatedly that the tragic death had marked the end of any 'perfect happiness on earth', iv. 382. Was henceforth to keep the date 6 January as a day of remembrance and prayer.

Withdraws 'Love and Fashion' from production, iv. 396–7.

II. Biographical Data

1. *Marriage, happiness of, reviewed*: iii. 9, 74, 84, 91–2, 148, 264; iv. 12–13;
   illness, iii. 22, 24, 32, 35;

Index

525

Index

Index

Cholmley, Anne Jesse, *née* Smelt (*c.* 1750–*post* 1812), wife of the following, iv. 260.

Cholmley, Nathaniel (1721–91), M.P., iv. 260 n.

Cicero, Marcus Tullius (106–43 B.C.), iii. 163.

Clarence, Duke of. *See* William IV, H.R.M.

Clarke, the Revd. Samuel (1684–1750), D.D., iv. **131 n.**

Clarke, Sarah. *See* Rose, Sarah.

Clay, Sophia (Burrell), *née* Raymond (1750–1802), Lady Burrell, poetess: visits d'Arblays, iv. 179, 211; *Telemachus*, iii. 16 n.; *Theodora*, iii. 16 n.; mentioned, iii. 128, **354**; iv. 80, 412.

Clay, the Revd. William (*c.* 1766–1836), 2nd husband of the preceding, iii. **354**; iv. 179.

Cléry, Jean-Baptiste Cant Hanet de (1759–1809), *Journal . . . pendant la captivité de Louis XVI*, iv. 132–3, 145.

Clifton, Glos., iii. 123, 125, 133; iv. 471.

Clonfert, Bishop of. *See* Marlay, Richard.

Clootz, Jean-Baptiste (1755–94), Baron von Gnadenthal: arrest, death of, iii. 38, **52**.

Cloyne, Bishop of. *See* Hervey, Frederick Augustus.

Coblentz, iv. 68 n.

Cocks, Anne, *née* Pole (d. 1833), Lady Somers, iii. 102 n.

Coigny, comte de. *See* Franquetot, Augustin-Gabriel de.

Coke, Anne Margaret. *See* Anson, Anne Margaret.

Coke, Thomas William (1754–1842), M.P., 1st Earl of Leicester of Holkham, iii. 42 n., 91.

Coleridge, Ernest Hartley, *Life of Thomas Coutts, Banker*, iv. 84 n.

Colman, George (1762–1836), dramatist, *The Heir at Law*, iv. 88, 90, 129.

Colombier, Charlotte. *See* Milner, Charlotte.

Cone, Carl B., *Burke and the Nature of Politics*, iii. 75 n.

Connaught, Duke of. *See* William Henry, H.R.H.

Conolly, Lady Louisa Augusta, *née* Lennox (1743–1821), iii. **241.**

Conolly, the Rt. Hon. Thomas (1738–1803), iii. **241 n.**

Constantinople, iii. 23, 333 n.

Constitutionalists, iii. 21, 26–7, 45 n., 46 n., 349 n.

Cook, Elizabeth (*fl.* 1796), CB's servant, iii. 155.

Cook, James (1728–79), circumnavigator, iii. 62 n.

COOKE, the Revd. Samuel (1741–1820), M.A., iii. **2–3**, 40–1, 56–7, 63, 64, 137, 255, 335; iv. **50**, 191, 223, 262, 408 n., 409, 493, 508.

Cooke, Cassandra, *née* Leigh (1744–1826), wife of the preceding, iii. **3**; visits FBA, iii. 204; iv. 191, 192; *re* Charlotte Twistleton, iii. 41; mentioned, iii. 8, 46, 56–7, 63, 137, 140, 144, 199, 255, 274; iv. 45, **50**, 223, 262, 277, 408–9, 493, 495–6, 508.

Cooke, Theophilus Leigh (1778–1846), M.A., son of the above, iv. **50.**

Cooke, George (1779–1853), M.A., brother of the preceding, iv. **50.**

Cooke, Mary (1781–*post* 1820), sister of the preceding, iv. **50**, 192, 262.

Cooke, Papilian Catherine (*c.* 1731–97): death, iii. 353–4, 363; iv. 25; her legacies to Burneys, iii. 353; mentioned, iii. 274, 322, 331.

Cooper, Margaret. *See* de Luc, Margaret.

Copeland, Professor Thomas W., iii. 164 n., 248 n.

Copenhagen, battle of, iv. 481 n.

Cornwallis, General Sir Charles (1738–1805), 2nd Earl, 1st Marquess, iv. 197 n.

Cosway, Richard (1745–1821), artist, iv. 225 n.

Cottrell-Dormer, Sir Clement (1686–1758), Master of the King's Ceremonies, iv. **291.**

Courtenay, John (1738–1816), M.P., *Present State of Manners, Arts, and Politics*, iii. **77**; cites CB, iii. 112–13 n., 256.

Courtenay, William (1777–1859), 10th Earl of Devon, iii. **215 n.**

537

Index

553

Index

Rushout, Rebecca, *née* Bowles (d. 1818), wife of the preceding, iv. **134**.

Russell, Caroline. *See* Spencer, Caroline.

Russell, Francis (1765–1802), 5th Duke of Bedford, iv. 84–5.

Russia, iv. 166.

Rutland, 2nd Duke of. *See* Manners, John.

Ryan, Mary, journalist, 'A Stone for Susanna', iv. 383 n.

Ryder, the Hon. Dudley (1762–1847), M.P., iv. **338 n.**

Ryder, Lady Susan, *née* Leveson-Gower (1772–1838), iv. **338**, 340 n.

Sablonkoff, Juliana, *née* Angerstein (1772–1846), iv. 441;
engagement to Charles Locke, iii. **181 n.**; iv. 98–9.

Sablonkoff, Nicholas (1776–1848), Russian general, iii. **181 n.**

Sacchini, Antonio-Maria-Gasparo (1734–86), composer, *Arvire et Evelina*, iii. 266.

'Safe', a, iii. 225 n.

Sainte-Marie, Jean-Jacques-René (b. 1730), seigneur d'Agneaux, marquis de, *émigré*, iv. **236**, 238.

Sainte-Marie, Louise-Françoise, *née* de Pestalozzy (*fl.* 1774–99), marquise de, wife of the preceding, iv. 236, 238, 300.

Saint-Méry, Médéric-Louis-Elie Moreau de (1750–1819), *Voyage aux Etats-Unis*, ed. Stewart L. Mims, iii. **26 n.**; iv. 495 n.

Saint-Pol-de-Léon, comte de. *See* La Marche, Jean-François de.

Saint-Priest, François-Emmanuel Guignard (1735–1821), comte de, iii. **333 n.**

Saint-Priest, Constance (de Ludolph) Guignard, *née* Guillelmine (*fl.* 1775–1807), comtesse de, iii. 333.

St. Vincent, Viscount of, Earl. *See* Jervis, John.

Salisbury, Bishops of. *See* Barrington, Shute; Douglas, John; Fisher, John.

Salle, Jean-Baptiste (*c.* 1759–94), *conventionnel*, iii. 25.

Salomon, Johann Peter (1745–1815), musician, concerts of, iii. 50 n.; iv. 493.

Saltersford, Baron and Baroness. *See* Stopford.

Salusbury, Hester Lynch. *See* Piozzi, Hester Lynch (Thrale).

Sam, CB's coachman, iii. 47.

Sandford, Rebecca, *née* Burney (1758–1835), FBA's cousin, iv. 417, 438 n.

Sandwich, Earls of. *See* Montagu, John (1718–92); Montagu, John (1742/3–1814).

San Fiorenzo, H.M.S., iv. 8, 9.

Sansom, James (d. 1823), iv. 175.

Saunders, Sir Charles (*c.* 1713–75), M.P., Admiral, iv. **504**.

Saurin, Bernard-Joseph (1706–81), *Le mariage de Julie*, iv. 495.

Saye and Sele, Lord and Lady. *See* Twistleton.

Sayer, Edmund. *See* Poulter, Edmund.

SCHAUB, Sir Luke (1690–1758), iii. **2 n.**; MS. correspondence of, iv. 3.

Schaub, Marguerite (de Pesne), *née* de Ligonier du Buisson (*c.* 1713–93), wife of the preceding, death, iii. 1, **2**, 8.

Schaub, Frederica Augusta, daughter of the above. *See* Locke, Frederica Augusta.

Schérer, Barthélemy-Louis-Joseph (1747–1804), *général*, iv. 298 n.

Schwellenberg, Elizabeth Juliana (*c.* 1728–97), Keeper of the Robes to Queen Charlotte:
Letters by, quoted, iii. 11 n., 158, 161; death, iii. 314 n., 333 n.; iv. 13; MS. correspondence, iii. 11 n.; mentioned, iii. 62, 93 n., 265 n., 282; iv. 88, 102, 507.

Scott, Elizabeth, *née* Montagu (1743–1827), Duchess of Buccleuch, subscribes to *Camilla*, iii. 143 n.

Scott, Frances. *See* Douglas, Frances.

Scott, George L. (1708–80), iii. **8 n.**

Scott, Sarah, *née* Robinson (1723–95), wife of the preceding, iii. **8**.

Scott, J. M., *The Book of Pall Mall*, iv. 330 n.

Scott, the Revd. James (1733–1814), and the French clergy, iii. **15 n.**

Scott, Sir Walter (1771–1832), translation of Bürger's 'Lenore', iv. 40 n.

Scott-Waring, John (1747–1819), Major, *re* Warren Hastings, iv. **259 n.**

Index

aids *émigrés*, iii. 19;

MS. correspondence, iii. 66 n.;

De l'influence des passions, iii. 312;

Correspondence, ed. Jasinski, iii. 26 n., 66 n.;

Lettres à Narbonne, ed. Solovieff, iii. 19 n., 26 n., 66 n., 346 n., 350 n.;

Lettres à Ribbing, ed. Balayé, iii. 274 n.

Stafford, Marquess of. *See* Leveson-Gower, Granville.

Stanhope, Anne Maria. *See* Pelham-Clinton, Anne Maria.

Stanhope, Charles (1753–1816), *styled* Viscount Mahon, 3rd Earl Stanhope, M.P.:

and the French constitution, iii. 37–8;

and constitutional reform in England, iii. 63, 64 n.

Stanley, Sir John Thomas (1766–1850), author, 1st Baron Stanley of Alderley, iv. 40 n.

Steele, Sir Richard (1672–1729), author, iii. 57 n.

Steibalt, Daniel (*c.* 1756–1823), pianist and composer, iii. **251**.

Stephenson, Alexander (d. 1774), iii. **362–3 n.**

Stephenson, Ann, sister of the preceding. *See* Farquhar, Ann.

Sterkey, the Revd. Alexander (*c.* 1767–1838), iv. **101 n.**

Sterkey, *Charlotte*-Adrienne, *née* Peschier (1774–1849), wife of the preceding, iv. **101 n.**

Stewart, Harriet, *née* Wainwright (*c.* 1760–1843), vocalist and composer:

Comâla, iv. **499–500 n.**;

Critical Remarks on the Art of Singing, iv. 500 n.;

Seringapatam Chorus, and CB's opinion of, iv. 500 n.

Stewart, John (d. 1807), Lt.-Col., iv. **500 n.**

Stopford, James (1731–1810), 2nd Earl of Courtown, 1st Baron Saltersford, iv. **83 n.**

Stopford, Mary, *née* Powys (*c.* 1737–1810), wife of the preceding, Lady-in-Waiting, iv. 83.

Strahan, William (1715–85), King's printer, iv. **190 n.**;

'The Cash accompt books of', iii. 111 n.

Strahan, Andrew (1750–1831), King's printer, M.P., son of the preceding, iv. **190–1**;

will of, iv. 189 n.–190 n.

Strange, Sir Robert (1721–92), engraver, iv. 109 n.

Strange, Isabella, *née* Lumisden (1719–1806), wife of the preceding, FBA visits, iv. 108–9.

Strange, Isabella Katherina (*c.* 1759–1849), daughter of the above, iv. 108.

Strange, James Charles Edward Stuart (1753–1840), M.P., brother of the preceding, iv. 108.

Strange, Margaret, *née* Durham (d. *pre* Oct. 1791), 1st wife of the preceding, iv. 108 n.

Strange, Isabella, daughter of the preceding. *See* Murray, Isabella.

Strange, Anne (Drummond), *née* Dundas (1767–1852), 2nd wife of James (*supra*), iv. 108 n.

Stratton, Anne, *née* Dewes (1778–1861), iii. 11; iv. **194–5**.

Streater, Elizabeth. *See* Halford, Elizabeth.

Stryienski, Casimir, *Mesdames de France*, iv. 296 n.

Stuart, Catherine-Juliana, *née* Anson (1780–1843), iii. 421.

Stuart, Dorothy Margaret, *Dtrs. Geo. III*, iii. 187 n., 314 n.; iv. 308 n.

Stuart, the Hon. William (1755–1822), Archbishop of Armagh and Primate of Ireland, iv. **506**, 510.

Stuart, Sophia Margaret, *née* Penn (*c.* 1765–1847), wife of the preceding, employs Susan Adams, iv. 506, **507**.

Stuart, Louisa (1801–23), daughter of the above, iv. **506**.

Stuart Jones, E. H.:

An Invasion that Failed, iii. 253 n.;

The Last Invasion of Britain, iii. 287 n.

Styleman, Nicholas (1721–88), of Snettisham Hall, iii. 8 n.;

biography of, by Jamesina Waller, iii. 8 n.

Styleman, Catharine, *née* Henley (*c.* 1724–93), death, iii. 8.

575